Evaluating Learning Algorithms

The field of machine learning has matured to the point where many sophisticated learning approaches can be applied to practical applications. Thus it is of critical importance that researchers have the proper tools to evaluate learning approaches and understand the underlying issues.

This book examines various aspects of the evaluation process with an emphasis on classification algorithms. The authors describe several techniques for classifier performance assessment, error estimation and resampling, and obtaining statistical significance, as well as selecting appropriate domains for evaluation. They also present a unified evaluation framework and highlight how different components of evaluation are both significantly interrelated and interdependent. The techniques presented in the book are illustrated using R and WEKA, facilitating better practical insight as well as implementation.

Aimed at researchers in the theory and applications of machine learning, this book offers a solid basis for conducting performance evaluations of algorithms in practical settings.

Nathalie Japkowicz is a Professor of Computer Science at the School of Information Technology and Engineering of the University of Ottawa. She also taught machine learning and artificial intelligence at Dalhousie University and Ohio State University. Along with machine learning evaluation, her research interests include one-class learning, the class imbalance problem, and learning in the presence of concept drifts.

Mohak Shah is a Postdoctoral Fellow at McGill University. He earned a PhD in Computer Science from the University of Ottawa in 2006 and was a Postdoctoral Fellow at CHUL Genomics Research Center in Quebec prior to joining McGill. His research interests span machine learning and statistical learning theory as well as their application to various domains.

Evaluating Learning Algorithms

A Classification Perspective

NATHALIE JAPKOWICZ

University of Ottawa

MOHAK SHAH

McGill University

CAMBRIDGE
UNIVERSITY PRESS

CAMBRIDGE UNIVERSITY PRESS
Cambridge, New York, Melbourne, Madrid, Cape Town, Singapore,
São Paulo, Delhi, Dubai, Tokyo, Mexico City

Cambridge University Press
32 Avenue of the Americas, New York, NY 10013-2473, USA

www.cambridge.org
Information on this title: www.cambridge.org/9780521196000

First published 2011

Printed in the United States of America

A catalog record for this publication is available from the British Library.

Library of Congress Cataloging in Publication data
Japkowicz, Nathalie.
Evaluating Learning Algorithms : A Classification Perspective / Nathalie Japkowicz, Mohak Shah.
p.   cm.
Includes bibliographical references.
ISBN 978-0-521-19600-0
1. Machine learning.   2. Computer algorithms – Evaluation.   I. Shah, Mohak.   II. Title.
Q325.5.J37   2011
006.3′1–dc22   2010048733

ISBN 978-0-521-19600-0 Hardback

This book is dedicated to the memory of my father, Michel Japkowicz (1935–2008), who was my greatest supporter all throughout my studies and career, taking a great interest in any project of mine. He was aware of the fact that this book was being written, encouraged me to write it, and would be the proudest father on earth to see it in print today.

Nathalie

This book is dedicated to the loving memory of my father, Upendra Shah (1948–2006), who was my mentor in life. He taught me the importance of not falling for means but looking for meaning in life. He was also my greatest support through all times, good and bad. His memories are a constant source of inspiration and motivation. Here's to you Dad!

Mohak

Contents

Preface

This book was started at Monash University (Melbourne, Australia) and Laval University (Quebec City, Canada) with the subsequent writing taking place at the University of Ottawa (Ottawa, Canada) and McGill University (Montreal, Canada). The main idea stemmed from the observation that while machine learning as a field is maturing, the importance of evaluation has not received due appreciation from the developers of learning systems. Although almost all studies make a case for the evaluation of the algorithms they present, we find that many (in fact a majority) demonstrate a limited understanding of the issues involved in proper evaluation, despite the best intention of their authors. We concede that optimal choices cannot always be made due to limiting circumstances, and trade-offs are inevitable. However, the methods adopted in many cases do not reflect attention to the details warranted by a proper evaluation approach (of course there are exceptions and we do not mean to generalize this observation).

Our aim here is not to present the readers with yet another recipe for evaluation that can replace the current default approach. Rather, we try to develop an understanding of and appreciation for the different concerns of importance in the practical application and deployment of learning systems. Once these concerns are well understood, the other pieces of the puzzle fall quickly in place since the researcher is not left shooting in the dark. A proper evaluation procedure consists of many components that should all be considered simultaneously so as to correctly address their interdependence and relatedness. We feel that the best (read most easily understood) manner to bring this holistic view of evaluation to the fore is in the classification setting. Nonetheless, most of the observations that we make with regard to the various evaluation components extend just as well to other learning settings and paradigms since the underlying evaluation principles and objectives are essentially the same.

Altogether, this book should be viewed not only as a tool designed to increase our understanding of the evaluation process in a shared manner, but also as a first step in the direction of stimulating a community-wide debate on the relevance and importance of the evaluation of learning algorithms.

Incorporating concepts from both machine learning and statistics proved to be a bit more involved than we had first imagined. The main challenge was to integrate the ideas together and present them in a coherent manner. Indeed, sometimes the same terms are used in the two fields to mean different quantities while at other times, the same quantities are referred to by multiple names and notations. We have tried to put some aspects under a unified scheme (of both terminology and notation) but have left others to their more conventional usage, just to make sure that the reader can relate these to other texts. For instance, while we have used α for the confidence parameter in the statistical significance testing, we have also, in some places, used the common notion of p-value to relate to other discussions. Similarly, both P and Pr frequently appear in probabilistic contexts. We have used both these terms, keeping in mind their common use as well as a better readability of the text. To achieve this, we have used Pr when referring to events or probabilities for discrete variables. For other cases, e.g., distributions over continuous variables and priors, we use P or other symbols, as indicated in the text. However, with some exceptions, most notations are used locally and explained in their proper context to avoid confusion.

We have tried to illustrate the various methods and tests presented in the book with the use of the freely available R statistical package and WEKA machine learning toolkit. Our code, however, is in no sense optimal. Our main aim here was to illustrate the concepts in the simplest possible manner so that even the least experienced programmers could apply the code easily in order to immediately utilize the tools presented in the book. We hope to post better optimized code on the book Web page in the near future.

While our names figure on the cover, we cannot claim complete credit for the work presented in this book. This work was made possible thanks to the support of many people. The deficiencies or errors, however, are solely due to us. We would now like to take some space to thank them and acknowledge their support, advice, and understanding.

We would like to thank all our colleagues at the various institutions that hosted us while this book was in progress. They helped us form and develop our ideas on evaluation and stimulate our thoughts on various aspects of the problem, either directly or indirectly. These include: Peter Tischer, Ingrid Zuckerman, and Yuval Marom at Monash; Mario Marchand, Jacques Corbeil, and Francois Laviolette at Laval; Stan Matwin and Marcel Turcotte at the University of Ottawa; Chris Drummond and Peter Turney at the University of Ottawa and the National Research Council of Canada; Tal Arbel, D. Louis Collins, Doina Precup, and Douglas L. Arnold at McGill; the graduate students and postdoctoral Fellows William Klement, Guichong Li, Lisa Gaudette, Alex Kouznetsov, and Shiven Sharma at the University at Ottawa; Heidar Pirzadeh and Sara Shanian at Laval; and Dante De Nigris and Simon Francis at McGill. William, Alex,

Guichong, and Shiven were also instrumental in running certain experiments, checking some of our formulas and code, and helping with the presentation, in various parts of the book. We also benefited greatly from discussions with Rocio Alaiz-Rodriguez during her visit to the University of Ottawa and, later, on-line. Conversations held about evaluation in the context of a collaboration with Health Canada were also quite enlightening and helped shape some of the ideas in this book. In particular, we would like to thank Kurt Ungar, Trevor Stocki, and Ian Hoffman for sharing their thoughts with us, as well as for providing us with data on Radioxenon Monitoring for the Detection of Nuclear Explosions.

Nathalie would like to thank, most particularly, James Malley of the National Institute of Health for helping her recognize the inadequacy of current evaluation practices in machine learning and the repercussions they may have in collaborative settings; and Chris Drummond with whom she had numerous discussions on evaluation, some of which have been ongoing for the past ten years.

Mohak would also like to extend a note of thanks to Ofer Dekel and Microsoft Research, Seattle, for hosting him there and the immensely productive discussions that helped invoke novel thoughts and ideas.

We would also like to acknowledge financial support from the Natural Science and Engineering Research Council of Canada.

Many thanks to our first editor at Cambridge University Press, Heather Bergman, whose confidence in our project was very uplifting. She made contract negotiations very easy, with her dynamism and encouragement. Lauren Cowles, who succeeded her as our editor, has been equally competent and helpful. Lauren indeed made the administrative process extremely easy and efficient, allowing us to devote more time to the ideas and contents of the book. Our copy editor Victoria Dahany deserves a special thank you for her meticulous work and the painstaking effort to refine our discussion without which this book would not have been in its present form. We would also like to thank Victoria for her encouraging notes during the copyediting phase that reinforced our belief in both the importance and pertinence of the subject matter. We would also like to thank David Jou, Marielle Poss, Katy Strong, and the Cambridge marketing team for their thorough professionalism and help with processing the book and disseminating the information as well as with design aspects of the marketing material. Also, the team at Aptara, especially Sweety Singh, Tilak Raj, and Pushpender Rathee, has been thoroughly professional in taking the book publication forward from copyediting to its final version.

Nathalie would also like to thank her husband, Norrin Ripsman, for sharing his experience with writing and publishing books. His advice on dealing with presses and preparing our material was particularly helpful. On a more personal note, she appreciated him for being there every step of the way, especially at times when the goal seemed so far away. Her daughter Shira also deserves great thanks for being the excellent girl that she is and bearing with her Mum's work all along. The baby-to-be, now lovely little Dafna, showed tremendous patience (in both her fetal and infant states), which made it possible for Nathalie to continue working on the project prior to and after her birth. Nathalie's father, Michel Japkowicz, and her mother, Suzanne Japkowicz, have also always been an unconditional source of loving support and understanding. Without their constant interest in her work, she would not be where she is today. Nathalie is also grateful to her in-laws, Toba and Michael Ripsman, for being every bit as supportive as her own parents during the project and beyond.

On the personal front, Mohak would like to acknowledge his mother Raxika Shah and his sister Tamanna Shah for their unconditional love, support, and encouragement. It is indeed the unsung support of family and friends that motivates you and keeps you going, especially in difficult times. Mohak considers himself exceptionally fortunate to have friends like Sushil Keswani and Ruma Paruthi in his life. He is also grateful to Rajeet Nair, Sumit Bakshi, Arvind Solanki, and Shweta (Dhamani) Keswani for their understanding, support, and trust.

Finally, we heartily apologize to friends and colleagues whose names may have been inadvertently missed in our acknowledgments.

Nathalie Japkowicz and Mohak Shah
Ottawa and Montreal
2010

Acronyms

2D	two-dimensional	Inf	infimum
3D	three-dimensional	KDD	Knowledge Discovery in
ALL	acute lymphoblastic		Databases (Archive)
	leukemia	KL	Kullback–Leibler
AML	acute myloid leukemia	KS	Kolmogorov–Smirnov
ANOVA	analysis of variance	LOO	leave-one-out
ARI	adjusted Rand index	MAP	maximum a posteriori
AUC	area under the (ROC)	MDS	multidimensional scaling
	curve	MRI	Magnetic Resonance
Bin	Binomial (distribution)		Imaging
BIR	Bayesian information	NEC	normalized expected
	reward		cost
CD	critical difference	NHST	null hypothesis statistical
CDF	cumulative distribution		testing
	function	NPV	negative predictive value
CTBT	Comprehensive Nuclear	PAC	probably approximately
	Test Ban Treaty		correct
CV	cross-validation	PPV	positive predictive value
DEA	data envelopment analysis	PR	precision-recall
DET	Detection Error Trade-Off	RMSE	root-mean-square error
ERM	empirical risk minimization	ROC	receiver operating
exp	exponential		characteristic (curve)
HSD	honestly significant	ROCCH	ROC convex hull
	difference	ROCR	ROC in R package
IBSR	Internet Brain	SAR	metric combining squared
	Segmentation Repository		error (S), accuracy (A),
iff	if and only if		and ROC area (R)
i.i.d.	independently and	SAUC	scored AUC
	identically distributed	SCM	set covering machine

SIM	simple and intuitive	SVM	support vector machine
	measure	UCI	University of California,
SRM	structural risk		Irvine
	minimization	VC	Vapnik–Chervonenkis
SS	sums of squares	w.r.t.	with regard to

Algorithms

1NN	1-nearest-neighbor	NN	nearest neighbor
ADA	AdaBoost using decision	RF	random forest
	trees	RIP	Ripper
C45	decision tree (c4.5)	SCM	set covering machine
NB	naive Bayes	SVM	support vector machine

Algorithms are set in small caps to distinguish them from acronyms.

Acronyms used in tables and math

CI	confidence interval	LR	likelihood ratio
FN	false negative	Pr	probability
FP	false positive	TN	true negative
FPR	false-positive rate	TP	true positive
IR	information reward	TPR	true-positive rate

These are not acronyms, although sometimes TPR and FPR will appear as
such. Authors' preferences were followed in this case.

1

Introduction

Technological advances in recent decades have made it possible to automate many tasks that previously required significant amounts of manual time, performing regular or repetitive activities. Certainly, computing machines have proven to be a great asset in improving human speed and efficiency as well as in reducing errors in these essentially mechanical tasks. More impressive, however, is the fact that the emergence of computing technologies has also enabled the automation of tasks that require significant understanding of intrinsically human domains that can in no way be qualified as merely mechanical. Although we humans have maintained an edge in performing some of these tasks, e.g., recognizing pictures or delineating boundaries in a given picture, we have been less successful at others, e.g., fraud or computer network attack detection, owing to the sheer volume of data involved and to the presence of nonlinear patterns to be discerned and analyzed simultaneously within these data. Machine learning and data mining, on the other hand, have heralded significant advances, both theoretical and applied, in this direction, thus getting us one step closer to realizing such goals.

Machine learning is embodied by different learning approaches, which are themselves implemented within various frameworks. Examples of some of the most prominent of these learning paradigms include supervised learning, in which the data labels are available and generally discrete; unsupervised learning, in which the data labels are unavailable; semisupervised learning, in which some, generally discrete, data labels are available, but not all; regression, in which the data labels are continuous; and reinforcement learning, in which learning is based on an agent policy optimization in a reward setting. The plethora of solutions that have been proposed within these different paradigms yielded a wide array of learning algorithms. As a result, the field is at an interesting crossroad. On the one hand, it has matured to the point where many impressive and pragmatic data analysis methods have emerged, of course, with their respective strengths and limitations.[1] On the other hand, it is now overflowing with hundreds of studies trying to improve the basic methods, but only marginally succeeding in doing so (Hand, 2006).[2] This is especially true on the applied front. Just as in any scientific field, the practical utility of any new advance can be accepted only if we can demonstrate beyond reasonable doubt the superiority of the proposed or novel methods over existing ones in the context in which it was designed.

This brings the issue of evaluating the proposed learning algorithms to the fore. Although considerable effort has been made by researchers in both developing novel learning methods and improving the existing models and approaches, these same researchers have not been completely successful at alleviating the users' scepticism with regard to the worth of these new developments. This is due, in big part, to the lack of both depth and focus in what has become a ritualized evaluation method used to compare different approaches. There are many issues involved in the question of designing an evaluation strategy for a learning machine. Furthermore, these issues cover a wide range of concerns pertaining to both the problem and the solution that we wish to consider. For instance, one may ask the following questions: What precise measure is best suited for a quantified assessments of different algorithms' property of interest in a given domain? How can these measures be efficiently computed? Do the data from the domain of interest affect the efficiency of this calculation? How can we be confident about whether the difference in measurement for two or more algorithms denotes a statistically significant difference in their performance? Is this statistical difference practically relevant as well? How can we best use the available data to discover whether such differences exist? And so on. We do not claim that all these issues can be answered in a definitive manner, but we do emphasize the need to understand the issues we are dealing with, along with the various approaches available to tackle them. In particular, we must understand the strengths and limitations of these approaches as well as the proper manner in which they should be applied. Moreover, we also need to understand what these methods offer and how to properly interpret the results of their application. This is very different from the way evaluation has been perceived to date in the machine learning community, where we have been using a routine, de facto, strategy, without much concern about its meaning.

In this book, we try to address these issues, more specifically with regard to the branch of machine learning pertaining to classification algorithms. In particular, we focus on evaluating the performance of classifiers generated by supervised learning algorithms, generally in a binary classification scenario. We wish to emphasize, however, that the overall message of the book and the

---

[1] These developments have resulted both from empirically studied behaviors and from exploiting the theoretical frameworks developed in other fields, especially mathematics.

[2] Although the worth of a study that results in marginal empirical improvements sometimes lies in the more significant theoretical insights obtained.

insights obtained should be considered in a more general sense toward the study of all learning paradigms and settings. Many of these approaches can indeed be readily exported (with a few suitable modifications) to other scenarios such as unsupervised learning, regression and so on. The issues we consider in the book deal not only with evaluation measures, but also with the related and important issues of obtaining (and understanding) the statistical significance of the observed differences, efficiently computing the evaluation measures in as unbiased a manner as possible, and dealing with the artifacts of the data that affect these quantities. Our aim is to raise an awareness of the proper way to conduct such evaluations and of how important they are to the practical utilization of the advances being made in the field. While developing an understanding of the relevant evaluation strategies, some that are widely used (although sometimes with little understanding) as well as some that are not currently too popular, we also try to address a number of practical criticisms and philosophical concerns that have been raised with regard to their usage and effectiveness and examine the solutions that have been proposed to deal with these concerns.

Our aim is not to suggest a recipe for evaluation to replace the previous de facto one, but to develop an understanding and appreciation of the evaluation strategies, of their strengths, and the underlying caveats. Before we go further and expand our discussion pertaining to the goals of this book by bringing forth the issues with our current practices, we discuss the de facto culture that has pervaded the machine learning community to date.

1.1 The De Facto Culture

For over two decades now, with Kibler and Langley (1988) suggesting the need for a greater emphasis on performance evaluation, the machine learning community has recognized the importance of proper evaluation. Research has been done to both come up with novel ways of evaluating classifiers and to use insights obtained from other fields in doing so. In particular, researchers have probed such fields as mathematics, psychology, and statistics among others. This has resulted in significant advances in our ability to track and compare the performance of different algorithms, although the results and the importance of such evaluation has remained underappreciated by the community as a whole because of one or more reasons that we will soon ponder. More important, however, is the effect of this underappreciation that has resulted in the entrenchment of a *de facto* culture of evaluation. Consider, for example, the following statement extracted from (Witten and Frank, 2005b, p. 144), one of the most widely used textbooks in machine learning and data mining:

The question of predicting performance based on limited data is an interesting, and still controversial one. We will encounter many different techniques, of which one – repeated cross-validation – is gaining ascendance and is probably the evaluation method of choice in most practical limited-data situations.

This, in a sense, prescribes repeated cross-validation as a de facto method for *most practical limited data situations*. And therein lies the problem. Although cross-validation has indeed appeared to be a strong candidate among resampling methods in limited data situations, generalizing its use to most practical situations is pushing our luck a bit too far. Most of the practical data situations warrant looking into broader and deeper issues before zeroing in on an evaluation strategy (or even an error-estimation method such as cross-validation). We will soon look into what these issues are, including those that are generally obvious and those that are not.

The preceding take on choosing an evaluation method makes the implicit statement that cross-validation has been adopted as a standard. This implication is quite important because it molds the mindset of both the researcher and the practitioner as to the fact that a standard recipe for evaluation can be applied without having to consider the full context of that evaluation. This context encompasses many criteria and not simply, as is sometimes believed, the sample size of the application. Other important criteria are the class distribution of the data, the need for parameter selection (also known as model selection), the choice of a relevant and appropriate performance metric, and so on. Witten and Frank (2005b, pp. 144) further state,

> Comparing the performance of different machine learning methods on a given problem is another matter that is not so easy as it sounds: to be sure that apparent differences are not caused by chance effects, statistical tests are needed.

Indeed, statistical tests are needed and are even useful so as to obtain "confidence" in the difference in performance observed over a given domain for two or more algorithms. Generally the machine learning community has settled on merely rejecting the null hypothesis that the apparent differences are caused by chance effects when the t test is applied. In fact, the issue is a lot more involved.

The point is that no single evaluation strategy consisting of a combination of evaluation methods can be prescribed that is appropriate in *all* scenarios. A de facto – or perhaps, more appropriately, a panacea – approach to evaluation, even with minor variations for different cases, is hence neither appropriate nor possible or even advisable. Broader issues need to be taken into account.

Getting back to the issue of our general underappreciation of the importance of evaluation, let us now briefly consider this question: *Why and how has the machine learning community allowed such a de facto or panacea culture to take root?* The answer to this question is multifold. Naturally we can invoke the argument about the ease of comparing novel results with existing published ones as a major advantage of sticking to a very simple comparison framework. The reasons for doing so can generally be traced to two main sources: (i) the unavailability of other researchers' algorithm implementations, and (ii) the ease of not having to replicate the simulations even when such implementations are available. The first concern has actually encouraged various researchers to come together in calling for the public availability of algorithmic implementations under general public licenses (Sonnenburg et al., 2007). The second concern should not be mistaken for laziness on the part of researchers. After all, there can be no better reward in being able to demonstrate, fair and square – i.e., by letting the creators of the system themselves demonstrate its worth as best as they can – the superiority of one's method to the existing state of the art.

Looking a little bit beyond the issues of availability and simplicity, we believe that there are more complex considerations that underlie the establishment of this culture. Indeed, the implicit adoption of the de facto approach can also be linked to the desire of establishing an "acceptable" scientific practice in the field as a way to validate an algorithm's worth. Unfortunately, we chose to achieve such acceptability by using a number of shortcuts. The problem with this practice is that our comparisons of algorithms' performance, although appearing acceptable, are frequently invalid. Indeed, many times, validity is lost as a result of the violation of the underlying assumptions and constraints of the methods that we use. This can be called the "politically correct" way of doing evaluations. Such considerations are generally, and understandably, never stated as they are implicit.

Digging even deeper, we can discover some of the reasons for this standard adoption. A big part of the problem is attributable to a lack of understanding of the evaluation approaches, their underlying mode of application, and the interpretation of their results. Although advances have been made in finding novel evaluation approaches or their periodic refinements, these advances have not propagated to the mainstream. The result has been the adoption of a "standard" simple evaluation approach comprising various elements that are relatively easily understood (even intuitive) and widely accepted. The downside of this approach is that, even when alternative (and sometimes better-suited) evaluation measures are utilized by researchers, their results are met with scepticism. If we could instill a widespread understanding of the evaluation methodologies in the community, it would be easier to not only better evaluate our classifiers but also to better appreciate the results that were obtained. This can further result in a positive-feedback loop from which we can obtain a better understanding of various learning approaches along with their bottlenecks, leading in turn to better learning algorithms. This, however, is not to say that the researchers adopting alternative, relatively less-utilized elements of evaluation approaches are completely absolved of any responsibility. Instead, these researchers also have the onus of making a convincing case as to why such a strategy is more suitable than those in current and common use. Moreover, the audience – both the reviewers and the readers – should be open to better modes of evaluation that can yield a better understanding of the learning approaches applied in a given domain, bringing into the light their respective strengths and limitations. To realize this goal, it is indeed imperative that we develop a thorough understanding of such evaluation approaches and promote this in the basic *required* machine learning and data mining courses.

1.2   Motivations for this Book

As just discussed, there is indeed a need to go beyond the de facto evaluation approaches. There are many reasons why this has not happened yet. However, the core reasons can be traced to a relative lack of proper understanding of the procedures. Progress toward realizing the goal of more meaningful classifier evaluation and consequently better understanding of the learning approaches themselves can take place only if both the researchers involved in developing novel learning approaches and the practitioners applying these are better aware of not only the evaluation methods, but also of their strengths and limitations together with their context of application.

There have also been criticisms of specific evaluation methods that were condemned for not yielding the desired results. These criticisms, in fact, arise from unreasonable expectations from the evaluation approaches. It is important to understand what a given evaluation method promises and how the results it obtained should be interpreted. One of the widest criticisms among these has fallen on the statistical significance testing procedure, as we will see later in the book. Although some of these criticisms are genuine, most of them result from a mistaken interpretation. The tests are not definitive, and it is important that both their meaning and the results they produce be interpreted properly. These will not only help us develop a better understanding of the learning algorithms, but they will also lead to a raised awareness in terms of what the tests mean and hence what results should (and can) be expected. A better understanding of the overall evaluation framework would then enable researchers to ask the right questions before adopting the elements of that evaluation framework. Summarizing the goals toward this raised awareness, we need to make sure that both the researchers and practitioners follow these guidelines:

1. To have a better understanding of the entire evaluation process so as to be able to make *informed decisions* about the strategies to be employed.
2. To have *reasonable* expectations from the evaluation methods: For instance, the t test only helps us guard against the claim that one algorithm is better than others when the evidence to support this claim is too weak. It doesn't help us *prove* that one algorithm is better than other in *any* case.

3. To possess a knowledge of the right questions to be asked or addressed before
   adopting an evaluation framework.

Note that the *de facto* method, even if suitable in many scenarios, is not a
panacea. Broader issues need to be taken into account. Such awareness can be
brought about only from a better understanding of the approaches themselves.
This is precisely what this book is aimed at. The main idea of the book is
not to prescribe specific recipes of evaluation strategies, but rather to educate
researchers and practitioners alike about the issues to keep in mind when adopting an evaluation approach, to enable them to objectively apply these approaches
in their respective settings.

While furthering the community's understanding of the issues surrounding evaluation, we also seek to simplify the application of different evaluation
paradigms to various practical problems. In this vein, we provide simple and
intuitive implementations of all the methods presented in the book. We developed these by using WEKA and R, two freely available and highly versatile
platforms, in the hope of making the discussions in the book easily accessible
to and further usable by all.

Before we proceed any further, let us see, with the help of a concrete example,
what we mean by the de facto approach to evaluation and what types of issues
can arise as a result of its improper application.

1.3   The De Facto Approach

As we discussed in Section 1.1, a de facto evaluation culture has pervaded a big
part of experimental verification and comparative evaluation of learning algorithms. The approaches utilized to do so proceed along the following lines, with
some minor variations: Select an evaluation metric, the most often used one
being accuracy; select a large-enough number of datasets [the number is chosen
so as to be able to make a convincing case of apt evaluation and the datasets are
generally obtained from a public data repository, the main one being the University of California, Irvine, (UCI) machine learning repository]; select the best
parameters for various learning algorithms, a task generally known as model
selection but mostly inadvertently interleaved with evaluation; use a k-fold
cross-validation technique for error estimation, often stratified 10-fold cross-
validation, with or without repetition; apply paired t tests to all pairs of results
or to the pairs deemed relevant (e.g., the ones including a possibly new algorithm of interest) to test for statistical significance in the observed performance
difference; average the results for an overall estimate of the algorithm's performance or, alternatively, record basic statistics such as win/loss/ties for each algorithm with respect to the others. Let us examine this de facto approach with an
illustration.

Table 1.1. *Datasets used in the illustration of the* de facto *evaluation approach*

Datasets	#attr	#ins	#cls
Anneal	39	898	5
Audiology	70	226	24
Balance scale	5	625	3
Breast cancer	10	286	2
Contact lenses	5	24	3
Diabetes	9	768	2
Glass	10	214	6
Hepatitis	20	155	2
Hypothyroid	30	3772	4
Mushroom	23	8124	2
Tic-tac-toe	10	958	2

1.3.1 An Illustration

Consider an experiment that consists of running a set of learning algorithms on a number of domains to compare their generic performances. The algorithms used for this purpose include naive bayes (NB), support vector machines (SVMs), 1-nearest neighbor (1NN), AdaBoost using decision trees (ADA), Bagging (BAG), a C4.5 decision tree (C45), random forest (RF), and Ripper (RIP).

Tables 1.2 and 1.3 illustrate the process just summarized with actual experiments. In particular, Table 1.1 shows the name, dimensionality (#attr), size (#ins), and number of classes (#cls) of each domain considered in the study. Table 1.2 shows the results obtained by use of accuracy, 10-fold stratified cross-validation, and *t* tests with 95% confidence, and averaging of the results obtained by each classifier on all the domains. In Table 1.2, we also show the results of the *t* test with each classifier pitted against NB. A "v" next to the result indicates the significance test's success of the concerned classifier against NB, a "*" represents a failure, against NB (i.e. NB wins) and no symbol signals a tie (no statistically significant difference). The results of the *t* test are summarized at the bottom of the table. Table 1.3 shows the aggregated *t*-test results obtained by each classifier against each other in terms of wins–ties–losses on each domain. Each classifier was optimized prior to being tested by the running of pairwise *t* tests on different parameterized versions of the same algorithm on all the domains. The parameters that win the greatest numbers of *t* tests among all the others, for one single classifier, were selected as the optimal ones.

As can be seen from these tables, results of this kind are difficult to interpret because they vary too much across both domains and classifiers. For example, the SVM seems to be superior to all the other algorithms on the balance scale and it apparently performs worst on breast cancer. Similarly, bagging is apparently

Table 1.2. Accuracy results of various classifiers on the datasets of Table 1.1

Dataset	NB	SVM	1NN	ADA(DT)	BAG(REP)	C45	RF	RIP
Anneal	96.43	99.44 v	99.11 v	83.63 *	98.22	98.44 v	99.55 v	98.22 v
Audiology	73.42	81.34	75.22	46.46 *	76.54	77.87	79.15	76.07
Balance scale	72.30	91.51 v	79.03	72.31	82.89 v	76.65	80.97 v	81.60 v
Breast cancer	71.70	66.16	65.74 *	70.28	67.84	75.54	69.99	68.88
Contact lenses	71.67	71.67	63.33	71.67	68.33	81.67	71.67	75.00
Pima diabetes	74.36	77.08	70.17	74.35	74.61	73.83	74.88	75.00
Glass	70.63	62.21	70.50	44.91 *	69.63	66.75	79.87	70.95
Hepatitis	83.21	80.63	80.63	82.54	84.50	83.79	84.58	78.00
Hypothyroid	98.22	93.58 *	91.52 *	93.21 *	99.55 v	99.58 v	99.39 v	99.42
Tic-tac-toe	69.62	99.90 v	81.63 v	72.54 v	92.07 v	85.07 v	93.94 v	97.39 v
Average	78.15	82.35	77.69	71.19	81.42	81.92	83.40	82.05 v
t test		3/6/1	2/6/2	1/5/4	3/7/0	3/7/0	4/6/0	4/6/0

Note: The final row gives the numbers of wins/ties/losses for each algorithm against the NB classifier.

Notes: A "v" indicates the significance test's success in favor of the corresponding classifier against NB while a "*" indicates this success in favor of NB. No symbol indicates the result between the concerned classifier and NB were not found to be statistically significantly different.

Table 1.3. *Aggregate number of wins/ties/losses of each algorithm against the others over the datasets of Table 1.1*

Algorithm	NB	SVM	1NN	ADA	BAG	C45	RF	RIP
NB		3/6/1	2/6/2	1/5/4	3/7/0	3/7/0	4/6/0	4/6/0
SVM	1/6/3		0/6/4	0/5/5	2/5/3	2/6/2	2/6/2	1/7/2
1NN	2/6/2	4/6/0		0/5/5	2/8/0	2/8/0	3/7/0	2/8/0
ADA	4/5/1	5/5/0	5/5/0		6/4/0	5/5/0	6/4/0	6/4/0
BAG	0/7/3	3/5/2	0/8/2	0/4/6		1/7/2	1/9/0	1/8/1
C45	0/7/3	2/6/2	0/8/2	0/5/5	2/7/1		3/7/0	2/7/1
RF	0/6/4	2/6/2	0/7/3	0/4/6	0/9/1	0/7/3		1/8/1
RIP	0/6/4	2/7/1	0/8/2	0/4/6	1/8/1	1/7/2	1/8/1	

the second best learner on the hepatitis dataset and is average, at best, on breast cancer. As a consequence, the aggregation of these results over domains is not that meaningful either. Several other issues plague this evaluation approach in the current settings. Let us look at some of the main ones.

1.3.2 Issues with the Current Illustration

Statistical Validity – I.   First we focus on the sample size of the domains. With regard to the sample size requirement, a rule of thumb suggests a minimum of 30 examples for a paired t test to be valid (see, for instance, Mitchell, 1997).[3] When 10-fold cross-validation experiments on binary datasets are run, this amounts to datasets of at least 300 samples. This assumption is violated in breast cancer and hepatitis. For the multiclass domains, we multiply this requirement by the number of classes and conclude that the assumption is violated in all cases but balance scale and hypothyroid. That is, at the outset, the assumption is violated in 6 out of 11 cases. This, of course, is only a quick rule of thumb that should be complemented by an actual visualization of the data that could help us determine whether the estimates are normally distributed (specific distributional oddities in the data could falsify the quick rule of thumb). In all cases for which the data is too sparse, it may be wiser to use a nonparametric test instead.

Statistical Validity – II.   In fact, the dearth of data is only one problem plaguing the validity of the t test. Other issues are problematic as well, e.g., the inter-dependence between the number of experiments and the significance level of a statistical test. As suggested by Salzberg (1997), because of the large number of experiments run, the significance level of 0.05 used in our t test is not stringent enough: It is possible that, in certain cases, this result was obtained by chance. This is amplified by the fact that the algorithms were tuned on the same datasets

---

[3] We examine the sample size requirements later in the book.

as they were tested on and that these experiments were not independent. Such problems can be addressed to a considerable extent by use of well-known procedures such as analysis of variance (ANOVA) or other procedures such as the Friedman test (Demšar, 2006) or the Bonferroni adjustment (Salzberg, 1997).

Evaluation Metric.   Regarding the use of "accuracy" as an evaluation metric, it should be noted that a number of domains used in this study are imbalanced. For example, the hepatitis domain contains 123 examples of one class ("live") and 32 of the other ("die"), i.e., the small class represents about 21% of all the data. This means that a trivial classifier issuing class "live" systematically would obtain an accuracy of 79%. Hence the accuracy estimate does not give the real picture of how good the classifier is in discerning one class from the others and is clearly unacceptable in such cases.

Aggregating the Results.   The averaging of the results shown in Table 1.2 is not meaningful either. Consider, for example, ADA and NB on audiology and breast cancer. Although, in audiology, ADA's performance with respect to 1NN's is dismal and rightly represented as such with a drop in performance of close to 30%, ADA's very good performance in breast cancer compared with 1NN's is represented by only a 5% increase in performance. Averaging such results (among others) does not weigh the extent of performance differences between the classifiers. On the other hand, the win/tie/loss results give us quantitative but not qualitative assessments: We know how many times each algorithm won over, tied with, or lost against each other, but not by how much. Alternative approaches as well as appropriate statistical tests have been proposed for this purpose that may prove to be helpful.

Dataset Selections.   There have been a number of criticisms related to the datasets on which machine learning experiments are undertaken. For example, a study by Holte (1993) suggested that the University of California, Irvine (UCI) datasets are relatively easy to classify and are not necessarily representative of the type of problems to which algorithms are applied in actual practical settings. This criticism is echoed by Salzberg (1997) and Saitta and Neri (1998), who also add that researchers become overreliant on community datasets and may start, unwittingly, to overfit their classifiers to these particular domains. The acquisition of new datasets and the creation of artificial domains may be ways to ease this overreliance.

Model Selection versus Evaluation.   An additional problem with the de facto approach to evaluation is the fact that the purpose of the evaluation procedure is rarely clarified. Evaluation could be done with the purpose of selecting appropriate parameters for the different classifiers considered (model selection) or selecting one or several classifiers from among a number of classifiers available. This exploratory pursuit, though, is different from the issue of deciding what classifier is best for a task or for a series of tasks (the primary purpose of evaluation in learning experiments). Yet the two processes are usually merged into a gray area with no attempt to truly subdivide them – and hence minimize the biases in evaluation estimates. This is mainly due to the fact that machine learning researchers are both the designers and the evaluators of their systems. In other areas, as will be touched on later, these two processes are subdivided.

Internal versus External Validation.   The last issue we wish to point out has to do with the fact that, although we carefully use cross-validation to train and test on different partitions of the data, at the end of the road, these partitions all come from the same distribution because they belong to the same dataset. Yet the designed classifiers are applied to different, even if related, data. This is an issue discussed by Hand (2006) in the machine learning community; it was also considered in the philosophy community by Forster (2000) and Busemeyer and Wang (2000). We discuss some of the solutions that were proposed to deal with this issue.

This short discussion illustrates some of the reasons why the de facto approach to evaluation cannot be applied universally. As we can see, some of these reasons pertain to the evaluation measures considered, others pertain to the statistical guarantees believed to have been obtained, and still others pertain to the overall evaluation framework. In all cases, the issues concern the evaluator's belief that the general worth of the algorithm of interest has been convincingly and undeniably demonstrated in comparison with other competitive learning approaches. In fact, critics argue, this belief is incorrect and the evaluator should be more aware of the controversies surrounding the evaluation strategy that has been utilized.

1.4   Broader Issues with Evaluation Approaches

We now expand on the preceding discussion by bringing in more formal arguments to each of the issues considered. This section represents the basis for this book and is further expanded in the subsequent chapters.

1.4.1 Evaluation Metrics

In the realm of all the issues related to classifier evaluation, those concerning evaluation metrics have, by far, received the most attention. Two different aspects related to evaluation metrics are of significance: the choice of a metric and the aggregation of its results.

The most widely used metric for quantitatively assessing the classifier performance is accuracy. However, accuracy suffers from a serious shortcoming in that it does not take asymmetric misclassification costs into consideration. This limitation, as it turns out, can have serious implications in that in most practical scenarios there is almost always an unequal misclassification cost associated with each class. This problem was recognized early. Kononenko and Bratko (1991) proposed an information-based approach that takes this issue into consideration, along with the questions of dealing with classifiers that issue different kinds of answers (categorical, multiple, no answer or probabilistic) and comparisons on different domains. Although their method generated some interest and a following in some communities, it did not receive large-scale acceptance. Perhaps this is due to the fact that it relies on knowledge of the cost matrix and prior class probabilities, which cannot generally be estimated accurately.

More successful has been the effort initiated by Provost et al. (1998), who introduced ROC analysis to the machine learning community. ROC analysis allows an evaluator to commit neither to a particular class prior distribution nor to a particular cost matrix. Instead, it analyzes the classifier's performance over all the possible priors and costs. Its associated metric, the AUC, has started to be used relatively widely, especially in cases of class imbalances. There have been standard metrics adopted by other related domains as well to take into account the class imbalances. For instance, the area of text categorization often uses metrics such as precision, recall, and the F measure. In medical applications, it is not uncommon to encounter results expressed in terms of sensitivity and specificity, as well as in terms of positive predictive values (PPVs) and negative predictive values (NPVs).

As mentioned previously, although accuracy remains overused, many researchers have taken note of the fact that other metrics are available and easy to use. As a matter of fact, widely used machine learning libraries such as WEKA (Witten and Frank, 2005a) contains implementations of many of these metrics whose results can be obtained in an automatically generated summary sheet. Drummond (2006) also raised an important issue concerning the fact that machine learning researchers tend to ignore the kind of algorithmic properties that are not easy to measure. For example, despite its noted interest, the comprehensibility of a classifier's result cannot be measured very convincingly and thus is often not considered in comparison studies. Other properties that are similarly perhaps better formulated qualitatively than quantitatively are also usually ignored. We discuss these and related issues in greater depth in Chapters 3, 4, and 8.

1.4.2 Aggregating the Results

Performance evaluation of different classifiers is usually carried out across a number of different domains in order to assess how a given classifier of interest fares compared with the other competitive approaches. Typically this leads to aggregating the results on various domains for each classifier, with the aggregation quantitatively summarized in a single number. This is problematic, given that the same value may take different meanings, depending on the domain. Recognizing this problem, researchers sometimes use a win/tie/loss approach, counting the number of times each classifier won over all the others, tied with the best, or lost against one or more. This, however, requires that the performance comparison be deterministically categorized as a win, tie, or loss without the margins being taken into account. That is, any information pertaining to how close classifiers were to winning or tieing is essentially ignored. We discuss the issue of aggregation in Chapter 8.

1.4.3 Statistical Significance Testing

One of the most widely used statistical significance measures currently adopted in the context of classifier evaluation is the t test. However, this is not the only option, and, in fact, the t test is by no means applicable to all scenarios. An in-depth analysis of algorithms and their behavior is required when experiments are performed in wide settings involving multiple domains and multiple datasets. Tests such as the t test that are suitable for comparing the performance of two classifiers on a single domain are certainly not suitable in the cases in which such testing is to be performed over multiple classifiers and domains. Moreover, there are also nonparametric alternatives that can in some situations be more apt for comparing two classifiers on a single domain. Some studies have appeared for a subset of these statistical tests (mostly the ones suitable to compare two classifiers on a single domain) and have based their analysis on two quantities: the *type I error* of the test, which denotes the probability of incorrectly detecting a difference when no such difference between two classifiers exists; and the *power of the test*, signifying the ability to detect differences when they do exist. See, for instance, (Dietterich, 1998) and (Demšar, 2006).

We will develop an understanding of both these criteria of assessing a significance test as well as of particular tests, both parametric and nonparametric, that can be utilized under different settings in Chapter 6.

1.4.4 Error Estimation and Resampling Statistics

Limited data availability in most practical scenarios today, especially in the newly emerging fields in which learning techniques are applied, necessitates the use of resampling methods such as k-fold cross-validation for the purpose of error estimation. A natural question then is whether error-estimation methods affect the statistical testing. Evidence suggests so. For instance, the use of cross-validation causes accrued uncertainty in the ensuing t test because the learned classifiers are not independent of each other. When cross-validation is further repeated (e.g., as suggested by Witten and Frank, 2005b), the independence assumption between the test sets is then violated in addition to the one concerning the classifiers. The meaning of the t test is thus gravely affected, and a researcher should, at the least, be aware of all the assumptions that are violated and the possible consequences of this action.

Alternatives to cross-validation testing in such scenarios in which statistical significance testing effects are kept in mind have been suggested. Two of the main resampling statistics that have appeared to be useful, but have so far eluded the community, are *bootstrapping* and *randomization*. Bootstrapping has attracted a bit of interest in the field (e.g., Kohavi, 1995, and Margineantu and Dietterich, 2000), but is not, by any means, widely used. Randomization, on the other hand, has gone practically unnoticed except for rare citings (e.g., Jensen and Cohen, 2000).

Resampling tests appear to be strong alternatives to parametric tests for statistical significance too, in addition to facilitating error estimation. We believe that the machine learning community should engage in more experimentation with them to establish alternatives in case the assumptions, constraints, or both, of the standard tests such as the t test are not satisfied, rendering them inapplicable. Error-estimation methods are the focus of our discussions in Chapter 5.

1.4.5 Datasets

The experimental framework used by the machine learning community often consists of running large numbers of simulations on community-shared domains such as those from the UCI Repository for Machine Learning. There are many advantages to working in such settings. In particular, new algorithms can easily be tested under real-world conditions; problems arising in real-world settings can thus be promptly identified and focused on; and comparisons between new and old algorithms are easy because researchers share the same datasets. Unfortunately, along with these advantages, are also a couple of disadvantages: such as the multiplicity effect and the issues with community experiments. We discuss these in detail in Chapter 7.

1.4.6 Other Issues

Repeated Tuning.   One of the main cautions to be exerted in tuning an algorithm, i.e., choosing the best learning parameters, alternatively known as model selection, is that such parameter selection should be performed *independently of the test set*. This, however, is seldom the case with the situation being aggravated in the case of repeated experimental runs. Unfortunately, the adjustments to the statistical tests necessary in such a situation are usually not made.

Generalizing Results.   It might not necessarily be correct to generalize the results obtained in the domains of the UCI Repository to any other datasets, given that these datasets represent only a small portion of all the datasets encountered in the real world and may not be the most representative domains.

Properly Defining the Evaluation Problem. The definition of the specific evaluation problems we seek to tackle is important because different goals will give rise to different choices. In particular, it is important to know whether we will be comparing a new algorithm with one or several existing ones; whether this comparison will take place in one domain of interest or more; whether we are looking for specific properties of the algorithms we are testing or general ones; and so on. In the absence of such goal-oriented definitions, we may be able to generate results showing advantages or disadvantages of different methods, but it is unclear how these results relate to reality.

Exploratory pursuit versus Final Evaluation. The division between the two kinds of research is problematic. Although it is clear that they should be separated, some researchers (e.g., Drummond, 2006) recognize that they cannot be, and that, as a result, we should not even get into issues of statistical validation of our results and so on, because we are doing only exploratory research that does not demand such formal testing. This is a valid point of view, although we cannot help but hope that the results we obtain be more definitive than those advocated by this point of view.

Internal versus External Validity. As suggested by Forster (2000), when faced with the question of how a classifier will extrapolate to new data, the answer often is that there is no way to know this. Indeed, how can one predict the future without any glimpse of what that future looks like? Busemeyer and Wang (2000), however, believe that it is possible, through induction, to at least partly answer this question. In particular, they suggest a technique based on the following principle: Successful extrapolation in the past may be a useful indicator of future performance. Their idea is thus to find out whether there are situations in which past extrapolation is a useful indicator of future extrapolation and whether this empirical information can be exploited.

There also is a significant contribution made to this question by the research done in the field of statistical learning theory. Theoretical guarantees on the future performance of the learning algorithms in the form of upper (and lower) bounds on the generalization error of a classifier can be obtained. Some of these approaches have also met with considerable success, showing promise in furthering the objective of studying the generalization behavior of learning approaches. We study in detail these questions, concerns, and available solutions in their respective contexts later in the book.

1.5   What Can We Do?

There are inherent dangers associated with too stringent a criticism of our evaluation procedure that should not go unnoticed. As mentioned in (Witten and Frank, 2005b), philosophers have been debating for 2000 years the question of how to evaluate scientific theories. Some philosophers or statisticians remain very critical of the process because of the many assumptions it necessarily breaks due to the dearth of data, the complexity of its behavior, and the fact that its purpose is essentially to try to predict the future, which is, of course, unknown. Despite all the imperfections of the evaluation process, very impressive discoveries have been made over the years. This also applies to the our field of research and suggests that our criticisms of evaluation should remain balanced. Drummond and Japkowicz (2010) present a discussion of the two extreme views, which can be helpful in weighting the two sets of arguments.

That being said, we believe that we could (and should) improve on the current de facto evaluation method used in machine learning by applying some of the tools that were suggested in the past and that were just summarized. This could resolve the deadlock the machine learning community is currently in and steer it in a new, more exciting, and promising direction. Immediate steps in these direction can be summarized as follows:

Better Education. The purpose of better educating students interested in machine learning would be to sensitize them to the uncertainties associated with the evaluation procedure and give them the tools necessary to decrease this uncertainty. The education process could involve the inclusion of more material on evaluation in introductory course(s) on machine learning or, alternatively, the creation of an advanced course on machine learning devoted entirely to the topic of classifier evaluation. The purpose of this book is to provide a basis for such courses or self-study.

Better Division Between Exploratory Research and Evaluation. In the pharmaceutical industry, we observe that the researchers involved in drug design are not typically involved in drug testing. The tests are usually performed independently once the drug design process is completed. In other words, the drug designers do not keep on formally testing and tweaking their product until their results are acceptable. They conduct informal prototypical tests to guide their research, but leave the formal testing to other researchers better trained in statistical methods.

Machine learning researchers have a very distinct advantage over drug designers: Our experiments are fast, cheap, and do not cost lives. We thus have much more freedom when it comes to customizing our algorithms than they do when it comes to customizing their products. With this advantage, however, comes the disadvantage of believing that we can engage in formal testing by ourselves. This, we believe, is not necessarily correct. Any such testing will essentially be biased.

Based on these observations, it would be interesting to consider the division of our experimental process in three branches. The first is the exploratory research essentially emphasizing the *innovative* aspect that could be involved, at best, only in prototypical testing of these strategies. The second corresponds to the *evaluative* aspect of the research, focusing on efficiency and rigorously evaluating and comparing the various learning strategies. Finally, one branch of research could focus on the *evaluation design*, emphasizing the further study, innovation, refinement, and improvement of the evaluation approaches themselves.

Better Data Exchanges Between Applied Fields and Machine Learning. The view taken here is that we need to strongly encourage the collection of real datasets to test our algorithms. A weakness in our present approach that needs to be addressed is the reliance on old data. The old data have been used too frequently and for far too long; hence results based on these may be untrustworthy. The UCI repository was a very good innovation, but despite being a nonstatic collection with new datasets being collected over time, it does not grow at a fast-enough pace, nor does it discriminate among the different domains that are contributed. What the field lacks, mainly, are data focused on particular topics. It would be useful to investigate the possibility of a data-for-analysis exchange between practitioners in various fields and machine learning researchers.

Better Reliance on Artificial Data. Although there is unquestionable value in real data, this does not diminish the unique advantages that might be obtained from using artificial data to obtain insights into the behavior of the algorithms. Real data are good at informing us about different aspects of the world, some of which we may have overlooked. Artificial data, on the other hand, allow us to explore variabilities not found in the real data we have collected that yet can reasonably be expected in practice. Artificial data can also be designed in a controlled manner to study specific aspects of the performance of algorithms. Consequently such data may allow for tighter control, which gives rise to more carefully constructed and more enlightening experiments. Although, on the one hand, real data are hard to come by, on the other hand, artificial data present the danger of oversimplifying the problem. The debate between limited but real datasets versus artificial data is likely to continue. However, an argument can be made to utilize the two in tandem for better evaluation.

1.6   Is Evaluation an End in Itself?

Certainly not. Evaluation approaches should not be perceived as ends in themselves. Our ultimate goal is the pursuit of learning algorithms that can approach the behavior of the domains that they model. Evaluation methods should be a step further in the direction of developing an understanding of the approaches at hand, along with their strengths and limitations in the domain in which they are applied. On the front of developing generic theoretical advancements toward a learning paradigm, the evaluation studies should provide us with feedback on how the algorithmic theories should be refined or, possibly, how innovations should be made on them.

It is important to note that evaluation approaches are our currently best available tools that enable us to notice the anomalies in algorithmic behavior in addition to studying their positive characteristics. This is not to assert that the approaches in use now or suggested in this text are, or will be, even in the near future, the only means to study learning algorithms. It is entirely possible that these will be swept off by better-refined and more apt methods of studying our learning strategies. But the underlying philosophy would remain the same: There lies a need to stringently, meticulously, and objectively study the behavior of learning strategies, compare these with the competitive approaches, improve, refine, or replace them, and hence utilize them as best as possible in the contexts of concern. The goal of the evaluation exercise therefore should be to enable us to ask the right questions about the applicability of learning approaches and further know and understand their limitations, thus resulting in a positive feedback to improved algorithmic designs.

1.7 Purpose of the Book

The purpose of this book is to bring both researchers and practitioners to a level of sophistication in statistical analysis and choices of evaluation methods and metrics sufficient to conduct proper evaluation of algorithms. To date, aside from a small group of scholars, data mining practitioners as well as researchers have not been questioning the way they conduct the evaluation of their classifiers to the extent and with the rigor that this issue warrants. A relatively sophisticated methodology is simply adopted and applied to all cases indiscriminately. On the choice of performance measures, we have been a little more careful, noting that, in certain domains, accuracy has its drawbacks, and we move on to alternative measures. Yet a look at several recently published studies points to a number of important issues that should be put on the table when evaluating algorithms. Criticisms go as far as claiming that the improvements observed by our current evaluation methods are in fact much less impressive than they appear (Hand, 2006).

The purpose of this book is to bring the discussions that have taken place in the small subcommunity of statistically aware researchers to the forefront. Although we are not ready to answer the question of how best to evaluate classifiers, we believe that it is important to understand what issues are at hand and what choices and assumptions are implicitly being made by proceeding with evaluation the way we have chosen to. This will help us focus on real advances rather than tweaking the approaches that result, at best, in marginal improvements. We are not suggesting that we all become statistical experts, deriving new methodologies and mathematically proving their adequacies. Instead, we are proposing that we develop a level of understanding and awareness in these issues similar to those that exist in empirically stringent fields such as psychology or economics that can enable us to craft experiments and validate models more rigourously.

1.8 Other Takes on Evaluation

The view of evaluation presented in this book is not necessarily shared by everyone in the community. Two notable voices in apparent disagreement are those of Chris Drummond and Janez Demšar (see Drummond, 2006; Demšar, 2008; Drummond, 2008). Favoring a less-rigorous approach to evaluation, they argue that it is not the machine learning researcher's job to perform such strict evaluation. Rather, the researcher should follow an exploratory approach to machine learning and have recourse to only light methods of evaluation, mainly to guide the research. This comes from Drummond's and Demšar's belief that error estimation and statistical testing is often not meaningful as their results are typically wrongly interpreted or, even when not misinterpreted, either obvious or otherwise uninteresting. This position, by the way, is based on similar points of view that have appeared in other fields. Another fear Drummond and Demšar expressed is the fact that, by their stringency, formal statistical testing or rigid clockwise evaluation in general may disqualify perfectly interesting ideas that would be worthy of dissemination and further examination.

Although their argument does have merit, we still feel that a need for better education in evaluation methods for the members of the machine learning community and the structured application of well-thought-out evaluation methods are a necessary first step. This would enable researchers to make informed choices even when performing limited and relatively less-rigorous evaluation. The purpose of the book is to provide the information necessary to every researcher or practitioner in the field so as to enable and initiate a broader debate with a wider community-wide participation.

1.9 Moving Beyond Classification

The fields of machine learning and data mining encompass many other sub-disciplines beside classification. Furthermore, the data analysis community as a whole spans many academic fields such as business, psychology, medicine, library science, and so on, each with specific tasks related to machine learning, including forecasting and information retrieval. In this view, the focus of the book on classification algorithms may seem narrow. However, this is not the case. The main motivations behind using classification algorithms as a basis for discussing evaluation come in part because of their relative ease of evaluation and their wide use for various learning tasks and in part because of the ease of illustrating various concepts in their context. However, we wish to make the point that, despite its relative simplicity, the evaluation of classifiers is not an easy endeavor, as evidenced by the mere length of this book. Many techniques needed to be described and illustrated within the context of classification alone. Providing a comprehensive survey of evaluation techniques and methodologies, along with their corresponding issues, would have indeed been prohibitive.

Further, it is extremely important to note that the insights obtained from the discussion of various components of the evaluation framework over classification algorithms are not limited to this paradigm but readily generalize to a significantly wider extent. Indeed, although the performance metrics or measures differ from task to task (e.g., unsupervised learning is concerned about cluster tightness and between-cluster distance; association rule mining looks at the notions of support and confidence), error estimation and resampling, statistical testing and dataset selection can make use of the techniques that apply to classifier evaluation. This book should thus be useful for researchers and practitioners in any data analysis task because most of its material applies to the different learning paradigms they may consider. Because performance metrics are typically the best-known part of evaluation in every learning field, the book will remain quite useful even if it does not delve into this particular topic for the specific task considered.

1.10   Thematic Organization

The remainder of the book is divided into eight chapters: Chapter 2 gives a quick review of the elements of machine learning and statistics necessary to follow the discussions in the subsequent chapters. The following two chapters look at the issue of performance metrics. Chapter 3 presents a broad ontology of performance metrics and studies the ones based solely on the confusion matrix. Chapter 4 then advances the discussion, taking into account additional information such as costs, priors, and uncertainty along with the confusion matrix to design performance measures. Chapter 5 discusses various error-estimation methods, taking into account the issue of model selection in each setting. We then move on to the issue of statistical significance testing in Chapter 6 and discuss the inherent assumptions, constraints, and the general application settings of these tests. Chapter 7 focuses on the issues of dataset selection and the experimental frameworks, bringing into discussion issues such as community experiments as well as the criticisms and proposed solutions surrounding them. Chapter 8 gives a glimpse of some recent developments on various fronts that are directly relevant to classifier evaluation as well as some that have an indirect but nevertheless significant impact. The book concludes with Chapter 9, which presents a general evaluation framework providing a unified view of the various aspects of the classifier evaluation approach. All the methods discussed in the book are also illustrated using the R and WEKA packages, at the end of their respective chapters. In addition, the book includes three appendices. Appendix A contains all the statistical tables necessary to interpret the results of the statistical tests of Chapters 5 and 6. Appendix B lists details on some of the data we used to illustrate our discussions, and, finally, Appendix C illustrates the framework of Chapter 9 with two case studies.

2

Machine Learning and Statistics Overview

This chapter is aimed at establishing the conceptual foundation of the relevant aspects of machine learning and statistics on which the book rests. This very brief overview is in no way exhaustive. Rather, our main aim is to elucidate the relationship of these concepts to the performance evaluation of learning algorithms. The chapter is composed of two parts. The first part discusses concepts most specific to machine learning; the second part focuses on the statistical elements. Even though these may seem like two disparate parts, they are not entirely independent. We try to highlight the relationship between the concepts discussed in one field to the problems at hand in the other. Let us start with a brief discussion of the important concepts of machine learning.

2.1 Machine Learning Overview

Learning is the human process that allows us to acquire the skills necessary to adapt to the multitude of situations that we encounter throughout our lives. As human beings, we rely on many different kinds of learning processes at different stages to acquire different functionalities. We learn a variety of different skills, e.g., motor, verbal, mathematical, and so on. Moreover, the learning process differs with the situations and time, e.g., learning how to speak as a toddler is different from learning similar skill sets in a given profession. Variations in learning are also visible in terms of contexts and the related tools, e.g., classroom learning differs from social contexts, rote learning may be more suitable for memorizing but differs from learning how to reason.

Machine learning aims at analogizing this learning process for computers. Efforts to automate learning have largely focused on perfecting the process of *inductive inference*. Inductive inference, basically refers to observing a phenomenon and generalizing it. Essentially, this is done by characterizing the observed phenomenon and then using this model to make predictions over future phenomena. In this book, we focus on a very useful, although much more specific, aspect of inductive inference: *classification*.

2.1.1 The Learning Problem

The general model of learning can be described using the following three components:

1. An instance space $\mathcal{X}$ from which random vectors $\mathbf{x} \in \mathbb{R}^n$ can be drawn independently according to some fixed but unknown distribution.
2. A label $y \in \mathcal{Y}$ for every vector $\mathbf{x}$ according to some fixed but unknown conditional distribution. In the more general setting, y need not be scalar but can annotate the example $\mathbf{x}$ with a set of values in the form of a vector $\mathbf{y}$.
3. A learning algorithm A that can implement a set of functions f from some function class $\mathcal{F}$ over the instance space.

Given our three components, the problem of learning is that of choosing the best classifier from the given set of functions that can most closely approximate the labels of the vectors. This classifier is generally selected based on a training set S of m training examples drawn according to $\mathcal{X}$ with their respective labels. Each tuple of a vector $\mathbf{x}$ and its label y can be represented by $\mathbf{z} = (\mathbf{x}, y)$ which can be assumed to be drawn independently from a joint distribution D.

The space of classifiers or functions $\mathcal{F}$ is referred to as the *hypothesis space* or *classifier space*. However, we reserve the term hypothesis for its more conventional usage in statistical significance testing and use the term classifier space from here onward when referring to the space of functions explored by a learning algorithm. Each training example $\mathbf{x}$ is basically an instantiation of a random vector in $\mathcal{X}$, and hence we also refer to these as instances.

Different configurations of the preceding setting yield different learning problems. When the learning algorithm has access to the labels y for each example $\mathbf{x}$ in the training set, the learning is referred to as *supervised learning*; the term *unsupervised learning* is used otherwise. The availability of the labels for input examples also dictates the goals of these two learning methods. The first aims to obtain a model that can provide an output based on the observed inputs (e.g., to provide a diagnosis based on a set of symptoms). The latter, on the other hand, tries to model the inputs themselves. This can be thought of as grouping together (or clustering) instances that are similar to each other, e.g., patients with similar sets of symptoms.

Please note that the preceding formulation for learning, although quite general, is constrained by the type of information that the learning algorithm A can get. That is, we consider this information in terms of training examples that are vectors in the n-dimensional Euclidean space. Providing information in terms of examples is arguably the most widely practiced methodology. However, other approaches exist, such as providing learning information via relations, constraints, functions, and even models. Moreover, there have recently been attempts to learn from examples with and without labels together, an approach largely known as semisupervised learning.

In addition, the mode of providing the learning information also plays an important role that gives rise to two main models of learning: *active learning* (a learner can interact with the environment and affect the data-generation process) and *passive learning* (in which the algorithm is given a fixed set of examples as a way of observing its environment, but lacks the ability to interact with it). It should be noted that active learning is different from online learning in which a master algorithm uses the prediction of competing hypotheses to predict the label of a new example and then learns from its actual label. In this book, the focus is on passive learning algorithms; more specifically, classification algorithms in this paradigm. We illustrate the classification problem with an example. We further characterize this problem concretely a bit later.

A Classification Example

The aim of classification algorithm A is to obtain a mapping from examples $\mathbf{x}$ to their respective labels y in the form of a classifier f that can also predict the labels for future unseen examples. When y takes on only two values as labels, the problem is referred to as a binary classification problem. Although restricting our discussions to this problem makes it easier to explain various evaluation concepts, in addition to the fact that these algorithms are those that are the most familiar to the researchers, enabling them to put the discussion in perspective, this choice in no way limits the broader understanding of the message of the book in more general contexts. Needless to say, many of the proposed approaches extend to the multiclass case as well as to other learning scenarios such as regression, and our focus on binary algorithms in no way undermines the importance and contribution of these paradigms in our ability to learn from data.

Consider the following toy example of concept learning aimed at providing a flu diagnosis of patients with given symptoms. Assume that we are given the database of Table 2.1 of imaginary patients. The aim of the learning algorithm here is to find a function that is consistent with the preceding database and can then also be used to provide a flu or no-flu diagnosis on future patients based on their symptoms. Note that by consistent we mean that the function should agree with the diagnosis, given the symptoms in the database provided. As we will see later, this constraint generally needs to be relaxed to avoid overspecializing the function that, even though agrees on the diagnosis of every patient in the database, might not be as effective in diagnosing future unseen patients.

From the preceding data, the program could infer that *anyone with a body temperature above 38 °C and sinus pain has the flu*. Such a formula can then be

Table 2.1. *Table of imaginary patients*

Patient	Temperature (°C)	Cough	Sore throat	Sinus pain	Diagnosis
1	37	Yes	No	No	No-flu
2	39	No	Yes	Yes	Flu
3	38.8	No	No	No	No-flu
4	36.8	No	Yes	No	No-flu
5	38.5	Yes	No	Yes	Flu
6	39.2	No	No	Yes	Flu

applied to any new patient whose symptoms are described according to the same four parameters used to describe the patients from the database (i.e., temperature, cough, sore throat, and sinus pain) and a diagnosis issued.[1]

Several observations are worth making at this point from this example: First, many formulas could be inferred from the given database. For example, the machine learning algorithm could have learned that *anyone with a body temperature of 38.5 °C or more and cough, a sore throat, or sinus pain has the flu* or it could have learned that *anyone with sinus pain has the flu.*

Second, as suggested by our example, there is no guarantee that any of the formulas inferred by the machine learning algorithm is correct. Because the formulas are inferred from the data, they can be as good as the data (in the best case), but not better. If the data are misleading, the result of the learning system will be too.

Third, what learning algorithms do is different from what a human being would do. A real (human) doctor would start with a theoretical basis (a kind of rule of thumb) learned from medical school that he or she would then refine based on his or her subsequent observations. He or she would not, thankfully, acquire all his or her knowledge based on only a very limited set of observations.

In terms of the components of learning described in the preceding formulation, we can look at this illustration as follows. The first component corresponds to the set of all the potential patients that could be represented by the four parameters that we listed (temperature, cough, sore throat, and sinus pain). The example database we use lists only six patients with varying symptoms, but many more could have been (and typically are) presented.

The second component, in our example, refers to the diagnosis, flu and no-flu, associated with the symptoms of each patient. A classification learning algorithm's task is to find a way to infer the diagnosis from the data. Naturally, this can be done in various ways.

The third component corresponds to this choice of the classification learning algorithm. Different algorithms tend to learn under different learning paradigms to obtain an optimal classifier and have their own respective learning biases.

---

[1] In fact, choosing such a formula would obviate the need to measure symptoms other than temperature and sinus pain.

Before we look at different learning strategies, let us define some necessary notions.

2.1.2 The Loss Function and the Notion of Risk

The choice of the best classifier is often based on the measure of *risk*, which is nothing but the degree of disagreement between the true label y of a vector $\mathbf{x}$ and the one assigned by the classifier $f : \mathcal{X} \to \mathcal{Y}$ that we denote by $f(\mathbf{x})$. Before defining the *risk* of a classifier, let us define the *loss function*. A loss function is a quantitative measure of the loss when the label y of the vector $\mathbf{x}$ is different from the label assigned by the classifier. We denote the generic loss function by $L(y, f(\mathbf{x}))$ that outputs the loss incurred when y differs from $f(\mathbf{x})$. We can now define "the *risk* or *expected risk* of the classifier f" as

$$R(f) = \int L(y, f(\mathbf{x}))\, dD(\mathbf{x}, y), \tag{2.1}$$

where the probability measure $D(\mathbf{z}) = D(\mathbf{x}, y)$ is unknown. This risk is often referred to as the *true risk* of the classifier f. For the zero–one loss, i.e., $L(y, f(\mathbf{x})) = 1$ when $y \neq f(\mathbf{x})$ and 0 otherwise, we can write the *expected risk* as

$$R(f) \stackrel{\text{def}}{=} \Pr_{(\mathbf{x}, y) \sim D} (y \neq f(\mathbf{x})) \tag{2.2}$$

Note that the classifier f in question is defined given a training set. This makes the loss function a training-set-dependent quantity. This fact can have important implications in studying the behavior of a learning algorithm as well as in making inferences on the true risk of the classifier. We will see this in some more concrete terms in Subsection 2.1.7.

Empirical Risk

It is generally not possible to estimate the true or expected risk of the classifier without the knowledge of the true underlying distribution of the data and possibly their labels. As a result, the expected risk takes the form of a measurable quantity known as the empirical risk. Hence the learner often computes the *empirical risk* $R_S(f)$ of any given classifier $f = A(S)$ induced by the algorithm A on a training set S of size m according to

$$R_S(f) \stackrel{\text{def}}{=} \frac{1}{m} \sum_{i=1}^{m} L(y_i, f(\mathbf{x}_i)), \tag{2.3}$$

which is the risk of the classifier with respect to the training data. Here, $L(y, f(\mathbf{x}))$ is the specific loss function that outputs the loss of mislabeling an example. Note that this function can be a binary function (outputting only 1 or 0) or a continuous function, depending on the class of problems.

Illustration of the Notion of Empirical Risk

In the example of Subsection 2.1.1, let us assume that the classifier f was *anyone with a cough or a sore throat has the flu*. Such a classifier would guess that patients 1, 2, 4, and 5 in Table 2.1 have the flu, whereas patients 3 and 6 do not have the flu. However, our data show that patients 2, 5, and 6 have the flu, whereas patients 1, 3, and 4 do not. In the case in which each class is given the same importance (i.e., diagnosing a flu patient as a no-flu patient is as detrimental as diagnosing a no-flu patient with the flu), we will have $L(y_i, f(\mathbf{x}_i)) = 1$ and $L(y_j, f(\mathbf{x}_j)) = 0$ for $i = \{1, 4, 6\}$ and $j = \{2, 3, 5\}$, respectively. We cannot measure the true risk in the absence of the true underlying distribution. The empirical risk, aimed at approximating this for the chosen classifier, would then be $R_S(f) = 1/6 \times 3 = 0.5$. Interestingly, this risk estimate basically represents the probability of the classifier's being wrong to be the same as a coin toss, which would be the same as choosing a classifier that generates the labels randomly with a probability of 0.5 for each class.

2.1.3 Generalization Error

The *generalization error* is a measure of the deviation of the expected risk of the classifier $f = A(S)$ learned from the overall minimum expected risk. Hence the generalization error of algorithm A over a sample S is

$$R(A, S) \overset{\text{def}}{=} R(f) - \inf_{f' \in \mathcal{F}} R(f'),$$

where inf denotes the infimum.[2]

In other words, it is understood that the data on which the classifier is trained, although representative of the true distribution, may not lead the algorithm to learn the classifier f' with minimum possible risk. This can be mainly due to two reasons. First, there might not be enough data for the algorithm to make an inference on the full underlying distribution. And second, the limited data that are available can further be affected by noise occurring from various sources, such as errors in measurement of various values, data entry, or even label assignment. As a result, the best classifier output by the algorithm given the training data is generally not the best overall classifier possible. The additional risk that the classifier f output by the algorithm has over and above that of the best classifier in the classifier space f' is referred to as the generalization error. Note that the classifier f can have a zero training error and still might not be the best possible classifier because the true risk of f would still be greater than that of f'.

Hence a learning algorithm basically aims at minimizing this generalization error. Given a training set $S = (\mathbf{z}_1, \ldots, \mathbf{z}_m)$ of m examples, the task of a learning algorithm is to construct a classifier with the smallest possible risk without any

---

[2] Infimum indicates the function f' that minimizes $R(f')$ but f' need not be unique.

information about D, the underlying distribution. However, computing the true risk of a classifier as just given can be quite difficult. In our toy domain, for example, it is possible that the true formula for the flu concept is *anyone with a sore throat or sinus pain and a body temperature above 37.5°C has the flu.* Of course, this formula could not necessarily be inferred from the given data set, and thus the classifier output by the algorithm based on the training data would not perform as the desired ideal classifier because some instances of patients with the flu, in the true population, necessarily include patients with high body temperatures and sore throats only.

Obtaining a classifier with minimum generalization error from the training data is a difficult task. There are some results in learning theory that, for a given formulation of the learning algorithm, can demonstrate that this can be achieved by minimizing the empirical risk, and, in some cases, additional quantities calculated from the data. For instance, the uniform risk bounds tie the minimization of generalization error to studying the convergence of empirical risk to the true risk uniformly over all classifiers for the class of empirical risk minimization algorithms discussed in the next subsection.

2.1.4 Learning Algorithms

The issue of modeling the data (or its label-generation process) by choosing the best classifier that not only describes the observed data but can also generalize well is the core of the learning process. To explore the classifier space and choose the best possible classifier given some training data, various learning approaches have been designed. These vary in both the classifier space that they explore and the manner in which they select the most suitable classifier from a given classifier space with respect to the training data. This latter optimization problem is the problem of *model selection.* This optimization is generally based on finding the minimum empirical risk on the training data or the best trade-off of the empirical risk and the complexity of the classifier chosen. The model selection criterion of a learning algorithm is an essential part of the algorithm design. There are three main categories into which most of the learning algorithms can be categorized with regard to the model selection criterion that they utilize. These are the algorithms that learn by empirical risk minimization (ERM), structural risk minimization (SRM), and regularization. These approaches, by themselves, have been proven to be quite effective and have also paved the way for other approaches that exploit these to yield better ones. Note, however, that, unlike the SRM, the ERM approaches focus on one classifier space and hence are relatively restrictive. Let us briefly look at these categories individually.

Empirical Risk Minimization (ERM)

The class of learning algorithms that learn by ERM makes the most direct use of the notion of risk as their optimization criterion to select the best classifier from the classifier space being explored. Given some training set S, the ERM algorithm A_{erm} basically outputs the classifier that minimizes the empirical risk on the training set. That is,

$$A_{\text{erm}}(S) = f' \stackrel{\text{def}}{=} \operatorname*{argmin}_{f \in \mathcal{F}} R_S(f).$$

Structural Risk Minimization (SRM)

This class of learning algorithms goes beyond the use of merely the empirical risk as the optimization criterion. The underlying intuition here is that more complex classifiers generalize poorly (possibly because of overfitting). Hence the idea is to discover classifiers that not only have acceptable empirical risk but are also not unreasonably complex. By definition the class of SRM algorithms explores classifier spaces of increasing complexities and might not be restricted to one classifier space as we mentioned earlier. However, it should be noted that these classifier spaces of increasing complexity nevertheless belong to the same class. For instance, a learning algorithm that learns linear classifiers will learn only linear classifiers of increasing complexity (sometimes imposed implicitly using kernels, for instance, in the case of a SVM) but not other classes such as decision trees.

An SRM algorithm aims at selecting a classifier (or model) with the least complexity (also referred to as *size* or *capacity*) that achieves a small empirical risk. For this, $\mathcal{F}$ is represented by a sequence of classifier spaces of increasing sizes $\{\mathcal{F}_d : d = 1, 2 \ldots\}$ and the SRM algorithm A_{srm} is such that:

$$A_{\text{srm}}(S) = f' \stackrel{\text{def}}{=} \operatorname*{argmin}_{f \in \mathcal{F}_d, d \in \mathbb{N}} \left[R_S(f) + p(d, |S|) \right],$$

where $p(d, |S|)$ is a function that penalizes the algorithm for classifier spaces of increasing complexity.

Let cm be some complexity measure on classifier space. We would have a set of classifier spaces $\mathcal{F} = \{\mathcal{F}_1, \ldots, \mathcal{F}_k\}$ such that the complexity of classifier space $\mathcal{F}_i$ denoted as $cm_{\mathcal{F}_i}$ is greater than or equal to $cm_{\mathcal{F}_{i-1}}$. Then the SRM algorithm would be to compute a set of classifiers minimizing the empirical risk over the classifier spaces $\mathcal{F} = \{\mathcal{F}_1, \ldots, \mathcal{F}_k\}$ and then to select the classifier space that gives the best trade-off between its complexity and the minimum empirical risk obtained over it on the training data.

Regularization

There are other approaches that extend the preceding algorithms, such as regularization, in which one tries to minimize the regularized empirical risk. This is done by defining a *regularizing term* or a *regularizer* (typically a norm on the classifier $||f||$) over the classifier space $\mathcal{F}$ such that the algorithm outputs a classifier f':

$$f' = \underset{f \in \mathcal{F}}{\text{argmin}} \ R_S(f) + \lambda ||f||^2.$$

The regularization in this case can also be seen in terms of the complexity of the classifier. Hence a regularized risk criterion restricts the classifier space complexity. Here it is done by restricting the norm of the classifier. Other variants of this approach also exist such as normalized regularization. The details on these and other approaches can be found in (Hastie et al., 2001), (Herbrich, 2002), and (Bousquet et al., 2004b), among others.

Learning Bias and Algorithm Formulation

Many early learning algorithms and even some novel ones have adopted the ERM principle. Among them are approaches such as decision tree learning, naive Bayes, and set covering machine (SCM; Marchand and Shawe-Taylor, 2002; Shah, 2006). However, further modifications and refinements of algorithms exploring the same classifier space have also since appeared that incorporate other considerations accounted for by the SRM and regularization frameworks. That is, the underlying learning bias that an algorithm explores need not depend on the principle that it utilizes to learn. A linear discriminant function, for instance, can work purely in an ERM manner if it does not take into account any constraints on the weight vector that it learns (e.g., the norm of this vector) and focuses solely on the empirical risk on the training data. Early perceptron learning algorithms are an example of such an approach. However, learning linear discriminants can also take on the form of support vector machines (SVMs) in the SRM framework. Even on top of these, there have been regularized versions of linear discriminants available that take into account some regularization of the classifier space. For instance, some attempts have been made to incorporate such regularization in the case of SVM to obtain sparse classifiers (SVMs with a small number of support vectors). Hence it might not be a good idea to tie particular learning biases to learning strategies in definitive form. A learning bias such as a linear discriminant or decision trees can be learned by use of more than one strategy.

2.1.5 The Classification Problem

Let us now concretely characterize the binary classification problem that we illustrated in Subsection 2.1.1. Although we focus on the binary classification algorithms, the general techniques of evaluation discussed have much wider significance and implications. In a binary classification problem the label y corresponding to each example $\mathbf{x}$ is binary, i.e., $y \in \{0, 1\}$. Hence the aim of a

binary classification algorithm is to identify a classifier that maps the examples
to either of the two classes. That is, $f : \mathcal{X} \longrightarrow \{0, 1\}$. The risk of misclassifying
each example by assigning a wrong class label is typically modeled as a zero–
one loss. That is, the classifier incurs a loss of 0 whenever the output of the
classifier matches the true label y of the instance vector $\mathbf{x}$ and 1 otherwise (i.e.,
when the classifier makes an error).

Hence the classification problem is to minimize the probability of the misclassification error over the set S of training examples while making a promising
case of good generalization. The true error in the case of a zero–one loss can be
represented as shown in Equation (2.4):

$$R(f) \overset{\text{def}}{=} \Pr_{(\mathbf{x}, y) \sim D} (y \neq f(\mathbf{x})) = \mathbf{E}_{(\mathbf{x}, y) \sim D} I(y \neq f(\mathbf{x})), \qquad (2.4)$$

where the indicator function $I(a)$ represents the zero–one loss such that $I(a) = 1$
if predicate a is true and 0 otherwise.

Similarly, the empirical risk $R_S(f)$ can be shown to be

$$R_S(f) \overset{\text{def}}{=} \frac{1}{m} \sum_{i=1}^{m} I(y_i \neq f(\mathbf{x}_i)) \overset{\text{def}}{=} \mathbf{E}_{(\mathbf{x}, y) \sim S} I(y \neq f(\mathbf{x})). \qquad (2.5)$$

Note that the loss function $L(\cdot, \cdot)$ in Equation (2.3) is replaced with the
indicator function in the case of Equation (2.5) for the classification problem.

Given this definition of *risk*, the aim of the classification algorithm is to find a
classifier f given the training data, such that, the risk of f is as close as possible
to that of the optimal classifier $f' \in \mathcal{F}$ (minimizing the generalization error).
This problem of selecting the best classifier from the classifier space given the
training data is sometimes also referred to as *model selection*.

Recall our toy example from Subsection 2.1.1. A classifier based on the
criterion *anyone with a cough or a sore throat and a temperature at or above
38.5 °C has the flu* would have an empirical risk of $1/6$, whereas another based
on the criterion *anyone with a cough or a sore throat has the flu* would have
an empirical risk of $1/2$ on the data of Table 2.1. Hence, given the two criteria,
ERM learning algorithms would select the former. How does model selection,
i.e., choice of a classifier based on the training data, affect the performance of
the classifier on future unseen data (also referred to as classifier's generalization
performance)? This can be intuitively seen easily in the case of the regression
problem, as follows.

2.1.6 The Challenges of Learning

There are always certain trade-offs involved in selecting the best classifier. Let us
take a look at the issues involved from a model-fitting perspective also known as
the problem of *regression*. A model f that fits the data too closely might lead to
overfitting. Overfitting refers to the problem of making a solution (function) too

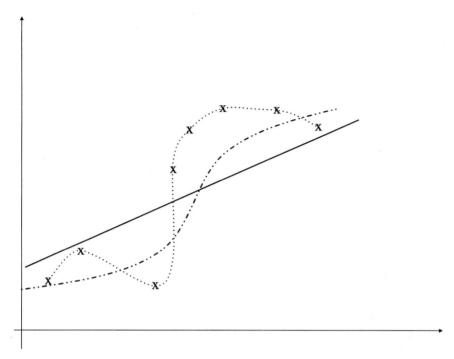

Figure 2.1. A simple example of overfitting and underfitting problems. Consider the problem of fitting a function to a set of data points in a two-dimensional plane, known as the *regression problem*. Fitting a curve passing through every data point leads to overfitting. On the other hand, the other extreme, approximation by a line, might be a misleading approximation and underfits if the data are sparse. The issue of overfitting is generally addressed by use of approaches such as pruning or boosting. Approaches such as *regularization* and Bayesian formulations have also shown promise in tackling this problem. In the case of sparse datasets, we use some kind of smoothing or back-off strategy. A solution in between the two extremes, e.g., the dash-dotted curve, might be desirable.

specific to generalize well in the future. Such a solution is hence not generally preferred. Similar is the problem in which f underfits the data, that is, f is too general. See Figure 2.1 for an example.

In our previous example, it is possible that the formula *anyone with a cough or a sore throat and a temperature at or above 38.5 °C has the flu* overfits the data in that it closely represents the training set, but may not be representative of the overall distribution. On the other hand, the formula *anyone with a cough or a sore throat has the flu* underfits the data because it is not specific enough and, again, not representative of the true distribution.

Generally speaking, we *do not* focus on the problem of model selection when we refer to comparison or evaluation of classifiers in this book. We assume that the learning algorithm A has access to some method that is believed to enable it to choose the best classifier f from $\mathcal{F}$ based on the training sample S. The method on which A relies is what is called the *learning bias* of an algorithm.

This is the preferential criterion used by the learning algorithm to choose one classifier over others from *one* classifier space. For instance, an ERM algorithm would select a classifier $f \in \mathcal{F}$ if it outputs an empirical risk that is lower than any other classifier in $\mathcal{F}$ *given* a specific training sample S. Even though our primary focus in this book is on evaluation, we explore some concepts that also have implications in the model selection.

Finally, in the case of most of the algorithms, the classifier (or a subspace of the classifier space) is defined in terms of the user-tunable parameters. Hence the problem of model selection in this case also extends to finding the best values for the user-tunable parameters. This problem is sometimes referred to separately as that of *parameter estimation*. However, this is, in our opinion, a part of the model selection problem because these parameters are either used to characterize or constrain the classifier class (e.g., as in the case of regularization) or are part of the model selection criterion (e.g., penalty on the misclassification). We use the terms model selection and parameter estimation interchangeably.

Generalization and Specialization

Let us go back to the example of Figure 2.1. Adopting a model, such as the preceding straight line, leads to a model that describes the data through their common behavior and does not focus on explaining individual or clusters of data points. This is a more general model. On the other hand, the dotted curve, for instance, aims at describing each and every data point. That is, it yields a highly specialized model. The more general the model, the higher the chances that it can underfit. That is, it can lead to too general a description of the data. The more specialized the model, the higher the chances that it can overfit. This is because it aims at explaining each individual data point, leading to poor generalization. A successful learning strategy would aim at finding a solution that lies somewhere between the two, trading off some specialization so as to obtain better generalization. We look into another intuitive take on this in the next subsection on bias and variance analysis.

2.1.7 Bias–Variance Trade-Off

The bias–variance analysis of the classifier risk has become a major source for understanding the behavior of learning algorithms. There have been various attempts at characterizing the bias–variance behavior of a classifier's risk given a fixed loss function. Even though the underlying principle relies on the idea that a nontrivial trade-off between the bias and the variance behavior of a loss function (and hence classifier risk) is desirable so as to obtain classifiers with better generalization performance, a unified framework that can bring together a formulation for understanding such behavior over a variety of loss functions is not yet available. One of the commendable attempts in proposing such a framework that incorporates prominent loss functions is due to Domingos (2000), which we follow here.

Bias–Variance Decomposition

In this subsection, we describe the notion of bias and variance of arbitrary loss functions along the lines of Domingos (2000). More precisely, given an arbitrary loss function, we are concerned with its bias–variance decomposition. As we will see, studying the bias–variance decomposition of a loss function gives important insights into both the behavior of the learning algorithm and the model selection dilemma. Moreover, as we will see in later chapters, this analysis also has implications for the evaluation because the error-estimation methods (e.g., resampling) can have significant effects on the bias–variance behavior of the loss function, and hence different estimations can lead to widely varying estimates of the empirical risk of the classifier.

We described the notion of the loss function in Subsection 2.1.2. Let L be an arbitrary loss function that gives an estimate of the loss that a classifier incurs as a result of disagreement between the assigned label $f(\mathbf{x})$ and the true label y of an example $\mathbf{x}$. Then we define the notion of *main prediction* of the classifier as follows.

Definition 2.1. *Given an arbitrary loss function L and a collection of training sets* **S**, *the* main prediction *is the one that minimizes the expectation* **E** *of this loss function over the training sets* **S** *(denoted as* $\mathbf{E_S}$*). That is,*

$$\overline{y} = \underset{y'}{\operatorname{argmin}}\ \mathbf{E_S}[L(y', f(\mathbf{x}))].$$

That is, the main prediction of a classifier is the one that minimizes the expected loss of the classifier on training sets **S**. In the binary classification scenario, this will be the most frequently predicted label over the examples in the training sets $S \in \mathbf{S}$. That is, the main prediction characterizes the label predicted by the classifier that minimizes the average loss relative to the true labels over all the training sets. Hence this can be seen as the most likely prediction of the algorithm A given training sets **S**.

Note here the importance of a collection of training sets **S**, recalling the observation that we previously made in Subsection 2.1.2 on the nature of the loss function. The fact that a classifier is defined given a training set establishes a dependency of the loss function behavior on a specific training set. Averaging over a number of training sets can alleviate this problem to a significant extent. The size of the training set has an effect on the loss function behavior too. Consequently, what we are interested in is averaging the loss function estimate over several training sets of the same size. However, such an averaging is easier said than done. In practice, we generally do not have access to large amounts of data that can enable us to have several training sets. A solution to this problem can come in the form of data resampling. We explore some of the prominent techniques of data resampling in Chapter 5 and also study the related issues.

Let us next define the optimal label $y^\dagger$ of an example $\mathbf{x}$ such that $y^\dagger = \operatorname*{argmin}_{y'} \mathbf{E}_y[L(y, y')]$. That is, if an example $\mathbf{x}$ is sampled repeatedly then the associated label y need not be the same because y is also sampled from a conditional distribution[3] $\mathcal{Y}|\mathcal{X}$. The optimal prediction $y^\dagger$ denotes the label that is closest to the sampled labels over these repeated samplings. This essentially suggests that, because there is a nondeterministic association between the examples and their respective labels (in an ideal world this should not be the case), the sampled examples are essentially noisy, with their noise given by the difference between the optimal label and the sampled label.

Definition 2.2. *The noise of an example* $\mathbf{x}$ *is defined as*

$$N(\mathbf{x}) = \mathbf{E}_y[L(y, y^\dagger)].$$

Hence the noise of the example can basically be seen as a measure of misleading labels. The more noisy an example is, the higher the divergence, as measured by the loss function, of its label from the optimal label.

An optimal model would hence be the one that has $f(\mathbf{x}) = y^\dagger$ for all $\mathbf{x}$. This is nothing but the Bayes classifier in the case of classification with zero–one loss function. The associated risk is called the Bayes risk.

We can now define the bias of a learning algorithm A.

Definition 2.3. *Given a classifier* f, *for any example* $\mathbf{z} = (\mathbf{x}, y)$, *let* $y^\dagger$ *be the optimal label of* $\mathbf{x}$; *then the bias of an algorithm* A *is defined as*

$$B_A(\mathbf{x}) = L(y^\dagger, \overline{y}).$$

The average bias consequentally is

$$\overline{B}_A = \mathbf{E}_\mathbf{x}[B_A(\mathbf{x})].$$

The bias of algorithm A can hence be seen as a measure of the overall behavior of the algorithm, dependent of course on the chosen loss function, on example $\mathbf{x}$. That is, this gives a quantification over the difference between the average prediction of the algorithm and the optimal label of the example $\mathbf{x}$. This is basically a measure of the systematic loss of algorithm A and is independent of the training set. If an algorithm can always predict the optimal label, then the bias reduces to zero. Hence, in the classification case, the expected bias of an algorithm can be seen as the difference in the most frequent prediction of the algorithm and the optimal label of the examples.

---

[3] Recall that the examples and the respective labels are sampled from a joint distribution $\mathcal{X} \times \mathcal{Y}$.

Accordingly, we can also define the variance of an algorithm:

Definition 2.4. *The variance of an algorithm A on an example* **x** *is defined as*

$$V_A(\mathbf{x}) = \mathbf{E_S}[L(\overline{y}, f(\mathbf{x}))],$$

and hence the average variance is denoted as

$$\overline{V}_A = \mathbf{E_x}[V_A(\mathbf{x})].$$

Unlike the bias of the algorithm, the variance is not independent of the training set, even though it is independent of the true label of each **x**. The variance of the algorithm can be seen as a measure of the stability, or lack thereof, of the algorithm from the average prediction in response to the variation in the training sets. Hence, when averaged, this variance gives an estimate of how much the algorithm diverges from its most probable estimate (the average prediction). Finally, the bias and variance are nonnegative if the loss function is nonnegative.

With the preceding definitions in place, we can decompose an arbitrary loss function into its bias and variance components as follows.

We have an example **x** with true label y and a learning algorithm predicting $f(\mathbf{x})$ given a training set $S \in \mathbf{S}$. Then, for an arbitrary loss function L, the expected loss over the training sets **S** and the true label y can be decomposed as

$$\mathbf{E_{S,y}}[L(y, f(\mathbf{x}))] = \lambda_1 N(\mathbf{x}) + B_A(\mathbf{x}) + \lambda_2 V_A(\mathbf{x}),$$

where λ_1 and λ_2 are loss-function-based factors and the other quantities are as previously defined.

Let us now look at the application of this decomposition on two specific loss functions in the context of regression and classification respectively. We start with the regression case where the loss function of choice is the squared loss. The squared loss is defined as

$$L_{\text{sqr}}(y, f(\mathbf{x})) = (y - f(\mathbf{x}))^2,$$

with both y and $f(\mathbf{x})$ being real valued. It can be shown that, for squared loss, $y^\dagger = \mathbf{E_y}[y]$ and $\overline{y} = \mathbf{E_S}[f(\mathbf{x})]$ and further that $\lambda_1 = \lambda_2 = 1$.

Hence, in the case of squared loss, the following decomposition holds, with $\lambda_1 = \lambda_2 = 1$:

$$
\begin{aligned}
\mathbf{E_{S,y}}[(y - f(\mathbf{x}))^2] &= N(\mathbf{x}) + B_A(\mathbf{x}) + V_A(\mathbf{x}) \\
&= \mathbf{E_y}[L(y, y^\dagger)] + L(y^\dagger, \overline{y}) + \mathbf{E_S}[L(\overline{y}, f(\mathbf{x}))] \\
&= \mathbf{E_y}[(y - \mathbf{E_y}[y])^2] + (\mathbf{E_y}[y] - \mathbf{E_S}[f(\mathbf{x})])^2 \\
&\quad + \mathbf{E_S}[(\mathbf{E_S}[f(\mathbf{x})] - f(\mathbf{x}))^2].
\end{aligned}
$$

Coming to the focus of the book, the binary classification scenario, we can define the bias–variance decomposition for both the asymmetric loss (unequal loss in misclassifying an instance of class 0 to class 1 and vice versa) and symmetric loss (equal loss of misclassification of both classes) scenarios, as follows:

Theorem 2.1. *Given any real-valued asymmetric loss function L such that for labels y_1 and y_2, $L(y_1, y_2) \neq 0$, $\forall y_1 \neq y_2$, then, for a two-class classification algorithm A giving a classifier f,*

$$\mathbf{E}_{\mathbf{S},y}[L(y, f(\mathbf{x}))] = \left[\Pr_{\mathbf{S}}(f(\mathbf{x}) = y^{\dagger}) - \frac{L(y^{\dagger}, f(\mathbf{x}))}{L(f(\mathbf{x}), y^{\dagger})}\Pr_{\mathbf{S}}(y \neq y^{\dagger})\right] \cdot N(\mathbf{x})$$
$$+ B_A(\mathbf{x}) + \lambda_2 V_A(\mathbf{x}), \tag{2.6}$$

with $\lambda_2 = 1$ if $\overline{y} = y^{\dagger}$ and $\lambda_2 = -\frac{L(y^{\dagger}, \overline{y})}{L(\overline{y}, y^{\dagger})}$ if $\overline{y} \neq y^{\dagger}$.
Moreover, for a symmetric loss function we have

$$\mathbf{E}_{\mathbf{S},y}[L(y, f(\mathbf{x}))] = [2 \cdot \Pr_{\mathbf{S}}(f(\mathbf{x}) = y^{\dagger}) - 1] \cdot N(\mathbf{x}) + B_A(\mathbf{x}) + \lambda_2 V_A(\mathbf{x}),$$

with $\lambda_2 = 1$ if $L(\overline{y}, y^{\dagger}) = 0$ and $\lambda_2 = -1$ if $L(\overline{y}, y^{\dagger}) = 1$; where $\Pr$ denotes the probability.

In the more general multiclass case, we can obtain a bias–variance decomposition for zero–one loss as follows.

Theorem 2.2. *For a zero–one loss function (that is, the indicator loss function) in the multiclass classification scenario, the bias–variance decomposition can be shown to be*

$$\mathbf{E}_{\mathbf{S},y}[L(y, f(\mathbf{x}))] = \left[\Pr_{\mathbf{S}}(f(\mathbf{x}) = y^{\dagger}) - \Pr_{\mathbf{S}}(f(\mathbf{x}) \neq y^{\dagger})\right.$$
$$\left. \times \Pr_y(f(\mathbf{x}) = y|y^{\dagger} \neq y)\right] \cdot N(\mathbf{x})$$
$$+ B_A(\mathbf{x}) + \lambda_2 V_A(\mathbf{x}), \tag{2.7}$$

with $\lambda_2 = 1$ if $\overline{y} = y^{\dagger}$ and $\lambda_2 = -\Pr_{\mathbf{S}}(f(\mathbf{x}) = y^{\dagger}|f(\mathbf{x}) \neq \overline{y})$ otherwise.

The bias–variance decomposition leads to some interesting observations about the behavior of the learning algorithm. With regard to the classification scenario, there are two main observations that warrant elaboration in the current context:

- When the algorithm is not biased on an example, the variance is additive. For biased examples, the variance is substractive. We note this by looking at the bias–variance decomposition of Theorem 2.1. Note that, when $B_A(\mathbf{x}) = 0$, λ_1 reduces to zero and $\lambda_2 = 1$. Similarly, λ_2 is negative when $B_A(\mathbf{x}) \neq 0$, i.e., $L(\overline{y}, y^{\dagger}) = 1$. The preceding behavior suggests that the loss of an algorithm is reduced by increasing the variance in the case in which the learner is biased on an example. That is, in this case, it is advisable to specialize the learner more. In an analogous manner, it pays to generalize the algorithm in response to an unbiased learner by reducing the variance because, in this case, the parameter λ_2 becomes positive, resulting in the variance being additive. These observations give a useful guide to model selection. A nontrivial trade-off between the bias and variance components can yield a classifier that can avoid overfitting and underfitting as a result. The next subsection discusses this in greater detail on a more qualitative level.

- The first parameter λ_1 plays an important role. As defined in the case of zero–one loss, it suggests that, when the prediction $f(\mathbf{x})$ of the classifier is not the same as the optimal prediction $y^\dagger$ (which minimizes the overall loss), then increasing the noise of the example can have the effect of reducing the average error of the algorithm. This is indeed an interesting property and can help explain the good performance of complex classification algorithms in the limited, noisy, or both, data scenarios. In summary, the zero–one loss is relatively robust to the variance of the algorithm, and in some cases can even benefit as a result of increased variance. However, in the case of multiclass classification, it can be shown that the tolerance to variance reduces as the number of classes increases.[4]

Note that this behavior holds in the case of zero–one loss, that is, the classification case. However, the preceding decomposition of the error also gives appropriate behavior traits (and hence a guide to optimizing the model) of the algorithm in the regression case when the zero–one loss is replaced with a squared loss.

Model Selection and Bias–Variance Trade-Off

Let us now look at the issue of model selection as well as the issues of generalization (underfitting) and specialization (overfitting) of the algorithm from a bias–variance perspective. Recall our discussion of Subsection 2.1.6 on the challenges of learning. More specifically, recall Figure 2.1. Let us again consider the two extreme models that can be fit to the data. The first is the case of a straight line. This is generally done in the case of linear regression. As can be seen, fitting a line can result in too simple a model. The error of this model is mainly attributable to its intrinsic simplicity rather than the dependence on the training data on which the model is obtained. As a result, the predominant factor in the resulting error of the classifier is its bias with respect to the examples. The other extreme in our case is the curve that aims at fitting each and every individual data point. This model too might not generalize well because it has extremely high dependence on the training data. As a result the model will have a very high variance and will be very sensitive to the changes in the training data. Hence, in this case, the main source of the error of the model is its variance. Moreover, the problem of a high error that is due to high variance of the model

---

[4] This can be seen by analyzing the behavior of the bias and variance in Theorem 2.2 in an analogous manner.

can further be aggravated if the data are sparse. This explains why too complex a model can result in a very high error in the regression case (squared loss) when the data are sparse.

It does not mean that the contribution of the variance term in the case of too simple a model and the bias term in the case of too complex a model is zero. However, in the two cases, the bias and the variance terms, respectively, are very dominant in their contribution of the error, rendering the contribution of the other terms relatively negligible. A model that can both fit the training data well and generalize successfully at the same time can essentially be obtained by a nontrivial trade-off of the bias and the variance of the model. A model with a very high bias can result in underfitting whereas a model with a very high variance results in overfitting. The best model would depend on an optimal bias–variance trade-off and the nature of the training data (mainly sparsity and size).

Classifier Evaluation and Bias–Variance Trade-Off

In our preceding analysis we saw how we can analyze a learning algorithm by means of decomposing its risk into the bias and the variance (and of course systematic noise) components. We also saw how various components affect the type of a classifier an algorithm chooses. That is, we saw how the bias–variance behavior affects the process of model selection. However, the bias–variance analysis also allows us to look into the interactions between the training data and the error estimates of the algorithm. It allows us to explore the relationship on the nature of the error estimate that can be obtained (whether more conservative or liberal) given the size of the training data as well as the sampling performed. We explore these issues in Chapter 5.

2.1.8 Classifier Evaluation: Putting Components in Perspective

We have shown how the issues of model selection and parameter settings, the loss function, and the bias–variance trade-off of the error of the learning algorithm are all intimately related. Let us briefly put these elements in perspective by looking at the overall learning process.

Given a learning problem, we select a classifier or function class from which we hope to discover a model that can best describe the training data as well as generalize well on future unseen data obtained from the same distribution as the training data.[5] The learning algorithm is then applied to the training data, and a classifier that best describes the training data is obtained.

The algorithm selects this classifier based on some quantitative measure, taking into account the error of the classifiers on the training data and possibly

---

[5] It should be noted that there have also been recent attempts at designing algorithms in which this restriction on both the training and the test data coming from the same distribution is not imposed.

trading this accuracy off in favor of a better measure over classifier complexity. The behavior of the error of the learning algorithm can be analyzed by decomposing it into its components, mainly bias and variance. The study of bias and variance trade-off also gives insight into the learning process and preferences of a learning algorithm. However, explicit characterization of the bias and variance decomposition behavior of the learning algorithm is difficult owing to two main factors: the lack of knowledge of the actual data generating distribution and a limited availability of data. The first limitation is indeed the final goal of the learning process itself and hence cannot be addressed in this regard. The second limitation is important in wake of the first. In the absence of the knowledge of the actual data-generating distribution, the quantities of interest need to be estimated empirically by use of the data at hand. Naturally, the more data at hand, the closer the estimate will be to the actual value. A smaller dataset size can significantly hamper reliable estimates. Limited data availability plays a very significant role both in the case of model selection and in assessing the performance of the learning algorithm on test data. However, this issue can, to some extent, be ameliorated by use of what are known as data resampling techniques. We discuss various resampling techniques, their use and implications, and their effect on the performance estimates of the learning algorithm in detail in Chapter 5. Even though our main focus is not on the effect of resampling on model selection, we briefly discuss the issue of model selection, where pertinent, while discussing some of the resampling approaches.

In this book, we assume that, given a choice of the classifier space, we have at hand the means to discover a classifier that is best at describing the given training data and a guarantee on future generalization over such data.[6] Now every learning algorithm basically explores a different classifier space. Consider another problem then. What if the classifier space that we chose does not contain such a classifier? That is, what if there is another classifier space that can better explain the data at hand? Let us go a step further. Assume that we have k candidate classifier spaces each available with an associated learning algorithm that can discover the classifier in each case that best describes the data. How do we choose the best classifier space from among all these? Implicitly, how do we choose the best learning algorithm given our domain of learning? Looked at in another way, how can we decide which of the k algorithms is the best on a set of given tasks? *This problem, known as the evaluation of the learning algorithm, is the problem that we explore in this book.*

---

[6] We use the term guarantee loosely here. Indeed there are learning algorithms that can give a theoretical guarantee over the performance of the classifier on future data. Such guarantees, known as risk bounds or generalization error bounds, have even been used to guide the model selection process. However, in the present case, we also refer to implicit guarantees obtained as a result of optimizing the model selection criterion such as the ERM or SRM.

We can look at evaluating learning algorithms from a different perspective. Instead of having a domain of interest in which to find the best-suited approach to learning, let us say that we have designed a generic learning algorithm. We now wish to evaluate how good our learning algorithm is. We can measure this "goodness" in various respects. For instance, what are the domains that are most suitable for our learning algorithm to apply to? How good is our learning algorithm compared with other such generic learning algorithms? On what domains? And so on. Two of the main issues underlying such evaluations are those of evaluation metrics and dataset selection and the concerns surrounding them. We discuss various possibilities for evaluation metrics in Chapters 3 and 4 and overview some of the main aspects of dataset selection in Chapter 7. We also look at philosophical as well as qualitative concerns surrounding issues such as synthetic versus real-world data for evaluation, community datasets, and so on. In Chapter 6, we also look at how confident we can be about the results of our evaluation. To conduct such an analysis we need to use statistical tools whose basic aspects are reviewed in the next part of this chapter.

2.2   Statistics Overview

Changing gears now, this part aims to introduce the basic elements of statistics necessary to understand the more advanced concepts and procedures that are introduced in Chapters 5 and 6. Needless to say, rather than trying to be exhaustive, we discuss the most relevant concepts just as we did in the first part of this chapter. Furthermore, this overview has more of a functional than an analytical bias, our goal being to encourage better practice. In certain cases, this chapter gives a brief introduction to a topic, which is then developed in more detail in Chapters 5 and 6.

This section is divided into four subsections. In the first subsection, we define the notion of random variables and their associated quantities. The second subsection then introduces the concept of probability distributions and then discusses one of the extremely important results in statistics theory, the central limit theorem. The third subsection then discusses the notion of confidence intervals, and the last subsection briefly covers the basics behind hypothesis testing and discusses the concepts of type I and type II errors and the power of a test.

In the remainder of this chapter and the subsequent chapters, statistical concepts are defined formally and their computation illustrated, mainly by use of the R Project for Statistical Computing, commonly known as the R Package (R Development Core Team, 2010) because of its ease of use and free availability that enable the readers to replicate the results.

Let us begin with an example that will serve as an illustration basis for the rest of this part of the chapter.

Table 2.2. *Results of running three learning algorithms on the labor dataset from the UCI Repository*

Trial No.	Classifiers	$f1$	$f2$	$f3$	$f4$	$f5$	$f6$	$f7$	$f8$	$f9$	$f10$	Trial error (sum)
1	c4.5	3	0	2	0	2	2	2	1	1	1	14
	RIP	2	3	0	0	2	3	1	0	1	0	12
	NB	1	0	0	0	0	1	0	2	0	0	4
2	c4.5	2	1	1	2	2	0	0	0	1	1	10
	RIP	2	1	0	0	2	1	0	1	1	0	8
	NB	2	0	1	1	0	0	0	0	0	0	4
3	c4.5	0	0	2	2	1	2	1	0	1	1	10
	RIP	0	0	1	2	1	1	1	1	2	1	10
	NB	0	0	0	0	0	1	0	0	0	0	1
4	c4.5	3	1	2	1	0	1	3	1	1	2	15
	RIP	2	0	1	1	1	0	4	1	1	1	12
	NB	2	0	0	1	0	0	0	0	0	1	4
5	c4.5	0	1	2	1	0	1	0	1	2	1	9
	RIP	2	1	1	1	0	1	0	2	0	1	9
	NB	0	1	0	0	1	0	0	0	0	2	4
6	c4.5	2	1	1	1	4	1	2	1	1	0	14
	RIP	0	0	2	0	3	0	0	0	1	0	6
	NB	0	0	1	0	1	1	0	0	0	0	3
7	c4.5	1	2	1	2	1	1	2	1	0	1	12
	RIP	1	1	1	2	1	1	2	2	0	1	12
	NB	1	1	1	0	1	2	2	0	1	0	9
8	c4.5	0	1	1	0	0	0	1	0	3	2	8
	RIP	1	1	1	0	0	1	0	0	1	1	6
	NB	0	0	0	0	0	0	0	0	1	1	2
9	c4.5	1	2	1	2	2	2	0	3	1	1	15
	RIP	0	0	1	0	0	1	0	2	0	1	5
	NB	0	0	0	1	0	0	0	0	0	1	2
10	c4.5	3	1	1	3	3	2	0	2	2	0	17
	RIP	3	1	1	1	0	2	2	1	1	1	13
	NB	0	1	0	0	0	0	1	1	1	0	4

An Example

Consider the results of Table 2.2 obtained by running three learning algorithms on the labor dataset from the UCI Repository for Machine Learning. The learning algorithms used were the C4.5 decision trees learner (c45), naive Bayes (NB), and Ripper (RIP). All the simulations were run by a 10-fold cross-validation over the labor dataset and the cross-validation runs were repeated 10 times on different permutations of the data.[7] The dataset contained 57 examples. Accordingly,

[7] This practice is discussed in Bouckaert (2003). We overview this technique in Chapter 5.

reported results of the classifier errors on the test folds pertain to the ones on six examples in the first seven folds in the table, and the reported errors are over five examples in the last three test folds. The training and test folds within each run of cross-validation and for each repetition were the same for all the algorithms. All the experiments that involve running classifiers in this and the subsequent chapters, unless otherwise stated, are done with the WEKA machine learning toolkit (Witten and Frank, 2005a).

With these results in the background, let us move on to discussing the concept of random variables.

2.2.1 Random Variables

In this subsection, we present both the familiar, analytical definition of a random variable and associated concepts that can be found in the standard statistics literature and the more functional description emphasizing their utilization in the context of classifier performance modeling and evaluation.

A random variable is a function that associates a unique numerical value with every outcome of an experiment. That is, a random variable can be seen as a measurable function that maps the points from a probability space to a measurable space. Here, by probability space, we mean the space in which the actual experiments are done and the outcomes achieved. This need not be a measurable space, that is, the outcomes of an experiment need not be numeric. Consider the most standard example of a coin toss. The outcomes of a coin toss can be "heads" or "tails." However, we often need to map such outcomes to numbers, that is, measurable space. Such a quantification allows us to study their behavior. A random variable does precisely this. Naturally the range of the values that a random variable can take would also depend on the nature of the experiment that it models. For a fixed set of outcomes of an experiment, such as the coin toss, a random variable results in discrete values. Such a random variable is known as a discrete random variable. On the other hand, a continuous random variable can model experiments with infinite possible outcomes.

The probabilities of the values that a random variable can take are also modeled accordingly. For a random variable x, these probabilities are modeled with a probability distribution, denoted by $\Pr(x)$ when x is discrete and with a probability density function, denoted by $p(x)$, when x is continuous. A probability distribution hence associates a probability with each of the possible values that a discrete random variable can take. It can thus be seen as a list of these probability values.

In the case of a continuous random variable, which can take on an infinite number of values, we need a function that can yield the probability of the variable taking on values in a given interval. That is, we need an integrable function. The probability density function fulfills these requirements.

To look at this closely, we first take a look at the cumulative distribution function (CDF). With every random variable, there is an associated CDF that gives the probability of the variable taking a value less than or equal to a value x_i for every x_i. That is, the cumulative distribution function $p_{cdf}(x)$ is

$$p_{cdf}(x) = \Pr(x \le x_i), \forall -\infty < x_i < \infty.$$

Given a CDF, we can define the probability density function $p(\cdot)$ associated with a continuous random variable x. The probability density function $p(x)$ is just the derivative of the CDF of x:

$$p(x) = \frac{d}{dx} p_{cdf}(x).$$

If x_a and x_b are two of the possible values of x, then it follows that

$$\int p(x)dx = p_{cdf}(x_b) - p_{cdf}(x_a) = \Pr(x_a < x < x_b).$$

Hence $p(x)$ can be a probability density function of x if and only if

$$\int p(x)dx = 1$$

and

$$p(x) > 0, \forall x.$$

The expected value of a random variable x denotes its central value and is generally used as a summary value of the distribution of the random variable. The expected value generally denotes the average value of the random variable. For a discrete random variable x taking m possible values $x_i, i \in \{1, \ldots, m\}$, the expected value can be obtained as

$$\mathbf{E}[x] = \sum_{i=1}^{m} x_i \Pr(x_i),$$

where $\Pr(\cdot)$ denotes the probability distribution, with $\Pr(x_i)$ denoting the probability of x taking on the value x_i. Similarly, in the case in which x is a continuous random variable with $p(x)$ as the associated probability density function, the expected value is obtained as

$$\mathbf{E}[x] = \int x p(x)dx.$$

In most practical scenarios, however, the associated probability distribution or the probability density functions are unknown, as we will see later. What is available is a set of values that the random variables take. In such cases we can consider, when the size of this set is acceptably large, this sample to be representative of the true distribution. Under this assumption, the sample mean can then be used to estimate the expected value of the random variable. Hence, if S_x is the set of values taken by the variable x, then the sample mean can be calculated as

$$\bar{x} = \frac{1}{|S_x|} \sum_{i=1}^{|S_x|} x_i,$$

where $|S_x|$ denotes the size of the set S_x.

Although, the expected value of a random variable summarizes its central value, it does not give any indication about the distribution of the underlying variable by itself. That is, two random variables with the same expected value can have entirely different underlying distributions. We can obtain a better sense of a distribution by considering the statistics of variance in conjunction with the expected value of the variable.

The variance is a measure of the spread of the values of the random variable around its central value. More precisely, the variance of a random variable (probability distribution or sample) measures the degree of the statistical dispersion or the spread of values. The variance of a random variable is always nonnegative. Hence, the larger the variance, the more scattered the values of the random variable with respect to its central value. The variance of a random variable x is calculated as

$$\text{Var}(x) = \sigma^2(x) = \mathbf{E}[x - \mathbf{E}[x]]^2 = \mathbf{E}[x^2] - \mathbf{E}[x]^2.$$

In the continuous case, this means:

$$\sigma^2(x) = \int (x - \mathbf{E}[x])^2 p(x)dx,$$

where $\mathbf{E}[x]$ denotes the expected value of the continuous random variable x and $p(x)$ denotes the associated probability density function. Similarly, for the discrete case,

$$\sigma^2(x) = \sum_{i=1}^{m} \text{Pr}(x_i)(x_i - \mathbf{E}[x])^2,$$

where, as before, $\text{Pr}(\cdot)$ denote the probability distribution associated with the discrete random variable x.

Given a sample of the values taken by x, we can calculate the sample variance by replacing the expected value of x with the sample mean:

$$\text{Var}_S(x) = \sigma_S^2 = \frac{1}{|S_x| - 1} \sum_{i=1}^{|S_x|} (x_i - \bar{x})^2.$$

Note that the denominator of the preceding equation is $|S_x| - 1$ instead of $|S_x|$.[8] The preceding estimator is known as the unbiased estimator of the variance of

---

[8] This correction is known as Bessel's correction.

a sample. For large $|S_x|$, the difference between $|S_x|$ and $|S_x| - 1$ is rendered insignificant. The advantage of $|S_x| - 1$ is that in this case it can be shown that the expected value of the variance $\mathbf{E}[\sigma^2]$ is equal to the true variance of the sampled random variable.

The variance of a random variable is an important statistical indicator of the dispersion of the data. However, the unit of the variance measurement is not the same as the mean, as is clear from our discussion to this point. In some scenarios, it can be more helpful if a statistic is available that is comparable to the expected value directly. The standard deviation of a random variable fills this gap. The standard deviation of a random variable is simply the square root of the variance. When estimated on a population or sample of values, it is known as the sample standard deviation. It is generally denoted by $\sigma(x)$. This also makes it clear that using $\sigma^2(x)$ for variance denotes that the unit of the measured variance is the square of the expected value statistic. $\sigma(x)$ is calculated as

$$\sigma(x) = \sqrt{\mathrm{Var}(x)}.$$

Similarly, we can obtain the sample standard deviation by considering the square root of the sample variance. One point should be noted. Even when an unbiased estimator of the *sample* variance is used (with $|S_x| - 1$ in the denominator instead of $|S_x|$), the resulting estimator is still *not* an unbiased estimator of the *sample* standard deviation.[9] Furthermore, it underestimates the true sample standard deviation. A biased estimator of the sample variance can also be used without significant deterioration. An unbiased estimator of the sample standard deviation is not known except when the variable obeys a normal distribution.

Another significant use of the standard deviation will be seen in terms of providing confidence to some statistical measurements. One of the main such uses involves providing the confidence intervals or margin of error around a measurement (mean) from samples. We will subsequently see an illustration.

Performance Measures as Random Variables
The insights into the random variables and the related statistics that we just presented are quite significant in classifier evaluation. The performance measure of a classifier on any given dataset can be modeled as a random variable and much of the subsequent analysis follows, enabling us to understand the behavior of the performance measure in both absolute terms and in terms relative to other performance measures or even the same performance measure across different learning settings. Various learning strategies have varying degrees of assumptions on the underlying distribution of the data. Given a classifier f resulting from applying a learning algorithm A to some training data S_{train}, we can test f on previously unseen examples from a test data. Learning from

---

[9] This can be seen by applying Jensen's inequality to the standard deviation, which is a concave function, unlike its square, the variance. We do not discuss these issues in detail as they are beyond the scope of this book.

inductive inference does make the underlying assumption here that the data for both the training as well as the test set come from the same distribution. The examples are assumed to be sampled in an independently and identically distributed (i.i.d.) manner. The most general assumption that can be made is that the data (and possibly their labels) are assumed to be generated from some arbitrary underlying distribution. That is, we have no knowledge of this true distribution whatsoever. This is indeed a reasonable assumption as far as learning is concerned because the main aim is to be able to model (or approximate) this distribution (or the label-generation process) as closely as possible. As a result, each example in the test set can be seen as being drawn independently from some arbitrary but fixed data distribution. The performance of the classifier applied to each example can be measured for the criterion of interest by use of corresponding performance measures. The criterion of interest can be, say, how accurately the classifier predicts the label of the example or how much the model depicted by the classifier errs in modeling the example. As a result, we can, in principle, also model these performance measures as random variables, again from an unknown distribution possibly different from the one that generates the data and the corresponding labels. This is one of the main strategies behind various approaches to classifier assessment as well as to evaluation.

Example 2.1. Recall Table 2.2 that presented results of running 10 runs of 10-fold cross-validation on the labor dataset from the UCI Repository. Now a classifier run on each test example (in each fold of each run) for the respective learning algorithms gives an estimate of its empirical error by means of the indicator loss function. The classifier experiences a unit loss if the predicted label does not match the true label. The empirical risk of the classifier in each fold can then be obtained by averaging this loss over the number of examples in the corresponding fold. Table 2.3 gives this empirical risk for all the classifiers. The entries of Table 2.3 correspond to the entries of Table 2.2 but are divided by the number of examples in the respective folds. That is, the entries in the first seven columns are all divided by six, whereas those in the last three columns are each divided by five. Then we can model the empirical risk of these classifiers as random variables with the estimates obtained over each test fold and in each trial run as their observed values. Hence we have 100 observed values for each of the three random variables used to model the empirical risk of the three classifiers. Note that the random variable used for the purpose can have values in the [0, 1] range, with 0 denoting no risk (all the examples classified correctly) and 1 denoting the case in which all the examples are classified incorrectly.

Let us denote the empirical risk by $R_S(\cdot)$. Then the variables $R_S(\text{c45})$, $R_S(\text{rip})$, and $R_S(\text{nb})$ denote the random variables representing the empirical risks for the decision tree learner, Ripper, and the naive Bayes algorithm, respectively. We can now calculate the sample means for the three cases from the population of 100 observations at hand.

Table 2.3. *Empirical risks for the classifiers in [0,1] range from Tab. 2.2*

Trial No.	Classifiers	f1	f2	f3	f4	f5	f6	f7	f8	f9	f10
1	c4.5	0.5	0	0.3333	0	0.3333	0.3333	0.3333	0.2	0.2	0.2
	RIP	0.3333	0.5	0	0	0.3333	0.5	0.1667	0	0.2	0
	NB	0.1667	0	0	0	0	0.1667	0	0.4	0	0
2	c4.5	0.3333	0.1667	0.1667	0.3333	0.3333	0	0	0	0.2	0.2
	RIP	0.3333	0.1667	0	0	0.3333	0.1667	0	0.2	0.2	0
	NB	0.3333	0	0.1667	0.1667	0	0	0	0	0	0
3	c4.5	0	0	0.3333	0.3333	0.1667	0.3333	0.1667	0	0.2	0.2
	RIP	0	0	0.1667	0.3333	0.1667	0.1667	0.1667	0.2	0.4	0.2
	NB	0	0	0	0	0	0.1667	0	0	0	0
4	c4.5	0.5	0.1667	0.3333	0.1667	0	0.1667	0.5	0.2	0.2	0.4
	RIP	0.3333	0	0.1667	0.1667	0.1667	0	0.6667	0.2	0.2	0.2
	NB	0.3333	0	0	0.1667	0	0	0	0	0	0.2
5	c4.5	0	0.1667	0.3333	0.1667	0	0.1667	0	0.2	0.4	0.2
	RIP	0.3333	0.1667	0.1667	0.1667	0	0.1667	0	0.4	0	0.2
	NB	0	0.1667	0	0	0.1667	0	0	0	0	0.4
6	c4.5	0.3333	0.1667	0.1667	0.1667	0.6667	0.1667	0.3333	0.2	0.2	0
	RIP	0	0	0.3333	0	0.5	0	0	0	0.2	0
	NB	0	0	0.1667	0	0.1667	0.1667	0	0	0	0

(continued)

Table 2.3 *(cont.)*

Trial No.	Classifiers	f1	f2	f3	f4	f5	f6	f7	f8	f9	f10
7	c4.5	0.1667	0.3333	0.1667	0.3333	0.1667	0.1667	0.3333	0.2	0	0.2
	RIP	0.1667	0.1667	0.1667	0.3333	0.1667	0.1667	0.3333	0.4	0	0.2
	NB	0.1667	0.1667	0.1667	0	0.1667	0.3333	0.3333	0	0.2	0
8	c4.5	0	0.1667	0.1667	0	0	0	0.1667	0	0.6	0.4
	RIP	0.1667	0.1667	0.1667	0	0	0.1667	0	0	0.2	0.2
	NB	0	0	0	0	0	0	0	0	0.2	0.2
9	c4.5	0.1667	0.3333	0.1667	0.3333	0.3333	0.3333	0	0.6	0.2	0.2
	RIP	0	0	0.1667	0	0	0.1667	0	0.4	0	0.2
	NB	0	0	0	0.1667	0	0	0	0	0	0.2
10	c4.5	0.5	0.1667	0.1667	0.5	0.5	0.3333	0	0.4	0.4	0
	RIP	0.5	0.1667	0.1667	0.1667	0	0.3333	0.3333	0.2	0.2	0.2
	NB	0	0.1667	0	0	0	0	0.1667	0.2	0.2	0

The *sample mean* for these random variables would then indicate the overall average value taken by them over the folds and runs of the experiment. We can compute these means, indicated by an overline bar, by averaging the values in the respective cells of Table 2.3. The values can be recorded as vectors in R and the mean can then be calculated as follows:

Listing 2.1: Sample R command to input the sample values and calculate the mean.

```
> c45= c(.5,0,.3333,0,.3333,.3333,.3333,.2,.2,.2,
         .3333,.1667,.1667,.3333,.3333,0,0,0,.2,.2,
         0,0,.3333,.3333,.1667,.3333,.1667,0,.2,.2,
         .5,.1667,.3333,.1667,0,.1667,.5,.2,.2,.4,
         0,.1667,.3333,.1667,0,.1667,0,.2,.4,.2,
         .3333,.1667,0.1667,0.1667,.6667,.1667,.3333,.2,.2,0,
         .1667,.3333,.1667,.3333,.1667,.1667,.3333,.2,0,.2,
         0,.1667,.1667,0,0,0,.1667,0,.6,.4,
         .1667,.3333,.1667,.3333,.3333,.3333,0,.6,.2,.2,
         .5,.1667,.1667,.5,.5,.3333,0,.4,.4,0)
> mean(c45)
[1] 0.217668

> jrip=    c(.3333,.5,0,0,.3333,.5,.1667,0,.2,0,
            .3333,.1667,0,0,.3333,.1667,0,.2,.2,0,
            0,0,.1667,.3333,.1667,.1667,.1667,.2,.4,.2,
            .3333,0,.1667,.1667,.1667,0,.6667,.2,.2,.2,
            .3333,.1667,.1667,.1667,0,.1667,0,.4,0,.2,
            0,0,.3333,0,.5,0,0,0,.2,0,
            .1667,.1667,.1667,.3333,.1667,.1667,.33,.4,0,.2,
            .1667,.1667,.1667,0,0,.1667,0,0,.2,.2,
            0,0,.1667,0,0,.1667,0,.4,0,.2,
            .5,.1667,.1667,.1667,0,.3333,.3333,.2,.2,.2)
> mean(jrip)
[1] 0.163306

> nb=c(.1667,0,0,0,0,.1667,0,.4,0,0,
       .3333,0,.1667,.1667,0,0,0,0,0,0,
       0,0,0,0,0,.1667,0,0,0,0,
       .3333,0,0,.1667,0,0,0,0,0,.2,
       0,.1667,0,0,.1667,0,0,0,0,.4,
       0,0,.1667,0,.1667,.1667,0,0,0,0,
       .1667,.1667,.1667,0,.1667,.3333,.3333,0,.2,0,
       0,0,0,0,0,0,0,0,.2,.2,
       0,0,0,.1667,0,0,0,0,0,.2,
       0,.1667,0,0,0,0,.1667,.2,.2,0)
> mean(nb)
[1] 0.065338
```

Note here that c() is a method that combines its arguments to form a vector; mean() computes the sample mean of the vector passed to it.

What we essentially just did was model the empirical risk as a continuous random variable that can take values in the [0, 1] interval and obtain the statistic of interest. An alternate to this was modeling the risk as a binary variable that can take values in {0, 1}. Applying the classifier on each test example in each of the test folds would then give an observation. These values can then be averaged over to obtain the corresponding sample means. Hence, by adding the errors made in each test fold and then further over all the trials, we would end up with a population of size $10 \times 57 = 570$. The sample means can then be calculated as

$$\overline{R}(\text{c45}) = R_S(\text{c45}) = \frac{14 + 10 + 10 + 15 + 9 + 14 + 12 + 8 + 15 + 17}{570}$$

$$= 0.2175,$$

$$\overline{R}(\text{RIP}) = R_S(\text{RIP}) = \frac{12 + 8 + 10 + 12 + 9 + 6 + 12 + 6 + 5 + 13}{570}$$

$$= 0.1632,$$

$$\overline{R}(\text{NB}) = R_S(\text{NB}) = \frac{4 + 4 + 1 + 4 + 4 + 3 + 9 + 2 + 2 + 4}{570} = 0.0649.$$

Note the marginal difference in the estimated statistic as a result of the round-off error. Both the variations of modeling the performance as a random variable are equivalent (although in the case of discrete modeling, it can be seen that, instead of modeling the empirical risk, we are modeling the indicator loss function).

We will use the continuous random variables for modeling as in the preceding first case because this allows us to model the empirical risk (rather than the loss function). Given that these sample means represent the mean empirical risk of each classifier, this suggests that NB classifies the domain better than RIP, which in turn classifies the domain better than c4.5. However, the knowledge of only the average performance, via the mean, of classifier performance is not enough to give us an idea of their relative performances. We are also interested in the spread or deviation of the risk from this mean. The standard deviation, by virtue of representation in the same units as the data, is easier to interpret. It basically tells us whether the elements of our distribution have a tendency to be similar or dissimilar to each other. For example, in a population made up of 22-year-old ballerinas, the degree of joint flexibility is much more tightly distributed around the mean than it is in the population made up of all the 22-year-old young ladies (ballerinas and nonballerinas included). Thus the standard deviation, in the first case, will be smaller than in the second. This is because ballerinas have to be naturally flexible and must train to increase this natural flexibility further, whereas in the general population, we will find a large mixture of young ladies with various degrees of flexibility and different levels of training. Let us then compute the standard deviations with respect to the mean empirical risks, in each case using R [the built-in sd( ) function can be used for the purpose]:

Listing 2.2: Sample R command to computer standard deviation.

```
> sd(c45)
[1]  0.1603415
> sd(jrip)
[1]  0.1492936
> sd(nb)
[1]  0.1062516
>
```

So what do these values tell us in terms of how to compare the performances of c4.5, NB, and RIP on our labor dataset? The relatively high standard deviations exhibited by c4.5 and RIP tell us that the distribution of values around the sample means of these two experiments varies a great deal. That is, over some folds these two classifiers make very few errors (lower risk) compared with NB, whereas on others this number is relatively very high (and hence higher risk). Indeed, this behavior can be seen in Table 2.3. On the other hand, NB appears to be relatively more stable. Another take on the spread is given by the variance calculated with the var( ) function in the R Package:

Listing 2.3: Sample R command to computer variance.

```
> var(c45)
[1]  0.02570940
> var(jrip)
[1]  0.02228859
> var(nb)
[1]  0.01128940
>
```

2.2.2 Distributions

We introduced the notions of probability distributions and density functions in the previous subsection. Let us now focus on some of the main distributions that have both a significant impact on and implications for the approaches currently used in assessing and evaluating the learning algorithms. Although we can model data by using a wide variety of distributions, we would like to focus on two important distributions most relevant to the evaluation of learning algorithms: the Normal or Gaussian distribution and the binomial distribution. Among these, the normal distribution is the most widely used distribution for modeling classifier performance for a variety of reasons, such as the analytical tractability of the results under this assumption, asymptotic analysis capability owing to the central limit theorem subsequently discussed, asymptotic ability to model a wide variety of other distributions, and so on. As we will see later, many approaches impose a normal distribution assumption on the performance measures (or some function of the performance measures). For instance, the standard *t* test assumes the difference in the performance measure of two algorithms to be normally distributed around the zero mean.

The binomial distribution has recently earned more significance. It models a discrete random variable and can aptly be applied to model the number of successes in a series of experiments. This is hence the model of choice when we wish to model how frequently an algorithm succeeds in classifying an instance from the test set correctly (modeling the empirical risk using the indicator loss, especially when this risk is, as is typically the case, closer to zero). Modeling of the classification error in terms of the binomial distribution enables us to obtain very tight guarantees on the generalization error of the learning algorithm. We will see some such results later in the book with regard to the empirical risk minimization algorithms. For now, let us start with the normal distribution.

The Normal Distribution

The normal or Gaussian distribution is used to model a continuous random variable. A continuous random variable x taking any value in the interval $[-\infty, \infty]$ is said to be normally distributed with parameters μ and σ^2 if the probability density function of x can be denoted by

$$p(x) = \frac{1}{\sqrt{2\pi\sigma^2}} \exp\left[-\frac{1}{2}\left(\frac{(x-\mu)^2}{\sigma^2}\right)\right] \tag{2.8}$$

where exp denotes exponential.

The parameter μ, called the mean here, refers to the expected value $E[x]$, and σ^2 represents the variance of the random variable around the mean. Note that we avoid denoting μ and σ^2 as functions of x because it is clear from the context. A variable x that is normally distributed with mean μ and variance σ^2 can be denoted as $x \sim N(\mu, \sigma^2)$, which has the same meaning as Equation (2.8). One important type of normal distribution is called the standard normal distribution. A random variable x distributed according to a standard normal distribution has mean $\mu = 0$ and the variance $\sigma^2 = 1$, and is denoted as $x \sim N(0, 1)$. The normal distribution, when plotted, results in the famous symmetric bell-shaped curve around the mean. The characteristics of this curve, especially the center and width, are decided by the two parameters μ and σ^2 defining the normal distribution. With increasing variance, one would obtain a wider bell curve. Figure 2.2 shows the shape of the standard normal distribution, along with two normal distributions also centered around 0, but with standard deviations of 0.5 and 2. Note the effect of increasing the variance (and hence the standard deviation).

The Binomial Distribution

The binomial distribution is used to model discrete random variables that generally take on binary values. Consider a hypothetical trial that can have two outcomes, success and failure. The probability of success in any given trial (or

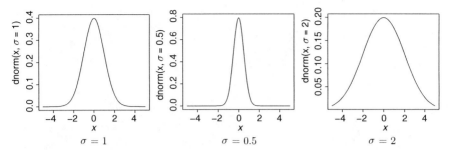

Figure 2.2. Normal distributions centered around 0 with standard deviations (sd) $= \sqrt{\sigma^2}$ of 1 (the standard normal distribution), 0.5, and 2.

experiment) is denoted by p_s. Such trials are typically referred to as Bernoulli trials. Then the binomial distribution models the number of successes in a series of experiments with the probability of success in each experiment being p_s. An important assumption here is that the number of trials is fixed in advance. Furthermore, the probability of success in each trial is assumed to be the same. That is, p_s is fixed across various trials. Each trial is further assumed to be statistically independent of all other trials. That is, the outcome of any given trial does not depend on the outcome of any other trial.

Given the preceding setting, a random variable x is said to be binomially distributed with parameters m and p_s, denoted as $x \sim \text{Bin}(m, p_s)$, if it obeys the following probability distribution:

$$\text{Pr}(x) = \binom{m}{k} p_s^k (1 - p_s)^{(m-k)},$$

which is nothing but the probability of exactly k successes in m trials.

Consider a classifier that maps each given example to one of a fixed number of labels. Each example also has an associated true label. We can model the event as a success when the label identified by the classifier matches the true label of the example. Then the behavior of the classifier prediction over a number of different examples in a test set can be modeled as a binomial distribution. The expected value $\mathbf{E}[x]$ of a binomial distribution can be shown to be mp_s and its variance to be $mp_s(1 - p_s)$. In the extreme case of $m = 1$, the binomial distribution becomes a Bernoulli distribution, which models the probability of success in a single trial. On the other hand, as $m \longrightarrow \infty$, the binomial distribution approaches the Poisson distribution when the product mp_s remains fixed. The advantage of sometime using a Poisson distribution to approximate a binomial distribution can come from the reduced computational complexity. However, we do not delve into these issues, as these are beyond the scope of this book.

Let us then see the effect of m on the binomial distribution. Figure 2.3 shows three unbiased binomial distributions (an unbiased binomial distribution has

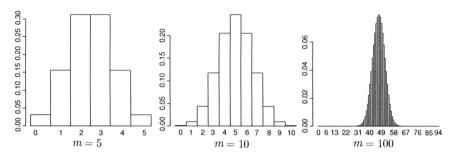

Figure 2.3. Binomial distributions with a probability of 0.5 (unbiased) and trial sizes $m = 5$, $m = 10$, and $m = 100$. As the trial size increases, it is clear that the binomial distribution approaches the normal distribution.

$p_s = 0.5$) with increasing trial sizes. It can be seen that as the trial size increases the binomial distribution approaches the normal distribution (for fixed p_s).[10] The probability of a success in a Bernoulli trial also affects the distribution. Figure 2.4 shows two biased binomial distributions with success probabilities of 0.3 and 0.8 over 10 trials. In these cases, the graph is asymmetrical.

Other Distributions

Many other distributions are widely used in practice for data modeling in various fields. Some of the main ones are the Poisson distribution, used to model the number of events occurring in a given time interval, the geometric distribution, generally used to model the number of trials required before a first success (or failure) is obtained, and the uniform distribution, generally used to model random variables whose range of values is known and that can take any value in this range with equal probability. These, however, are not directly relevant to the subject of this book. Hence we do not devote space to discussing these distributions in detail. Interested readers can find these details in any standard statistics text.

The Central Limit Theorem

Let us now discuss a very important result known as the central limit theorem or the second fundamental theorem of probability. This theorem is subsequently given without a proof.

Theorem 2.3. The central limit theorem: *Let $x_1, x_2, \ldots, x_m$ be a sequence of m i.i.d. random variables, each with a finite expectation μ and variance σ^2. Then, as m increases, the distribution of the sample means of $x_1, x_2, \ldots, x_m$ approaches the normal distribution with a mean μ and variance σ^2/m irrespective of the original distribution of $x_1, x_2, \ldots, x_m$.*

---

[10] Note that a continuity correction, such as one based on the Moivre–Laplace theorem, is recommended in the case in which a normal approximation from a binomial is used for large m's.

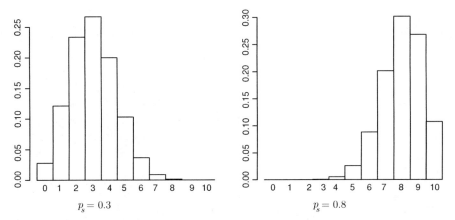

Figure 2.4. Binomial distributions with probabilities of success $p_s = 0.3$ and $p_s = 0.8$ with $m = 10$. For these biased distributions, the graph has become asymmetrical.

Let us denote by S_m the sum of m random variables. That is,

$$S_m = x_1 + x_2 + \cdots + x_m.$$

Then the random variable r_m defined as

$$r_m = \frac{S_m - m\mu}{\sigma\sqrt{m}}$$

is such that its distribution converges to a standard normal distribution as m approaches ∞.

The normal distribution assumption over certain variables of interest or even statistics of interest (see the following subsection on sampling distribution) is one of the most common assumptions made to analyze the behavior of various aspects of learning algorithms, especially their performance on data. This assumption appears as an important consequence of the central limit theorem. The sample mean appears as a statistics of choice to investigate with the normal distribution assumption, as we will see later. We will also see how this assumption plays a central role in not only establishing a basis of analysis, but also in affecting the results obtained as a consequence.

The central limit theorem can be used to show that the sampling distribution of the sample mean can be approximated to be normal even if the distribution of the population from which the samples are obtained is not normal but well behaved when the size of the samples is sufficiently large. This observation will have important implications especially in the case of statistical significance testing, in which such results with the normality distribution assumption of the sample means are frequently put into practice but the necessary factors for such assumption to hold, i.e., the required sample size and the underlying population distribution, are often neglected.

Sampling Distribution

Consider a sample obtained from sampling data according to some given distribution. We can then calculate various kinds of statistics on this sample (e.g., mean, variance, standard deviation, etc.). These are called sample statistics. The sampling distribution denotes the probability distribution or a probability density function associated with the sample statistic under repeated sampling of the population. This sampling distribution then depends on three factors, viz., the size of the sample, the statistic itself, and the underlying distribution of the population. In other words, the *sampling distribution* of a statistic (for example, the mean, the median, or any other description or summary of a dataset) is the distribution of values obtained for those statistics over all possible samplings of the same size from a given population.

For instance, we obtain m samples for a random variable x denoted $\{x_1, x_2, \ldots, x_m\}$ with known probability distribution and calculate the sample mean $\bar{x} = \frac{1}{m} \sum_{i=1}^{m} x_i$. When using x to model the empirical risk, we can obtain the average empirical risk on a dataset of m examples by testing the classifier on each of these. Further, because this average empirical risk is a statistic, repeated sampling of the m data points and calculating the empirical risk in each case will enable us to obtain a sampling distribution of the empirical risk estimates. There can be a sampling distribution associated with any sample statistic estimated (although not always computable). For instance, in the example of Table 2.3, we use a random variable to model the empirical risk of each classifier and calculate the average (mean) empirical risk on each fold. Hence, the 10 runs with 10 folds each give us 100 observed values of $R_S(\cdot)$ for each classifier over which we calculate the mean. This, for instance, results in the corresponding sample mean of the empirical risk in the case of c4.5 to be $\bar{R}(\text{c45}) = 0.217668$.

Because the populations under study are usually finite, the true sampling distribution is usually unknown (e.g., note that the trials in the case of Table 2.3 are interdependent). Hence it is important to understand the effect of using a single estimate of sampling distribution based on one sampling instead of repeated samplings. Typically, the mean of the statistic is used as an approximation of the actual mean obtained over multiple samplings. The central limit theorem plays an important role in allowing for this approximation. Let us see the reasoning behind this.

Denote a random variable x that is normally distributed with mean μ and variance σ^2 as $x \sim N(\mu, \sigma^2)$. Then the sampling distribution of the sample mean $\bar{x}$ coming from m-sized samples is

$$\bar{x} \sim N(\mu, \frac{\sigma^2}{m}). \tag{2.9}$$

Moreover, if x is sampled from a finite-sized population of size N, then the sampling distribution of the sample mean becomes

$$\bar{x} \sim N(\mu, \frac{N-m}{N-1} \times \frac{\sigma^2}{m}). \tag{2.10}$$

Note here the role of the central limit theorem just described. With increasing N, Approximation (2.10) would approach Approximation (2.9). Moreover, note how the sample mean in Approximations (2.9) and (2.10) is basically the actual mean.

Another application of the sampling distribution is to obtain the sampling distribution of difference between two means. We will see this in the case of hypothesis testing. Let x_1 and x_2 be two random variables that are normally distributed with means μ_1 and μ_2, respectively. Their corresponding variances are σ_1^2 and σ_2^2. That is, $x_1 \sim N(\mu_1, \sigma_1^2)$ and $x_2 \sim N(\mu_2, \sigma_2^2)$. We are now interested in the sampling distribution of the sample mean of x_1 over m_1-sized samples, denoted as $\overline{x_1}$, and the sample mean of x_2 over m_2-sized samples, denoted as $\overline{x_2}$. Then it can be shown that the difference of the sampling means is distributed as

$$\overline{x_1} - \overline{x_2} \sim N(\mu_1 - \mu_2, \frac{\sigma_1^2}{m_1} + \frac{\sigma_2^2}{m_2}).$$

Finally, consider a variable x that is binomially distributed with parameter p. That is, $x \sim \text{Bin}(p)$; then it can be shown that the sample proportion $\overline{p}$ also follows a binomial distribution parameterized by p, that is, $\overline{p} \sim \text{Bin}(p)$.[11]

2.2.3 Confidence Intervals

Let us now discuss one of the important concepts in which the sampling distribution of a population statistic plays a significant role. Consider a set of observations sampled according to some population distribution. This sample can serve to estimate a sample statistic of interest that can then be used to approximate the true statistic of the underlying distribution. The sample statistics previously discussed, such as the sample mean, essentially give the point estimate of such statistics. Confidence intervals, on the other hand, give interval estimates in the form of a range of values in which the true statistic is likely to lie.

Hence a confidence interval gives an estimated range of values that is likely to include an unknown population parameter, the estimated range being calculated from a given sample of data. This, in a sense, then associates reliability to the point estimates of the true statistic obtained from the sample. Accordingly, associated with this estimated range is a confidence level that determines how likely the true statistic is to lie in the confidence interval. This confidence level is generally denoted in the form of $(1 - \alpha)$, where $\alpha \in [0, 1]$ is called the confidence parameter (or confidence coefficient). The most common value used for α is 0.05, referring to a confidence level of $1 - 0.05 = 0.95$ or 95%. Note that this is not the same as giving the probability with which the true statistic will lie in the interval. Rather, what this conveys is that, if we were

---

[11] Note that this notation differs from the previous one for binomial distribution for the sake of simplicity since the number of trials is assumed to be fixed and uniform across trials.

to obtain multiple samples repeatedly from the population according to the underlying distribution, then the true population statistic is likely to lie in the estimated confidence interval $(1 - \alpha)100\%$ of times. As can be easily noted, reducing the value of α will have the effect of increasing the confidence level on the estimated range's likelihood of containing the true population statistic, and hence will widen the confidence interval. Similarly, increasing α would tighten the confidence interval. When computed over more than one statistic, the confidence interval becomes a confidence region.

Note that the preceding interpretation of the confidence interval is strictly a statistical interpretation and should not be confused with its Bayesian counterpart, known as the *credible intervals*. The two can be identical in some cases; however, the credible intervals can differ significantly when these are applied in a strong Bayesian sense with prior information integrated. We do not discuss the credible intervals here. Interested readers can obtain more information from any standard Bayesian statistical inference text.

Getting back to our ballerinas, if we compute, from our ballerina sample, the average degree of joint flexibility, we may not trust that this value is necessarily the true average for all ballerinas, but we can build a 95% confidence interval around this value and claim that the true average is likely to fall in this interval with 95% confidence level. This confidence level is also related to the statistical hypothesis testing, as we will see later. However, the two notions do not necessarily have the same interpretation.

Although the idea of providing interval estimates over the true statistic seems appealing, there are some caveats to this approach that should be taken into account. The most important of these is that the intervals are obtained based on a strong parametric assumption on the statistic of interest. In the most general form that we subsequently describe, the statistic is assumed to be distributed according to a Gaussian distribution around the sample mean. Let us see this most common case.

As we already saw, the sample mean can be relatively reliably used to compute the true mean. Hence, by making use of the standard error (sample standard deviation) obtained from the sample, we can obtain a value Z_P that would determine the confidence limits (the end points of confidence intervals). Consider a random variable x distributed according to a normal distribution with true mean μ and variance σ^2. Let S_x be the sample of a set of values for x. We denote the sample mean by $\overline{x}$, calculated as

$$\overline{x} = \frac{1}{|S_x|} \sum_{i=1}^{|S_x|} x_i,$$

with each x_i denoting an observed value of x in the sample S_x and $|S_x|$ denoting the size of the set S_x. Similarly, we can calculate the standard error (sample standard deviation) that according to our assumption will approximate $\sigma/\sqrt{|S_x|}$ (see

Subsection 2.2.2). Next we can standardize the statistic to obtain the following random variable:

$$Z = \frac{\overline{x} - \mu}{\frac{\sigma}{\sqrt{|S_x|}}}.$$

Now we wish to find, at probability $1 - \alpha$, the lower and upper bounds on the values of Z. That is, we wish to find Z_P such that

$$\Pr(\overline{x} + Z_P \leq Z \leq \overline{x} - Z_P) = 1 - \alpha.$$

The value of Z_P can be obtained from the CDF of Z. Once Z_P is obtained, the confidence interval around $\overline{x}$ can be given as $(\overline{x} - Z_P \frac{\sigma}{\sqrt{|S_x|}}, \overline{x} + Z_P \frac{\sigma}{\sqrt{|S_x|}})$. Note that we do not know the true standard deviation σ. In this case, we use the sample standard deviation or standard error $\sigma(x)$ for the purpose. That is, at confidence level $1 - \alpha$, the value of the true mean μ lies between the lower and upper bounds of the confidence intervals (also known as confidence limits) denoted as CI_{lower} and CI_{upper} such that

$$\text{CI}_{\text{lower}} = \overline{x} - Z_P \frac{\sigma(x)}{\sqrt{|S_x|}},$$

$$\text{CI}_{\text{upper}} = \overline{x} + Z_P \frac{\sigma(x)}{\sqrt{|S_x|}}.$$

Note that this is essentially the two-sided confidence interval, and hence we have considered a confidence parameter of $\alpha/2$ to account for the upper and the lower bounds each while considering the CDF. This will have important implications in statistical hypothesis testing, as we will see later. The discussion up until here on the manner of calculating the confidence intervals was aimed at elucidating the process. However, tables with Z_P values corresponding to the desired level of significance are available (see Table A.1 in Appendix A). Hence, for desired levels of confidence, these values can be readily used to give the confidence intervals.

Let us go back to our example from Table 2.3. We calculated the mean empirical risk of the three classifiers on the labor dataset. Using the sample standard deviation, we can then obtain the confidence intervals for the true risk. The value of Z_P corresponding to $\alpha = 0.05$ (95% confidence level) is found to be 1.96 from Table A.1 in Appendix A. Hence we can obtain, for c4.5,

$$\text{CI}_{\text{lower}}^{R(c45)} = \overline{R}(c4.5) - Z_P \frac{\sigma(x)}{\sqrt{|S_x|}}$$

$$= 0.217668 - 1.96 \frac{0.1603415}{\sqrt{100}}.$$

Similarly,

$$CI_{upper}^{R(c45)} = \overline{R}(c4.5) + Z_P \frac{\sigma(x)}{\sqrt{|S_x|}}$$

$$= 0.217668 + 1.96 \frac{0.1603415}{\sqrt{100}}.$$

The confidence limits for the other two classifiers can be obtained in an analogous manner.

As we mentioned earlier, the confidence interval approach has also been important in statistical hypothesis testing. One of the most immediate applications of this approach employing the assumption of normal distribution on the statistic can be found in the commonly used significance test, the t test. The confidence interval calculation is implicit in the t test that can be used to verify if the statistic differs from the one assumed by the null hypothesis. There are many variations of the t test. We demonstrate the so-called one-sample t test on the empirical risk of the three classifiers in our example of Table 2.3. Here the test is used to confirm if the sample mean differs from 0 in a statistically significant manner. This can be done in R for the empirical risks of the three classifiers, also giving the confidence interval estimates, as follows:

Listing 2.4: Sample R command for executing the t test and thereby obtain the confidence interval for the means of the sample data.

```
> t.test(c45)

        One Sample t-test

data:   c45
t = 13.5753, df = 99, p-value < 2.2e-16
alternative hypothesis: true mean is not equal to 0
95 percent confidence interval:
 0.1858528 0.2494832
sample estimates:
mean of x
 0.217668


> t.test(jrip)

        One Sample t-test

data:   jrip
t = 10.9386, df = 99, p-value < 2.2e-16
alternative hypothesis: true mean is not equal to 0
95 percent confidence interval:
 0.1336829 0.1929291
sample estimates:
mean of x
```

```
     0.163306

> t.test(nb)

        One Sample t-test

data:   nb
t = 6.1494, df = 99, p-value = 1.648e-08
alternative hypothesis: true mean is not equal to 0
95 percent confidence interval:
 0.04425538 0.08642062
sample estimates:
mean of x
 0.065338


>
```

These confidence intervals can be plotted using the `plotCI` command available in the `gplot` package, as follows:

Listing 2.5: Sample R command for plotting the confidence intervals of c4.5, RIP, and NB means when applied to the labor data

```
> means <- c(.217668, .163306, .065338)
> stdevs <- c(.1603415, .1492936, .1062516)
> ns <- c(100, 100, 100)
> qt(.95, ns)
> ciw   <- qt(0.95, ns) * stdevs / sqrt(ns)
> plotCI(x=means, uiw=ciw, col="black", labels=round(means,-3),
    xaxt="ns", xlim=c(0,5))
> axis(side=1, at=1:3, labels=c('c45', 'jrip', 'nb'), cex=0.7)
```

The result is shown in Figure 2.5, where the 95% confidence intervals for the three classifiers are shown around the mean. The figure shows that the true means of the error rates of these classifiers are probably quite distinct from one another, given the little, if any, overlap displayed by the graphs (an effect enhanced by the scale on the vertical axis too). In particular, the NB interval does not overlap with either the c4.5's or RIP's, and there is only a marginal overlap between the intervals of c4.5 and RIP. It is worth noting that, although our conclusions may seem quite clear and straightforward, the situation is certainly not as simple as it appears. For starters, recall that these results have a 95% confidence level, indicating that there still is some likelihood of the true mean not falling in the intervals obtained around the sample mean empirical risks. Moreover, the results and subsequent interpretations obtained here rely on an important assumption that the sampling distribution of the empirical risk can be approximated by a normal distribution. Finally, there is another inherent assumption, which we did not state explicitly earlier and indeed is more often than not taken for granted, that of the i.i.d. nature of the estimates of risk in the sample. This final assumption

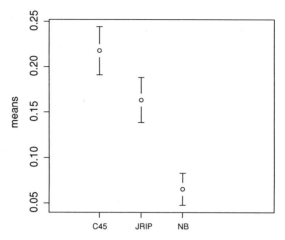

Figure 2.5. The confidence intervals for C4.5, NB, and RIP.

is obviously violated, given that the repeated runs of the 10-fold cross-validation are done by sampling from the same dataset. Indeed, these assumptions can have important implications. The normality assumption in particular, when violated, can yield inaccurate or even uninterpretable estimates of the confidence intervals, as we will see later in the book (Chapter 8). We will also discuss the effects of such repeated sampling from the same set of instances (Chapter 5).

Another issue has to do with the importance that confidence intervals have started gaining in the past decade, vis-à-vis the hypothesis testing approach discussed in the next subsection. Indeed, in recent years, arguments in favor of using confidence intervals over hypothesis testing have appeared (e.g., Armstrong, 2007). The reasoning behind the recommendation goes along the following two lines:

- First, the meaning of the significance value used in hypothesis testing has come under scrutiny and has become more and more contested. In contrast, confidence intervals have a simple and straightforward interpretation.
- Second, significance values allow us to accept or reject a hypothesis (as we will see in the next subsection), but cannot help us decide by how much to accept or reject it. That is, the significance testing approach does not allow quantification of the extent to which a hypothesis can be accepted or rejected. Conversely, confidence intervals give us a means by which we can consider such degrees of acceptance or rejection.

Even though there is some merit to the preceding arguments with regard to the limitations of hypothesis testing, these shortcomings do not, by themselves, make confidence intervals a de facto method of choice. The confidence interval approach also makes a normal assumption on the empirical error that is often violated. As we will see in Chapter 8, this can result in unrealistic estimates.

Moreover, statistical hypothesis testing, when applied taking into account the underlying assumptions and constraints, can indeed be helpful. To make this discussion clearer, let us now discuss the basics of statistical hypothesis testing.

2.2.4 Hypothesis Testing

Our discussion so far has focused on modeling and estimating the statistic of interest on any given sample and mapping these ideas to the problem of evaluating learning algorithms. Essentially we can model the performance of the classifier, commonly its empirical risk, as a random variable and study its behavior. Just as we did previously, a typical approach would be to study the average performance of the classifier by obtaining the mean empirical risk (or any other monotonic performance measure). Given an estimate of the mean performance, the next question is, how reliable is this estimate? That is, how representative of the true statistic is this estimate of the expected value of the random variable? When put in the context of comparing two classifiers, the natural question to ask would be this: Given the difference between the mean performances of two classifiers on a given dataset, how representative is this empirical difference of the difference in their true values? Statistical hypothesis testing is aimed at addressing these questions.

Statistical hypothesis testing, sometimes referred to as just hypothesis testing, plays a very important role in statistical inference. It is part of the branch of statistics known as *confirmatory data analysis*. Hence, as the name suggests, the main concern of its application is to *confirm* whether the observed behavior is representative of the true behavior. As soon as we interpret the confirmatory data analysis in this manner, it becomes clear that there is indeed an assumption of the true behavior (how much ever weak) of the data at hand. Such an analysis is essentially a deductive approach in which we assume the existence of a hypothesis (called the "null hypothesis") and then proceed to reject or accept (more appropriately "fail to reject") this hypothesis. Further, as a result of this null-hypothesis existence requirement, we make (sometimes strong) assumptions on the behavior of the data at hand that might not be verifiable. For instance, recall how, as we discussed briefly, the t test assumes the empirical risk to be distributed according to a normal distribution in our example. Such assumptions are a source of considerably opposing viewpoints on the use of hypothesis testing. Indeed, there can be significant disadvantages to such an approach. Because assumptions on hypothesis are made a priori, this could lead to performing statistical testing in a preconceived framework. An immediate consequence of such assumptions is that conditions and results that might not be explained by the assumed models are left unaccounted for (in fact, even neglected). Finally, the outcomes of such testing can become uninterpretable, and in many cases even misleading, if the initial assumptions are violated. What, then, are the advantages of using such approaches? The first and foremost is the existence of strong, well-established, and analytically tractable techniques for testing as a result of the modeling assumptions. This results in statistical testing methods that are theoretically justified. Consequently this yields strong verifiable results when the underlying assumptions are satisfied.

This is different from the inductive nature of the *exploratory data analysis* approaches in which the observations and calculations on the data are used to obtain insights without any a priori assumptions. However, the downside of this approach, naturally, is that it may not yield concrete results, especially in the wake of limited data to support strong conclusions.

As we previously mentioned, much of the hypothesis testing, especially that relevant to our context, is centered around the idea of null-hypothesis testing. Let us look at null-hypothesis testing in its general form. A null hypothesis characterizes, generally quantitatively, an a priori assumption on the behavior of the data at hand. For instance, this can be some statistic of interest such as the empirical mean of the data. By a priori assumption on behavior, we mean that the behavior of the data (or a statistic on this data) is assumed to always hold, unless the observed statistic from the data contradicts it, in which case we have to reject this assumption (possibly in favor of an alternative explanation). The goal of this hypothesis testing is then to find the probability with which the data statistic of interest is at least as extreme as the one measured from the data (observed). For instance, recall when we applied the one sample t test (Listing 2.4). This test assumed that the true mean empirical risk was zero and the observed mean seemed highly improbable (exceptionally low p value), leading us to reject this null hypothesis in all three cases.[12]

A typical statistical hypothesis testing procedure can be summarized as follows:

1. State the a priori hypothesis, the null hypothesis H_0, and possibly an alternative research hypothesis. This is an extremely important step because it has implications for the rest of the hypothesis testing procedure.
2. The null hypothesis that one typically wishes to refute is the opposite of the research hypothesis in which one is interested. Consider the assumptions made by this hypothesis on the data.
3. Decide on the suitable statistical test and the corresponding statistic (the one used to reject the null hypothesis).
4. Calculate the observed test statistic from the data and compare against the value expected according to the null-hypothesis assumptions.
5. Decide on a critical region needed for the observed test statistic to lie in under the null hypothesis for it to be considered sufficiently extreme (that is, has extremely low probability) to be able to reject the null hypothesis.

---

[12] Note that this is not to say that this assumption was the *best* choice. One might more realistically wish to assume that the empirical risk is 0.5, i.e., the classifier is a random classifier, and to test the observed risk against this assumption instead. However, this does not affect the point we wish to make about the basic methodology here.

6. If the observed test statistic lies in the critical region (has extremely low probability of being observed under the null-hypothesis assumption), reject the null hypothesis H_0. However, note that, when this is not the case, one would fail to reject the null hypothesis. This does not lead to the conclusion that one can accept the null hypothesis.

Step 6 makes an important point. In the case in which the null hypothesis cannot be rejected based on the observed value of the test statistic, the conclusion that it must be accepted necessarily does not hold. Recall that the null hypothesis was *assumed*. Hence not being able to disprove its existence does not necessarily confirm it.

We are interested in comparing the performance of two learning algorithms. In our case then the null hypothesis can, for instance, assume that the difference between the empirical risks of the two classifiers is (statistically) insignificant. That is, the two estimates come from a similar population. Because the errors are estimated on the same population, the only difference being the two classifiers, this then translates to meaning that the two classifiers behave in a more or less similar manner. Rejecting this hypothesis would then mean that the observed difference between the classifiers' performances is indeed statistically significant (technically this would lead us to conclude that the difference is not statistically insignificant; however, our null-hypothesis definition allows us to draw this conclusion).

One- and Two-Tailed Tests

In the statistics literature, the one-tailed and two-tailed tests are also referred to as one-sided and two-sided tests, respectively. A statistical hypothesis test is called one sided if the values that can reject the null hypothesis are contained wholly in one tail of the probability distribution. That is, these values are all either lower than the threshold of the test (also known as the critical value of the test) or higher than the threshold, but not both. On the other hand, a two-tailed test enables rejecting the null hypothesis, taking into account both the tails of the probability distribution.

In other words, an H_0 expressed as an equality can be rejected in two ways. For instance, we formulate H_0 to say that the difference between two sample means is equal to zero. Then we can reject this hypothesis in two ways: first, if the difference is less than zero, and second, if the difference is greater than zero. If we are concerned about either only the lower or the higher statistic, a one-tailed test would suffice. However, when both manners of hypothesis rejection are significant, a two-tailed test is used.

For example, let us assume that we are comparing the results between c4.5 and NB from Table 2.3, and let us assume that we already know that NB is never a worse classifier than c4.5 on data similar to the labor data that we are using here. The hypothesis that we want to test is that, on this particular labor domain, C4.5 is once again not as accurate as NB. In such a case, we hypothesize that the difference between the true risk of C4.5 [$R(\text{C45})$] and that of NB [$R(\text{NB})$] has a mean of 0. Note that our assumption says that NB is never worse than C4.5, and hence this difference is never considered to be less than zero. Under these assumptions, we can obtain the observed difference in the mean empirical risk of the two classifiers $\overline{R}(\text{C45}) - \overline{R}(\text{NB})$ and apply a one-tailed test to verify if the observed difference is significantly greater than 0. On the other hand, we may not have any a priori assumption over the classifiers' performance difference, e.g., in the case of C4.5 and RIP in the preceding example. In such cases, we might be interested in knowing, for instance, only whether the observed difference between their performance is indeed significant. That is, this difference (irrespective of what classifier is better) would hold if their true distribution were available. We leave the details of how such testing is performed in practice and under what assumptions to a more elaborate treatment in Chapter 6.

Parametric and Nonparametric Approaches to Hypothesis Testing

There are mainly two approaches to statistical hypothesis testing, parametric and nonparametric, which come from the type of assumptions made to establish the null hypothesis. The parametric approach assumes a well-defined underlying distribution over the statistic of interest under this null hypothesis. Hence it is assumed that the sample statistic is representative of the true statistic according to a well-defined distribution model such that its true defining statistic can be characterized systematically. The hypothesis test then aims at confirming or, more appropriately, rejecting the assumption that the behavior of the observed statistic of interest resembles that of the true statistic. A common example would be the Student's t test over the difference of true empirical risks of two classifiers. The test, as a null hypothesis, assumes that the two classifiers perform in a similar manner (that is, the two estimates of the observed empirical risks come from the same population). As a result, the difference between them is assumed to be distributed according to a normal distribution centered at zero (the mean of the normal distribution). As can be noted, here again there is a correlation between the confidence interval approach and the normal distribution assuming hypothesis tests over the mean empirical error, in that confidence intervals can be obtained over the means simply by reversing the hypothesis testing criterion.

In contrast to parametric hypothesis testing, the nonparametric approaches do not rely on any fixed model assumption over the statistic of interest. Such tests often take the form of ranking-based approaches because this enables the characterization of two competing hypotheses in terms of their comparative ability to explain the sample at hand. An example would be McNemar's test for the comparison of two populations, which we detail in Chapter 6 along with other statistical testing methods in the context of evaluating learning algorithms.

Of course, there are advantages and limitations to both the parametric and the nonparametric approaches. The nonparametric tests, as a result of independence from any modeling assumption, are quite useful in populations for which outliers skew the distribution significantly (not to mention, in addition, the case in which no distribution underlies the statistics). However, the consequence of this advantage of model independence is the limited power (see the discussion on the type II error in the following subsection) of these tests because limited generalizations can be made over the behavior or comparison of the sample statistic in the absence of any concrete behavior model. Parametric approaches, on the other hand, are useful when the distributional assumption are (even approximately) met because, in that case, strong conclusions can be reached. However, in the case in which the assumptions are violated, parametric tests can be grossly misleading.

Let us now see how we can characterize the hypothesis tests themselves in terms of their ability to reject the null hypothesis. This is generally quantified by specifying two quantities of interests with regard to the hypothesis test, its type I error and its type II error, the latter of which also affects the power of the test, as we subsequently discuss.

Type I and Type II Errors, Power of a Test
The type I and type II errors and the associated power of a statistical test can be defined as follows:

Definition 2.5. *A type I error (α) corresponds to the error of rejecting the null hypothesis H_0 when it is, in fact, true (false positive). A type II error (β) corresponds to the error of failing to reject H_0 when it is false (false negative).*

Note that the type II error basically quantifies the extent to which a test validates the null hypothesis when it in fact does not hold. Hence we can define the power of test by taking into account the complement of the type II error, as follows:

Definition 2.6. *The power of a test is the probability of rejecting H_0, given that it is false:*

$$\text{Power} = 1 - \beta.$$

The preceding two types of errors are generally traded off. That is, reducing the type I error makes the hypothesis test more sensitive in that it does not reject H_0 too easily. As a result of this tendency, the type II error of the test, that of failing to reject H_0, even when it does not hold, increases. This then gives us a test with low power. A low-power test may be insufficient, for instance, in finding the difference in classifier performance as significant, even when it is so. The parametric tests can have more power than their nonparametric counterparts because they can characterize the sample statistic in a well-defined manner.

However, this is true only when the modeling assumption on the distribution of the sample statistics holds. The α parameter is the confidence parameter in the sense that it specifies how unlikely the result must be if one is to reject the null hypothesis. A typical value of α is 0.05 or 5%. Reducing α then amounts to making the test more rigorous. We will see in Chapter 5 how this α parameter also affects the sample size requirement for the test in the context of analyzing the holdout method of evaluation.

In addition to these characteristics arising from the inherent nature of the test, the power of tests can be increased in other manners too (although with corresponding costs), as follows:

- **Increasing the size of the type I error:** As just discussed, the first and simplest way to increase power or lower the type II error is to do so at the expense of the type I Error. Although we usually set α to 0.05, if we increased it to 0.10 or 0.20, then β would be decreased. An important question, however, is whether we are ready to take a greater chance at a type I error; i.e., whether we are ready to take the chance of claiming that a result is significant when it is not, to increase our chance of finding a significant result when one exists. Often this is not a good alternative, and it would be preferable to increase power without having to increase α.
- **Using a one-tailed rather than a two-tailed test:** One-tailed tests are more powerful than two-tailed tests for a given α level. Indeed, running a two-tailed test for $\alpha_2 = 0.05$ is equivalent to running two one-tailed test for $\alpha_1 = 0.025$. Because α_1 is very small in this case, its corresponding β_1 is large, and thus the power is small. Hence, in moving from a two-tailed $\alpha_2 = 0.05$ test to a one-tailed $\alpha'_1 = 0.05$ test, we are doubling the value of α_1 and thus decreasing the value of β'_1, in turn increasing the power of the test. Of course, this can be done only if we know which of the two distribution means considered in the test are expected to be higher. If this information is not available, then a two-tailed test is necessary and no power can be gained in this manner.
- **Choosing a more sensitive evaluation measure:** One way to separate two samples, or increase power, is to increase the difference between the means of the two samples. We can do this, when setting up our experiments, by selecting an evaluation measure that emphasizes the effect we are testing. For example, let us assume that we are using the balanced F measure (also called the F_1 measure) to compare the performance of two classifiers, but let us say that precision is the aspect of the performance that we care about the most. (Both of these performance measures are discussed in Chapter 3.) Let us assume that, of the two classifiers tested, one was specifically designed to improve on precision at the expense of recall (complementary measure of precision used to compute the F measure, also discussed in Chapter 3). If F_1 is the measure used, then the gains in precision of the more precise

algorithm would be overshadowed by its losses in recall, given that both measures are weighed equally. If, however, we used the $F_{0.5}$ measure that weighs precision more than recall, the expected gains in precision would be more noticeable.[13] This would also have the effect of increasing the power of the statistical test.

- **Increasing the sample size:** Another way to separate two samples is to decrease their spread, or standard deviation. This is feasible by increasing the size of the sample. One way of doing so would be to use resampling methods such as a 10-fold-cross-validation or its repeated runs. Of course, this is generally accompanied by additional computational costs, not to mention the bias in the resulting performance estimates as a result of relaxation of the data independence assumption and reuse of data in various runs.

Before wrapping this review of statistical concepts, let us see one final notion, that of the effect size of a statistical test.

Effect Size

The idea of separating the two samples in order to increase power comes from the fact that power is inextricably linked to the amount of overlap that occurs between two distributions. Let us see what we mean by this in the context of comparing classifier performance. If we are interested in characterizing the difference in risk of two classifiers, then, in the parametric case, our null hypothesis can assume this difference to be distributed according to a normal distribution centered at zero. Let us call this the standard distribution. We would then calculate the parameters of the distribution of the statistics of interest from the data. Let us denote this as the empirical distribution. Then, the farther the empirical distribution is from the standard distribution, the more confidence we would have in rejecting the null hypothesis. The strength with which we can reject the null hypothesis is basically the effect size of the test. Figure 2.6 illustrates this notion graphically. The distribution on the left is the standard distribution, and the one on the right is the empirical distribution with the straight vertical line denoting the threshold of the hypothesis test beyond which the null hypothesis is rejected. The overlap to the right of the threshold basically signifies the probability that we reject the null hypothesis even when it holds (type I error, α). The tail of the standard distribution is nothing but α. Similarly, the overlap to the left of the threshold denotes the probability that we do not reject the null hypothesis even though it does not hold (type II error, β). It is clear that moving the separating line to the left increases α while decreasing β. In fact, choosing any significance level α implicitly defines a trade-off in terms of increasing β. Note, however, that in the event of very large samples, these trade-offs can be

---

[13] We assume here that we do not wish to disregard recall altogether because otherwise we would use the precision measure directly.

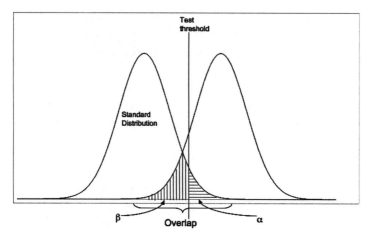

Figure 2.6. Type I and type II errors.

deemed relatively unnecessary. Note here that we assumed in Figure 2.6 that the standard distribution lies on the left of the empirical distribution. This need not always be the case. If such a direction of the effect is known, we can use a one-tailed test. However, if we do not know this directionality, a two-tailed test should be employed. Finally, it can be seen that the two types of errors depend on the overlap on either side of the test threshold between the two distributions. Hence, if one were to reduce the standard deviations of the (one or) two distributions, this would lead to a reduction in the corresponding overlaps, thereby reducing the respective errors. This would in turn result in increased power.

Hence we can see that a parametric modeling on the two distributions would rely on their overlap. Reporting the amount of overlap between two distributions would thus be a good indicator of how powerful a test would be for two populations. Quantifying this overlap would then be an indicator of the test's *effect size*. Naturally, a large effect size indicates a small overlap whereas a small effect size indicates a large overlap. In the literature, several measures have been proposed to quantify the effect size of a test depending on the hypothesis test settings. With regard to the more common case of comparing two means over the difference of classifier performance, Cohen's *d* statistic has been suggested as a suitable measure of the effect size. It is discussed in Chapter 6.

2.3 Summary

This chapter was aimed at introducing the relevant concepts of machine learning and statistics and placing them in the context of classifier evaluation. Even though the book assumes familiarity on the part of the reader with the machine learning basics, especially classification algorithms, we believe that the discussion in this chapter will enable the reader to relate various notions not only to the context of evaluation, but also with regard to the associated statistics perspective. The statistical concepts surveyed in the second section of this chapter recur frequently in the context of various aspects of evaluation. Together with the different concepts introduced in this chapter and those that will be reviewed further, we pointed out two important and free Web-based packages for use in both machine learning research and its evaluation. The first one was the WEKA machine learning toolkit, which implements a large number of machine learning algorithms, as well as preprocessing and postprocessing techniques. The second one was the R Project for Statistical Computing, which is a free implementation of statistical routines [closely related to the (commercial) S Package]. This package implements, among other things, a large number of statistical tests, whose use is demonstrated more thoroughly in Chapter 6.

Chapters 3–7 focus on specific aspects of the evaluation procedure in the context of comparing the performances of two or more learning algorithms. The most fundamental aspect of evaluating the performances is deciding on how to assess or measure these in the first place. Chapters 3 and 4 discuss various alternatives for such performance measures.

2.4 Bibliographic Remarks

Most of the concepts discussed in this chapter can be found in standard machine learning and statistics theory texts. We give specific references at the end of later chapters as we delve into the details of various components of the evaluation framework.

3

Performance Measures I

The evaluation of learning algorithms both in absolute terms and in relation to other algorithms involves addressing four main components:

- performance measures,
- error estimation,
- statistical significance testing, and
- test benchmark selection.

The first component concerns the property of the algorithm's performance that one wishes to measure. The answers are sought for questions such as these: Do we measure how accurate the algorithm is? If so, how do we define accuracy? Do we value one aspect of the algorithm's performance more than other? These and related issues are the focus of this and the next chapter. Once a performance measure is chosen, the next big concern is to estimate it in as unbiased a manner as possible, making the best possible use of the available data. This is the focus of Chapter 5, on performance estimation. Chapter 6 then focuses on investigating whether the differences in the performances obtained by the algorithm alone or in relation to others are statistically significant. Finally, we try to complete the puzzle with a discussion on what domains can be deemed suitable as benchmarks to evaluate learning approaches. This is the focus of Chapter 7.

Performance measures have arguably received the greatest amount of attention in the field. As a consequence of the inherent multidisciplinary nature of the machine learning tasks, different variants of these performance measures have been influenced by approaches from a variety of disciplines, including statistics, medicine, and information retrieval. Having been studied extensively, the aspect of evaluation pertaining to the choice of a possible performance measure has reached enough maturity for studies to have surfaced that propose frameworks for evaluating and combining existing performance measures. See Section 3.8 as well as Chapter 8 for some pointers.

This chapter and the next review various prominent performance measures and touch on the different issues one encounters when selecting these for evaluation studies. Different dichotomies of performance measures can be formed. We decided to use a simple and intuitive, though a bit approximate, one based on the so-called confusion matrix. This chapter focuses on the performance measures whose elements are based on the information contained in the confusion matrix alone. In the next chapter, we extend our focus to take into account measures incorporating information about (prior) class distributions and classifier uncertainties.

3.1 Overview of the Problem

When the issue of choosing an appropriate performance evaluation measure for an experimental study is considered, several questions come into play. The first issue naturally concerns the type of learning algorithm to be evaluated. With regard to the performance on the training or test instances, the algorithms can essentially be categorized into deterministic and probabilistic algorithms. The deterministic algorithms output a fixed class label for each instance and hence can be better measured in terms of the zero–one loss. That is, the loss of misclassifying an example (assigning a wrong class label to the instance) is one; and zero otherwise. Probabilistic classifiers, on the other hand, issue a probability estimate on the class membership of the example for various classes. In such a case, a zero–one loss function is generally not an appropriate measure of classifier's performance. To obtain deterministic class assignments from probabilistic classifiers, typically either a maximum a posteriori (MAP) or a Bayesian estimate is considered. Typically the classifiers are tested once a deterministic labeling of the test instances is obtained. As a result, this can be organized in the form of a confusion matrix. This is our starting point in this analysis.

Another class of learning algorithms yields a score (typically continuous) on each test instance. These scoring classifiers are then generally thresholded so as to obtain deterministic labels for test examples. Examples of such algorithms can include neural networks, decision trees, and so on. In a binary classification scenario, a classifier that outputs scores on each test instance in a fixed interval $[a, b]$ can be thresholded at some point $s_t \in [a, b]$ such that all the examples with a score greater than s_t are classified as positive whereas the examples scoring less than s_t are labeled as negative. In this sense of continuous scores, these classifiers are also referred to as ranking classifiers. However, we avoid this term to avoid confusion with ranking algorithms (which obtain the ordering of a given set of instances). Note that the scoring algorithms can be treated as ranking algorithms, but the opposite does not necessarily hold. The scoring algorithms make an even more interesting case in terms of performance measurement because the resulting labeling depends on choosing an appropriate threshold.

This can be considered similar to parameter selection (model selection) in other algorithms. However, scoring algorithms typically operate in a continuous space, and hence their behavior can be tracked over the space of all possible thresholds.

Scoring classifiers, in a sense, then output, instead of a discrete label, a real-valued score, possibly signifying the extent to which the example is found to be representative of a certain class. We refer to performance measures that take this space into consideration as scoring measures. In an analogous manner, the performance evaluation of probabilistic classifiers should also take into account their output in terms of probability estimates (and not merely the resulting MAP or Bayesian labels) to better reflect the classifier's weighting on each class label for the given instance. Metrics that take these aspects into account can be categorized as reliability metrics. There are certainly other classifiers for which specialized performance measures should be utilized. For instance, we do not discuss, here, the class of probably approximately correct (PAC) Bayesian classifiers that output a posterior probability on the space of classifiers. Hence the resulting labels on the test set are typically obtained by either a Bayesian (majority) classifier over this posterior or a Gibbs classifier that picks a deterministic classifier based on the posterior distribution over classifiers. Bayesian or Gibbs performance estimates are more suitable in such cases. In this book, we limit our discussion to the most common classifiers whose performances can be characterized in terms of the confusion matrix and possibly some additional information. Throughout the book, however, we provide pointers to other metrics and even briefly discuss metrics for some common cases such as regression.

In this chapter and the next, we discuss different measures for assessing the performance of the learning algorithms, their respective strengths and limitations, and their suitability to particular training or test settings. For the purpose of making the discussion more intuitive, we divide these performance measures into two categories. First, we discuss the measures that take information solely from the confusion matrix resulting from the application of a learning algorithm (or the resulting classifier) on training (or test) data. These measures are typically applied in the case of deterministic classification algorithms. Second, we discuss the measures that take into account, in addition to the confusion matrix, information about the class distribution priors and classifier uncertainty. Such metrics are useful with regard to the scoring classifiers previously discussed. We also briefly discuss some Bayesian measures to account for probabilistic classifiers and measures for regression algorithms. This chapter focuses on the first group of performance measures, the ones that take into account information solely from the confusion matrix. We cover the second group in the next chapter.

Other issues that arise while we measure the algorithms' performance are the possibly asymmetric costs of misclassification (in which a classifier's error on examples of a certain class is deemed more serious than that on examples of other classes), taking into consideration prior class distributions to account for class imbalances and robustness in the presence of concept drift or noise. We also briefly discuss these aspects. Finally, we also see how the representation of the various performance measures affects the type and amount of information they convey as well as their interpretability and understandability. For instance, we will see how graphical measures such as those used for scoring algorithms as discussed in the next chapter result in the visualization of the algorithms' performance over different settings. The scalar measures, on the other hand, have the advantage of being concise and allow for clear comparisons of different learning methods. However, because of their conciseness, they lack informativeness because they summarize a great deal of information into a scalar metric. The disadvantage of the graphical measures appears in the form of a lack of ease in implementation and a possibly increased time complexity. In addition, results expressed in this form may be more difficult to interpret than those reported in a single measure.

3.1.1 Monotonic and Nonmonotonic Measures

While discussing the performance measures in this and the next chapter, unless otherwise specified, we discuss only the monotonic measures of performance. A monotonic performance measures $pm(\cdot)$ is such that, over the range of $pm(\cdot)$, either the relationship "$pm(f_1) > pm(f_2)$ implies that f_1 is 'better' than f_2, and vice versa" or "$pm(f_1) > pm(f_2)$ implies that f_2 is 'better' than f_1, and vice versa" holds. That is, a strict increase (or decrease) in the value of $pm(\cdot)$ indicates a better (or worse) classifier throughout the range of the function $pm(\cdot)$, or vice versa. Some measures that are not strictly monotonic can be thought of [e.g., using ideas such as Kolmogorov complexity which is a nonmonotonic measure over strings (Li and Viťanyi, 1997)] as the class-conditional probability estimate discussed in (Kukar et al., 2002) in the context of a multiclass problem.

3.1.2 The Confusion Matrix

The performance measures that we discuss in this chapter draw information from the confusion matrix. Let us start then by discussing what a confusion matrix is, in the general case, for a classifier f. We then focus on the performance measures available in binary classification, mainly for two reasons. First, this is the domain where the measures have largely been applied. Second, the strengths and limitations of performance measures in the two-class scenario are relatively easy to understand and are quite illustrative of their behavior in the more general context.

Let us denote the confusion matrix by $\mathbf{C}$. Then $\mathbf{C} = \{c_{ij}\}$, $i, j \in \{1, 2, \ldots, l\}$, where i is the row index and j is the column index. Generally, $\mathbf{C}$ is defined with respect to some fixed learning algorithm. There are two facts worth a mention here. First, the confusion matrix can indeed be extended to incorporate information for the performance of more than one algorithm. This will result in a higher-dimensional tensor. We do not, however, delve into this owing to the more prominent use of the confusion matrix in the current formulation as well as the ease of understanding various aspects under this formulation. Another aspect worth noting is that, given a training dataset and a test dataset, an algorithm learns on the training set, outputting a fixed classifier f. The test-set performance of f is then typically recorded in the confusion matrix. This is why we define our confusion matrix entries as well as the measures derived from these with respect to a fixed classifier f. However, in the cases in which the size of the overall data at hand is limited, resampling approaches are utilized that divide the data into training sets and test sets and perform runs over these divisions multiple times. In this case, the confusion matrix entries would be the combined performance of the learning algorithm on the test sets over all such runs (and hence represent the combined performance of classifiers in each run). Of course, there are concerns with regard to the reliability of these estimates in the resampling scenario, but we postpone the discussion of resampling techniques and their associated issues to Chapter 5.

For the present case, assuming a fixed classifier f, let us denote the confusion matrix with respect to f as $\mathbf{C}(f)$. Then $\mathbf{C}(f)$ is a square $l \times l$ matrix for a dataset with l classes. Each element $c_{ij}(f)$ of the confusion matrix denotes the number of examples that actually have a class i label and that the classifier f assigns to class j. For instance, the entry $c_{13}(f)$ denotes the number of examples belonging to class 1 that are assigned to class 3 by classifier f.

Hence, for a test set T of examples and a classifier f, the confusion matrix $\mathbf{C}(f)$ can be defined as

$$\mathbf{C}(f) = \left\{ c_{ij}(f) = \sum_{\mathbf{x} \in T} [(y = i) \wedge (f(\mathbf{x}) = j)] \right\},$$

where $\mathbf{x}$ is a test example and y is its corresponding label such that $y \in \{1, 2, \ldots, l\}$.

We can easily make the following observations:

- $\sum_{j=1}^{l} c_{ij}(f) = c_{i.}(f)$ denotes the total number of examples of class i in the test set.
- $\sum_{i=1}^{l} c_{ij}(f) = c_{.j}(f)$ denotes the total number of examples assigned to class j by classifier f.
- All the diagonal entries c_{ii} denotes the correctly classified examples for class i. Hence $\sum_{i=1}^{l} c_{ii}(f)$ denotes the total number of examples classified correctly by classifier f.
- All the nondiagonal entries denote misclassifications. Hence $\sum_{i,j:i \neq j} c_{ij}(f)$ denotes the total number of examples assigned to wrong classes by classifier f.

Table 3.1. *Confusion matrix for the binary classification case*

f	Pred_Negative	Pred_Positive
Act_Negative	$c_{11}(f)$	$c_{12}(f)$
Act_Positive	$c_{21}(f)$	$c_{22}(f)$

As can be seen in the preceding case, the entries of **C** deal with a deterministic classification scenario for the symmetric loss case. That is, f deterministically assigns a label to each instance with a unit probability instead of making a probabilistic statement on its membership for different classes. Moreover, the cost associated with classifying an instance **x** to class j, $j \in \{1, \ldots, l\}$, is the same as classifying it to class k such that $k \in \{1, \ldots, l\}$, $k \neq j$. We will see a bit later how we can incorporate these considerations into the resulting performance measures.

3.1.3 The Binary Classification Case

The binary classification case is the most common setting in which the performance of the learning algorithm is measured. Also, this setting serves well for illustration purposes with regard to the strengths and limitations of the performance measures. For $l = 2$ classes, the confusion matrix is obviously a 2×2 matrix and is generally of the following form. With the two classes called "negative" and "positive," respectively, $\mathbf{C}(i)$ for the binary classification case can be written as in Table 3.1

Here the rows represent the actual class of the test examples whereas the columns represent the class assigned (or predicted) by the classifier f. Hence c_{11} denotes the element in the first row and first column and is equal to the total number of examples whose actual labels are negative and that are also assigned a negative label by the classifier f.

We can describe the binary confusion matrix in the more intuitive form shown in Table 3.2. This confusion matrix contains four characteristic values: the numbers of true positives (TPs), false positives (FPs), false negatives (FNs), and true negatives (TNs). TP and TN thus stand for the number of examples from the testing set that were correctly classified as positive and negative, respectively. Conversely, FN and FP stand for the positive and negative examples that were erroneously classified as negative and positive, respectively.

Table 3.2. *Alternative representation of the confusion matrix*

	Pred_Negative	Pred_Positive	
Act_Negative	True negative (TN)	False positive (FP)	$N = \text{TN} + \text{FP}$
Act_Positive	False negative (FN)	True positive (TP)	$P = \text{FN} + \text{TP}$

Table 3.3. *Confusion matrix for NB applied to the breast cancer domain*

NB	Pred_Negative	Pred_Positive
Act_Negative	168	33
Act_Positive	48	37

Let us illustrate this with an example. Consider applying a naive Bayes (NB) classifier to the breast cancer dataset (we discuss this and some other experiments in Section 3.3). The domain refers to the application of the classifier to predict, from a set of patients, whether a recurrence would occur. Hence the two class labels refer to "positive" (recurrence occurred) and "negative" (recurrence did not occur). On applying the NB classifier to the test set, we obtain the confusion matrix of Table 3.3.

Let us now interpret the meaning of the values contained in the confusion matrix. Relating the matrix of Table 3.3 to that of Table 3.2, we see that TP = 37, TN = 168, FP = 33, and FN = 48. The confusion matrix shows that out of the $37 + 48 + 33 + 168 = 286$ patients in our test set who previously had breast cancer, TP + FN = $37 + 48 = 85$ suffered a new episode of the disease whereas FP + TN = $33 + 168 = 201$ had remained disease free at the time the data were collected. Our trained NB classifier (we do not worry for now about the issue of how the algorithm was trained and tested so as to obtain the performance estimates; we will come back to this in Chapter 5) predicts results that differ from the truth in terms of both numbers of predictions and predicted class distributions. It predicts that only TP + FP = $37 + 33 = 70$ patients suffered a new episode of the disease and that FN + TN = $48 + 168 = 216$ did not suffer from any new episode. It is thus clear that NB is a generally optimistic classifier (for this domain, in which "optimistic" refers to fewer numbers of recurrences) in the sense that it tends to predict a negative result with a higher frequency relative to the positive prediction. The confusion matrix further breaks these results up into their correctly predicted and incorrectly predicted components for the two prediction classes. That is, it reports how many times the classifier predicts a recurrence wrongly and how many times it predicts a nonrecurrence wrongly. As can be seen, of the 70 recurrence cases predicted overall by NB, 37 were actual recurrence cases, whereas 33 were not. Similarly, out of the 216 cases for which NB predicted no recurrence, 168 cases were actual nonrecurrence cases, whereas 48 were recurrence cases.[1]

---

[1] Note, however, that the data were collected at a particular time. At that time, the people wrongly diagnosed by NB, did not have the disease again. However, this does not imply that they did not develop it at any time after the data were collected, in which case NB would not be that wrong. We restrain ourselves from delving into this issue further for now. But this highlights an inherent limitation of our evaluation strategy and warns the reader that there may be more variables in play when a learning algorithm is applied in practice. Such application-specific considerations should always be kept in mind.

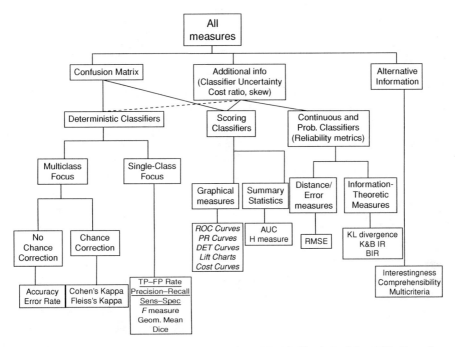

Figure 3.1. An ontology of performance metrics. (KL, Kullback–Leibler; BIR, Bayesian information reward; K & B IR, Kononenko and Bratko information reward.)

3.2 An Ontology of Performance Measures

From the preceding discussion and the information a performance measure is expected to take into account, we can design an ontology of these measures, as we subsequently discuss. We mainly cover the measures currently used with regard to classifier evaluation in machine learning. Novel measures can certainly arise and either fit in appropriate places in the proposed ontology or extend its design. The measures presented in this ontology are discussed in more detail in Sections 3.4 and 3.5, as well as in Chapter 4.

Figure 3.1 presents an ontology of various performance measures widely used in the field relevant to our context. Our discussion of the performance measures in this and the next chapter follows this conceptual framework. Where relevant, we also discuss some other measures of performance, albeit briefly.

The ontology has been built according to three dimensions. The first dimension concerns the type of information taken into consideration: the confusion matrix alone, the confusion matrix in conjunction with additional information, and information in forms other than the confusion matrix altogether.

The second dimension is dependent on the category of classifier that has implications for the choice of metric. It distinguishes among the evaluation of deterministic classifiers, scoring classifiers, and continuous or probabilistic classifiers. For measures that consider the confusion matrix alone and focus on deterministic classifiers,[2] the ontology considers whether the metric focuses on all the classes in the domain, or whether it focuses on a single class of interest. The measures corresponding to these two categories are covered in this chapter.

In the case of metrics that consider the confusion matrix together with extra information, the ontology differentiates between the scoring and the continuous or probabilistic classification algorithms. These metrics are discussed in Chapter 4. With regards to measures using information in other forms, we concern ourselves with whether the measure in question attempts to capture interestingness, comprehensibility, or whether it is a multicriteria measure. These types of measures are more experimental and more seldom used in machine learning. Their discussion is thus relegated to Chapter 8, which surveys recent developments.

The third dimension, indicated in respective typefaces, concerns the format returned by the evaluation metric or its output. In particular, we interest ourselves in how compressed the returned information is. Performance methods that return a scalar value are those that compress their information the most. They are thus practical metrics that make comparisons among learning methods quick and easy, but at the same time are the least informative because of their high compression rate. These are represented in regular roman type. Methods that return two values, like Precision–Recall or sensitivity–Specificity (abbreviated Sens.–Spec.) are more informative because of their lower compression rate, but can make comparisons between algorithms more difficult. Indeed, what if one metric ranks one classifier better than the other and the other metric does the opposite? In fact, combination metrics such as the F measure were created exactly for this reason, but, as a single scalar, they fall back into the less-informative category of metrics. The two-valued output metrics are all shown underlined. Finally, we consider methods that return a graph such as ROC Curves or Cost Curves as the most informative format of all, but also the most complex to handle practically. In fact, as in the case of the F Measure, the AUC is used to summarize the ROC graph (and thus, once again, falls back into the category of least-informative metrics). The graphical methods are represented in italics in our graph.

3.3   Illustrative Example

Before proceeding to discuss different performance measures themselves, let us illustrate how these focus on different aspects of the effectiveness of the learning process and differ in their comparative assessments of the algorithms. In many practical applications, in fact, there is an inevitable trade-off between

---

[2] The confusion matrix alone can also be used for classifiers other than deterministic ones (e.g., by thresholding the decision function) or can, at least in theory, incorporate partial-loss information. However, it is conventionally used for deterministic classifiers, which is why we focus on this use here. Similarly, measures over deterministic classifiers can also take into account additional information (e.g. skew). We indicate this possibility with a dashed line.

Table 3.4. *A study of the UCI breast cancer domain*

Algorithm	Acc	RMSE	TPR	FPR	Prec	Rec	F	AUC	K & B
NB	71.7	0.4534	0.44	0.16	0.53	0.44	0.48	0.7	48.1118
C45	75.5	0.4324	0.27	0.04	0.74	0.27	0.4	0.59	34.2789
3NN	72.4	0.5101	0.32	0.1	0.56	0.32	0.41	0.63	43.3682
RIP	71	0.4494	0.37	0.14	0.52	0.37	0.43	0.6	22.3397
SVM	69.6	0.5515	0.33	0.15	0.48	0.33	0.39	0.59	54.8934
Bagging	67.8	0.4518	0.17	0.1	0.4	0.17	0.23	0.63	11.3004
Boosting	70.3	0.4329	0.42	0.18	0.5	0.42	0.46	0.7	34.4795
RF	69.23	0.47	0.33	0.15	0.48	0.33	0.39	0.63	20.7763

Note: See text for definitions of abbreviations used in the table.

these performance measures. That is, making a classifier "better" in terms of a particular measure can result in a relatively "inferior" classifier in terms of another.

Tables 3.4 and 3.5 present the results of applying eight different learning algorithms to two UCI domains: the breast cancer and the liver dataset. Both domains are binary. The breast cancer dataset comprises 286 instances (201 negative, i.e., nonrecurrence events; and 85 positive, i.e., recurrence events), with each instance containing nine nominal-valued attributes. The liver dataset consists of 345 instances (145 positive and 200 negative) with six nominal-valued attributes.

The eight learning algorithms considered, all from the WEKA machine learning toolkit, are NB, decision tree (C45), 3 nearest neighbor (3NN), Ripper (RIP), SVM (in WEKA, this is called SMO), bagging, boosting, and random forest (RF). This represents a diverse set of well-known learning strategies and is illustrative of the diverse features of different performance metrics. We use the default parameter values in each case because our main aim is to highlight the differences between performance measures here, and not classifier optimization.

Table 3.5. *A study of the UCI liver domain*

Algorithm	Acc	RMSE	TPR	FPR	Prec	Rec	F	AUC	K & B
NB	55.36	0.5083	0.766	0.6	0.481	0.766	0.59	0.64	17.96
C45	68.7	0.5025	0.531	0.2	0.658	0.531	0.588	0.67	87.72
3NN	62.9	0.6072	0.566	0.325	0.558	0.566	0.562	0.63	77.56
RIP	64.64	0.4835	0.469	0.225	0.602	0.469	0.527	0.65	57.12
SVM	58.26	0.6461	0.007	0	1.0	0.007	0.014	0.5	45.38
Bagging	71.01	0.4513	0.572	0.19	0.686	0.572	0.624	0.73	71.48
Boosting	66.09	0.4683	0.462	0.195	0.632	0.462	0.534	0.68	43.3
RF	68.99	0.456	0.648	0.28	0.627	0.648	0.637	0.74	84.31

Note: See text for definitions of abbreviations used in the table.

The results are reported with the following performance measures: accuracy (Acc), the root-mean-square error (RMSE), the true-positive and false-positive rates (TPR and FPR), precision (Prec), recall (Rec), the F Measure (F), the area under the ROC curve (AUC), and Kononenko and Bratko's information score (K & B). All the results were obtained with the WEKA machine learning toolkit whose advanced options allow for a listing of these metrics. The reported results are averaged over a 10-fold cross-validation run of the learning algorithm on the dataset. However, for now, we do not focus on what each of these measures means and how they were calculated. Our aim here is to emphasize that different performance measures, as a result of assessing different aspects of algorithms' performances, yield different comparative results. We do not delve into the appropriateness of the 10-fold cross-validation method either. We discuss this and other error-estimation methods in detail in Chapter 5.

Let us look into the results. If we were to rank the different algorithms based on their performance on the dataset (rank 1 denoting the best classifier) we would end up with different rankings depending on the performance measures that we use. For example, consider the results obtained by accuracy and the F measure on the breast cancer domain (Table 3.4). Accuracy ranks c45 as the best classifier whereas the AUC ranks it as the worst, along with svm. Similarly, the F measure ranks nb as the best classifier, whereas accuracy ranks it somewhere in the middle. Across categories, AUC is in agreement with RMSE when it comes to c45's rank, but the two metrics disagree as to where to rank boosting. When ranked according to the AUC, boosting comes first (tied with nb) whereas it is ranked lower for Acc. Similar disagreements can also be seen between K & B and AUC as, for example, with respect to their ranking of svm.

Of course, this is a serious problem because a user is left with the questions of which evaluation metric to use and what their results mean. However, it should be understood that such disagreements do not suggest any inherent flaw in the performance measures themselves. This, rather, highlights two main aspects of such an evaluation undertaking: (i) different performance measures focus on different aspects of the classifier's performance on the data and assess these specific aspects; (ii) learning algorithms vary in their performance on more than one count. Taken together, these two points suggest something very important:

> The algorithm's performance needs to be measured on one or a few of the most relevant aspects of the domain, and the performance measures considered should be the ones that focus on these aspects.

Such varying conclusions can be partly attributed to the lack of comprehensive performance measures that take into account most or all of the relevant aspects of the algorithms' performances. However, perhaps a more important aspect is that of the relevance of the performance criteria. For instance, consider a scenario in which a learning algorithm is deployed in a combat vehicle for the critical and sensitive task of assessing the possibility that land mines are present, based on certain measurements. Obviously the most critical performance criterion here is the detection of *all* the mines even if this comes at a cost of some false alarms. Hence a criterion that assesses performance on such comprehensive detection is more important than the overall accuracy of prediction. In an analogous manner, different learning tasks or domains impose different performance requirements on the learning algorithms that, in turn, require performance measures capable of assessing the algorithms' performance on these criteria of interest.

To utilize an appropriate performance measure, it is hence necessary to learn their focus, strengths, and limitations. The rest of the chapter focuses on studying the aspects of various performance measures that rely on the information conveyed solely by the confusion matrix. We then extend our analysis to measures that take into account additional information such as classifier uncertainty. The various performance metrics that we study focus on the binary classification scenario. However, the observations and findings with regard to their strengths and limitation extend to multiclass classification settings as well. Let us start our discussion with metrics that have a multiple-class focus.

3.4 Performance Metrics with a Multiclass Focus

The metrics described in this section focus on the overall performance of the learning algorithm on all the classes in the dataset. These hence focus on the accuracy (or, equivalently, the error rate) of the algorithm in classifying the examples of the test data and measures derived from these quantities.

Recall from Chapter 2 our definition of the empirical risk $R_T(f)$ of classifier f on test set T, defined as

$$R_T(f) = \frac{1}{|T|} \sum_{i=1}^{|T|} I(y_i \neq f(\mathbf{x}_i)), \tag{3.1}$$

where $I(a)$ is the indicator function that outputs 1 if the predicate a is true and zero otherwise, $f(\mathbf{x}_i)$ is the label assigned to example $\mathbf{x}_i$ by classifier f, y_i is the true label of example $\mathbf{x}_i$, and $|T|$ is the size of the test set.

In terms of the entries of the confusion matrix, the empirical error rate of Equation (3.1) can be computed as[3]

$$R_T(f) = \frac{\sum_{i,j:i \neq j} c_{ij}(f)}{\sum_{i,j=1}^{l} c_{ij}(f)} = \frac{\sum_{i,j=1}^{l} c_{ij}(f) - \sum_{i=1}^{l} c_{ii}(f)}{\sum_{i,j=1}^{l} c_{ij}(f)}.$$

---

[3] Note that while we use single summation signs for notational simplicity (e.g. $\sum_{i,j=1}^{l}$), it indicates iteration over both the indices (i.e. $\sum_{i=1}^{l} \sum_{j=1}^{l}$), for this and subsequent uses.

Error rate, as also discussed in the last chapter, measures the fraction of the instances from the test set that are misclassified by the learning algorithm. This measurement further includes the instances from all classes.

A complement to the error-rate measurement naturally would measure the fraction of correctly classified instances in the test set. This measure is referred to as *accuracy*. Reversing the criterion in the indicator function of Equation (3.1) leads to the accuracy measurement $\text{Acc}_T(f)$ of classifier f on test set T, i.e.,

$$\text{Acc}_T(f) = \frac{1}{|T|} \sum_{i=1}^{|T|} I(f(\mathbf{x}_i) = y_i).$$

This can be computed in terms of the entries of the confusion matrix as

$$\text{Acc}_T(f) = \frac{\sum_{i=1}^{l} c_{ii}(f)}{\sum_{i,j=1}^{l} c_{ij}(f)}$$

For the binary classification case, our representations of the confusion matrix of Table 3.1 and subsequently Table 3.2 yield

$$\text{Acc}_T(f) = \frac{c_{11}(f) + c_{22}(f)}{c_{11}(f) + c_{12}(f) + c_{21}(f) + c_{22}(f)} = \frac{\text{TP} + \text{TN}}{P + N},$$

$$R_T(f) = 1 - \text{Acc}_T(f) = \frac{c_{12}(f) + c_{21}(f)}{c_{11}(f) + c_{12}(f) + c_{21}(f) + c_{22}(f)} = \frac{\text{FN} + \text{FP}}{P + N}$$

Example 3.1. In the example of NB applied to the breast cancer domain, the accuracy and error rates are calculated as

$$\text{Acc}_T(f) = \frac{37 + 168}{37 + 48 + 33 + 168} = 0.7168,$$

$$R_T(f) = 1 - 0.7168 = 0.2832$$

These results tell us that NB makes a correct prediction in 71.68% of the cases or, equivalently, makes prediction errors in 28.32% of the cases. How should such a result be interpreted? Well, if a physician is happy being right with approximately 7 out of 10 of his patients, and wrong in 3 out of 10 cases, then he or she could use NB as a guide. What the physician does not know, however, is whether he or she is overly pessimistic, overly optimistic, or a mixture of the two, in terms of telling people who should have no fear of recurrence that they will incur a new episode of cancer or in telling people who should worry about it not to do so. This is the typical context in which accuracy and error rates can result in misleading evaluation, as we will see in the next subsection.

3.4.1 Strengths and Limitations

Accuracy and *error rate* effectively summarize the overall performance, taking into account all data classes. Moreover, they give great insight, in learning

Table 3.6. *Hypothetical confusion matrix I for hypothetical classifier H_A*

H_A	Pred_Negative	Pred_Positive	
Act_Negative	400	100	$N = 500$
Act_Positive	300	200	$P = 500$

theoretic terms, into the generalization performance of the classifier by means of studying their convergence behaviors, as we will see in Chapter 8. As a result of trying to summarize the information in a scalar metric, there are inevitable limitations to both the information that these metrics can encompass and their effectiveness in different settings. In particular, this strength of summarizing can result in significant limitations when either the performance on different classes is of varying importance or the distribution of instances in the different classes of the test data is skewed. The first limitation results in the lack of information conveyed by these measures on the varying degree of importance on the performance on different classes. This limitation and the interest in class-specific performance estimate are addressed with the single-class focus measures that we discuss in the next subsection. The second limitation regards these metrics' inability to convey meaningful information in the case of skewed class distribution. Accuracy and error rates can be effective measures when the proportion of instances belonging to different classes in the test set is more or less balanced (i.e., similar for different classes). As soon as this distribution begins to skew in the direction of a particular class, the more-prevalent class dominates the measurement information in these metrics, thereby making them biased. This limitation is addressed to some extent by the scoring and reliability methods and metrics discussed in Chapter 4.

Another limitation of these metrics appears in the form of different misclassification costs. This is in line with the first limitation we previously discussed but addresses a slightly different concern. Differing misclassification costs can be relevant in the case of both balanced and skewed class distributions. The problems in the case of skewed class distributions are related to the fact that accuracy (or error rate) does not distinguish between the *types* of errors the classifier makes (on one class as opposed to the other classes). On the other hand, the problems in the case of unequal misclassification costs relate to the fact that accuracy (or error rate) does not distinguish between the *importance* of errors the classifier makes over instances of one class in comparison with those of other classes. Let us illustrate the problems more specifically with the following hypothetical example.

Example 3.2. Consider two classifiers represented by the two confusion matrices of Tables 3.6 and 3.7. These two classifiers behave quite differently from one another. The one symbolized by the confusion matrix of Table 3.6 does

Table 3.7. *Hypothetical confusion matrix II for hypothetical classifier H_B*

H_B	Pred_Negative	Pred_Positive	
Act_Negative	200	300	$N = 500$
Act_Positive	100	400	$P = 500$

not classify positive examples very well, getting only 200 out of 500 right. On the other hand, it does not do a terrible job on the negative data, getting 400 out of 500 well classified. The classifier represented by the confusion matrix of Table 3.7 does the exact opposite, classifying the positive class better than the negative class, with 400 out of 500 versus 200 out of 500 correct classifications. It is clear that these classifiers exhibit quite different strengths and weaknesses and should not be used blindly on a dataset such as the medical domain we previously used. Yet both classifiers exhibit the same accuracy of 70%.[4]

Now let us consider the issues of class imbalance and differing costs. Let us assume an extreme case in which the positive class contains 50 examples and the negative class contains 950 examples. In this case, a trivial classifier incapable of discriminating between the positive and the negative class, but blindly choosing to return a "negative" class label on all instances, would obtain a 95% accuracy. This indeed is not representative of the classifier's performance at all. Because many classifiers, even nontrivial ones, take the prior class distributions into consideration for the learning process, the preference for the more-dominant class would prevail, resulting in their behaving the way our trivial classifier does. Accuracy results may not convey meaningful information in such cases.

This also brings us to the question of how important it is to correctly classify the examples from the two classes in relation to each other. That is, how much cost do we incur by making the classifier more sensitive to the less-dominant class while incurring misclassification of the more-dominant class? In fact, such costs can move either way, depending on the importance of (mis)classifying instances of either class. This is the issue of misclassification costs. However, the issues of misclassification costs can also be closely related to, although definitely not limited to, those of class distribution.

Consider the case in which the classes are fully balanced, as in the two previous confusion matrices. Assume, however, that we are dealing with a problem for which the misclassification costs differ greatly. In the critical example of breast cancer recurrence (the positive class) and nonrecurrence (the negative class), it is clear, at least from the patient's point of view, that false-positive errors have a lower cost because these errors consist of diagnosing recurrence when

---

[4] Of course, one can think of reversing the class labels in such cases. However, this may not exactly invert the problem mapping. Also, this trick can become ineffective in the multiclass case.

the patient is, in fact, not likely to get the disease again; whereas false-negative errors are very costly, because they correspond to the case in which recurrence is not recognized by the system (and thus is not consequently treated the way it should be). In such circumstances, it is clear that the system represented by the preceding first confidence matrix is much less appropriate for this problem because it issues 300 nonrecurrence diagnostics in cases in which the patient will suffer a new bout of cancer, whereas the system represented by the second confidence matrix makes fewer (100) mistakes (needless to say that, in practical scenarios, even these many mistakes will be unacceptable).

Clearly the accuracy (or the error-rate measures) does not convey the full picture and hence does not necessarily suffice *in its classical form* in domains with differing classification costs or wide class imbalance. Nonetheless, these measures do remain simple and intuitive ways to assess classifier performance, especially when the user is aware of the two issues just discussed. These metrics serve as quite informative measures when generic classifiers are evaluated for their overall performance-based comparative evaluation. We will come back to the issue of dealing with misclassification costs (also referred to as the asymmetric loss) a bit later in the chapter.

When assessing the performance of the classifier against the "true" labeling of the dataset, it is implicitly assumed that the actual labels on the instances are indeed unbiased and correct. That is, these labels do not occur by chance. Although such a consideration is relatively less relevant when we assume a perfect process that generates the true labels (e.g., when the true labeling can be definitively and unquestionably established), it is quite important when this is not the case (in most practical scenarios). This can be the case, for instance, in which the result from the learning algorithm is compared against some silver standard (e.g., labels generated from an approximate process or a human rater). An arguable fix in such cases is the correction for chance, first proposed by Cohen (1960) for the two-class scenario with two different processes generating the labels. Let us look into some such chance-correction statistics.

3.4.2 Correcting for Chance: Agreement Statistics

It has been widely argued that the conventional performance measures, especially the accuracy estimate, do not take into account the correct classification as a result of a mere coincidental concordance between the classifier output and the "true" label-generation process. Typically, at least in the case of classifier assessment, it is assumed that the true class labels of the data examples are deterministically known, even though they are the result of an arbitrary unknown distribution that the algorithm aims to approximate. These true labels are sometimes referred to as ground truth. However, this assumption makes it impossible to take into account the inherent bias of the label-generation process. Consider, for instance, a dataset with 75% positive examples and the rest negative. Clearly this is a case of imbalanced data, and the high number of positive instances can be an indicator of the bias of the label-generation process in labeling instances as positive with a higher frequency. Hence, if we have a classifier that assigns a positive label with half the frequency (an unbiased coin toss), then, even without learning on the training data, we would expect its positive label assignment to agree with the true labels in $0.5 \times 0.75 = 0.375$ proportion of the cases. Conventional measurements such as accuracy do not take such accurate classifications into consideration that can be the result of mere chance agreement between the classifier and the label-generation process. This concern is all the more relevant in applications such as medical image segmentation in which the true class labels (i.e., the ground truth) are not known at all. Experts assign labels to various segments of images (typically pixels) against which the learning algorithm output is evaluated. Not correcting for chance, then, ignores the bias inherent in both the manual labeling and the learned classifier, thereby confusing the accurate segmentation achieved merely by chance for an indication of the efficiency of the learning algorithm.

It has hence been argued that this chance concordance between the labels assigned to the instances should be taken into account when the accuracy of the classifier is assessed against the true label-generation process. Having their roots in statistics, such measures have been used, although not widely, in the machine learning and related applications. These measures are popularly known as agreement statistics.[5] We very briefly discuss some of the main variations with regard to the binary classification scenario. Most of these agreement statistics were originally proposed in an analogous case of measuring agreement on class assignment (over two classes) to the samples in a population by two raters (akin to label assignment to instances of the test set in our case by the learning algorithm and the actual underlying distribution). These measures were subsequently generalized to the multiclass, multirater scenario under different settings. We provide pointers to these generalizations in Section 3.8.

As a result of not accounting for such chance agreements over the labels, it has been argued that accuracy tends to provide an overly optimistic estimate of correct classifications when the labels assigned by the classifier are compared with the true labels of the examples. The agreement measures are offered as a possible, although imperfect, fix. We will come to these imperfections shortly. We discuss three main measures of agreement between the two label-generation processes that aim to obtain a chance-corrected agreement: the S coefficient (Bennett et al., 1954), Scott's π (pi) statistic (Scott, 1955), and Cohen's κ (kappa) statistic. The three measures essentially differ in the manner in which they account for chance agreements.

---

[5] The statistics literature refers to these as interclass correlation statistics or interrater agreement measures.

Table 3.8. *The two-class confusion matrix*

	Pred_Negative	Pred_Positive	
Act_Negative	True negative (TN)	False positive (FP)	$Y_N = \text{TN} + \text{FP}$
Act_Positive	False negative (FN)	True positive (TP)	$Y_P = \text{FN} + \text{TP}$
	$f_N = \text{TN} + \text{FN}$	$f_P = \text{FP} + \text{TP}$	

Let the actual process of label-generation (the true label-assigning process) be denoted as Y. Let Y_P and Y_N denote the number of examples to which this process assigns a positive and a negative label, respectively. Similarly, let us denote the classifier by f and accordingly denote by f_P and f_N the number of examples to which f assigns a positive and a negative label, respectively. The empirical estimates of these quantities can be obtained from the confusion matrix, as shown in Table 3.8.

Similarly, we can denote the probability of overall agreement over the label assignments between the classifier and the true process by P_o. The empirical estimate of P_o can also be obtained from the confusion matrix of Table 3.8 as $P_o = \frac{\text{TN} + \text{TP}}{m}$, where $m = \text{TN} + \text{FP} + \text{FN} + \text{TP}$. Given these empirical estimates of the probabilities, the S coefficient is defined as

$$S = 2P_o - 1.$$

The other two statistics, that is, Scott's π and Cohen's κ, have a common formulation in that they take the ratio of the difference between the observed and chance agreements and the maximum possible agreement that can be achieved over and beyond chance. However, the two measures treat the chance agreement in different manners. Whereas Scott's π estimates the chance that a label (positive or negative) is assigned given a random instance *irrespective* of the label-assigning process, Cohen's κ considers this chance agreement by considering the two processes to be fixed. Accordingly, Scott's π is defined as

$$\pi = \frac{P_o - P_e^S}{1 - P_e^S},$$

where the chance agreement over the labels, denoted as P_e^S, is defined as

$$P_e^S = P_P^2 + P_N^2 \tag{3.2}$$

$$= \left[\frac{(f_P + Y_P)/2}{m} \right]^2 + \left[\frac{(f_N + Y_N)/2}{m} \right]^2. \tag{3.3}$$

Cohen's κ, on the other hand, is defined as

$$\kappa = \frac{P_o - P_e^C}{1 - P_e^C},$$

Table 3.9. *Hypothetical confusion matrix to illustrate the calculation of Cohen's κ*

H_k	Pred-a	Pred-b	Pred-c	Total
Act-a	60	50	10	120
Act-b	20	90	40	150
Act-c	40	10	80	130
Total	120	150	130	

where the chance agreement over the labels in the case of Cohen's κ, denoted as P_e^C, is defined as

$$P_e^C = P_P^Y P_P^f + P_N^Y P_P^f$$
$$= \frac{Y_P}{m} \frac{f_P}{m} + \frac{Y_N}{m} \frac{f_N}{m}.$$

As can be seen, unlike Cohen's κ, Scott's π is concerned with the overall propensity of a random instance being assigned a positive or negative label and hence marginalizes *over the processes*. Therefore, in the case of assessing a classifier's chance corrected accuracy against a "true" label-generating process (whether unknown or by, say, an expert), Cohen's κ is a more-relevant statistic in our settings, which is why it is the only agreement statistic included in WEKA. We illustrate it here by the following example.

Example 3.3. Consider the confusion matrix of Table 3.9 representing the output of a hypothetical classifier H_k on a three-class classification problem. The rows represent the actual classes, and the columns represent the outputs of the classifier. Now, just looking at the diagonal entries will give us an estimate of the accuracy of the classifier $\text{Acc}(H_k)$. With regard to the preceding agreement statistics framework, this is basically the observed agreement P_o. Hence, $P_o = (60 + 90 + 80)/400 = 0.575$.

Let us see how we can generalize Cohen's κ to this case. For this we need to obtain a measure of chance agreement. Recall that we previously computed the chance agreement in the case of Cohen's κ as the sum of chance agreement on the individual classes. Let us extend that analysis to the current case of three classes. The chance that both the classifier and the actual label assignment agree on the label of any given class is the product of their proportions of the examples assigned to this class. In the case of Table 3.9, we see that the classifiers H_k assigns a proportion 120/400 of examples to class a (sum of the first column). Similarly, the proportion of true labels of class a in the dataset is also 120/400 (sum of first row). Hence, given a random example, both the classifier and the true label of the example will come out to be a, with probability $(120/400) \times (120/400)$. We can calculate the chance agreement probabilities for classes b and c in similar fashion. Adding these chance agreement probabilities for the three classes will give us the required P_e^C. That is,

$$P_e^C = \frac{120}{400} \times \frac{120}{400} + \frac{150}{400} \times \frac{150}{400} + \frac{130}{400} \times \frac{130}{400}$$
$$= 0.33625.$$

Hence, we get Cohen's κ agreement statistic for classifier H_k with the previously calculated values as

$$\kappa(H_k) = \frac{P_o - P_e^C}{1 - P_e^C}$$
$$= \frac{0.575 - 0.33625}{1 - 0.33625}$$
$$= 0.3597.$$

As we can see, the accuracy estimate of 57.5% for classifier H_k may be overly optimistic because it ignores the coincidental concordance of the classifier with the true labels. Indeed, it can be seen that the classifier mimics the class distribution of the actual labels when assigning labels to the instances (even though the overlap on the instances assigned the correct labels is less). Hence, for a random instance, the classifier will assign a class label with the same proportion as that of the true class distribution (empirically over the dataset). This will result in the classifier being right, merely by chance, in about 33.6% cases as previously calculated over all classes (the P_e^C value). A more realistic estimate of classifier effectiveness is then the proportion of labels that the classifier gets right over and above this chance agreement, which is what Cohen's κ represents.

In summary, the agreement measures take the marginal probability of label assignments into account to correct the estimated accuracy for chance. There have been arguments against the measures, mainly with regard to the imperfect accounting for chance as a result of the lack of knowledge of the true marginals. Moreover, the limitations with respect to the sensitivity of these measures to issues such as class imbalance (generally referred to as bias), prevalence, and misclassification costs still appear in the case of these chance-corrected measures. In Section 3.8, we provide pointers to the measures that address these issues to some extent by proposing modified agreement measures that account for bias and prevalence as well as to other measures that generalize the ones discussed here to the multiclass scenarios (though we show how this can be done in a simple case in the preceding example). One of the most popular generalizations has appeared in the form of Fleiss's kappa statistic, which generalizes the Scott's π measure. Even though the critiques with regard to the bias and prevalence behaviors of the preceding agreement measures are well justified and should be taken note of, it should also be kept in mind that these agreement measures are proposed as summary measures and hence can provide, within the proper context (generally the same that applies to reliable accuracy estimation), acceptable and reasonable performance assessment.

Let us now shift our attention to measures that are aimed at assessing the effectiveness of the classifier on a single class of interest.

3.5 Performance Metrics with a Single-Class Focus

The metrics discussed in the previous section generally aim at characterizing the overall performance of the classifier on instances of all the classes. These metrics can be effective when the user is interested in observing such general behavior and when other constraints with regard to the effectiveness of these metrics are met (e.g., when the class distributions are balanced or the performance on different classes are equally important). However, depending on the application domain of the learning algorithm, there can be different concerns in play. One of the most prominent of such concerns appears in the form of the greater relevance of the algorithms' performance on a single class of interest. This performance on the single class can be relevant either with regard to the instances of this class itself or with regard to the instances of other classes in the training data. It can also serve the purpose of measuring the overall performance of the classifier with an emphasis on the instances of each individual class as opposed to an all encompassing measurement resulting from accuracy or error rate. Of course, this necessitates reporting the statistics over all the classes of interest. This section focuses on some of the most prominent measures that address these concerns. We further focus on the binary classification scenario in which such measures are mostly applied and also appear in conjunction with their complement measurements.

3.5.1 True- and False-Positive Rates

The most natural metric aimed at measuring the performance of a learning algorithm on instances of a single class is arguably its true-positive rate. Although the nomenclature can be a bit misleading in the multiclass scenario (indeed, what class can be considered "positive" among the many classes?), it is relatively more intuitive in the binary classification scenario, in which typical references to the instances of the two classes are made as "positive" and "negative." In its general form, this measure refers to the proportion of the examples of some class i of interest actually assigned to class i by the learning algorithm. In terms of the entries of the general confusion matrix $\mathbf{C}$ described in Subsection 3.1.2, the true-positive rate of a classifier f with regard to (w.r.t) class i (that is, when the class of interest, the "positive" class, is class i) is defined as

$$\mathrm{TPR}_i(f) = \frac{c_{ii}(f)}{\sum_{j=1}^{l} c_{ij}(f)} = \frac{c_{ii}(f)}{c_{i.}(f)}.$$

In an analogous manner, one can also be interested in the instances assigned to class i of interest that actually do not belong to this class. The false-positive rate of a classifier quantifies this proportion. The false-positive rate of classifier f w.r.t. class i is defined in terms of $\mathbf{C}$'s entries as

$$\text{FPR}_i(f) = \frac{\sum_{j:j\neq i} c_{ji}(f)}{\sum_{j,k:j\neq i} c_{jk}(f)}.$$

Hence $\text{FPR}_i(f)$ measures the proportion of examples not belonging to class i that are nonetheless erroneously classified as belonging to class i.

In the binary classification case, the preceding metrics, for the class of interest termed positive in accordance with the confusion matrix representations of Tables 3.1 and 3.2, simplify to

$$\text{TPR}(f) = \frac{c_{22}(f)}{c_{21}(f) + c_{22}(f)} = \frac{\text{TP}}{\text{TP} + \text{FN}},$$

$$\text{FPR}(f) = \frac{c_{12}(f)}{c_{11}(f) + c_{12}(f)} = \frac{\text{FP}}{\text{FP} + \text{TN}}.$$

True- and false-positive rates generally form a complement pair of reported performance measures when the performance is measured over the positive class in the binary classification scenario. Moreover, we can obtain the same measures on the "negative" class (the class other than the "positive" class) in the form of true-negative rate $\text{TNR}(f)$ and false-negative rate $\text{FNR}(f)$, respectively. Our representations of Tables 3.1 and 3.2 yield

$$\text{TNR}(f) = \frac{c_{11}(f)}{c_{11}(f) + c_{12}(f)} = \frac{\text{TN}}{\text{TN} + \text{FP}},$$

$$\text{FNR}(f) = \frac{c_{21}(f)}{c_{21}(f) + c_{22}(f)} = \frac{\text{FN}}{\text{FN} + \text{TP}}.$$

In signal detection theory, the true-positive rate is also known as the *hit rate*, whereas the false-positive rate is referred to as the *false-alarm rate* or the *fallout*. Next we discuss another complement metric that generally accompanies the true-positive rate.

3.5.2 Sensitivity and Specificity

The true-positive rate of a classifier is also referred to as the *sensitivity* of the classifier. The term has its origin in the medical domain, in which the metric is typically used to study the effectiveness of a clinical test in detecting a disease. The process of evaluating the test in the context of detecting a disease is equivalent to investigating how sensitive the test is to the presence of the disease. That is, how many of the positive instances (e.g., actual disease cases) can the test successfully detect? The complement metric to this, in the case of the two-class scenario, would focus on the proportion of negative instances (e.g., control cases or healthy subjects) that are detected. This metric is called the *specificity* of the learning algorithm. Hence specificity is the true-negative rate in the case of the binary classification scenario. That is, sensitivity is generally considered in terms of the positive class whereas the same quantity, when measured over the negative class, is referred to as specificity.

Again, from the binary classification confusion matrix of Table 3.2, we can define the two metrics as

$$\text{Sensitivity} = \frac{\text{TP}}{\text{TP} + \text{FN}},$$

$$\text{Specificity} = \frac{\text{TN}}{\text{FP} + \text{TN}}.$$

As can be seen, sensitivity is nothing but $1 - \text{FNR}(f)$, whereas specificity is the true-negative rate $\text{TNR}(f)$. Just as TNR and FNR, these two metrics are functions of the classifier f too, but we omit this when the context is clear.

In the multiclass scenario, sensitivity measurements essentially study the accuracy of the classifier over individual classes. Hence this ameliorates the effect of class imbalance arising in the accuracy or error-rate measurements thereby skewing these estimates. We will see another measure, the geometric mean, that aims at addressing this problem too.

In the example of NB applied to the breast cancer domain (Table 3.3), we obtain Sensitivity(NB) $= 37/(37 + 33) = 0.53$ and Specificity(NB) $=$ $168/(48 + 168) = 0.78$. The 0.53 sensitivity value obtained tells us that NB rightly predicted only 53% of the actual recurrence cases. On the other hand, the specificity of 0.78 shows that, in 78% of all cases of actual nonrecurrence, NB made the right prediction.

So what does this mean? To answer this question, we considered the situation of a patient who wants to put all the chances of survival on her side. A sensitivity of 0.53 tells us that NB missed $100 - 53 = 47\%$ of the actual recurrence cases, meaning that if a physician chose not to administer the treatment reserved for patients with the greatest chances of recurrence, based on NB results, there is 47% of a chance that the physician denied a potentially lifesaving treatment to a patient who needed it. The specificity of 0.78 tells the patient that she may receive unnecessary treatment in $100 - 78 = 22\%$ of the cases. Altogether, these results would tell a proactive patient not to rely on NB.

Recall our hypothetical example of Tables 3.6 and 3.7, which yielded the same accuracy in both cases. For the confusion matrix in the first case, we have Sensitivity $(H_A) = 200/(200 + 300) = 0.4$ and Specificity $(H_A) = 400/(400 + 100) = 0.8$. However, for the second case, we get Sensitivity $(H_B) = 400/(400 + 100) = 0.8$ and Specificity $(H_B) = 200/(200 + 300) = 0.4$.

In essence, the tests, together, identify the proportion of the two classes correctly classified. However, unlike accuracy, they do this separately in the context of each individual class of instances. As a result of the class-wise treatment, the measures reduce the dependency on uneven class distribution in the test data. However, the cost of doing so appears in the form of a metric for each single class. In the case of a multiclass classification problem, this would lead to as many metrics as there are classes, making it difficult to interpret. There are also other aspects that one might be interested in but that are missed by this metric pair. One such aspect is the study of the proportion of examples assigned to a certain class by the classifier that actually belong to this class. We will study this and the associated complementary metric soon. But before that, let us describe a metric that aims to combine the information of sensitivity and specificity to yield a metric-pair that studies the class-wise performance in a relative sense.

Likelihood Ratio

An important measure related to the sensitivity and specificity of the classifier, known as the likelihood ratio, aims to combine these two notions to assess the extent to which the classifier is effective in predicting the two classes. Even though the measure combines sensitivity and specificity, there are two versions, each making the assessment for an individual class. For the positive class,

$$\text{LR}_+ = \frac{\text{Sensitivity}}{1 - \text{Specificity}},$$

whereas for the negative class,

$$\text{LR}_- = \frac{1 - \text{Sensitivity}}{\text{Specificity}}.$$

In our breast cancer domain, LR_+ summarizes how many times *more* likely patients whose cancer did recur are to have a positive prediction than patients without recurrence: LR_- summarizes how many times *less* likely patients whose cancer did recur are to have a negative prediction than patients without recurrence. In terms of probabilities, LR_+ is the ratio of the probability of a positive result in people who do encounter a recurrence to the probability of a positive result in people who do not. Similarly, LR_- is the ratio of the probability of a negative result in people who do encounter a recurrence to the probability of a negative result in people who do not.

A higher positive likelihood and a lower negative likelihood mean better performance on positive and negative classes, respectively, so we want to maximize LR_+ and minimize LR_-. A likelihood ratio higher than 1 indicates that the test result is associated with the presence of the recurrence (in our example), whereas a likelihood ratio lower than 1 indicates that the test result is associated with the absence of this recurrence. The further likelihood ratios are from 1, the stronger the evidence for the presence or absence of the recurrence. Likelihood ratios reaching values higher than 10 and lower than 0.1 provide acceptably strong evidence (Deeks and Altman, 2004).

When two algorithms, A and B are compared, the relationships between the positive and the negative likelihood ratios of both classifiers can be interpreted in terms of comparative performance as follows, for $LR_+ \geq 1$:[6]

- $LR_+^A > LR_+^B$ and $LR_-^A < LR_-^B$ imply that A is superior overall.
- $LR_+^A < LR_+^B$ and $LR_-^A < LR_-^B$ imply that A is superior for confirmation of negative examples.
- $LR_+^A > LR_+^B$ and $LR_-^A > LR_-^B$ imply that A is superior for confirmation of positive examples.

Example 3.4. Applying this evaluation method to the confusion matrix that was obtained from applying NB to the breast cancer domain, we obtain the following values for the likelihood ratios of a positive and a negative test, respectively:

$$LR_+ = \frac{0.53}{1 - 0.78} = 2.41,$$

$$LR_- = \frac{1 - 0.53}{0.78} = 0.6.$$

This tells us that patients whose cancer recurred are 2.41 times more likely to be predicted as positive by NB than patients whose cancer did not recur; and that patients whose cancer did recur are 0.6 times less likely to be predicted as negative by NB than patients whose cancer did not recur. This is not a bad result, but the classifier would be more impressive if is positive likelihood ratio were higher and its negative likelihood ratio smaller.

Following our previously discussed hypothetical example, we find that the classifier represented by Table 3.6, denoted as classifier H_A, yields $LR_+^{H_A} = 0.4/(1 - 0.8) = 2$ and $LR_-^{H_A} = (1 - 0.4)/0.8 = 0.75$, whereas the classifier represented by Table 3.7, denoted as classifier H_B, yields $LR_+^{H_B} = 0.8/(1 - 0.4) = 1.33$ and $LR_-^{H_B} = (1 - 0.8)/0.4 = 0.5$.

We thus have $LR_+^{H_A} > LR_+^{H_B}$ and $LR_-^{H_A} > LR_-^{H_B}$, meaning that classifier H_A is superior to classifier H_B for confirmation of positive examples; but that classifier H_B is better for confirmation of negative examples.

Note that, when interpreted in a probabilistic sense, the likelihood ratios used together give the likelihood in the Bayesian sense, which, along with a prior over the data, can then give a posterior on the instances' class memberships. The preceding discrete version has found wide use in clinical diagnostic test assessment. In the Bayesian or probabilistic sense, however, the likelihood ratios are used in the context of nested hypothesis, that is, on hypotheses that belong

---

[6] If an algorithm does not satisfy this condition, then "positive" and "negative" likelihood values should be swapped.

to the same class of functions but vary in their respective complexities. This is basically model selection with regard to choosing a more (or less) complex classifier depending on their respective likelihoods given the data at hand.

3.5.3 Positive and Negative Predictive Values

Another aspect of assessment is the question of what the proportion of examples that truly belong to class i is from among all the examples assigned to (or classified as) class i. The positive predictive value (PPV) measures this statistic over the learning algorithm's performance on a test set (considering the class of interest i to be the "positive" class). Hence this metric measures how "precise" the algorithm is when identifying the examples of a given class. PPV therefore is also referred to as *precision*. PPV has its origin in medical evaluation. The usage of the term precision for the metric is more common in the information-retrieval domain.

In the context of the example of clinical test efficacy on patients, used to introduce the concepts of sensitivity and specificity, we can imagine that a clinician would also be interested in learning the proportion of positive tests that indeed detect the genuine presence of some pathology or condition of interest. Being typically applied in the binary class scenario, the PPV can be measured with respect to both the classes of the test domain. By convention, PPV measures the proportion of correctly assigned positive examples. The complement of PPV in this context appears in the form of the negative predictive value (NPV), which measures the proportion of correctly assigned negative examples. For example, when two clinical conditions are distinguished based on a test, it is desired that the test be highly effective in detecting both the conditions, i.e., have high PPV and NPV values.

The *precision* or PPV of a classifier f on a given class of interest i (the "positive" class), in terms of the entries of $\mathbf{C}$, is defined as

$$\mathrm{PPV}_i(f) = \mathrm{Prec}_i(f) = \frac{c_{ii}(f)}{\sum_{j=1}^{l} c_{ji}(f)} = \frac{c_{ii}(f)}{c_{\cdot i}(f)}.$$

The counterpart of PPV in the binary classification scenario is the NPV. PPV in this case typically refers to the class of interest (positive) whereas NPV measures the same quantity with respect to the negative (e.g., control experiments in medical applications) class.

In terms of the binary classification confusion matrix of Table 3.2, we can define the two metrics as

$$\mathrm{Prec}(f) = \mathrm{PPV}(f) = \frac{\mathrm{TP}}{\mathrm{TP} + \mathrm{FP}},$$

$$\mathrm{NPV}(f) = \frac{\mathrm{TN}}{\mathrm{TN} + \mathrm{FN}}.$$

For the breast cancer prediction domain as predicted by NB, we obtain PPV(NB) $= 37/(37 + 48) = 0.44$ and NPV(NB) $= 168/(168 + 33) = 0.84$, which can be interpreted in the following way.

The 0.44 PPV value suggests that a positive prediction by NB should be taken with a grain of salt, given that it will be true in only 44% of the cases, whereas the NPV value of 0.84 suggests that a negative prediction by NB is relatively more reliable because such predictions were shown to be true in 84% of the cases. Hence NB can function as a preliminary screening tool to look relatively reliably for negative conformance.

Coming back to our hypothetical examples of Tables 3.6 and 3.7, we obtain, for the first table, PPV(H_A) $= 200/(200 + 100) = 0.667$ and NPV(H_A) $= 400/(400 + 300) = 0.571$. Similarly, the second table yields PPV(H_B) $= 400/(400 + 300) = 0.571$ and NPV(H_B) $= 200/(200 + 100) = 0.667$.

In this case, as we can see, a concrete judgment call on the superiority of the classifier in one case or the other is almost impossible based on the two metrics of PPV and NPV alone. Hence, even though we can study the class-wise performance of the classifier, in the case of identical precision achieved by the classifiers on two classes (even though the actual number of class predictions varies), the PPV and NPV might not provide enough information. On the other hand, with a reliability perspective, these metrics give an insight into how reliable the class-wise predictions of a classifier is (as in the previous example of NB).

This analysis together with that for sensitivity–specificity is starting to suggest that there is an information trade-off carried through the different metrics. In fact, a practitioner has to choose, quite carefully, the quantity he or she is interested in monitoring while keeping in mind that other values matter as well and that classifiers may rank differently, depending on the metrics along which they are being compared. Let us look at another approach to addressing the class imbalance issue.

Geometric Mean

As discussed previously, the informativeness of accuracy acc(f) generally reduces with increasing class imbalances. It is hence desirable to look at the classifier's performance on instances of individual classes. One way of addressing this concern is the sensitivity metric. Hence, in the two-class scenario, we use sensitivity and specificity metrics' combination to report the performance of the classifier on the two classes. The geometric mean proposes another view of the problem. The original formulation was proposed by Kubat et al. (1998) and is defined as

$$Gmean_1(f) = \sqrt{TPR(f) \times TNR(f)}.$$

As can be seen, this measure takes into account the relative balance of the classifier's performance on both the positive and the negative classes. $Gmean_1(f)$ becomes 1 only when TPR(f) $=$ TNR(f) $= 1$. For all other combinations of the classifier's TPR(f) and TNR(f), the measures weigh the resulting statistic by the relative balance between the two. In this sense, this measure is closer to the multiclass focus category of the measures discussed in the previous section.

Another version of the measures, focusing on a single class of interest, can similarly take the precision of the classifier Prec(f) into account. In the two-class scenario, with the class of interest being the "positive" class, this yields

$$G\, \mathrm{mean}_2(f) = \sqrt{\mathrm{TPR}(f) \times \mathrm{Prec}(f)}.$$

Hence the $G\mathrm{mean}_2$ takes into account the proportion of the actual positive examples labeled as positive by the classifier as well as the proportion of the examples labeled by the classifier as positive that are indeed positive.

3.5.4 Precision, Recall, and the F Measure

Finally, we can focus on both the PPV over a class of interest in conjunction with the sensitivity of the classifier over this class. These are typical statistics of interest in domains such as information retrieval in which we are interested not only in the proportion of relevant information identified, but also in investigating the actually relevant information from the information tagged as relevant. As we have seen earlier, the first of these two statistics is nothing but the sensitivity or the TPR, whereas the second statistic is the PPV. In the information-retrieval domain, these are generally referred to as *recall* and *precision*, respectively. At the risk of repeating ourselves, we restate the two metrics for the binary classification scenario:

$$\mathrm{Prec}(f) = \mathrm{PPV}(f) = \frac{\mathrm{TP}}{\mathrm{TP} + \mathrm{FP}},$$

$$\mathrm{Rec}(f) = \mathrm{TPR}(f) = \frac{\mathrm{TP}}{\mathrm{TP} + \mathrm{FN}}.$$

In the case of NB applied to the breast cancer recurrence prediction problem, we have, as calculated earlier, Prec(NB) = TP/(TP + FP) = 37/(37 + 48) = 0.4353 and Rec(NB) = TP/(TP + FN) = 37/(37 + 33) = 0.5286. This means that, of all the patients who were classified as recurrence cases, only 43.53% indeed had lived through recurrences of their breast cancer, i.e., this tells us that NB is not very precise when establishing a positive diagnostic. It also means that, of all the patients it should have identified as recurrence cases, it identified only 52.85% of them as such, i.e., NB recalled only slightly more than half all the patients it should have recalled as recurrence cases. In this light, this further confirms our earlier observation of the very limited utility of NB with regard to positive recurrence cases.

With regard to our hypothetical examples of Tables 3.6 and 3.7 we obtain Prec(H_A) = 200/(200 + 100) = 0.667 and Rec(H_A) = 200/(200 + 300) = 0.4

Table 3.10. *Hypothetical confusion*
matrix III over hypothetical classifier H_C

H_C	Pos	Neg
Yes	200	100
No	300	0
	$P = 500$	$N = 100$

in the first case and $\text{Prec}(H_B) = 400/(400 + 300) = 0.572$ and $\text{Rec}(H_B) = 400/(400 + 100) = 0.8$ in the second.

These results reflect the strength of the second classifier on the positive data compared with that of the first classifier. However, the disadvantage in the case of this metric pair is that precision and recall do not focus on the performance of the classifier on any other class than the class of interest (the "positive" class). It is possible, for example, for a classifier trained on our medical domain to have respectable precision and recall values even if it does very poorly at recognizing that a patient who did not suffer a recurrence of her cancer is indeed healthy. This is disturbing because the same values of precision and recall can be obtained no matter what proportion of patients labeled as healthy are actually healthy, as in the example confusion matrix of Table 3.10. This is similar to the confusion matrix in Table 3.6, except for the true-negative value, which was set to zero (and the number of negative examples N, which was consequently decreased to 100). In the confusion matrix of Table 3.10, the classifier H_C obtains the same precision and recall values as in the case of H_A of Table 3.6. Yet it is clear that the H_C presents a much more severe shortcoming than H_A because it is incapable of classifying true-negative examples as negative (it can, however, wrongly classify positive examples as negative!). Such a behavior, by the way, as mentioned before, is reflected by the accuracy metric, which assesses that the classifier H_C is accurate in only 33% of the cases whereas H_A is accurate in 60% of the cases. Specificity also catches the deficiency of precision and recall in actually a much more direct way because it obtains 0 for H_C.

Hence, to summarize, the main advantage of single-class focus metrics lies in their ability to treat performance of the classifier on an individual class basis and thus account for shortcomings of multiclass measures, such as accuracy, with regard to class imbalance problems, all the while studying the aspects of interest within the individual class performance. However, this advantage comes at certain costs. First, of course, is that no single metric is capable of encapsulating all the aspects of interest, even with regard to the individual class (see for instance the case of sensitivity and precision). Second, two (multiple) metrics need to be reported to detail the classifier performance over two (multiple) classes, even for a single aspect of interest. Increasing the number of metrics being reported makes it increasingly difficult to interpret the results. Finally, we do not yet know of a principled way of combining these measures to yield a summary measure. Further, an argument against combining these three metrics is that evaluation methods are supposed to summarize the performance. If we must report the values of these metrics (over individual classes), then why not simply return the confusion matrix, altogether? With regards to TPR and TNR, we previously discussed their geometric mean $Gmean_1(f)$ as a way to obtain a single measure to summarize them. We now describe a metric that attempts to combine the precision and recall observation, instead, in a scalar statistic, by way of their weighted combination.

F Measure

The F measure attempts to address the issue of convenience brought on by a single metric versus a pair of metrics. It combines precision and recall in a single metric. More specifically, the F measure is a weighted harmonic mean of precision and recall. For any $\alpha \in \mathbb{R}, \alpha > 0$, a general formulation of the F measure can be given as[7]

$$F_\alpha = \frac{(1 + \alpha)[\text{Prec}(f) \times \text{Rec}(f)]}{\{[\alpha \times \text{Prec}(f)] + \text{Rec}(f)]\}}.$$

There are several variations of the F measure. For instance, the *balanced F measure* weights the recall and precision of the classifier evenly, i.e., $\alpha = 1$:

$$F_1 = \frac{2[\text{Prec}(f) \times \text{Rec}(f)]}{[\text{Prec}(f) + \text{Rec}(f)]}.$$

Similarly, F_2 weighs recall twice as much as precision and $F_{0.5}$ weighs precision twice as much as recall. The weights are generally decided based on the acceptable trade-off of precision and recall.

In our NB-classified breast cancer domain, we obtain

$$F_1 = \frac{2(0.4353 \times 0.5286)}{(0.4353 + 0.5286)} = \frac{0.46}{0.96} = 0.48,$$

$$F_2 = \frac{3(0.4353 \times 0.5286)}{[(2 \times 0.4353) + 0.5286]} = \frac{0.69}{1.4} = 0.49,$$

$$F_{0.5} = \frac{1.5(0.4353 \times 0.5286)}{[(0.5 \times 0.4353) + 0.5286]} = \frac{0.345}{0.74625} = 0.46.$$

This suggests that the results obtained on the positive class are not very good and that NB favors neither precision nor recall.

---

[7] Note that this α is different from the one used in statistical significance testing. However, because it is a conventional symbol in the case of F measure, we retain it here. The different context of the two usages of α will disambiguate the two, helping avoid confusion.

For our hypothetical example from Tables 3.6 and 3.7, we have $F_1^{H_A} = 2 \times 0.67 \times 0.4/[(2 \times 0.67) + 0.4] = 0.31$ and $F_1^{H_B} = 2 \times 0.572 \times 0.8/[(2 \times 0.572) + 0.8] = 0.47$. This shows that, with precision and recall weighed equally, H_B does a better job on the positive class than H_A. On the other hand, if we use the F_2 measure, we get $F_2^{H_A} = 0.46$ and $F_2^{H_B} = 0.7$, which emphasizes that recall is a greater factor in assessing the the quality of H_B than precision.

Similarly, the use of $F_{0.5}$ measure results in $F_{0.5}^{H_A} = 0.55$ and $F_{0.5}^{H_B} = 0.632$, indicating that recall is indeed very important in the case of H_B. Indeed, when precision counts for twice as much as recall, the two metrics obtain results that are relatively close to one another.

This goes on to show that choosing the relative weight for combining the precision and recall is very important in the F-measure calculations. However, in most practical cases, appropriate weights are generally not known, resulting in a significant limitation with regard to the use of such combinations of measures. We revisit this issue when discussing the weighted versions of other performance measures a bit later. Another limitation of the F measure results from the limitation of its components. Indeed, just as the precision–recall metric pair, the F measure leaves out the true-negative performance of the classifier.

Skew and Cost Considerations

The entries of the confusion matrix are quite informative. However, each entry by itself can be misleading, and hence an attempt is generally made to take into account the information conveyed by these entries in relation to other relevant entries of the matrix. Different performance measures aim at addressing these relationships in different ways. For instance, while considering accuracy or error rates, the measures combine the diagonal entries to obtain an overall evaluation on all classes (and not just on one particular class). On the other hand, measures such as sensitivity are typically studied in relation to their respective complements (e.g., specificity in the binary classification scenario) to present a relatively unbiased picture. This is important because partial information can be quite misleading.

However, even when such care is taken, there can be other confounding issues. These issues may need to be addressed at different stages of learning. In particular, the distinction between the solutions that can be offered *during* learning and the ones that can be applied *after* learning is important. We will briefly ponder on this shortly. But before that, let us talk about the two issues that can be important in interpreting the results of the classifier on the test data as conveyed by the confusion matrix. The first is that of the class distributions. By class distribution, we mean the distribution of instances belonging to various classes in the test set. Alternatively, this is referred to as class imbalance. We confronted this issue earlier in the chapter while studying different performance measures, and we also saw some attempts to take it into consideration while interpreting the results. Another solution to the class imbalance problem has been proposed that takes into account *class ratios* instead of fixing the measurements with regard to the class size of a particular class. *Class ratio* for a given class i refers to the number of instances of class i as opposed to those of other classes in the dataset. Hence, in the two-class scenario, the class ratio of the positive class as opposed to the negative class, denoted as ratio$_+$, can be obtained as

$$\text{ratio}_+ = \frac{(\text{TP} + \text{FN})}{(\text{FP} + \text{TN})}.$$

In the multiclass scenario, for the class of interest i, we get

$$\text{ratio}_i = \frac{\sum_j c_{ij}}{\sum_{j, j \neq i} c_{ji} + \sum_{j, j \neq i} c_{jj}}.$$

The entries can then be weighted by their respective class ratios. For instance, in the binary case, the TPR can be weighed by ratio$_+$ whereas the TNR can be weighed by *ratio$_-$*, the class ratio of the negative class. Such an evaluation that takes into account the differing class distributions is referred to as a skew-sensitive assessment.

The second issue that confounds the interpretation of the entries of the confusion matrix that we wish to discuss here is that of asymmetric misclassification costs. There are two dimensions to this. Misclassifying instances of a class i can have a different cost than misclassifying the instances of class j, $j \neq i$. Moreover, the cost associated with the misclassification of class i instances to class j, $j \neq i$ can differ from the misclassification of class i instances to class j', $j' \neq j$. For instance, consider a learning algorithm applied to the tasks of differentiating patients with acute lymphoblastic leukemia (ALL) or acute myloid leukemia (AML) and healthy people based on their respective gene expression analyses (see Golub et al., 1999, for an example of this). In such a scenario, predicting one of the pathologies for a healthy person might be less costly than missing some patients (with ALL or AML) by predicting them as healthy (of course, contingent on the fact that further validation can identify the healthy people as such). On the other hand, missing patients can be very expensive because the disease can go unnoticed, resulting in devastating consequences. Further, classifying patients with ALL as patients with AML and vice versa can also have differing costs.

The asymmetric (mis)classification costs almost always exist in real-world problems. However, in the absence of information to definitively establish such costs, a comforting assumption, that of symmetric costs, is made. As a result, the confusion matrix, by default, considers all errors to be equally important. The question then becomes this: How can we effectively integrate cost considerations when such knowledge exists? Incorporating such asymmetric costs can be quite important for both effective learning on the data and sensible evaluation. This brings us back to our discussion on the distinction of solutions applied *during* the learning process and *after* the learning is done. The asymmetric cost of misclassification can be integrated into the learning process itself so as to make the learning algorithm sensitive to such costs. This would require the incorporation of an asymmetric loss function that would replace, for instance, the zero–one loss function in the classification case. This is easier said than done. Such asymmetric loss incorporation introduces its own set of challenges to the underlying learning-theoretic model. However, we concern ourselves with the more relevant aspect, in the context of this book, of incorporating these costs in the assessment phase. Accounting for misclassification costs during the evaluation phase is useful for many reasons. First, incorporating the costs in the learning process is difficult. Moreover, different learning algorithms may deal with such asymmetric losses in different ways (and with differing efficiency). The second, and perhaps more important, reason is that such costs might not be available during learning. Also, these costs can be time sensitive. That is, such misclassification costs can change over time. The most direct approach for incorporating misclassification costs is to weight the nondiagonal entries of the confusion matrix accordingly. These cost estimates can either be known a priori or come from domain experts. Doing so results in the weighted variants of different performance measures. For instance, the empirical error refers to the proportion of examples in the test set that appear in the nondiagonal entries of the confusion matrix. In the weighted estimate, each of the nondiagonal entries $c_{ij}, i \neq j$, of $\mathbf{C}$ is weighted by a respective cost, say, w_{ij}. The empirical error estimate is then obtained as a combination of these weighted proportions of the misclassified entries.

Note that cost considerations in the evaluation need not be the same as the skew or class distribution considerations previously discussed. The cost of misclassification may or may not overlap with the presence or not of class imbalance. Although attempts have been made to integrate the two by way of introduction of *cost ratios*, we do not discuss these here. Interested readers are referred to the pointers in Section 3.8.

3.5.5 Classification Uncertainty

Another issue worth considering when looking at misclassifications is that of classifier uncertainty. Let us see this with an illustration. Consider the output of a probabilistic classifier on a hypothetical test set of 10 instances (too small and never recommended in practice), with two classes as shown in Table 3.11. The classifier outputs the class labels for each instance with associated probabilities. The table shows the predicted class as the one with a higher probability.

This is in contrast to a deterministic classifier that outputs a fixed class label on a test instance without making any implicit certainty statements. When considered in this sense – considering the output labels without (un)certainty information – the classifier of Table 3.11 makes three classification errors. However, this deterministic consideration, as done by the confusion matrix,

Table 3.11. *The output of a probabilistic classifier on a hypothetical test set with two classes,* P *and* N

Instance	Actual class	Predicted class	Probability
1	*P*	*P*	0.80
2	*P*	*N*	0.55
3	*P*	*P*	0.70
4	*P*	*P*	0.90
5	*N*	*N*	0.85
6	*N*	*P*	0.90
7	*N*	*N*	0.60
8	*N*	*N*	0.80
9	*N*	*P*	0.75
10	*N*	*N*	0.95

loses the uncertainty information of the classifier. That is, it suggests that we should be equally confident in all the class labels predicted by the classifier or alternatively that the labels output by the classifier are all perfectly certain. Nonetheless, when looked at closely, the information in the table gives us a more detailed picture. In particular, instances that are misclassified with little certainty (e.g., Instance 2) can quite likely correspond to instances often called boundary examples. On the other hand, when misclassifications are made with high certainty (e.g., Instance 6), then either the classifier or the examples need to be studied more carefully because such a behavior can be due to a lack of proper learning or to the presence of noise or outliers, among other reasons. There can also be other cases in which uncertainty is introduced in the performance estimates (e.g., stochastic learning algorithms) and for which it is not trivial to measure the performance of the learning algorithm on the test data. Altogether, the point we wish to make here is that information about a classifier's certainty or uncertainty can be very important. As can be clearly seen, the confusion matrix, at least in its classical form, does not incorporate this information. Consequently the lack of classifier uncertainty information is also reflected in all the performance measures that rely solely on the confusion matrix. The next chapter discusses the issue in more depth as it moves away from performance measures that rely solely on the confusion matrix.

3.6   Illustration of the Confusion-Matrix-Only-Based Metrics Using WEKA

We now illustrate how to obtain the computations of the metrics discussed in Sections 3.4 and 3.5 by using WEKA. All these metrics are calculated by WEKA, but not necessarily called by the same name as the one we used here.

The first step in obtaining the value of the metrics in WEKA is to ensure that the option "Output per-class stats" is checked in the "More options" menu of

WEKA's classification screen. The following listing shows the WEKA summary output obtained on the labor dataset with c45 with the preceding option checked.

Listing 3.1: WEKA's extended output.

```
=== Summary ===

Correctly Classified Instances          42              73.6842 %
Incorrectly Classified Instances        15              26.3158 %
Kappa statistic                          0.4415
Mean absolute error                      0.3192
Root mean squared error                  0.4669
Relative absolute error                 69.7715 %
Root relative squared error             97.7888 %
Total Number of Instances               57

=== Detailed Accuracy By Class ===

TP Rate   FP Rate   Precision   Recall  F−Measure   ROC Area   Class
  0.7      0.243      0.609      0.7      0.651       0.695      bad
  0.757    0.3        0.824      0.757    0.789       0.695      good

=== Confusion Matrix ===

  a   b    <— classified as
 14   6  |   a = bad
  9  28  |   b = good
```

We now link the WEKA terminology to our terminology and indicate the values obtained by the classifier on this dataset in Table 3.12. All these correspondences can be established by getting back to the formulas previously listed in Sections 3.4 and 3.5 and comparing them with the values output by WEKA.

3.7   Summary

In this chapter, we focused on the measures that take into account, in some form or other, information extracted solely from the confusion matrix. Indeed, these are some of the most widely utilized measures – despite the limitations that we discussed – and they are shown to perform reasonably well when used in the right context. The measures that we discussed here, at least in their classical form, generally address the performance assessment of a deterministic classifier. There is also a qualitative aspect to the limitation of the information conveyed by the confusion matrix. Because the entries of the confusion matrix report the "numbers" of correctly or incorrectly classified examples in trying to provide the information succinctly, there is another loss incurred by the confusion-matrix-based metrics: the loss incurred by not looking at overlapping sets of examples, rather than just numbers, classified correctly or missed by respective (two or more) algorithms. Indeed, algorithms that have a highly overlapping set

Table 3.12. *Relating WEKA terminology to our case*[8]

Metric name	WEKA's teminology	Value in the example
Accuracy	Correctly classified instances (percentage)	73.6842
Error rate	Incorrectly classified instances	26.3158
TPR	DABC[a]: "good" TPR	0.757
TNR	DABC: "bad" recall	0.7
FPR	DABC: "good" FPR	0.3
FNR	DABC: "bad" FPR	0.243
Cohen's Kappa statistics	Kappa statistic	0.4415
Sensitivity	DABC: "good" TPR	0.757
Specificity	DABC: "bad" recall	0.7
PPV	DABC: "good" precision	0.824
NPV	DABC: "bad" precision	0.609
Precision	DABC: "good" precision	0.824
Recall	DABC: "good" recall	0.757
F Measure	DABC: "good" F Measure	0.789

[a] DABC stands for the part of the output titled "Detailed Accuracy By Class."

of instances on which they perform similarly can have learned more accurate models of the data than the ones achieving the same numbers but on nonoverlapping sets of instances. Another limiting aspect of the confusion-matrix-based measures follows from the fact that they do not allow users to visualize the performance of the learning algorithm with varying decision thresholds. On a similar account, the measures resulting from such information also tend to be scalar. Such an attempt to obtain a succinct single-measure description of the performance results in the loss of information. Although pairs of measures are sometimes used to compensate for this (e.g., sensitivity and specificity), this does not address the issue completely. In the next chapter, we extend our discussion of performance measures to the ones that do not rely only on the information from a confusion matrix (at least, not just a single confusion matrix). In particular, we look into graphical measures that allow the user to visualize the performance of the classifier, for a given criterion, over its full operating range (range of possible values of the classifier's decision threshold).

3.8   Bibliographic Remarks

Concerns about what aspects of a classifier's performance to evaluate were expressed by Caruana and Niculescu-Mizil (2004) and Ferri et al. (2009) who identify *classification, ranking,* and *reliability* as three major criteria. Issues about traits distinguishing performance measures from one another and their robustness in the presence of concept drift and noise were all discussed in

[8] Note that WEKA reports Fleiss's Kappa for the multiclass case.

(Ferri et al., 2009) and are very important because they affect our choices of a performance metric, given what we know of the domain to which it will be applied.

Various studies about evaluating and combining the performance measures themselves have appeared, such as those of Ling et al. (2003); Caruana and Niculescu-Mizil (2004); Huang and Ling (2007); and Ferri et al. (2009). We will see some of the interesting aspects of this research in Chapter 8.

WEKA has become one of the most widely used machine learning tool. The relevant sources are (Witten and Frank, 2005a, 2005b).

With regard to combining the prior class distribution and the asymmetric classification costs, the concept of cost ratios was proposed. In general, Flach (2003) suggests that we use the neutral term skew-sensitive learning rather than cost-sensitive learning to refer to adjustments to learning or evaluation pertaining to either the class distribution or the misclassification cost. Using cost ratios for classifier performance assessment was also discussed by Ciraco et al. (2005). The first prominent criticism against the use of accuracy and empirical error rate in the context of learning algorithms was made by Provost et al. (1998). Adapting binary metrics to multiclass classification and skew-ratio considerations was also discussed by Lavrač et al. (1999), who propose weighted relative accuracy. Examples of stochastic algorithms measuring Gibbs and Bayes risk can be found in (Marchand and Shah, 2005) and (Laviolette et al., 2010).

One of the most widely used agreement statistic has been Cohen's κ (Cohen, 1960). Scott's π statistics was proposed in (Scott, 1955), and Bennett's S coefficient was proposed in (Bennett et al., 1954). Earlier attempts to find agreement included Jaccard's index (Jaccard, 1912) and the Dice coefficient (Dice, 1945), among others. However, these did not take into account chance correction. Many generalizations with regard to Cohen's κ agreement statistic have appeared with their applicability in respective contexts. Some of the relevant readings include those of Fleiss (1971), Kraemer (1979), Schouten (1982), and Berry and Mielke (1988). Issues with regard to the behavior of Cohen's κ in the presence of bias and prevelance were also identified and corresponding corrected measures proposed. See, for instance (Byrt et al., 1993). Finally, Gwet (2002a, 2002b) noted the issues with Cohen's κ measures and introduced the AC_1 statistic, defined as

$$\frac{P_o - P_e^G}{1 - P_e^G},$$

where $P_e^G = 2P_P(1 - P_P)$ and P_P is defined in Equation (3.3) in Subsection 3.4.2.

4

Performance Measures II

Our discussion in the last chapter focused on performance measures that relied solely on the information obtained from the confusion matrix. Consequently it did not take into consideration measures that either incorporate information in addition to that conveyed by the confusion matrix or account for classifiers that are not discrete. In this chapter, we extend our discussion to incorporate some of these measures. In particular, we focus on measures associated with scoring classifiers. A scoring classifier typically outputs a real-valued score on each instance. This real-valued score need not necessarily be the likelihood of the test instance over a class, although such probabilistic classifiers can be considered to be a special case of scoring classifiers. The scores output by the classifiers over the test instances can then be thresholded to obtain class memberships for instances (e.g., all examples with scores above the threshold are labeled as positive, whereas those with scores below it are labeled as negative). Graphical analysis methods and the associated performance measures have proven to be very effective tools in studying both the behavior and the performance of such scoring classifiers. Among these, the receiver operating characteristic (ROC) analysis has shown significant promise and hence has gained considerable popularity as a graphical measure of choice. We discuss ROC analysis in significant detail. We also discuss some alternative graphical measures that can be applied depending on the domain of application and assessment criterion of interest. We also touch on metrics commonly known as reliability metrics that take partial misclassification loss into account. Such metrics also form the basis for evaluation measure design in continuous learning paradigms such as regression analysis. We briefly discuss the root-mean-square-error metric as well as metrics inspired from information theory, generally utilized in the Bayesian analysis of probabilistic classifiers.

Let us start with the commonly used graphical metrics for performance evaluation of classifiers.

4.1   Graphical Performance Measures

It is desirable for a performance measure not only to take into account the information contained in the confusion matrix, but also to incorporate considerations such as skew and prior class distributions. Moreover, when dealing with a scoring classifier, it is often desirable that the measure enables an assessment of classifier performance over its full operating range (of possible scores). Typically, information related to skew, cost, or prior probabilities (other than the class distribution in the training set) of the data is generally not known. Even when the asymmetric nature of the misclassification cost is known, it is not easily quantifiable. Graphical performance measures are very useful in such cases because they enable visualization of the classifier performance over the full operating range and hence under different skew ratios and class distribution priors.

Being able to visualize the behavior of a classifier across its operating range is an obvious advantage of graphical measures. However, as we will see, even such measures have issues that might not be easily resolved when it comes to deciding which classifier is *generally* more appropriate among the ones studied, when no single classifier dominates all the others over the full operating range. On the other hand, if we have the information over the full operating range, it is significantly easier to discover zones of optimality. That is, it is easier to identify the skew ratios under which one classifier is superior to others. The question of choosing one single optimal classifier based on some quantification of the resulting graphs gives rise to measures that incorporate all the details into a scalar metric. Inevitably, compressing the information in a scalar metric results in significant information loss.

Let us start by discussing, arguably, the most widely used graphical performance analysis method in machine learning evaluation, the ROC analysis. We also discuss other evaluation methods such as cost curves, precision–recall (PR) curves, and lift charts as alternative graphical measures. As we will see, whereas some methods take into account the same information as ROC analysis, albeit in a different form, others address different criteria of interest in classifier assessment while still exploiting the visualization capabilities of graphical measures. Finally, we also illustrate these methods by using available specialized statistical analysis packages such as R and ROCR in Section 4.6.

4.2   Receiver Operating Characteristic (ROC) Analysis

Receiver operating characteristic (ROC) analysis has its origin in signal detection theory as a means to set a threshold or an operating point for the receiver to detect the presence or absence of signal. The signal is assumed to be corrupted by noise that in turn is assumed to be distributed according to a normal distribution. The choice of the best operating point depends on factors such as the variance of the noise that corrupts the signal, the strength of the signal itself, and the desired hit (detecting the signal when the signal is actually present) or false-alarm (detecting a signal when the signal is actually absent) rate. The selection of the best operating point is typically a trade-off between the hit rate and the false-alarm rate of a receiver.

In the context of learning algorithms, ROC graphs have been used in a variety of ways. ROC is a very powerful graphical tool for visualizing the performance of a learning algorithm over varying decision criteria, typically in a binary classification scenario. ROCs have been utilized not only to study the behavior of algorithms but also to identify optimal behavior regions, perform model selection, and perhaps most relevant to our context, for the comparative evaluation of learning algorithms. However, before we proceed with the evaluation aspect, it would be quite helpful to understand the ROC space, the meaning of the ROC curve, and its relation to other performance measures.

An ROC curve is a plot in which the horizontal axis (the x axis) denotes the false-positive rate FPR and the vertical axis (the y axis) denotes the true-positive rate TPR of a classifier. We discussed these measures in the last chapter. As you may recall, the TPR is nothing but the sensitivity of the classifier whereas the FPR is nothing but 1-TNR (TNR is the true negative rate) or equivalently $1 - specificity$ of the classifier. Hence, in this sense, ROC analysis studies the relationship between the sensitivity and the specificity of the classifier.

4.2.1 ROC Space

Because, for both the TPR and FPR, it holds that $0 \leq$ TPR ≤ 1 and $0 \leq$ FPR ≤ 1, the ROC space is a unit square, as shown in Figure 4.1. The output of a deterministic classifier results in a single point in this ROC space. The point $(0, 0)$ denotes a trivial classifier that classifies all the instances as negative and hence results in both the TPR and the FPR being zero. On the other end of the square, the point $(1, 1)$ corresponds to the trivial classifier that labels all the instances as positive and hence has both the TPR and the FPR values of unity. The diagonal connecting these two points $[(0, 0)$ and $(1, 1)]$ has TPR $=$ FPR at all the points. The classifiers falling along this diagonal can hence be considered to be random classifiers (that is, they assign positive and negative labels to the instances randomly). This resembles a biased coin toss at every point along the diagonal with bias $p =$ TPR $=$ FPR of assigning a positive label and $1 - p$ of assigning a negative label. It follows naturally that the classifiers lying above this diagonal perform better than random, whereas the ones below, perform worse than random (for instance, the classifier f in Figure 4.1 performs worse than random). As a rule of thumb, for two points f_a and f_b in the ROC space, f_a represents a better classifier than f_b if f_a is on the left of f_b *and* higher than f_b.

The points $(1, 0)$ and $(0, 1)$ give the other two extremes of the ROC space. The point $(1, 0)$ has FPR $= 1$ and TPR $= 0$, meaning that the classifier denoted

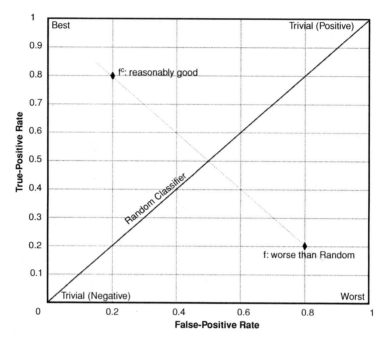

Figure 4.1. The ROC space.

by this point gets all its predictions wrong. On the other hand, the point (0, 1) denotes the ideal classifier, one that gets all the positives right and makes no errors on the negatives. The diagonal connecting these two points has TPR = 1 − FPR. Note that 1 − FPR is nothing but TNR, as discussed in the last chapter. This goes to show that the classifiers along this diagonal perform equally well on both the positive and the negative classes.

An *operating point* in the ROC space corresponds to a particular decision threshold of the classifier that is used to assign discrete labels to the examples. As just mentioned, the instances achieving a score above the threshold are labeled positive whereas the ones below are labeled negative. Hence, what the classifier effectively does is establish a threshold that discriminates between the instances from the two classes coming from two unknown and possibly arbitrary distributions. The separation between the two classes then decides the classifier's performance for this particular decision threshold. Hence each point on the ROC space denotes a particular TPR and FPR for a classifier. Now, each such point will have an associated confusion matrix summarizing the classifier performance. Consequently an ROC curve is a collection of various confusion matrices over different varying decision thresholds for a classifier.

Theoretically, by tuning the decision threshold over the continuous interval between the minimum and maximum scores received by the instances in the dataset, we can obtain a different TPR and FPR for each value of the scoring

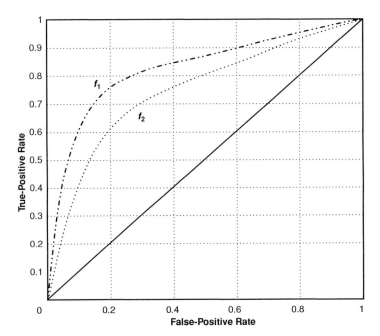

Figure 4.2. The ROC curves for two hypothetical scoring classifiers f_1 and f_2.

threshold, which should result in a continuous curve in the ROC space (such as
the one shown in Figure 4.2 for two hypothetical classifiers f_1 and f_2). However,
this is not necessarily the case in most practical scenarios. The reasons for this
are twofold. First, the limited size of the dataset limits the number of values
on the ROC curves that can be realized. That is, when the instances are sorted
in terms of the scores achieved as a result of the application of the classifier,
then all the decision thresholds in the interval of scores of any two consecutive
instances will essentially give the same TPR and FPR on the dataset, resulting
in a single point. Hence, in this case, the maximum number of points that can be
obtained are upper bounded by the number of examples in the dataset. Second,
this argument assumes that a continuous tuning of the decision threshold is
indeed possible. This is not necessarily the case for all the scoring classifiers, let
alone the discrete ones for which such tuning cannot be done at all. Classifiers
such as decision trees, for instance, allow for only a finite number of thresholds
(upper bounded by the number of possible labels over the leafs of the decision
tree). Hence, in the typical scenario of a scoring classifier, varying the decision
threshold results in a step function at each point in the ROC space. An ROC
curve can then be obtained by extrapolation over this set of finite points. Discrete
classifiers, the ones for which such a tuning of the decision threshold is not
possible, yield discrete points in the ROC space. That is, for a given test set T,
a discrete classifier f will generate one tuple [FPR(f), TPR(f)] corresponding

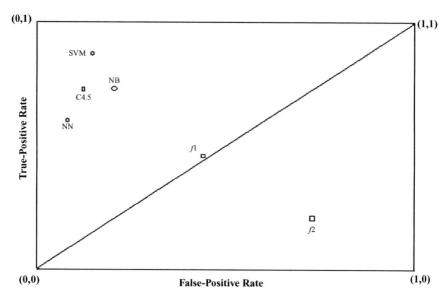

Figure 4.3. An example of a ROC plot for discrete classifiers in a hypothetical scenario.

to one point in the two-dimensional (2D) ROC space (for instance, the classifier f or f^c in Figure 4.1 represents such discrete classifiers). Figure 4.3 shows some examples of points given by six classifiers in the ROC space on some hypothetical dataset.

The classifiers appearing on the left-hand side on an ROC graph can be thought of as more *conservative* in their classification of positive examples, in the sense that they have small false-positive rates, preferring failure to recognize positive examples to risking the misclassification of negative examples. The classifiers on the right-hand side, on the other hand, are more *liberal* in their classification of positive examples, meaning that they prefer misclassifying negative examples to failing to recognize a positive example as such. This can be seen as quite a useful feature of ROC graphs because different operating points might be desired in the context of different application settings. For instance, in the classical case of cancer detection, labeling a benign growth as cancer leads to fewer negative consequences than missing to recognize a cancerous growth as such, whereas false negatives are not as serious in applications such as information retrieval.

Let us illustrate this in the plot of Figure 4.3. We see that the "best" overall classifier is svm because it is closest to point (0, 1). Nevertheless, if retaining a small false-positive rate is the highest priority, it is possible that, in certain circumstance, c4.5 or even NN would be preferred. There is no reason why NB should be preferred to c4.5 or svm, however, because both its false-positive and true-positive rates are worse than those of c4.5 or svm. We will come back to this a bit later. $f1$ is a very weak classifier, barely better than random guessing. As for $f2$, it can be made (roughly) equivalent to NB once its decisions are reversed in manner analogous to that of classifier f in Figure 4.1 that is the mirror of f^c along the center of the graph.

It should be noted that it is not trivial to characterize the performances of classifiers that are just slightly better than those of the random classifier (points just above the diagonal). A statistical significance analysis is required in such cases to ascertain whether the marginally superior performance of such classifiers, compared with that of a random classifier, is indeed statistically significant. Finally, each point on the ROC curve represents a different trade-off between the false positives and false negatives (also known as the *cost ratio*). The cost ratio is defined by the slope of the line tangent to the ROC curve at a given point.

A Note on Scoring Classifiers

The preceding description of the ROC space suggests that, to characterize the behavior of a classifier throughout its operating range, we implicitly assume that it issues a score on every instance. This score can then be thresholded so as to choose a decision boundary. The easiest way to conceptualize this kind of classifier is to think of a neural network. Indeed, a multilayer perceptron outputs a continuous value, typically in the interval [0, 1] rather than binary labels. A value close to 1 can be interpreted as assigning an instance to the positive class, whereas one near 0 would mean classification of the corresponding instance as negative. Details about the proximity to either ends of the interval are rarely discussed as criteria for classifying the corresponding instance as negative or positive. Instead, a decision threshold, typically 0.5, is assumed. However, obviously a threshold of 0.5 is not the only possibility. In principle, any value in the operating range [0, 1] can act as a decision threshold. Each such threshold will yield a different FPR and TPR.

Many discrete classifiers can be turned into scoring classifiers by referring to their respective decision or discriminative criteria rather than to the resulting labels. For instance, a decision tree can be converted to a scoring classifier by realizing various dichotomies on the labels over its leaf nodes. We do not go into the details of how to convert a discrete classifier into a scoring classifier here. Interested readers are referred to the pointers in Section 4.8. However, it should be noted that the techniques of converting (in most cases, reverting from) discrete to scoring classifiers are becoming standard. For instance, machine learning packages such as WEKA come with an ROC analysis capability for the set of implemented classifiers. For the present analysis, we work with the assumption that a scoring classifier is available at hand.

Typically, owing either to the limited number of instances in the test set or the inherent limitation of the learning algorithm, the classifier scores result in a discrete distribution. That is, even for a classifier that outputs continuous scores in a possible $[-\infty, +\infty]$ interval, in the event of a limited dataset size, only finite dichotomies over the label assignment to the test instances can be realized, and hence the score can be thresholded at a finite number of points (resulting in different performances). Hence this would yield a piecewise ROC graph as a consequence of a discrete score distribution. Similarly, as mentioned earlier, classifiers such as decision trees yield only a finite number of scores (and hence thresholding possibilities), again giving a discrete score distribution. An ROC curve is obtained by extrapolation of the resulting discrete points on the ROC graph. However, in the limit, the scores can be generalized to being probability density functions.

Another observation worth making in the case of ROC analysis is also that the classifier scores need to be only relative. The scores need not be in any predefined intervals, nor be likelihoods or probabilities over class memberships. What indeed matters is the label assignment obtained (and hence the resulting confusion matrix) when the score interval is thresholded. The overall hope is that the classifier typically scores the positive examples higher than the negative examples. In this sense, the scoring classifiers are sometimes also referred to as *ranking classifiers* in the context of ROC analysis. However, it is important to clarify that these algorithms need not be ranking algorithms in the classical sense. That is, they need not rank all the instances in a desired order. What is important is that the positive instances are generally ranked higher than the negative ones. Therefore we henceforward use the term scoring classifiers, avoiding the more confusing term of ranking classifiers.

4.2.2 Skew Considerations

As we can see, the ROC graphs are insensitive to class skews (or class imbalances). This is because ROC plots are measures of TPR and FPR of a classifier and do not take into account the actual class distributions of the positive and negative examples, unlike measures such as accuracy, empirical risk, or the F measure. However, this observation has both a significant underlying assumption and subsequent implications. An ROC curve is based on a 2×2 confusion matrix, which has 3 degrees of freedom. The points in the 2D ROC space hence are essentially projections of points from a three-dimensional (3D) space. The first two dimensions of the space correspond to the TPR and the FPR, as we discussed earlier. However, the third dimension generally depends on the specific performance measure used to evaluate the algorithm. For instance, measures such as accuracy and empirical risk are sensitive to class imbalances. Hence a useful third dimension to consider when the classifier is evaluated by use of these measures would be the class ratio. The performances of the algorithm on (possibly) different models will yield points in this 3D ROC space with the points in the same TPR $\times$ FPR slice corresponding to the performances with regard to the same class distribution. That is, this third dimension enables us to characterize the various TPRs and FPRs that can be realized by the classifier over its entire operating range and, further, over different class distributions.

Hence, in considering a 2D ROC space, we essentially relax this assumption. When considering performances on a 2D slice, we have the implicit assumption that the TPR and the FPR are independent of the empirical (or expected) class distributions. However, when this 2D ROC space is considered with respect to performance measures, such as accuracy, that are sensitive to such class imbalances, it is wise to incorporate this consideration into the performance measure itself. In addition, we can take misclassification costs in such cases into account by including the cost ratios.

More generally, the factors such as class imbalances, misclassification costs, and credits for correct classification can be incorporated by a single metric, the *skew ratio*. Note that a single metric can be used in many measures, not merely because it alone can account for all the different concerns previously mentioned. Rather, the rationale behind this is that the different factors have similar effects on the performance measures such as accuracy or empirical error rate, and hence a single metric can be used to signify this (possibly combined) effect. This does not have significant effect as long as the performance measure is used to compare various algorithms' performances under similar settings. However, the interpretation of the performance measure and the corresponding algorithm's performance with respect to it can vary significantly.

A skew ratio r_s can be utilized such that $r_s < 1$ if positive examples are deemed more important, for instance, because of a class imbalance with fewer positives in the test set compared with the negatives or because of a high misclassification cost associated with the positives. In an analogous manner, $r_s > 1$ if the negatives are deemed more important. Accounting for class imbalances, misclassification costs, credits for correct classification, and so on hence compels the algorithm to trade off the performance on positives and negatives in relation to each other. This trade-off can be represented, in the context of skewed scenarios, by the skew ratio. Let us see how, in view of the skew consideration by means of r_s, the classifier performance can be characterized with regard to some specific performance measure.

4.2.3 Isometrics

The optimal operating point (threshold) for the classifier will need to be selected in reference to some fixed performance measure. To select an optimal operating point on the ROC curve, any performance measure can be used as long as it can be formulated in terms of the algorithm's TPR and FPR. For instance, given a skew ratio r_s, we can define the (skew-sensitive) formulation of the accuracy of classifier f as

$$\text{Acc}(f) = \frac{\text{TPR}(f) + (1 - r_s)\text{FPR}(f)}{1 + r_s}, \tag{4.1}$$

where r_s is the skew ratio. In the case of symmetric misclassification cost (possibly because of the lack of knowledge of such costs), r_s can represent the *class ratio* such that

$$r_s = \frac{TN + FP}{TP + FN}.$$

Hence, in the event of r_s representing the class ratio, it can be seen that a value of r_s less than unity weighs the positive examples more than the negative ones and vice versa. Also, this is solely reflective of the class distribution in the test set (which can substantially differ from the actual importance of positive examples with regard to the negatives if the misclassification costs or other affecting factors are known).

Given the preceding definition of accuracy for a fixed r_s, the lines in the 2D ROC curve with the same value of accuracy are referred to as the *isoaccuracy lines*. More generally, for any performance measure or *metric*, such lines or curves denoting the same metric value for a given r_s are referred to as *isometrics* or *isoperformances* lines (or curves). In the case of a 3D ROC graph, isometrics form surfaces. Another example of a metric that can be represented in terms of the algorithm's TPR and FPR is the precision of classifier f:

$$\text{Prec}(f) = \frac{\text{TPR}(f)}{\text{TPR}(f) + r_s[\text{FPR}(f)]}. \tag{4.2}$$

Under the preceding definition of r_s, we can obtain *isoprecision lines* on the 2D ROC graph (and surfaces in the 3D ROC space). Figures 4.4 and 4.5 give some examples of the isoaccuracy and isoprecision lines, respectively, on a 2D ROC graph.

In an analogous manner, isoperformance lines can be drawn on the ROC space connecting the classifiers with the same *expected cost*. The expected cost of classification by a classifier f can be defined as

$$\text{cost}_{\exp}(f) = P[1 - \text{TPR}(f)]\text{cost}(P) + N[\text{FPR}(f)]\text{cost}(N),$$

where $\text{cost}(P)$ is the cost incurred for classifying a positive example as negative (i.e., misclassification of a positive example) and $\text{cost}(N)$ is the cost of misclassifying a negative example; P and N denote, respectively, the number of positive and negative examples in the test set.

Consider two classifiers f_1 and f_2 represented by the two points (FPR_1, TPR_1) and (FPR_2, TPR_2), respectively, in the ROC space. For f_1 and f_2 to have the same performance, the slope of the line segment connecting these two points in the ROC space should be proportional to the ratio of the expected costs of misclassification of negative examples to that of positive examples. That is, f_1 and f_2 have the same performance if

$$\frac{\text{TPR}_2 - \text{TPR}_1}{\text{FPR}_2 - \text{FPR}_1} = \frac{\frac{N}{P+N}\text{cost}(N)}{\frac{P}{P+N}\text{cost}(P)}.$$

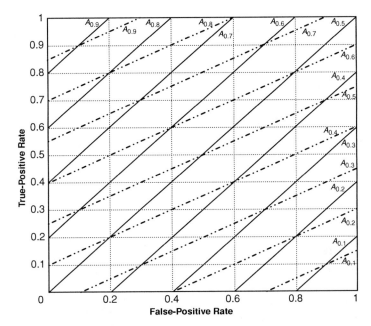

Figure 4.4. An ROC graph showing isoaccuracy lines calculated according to Equation (4.1). The subscripts following A denotes respective accuracies for $r_s = 1$ (black lines) and $r_s = 0.5$ (dash-dotted lines).

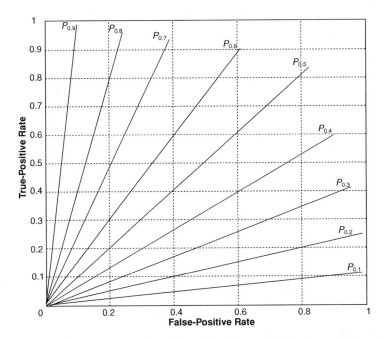

Figure 4.5. An ROC graph showing isoprecision lines calculated according to Equation (4.2) for $r_s = 1$. The subscripts following the P denote respective precisions.

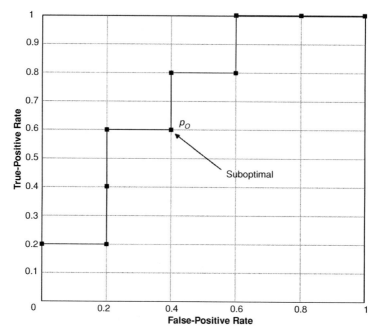

Figure 4.6. A Hypothetical ROC curve. Point p_c is a suboptimal point. That is, p_c is not optimal for any isoaccuracy line for any skew ratio.

Note here that this interpretation gives the isometrics in the expected cost scenario. The skew scenario is more general and the expected cost can be interpreted as its special case. However, analyzing expected skew can be more difficult, if at all possible, in most scenarios.

Although we do not show representative *isocurves* here, metrics such as entropy or the Gini coefficient yield *curves* on the 2D ROC graph. Interested readers are referred to the pointers in Section 4.8.

For a given performance measure, we can consider the highest point on the ROC curve that touches a given isoperformance line of interest (that is, with desired r_s) to select the desired operating point. This can be easily done by starting with the desired isoperformance line at the best classifier position in the ROC graph (FPR $= 0$, TPR $= 1$) and gradually sliding it down until it touches one or more points on the curve. The points thus obtained are the optimal performances of the algorithm for a desired skew ratio. We can obtain the value of the performance measure at this optimal point by looking at the intersection of the isoperformance line and the diagonal connecting the points (FPR $= 0$, TPR $= 1$) and (FPR $= 1$, TPR $= 0$). Naturally there are many points that are not optimal. That is, there is no skew ratio such that these points correspond to the optimal performance of the learning algorithm. We refer to all such points as suboptimal. For instance, the point p_o in Figure 4.6 is a suboptimal point. The set of points on the ROC curve that are not suboptimal forms the ROC *convex hull*, generally abbreviated as ROCCH (see Figure 4.7).

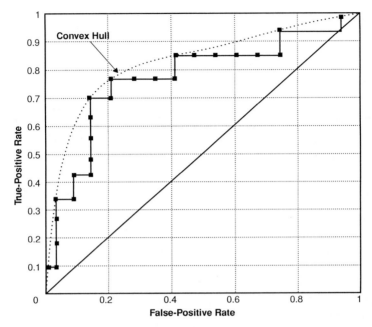

Figure 4.7. The ROCCH.

The notion of an ROCCH has important implications. The classifiers in the convex hull represent the optimal classifiers (under a given performance measure) for a given skew ratio. Hence the convex hull of the ROC curve of a classifier can identify regions of the scores that yield higher performance. With regard to our discussion on selecting the best operating point by sliding the isoperformance measure lines, Figure 4.8 shows how the optimal points for isoaccuracy lines for the ROC curve of Figure 4.7 lie on the ROCCH.

Moreover, in the case of multiple classifiers, the convex hull identifies the best classifier(s) for different operating points. The points on the ROC curve of a learning algorithm give a snapshot of the classifier performance for a given skew ratio. We discussed how these points can be compared in the ROC space. Similarly, we can also compare the overall behavior of the learning algorithms by means of the ROC curves. The convex hull of the ROC curves over all the classifiers can give important insights. The ROC curve of the classifier that lies on the convex hull for a given region of interest denotes the optimal classifier for that operating region. Generalizing this further, the ROCCH can also infer a hybrid classifier that can give optimal performance for different operating points by stochastically weighing different classifiers in the hybrid.

Consider two classifiers f_1 and f_2. We wish to compare the performances of these two classifiers by using the ROC curve visualization. We first plot the ROC curves for the performance of f_1 and f_2. There are two possible scenarios. First, the curve of one classifier lies strictly above the curve of the second classifier, as shown in Figure 4.2. In this case the convex hull of the hybrid classifier

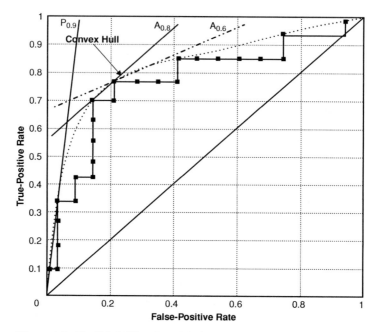

Figure 4.8. The ROCCH and model selection. See text for more details.

consisting of classifiers f_1 and f_2 will basically correspond to the convex hull of classifier f_1, because f_1 strictly dominates f_2 throughout the operating range over all skew ratios. The second scenario can be the one in which the ROC curves of the classifiers f_1 and f_2 intersect at one or more points. See, for instance, Figure 4.9. In this case f_1 is better for the cost ratios where its ROC curve lies above that of f_2, and vice versa. Accordingly, the convex hull of the hybrid classifier will consist of the points from the convex hull of f_1 in the regions where f_1 dominates, and from the convex hull of f_2, in the regions where f_2 is dominant, as shown in Figure 4.10.

Another example of suboptimal performance, in the case of discrete classifiers, is seen in the example of Figure 4.3 discussed earlier. The Naive Bayes (NB) classifier in this hypothetical example represents concavities in the classifier performance. If we were to construct the convex hull over the classifier performances of the discrete classifiers in the ROC graph of Figure 4.3, NB would lie below this convex hull and hence would, under no skew ratio, be optimal over the entire operating range. For an extended discussion on ROC convex hull and related issues, please refer to the pointers in Section 4.8.

4.2.4 ROC Curve Generation

Let us now come back to the specific issue of how ROC curves can be generated. We begin by describing the process used in the construction of a curve on a

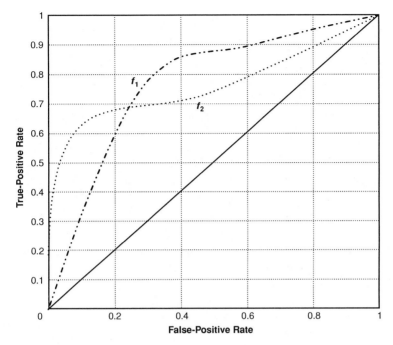

Figure 4.9. The ROC curves for two hypothetical scoring classifiers f_1 and f_2, in which a single classifier is not strictly dominant throughout the operating range.

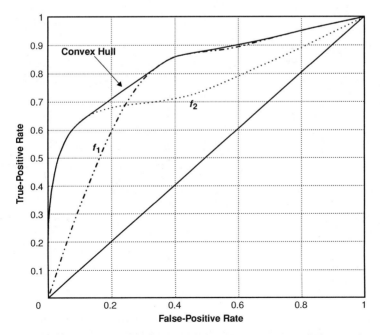

Figure 4.10. The convex hull over the classifiers f_1 and f_2 of Figure 4.9.

Table 4.1. *Points used to generate a ROC curve. See Example 4.1*

Instance #	1	2	3	4	5	6	7	8	9	10
Scores	0.95	0.9	0.8	0.85	0.68	0.66	0.65	0.64	0.5	0.48
True class	*p*	*n*	*p*	*p*	*n*	*p*	*n*	*p*	*n*	*n*

simple test domain, followed by the construction of curves in a resampling regimen.

Constructing an ROC Curve on a Simple Test Domain

Fawcett (2004, Algorithm 1, p. 8) describes the ROC curve generation as follows. Note that the version that we subsequently present is not the most efficient ROC curve-generation procedure but is indeed the simplest. We present it mainly because of its intuitive appeal in helping us elucidate the underlying rationale. For more efficient methods, the reader is encouraged to refer to (Fawcett, 2004, 2006). The efficient implementations of the ROC curve-generation process can also be found as a standard package in many machine learning toolkits such as WEKA and can be used off the shelf as we illustrate in our examples, too, later in the book.

Let T be the set of test instances, f be a scoring classifier, $f(i)$ be the continuous outcome of f for data point i, min and max be the smallest and largest values returned by f, respectively, and incr be the smallest difference between any two f values. Then the simple procedure of Listing 4.1 can be used to generate a ROC curve over the classifier's (limited) empirical operating range.[1]

Listing 4.1: Simple (but inefficient) algorithm for building an ROC curve.

```
for  t := min  to  max  by  incr  do
    FP := 0
    TP := 0
    for  i ∈ T  do
        if  f(i) ≥ t  then
            if i is a positive example then
                TP := TP + 1
            else
                FP := FP + 1
            endif
        endif
    endfor
    Add point (FP/N, TP/P) to ROC Curve
endfor
```

Let us now apply this in the following example.

Example 4.1. Table 4.1 shows the scores that a classifier assigns to the instances in a hypothetical test set along with their true class labels. According to the

[1] Note that we directly use index i to denote a data point instead of x_i. Since it directly corresponds to Listing 4.1 where i is typically used over iterations.

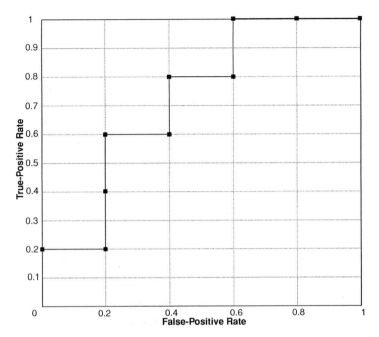

Figure 4.11. ROC analysis for the data of Table 4.1.

algorithm of Listing 4.1, the threshold will first be set at 0.48. At that threshold, we obtain TPR = FPR = 1 because every positive example has a score above or equal to 0.48, meaning that all the positive examples are well classified, but all the negative ones, with scores above 0.48 as well, are misclassified. This represents the first point on our curve. All the thresholds issued by increments of 0.05 until 0.5 yield the same results. At 0.5, however, we obtain TPR = 1 and FPR = 0.8. This represents the second point of our curve. The next relevant threshold is 0.64, which yields TPR = 1 and FPR = 0.6, giving the third point on the curve. We obtain the rest of the points in a similar fashion to obtain the graph of Figure 4.11.[2]

ROC Curves in the Resampling Regimen

With regard to the performance measure or method of interest, we obtain error estimates over the datasets by resampling the instances in which the dataset size is very small, as we will see in the next chapter. However, this poses an interesting issue with regard to studying the ROC behavior of the algorithm. For instance, when the commonly used k-fold cross-validation method is used for resampling, one question that comes up is that of how to combine the results of several cross-validation runs. As we have already briefly touched on, the

---

[2] Note that the plots obtained by varying the thresholds of *continuous* or *scoring* classifiers output a step function on a finite number of points. This would approximate the true curve of the form of Figure 4.2 in the limit of an infinite number of points because in principle the thresholds can be varied in the interval $[-\infty + \infty]$. We discussed this earlier in the chapter.

question of statistical validity is an important one when evaluating classifiers. Yet the procedure just discussed involves only a single testing set. How do we thus combine the results obtained on k testing sets in the case of cross-validation? With regard to the k-fold cross-validation, especially when $k = 10$, two main approaches have been proposed to deal with this issue. The first one consists of considering each different false-positive rate, i.e., each individual position on the horizontal axis, determining in each cross-validated set the smallest sample (starting from the highest-ranked) that allows us to reach this false-positive rate and averaging the true-positive rates obtained by the classifier in each of these subsets. The advantage of this approach is that it tends to smoothen the jagged ROC curve obtained from a single dataset. The second approach consists of running the 10-fold cross-validation experiments and then ranking the results of all the folds together, issuing a single curve for the 10 folds. The advantage of this method is its simplicity. It is not yet known definitively as to which of these two approaches is more representative of the learning algorithm's expected performance.

4.2.5 Summary Statistics and the AUC

Although the ROC analysis affords the advantage of being able to visualize the performance of classifiers over their operating ranges, it does not allow us to quantify this comparative analysis that can facilitate decision making with regard to the suitability or preference of one classifier over others in the form of an objective scalar metric. Various summary statistics have been proposed to address this shortcoming. Some such representative statistics include these:

- the area between the ROC curve and the diagonal of the ROC graph connecting the points FPR = TPR = 0 and FPR = TPR = 1,
- the intercept of the ROC curve with the diagonal connecting FPR = 1, TPR = 0 and FPR = 0, TPR = 1, and
- the total area under the ROC curve, abbreviated as AUC.

The first statistic aims at establishing the performance that a learning algorithm can achieve above the random classifier along TPR = FPR. The second signifies the operating range of the algorithm that yields classifiers with lower expected cost. The final and probably the most popular summary statistic for the ROC analysis is the AUC. Hence we discuss this metric in more detail.

The AUC represents the performance of the classifier averaged over all the possible cost ratios. Noting that the ROC space is a unit square, as previously discussed, it can be clearly seen that the AUC for a classifier f is such that $\text{AUC}(f) \in [0, 1]$, with the upper bound attained for a perfect classifier (one with TPR = 1 and FPR = 0). Morever, as can be noted, the random classifier represented by the diagonal cuts the ROC space in half and hence $\text{AUC}(f_{\text{random}}) = 0.5$. For a classifier with a reasonably better performance than random guessing, we would expect it to have an AUC greater than 0.5. An important point worth noting here is that an algorithm can have an AUC value of 0.5 also for reasons other than a random performance. If the classifier assigns the same score to all examples, whether negative or positive, we would obtain classifiers along the diagonal TPR = FPR. We can also obtain a similar curve if the classifier assigns similar distributions of the score. Consequently this would result in an AUC of approximately 0.5. We can also obtain such a metric value if the classifier performs very well on half of the examples of one class while at the same time performing poorly on the other half (that is, it assigns the highest scores to one half and the lowest to the other).

Another interpretation of an AUC can be obtained for ranking classifiers in that AUC represents the ability of a classifier to rank a randomly chosen positive test example higher than a negative one. In this respect, this is shown to be equivalent to Wilcoxon's Rank Sum test (also known as the Mann–Whitney U test). Wilcoxon's Rank Sum test is a nonparametric test to assess whether two samples (over orderings) of the observations come from a single distribution. It will be discussed at greater length in Chapter 6. With regard to the Gini coefficient (Gini), a measure of statistical dispersion popular in economics, it has been shown that AUC $= (\text{Gini} + 1)/2$.

Elaborate methods have been suggested to calculate the AUC. We illustrate the computation according to one such approach in Section 4.6. However, using Wilcoxon's Rank Sum statistic, we can obtain a simpler manner of estimating the AUC for ranking classifiers. To the scores assigned by the classifier to each test instance, we associate a rank in the order of decreasing scores. That is, the example with the highest score is assigned the rank 1. Then we can calculate the AUC as

$$\text{AUC}(f) = \frac{\sum_{i=1}^{|T_p|}(R_i - i)}{|T_p||T_n|},$$

where $T_p \subset T$ and $T_n \subset T$ are, respectively, the subsets of positive and negative examples in test set T, and R_i is the rank of the ith example in T_p given by classifier f.

AUC basically measures the probability of the classifier assigning a higher rank to a randomly chosen positive example than to a randomly chosen negative example. Even though AUC attempts to be a summary statistic, just as other single-metric performance measures, it too loses significant information about the behavior of the learning algorithm over the entire operating range (for instance, it misses information on concavities in the performance, or trade-off behaviors between the true-positive and the false-positive performances).

It can be argued that the AUC is a good way to get a score for the general performance of a classifier and to compare it with that of another classifier. This is particularly true in the case of imbalanced data in which, as discussed earlier, accuracy is strongly biased toward the dominant class. However, some criticisms have also appeared warning against the use of AUC across classifiers for comparative purposes. One of the most obvious is that, because the classifiers are typically optimized to obtain the best performance (in context of the given performance measure), the ROC curves thus obtained in the two cases would be similar. This then would yield uninformative AUC differences. Further, if the ROC curves of the two classifiers intersect (such as in the case of Figure 4.9), the AUC-based comparison between the classifiers can be relativly uninformative and even misleading. However, a more serious limitation of the AUC for comparative purposes lies in the fact that the misclassification cost distributions (and hence the skew-ratio distributions) used by the AUC are different for different classifiers. We do not delve into the details of this limitation here, but the interested reader is referred to the pointers in Section 4.8 and a brief related discussion in Chapter 8.

Nonetheless, in the event the ranking property of the classifier is important (for instance, in information-retrieval systems), AUC can be a more reliable measure of classifier performance than measures such as accuracy because it assesses the ranking capability of the classifier in a direct manner. This means that the measure will correlate the output scores of the classifier and the probability of correct classification better than accuracy, which focuses on determining whether all data are well classified, even if some of the data considered are not the most relevant for the application. The relationship between AUC and accuracy has also received some attention (see pointers in Section 4.8).

4.2.6 Calibration

The classifiers' thresholds based on the training set may or may not reflect the empirical realizations of labelings in the test set. That is, if the possible score interval is $[-\infty, +\infty]$, and if no example obtains a score in the interval $[t_1, t_2] \subset [-\infty, +\infty]$, then no threshold in the interval $[t_1, t_2]$ will yield a different point in the ROC space. The extrapolation between two meaningful threshold values (that is, ones that result in at least one different label over the examples in the test set) may not be very sensible. One solution to deal with this problem is *calibration*. All the scores in the interval $[t_1, t_2]$ can be mapped to the fraction of the positive instances obtained as a result of assigning any score in this interval. That is, for any threshold in the interval $[t_1, t_2]$, the fraction of instances labeled as positive remains the same, and hence all the threshold scores in the interval can be mapped to this particular fraction.

This is a workable solution as long as there are no concavities in the ROC curve. Concavity in the curve means that there are skew ratios for which the classifier is suboptimal. This essentially means that better classifier performance can be obtained for the skew ratios lying in the concave region of the curve although the empirical estimates do not suggest this. In the case of concavities, the behavior of the calibrated scores does not mimic the desired behavior of the slope of the threshold interval. The classifier obtained over calibrated scores can overfit the data, resulting in poor generalization. A solution for dealing with the issue of score calibration in the case of nonconvex ROCs has been proposed in the form of isotonic regression over the scores. The main idea behind the isotonic regression approach is to map the scores corresponding to the concave interval, say $[t_1^c, t_2^c]$, to an unbiased estimate of the slope of the line segment connecting the two points corresponding to the thresholds t_1^c and t_2^c. This in effect bypasses the concave segments by extrapolating a convex segment in the interval. Some pointers of interest with regard to calibration can be found in Section 4.8.

4.2.7 Extending the ROCs

Attempts have been made to extend ROC analysis to multiclass problems. However, ROC analysis in the multiclass case is much more complex than in the two-class case. The analysis in the two-class case is made especially convenient for two reasons: (i) the presence of only two classes makes the ROC plots easier to visualize and interpret; and (ii) the symmetry of the two-class classification as previously shown. In the case of more classes, say l, the confusion matrix becomes an $l \times l$ matrix with the l diagonal elements representing correct classification whereas the $l^2 - l$ nondiagonal elements represent classification errors. The next natural question that arises then is that of how to generalize the AUC statistic to the multiclass scenario. Attempts to generate multiclass ROCs have resulted in various formulations for obtaining the area under the multiclass ROC curves. Among the different proposed methods of generating multiclass ROCs and then obtaining their AUCs, the following formulation for obtaining the AUC proposed by Hand and Till (2001) is the most noteworthy:

$$ \text{AUC}_{\text{multiclass}}(f) = \frac{2}{l(l-1)} \sum_{l_i, l_j \in \mathcal{L}} \text{AUC}_{l_i, l_j}(f), $$

where $\text{AUC}_{\text{multiclass}}(f)$ is the total AUC of the multiclass ROC for the classifier f, $\mathcal{L}$ is the set of classes such that $|\mathcal{L}| = l$, and $\text{AUC}_{l_i, l_j}(f)$ is the AUC of the two-class ROC curve of f for the classes l_i and l_j.

Finally, as we discussed earlier, ROCs can be a significant tool to assist in evaluating the performance of hybrid classifiers designed to improve performance, in removing concavities from the individual classifiers' performance, or in the case of analyzing cascaded classifiers. The details are out of the scope of this book but some pointers are given in Section 4.8.

4.3 Other Visual Analysis Methods

Let us now discuss some other visualization techniques that can be beneficial in some specific scenarios and also explore, where relevant, their relation to the

ROC curves. In particular, we devote some space to discussing the cost curves. But, for now, let us start with the lift charts.

4.3.1 Lift Charts

Lift charts are a performance visualization technique closely related to the ROC curves. Lift charts plot the true positives against the dataset size required to achieve this number of true positives. That is, the vertical axis of the lift charts plots the true positives (and not the TPR) whereas the horizontal axis denotes the number of examples in the dataset considered for the specific true positives on the vertical axis. In other words, the ROC curve counts the number of negative examples that have slipped into the data sample for which the classifier issued a particular true-positive rate, whereas the lift chart counts both the positive and the negative examples in that set. In highly imbalanced datasets, in which, typically the number of positive examples is much smaller than that of negative examples, the horizontal axes of lift charts and ROC curves look very similar as do the curves.

The use of lift charts is more common in the business domains. A typical example for which lift charts are used in practice is in direct-mail advertising. Typically, very few people respond to this kind of advertising; yet the costs of mailing information to a large population can be high. The idea is to evaluate different classifiers whose goal is to identify the people most likely to respond to this kind of advertising. Lift charts allow a user to do so by expressing the result of classifiers in terms of curves similar to ROC curves that indicate which classifiers can identify actual respondents by using the smallest sample size (i.e., the smallest number of people to whom the information should be mailed and thus the smallest cost for the best response).

4.3.2 Precision–Recall (PR) Curves

Precision–recall Curves, sometimes abbreviated as PR curves, are similar to ROC curves and lift charts in that they explore the trade-off between the well-classified positive examples and the number of misclassified negative examples. As the name suggests, PR curves plot the precision of the classifier as a function of its recall. In other words, it measures the amount of precision that can be obtained as various degrees of recall are considered. For instance, in the domain of document-retrieval systems, PR curves would plot the percentage of relevant documents identified as relevant against the percentage of relevant documents deemed as such with respect to all the documents in the sample. The curves thus look different from ROC curves and lift curves because they have a negative slope. This is because precision decreases as recall increases. PR curves are a popular visualization technique in the information-retrieval field as illustrated by our earlier examples that discussed the notions of precision and recall. PR curves can sometimes be more appropriate than the ROC curves in the events of highly imbalanced data (Davis and Goadrich, 2006).

4.3.3 Cost Curves

Cost curves aim at plotting the relative costs directly instead of making use of ROC isometrics to do so in a surrogate fashion to determine the best classifier. Using the performance isometrics on the ROC curves can be tricky. Furthermore, in the cases of classifier comparisons, it can be difficult to determine the superiority of one classifier over the others, let alone quantifying the difference. In a sense, the information displayed by the cost curves is similar to that displayed by ROC curves. What makes cost curves attractive is their ease of use in determining the best classifier in situations in which the error cost, class distribution, or more generally the skew are known. For example, in Figure 4.9, although it is clear that the curve corresponding to classifier f_2 dominates the curve corresponding to classifier f_1 at first and that the situation is inverted afterward, this information cannot easily be translated into information telling us for what costs and class distributions classifier f_2 performs better than classifier f_1. Cost curves do provide this kind of information.

Cost-Curve Space

Cost curves plot the misclassification cost as a function of the proportion of positive instances in the dataset. Let us, for the moment, forget all about costs and focus just on the error rate. We can then graft the costs onto our explanations later. The important thing to keep in mind is that there is a point–line duality between cost curves and ROC curves. Cost curves are point–line duals of the ROC curves. In ROC space, a discrete classifier is represented by a point. The points representing several classifiers (produced by manipulating the threshold of the base classifier) can be joined (and extrapolated) to produce a ROC curve or the convex hull of the straight lines produced by joining each point together. In cost space, each of the ROC points is represented by a line and the convex hull of the ROC space corresponds to the lower envelope created by all the classifier lines. We illustrate the cost-curve space in Figure 4.12.

Figure 4.12 shows a space in which the error rate is plotted as a function of the probability of an example being from the positive class, $P(+)$. On the graph, we first focus on four lines: the three dashed straight lines and the x axis. Each of these lines represents a different ideal, terrible or trivial classifier: The x axis represents the perfect classifier, i.e., no matter what the value of $P(+)$ is, its error rate is always 0. The horizontal dashed line located on the y axis's value of 1 is the opposite classifier: the one that has a 100% error rate, no matter what $P(+)$ is. The two dashed diagonal lines represent the trivial classifiers. The one with an ascending slope is the one that always issues a negative classification, whereas the one with descending slope always issues a positive classification.

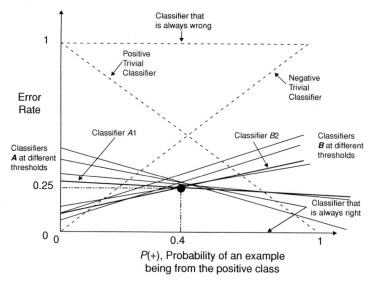

Figure 4.12. Illustration of a cost curve.

Clearly, the first of these classifiers gets a 100% error rate, when $P(+) = 1$ and a 0% error rate when $P(+) = 0$. Conversely, the second one obtains a 0% error rate when $P(+) = 1$ and a 100% error rate when $P(+) = 0$.

The graph also shows four full descending straight lines and four full ascending straight lines. By these lines, we mean to represent two families of (hypothetical) classifiers, say, A and B. Each of these lines would thus be represented by a point in ROC space, and the four A points would be used to generate classifiers A's ROC curve whereas the four B points would be used to generate B's ROC curve.

The first thing to note is that there are regions of the cost space in which each of classifiers from A and B are irrelevant. These represent all the areas of the lines that fall outside of the bottom triangle. These areas are irrelevant because, in those, the trivial positive or negative classifiers have lower error rates than classifiers from A or B. This lower triangle is called the *classifiers' operating region*. In this region, the line closest to the x axis is the best-performing classifier. It can be seen that, in certain parts of the operating region, one of the trivial classifiers is recommended whereas, in others, various classifiers from the A or B family are preferred.

Cost Curves versus ROC Curves

The question now becomes this: if cost curves are so similar to ROC curves, why bother using cost curves? The answer is that cost curves can provide more practical information than ROC curves in some cases. Consider, for example, the point located at position $(0.4, 0.25)$ in Fig. 4.12. This is a point where the dominating B classifier loses its performance to one of the A classifiers, which becomes the dominating classifier. This point is similar, in some ways, to the points at which two ROC curves cross, except that the ROC graph does not give us any practical information about when classifier A should be used over classifier B. Such practical information can, on the other hand, be read off the cost graph. In particular, we can read that for $0.26 \leq P(+) < 0.4$, classifier $B2$ should be used, but that for $0.4 \leq P(+) < 0.48$, classifier $A1$ should be used. This is practical information because $P(+)$ represents the class distribution of the domain in which the Classifier A and B compound system is deployed. In contrast, ROC graphs tell us that sometimes A is preferable to B, but we cannot read off when this is so from the graph.

Cost Considerations

The last point that we would like to discuss about cost curves is their use with different costs. Remember that, to simplify our discussion of cost curves, we chose to ignore costs. i.e., we assumed that each class had the same classification costs. When this is not the case, a very simple modification of the cost curves needs to be applied. This modification affects only the identity of the axes. The meaning of the curves and the reading of the graph remain the same. In this context, rather than representing the error rate, the y axis represents the normalized expected cost (NEC) or relative expected misclassification cost, defined as

$$\text{NEC} = \text{FNR} \times P_C[+] + \text{FPR} \times (1 - P_C[+]),$$

where FNR and FPR are the false-negative and false-positive rates, respectively, and $P_C[+]$, the probability cost function, a modified version of $P[+]$ that takes costs into consideration, is formally defined as

$$P_C[+] = \frac{P[+] \times C[+|-]}{P[+] \times C[+|-] + P[-] \times C[-|+]},$$

where $C[+|-]$ and $C[-|+]$ denote the cost of predicting a positive when the instance is actually negative and vice versa. $P[-]$ is the probability of an example belonging to the negative class.

4.3.4 Relative Superiority Graphs

Another method proposed to take cost into consideration while evaluating classifier performance has appeared in the form of relative superiority graphs that plot the ratio of costs, mapping them into the [0, 1] interval. The ratio of costs here refers to the relative expense of one type of error against another. That is, it refers to the relationship between the cost of making a false-positive error against a false-negative error. The rationale behind the relative superiority curve is that, although the precise costs of each type of error might either not be available or impossible to quantify, it may be the case that their relative costs are known. Mapping such relative costs then transforms the ROC curves into a set of parallel lines from which the superiority of classifiers in the regions of interest (of relative cost ratios) can be inferred. To replace the associated AUC, a loss comparison (LC) index is used in the case of relative superiority curves. In this context, sometimes interpreted as a binary version of the ROC curves, relative superiority curves can be used to identify whether a classifier is superior to the other with the LC index measuring the confidence in the inferred superiority.

4.3.5 DET Curves

Detection error trade-off (DET) curves can be interpreted as an alternative representation of the ROC curves in that, instead of plotting the TPR on the vertical axis, DET curves plot the FNR. The DET curves are typically log-scaled so that the area corresponding to the classifiers performing better than the random classifier is expanded. Note that, because of the change of vertical axis, this area is represented by the bottom-left region of the DET space. This is in contrast to the ROC space, where this area is represented by the upper left region. As a consequence of log-scaling, the surface area pertaining to these better-performing classifiers is expanded, enabling the user to obtain a better insight into their relative performances.

4.3.6 Limitations

We have discussed the limitations of the graphical analysis methods in the text in the preceding subsections. It is important that one keep these limitations in mind while drawing conclusions or making inferences based on these measures. Let us illustrate this point with one last example. ROC analysis suggests that an ideal classifier is achieved at point $(0, 1)$ in the ROC space (i.e., it has FPR $= 0$ and TPR $= 1$). Note the interesting aspect here: We make an implicit assumption that the classifier *always* generates either a positive or a negative label on *every* instance. This assumption can be problematic for the case of classifiers that can abstain from making a prediction. A classifier that can abstain can theoretically get TPR $= 1$ if it identifies all the positives correctly. However, instead of making errors on negatives, if it abstains from making predictions (whether positive or negative) on the set of negative instances totally, it can still achieve a FPR of zero even though, obviously, this classifier may be far from ideal.

In fact, such shortcomings result from the limitation of the confusion matrix itself and are reflected in all the measures and analysis methods that rely on the confusion matrix, including the ROC analysis.

4.4 Continuous and Probabilistic Classifiers

A continuous or scoring classifier outputs a real score on the test instances, which is then typically thresholded so as to obtain discrete class labels. In the case of probabilistic classifiers, that is, when the classifier score denotes the posterior on the class membership given the test instance, the output is more informative than the raw scores. This score generally signifies the extent of certainty in the classification decision. A probability close to 1, for instance, can signify how certain the classifier is that the actual label of the instance is indeed 1 in the case of the binary classification scenario. In the case of a more general continuous label scenario for regression, the distance of an instance's predicted class label to its actual label also gives a sense of the certainty of the classifier. Performance measures intended to assess the behavior of such continuous or probabilistic classifiers tend to take into account this aspect of certainty. We discuss some of these measures, also referred to as reliability metrics in some of the literature, in this section. With regard to the continuous classifiers, one of the most widely utilized metric is the RMSE metric. On the other hand, for probabilistic classifiers, the commonly used metrics can be grouped together as information-theoretic measures. Let us discuss these in turn.

4.4.1 Root-Mean-Square Error

The performance measure known as the root-mean-square error, commonly abbreviated as RMSE, is generally used to evaluate regression learning algorithms. As mentioned before, regression algorithms typically aim at fitting a function to the observed data and then generalize on unseen instances. Consequently, regression classifiers output a continuous valued label to each test instance with the aim of replicating the true labels. RMSE measures the "closeness" of the predicted labels to the true labels:

$$\text{RMSE}(f) = \sqrt{\frac{1}{m} \sum_{i=1}^{m} (f(\mathbf{x}_i) - y_i)^2},$$

where y_i is the true label of test instance $\mathbf{x}_i$ and $f(\mathbf{x}_i)$ represents the label predicted by the classifier f. Recall the definition of the risk of the classifier from Chapter 2. The RMSE measures the same classifier risk, the only difference being that of the loss function. Instead of using a zero–one loss function as in the case of classification, RMSE uses a squared loss function. Naturally, other notions of classifier risk can be defined under different settings by adapting the associated loss function. The squared loss, in a sense, quantifies the error (or alternatively closeness) of the predicted label to the true label. When specialized to the case of probabilistic classifiers, this then can be interpreted as a reliability measure.

Table 4.2. *Intermediate values for calculating the RMSE. See Example 4.2*

Inst. No.	Class 1 predicted	Actual	Diff^2/2	Class 2 predicted	Actual	Diff^2/2	SqrErr (sum of differences)
1	0.95	1.00000	0.00125	0.05	0.00000	0.00125	0.0025
2	0.6	0.00000	0.18	0.4	1.00000	0.18	0.36
3	0.8	1.00000	0.02	0.2	0.00000	0.02	0.04
4	0.75	0.00000	0.28125	0.25	1.00000	0.28125	0.5625
5	0.9	1.00000	0.005	0.1	0.00000	0.005	0.01

In the absence of any other information about the application domain and the specific evaluation needs, RMSE can serve as a good general-purpose performance measure because it has been shown to correlate most closely with both the classification metrics, such as accuracy, and the ranking metrics, such as the AUC, in addition to its suitability in evaluating probabilistic classifiers (Caruana and Niculescu-Mizil, 2004). Naturally it is reasonable to use it only in the case of continuous classifier predictions. The qualifications that we made in the beginning of this paragraph are indeed important; without these the RMSE need not necessarily be more suitable than any other metric in consideration.

Example 4.2. Here is an example of the way WEKA calculates the RMSE values. This example suggests how to handle continuous and multiclass data, although, for simplicity, it deals with only the binary case.[3] Let us assume that a classifier is trained on a binary dataset and that the test set contains five instances. We also assume that instances 1, 3, and 5 belong to class 1 whereas instances 2 and 4 belong to class 2. The results we obtained are listed in Table 4.2.

The columns titled "Class X predicted" ($X = 1$ or 2 in this example) show the numerical predictions obtained for each instance with respect to the class considered. The actual class value is shown in the next column. Columns Diff^2/2 squares the difference to the actual value for all class labels and divides it by the number of class labels (2, in this example, because this is a binary example). These are summed in the column "SqrErr" for each instance.

The five values of SqrErr are then summed to obtain 0.975. Finally, we compute the RMSE by dividing 0.975 by 5, the number of instances, and taking the square root of that ratio. In this example, we thus get RMSE = 0.4416.

4.4.2 Information-Theoretic Measures

Having their origins in physics and statistical mechanics, information-theory-based measures have proven to be useful, not only in measuring the performance

---

[3] The explanation was obtained from the WEKA mailing list at https://list.scms.waikato.ac.nz/pipermail/wekalist/2007-May/009990.html, but a new example was generated.

of the algorithms, but also in defining the optimization criteria for the learning problem itself. The main reason for their success is their intuitive nature. These measures *reward* a classifier upon correct classification relative to the (typically empirical) prior on the data. Note that, unlike the cost-sensitive metrics that we have discussed so far, including the ROC-based measures, the information-theoretic measures, by virtue of accounting for the data prior, are applicable to probabilistic classifiers. Further, these metrics are independent of the cost considerations and can be applied directly to the probabilistic output scenario. Consequently these measures have found a wide use in Bayesian learning. We discuss some of the main information-theoretic measures, starting with the classical Kullback–Leibler divergence.

Kullback–Leibler Divergence

We consider probabilistic classifiers where these measures can be applied most naturally. Let the true probability distribution over the labels be denoted as $p(y)$. Let the posterior distribution generated by the learning algorithm after seeing the data be denoted by $P(y|f)$. Note that, because f is obtained after looking at the training samples $\mathbf{x} \in S$, this empirically approximates $P(y|\mathbf{x})$, the conditional posterior distribution of the labels. Then the Kullback–Leibler divergence, also known as the KL divergence, can be utilized to quantify the difference between the estimated posterior distribution and the true underlying distribution of the labels:

$$
\begin{aligned}
\mathrm{KL}[p(y)||P(y|f)] &= \int [p(y)\ln p(y)dy] - \int p(y)\ln P(y|f)dy \\
&= -\int p(y)\ln P(y|f)dy - \left[-\int p(y)\ln p(y)dy \right] \\
&= -\int p(y)\ln \frac{P(y|f)}{p(y)}dy.
\end{aligned}
$$

The first equality basically denotes the difference between the entropies of the posterior and the prior distributions. For a given random variable y (labels in our case) and a given distribution $p(y)$, the entropy E, i.e., the average amount of information needed to represent the labels, is defined as:

$$
E[y] = -\int p(y)\log p(y)dy.
$$

Hence the KL divergence basically just finds the difference between the entropies of the two distributions $P(y|f)$ and $p(y)$. In view of this interpretation, the KL divergence is also known as the relative entropy. In information-theoretic terms, the relative entropy denotes the average additional information required to specify the labels by using the posterior distribution instead of the true underlying distribution of the labels. The base of the logarithm is 2 in this case, and hence the information content denoted by the entropy as well as the relative entropy should be interpreted in bits. Alternatively, the natural logarithm can also be used. This would result in an alternative unit called "nats" which, for all comparative purposes, is equivalent to the preceding unit except for a $\ln 2$ factor.

For a finite-size dataset S, this can be discretized to

$$\mathrm{KL}[p(y)\|P(y|f)] = -\sum_{x\in S} p(y) \ln \frac{P(y|f)}{p(y)} dy$$

$$= \sum_{x\in S} p(y) \ln \frac{p(y)}{P(y|f)} dy.$$

It can be shown that the KL divergence is minimized (equal to zero) if and only if (iff) the posterior distribution is the same as the prior, a situation referred to as *perfect calibration*, meaning that the classifier perfectly mimics the true underlying distribution of the labels. Also, it can be noted from the preceding definition that the KL divergence is asymmetrical; that is, $\mathrm{KL}[P(y)\|P(y|f)] \neq \mathrm{KL}[P(y|f)\|P(y)]$.

Even though the KL divergence is a very elegant way of measuring the difference between the posterior distribution obtained by the learner from the true distribution so as to gauge the quality of the obtained classifier, there is a significant drawback to it. The KL divergence necessitates the knowledge of the true underlying prior distribution of the labels, which is rarely, if at all, known in any practical application. This makes estimation of the KL divergence extremely difficult (although empirical estimations are sometimes done). With regard to the optimization of the learning algorithm on given data, that is, model selection, it can be shown that minimizing the KL divergence is equivalent to maximizing the likelihood function.

Let us then look into measures that, instead of relying on the true distribution of the labels, take into account a (typically empirically determined) prior distribution over the labels. This prior can come from the distribution of the samples of various classes in the training set for instance, or can also incorporate prior domain knowledge.

Kononenko and Bratko's Information Score

Kononenko and Bratko's information reward metric assumes a prior $P(y)$ on the labels. Note that this need not be the true distribution of the labels but can be an empirically determined prior distribution, such as the one based on the class distribution of the training data. Given the training set S, the learning algorithm outputs a probabilistic classifier, i.e., a posterior on the labels. Let $P(y|f)$ denote this posterior distribution on the labels conditional on the identified classifier f. Then the information score $\mathbf{I}$, of the prediction is defined as follows:

$$\mathbf{I}(x) = I[P(y|f) \geq P(y)]\{-\log[P(y)] + \log[P(y|f)]\}$$

$$+ I[P(y|f) < P(y)]\{-\log[1 - P(y)] + \log[1 - P(y|f)]\},$$

where $P(y)$ represents the prior probability of a label y, $P(y|f)$ denotes the posterior probability of the label y (after obtaining the classifier, that is, after seeing the data), and the indicator function $I(a)$ is equal to 1 iff the predicate a is true and zero otherwise.[4] Note that this single definition, in fact, represents two cases, which are instantiated depending on a correct or an incorrect classification. Note as well that, for simplification, log in this formula represents $\log_2$.

In the case in which $P(y|f) \geq P(y)$, the probability of class y has changed in the right direction. Let us understand the terms in the measure from an information-theoretic aspect. Recall from our previous discussion that the entropy of a variable (labels y in our case) denotes the *average* amount of information needed to represent the variables. This is nothing but an expectation over the entire distribution $P(y)$ over the variable. This basically means that, for a single instantiation of the variable y, the amount of information needed is nothing but $-\log P(y)$. That is, one needs $-\log P(y)$ bits of information to decide if a label takes on the value y. Similarly, the amount of information necessary to decide if the label does not take this particular value is nothing but $-\log[1 - P(y)]$. The metric hence measures the decrease in the information needed to classify the instances as a result of learning the classifier f.

Now, the average information score $\mathbf{I}_a$ of a prediction over a test set T is

$$\mathbf{I}_a = \frac{1}{m} \sum_{j=1}^{m} \mathbf{I}(\mathbf{x}_j), \quad \forall \mathbf{x} \in T, |T| = m$$

and the relative information score $\mathbf{I}_r$ is

$$\mathbf{I}_r = \frac{\mathbf{I}_a}{E(y)} 100\%,$$

where $E(y)$ is the entropy of the label distribution, which represents for k classes $\{y^1, \ldots, y^k\}$, the expected amount of information necessary to classify one instance, as discussed earlier. The discrete version of the entropy can be computed as

$$E(y) = - \sum_{i=1}^{k} P(y^i) \log P(y^i),$$

where $\sum_{i=1}^{k} P(y^i) = 1$.

As can be seen, the relative information score $\mathbf{I}_r$ can be used to compare the performance of different classifiers on the same domain (because it depends on the entropy of the label distribution for the given domain), whereas the average information score $\mathbf{I}_a$ can be used to compare the performance on different domains. Higher information score values correspond to better performance.

---

[4] Note that the notations for the information score and for the indicator function are slightly different: For the information score, we used a boldfaced $\mathbf{I}$, whereas we used an italic I for the indicator function.

Table 4.3. *Information score for the data in Table 2.2*

Class 1 predicted	Actual	Information score
0.95	1.00000	0.66297
0.6	0.00000	0
0.8	1.00000	0.415042
0.75	0.00000	0.32193
0.9	1.00000	0.58497

The information content interpretation of the score basically signifies that a less likely correct classification is held to be more valuable than a more likely one. This is because it denotes the effectiveness of the learning process over and above the information conveyed by the empirical priors. In an analogous manner, the classifier is also penalized more when a highly probable label is erred on.

Example 4.3. We consider the example in Table 4.2, previously used to illustrate the calculation of the RMSE assuming a probabilistic interpretation. In this table, the first instance is positive and $P(y_1 = 1) = 0.6 \le P(y_1 = 1|f) = 0.95$. Note that the $P(y)$'s are calculated empirically. Because, there are 3 out of 5 instances of class 1, we have $P(y = 1) = \frac{3}{5} = 0.6$. Similarly, we have $P(y = 0) = 0.4$. Therefore this instance's information score is calculated as $I = -\log(0.6) + \log(0.95) = 0.66297$. The fourth instance, on the other hand, is negative and $P(y_4 = 0) = 0.4 > P(y_4 = 0|f) = 0.25$. Therefore this instance's information score is calculated as $I = -\log(1 - 0.4) + \log(1 - 0.25) = 0.32193$. Altogether, the information scores obtained for the entire dataset are listed in Table 4.3. Using these values, we can calculate the average information score by averaging the information score values obtained for each instance. In the example, we get $I_a = 0.39698$.

We can also calculate the relative information score, first, by computing E as

$$E = -[0.6 \log(0.6) + 0.4 \log(0.4)] - (-0.4422 - 0.5288) = 0.971,$$

and second, by dividing I_a by E and turning the result into a percentage. i.e.,

$$I_r = \frac{I_a}{E} 100\% = 40.88\%$$

However, this measure too has some limitations, especially in multiclass scenarios. Because it considers the probability of only the true class, other classes are ignored. That is, each misclassification is weighted equally. Accordingly, a lack of calibration in such cases would not be penalized even though a correct one is rewarded (one sided). As a result, this might not lead toward an optimal posterior over the labels. Let us then look at a strategy proposed to deal with this issue.

Bayesian Information Reward

The Bayesian information reward (BIR) (Hope and Korb, 2004), in addition to retaining the qualities of the other information-theoretic measures, also takes into account the misclassified classes in the scoring criterion. It is claimed to reach maximal value under perfect calibration and is defined as

$$ \text{BIR} = \frac{\sum_i \text{IR}_i}{k}, $$

where

$$ \text{IR}_i = \begin{cases} \text{IR}_i^+ = \log \dfrac{P(y|f)}{P(y)} & \text{for correct class} \\[2ex] \text{IR}_i^- = \log \dfrac{1 - P(y|f)}{1 - P(y)} & \text{otherwise.} \end{cases} $$

The reward is zero when $P(y|f) = P(y)$ because this reflects an uninformative posterior as it simply mimics the empirical prior $P(y)$. Note here the contrast with the KL divergence that was maximized when the two distributions were alike, which should not be confused with the BIR. Whereas KL divergence measures the *distance* of the posterior obtained by the learning algorithm to the *true* underlying distribution of the labels, which is, indeed, the aim of learning, the BIR measures the *informativeness* of the posterior with regard to the *empirical prior* on the labels. Hence, in the case of KL divergence, a zero would indicate a perfect calibration, as previously mentioned. However, the lack of knowledge of the true underlying distribution of the labels makes the KL divergence difficult to use. The BIR evaluates the classifier on the overall distribution on the labels of all classes, unlike the previous measures that did so only on the true class. As a result, in the event of unavailability of the misclassification costs on the label combinations of different classes, BIR presents an empirical alternative for the cost-sensitive classification.

4.5 Specialized Metrics

We have mainly focused on the performance measures with regard to the evaluation of classification algorithms. Needless to mention, evaluation criteria have appeared in the context of other learning strategies too. Some of these resemble those discussed in this and the last chapter, whereas others address specific assessment criteria based on the type of learning strategy, as well as the domain of their application. Let us discuss some of these very briefly.

4.5.1 Metrics for Different Learning Strategies

Specialized metrics have appeared for evaluation with regard to learning strategies other than classification. Let us see some examples.

Regression analysis is basically a generalization of classification to real-valued class labels. Unlike classification, in which a classifier associates each instance with a discrete label, a regression algorithm associates a real-valued label to each instance. Accordingly, the evaluation of regression algorithms does not rely on the measures used to assess discrete classifiers. Two approaches have been widely used to assess regression algorithms: *residual-based loss functions* and *ranking metrics*. The RMSE that we previously discussed can be interpreted as a residual-based loss function. Alternatively, the mean-square error or the mean-absolute error is also used. Among the ranking metrics (metrics that treat the labels as ranking criteria for the instances), the better-known ones include the number of ranking-order switches and their weighted sum. This corresponds to Spearman's ρ (Spearman, 1904) and Kendall's τ (Kendall, 1938), nonparametric correlation coefficients.

Ordinal classification is closely related to multiclass classification, but carries an additional restriction on the classes. Namely, although the difference between two contiguous classes is not equal nor necessarily meaningful from a numeric point of view, there is an inherent ordering of the classes. This kind of classification is useful in domains in which examples have to be binned into human-generated scales, such as the case of medical diagnostic or product reviews. Evaluating such algorithms typically uses metrics such as linear correlation, normalized distance performance measure, and mean-absolute error in addition to the conventional measures such as accuracy, mean-squared error, and ROC for ordinal classification along with correlation.

Association rule mining refers to the process of discovering patterns of interest in a database. In such a problem, which is an unsupervised process, the training data are not arranged by classes, but instead, the process attempts to discover correlation among the descriptors or features of the data. Classification can be seen as a special case of this process in which the correlation has to be found between one set of features (the class) and all the others. The evaluation process in association rule mining is particularly important because such systems discover a lot of correlation among the features, many of which are meaningless. Discovering the meaningfulness of what has been learned is quite challenging. Consequently the performance measures used to evaluate such algorithms focus on this notion of "interestingness" of patterns and include measures such as novelty, diversity, coverage, utility, and applicability. More conventional notions, such as those used in Occam's razor criterion, also appear in the form of measures such as conciseness. Some of these measures are objective, whereas others are subjective. The most widely used metrics in association rule mining are support, coverage, and confidence.

Clustering is another unsupervised process that consists of grouping together patterns that are closely related. Once again, the training examples are not assigned to classes, and it is the clustering system's goal to regroup the patterns into categories that contain examples that are similar to each other and relatively dissimilar to all the other examples. Evaluating the quality of a clustering is difficult because the learned sets of clusters cannot be compared with any existing clustering (although in some cases, there is a gold standard that the system attempts to reach, and, in this case, the learned clustering can be compared to that gold standard, using measures similar to the ones used to assess regular classification methods). Often, however, it is unfair and perhaps even uninteresting to expect a clustering system to cluster the data in a way closely related to the gold standard. In such cases, evaluation needs to take a different form. Cluster compactness, cluster separation, cluster entropy, and class entropy are but a few measures that can be applied. The first two are based on cluster distribution and do not take into consideration the expectations set forth by the gold standard; the last two, on the other hand, are based on class conformation and do consider the expected classification outcome.

4.5.2 Domain-Specific Metrics

In addition to learning-specific evaluation metrics, different domains of application warrant specialized assessment criteria. Information retrieval and the medical domain are two areas in which impressive advances have been made with regard to the performance assessment of the learning algorithms.

Information retrieval is the process by which documents or parts thereof are identified as relevant to a particular query. It is very useful for searching through large databases of documents such as libraries or the World Wide Web. The field has been very active in identifying appropriate evaluation measures for a very long time. Some of the most important measures date back to the 1960s, many of which are still in prominent use. Many novel measures, however, have appeared in the past decade. We have already discussed three performance measures coming from the field in the form of precision, recall, and the F measure, all discovered in the 1960s. Among the more recent measures are fallout, expected search length, sliding ratio, novelty ratio, coverage ratio, satisfaction, frustration, and tolerance to irrelevance.

Similarly, in the medical domain, many evaluation metrics have appeared, many of which are in use in machine learning today. For example, both pairs of metrics called sensitivity and specificity and positive and negative predictive values come from the medical field. Other significant metrics include the likes of Youden's index and the discriminant power which are similar in intent to the F measure as they take into account, and combine, sensitivity and specificity.

4.5.3 Other Less-Common Ranking and Reliability Metrics

Information theory has led to some other related metrics that are used for both performance estimation and optimization. Some of these include the cross-entropy measures, which have also led to the so called cross-entropy-based optimization algorithms. Other related measures are offshoots from the entropy-based measures such as the mutual information and the Bayesian information criterion, which also take into account the complexity of the model in addition to the informativeness of the distributions. Because of this model-complexity-based reward (or penalization, as the case may be), these measures are sometimes not directly comparable across learners and domains. Other measures that have recently acquired some more prominence in distribution-based metrics includes the likes of probability calibration. The details on these and other metrics can be found by referring to the literature pointed to in Section 4.8.

4.6   Illustration of the Ranking and Probabilistic Approaches Using R, ROCR, and WEKA

In this section, we first discuss how to compute the graphical evaluation measures and methods discussed in this chapter, by using WEKA, R and the ROCR package. We then discuss how to obtain some of the reliability measures we consider by using WEKA.

4.6.1 WEKA and the ROCR package

To illustrate the graphical evaluation approaches, we make use of the WEKA machine learning toolkit, along with the "*ROCR Classifier Visualization in R*" package.[5] The instructions on how to download, install, and use the ROCR package are straightforward. To use the package, it is also necessary to install the following R packages: bitops, caTools, gdata, gplots, and gtools. These are all freely downloadable from the Web.

Once all the packages, including ROCR, have been installed, we load ROCR by typing "library(ROCR)". A demo and help pages are also available by typing the "demo" and "help" commands: shown below.

```
> library(ROCR)
> demo(ROCR)
> help(package=ROCR)
>
```

Even though we will not be making full use of the ROCR package, which is a sophisticated and easy-to-use one, the reader is encouraged to explore the measures and the features that are implemented in ROCR (see Howell, 2007).

---

[5] ROCR is freely downloadable from: http://rocr.bioinf.mpi-sb.mpg.de/ (2007) (also, see Sing et al., 2005).

4.6.2 Data Preparation

We begin by running WEKA on the labor data, using 10-fold cross-validation. To be able to extract ROC curves and the like from the WEKA run, we need to indicate to WEKA that it should output the classifier's predictions. We do so in the Explorer package by clicking on the "More Options" item in the Test Options area of the window and selecting, in the menu that appears, the item titled "Output predictions".

The predictions output by WEKA after running c45 on the labor data using 10-fold cross-validation will look as shown in Appendix B. Here, we reproduce a short segment of it for illustration purposes.

```
=== Predictions on test data ===

inst#,     actual,  predicted,  error,  probability distribution
   1       1:bad      2:good       +      0       *1
   2       1:bad      1:bad              *0.762    0.238
   3       2:good     2:good              0.082   *0.918
   4       2:good     1:bad        +     *0.762    0.238
   5       2:good     1:bad        +     *0.762    0.238
   6       2:good     2:good              0       *1
   1       1:bad      1:bad              *0.85     0.15
   2       1:bad      2:good       +      0       *1
   3       2:good     2:good              0       *1
   4       2:good     2:good              0.14    *0.86
   5       2:good     1:bad        +     *0.85     0.15
   6       2:good     2:good              0.14    *0.86
...
```

These data will be the basis for our plots in R. In particular, we will build a dataset containing, on the one hand, the numerical predictions made by the classifier (c45, in this case), and, on the other hand, the true labels of the data. We will do this by extracting the values in the last column of the preceding output (column 6), making them vectors, extracting the actual labels in the second column of the preceding output, converting them to values of 1 for positive and 0 for negative, and making them vectors as well. The two vectors thus created will be assigned to two elements of an R object, one called predictions and the other one called labels.

This can be done as in Listing 4.2.

Listing 4.2: Data preparation for ROCR (c45).

```
> laborDTpredictions = c(1,  0.238, .918,  .238,  .238,  1,  0.15,
    1,  1,  .86,  .15,  .86,  .17,  .17,  .815,  .815 ,  .815,  .815,
    .02,  .02,  .967,  .02,  .075,  .02 ,  .17,  .17,  .963,  .963,
    .963,  .963,  0.877,  .08,  0.877,  .08,  .764,  0.877,  .16,
    0.837,  0.837,  0.837,  0.837,  0.837,  .067,  .067,  .705,  .973,
    .803,  .203,  .86,  .86,  .86,  .86,  1,  .085,  .346,  1,  .346)
```

```
> laborDTlabels <- c
    (0,0,1,1,1,1,0,0,1,1,1,1,0,0,1,1,1,1,0,0,1,1,1,1,0,0,1,1,1,
     1,0,0,1,1,1,1,0,0,1,1,1,1,0,0,1,1,1,1,0,0,1,1,1,1,0,0,1,1,1)
> laborDTSingle <- c("predictions", "labels")
> laborDTSingle$predictions <- laborDTpredictions
> laborDTSingle$labels <- laborDTlabels
```

4.6.3 ROC Curves

We now illustrate how to plot an ROC curve by using WEKA and R. We first illustrate the simple case in which a simple ROC curve is built from the results obtained on a single test set. We then move on to the case in which 10-fold cross-validation has been performed and all 10 curves are plotted, along with their average. The last illustration concerns the comparison of two ROC curves coming from two different classifiers. For illustration purposes, we use the results from the decision tree (c45) and naive Bayes (nb) algorithms applied to the labor dataset from the UCI Repository.

Building a Single ROC Curve in the Case of Cross-Validated Data
The labor object created in Subsection 4.6.2 will now be used to build a ROC curve by use of the commands from the ROCR package. The R code for this follows, along with an illustration of the resulting graph.

Listing 4.3: Single ROC curve.

```
> pred <- prediction(laborDTSingle$predictions, laborDT$labels)
> perf <- performance(pred, "tpr","fpr")
> plot(perf, colorize=FALSE)
>
```

The result is illustrated in the graph of Figure 4.13.

This very simple solution for handling cross-validated data corresponds to the second of the solutions discussed in Subsection 4.2.4 on ROC curves in a cross-validated regimen. Indeed, as recommended in this situation, we pooled together the results of the 10 folds and built a single ROC curve from it. This pooling is evident from the first column of the WEKA results, which list the instance number. It can be seen, in that column, that there are 10 repetitions of instance numbers 1 to 6 or 1 to 5, each of these repetitions corresponding to a separate fold.

The next subsection instead considers the first of the recommended options from Subsection 4.2.4 on ROC curves in a cross-validated regimen in which the 10 curves drawn from the data at each fold are averaged into a single curve.

Building Multiple ROC Curves in the Case of Cross-Validated Data
To build multiple curves and average them, we need to present the data obtained from WEKA in a different format. In particular, we must separate the prediction

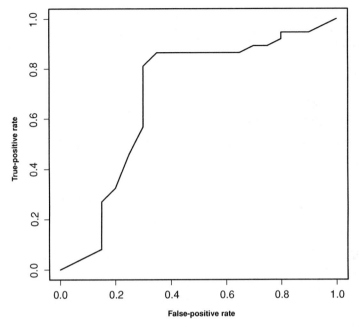

Figure 4.13. Single ROC curve for the labor data.

results of each fold as well as the label results of each fold. This can be done as follows.

Listing 4.4: Data preparation for multiple ROC curves.

```
> laborDT <- c("predictions", "labels")
> laborDT$predictions[[1]] <- c(1, 0.238, .918, .238, .238, 1)
> laborDT$predictions[[2]] <- c(0.15, 1, 1, .86, .15, .86)
> laborDT$predictions[[3]] <- c(.17, .17, .815, .815 , .815,
    .815)
> laborDT$predictions[[4]] <- c(.02, .02, .967, .02, .075, .02)
> laborDT$predictions[[5]] <- c(.17, .17, .963, .963, .963,
    .963)
> laborDT$predictions[[6]] <- c(0.877, .08, 0.877, .08, .764,
    0.877)
> laborDT$predictions[[7]] <- c(.16, 0.837, 0.837, 0.837,
    0.837, 0.837)
> laborDT$predictions[[8]] <- c(.067, .067, .705, .973, .803)
> laborDT$predictions[[9]] <- c(.203, .86, .86, .86, .86)
> laborDT$predictions[[10]] <- c(1, .085, .346, 1, .346)
>
> laborDT$labels[[1]] <- c(0,0,1,1,1,1)
> laborDT$labels[[2]] <- c(0,0,1,1,1,1)
> laborDT$labels[[3]] <- c(0,0,1,1,1,1)
> laborDT$labels[[4]] <- c(0,0,1,1,1,1)
> laborDT$labels[[5]] <- c(0,0,1,1,1,1)
> laborDT$labels[[6]] <- c(0,0,1,1,1,1)
> laborDT$labels[[7]] <- c(0,0,1,1,1,1)
```

```
> laborDT$labels[[8]] <- c(0,0,1,1,1)
> laborDT$labels[[9]] <- c(0,0, 1,1,1)
> laborDT$labels[[10]] <- c(0,0,1,1,1)
>
```

The data-entry operation just performed will create a data structure named "laborDT." (We do not discuss the warning messages output because these do not affect the results obtained.)

Given the "laborDT" object just constructed, 10 ROC plots and an 11th, vertical average plot can be built as follows.

Listing 4.5: Multiple ROC curves.

```
>
> pred <- prediction(laborDT$predictions, laborDT$labels)
> perf <- performance(pred,"tpr","fpr")
> plot(perf,col="black",lty=3)
> plot(perf,lwd=3,avg="vertical",spread.estimate="boxplot",add=
    TRUE)
>
```

This creates the plot of Figure 4.14.[6] The 10 ROC curves constructed for each fold are shown as broken lines. The solid line in bold represents the average of these 10 lines. The box plots show the estimate of the spread of the 10 curves at each point (when averaged vertically).

Comparing the ROC Curves of Two Different Classifiers

To compare the ROC curves of two different classifiers, we need to prepare a database for a different classifier. Here we chose NB, whose predictions are also shown in Appendix B. We organize the data as in the previous section so as to obtain 10 ROC curves per classifier as well as an extra curve for each, representing the vertical average of these 10 curves. Namely, we type in Listing 4.6.

Listing 4.6: Data preparation for multiple ROC curves of two different classifiers.

```
> laborNB <- c("predictions", "labels")
> laborNB$predictions[[1]] <- c(0.649, 0.037, 1,1, .985, 1)
> laborNB$predictions[[2]] <- c(0.984, 0.031, 0.999,1, 0.489,
    1)
> laborNB$predictions[[3]] <- c(0.072, 0, 0.997, 0.997, 1,
    0.996)
> laborNB$predictions[[4]] <- c(0, 0.001, 0.996, 0.251, 0.944,
    0.353 )
> laborNB$predictions[[5]] <- c(0, .074, .65, .999, 1, 1 )
```

---

[6] Please note that, in the labor dataset, the technique illustrated here is far from ideal, especially because each fold contains only 5 or 6 test instances. On the other hand, this example is practical for illustration purposes, because it contains so few data points.

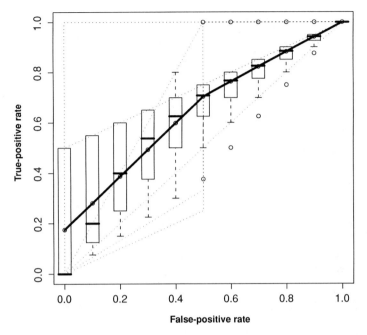

Figure 4.14. Multiple ROC curves for the labor data.

```
> laborNB$predictions[[6]] <- c(.004, 0,1,1,1,1 )
> laborNB$predictions[[7]] <- c( 0,0,1,0,1,1)
> laborNB$predictions[[8]] <- c(0.282, 0, .96,1,1 )
> laborNB$predictions[[9]] <- c(.02,0,.987,1,1 )
> laborNB$predictions[[10]] <- c(.002, .003,.667,.949,1 )
>
> laborNB$labels[[1]] <- c(0,0,1,1,1,1)
> laborNB$labels[[2]] <- c(0,0,1,1,1,1)
> laborNB$labels[[3]] <- c(0,0,1,1,1,1)
> laborNB$labels[[4]] <- c(0,0,1,1,1,1)
> laborNB$labels[[5]] <- c(0,0,1,1,1,1)
> laborNB$labels[[6]] <- c(0,0,1,1,1,1)
> laborNB$labels[[7]] <- c(0,0,1,1,1,1)
> laborNB$labels[[8]] <- c(0,0,1,1,1)
> laborNB$labels[[9]] <- c(0,0, 1,1,1)
> laborNB$labels[[10]] <- c(0,0,1,1,1)
>
```

We now plot the two series of curves as follows.

Listing 4.7: Plotting multiple ROC curves for two different classifiers.

```
>
> pred.DT <- prediction(laborDT$predictions, laborDT$labels)
> perf.DT <- performance(pred.DT,"tpr","fpr")
> pred.NB <- prediction(laborNB$predictions, laborNB$labels)
```

c.45's and Naive Bayes's performance on the UCI Labor Data

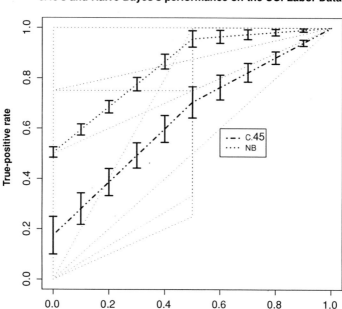

Figure 4.15. Single ROC curves for c45 and nb on the labor data.

```
> perf .NB <- performance ( pred .NB, "tpr", "fpr")
> plot ( perf .DT, lty =3, col="red",main="J.48's and Naive
       Bayes's performance on the UCI Labor Data")
> plot ( perf .NB, lty =3, col="blue", add=TRUE)
> plot ( perf .DT, lwd=3,avg="vertical", col="red", spread.estimate=
       "stderror",
         plotCI . lwd=2, add=TRUE)
> plot ( perf .NB, lwd=3,avg="vertical", col="blue", spread.estimate
       ="stderror",
         plotCI . lwd=2, add=TRUE)
> legend (0.6, 0.6, c ( ' J.48 ', 'NB') , col=c('red ', 'blue '),
  lwd=3)
>
```

This creates the plot of Figure 4.15, which can be interpreted like the plot of Figure 4.14, but with two averaged curves instead of a single one.

Please note that R and ROCR come with a large number of options. The purpose of this section is to introduce the readers to the R tools that are immediately useful for graphical classifier evaluation. However, we encourage the reader to explore the various options in greater depth.

Computing the AUC

In ROCR, many performance measures have been implemented by the command "performance" and calling it with the performance measure of interest. Here we call this function with performance measure AUC.

Listing 4.8: Computing AUC.

```
> laborDTpred <- prediction(laborDT$predictions, laborDT$labels)
> aucDT <- performance(laborDTpred, 'auc')
> laborNBpred <- prediction(laborNB$predictions, laborNB$labels)
> aucNB <- performance(laborNBpred, 'auc')
```

Both sets of commands return the 10 different AUC values obtained at each fold by c.45 and NB: 0.4375, 0.5, 1, 0.75, 1, 0.5625, 0.75, 1, 0.75 and 0.5833333 for c45 and 1, 0.875, 1, 1, 1, 1, 0.875, 1, 1, 1 for NB. It is clear from these values, as it is from the previous graph and from the results obtained in previous chapters, that NB performs much better on this dataset than c.45.

4.6.4 Lift Curves

Lift curves can be obtained in a fashion similar to that for the ROC curves, by use of the ROCR package. The following code shows how to plot a single lift curve for c45, a single lift curve for NB, and how to juxtapose them in the same graph (using "add=TRUE" in the second plot command). The principal modification appears in the "performance" function, where "tpr" and "fpr" are replaced with "lift" and "rpp," respectively. We used single curves to represent the 10 folds as the representation using 10 different folds is not as straightforward. To do so, we begin by creating an object representing the predictions by NB in a single curve. (We had previously done that for c45, but not for NB, for which we only represented the 10 separate folds case.)

Listing 4.9: Data preparation for ROCR (NB).

```
> laborNBpredictions = c
    (0.649,0.037,1,1,0.985,1,0.984,0.031,0.999,1,0.489,1,0.072,
    0,0.997,0.997,1,0.996,0, 0.001, 0.996, 0.251, 0.944,
    0.353, 0, .074, .65, .999, 1, 1, .004, 0,1,1,1,1,
    0,0,1,0,1,1, 0.282, 0,
    .96,1,1,0.02,0,0.987,1,1,0.002,0.003,0.667,0.949,1)
> laborNBlabels <- c
    (0,0,1,1,1,1,0,0,1,1,1,1,0,0,1,1,1,1,0,0,1,1,1,1,0,0,1,1,1,
    1,0,0,1,1,1,1,0,0,1,1,1,1,0,0,1,1,1,0,0, 1,1,1,0,0,1,1,1)
> laborNBSingle <- c("predictions", "labels")
> laborNBSingle$predictions <- laborNBpredictions
> laborNBSingle$labels <- laborNBlabels
```

The lift curves are then plotted as follows.

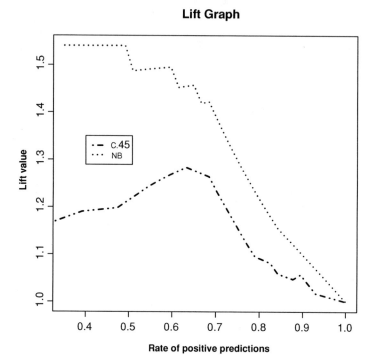

Figure 4.16. Single lift curves for C45 and NB on the labor data.

Listing 4.10: Plotting the lift curves of two different classifiers.

```
>
> pred.DT <- prediction ( laborDTSingle$predictions ,
     laborDTSingle$labels )
> perf.DT <- performance ( pred.DT, "lift" , "rpp" )
> pred.NB <- prediction ( laborNBSingle$predictions ,
     laborNBSingle$labels )
> perf.NB <- performance ( pred.NB, "lift" , "rpp" )
> plot (perf.NB, lwd=3, col="blue", main= "Lift  Graph")
> plot (perf.DT, col="red", lwd= 3, add=TRUE)
> legend (0.4, 1.35, c('J.48', 'NB'), col=c('red', 'blue'),
     lwd=3)
>
```

This creates the plot of Figure 4.16, which again shows NB's clear superiority over C45 on this domain.

Note that even though the lift charts in their conventional form resemble ROC curves, a more common usage includes lift value (ratio of the probability of positive prediction given the classifier and that in the absence of the classifier) on the y-axis and the rate of positive prediction on the x-axis. This shows increased likelihood of true positives as a result of using the respective classifier against a random model. This is hence the version illustrated here.

4.6.5 Precision–Recall Curves

To plot precision–recall (PR) curves, as for the lift curves, all that is needed is to alter the measures in the "performance" function from "tpr" and "fpr" to "prec" and "rec," respectively. This is done as follows, with the comparison of two curves used as per the previous section on lift charts.

Listing 4.11: Plotting the PR curves of two different classifiers.

```
>
> pred.DT <- prediction(laborDTSingle$predictions, laborDTSingle
      $labels)
> perf.DT <- performance(pred.DT,"prec","rec")
> pred.NB <- prediction(laborNBSingle$predictions, laborNBSingle
      $labels)
> perf.NB <- performance(pred.NB,"prec","rec")
> plot(perf.NB, lwd=3, col="blue", main= "Precision/Recall graphs")
> plot(perf.DT, col="red", lwd= 3, add=TRUE)
> legend(0.6, 0.9, c('J.48', 'NB'), col=c('red', 'blue'), lwd=3)
>
```

This creates the plot of Figure 4.17, which, once again, shows clearly NB's superior performance over C45's on the labor domain.

4.6.6 Cost Curves

The following code, also obtained from Howell (2007), allows us to build cost curves for C45's performance on the labor data.

Listing 4.12: Plotting the cost curves for C45 on the labor data.

```
> plot(0,0, xlim=c(0,1), ylim=c(0,1), xlab='Probability cost
      function',
          ylab="Normalized expected cost", main='Cost curve for the
          performance of C45 on the Labor Dataset')
> pred<-prediction(laborDTSingle$predictions, laborDTSingle$
      labels)
> lines(c(0,1),c(0,1))
> lines(c(0,1),c(1,0))
> perf1 <- performance(pred,'fpr','fnr')
> for (i in 1:length(perf1@x.values)) {
+    for (j in 1:length(perf1@x.values[[i]])) {
          lines(c(0,1),c(perf1@y.values[[i]][j], perf1@x.values
             [[i]][j]), col="gray",lty=3)
+    }
+ }
> perf<-performance(pred,'ecost')
> plot(perf,lwd=3,xlim=c(0,1),ylim=c(0,1), add=T)
```

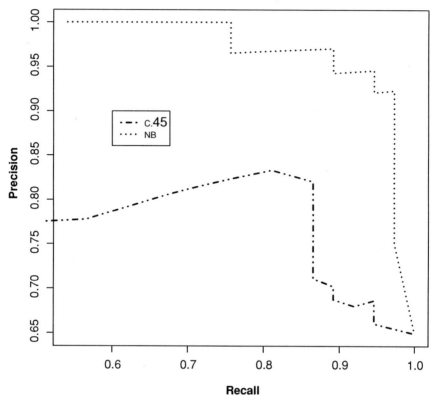

Figure 4.17. Single PR curves for c45 and NB on the labor data.

We can do the same thing with NB's performance by simply replacing

```
>   pred<-prediction(laborDTSingle$predictions, laborDTSingle$
    labels)
```

with

```
>   pred<-prediction(laborNBSingle$predictions, laborNBSingle$
    labels)
```

(note also the change in the graph title).

The two graphs are shown in the plots of Figure 4.18: It is clear, once again, that NB performs better than c.45 as its envelope is lower down.

We leave it to the reader as an exercise to investigate how other curves such as the relative superiority graphs and DET curves can be plotted.

4.6.7 Retrieving the Reliability Metrics From WEKA

Both the RMSE and Kononenko and Bratko's measures are reported in WEKA. Whereas the RMSE is reported as a standard measure, the Kononenko and Bratko measures need to be invoked by a special option. In particular, it is necessary to ensure that the option "Output entropy evaluation measures" is checked in the "More options" menu of WEKA's classification screen. Listing 4.13 shows the WEKA summary output obtained on the labor dataset with C45 with the preceding option checked.

Listing 4.13: WEKA's extended output.

```
=== Summary ===

Correctly Classified Instances          42               73.6842 %
Incorrectly Classified Instances        15               26.3158 %
Kappa statistic                         0.4415
K&B Relative Info Score                 1769.6451 %
K&B Information Score                    16.5588  bits     0.2905 bits/instance
Class complexity | order 0              53.3249  bits     0.9355 bits/instance
Class complexity | scheme             3267.2456  bits    57.3201 bits/instance
Complexity improvement    (Sf)       -3213.9207  bits   -56.3846 bits/instance
Mean absolute error                     0.3192
Root mean squared error                 0.4669
Relative absolute error                69.7715 %
Root relative squared error            97.7888 %
Total Number of Instances               57

=== Detailed Accuracy By Class ===

TP Rate    FP Rate    Precision    Recall    F-Measure    ROC Area    Class
0.7        0.243      0.609        0.7       0.651        0.695       bad
0.757      0.3        0.824        0.757     0.789        0.695       good

=== Confusion Matrix ===

 a    b    <-- classified as
14    6  |  a = bad
 9   28  |  b = good
```

As can be seen in the preceding output, the RMSE is reported under the name "Root mean squared error," and it has the value 0.4669 in the example. As well, the Kononenko and Bratko measures are also reported under the names "K and B Relative Info Score" (or I_r, in our notation) with a value of 1769.6451% in the current example and "K and B Information Score" with values of 16.5588 bits and 0.2905 bits/instance. In fact, the first of these values corresponds to the cumulative information score, or the sum of each instance's information score value, I, and the second one corresponds to I_a, the average information score, or the previous value divided by the number of instances.

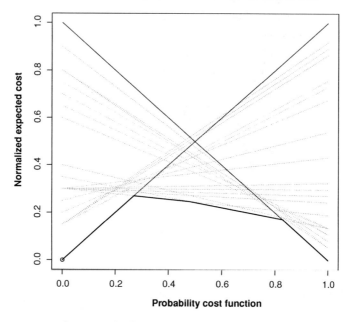

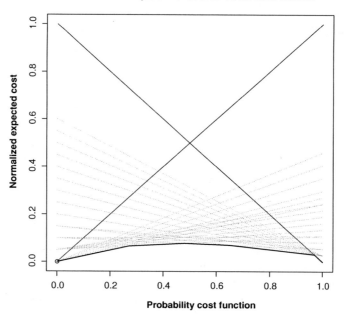

Figure 4.18. Cost curves for C45 (top) and NB (bottom) on labor data.

4.7 Summary

Complementing the last chapter that focused on performance measures based solely on information derived from a (single) confusion matrix, this chapter extended this discussion to measures that take into account criteria such as skew considerations and prior probabilities. To this end, we discussed various graphical evaluation measures that enable visualizing the classifier performance, possibly for a given measure, over its entire operating range under the scoring classifier assumption. In particular, we discussed in considerable detail the ROC analysis and also the cost curves. In addition to discussing the summary statistics with regard to these techniques, we also studied their relationship to other related graphical measures. We then briefly discussed the metrics generally employed in the case of continuous and probabilistic classifiers, focusing mainly on the information-theoretic measures. We concluded with a discussion on specialized metrics employed for learning problems other than classification as well as the ones customized for specific application domains. In the next chapter, we turn our focus to the issue of reliably estimating various performance measures, mainly with regard to considerations about the size of datasets.

4.8 Bibliographic Remarks

Very informative tutorial introductions to ROC analysis were presented in the context of machine learning by Flach (2003) and Fawcett (2004). They also discuss the issue of turning discrete classifiers into scoring ones. See (Witten and Frank, 2005b) for ROC curve construction in the 10-fold cross-validation case.

The relation between AUC optimization and empirical risk minimization was discussed by Cortes and Mohri (2004), who also proposed confidence intervals for the AUC (Cortes and Mohri, 2005). The relation between the Gini coefficient and the AUC was given by Hand and Till (2001), as was the succinct measure for calculating the AUC by using the Wilcoxon Rank Sum criterion shown in the text. Details on the Gini coefficient can be found in (Breiman et al., 1984). The R illustration for calculating the AUC is based on the algorithm proposed by Fawcett (2004). The relationship between the AUC and accuracy (or error-rate minimization) is a topic that was discussed by Ling et al. (2003) and Cortes and Mohri (2004). Other approaches for AUC computation can be found, for instance, in (Hanley and McNeil, 1982) and (Bradley, 1997). The limitations of the AUC were discussed by Hand and Till (2001). Hand (2009) also proposed an alternative metric in the form of the H measure that, he claims alleviates these limitations (see Hand, 2009). Forman (2002) suggested some methods for performing statistical significance analysis for classifiers that are slightly better than the random classifier in the context of ROC analysis. For more details on multiclass ROCs, some basic references include (Fawcett, 2006, Lachiche and

Flach, 2003, and Flach, 2003). Also, for a take on dealing with ROC concavities, see (Flach and Wu, 2005).

Calibration and isotonic regression was discussed by Zadrozny and Elkan (2002) and Fawcett and Niculescu-Mizil (2007).

PR curves are less used in machine learning, although Davis and Goadrich (2006) argue that they are more appropriate than ROC curves in the case of highly imbalanced datasets. Details on relative superiority graphs can be found in (Adams and Hand, 1999) and on DET curves in (Martin et al., 1997).

The relationship between RMSE and other metrics has been explored extensively. Caruana and Niculescu-Mizil (2004) opined that RMSE is a very good general-purpose metric because it correlates most closely with the classification and the ranking metrics, in addition to the probability metrics. Noting, however, that it can be applied only to continuous classifiers, Ferri et al. (2009) do not hold RMSE higher than any other metric. For performance measures for regression algorithms, see (Rosset et al., 2007). For a review and comparison of different evaluation metrics used in ordinal classification, please refer to (Gaudette and Japkowicz, 2009).

See (Geng and Hamilton, 2007) for more details on performance measures utilized in association rule mining. In addition to the measures mentioned in the text, Geng and Hamilton (2007) also define and discuss many others, including prevalence, relative risk, Jaccard, odds ratio, Gini index, and J Measure, and characterize them with respect to the criteria they defined. For some of the measures just named, original source references can also be found in the bibliographic remarks of the previous chapter.

See (He et al., 2002) for more details on performance measures for clustering algorithms. Demartini and Mizzaro (2006) give a nice overview and classification of the different metrics that were proposed in the field of information retrieval between 1960 and 2006. Finally, see (Deeks and Altman, 2004) for a discussion of performance measures used in the medical domain.

5

Error Estimation

We saw in Chapters 3 and 4 the concerns that arise from having to choose appropriate performance measures. Once a performance measure is decided upon, the next obvious concern is to find a good method for testing the learning algorithm so as to obtain as unbiased an estimate of the chosen performance measure as possible. Also of interest is the related concern of whether the technique we use to obtain such an estimate brings us as close as possible to the true measure value.

Ideally we would have access to the entire population and test our classifiers on it. Even if the entire population were not available, if a lot of representative data from that population could be obtained, error estimation would be quite simple. It would consist of testing the algorithms on the data they were trained on. Although such an estimate, commonly known as the *resubstitution error*, is usually optimistically biased, as the number of instances in the dataset increases, it tends toward the true error rate. Realistically, however, we are given a significantly limited-sized sample of the population. A reliable alternative thus consists of testing the algorithm on a large set of unseen data points. This approach is commonly known as the *holdout* method. Unfortunately, such an approach still requires quite a lot of data for testing the algorithm's performance, which is relatively rare in most practical situation. As a result, the holdout method is not always applicable. Instead, a limited amount of available data needs to be used and reused ingeniously in order to obtain sufficiently large numbers of samples. This kind of data reuse is called *resampling*. Together, resubstitution, hold-out and resampling constitute the area of error estimation. Error estimation is a complex issue as the results of our experiments may be meaningless if the data on which they were obtained are not representative of the actual distribution or if the algorithms are unstable and their performance unpredictable. Resampling must thus be done carefully.

Broadly, the resampling techniques can be divided into two categories: *simple resampling* and *multiple resampling*. The simple resampling techniques tend to use each data point for testing only once. Techniques such as *k-fold cross-validation* and *leave-one-out* are examples of simple resampling techniques (we may also include resubstitution in this category. However, we tend to use simple resampling to refer to the techniques that apply the algorithm multiple times, making the most use of the data). Multiple resampling techniques, on the other hand, do not refrain from testing data points more than once. Examples of such techniques include *random subsampling, bootstrapping, randomization, and repeated k-fold cross-validation*. In this chapter, we discuss various *error-estimation* techniques that might be suitable in offering better assurances with regard to the estimation of an algorithm's performance measure, especially in a limited data scenario.

Although both simple resampling and multiple resampling address the problem caused by the dearth of data, care needs to be taken with regard to the effect of using such approaches on the assumptions made by subsequent steps in the evaluation, mainly the statistical significance testing discussed in the next chapter. Recall that the independence of the data used to obtain the sample statistics is a fundamental assumption made by these tests. This chapter is aimed at highlighting the basic assumptions and context of application of various resampling approaches. In addition to studying the impact of using various resampling techniques on the resulting estimate in the context of their respective bias and variance behaviors in this chapter, we also see some specific approaches to deal with the issue of resampling in the context of statistical hypothesis testing. We also discuss the model selection considerations that should be made when applying these resampling techniques. We conclude the chapter with a series of examples in R that illustrate how to integrate resampling techniques into a practical evaluation framework.

Figure 5.1 shows an ontology of the various error-estimation methods discussed in this chapter. The discussion of various techniques is generally presented with regard to the error rate (risk) of the learning algorithm on the dataset as the performance measure. The main reason for adopting this performance measure is that a concrete bias–variance analysis is available in this case for classification, allowing us to explain the different aspects of the techniques more clearly. However, similar arguments would hold in the case of other performance measures as well.

Here is a roadmap for this chapter. Section 5.1 presents the context with respect to the risk estimates over the classifiers because this is the most common setting in which error-estimation methods are utilized (although some methods presented are more general and can be applied in the context of other performance measures too). Section 5.2 then presents the holdout method and also demonstrates how theoretically sound guarantees on the true risk can be obtained in this setting. This section also highlights the sample size requirement to do so and presents a motivation for using resampling techniques because only limited data instances are typically available in most practical scenarios. Before moving on to discussing the resampling techniques, Section 5.3 introduces a bias–variance

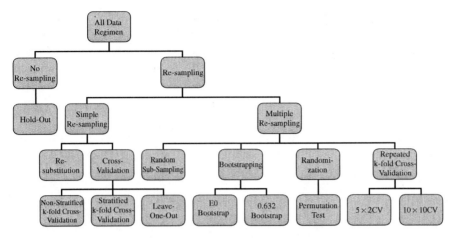

Figure 5.1. An Ontology of Error Estimation Methods

basis that is subsequently used to qualitatively analyze various error-estimation methods and also to develop an understanding of their comparative advantages and limitations. Section 5.4 then discusses the simple resampling methods, and Section 5.5 discusses the issue of model selection in the resampling regimen. Section 5.6 then discusses various multiple resampling methods, followed by a discussion of all the presented resampling approaches in Section 5.7. The illustration of various error-estimation techniques discussed in Sections 5.4 and 5.6 is presented in Section 5.8, using R and WEKA packages.

5.1   Introduction

Recall from Chapter 2 our definition of the *true or expected risk* of the classifier f:

$$R(f) = \int L(y, f(\mathbf{x})) d D(\mathbf{x}, y), \tag{5.1}$$

where $L(y, f(\mathbf{x}))$ denotes the loss incurred on the label $f(\mathbf{x})$ assigned to the example $\mathbf{x}$ by f and the true label of $\mathbf{x}$ is y; the probability measure $D(\mathbf{z}) = D(\mathbf{x}, y)$ here is unknown.

For the zero–one loss, i.e., $L(y, f(\mathbf{x})) = 1$ when $y \neq f(\mathbf{x})$ and 0 otherwise, we can write the expected risk as

$$R(f) = \Pr_{(\mathbf{x}, y) \sim D} (f(\mathbf{x}) \neq y). \tag{5.2}$$

However, in the absence of knowledge of the true distribution, the learner often computes the *empirical risk* $R_S(f)$ of any given classifier f on some training data S with m examples according to

$$R_S(f) = \frac{1}{m} \sum_{i=1}^{m} L(y_i, f(\mathbf{x}_i)). \tag{5.3}$$

Because the empirical risk of the classifier is used to approximate its true risk, the goal of error estimation is cut out in a straightforward manner: to obtain as unbiased an estimate of empirical risk as possible. This empirical risk on the training set can be measured in a variety of ways, as we will see shortly. Naturally the simplest approach to risk estimation would be to measure the empirical risk of a classifier f_S trained on the full training data S on the same dataset S. This measure is often referred to as the resubstitution risk (or resubstitution error rate). We denote it as $R_S^{\text{resub}}(f_S)$. As can be easily seen, this results in judging the performance of a classifier on the data that were used by the algorithm to induce that classifier. Consequently, such an estimate is essentially optimistically biased. The best way to obtain a minimum resubstitution error estimate is to overfit the classifier to each and every training point. However, this would essentially lead to poor generalization, as we saw in Chapter 2.

Before we look into other ways of obtaining empirical risk estimates, we need to consider various factors that should be taken into account in this regard. The effect that the learning settings can have on the empirical risk estimate can arise from the following main sources:

- random variation in the testing sets,
- random variation in the training sets,
- random variation within the learning algorithm, and
- random variation with respect to class noise in the dataset.

An effective error-estimation method should take into considerations these different sources of random fluctuations. In the simplest case, if we have enough training data, we can consider a separate set of examples to test the classifier performance. This test set is not used in any way while training the learning algorithm. Hence, assuming that the test set is representative of the domain in which the classifier is to be applied, we can obtain a reliable risk estimate, given enough training data. However, the qualification regarding enough training data availability is serious. We will exemplify this a bit later. But first, let us go ahead and look at this method of estimating risk on a separate testing set. This method has some very important advantages because concrete guarantees on the risk estimate can be obtained in this case.

5.2   Holdout Approach

In this method, as previously explained, a separate set of instances is reserved to assess the classifier's performance. This set is different from the training set used by the learning algorithm. The learning algorithm takes as input a labeled set of instances from the training set and outputs a classifier. This classifier is then given the unlabeled set of instances from the testing set. The classifier outputs labels for each of these instances and the estimate of the empirical error is obtained. In the case of a discrete binary classifier, this is basically the fraction of test instances that the classifier misclassifies. Conversely, the accuracy of the classifier is the fraction of the test instances that the classifier classifies correctly. Performance of the classifier on a separate test set is generally a good indicator of its generalization performance. Formal guarantees over the test-set performance in terms of theoretical confidence intervals can be provided in this case, as subsequently shown.

More formally, if we have a test set T with examples drawn i.i.d. from $D(\mathbf{z})$, then the empirical risk takes the form

$$R_T(f) = \int L(y, f_S(\mathbf{x}))dD(\mathbf{x}, y), \qquad (5.4)$$

where $f_S(\cdot)$ denotes the classifier output by the learning algorithm when given a training set S and with the underlying assumption that the test set T is representative of the distribution generating the data.

One of the biggest advantages of a holdout error estimate lies in its independence from the training set. Because the estimate is obtained on a separate test set, some concrete generalizations on this estimate can be obtained. Moreover, there is another crucial difference between a holdout error estimate and a resampled estimate. A holdout estimate pertains to the classifier output by the learning algorithm, given the training data. Hence any generalizations made over this estimate will essentially apply to any classifier with the given test-set performance. We will see later that this is not the case for the resampled error estimate. Let us now discuss the general behavior of the test-set error estimate.

5.2.1 Confidence Intervals

We saw one approach to determine the confidence intervals around the empirical risk estimate in Chapter 2. That approach relied on the assumption that the empirical risk of the classifier on the test data can be modeled, in the limit, as a Gaussian. Based on this assumption, the mean empirical risk and the corresponding variance on the test examples were obtained. A confidence interval was then provided in terms of a Gaussian around the mean empirical risk with its tails removed at Z_P multiples of standard deviation σ on either side, with Z_P defining the critical region for a given confidence level α. However, this did not allow us to make any probabilistic statements on the true risk (recall the discussion in Subsection 2.2.3).

It turns out that an asymptotic Gaussian assumption might not be the best way to provide confidence intervals, especially when modeling empirical risks closer to zero. We discuss this issue at greater length in Chapter 8. For now, it suffices to say that a binomial distribution can be used more effectively to model the empirical risk in the case of a discrete binary classifier leading us to make probabilistic statement on the upper and lower bounds for the true risk. An example is subsequently given of such bounds obtained by modeling the error as a Bernoulli variable. Using this observation and by applying Hoeffding's bound, we can get the following guarantee (proof is given in the appendix to this chapter).

For any classifier f, the true risk $R(f)$, with probability $1 - \delta$ and test error $R_T(f)$ on some test set T of m' examples, satisfies

$$\left| R_T(f) - R(f) \right| \leq t_{1-\delta} = \epsilon = \sqrt{\frac{1}{2m'} \ln\left(\frac{2}{\delta}\right)}. \tag{5.5}$$

Therefore, with probability $1 - \delta$,

$$R(f) \approx R_T(f) \pm t_{1-\delta}.$$

This bound basically gives the confidence interval within which we expect the true risk to fall with confidence $1 - \delta$ for some $\delta \in (0, 1]$. For example, fixing δ at 0.05, we can obtain a 95% confidence interval. Note the similarity between the parameter δ and the confidence parameter α of Subsection 2.2.3. However, the two are not essentially the same in terms of their interpretation, as should be clear from the earlier discussion of α and the appendix at the end of this chapter showing the proof of the preceding bound. We come back to this issue in Chapter 8, where we also provide a tighter version of the preceding bound. In the present context, let us see how this observation affects the sample size requirement.

5.2.2 The Need for Resampling

It can be seen from Equation (5.5) that the convergence of empirical risk to the true risk depends on the sample size m' and the true risk $R(f)$. This highlights the most prominent limitation of this method, which is its dependence on the size of the training data. A holdout estimate, to generalize well, requires a large sample size. This can be readily seen from the preceding analysis. Rearranging Equation (5.5) and solving for sample size m' gives us the bound on the required sample complexity as

$$m' \geq \frac{1}{2\epsilon^2} \ln\left(\frac{2}{\delta}\right).$$

This bound gives the minimum number of examples required for a given ϵ and δ. The sample size bound grows very quickly for small ϵ and δ. That is, for the confidence intervals to be any indicator of the classifier's performance, the required number of training examples is too large. With a single train and test partition, too few cases in the training group can lead to learning a poor classifier and too few test cases can lead to erroneous error estimates.

Ironically, one of the most common difficulties in machine learning problems is the unavailability of enough data. Hence, as previously discussed, if we use all the available data for training, it is not possible to have a reliable future performance measure estimate of the classifier. Second, if we divide this already small dataset into training and testing sets, then reliable learning is not possible.

Moreover, the sample size requirement grows exponentially with falling ϵ and δ, limiting the utility of this approach in most learning scenarios for which the overall availability of examples is limited. In such cases, researchers often make use of what are called *resampling* methods.

As the name suggests, these methods are based on the idea of being able to reuse the data for training and testing. Resampling has some advantages over the single-partition holdout method. Resampling allows for more accurate estimates of the error rates while allowing the learning algorithms to train on most data examples. Also, this method allows the duplication of the analysis conditions in future experiments on the same data. We discuss these methods in detail in Sections 5.4 and 5.6 from both applied and theoretical points of view. However, before proceeding to these, let us understand the bias–variance analysis that we introduced in Chapter 2 in the context of error estimation. This will be instrumental in helping us analyze various error-estimation methods with regard to their strengths, limitations, and applicability in practical scenarios. Although the discussion in the next section may seem a bit too theoretical, it will enable the reader to put the subsequent discussion in perspective and obtain practical insights about various resampling techniques.

5.3 What Implicitly Guides Resampling?

Of course there are many types of resampling schemes, possibly leading to a variety of error estimates on the training error of the algorithm. What distinguishes one from the other? More important, what should we care about when choosing one resampling method over another? When should we prefer one resampling method over others? These are the types of questions that we will be concerned with eventually. But it is probably better to see these issues in light of the resulting error estimate itself. What is it about the error estimate that is affected by resampling? Recall that we discussed in Chapter 2 how we can decompose the empirical error of a learning algorithm on the training data into its bias and variance components. We also discussed how this bias–variance decomposition affects the model selection problem. That is, how trading off bias and variance can help us avoid overfitting and underfitting. Let us now see the interrelationship between the empirical error estimate and the amount of training data on which (and the manner in which) these estimates are obtained. It is necessary to understand this interplay to achieve an appreciation for various resampling schemes and to understand how one might be more suitable in some scenarios than some others.

5.3.1 Estimating Bias and Variance

We have already seen how the error of an algorithm can be decomposed into bias and variance (and the noise component). Such a bias–variance decomposition enables us to understand the behavior of the algorithm as well as its model selection process. The bias and variance behavior of the algorithm's performance can be very useful in evaluating the algorithm both in absolute terms (how good the algorithm is, given the training sets, in terms of the chosen loss function) and in relative terms, with respect to other competing algorithms. However, as we saw earlier, the bias–variance decomposition of the algorithm's error necessitates knowing the true distribution of the data. That is, it requires a priori knowledge of the data-generation process. However, modeling or approximating this data-generation behavior is indeed the goal of designing the learning algorithm itself. As a result, it is impossible in practice to know the true values of the bias and the variance in the absence of the knowledge of the data distribution. Hence we would need to approximate these values by using some empirical estimates that can be obtained from the data at hand rather than having them depend explicitly on the true underlying data distribution.

Let us, very briefly, look at how this can be done for some given training data with an example. Recall the bias–variance analysis of the empirical error of a classifier from Chapter 2. The first quantity that needs to be estimated is the average prediction $\overline{y}$ of algorithm A. Note, however, that this should be done independently of the data on which the algorithm is to be subsequently tested. To achieve this, we can resort to resampling within the training examples when the data to train an algorithm are limited.

One way to perform such a division would be to divide the available training dataset S into two sets. One set is used to perform the training of the algorithm, call it S_{train} (say two-thirds of S), and the other is used to test the algorithm on examples not used in the training process (that is, previously unseen examples), denoted by S_{test}. The manner in which such a division is obtained leads to a variety of resampling techniques that further apply this partitioning repeatedly (with or without overlap), hence reusing these partitions for training and testing purposes, as we will see later. However, to keep the current discussion simple, we stick to a single partition.

To achieve the effect of multiple datasets, we can sample a collection $\mathbf{S}$ of n_{bs} training sets of some predefined size m from S_{train}. Training the algorithm on each training set yields a classifier whose loss on all examples can then be averaged, leading to an empirical estimate of the average prediction $\overline{y}$. Let f_i denote the classifier resulting from training algorithm A on a training set S_i sampled from S_{train}. When such a sampling is done with replacement, the process is known as bootstrap sampling (Efron and Tibshirani, 1993). We describe bootstrap resampling in detail in Subsection 5.6.2, but for our purpose now, it suffices to assume that we have some resampling of data that gives us a bunch of training sets. Then the average prediction can be estimated as

$$\overline{y} = \frac{1}{n_{\text{bs}}} \sum_{i=1}^{n_{\text{bs}}} \sum_{j=1}^{m} f_i(\mathbf{x}_j).$$

Then the error and the corresponding bias and variance terms can be estimated from the evaluation of the final classifier f (chosen after model selection, that is, generally with optimized parameters) on the test set S_{test}. The test error of the classifier is just the average loss of the classifier on each example:

$$R_{S_{\text{test}}}(f) = \mathbf{E}_{(\mathbf{x},y) \sim S_{\text{test}}}[L(y_i, f(\mathbf{x}_i))] = \frac{1}{|S_{\text{test}}|} \sum_{i=1}^{|S_{\text{test}}|} L(y_i, f(\mathbf{x}_i)),$$

where $(\mathbf{x}, y) \sim S_{|S_{\text{test}}|}$ denotes that $(\mathbf{x}, y)$ is drawn from S_{test}.

Note that, in the case of a zero–one loss, the previous equation reduces to the empirical error of Equation (2.5). However, we again run into the problem of estimating the decomposition terms in the absence of knowledge of the true data distribution. A common trick applied in such cases is the assumption of noiseless data. That is, we assume that the data have no noise and hence the noise term on the decomposition is zero. With this assumption, we can approximate the empirical estimates of the average bias as

$$\overline{B}_A = \mathbf{E}_{\mathbf{x}}[B_A(\mathbf{x})]$$

$$= \mathbf{E}_{\mathbf{x}}[L(y^{\dagger}, \overline{y})]$$

$$\cong \frac{1}{|S_{\text{test}}|} \sum_{i=1}^{|S_{\text{test}}|} L(y_i, \overline{y})$$

and the net variance as

$$V_A(\mathbf{x}) = \mathbf{E}_S[L(\overline{y}, f(\mathbf{x}))]$$

$$\cong \frac{1}{|S_{\text{test}}|} \sum_{i=1}^{|S_{\text{test}}|} L(y_i, f(\mathbf{x}_i)).$$

The zero-noise assumption just made can be deemed acceptable because the main interest in studying the bias–variance behavior of the algorithm's error is in their variation in response to various factors that affect the learning process. Hence we are interested in their relative values as opposed to the absolute values. However, in the case in which the zero-noise assumption is violated, the bias term previously estimated approximates the sum of the noise term and the bias term because we approximate the error of the average model.

5.3.2 Effect of Bias–Variance Trade-Off on Resampling-Based Error Estimation

The preceding method of (re)sampling the data is one of many options. Indeed what we have done previously is basically a variation of the holdout method to measure the empirical error rate to illustrate our point. Resampling typically performs such partitioning of the data multiple times, which further affects the estimates. We will see these specific issues in conjunction with the associated resampling methods. However, there are a few points worth noting here. The choice of a particular resampling method also affects the bias–variance characteristic of the algorithm's error. This then can have important implications for both the error estimation and subsequent evaluation of classifiers (both absolute evaluation and with respect to other algorithms) and its future generalization as a result of the impact of this choice on the process of model selection. As the approximations of the various terms in the bias–variance decomposition suggest, the size and the method of obtaining the training sets and the test sets can have important implications. Most prominently, note that the approximations are averaged over all samples. Moreover, in the case of average prediction, they are also sampled over different training sets. As soon as the sample size is limited, these approximations encounter variability in their estimates. Further, if we have a small number of training sets, the average prediction estimate cannot be reliably obtained. This then affects the bias behavior of the algorithm. On the other hand, having too few examples to test would result in high variance.

In practical scenarios, we invariably encounter the situation of a very limited dataset, let alone insufficient training sets and test sets individually. Resampling methods further aim at using the available data in a "smart" manner so as to obtain these estimates relatively reliably. However, various modes of resampling the data can introduce different limitations on the estimates for the bias and the variance and hence on the reliability of the error estimates obtained as a result.

For instance, when resampling is done with replacement, as in our previous example, we run the risk of seeing the same examples again (and missing some altogether). In such cases, the estimates can be highly variable (especially in the case of small datasets) because the examples in the training set might not be representative of the actual distribution. Another concern would arise when the partitioning of the data is done multiple times because in this case the error estimates are not truly independent if the different test-set partitions overlap. Similarly, the bias may be underestimated for cases in which the training sets overlap over multiple partitions. Although we do not focus on quantifying such effects for the various resampling methods we discuss here, we highlight the limitations and the effects of sample sizes on the reliability of the error estimate thus obtained.

While discussing the resampling methods, we frequently refer to their behavior in case of small, moderate, or large dataset sizes. However, mapping a concrete number to the sample size in these categories is nontrivial. The sample size bound in the case of a holdout test set gives us an idea of how the sample size is affected by the two parameters, ϵ and δ. The δ term there is fixed (to a desired confidence level). However, the ϵ takes into account implicitly the generalization error of the algorithm that in turn depends on a multitude of factors, including data dimensionality, classifier complexity, and data distribution. Throughout our discussion we assume that we do not have the required number of samples that would justify a holdout-based approach. Hence our reference to small-, moderate- or medium-, and large-sized datasets are all bounded by this constraint. These terms respectively denote ranges over the number of instances in the data farther from the sample size bound on the left in descending order. Interested readers can explore studies, referred to in the Bibliographic Remarks section at the end of the chapter, that have attempted to obtain more concrete quantifications over dataset sizes.

With the backdrop of different factors that play significant roles in the resulting reliability of the error estimates, let us now move on to the specific resampling methods, starting with the simple resampling techniques.

5.4 Simple Resampling

By simple resampling, we refer to the methods that test each and every point in the dataset and do so exactly once. We will relate this notion back to the resubstitution method introduced earlier too. The two methods that we discuss next in this category, the k-fold cross-validation and leave-one-out, are some of the most utilized methods for error estimation and for good reason, as we will see later. Prior to that, however, we design a formalization that allows us to unify various approaches that we discuss within a common framework.

5.4.1 A Resampling Framework

Consider a weight vector $\mathbf{w}$, each entry of which assigns a weight to each of the m examples $\mathbf{z}_i \in S$, $i \in \{1, \ldots, m\}$ in the training set S. In this subsection, we consider an ordered training set. Let $\mathbf{w} \in \{0, 1\}^m$. That is, $\mathbf{w}$ is a binary vector. The entries in $\mathbf{w}$ characterize the training set. A value of 1 at w_i, the ith position in the weight vector $\mathbf{w}$, denotes the presence of the corresponding example $\mathbf{z}_i$ in the resampled training-set partition.

Without loss of generality, let us say that there are k partitions. Then we can consider a distribution P_W on the sets W of $\mathbf{w}$'s such that each distribution would define a possible resampling over the training set. Each such resampling would consist of partitioning the training data into k partitions such that $1 \leq k \leq m$, with a weight vector $\mathbf{w}_k$ denoting the examples belonging to the kth partition. The number of possible sets of valid weight vectors would then give a possible partitioning of the data.

We can then, from the proportion of examples in a partition S_k of the training set S, characterize the resampled performance estimate of the classifier on the set S. Define the set $S_{\bar{k}}$ containing the examples in S that are not in S_k.

Given a set of weight vectors $W = \{\mathbf{w}_i\}$, $i \in \{1, 2, \ldots, k\}$ representing a valid partition over S, the resampled risk of the learning algorithm (that is, the risk is defined once a partition is decided) is denoted as[1]

$$R_S^{\text{resamp}}(f) = \mathbf{E_w} \int L(y, f_S^k(\mathbf{x})) d D^k(\mathbf{x}, y),$$

---

[1] We will see that the expectation of resampling risk over all possible partitions estimates the risk of multiple trial resamplings.

where $D^k(\mathbf{z}) = D^k(\mathbf{x}, y)$ denotes the distribution of the partition S_k. That is,

$$R_S^{\text{resamp}}(f) = \frac{1}{k} \sum_{i=1}^{k} \left[\frac{1}{|S_k|} \sum_{j=1}^{|S_k|} L(y_j, f_S^k(\mathbf{x}_j)) \right],$$

where f_S^k denotes the classifier learned from the set $S_{\overline{k}}$.

We now discuss some of the simple resampling schemes within this framework. In all cases, we present a more functional description followed by an analytical description within the preceding framework.

5.4.2 Resubstitution

As discussed earlier, resubstitution trains the classifier on the training set S and subsequently tests it over the same set S of examples. That is, we have the full mass of P_W on the weight vector $\mathbf{w} = \mathbf{1}$. Under our formalization, the case of $k = 1$ is the resubstitution case. We already discussed the fact that, as the classifier usually overfits the data it was trained on, the error estimate provided by this method is optimistically biased. This is why this approach is never recommended in practice for error-estimation purpose. We will see how more reliable estimates can be obtained that are less biased and hence better approximators of the true risk.

5.4.3 k-fold Cross-Validation

k-fold cross-validation (CV) is by far the most popular error-estimation approach in machine learning. *k-fold cross-validation* proceeds by dividing the dataset S containing m samples into k subsets of roughly equal sizes. Each subset is called a fold (hence the name of the method). The learning algorithm is then trained on $k - 1$ of these subsets taken together and tested on the kth subset. This is repeated k times with a different subset used for testing. Hence each of the k folds becomes a test set once. The experiment thus returns k estimates of the resulting classifier's error rate in each iteration. These estimates are then averaged together and constitute the resampled error estimate. Let us put the method in algorithmic form for better understandability:

Listing 5.1: k-fold CV.

```
−Divide the available training set S of size m in k
    nonoverlapping subsets Sᵢ, i = 1,...,k of size (approximately)
    m/k
−Initialize i = 1
−Repeat while i ≤ k
            − Mark the ith subset Sᵢ as test set
            − For the test set Sᵢ, generate the complement
                training dataset Sᵢ̄ containing all the examples
                from S except those in Sᵢ
```

       – Train and test the learning algorithm on $S_{\bar{i}}$ and S_i
          respectively
      –Obtain the empirical risk $R_{S_i}(f_i)$ (or any other
          performance measure of interest) of classifier f_i
          obtained by training the algorithm on $S_{\bar{i}}$ on S_i
      –Increment i by 1
– Average the $R_{S_i}(f_i)$ over all i's to obtain $R_S(f)$, the mean
    empirical risk of the k–fold cross validation.
–Report $R_S(f)$

Note that, in listing 5.1, even though we stick to the notation $R_S(f)$ to denote
the empirical risk of the k-fold CV, we refer to the averaged empirical risk over
the classifiers obtained in each of the k folds. It is important to note that the k
testing sets do not overlap. Each example is therefore used only once for testing
and $k - 1$ times for training.

     Let us formalize this technique. In the k-fold CV, we consider the case of $k \geq 2$
and $k < m(k = 1$ is the resubstitution case). The case of $k = m$ is a special case
called leave-one-out (LOO), and has achieved prominence in error estimation,
especially for small dataset sizes. We will discuss this shortly. Getting back to
$k \geq 2$, in the case in which m is even, we can easily characterize the distribution
P_W. For a given even m, the number n_k^W of possible sets of binary weight vectors
defining a valid partition of m examples in k subsets can be obtained with the
following formula:

$$n_k^W = \sum_{i=0}^{k-2} \binom{m - \frac{im}{k}}{\frac{m}{k}}.$$

     Then P_W would have $1/n_k^W$ mass on each of the possible n_k^W valid partitions
and zero mass elsewhere. This is basically resampling the set S into k partitions
without replacement.

     A bit more involved scheme can be thought of in the case of an odd m.
However, we can easily find an acceptable solution by subtracting 1 from m in
the case in which m is odd and utilize the preceding formulation to resample the
set S.

     The most common value used in the case of machine learning algorithms is
$k = 10$ with many empirical arguments in support of this number, especially
in large-size samples, owing mainly to the obtention of relatively less-biased
estimates as well as the observation of an acceptable computational complexity
in calculating these error estimates.

Stratified k-fold CV

Even if a careful resampling method such as k-fold CV is used, the split into a
training set and a testing set may be uneven. That is, the split may not take into
account the distribution of the examples of various classes while generating the
training and test subsets. This can result in scenarios in which examples of the

kind present in the testing set are either underrepresented in, or entirely absent
from, the training set. This can yield an even more pessimistic performance
estimate. A simple and effective solution to this problem lies in *stratifying* the
data. Stratification consists of taking note of the representation of each class in
the overall dataset and making sure that this representation is respected in both
the training set and the test set in the resulting partitions of data. For example,
consider a three-class problem with the dataset consisting of classes y_1, y_2 and
y_3. Let us assume, for illustration's sake, that the dataset is composed of 30%
examples of class y_1, 60% examples of class y_2, and 10% examples of class y_3.
A random split of the data into a training set and a testing set may very well
ignore the data of class y_3 in either the training or the testing set. This would lead
to an unfair evaluation. Stratification does not allow such a situation to occur
as it ensures that the training and testing sets in every fold or every resampling
event maintains the relative distribution with 30% of class y_1 examples, 60% of
class y_2 examples, and 10% of class y_3 examples.

Informally, in the case of binary data, a straightforward method to achieving
stratification is that of the following listing.

Listing 5.2: Stratified k-fold CV.

```
- Divide the training data into two sets (one for each class).
- Generate k subsets in each of the two sets.
- Combine one subset from each of the two sets to
    obtain k subsets that would maintain the original
    class distribution.
- Perform the classical k-fold cross validation over these
    k subsets.
```

In the case of multiclass classification with l classes, the preceding method
can easily be extended. Instead of dividing the data into two classes, divide the
training set into l sets, one for each class, and proceed as was previously done.
Stratification for use with CV has become a standard practice (for example, it is
hard-coded into WEKA).

Formalizing stratification in the case of binary classification, we would then
sample from two distributions. Let the training set S of m examples be such
that $m = m_p + m_n$, where m_p is the number of positive examples in the training set S and m_n is the number of negative examples. Hence we can have
$\mathbf{w} = \{w_1^p, w_2^p, \ldots, w_{m_p}^p, w_1^n, w_2^n, \ldots, w_{m_n}^n\}$. Then, for even m_p and m_n, we can
characterize the distribution P_W as follows. The number of possible sets W of
vectors $\mathbf{w}$ that partition the training set S in k stratified subsets can be calculated
as

$$
n_k^{\mathbf{w}} = \left\{ \sum_{i=0}^{k-2} \binom{(m_p - \frac{im_p}{k})}{\frac{m_p}{k}} \right\} \left\{ \sum_{i=0}^{k-2} \binom{(m_n - \frac{im_n}{k})}{\frac{m_n}{k}} \right\}.
$$

This distribution can be adapted to odd m_p, m_n, or both, analogous to the previous case of classical k-fold CV. Also, P_W will have equal mass on all the possible valid stratifications and zero mass elsewhere.

Discussion

k-fold CV is a very practical approach that has a number of advantages. First, it is very simple to apply and, in fact, is preprogrammed in software systems such as WEKA and can be invoked just by the touch of a button; it is not as computer intensive as LOO, discussed next, or the repeated resampling techniques that will be discussed later; it is not a repeated approach, thus guaranteeing that the estimates obtained from each fold are obtained on nonoverlapping subsets of the testing set.

On the other hand, whereas the testing sets used in k-fold CV are independent of each other, the classifiers built on the $k - 1$ folds in each iteration are not necessarily independent because the algorithm in each case is trained on a highly overlapping set of training examples. This can then also affect the bias of the error estimates. However, in the case of moderate to large datasets, this limitation is mitigated, to some extent, as a result of large-sized subsets. Another point worth noting here is that, unlike the holdout case that reports the error rate of a single classifier trained on the training set, the k-fold CV is an averaged estimate over the error rates of k different classifiers (trained and tested in each fold). In fact, this observation holds for almost all the resampling approaches.

5.4.4 Leave-One-Out Cross-Validation

Leave-One-Out (or the *Jackknife*) is an extreme case of k-fold CV. LOO is basically a k-fold CV performed with $k = m$. The procedure is the same as that in Listing 5.1 with $k = m$. Further, our formalization of the k-fold CV from the last section applies to the case of the LOO estimate as well with $k = m$.

Discussion

As can be seen easily, the error estimates obtained at each iteration of the LOO scheme refers to the lone testing example. As a result, this can yield estimates with high variances, especially in the case of limited data. However, the advantage of LOO lies in its ability to utilize almost the full dataset for training, resulting in a relatively unbiased classifier. Naturally, in the case of severely limited dataset size, the cost of highly varying risk estimates on test examples trumps the benefit of being able to use almost the whole dataset for training. This is because in the case of a very small dataset size, using even the whole set for training might not guarantee a relatively unbiased classifier. Almost analogically, the risk estimates would also not account for mitigating the high variance when averaged. However, as the dataset size increases, LOO can be quite advantageous except for its computational complexity. Hence LOO can be quite effective for moderate dataset sizes.

Indeed, for large datasets, LOO may be computationally too expensive to be worth applying, especially because a k-fold CV can also yield reliable estimates. Independent of the sample size, there are a couple of special cases, however, for which LOO can be particularly effective. LOO can be quite beneficial when there is wide dispersion of the data distribution or when the dataset contains extreme values. In such cases, the estimate produced by LOO is expected to be better than the one produced by k-fold CV.

5.4.5 Limitations of Simple Resampling Methods

Simple resampling methods can serve as good evaluation measures when the available data are limited. However, these methods also have some limitations. Resampling methods do not estimate the risk of a classifier but, rather, estimate the expected risk $E_S(A(S))$ of a learning algorithm A over samples S of the size of the partitions used for training. This is, for example, $m(1 - 1/k)$ for k-fold CV. Although, as previously mentioned, these methods do try to take the most out of the data by training on most cases, they suffer from the fact that no confidence intervals are known. It is thus currently impossible to provide rigorous formal guarantees over the risk of the classifier. This is in contrast to holdout methods, for which such guarantees and confidence intervals can be precisely stated. Even under the normality assumption, the sample standard deviation of the k-fold CV risk R_{CV}^k over the k different groups serves, at best, to give a rough idea of the uncertainty of the estimate. In contrast, the training-set bounds, an approach we discuss in Chapter 8, have been shown to provide acceptably good guarantees over the generalization behavior of the classifier in terms of its empirical performance on the training set in some cases.

Finally, as we noted previously, resampling provides the estimate of the average of the performances of (generally different) classifiers learned in various partitions. This is not the same as the estimate obtained in the case of the holdout case. This has both advantages and disadvantages. The advantage is that one can test the robustness of the algorithm by studying the stability of the estimates across various partitions (for the respective learned classifiers). The disadvantage is that, when reporting the results and comparing them against those of other algorithms, we tend to compare the average of the performance estimates rather than the estimate of a fixed classifier f, unlike in the case of the holdout approach.

In the context of applying resampling techniques, one must guard against the risk of confusing or intertwining model selection with error estimation. This can have potentially undesirable implications. Let us look at this issue in a bit more detail in the next section.

5.5   A Note on Model Selection

Recall that model selection basically refers to choosing the best parameters for the learning algorithm so as to obtain a classifier having minimum training error.[2] Once a classifier has reached the optimal value for the chosen criterion (e.g., a low training error), this classifier is then tested on the test set and its performance on that set is reported. To report as unbiased an estimate of classifier performance as possible, it is imperative that the model selection be carried out independently of the test instances. This is especially true for the resampling approaches because, in the wake of limited size datasets, the idea is to use as many examples for training as possible. However, if the instances put aside for testing in any given resampling run are used, even for validation, this would yield a classifier that is fine-tuned to obtain the best performance on this validation set, and hence result in an overly optimistic estimate of the classifier's performance.

5.5.1 Model Selection in Holdout

In the holdout scenario, a general approach to selecting the best hypothesis is to divide the data into three disjoint subsets (instead of two subsets as mentioned before): a training set, a validation set, and a test set. The learning algorithm is trained on the training set, yielding a set of candidate hypotheses (depending on, say, different parameter values that the algorithm takes as input). Each of these hypotheses is then tested on the validation set, and the one that performs best (e.g., makes the least number of errors) on this validation set is then selected. Testing of this *selected* hypothesis is done in the same manner as previously discussed, i.e., by the testing of its performance on the test set. Alternatively, a simple resampling can be run on the training set if only two partitions are used here. Model selection is performed by choosing the parameters giving the best resampled estimate of the chosen criterion.

5.5.2 Model Selection in Resampling

In the resampling scenario, it is necessary to hold the test partition independent of the learning bias. That is, any model selection necessary to tune the learning algorithm should be done independently of the test partition so as to obtain a relatively unbiased estimate of the classifier's performance on this test partition.

Consider, for instance, the case of k-fold CV. When trying to perform error estimation by using CV, the algorithm builds a classifier by using the $k - 1$ folds for training and tests it on the kth fold. However, if the algorithm also needs to perform model selection (i.e., find the best parameters for the classifier such as

---

[2] We are concerned here with the parameter selection to be precise and not with the optimization criteria used under different learning settings such as the ERM and SRM algorithms discussed in Chapter 2.

the kernel width for an SVM with a radial basis function kernel) then this should be done independently of the test fold as well because, otherwise, for each fold, the algorithm would have a positive bias toward obtaining the classifier performing best on the test fold. One solution is to use a *nested k-fold cross-validation*. The idea behind the nested k-fold CV is to divide the dataset into k disjoint subsets, just as was done in the k-fold CV method previously described. But now, in addition, we perform a separate k-fold CV *within* the $k-1$ folds during training in order to compare the different parameter instantiations of the algorithm. Once the best model is identified for that training fold, testing is, as usual, performed on the kth testing fold. The rationale behind this approach is to make the algorithm totally unbiased in parameter selection.

The simple resampling methods discussed so far may not yield the desired estimates in some scenarios such as extremely limited sample sizes, and more robust estimation methods are desired. Multiple resampling methods aim to do so (of course with some inherent costs). Let us then discuss some prominent multiple resampling methods.

5.6   Multiple Resampling

Multiple resampling refers to methods that potentially generate risk estimates based either on multiple samplings from the training set (e.g., bootstrap) or performing simple resampling multiple times (e.g., multiple k-fold CV). The advantage of multiple resampling over simple resampling is viewed in the additional stability of the estimates, resulting from a large number of repetitions of sampling. On the other hand, it should be kept in mind that this can also lead to other estimation problems because of the extreme reuse and thus loss of independence of the data used in various multiple resampling runs.

Let us very briefly look at the intuition behind multiple resampling in view of our resampling framework that would make this intuition over stability clearer. Recall that, when we partition the data into k subsets, then the resampled risk is basically an expectation over various $\mathbf{w} \in W$, where W is fixed. It is then natural to be interested in a relatively stable estimate of this resampled risk. A stable estimate is one with minimal (ideally none) dependency on any specific set of weight vectors W. We can obtain this by taking an expectation of the resampled risk over all possible sets of weight vectors. Hence the multiple-trial risk estimate of a resampling scheme, denoted as $R_S^{\mathrm{MT}}(f)$, is

$$R_S^{\mathrm{MT}}(f) = \mathbf{E}_W \mathbf{E}_{\mathbf{w}} \int L(y, f_S^k(\mathbf{x})) d D^k(\mathbf{x}, y),$$

where $D^k(\mathbf{z}) = D^k(\mathbf{x}, y)$ denotes the distribution of the partition S_k and the expectation with respect to $\mathbf{w}$ denotes the expectation over all the fixed partitioning defined by W, with each $\mathbf{w}$ defining a particular partition.

An empirical way to estimate this expectation is then to perform multiple trials over each resampling scheme. This observation gives rise to various multiple trial versions of the previously described simple resampling schemes as well as the introduction of some new ones. Let us look at some prominent multiple resampling techniques.

5.6.1 Random Subsampling

The first and probably the simplest multiple resampling technique is random subsampling. The technique can be summarized as in Listing 5.3.

Listing 5.3: Random subsampling.

- Initialize $i = 1$
- Repeat while $i \leq n$ (typically $n \geq 30$)
    - Randomly divide the dataset into a training set S^i_{train}, usually containing 2/3rd of the data, and a testing set $S^i_{\text{test}} = S \backslash S^i_{\text{train}}$ containing the examples from S not included in S^i_{train}.
    - Train the algorithm on S^i_{train} and obtain a classifier f_i.
    - Test f_i on S^i_{test} to obtain an estimate of the empirical risk $R_S(f_i)$.
    - Increment i by 1.
- Average the estimates $R_S(f_i)$ over the n repetitions to obtain the overall risk estimate $R_S(f)$.
- Report $R_S(f)$.

Random subsampling has an intuitive appeal. In the holdout framework, typically, the data are divided into two subsets, with one used for training (and validation) and the other one for testing purposes. Random subsampling, in the manner just described, basically extends this notion to the multiple resampling scenario. Moreover, it carries the advantage of being able to use a larger amount of data for training purposes, resulting in less-biased classifiers. However, in the limited data scenario, the variance in the estimates can still be significant because of the small test sets in each repetition. The problem is further aggravated for very small dataset sizes because, in this case, every iteration of the multiple runs would yield very similar classifiers.

5.6.2 Bootstrapping Approaches: The $\epsilon 0$ and .632 Bootstraps

The idea of bootstrapping comes from the question of what can be done when too little is known about the data. Bootstrapping works by assuming that the available sample is representative of the original distribution and creates a large number of new samples – the bootstrapped samples – by drawing, with replacement, from that population. Different variations of bootstrap have been proposed (see Chernik, 2007, for a review). We focus in particular on the $\epsilon 0$ and the .632

bootstrap, the two most common bootstrap techniques. Let us first summarize
the simpler $\epsilon 0$ bootstrap (also referred to as $e0$ bootstrap) estimate.

Listing 5.4: $\epsilon 0$ bootstrap.

- Given a dataset S with m examples
    - initialize $\epsilon 0 = 0$,
    - initialize $i = 1$.
- Repeat while $i \leq k$ (typically $k \geq 200$).
    - Draw, with replacement, m samples from S to obtain a training set S_{boot}^i.
    - Define $T_{\text{boot}}^i = S \backslash S_{\text{boot}}^i$, i.e., the test set contains the examples from S not included in S_{boot}^i.
    - Train the algorithm on S_{boot}^i to obtain a classifier f_{boot}^i.
    - Test f_{boot}^i on T_{boot}^i to obtain the empirical risk estimate $\epsilon 0_i$.
    - $\epsilon 0 = \epsilon 0 + \epsilon 0_i$.
    - Increment i by 1.
- Calculate $\epsilon 0 = \frac{\epsilon 0}{k}$.
- Report $\epsilon 0$.

Bootstrapping can be quite useful, in practice, in the cases in which the sample
is too small for CV or LOO approaches to yield a good estimate. In such cases,
a bootstrap estimate can be more reliable.

Let us formalize the $\epsilon 0$ bootstrap to understand better the behavior and the
associated intuition of not only the $\epsilon 0$ estimate but also of the .632 bootstrap
technique that it leads to. Going back to our resampling framework, let $\mathbf{w}$, in the
case of a bootstrap resampling, be such that

$$\mathbf{w}_{\text{boot}} \in \mathbb{N}^m,$$

such that

$$\forall i, 0 \leq w_i \leq m,$$

$$||\mathbf{w}||_1 = \sum_{i=1}^{m} w_i = m.$$

In this case, a weight vector $\mathbf{w}_{\text{boot}} = \{w_1, w_2, \ldots, w_m\}$ and its complement
$\mathbf{w}_{\text{boot}}^c = \{w_1^c, w_2^c, \ldots, w_m^c\}$ such that $w_i^c = 1$ if $w_i = 0$ and $w_i^c = 0$ otherwise.
That is, the set $\mathbf{w}_{\text{boot}}^c$ is defined as soon as $\mathbf{w}_{\text{boot}}$ is known. To find all possible
bootstrap sets, then, it suffices to identify the number of possible $\mathbf{w}_{\text{boot}}$. Hence a
distribution on W containing the vectors $\mathbf{w}_{\text{boot}}$ and $\mathbf{w}_{\text{boot}}^c$ is basically a distribution
on $\mathbf{w}_{\text{boot}}$, which is what we subsequently do.

For bootstrap sampling, P_W has equal mass on each of the possible $\mathbf{w}_{\text{boot}}$ in
this new distribution. This is basically sampling with replacement and, under
our original definition of $\mathbf{w}$, can be seen as follows.

Recall that we have $\mathbf{w} \in \{0, 1\}^m$. Let $\mathbf{w}_1, \mathbf{w}_2, \ldots, \mathbf{w}_m$ be the m basis vectors
such that each vector $\mathbf{w}_i$ has entry $w_i = 1$ and $w_j = 0 \, \forall j \neq i$. Now, let us

consider a uniform distribution on this set of basis vectors; that is, the probability of sampling each $\mathbf{w}_i$ is equal. Then we sample $\mathbf{w}_i$ from this distribution m times with each sampling, resulting in a weight vector $\mathbf{w}^i$ for $i = 1, 2, \ldots, m$. We can then obtain

$$\mathbf{w}_{\text{boot}} = \sum_i \mathbf{w}^i.$$

Bootstrap sampling relies on the assumption that the estimator obtained on a subsample (the sample obtained by bootstrapping) can approximate the estimate on the full sample. Let the size of our training sample S be m, i.e., $|S| = m$. Then, as previously mentioned, the bootstrap sampling method consists of sampling, *with replacement*, m examples *uniformly* from S. Let us call this resulting sample S_{boot}.

Because we sample the dataset with replacement, the probability of every example being chosen is uniform and is equal to $\frac{1}{m}$. Subsequently, the probability of an example not being chosen is $1 - \frac{1}{m}$. For any given example, the probability of it not being chosen after m samples hence is $(1 - \frac{1}{m})^m$. Now,

$$\left(1 - \frac{1}{m}\right)^m \approx \frac{1}{e} \approx 0.368.$$

Hence the expected number of distinct examples in the resulting sample of m instances is $(1 - 0.368)m = 0.632m$. The test set T_{boot} is then formed of all the examples from S not present in S_{boot}. A classifier f_{boot} is then obtained on S_{boot} and tested on T_{boot}. The empirical risk estimate of f_{boot} is obtained on T_{boot}. This process is repeated k times, and the respective risk estimates are averaged to obtain the $\epsilon 0$ estimate as

$$\epsilon 0 = \frac{1}{k} \sum_{i=1}^{k} \frac{1}{|T_{\text{boot}}^i|} \sum_{j=1}^{|T_{\text{boot}}^i|} I(f_{\text{boot}}^i(\mathbf{x}_j) \neq y_j),$$

where f_{boot}^i denotes the classifier obtained by training the algorithm on S_{boot}^i, the training sample obtained in the ith run, with T_{boot}^i being the corresponding test set.

The $\epsilon 0$ estimate obtained in the preceding manner, however, can be pessimistic because the classifier is typically trained only over 63.2% of data in each run. The next measure, the .632 estimate, aims to corrects for this pessimistic bias by taking into account the optimistic bias of the resubstitution error over the remaining fraction of $1 - 0.632 = 0.368$. The .632 bootstrap method is summarized in Listing 5.5.

Listing 5.5: .632 bootstrap.

```
– Given a dataset S with m examples:
– Train the learning algorithm on S to obtain a classifier fs.
– Test fs on S to obtain the resubstitution error rate err(f)
   (f) = R_S^resub(fs).
```

- Initialize the .632 risk estimate $e632 = 0$.
- Initialize $i = 1$.
- Repeat while $i \leq k$ (typically $k \geq 200$).
  - Draw, with replacement, m samples from S to obtain a training set S^i_{boot}.
  - Define $T^i_{boot} = S \backslash S^i_{boot}$, i.e., the test set contains the examples from S not included in S^i_{boot}.
  - Train the algorithm on S^i_{boot} to obtain a classifier f^i_{boot}.
  - Test f^i_{boot} on T^i_{boot} to obtain the empirical risk estimate $\epsilon 0_i$.
  - $e632 = e632 + 0.632 \cdot \epsilon 0_i$.
  - Increment i by 1.
- Calculate $e632 = \frac{e632}{k}$.
- Approximate the remaining proportion of the risk using $err(f)$ to give $e632 = e632 + 0.368 \times err(f)$.
- Return $e632$.

More formally, let the number of bootstrap samples generated be k. For each sample, we obtain a bootstrap sample S^i_{boot} and a corresponding bootstrap test set T^i_{boot}, $i \in \{1, 2, \ldots, k\}$. Moreover, a classifier f^i_{boot} is obtained on each S^i_{boot} and tested on T^i_{boot} to yield a corresponding estimate $\epsilon 0_i$. These estimates can together be used to obtain what is called the .632 bootstrap estimate, defined as

$$e632 = \frac{1}{k} \sum_{i=1}^{k} 0.632 \times \epsilon 0_i + 0.368 \times err(f)$$

$$= 0.632 \times \epsilon 0 + 0.368 \times err(f),$$

where $err(f)$ is the resubstitution error rate $R^{resub}_S(f_S)$, with f being the classifier f_S obtained by training the algorithm on the whole training set S.

Balanced Bootstrap Sampling

In balanced bootstrap sampling, the bootstrap samples are generated such that each example is present for a fixed number of times in all the samples altogether. Consider the case in which we wish to generate balanced bootstrap samples from m examples in S such that each element is present exactly m_b times. This will result in m_b bootstrap samples. An easy way to generate this is to first obtain a vector of $m \times m_b$ indices with m_b entries for each element of $\{1, 2, \ldots, m\}$. The next step is to scramble this vector randomly and then divide the resulting vector into m_b vectors of m indices each, sequentially. This procedure draws a parallel with stratified CV.

Discussion

In empirical studies, the relationship between the bootstrap and the CV-based estimates have received special attention. Bootstrapping can be a method of choice when more conventional resampling such as k-fold CV cannot be applied owing to small dataset sizes. Moreover, the bootstrap also, in such cases, results in estimates with low variance as a result of (artificially) increased dataset size. Further, the $\epsilon 0$ bootstrap has been empirically shown to be a good error estimator in cases of a very high true error rate whereas the .632 bootstrap estimator has been shown to be a good error estimator on small datasets, especially if the true error rate is small (i.e., when the algorithm is extremely accurate).

An interesting, perhaps at first surprising, result that emanates from various empirical studies is that the relative appropriateness of one sampling scheme over the other is classifier dependent. Indeed, it was found that bootstrapping is a poor error estimator for classifiers such as the NN or FOIL (Bailey and Elkan, 1993) that do not benefit from (or simply make use of) duplicate instances. In light of the fact that bootstrapping resamples with replacement, this result is not as surprising as it first appeared to be.

5.6.3 Randomization

The term randomization has been used with regard to multiple resampling methods in two contexts. The first is what is referred to as randomization over samples, that is, estimating the effect of different reorderings of the data on the algorithm's performance estimate. We refer to such randomization on training samples as permutation sampling or permutation testing. The second context in which randomization is used refers to the randomization over labels of the training examples. The purpose of this testing is to assess the dependence of the learning algorithm on the actual label assignment as opposed to obtaining the same or similar classifiers on chance label assignments. Like bootstrapping, randomization makes the assumption that the sample is representative of the original distribution. However, instead of drawing samples with replacement, as bootstrapping does, randomization reorders (shuffles) the data systematically or randomly a number of times. It calculates the quantity of interest on each reordering. Because shuffling the data amounts to sampling without replacement, it is one difference between bootstrapping and randomization.

In permutation testing, we basically look at the number of possible reorderings of the training set S to assess their effect on classifier performance. As we can easily see, there are a total of $m!$ possible reorderings of the entries of the vector $\mathbf{w}$ and hence those of the examples $\mathbf{z}$ in the training set S. We would then consider a distribution over these $m!$ orderings on unit vectors $\mathbf{w}$ and $P_{\mathbf{w}}$ that would have an equal probability $(= \frac{1}{m!})$ on each of the weight vectors.

Permutation testing can provide a sense of robustness of the algorithm to the ordering of the data samples and hence a sense of the stability of the performance estimate thus obtained. However, when it comes to comparing such estimates for two or more robust algorithms, permutation testing might not be very effective because the stability of estimates over different permutations is not the prominent criterion of difference between these approaches. Hence we are more interested in the randomization over labels.

Randomization Over Labels

We give an informal description of this technique for the binary label scenario, although extending it to the multilabel scenario is relatively trivial. The idea is to find out whether the error estimate obtained on the given data presents specific characteristics or whether it could have been obtained on similar but "bogus" data, and thus does not stand out as particularly significant. The "bogus" data are created by taking the genuine samples and randomly choosing to either leave its label intact or switch it. Once such a "bogus" dataset is created, the classifier is run on these data and its error estimated. This process is repeated a very large number of times in an attempt to establish whether the error estimate obtained on the true data is truly different from those obtained on large numbers of "bogus" datasets. In this sense, this overlaps to some extent with the hypothesis testing methodology that we discussed in Chapter 2. Let us summarize the basic technique.

Listing 5.6: Randomization over labels.

- Given: a dataset S with m examples.
- Decide on a performance measure pm.
- Calculate pm on the data (denoted as pm_{obt}).
- Repeat the following N times, where $N \in \mathbb{N}$ such that $N > 1000$:
  - Shuffle the data.
  - Assign the first m_1 samples to class 1 and the remaining m_2 samples to class 2, s.t. $m_1 + m_2 = m$ where $|s_p| = m_1$, $|s_n| = m_2$.
  - Calculate pm (here denoted pm_i^*) for the reshuffled data.
  - If $pm_i^* > pm_{obt}$, increment a counter by 1.
- Divide the value in the counter by N to get the proportion of times the pm on the randomized data exceeded the pm_{obt} on the data we actually obtained.
- This is the probability of a result such as pm_{obt} under the null hypothesis.
- Reject or retain the hypothesis stating that pm_{obt} is meaningful on the basis of this probability.

Note that this can be applied not only to validate a given classifier's performance against a random set of labelings, but also to characterize the difference of two classifiers in a comparative setting. In this regard, this resampling is generally used as a sanity check test to compare the classifiers' performance over random assignments of labels to the examples in S. Hence, keeping the ordering of the examples in the training set constant, we can randomize the labels while maintaining the label distribution. Alternatively, we can randomize the examples while keeping the label assignment constant, as shown in Listing 5.6. However, obtaining estimates over a large numbers of randomization on labels can be significantly computationally intensive.

5.6.4 Multiple Trials of Simple Resampling Methods

As we discussed earlier in the context of bootstrapping, one of the more straight-forward manners to obtain relatively stable estimates of the algorithm's performance to discount the dependence on the chosen set of weight vectors W (i.e., a particular partitioning) is to perform multiple runs over the simple resampling schemes. Moreover, single runs of simple resampling methods also suffer from the limitation of low replicability because they depend on factors such as the data permutation used when performing the original trials, as well as not having precisely the same training and testing sets when trying to replicate the results. *Replicability*, in this context, quantifies the probability of obtaining the same error estimate when running a learning algorithm on a given training dataset twice. This definition can be extended to the context of statistical significance testing (the original setting in which it was proposed) and gives some important insights, which we cover in the next chapter.

One solution to remedy the problem of low replicability is to report the exact setting of the trial with the data. This is neither frequently, if at all, done, nor practical to do in most cases. Multiple resamplings mitigate the variability effect over estimates to a certain extent in an indirect manner. Instead of trying to replicate the result over a single run of simple resampling, it averages the results over multiple runs (trials) in an attempt to obtain more stable estimates.

This then brings us to the question of how many runs of simple resampling methods to perform. Currently there is no convincing theoretical model to guide this choice. As a result, this is largely determined empirically. A couple of suggestions have been proposed. The most prominent ones include the $5 \times 2\,\mathrm{CV}$ (Dietterich, 1998) and $10 \times 10\,\mathrm{CV}$ (Bouckaert, 2003), performing 5 repetitions of twofold CV and 10 repetitions of 10-fold CV, respectively. The main motivation for proposing these approaches, however, lies in their subsequent role when the resulting error estimates are used to compare two learning algorithms on a given dataset. Hence we discuss the details and significance of these proposals in the next chapter, in their proper context.

5.7 Discussion

Choosing the best resampling method for a given task should be done carefully if an objective performance estimate is to be obtained. As we saw earlier, the bias–variance behavior of the associated loss is largely dependent on such choices and, in fact, also helps us guide this selection. For instance, it can be seen that increasing the number of folds in a k-fold CV approach would result in estimates that are less biased because a larger subset of the data is used for training. However, doing so would result in decreasing the size of the test partitions, thereby resulting in an increase in the variance of the estimates.

In addition to their effects on the bias–variance behavior of the resulting error estimate, selecting a resampling method also relies on some other factors. One such factor is the nature of the classifiers to be evaluated. For instance, more-stable classifiers would not need a permutation test. The less robust a classifier is, the more training data it would need to reach a stable behavior. In fact, it would also take multiple runs to approximate its average behavior. There are some dataset-dependent factors affecting the choice of resampling methods too. These include the size of the dataset as well as its spread (that is, the representative capability of the data) and the complexity of the domain that we wish to learn. A highly complex domain, for instance, in the presence of a limited dataset size, would invariably lead to a biased classifier. Hence the aim would be to use a resampling scheme that would allow it to use as much data for learning as possible. A multiple resampling scheme can also be useful in such scenarios.

Precisely quantifying various parameters involved in the choice of a resampling method is extremely difficult. Let us take an indirect approach in discussing some important observations by looking at them in a relative sense. One should read the following discussion while bearing in mind that the terms unbiased or almost unbiased are strictly relative with respect to the optimal classifier that can be obtained *given* the training data.

- The LOO cross-validation error estimate is almost unbiased because the training takes place on virtually all (all but one training example) of the available data and because the testing sets are completely independent. This estimate, however, suffers from high variance because of the extreme behavior of the tested classifiers on the one-case test sets. The problem is further aggravated in the binary classification zero–one loss scenario for discrete classifiers (which do not give probabilistic labels). LOO has a particularly high variance on small samples.
- Bootstrapping has been shown to perform well in the cases in which the sample is too small for CV or LOO approaches to yield a good estimate. In such cases, a bootstrap estimate shows less variance than simple resampling techniques (k-fold CV, for instance).
- In particular, the advantage of the $\epsilon 0$ bootstrap is its low variance, especially compared with 10-fold CV or the jackknife. On the other hand, it is more biased than the 10-fold CV estimator. $\epsilon 0$, however, is pessimistically biased on moderately sized samples. Nonetheless, it gives good results in the case of a high true error rate (Weiss and Kulikowski, 1991).
- Like the $\epsilon 0$ bootstrap, the .632 bootstrap is also a low-variance estimator. Unlike the $\epsilon 0$ estimator though, the .632 becomes too optimistic as the

sample size grows. However, it is a very good estimator on small datasets, especially if the true error rate is small (Weiss and Kulikowski, 1991).

- Although in cases of extremely small datasets, the k-fold CV often does not perform as well as bootstrapping (and using more folds does not help), it does not suffer from drastic problems the way bootstrapping does in terms of increased bias or when the true error expectations are not met.

Other concerns that should be taken into account while opting for a resampling method include the computational complexity involved in employing the resampling method of choice and the resulting gain in terms of more objective and representative estimates. For instance, increasing the folds in a k-fold CV all the way to LOO resampling would mean increasing the number of runs over the learning algorithm in each fold. Further, if model selection is involved, this would require nested runs to optimize the learning parameters, thereby further increasing the computational complexity. Bootstrapping, on the other hand, can also be quite expensive computationally. See the Bibliographic Remarks at the end of the chapter for observations from a specific study reported in (Weiss and Kulikowski, 1991).

As we noted earlier, the relative appropriateness of one sampling scheme over the other has also been found to be classifier dependent empirically. Kohavi (1995) further extends this observation to show that, not only are the resampling techniques sensitive to the classifiers under scrutiny, but they are also sensitive to the domains on which they are applied. In light of these observations, it would only be appropriate to end this discussion with the take-home message from the above observations echoed by Reich and Barai (1999, p. 11):

> The relations between the evaluation methods, whether statistically significantly different or not, varies with data quality. Therefore, one cannot replace one test with another and only evaluation methods appropriate for the context may be used.

5.8 Illustrations Using R

In this section, we illustrate the implementation of the various resampling techniques discussed in this chapter. For this, we make use of R in conjunction with the WEKA machine learning toolkit by way of the RWeka package (see the Bibliographic Remarks at the end of this chapter).

For simplicity, all our examples use the "Iris" dataset from the UCI repository. This set does not have missing values, which seem to cause problems with RWeka (we do not delve into the issue of optimizing RWeka, however). Similarly, to keep the R Code simple, certain aspects of the computation were hard-coded. For example, because the Iris data contain three classes, certain aspects of the code are tailored to the three-class case. Similarly, the number of classifiers compared (two) was also hard-coded, as was the choice of the metric returned (accuracy). Modifying these choices is not very difficult, as we will show when we do this for our experiments later in the book (see Appendix C).

Also note that we do not discuss the multiple trials of simple resampling methods mentioned in Subsection 5.6.4 here because these were mainly proposed with regard to comparing two classifiers and hence will be discussed in association with the appropriate statistical significance tests. Consequently we have relegated the description of the full versions of these multiple resampling trials to the next chapter, which is dedicated to statistical significance testing.

Although the resampling methods discussed in this chapter were designed in a more general framework than the multiple trials of simple resampling methods just mentioned, to make our illustrations interesting yet simple to follow, in all but one case, we applied them to the comparison of two classifiers on a single domain. More specifically, the case study we present here aims at comparing the performances of naive Bayes (NB) and and the C4.5 decision tree learner (C45) on the UCI Iris dataset. Even though we have not yet discussed it in depth, the resampling procedure is followed by a t test with an aim to illustrate the hypothesis testing principle discussed earlier in this context.

A different case study is used to illustrate randomization, however, to better explore the technique, given its less-frequent use in machine learning experiments. Let us start with cross-validation.

5.8.1 Cross-Validation

We first present the code for nonstratified cross-validation along with the paired t test for significance testing, followed by the stratified version of cross-validation in a similar manner. For this illustration, we do not use the cross-validation procedure provided by RWeka, however, because of the insufficient information it outputs. Indeed, this information would not enable us to perform either a significance test or an analysis over individual folds.

Nonstratified Cross-Validation

Listing 5.7 illustrates the nonstratified cross-validation procedure with the aim of comparing NB and C45 on the Iris dataset. The parameters and variables used are as follows: k denotes the number of folds desired, *dataSet* denotes the dataset on which the cross-validation study is performed, *setSize* refers to the number of samples in this dataset, and *dimension* denotes the number of attributes, including the class. Because the code is geared at comparing the performance of two classifiers, the parameters *classifier1* and *classifier2* indicating the two classifiers are included. For simplicity, we chose to assess the performances in terms of accuracy. The function thus reads the WEKA output and retrieves the accuracy figures in the form of two vectors, with entries in each vector referring to the accuracy obtained by *classifier1* and *classifier2*, respectively, on the individual test fold.

Listing 5.7: Sample R code for executing nonstratified *k*-fold cross-validation.

```
# Non-Stratified k-fold Cross-Validation
nonstratcv = function(k, dataSet, setSize, dimension,
                      classifier1, classifier2) {
# Initialize
numFolds <- k
testFoldSize <- setSize/numFolds
BaseSamp <- 1:setSize
shuffledInstanceLabels <- sample(setSize, setSize,
                                 replace=FALSE)
# Construct the Testing and Training Folds
TestList <- list()
TrainList <-list()
for(i in 1:numFolds) {
    SubSamp <- shuffledInstanceLabels[((i-1)*testFoldSize+1):
                                      (i*testFoldSize)]
    oneTest <- dataSet[SubSamp, 1:dimension]
    oneTrain <- dataSet[setdiff(BaseSamp,SubSamp), 1:dimension]
    TestList <- c(TestList, list(oneTest))
    TrainList <- c(TrainList, list(oneTrain))
}
# Perform k-Fold CrossValidation
classifier1ResultArray <- numeric(numFolds)
classifier2ResultArray <- numeric(numFolds)
for(i in 1:numFolds){
    oneTrain <- TrainList[i]
    oneTest <- TestList[i]
    classifier1Model <- classifier1(class~., data=oneTrain[[1]])
    classifier2Model <- classifier2(class~., data=oneTrain[[1]])
    classifier1Evaluation <- evaluate_Weka_classifier(
                            classifier1Model, newdata=oneTest[[1]])
    classifier1Accuracy <- as.numeric(substr(
                            classifier1Evaluation$string, 70,80))
    classifier2Evaluation <- evaluate_Weka_classifier(
                            classifier2Model, newdata=oneTest[[1]])
    classifier2Accuracy <- as.numeric(substr(
                            classifier2Evaluation$string, 70,80))
    classifier1ResultArray[i] <- classifier1Accuracy
    classifier2ResultArray[i] <- classifier2Accuracy
}
return(list(classifier1ResultArray, classifier2ResultArray))
}
```

Comparisons of classifier performances are often followed by testing the statistical significance of the observed difference in their performance. A simple *t* test is typically used, as illustrated in Listing 5.8 for the present case (available as a function implementation in R). We discuss in detail the issues as well as appropriateness of using this approach in the next chapter.

Listing 5.8: Sample R code for executing nonstratified *k*-fold cross-validation followed by a paired *t* test.

```
nonstratcvTtest = function(k, dataSet, setSize, dimension,
                           classifier1, classifier2) {
   allResults <- nonstratcv (k, dataSet, setSize, dimension,
                             classifier1, classifier2)
   print("mean accuracy of classifier 1:")
   print(mean(allResults[[1]]))
   print("mean accuracy of classifier 2:")
   print(mean(allResults[[2]]))
   t.test(allResults[[1]], allResults[[2]], paired=TRUE)
}
```

Now that the functions to perform the cross-validation and the associated R test are defined, let us see how to invoke these and look at their output (Listing 5.9).

Listing 5.9: Invocation and results of the nscv/*t*-test code.

```
> library(RWeka)
Loading required package: grid
> NB <- make_Weka_classifier("weka/classifiers/bayes/
      NaiveBayes")
> iris <- read.arff(system.file("arff", "iris.arff",
      package = "RWeka"))
> nonstratcvTtest(10, iris, 150, 5, NB, J48)
[1] "mean accuracy of classifier 1:"
[1] 95.998
[1] "mean accuracy of classifier 2:"
[1] 94.665


        Paired t-test

data:  allResults[[1]] and allResults[[2]]
t = 0.9996, df = 9, p-value = 0.3436
alternative hypothesis: true difference in means is not equal
    to 0
95 percent confidence interval:
 -1.683713   4.349713
sample estimates:
mean of the differences
                1.333
```

The mean accuracy of NB is 95.998% whereas that of c45 is 94.665%. The *p*-value output by the *t* test is found to be very large (0.3436), suggesting that the difference between the performance of the two classifiers on the Iris dataset cannot be deemed to be statistically significant at a 95% confidence level (more details in the next chapter).

Stratified Cross-Validation

The code for stratified cross-validation is a little bit more complex, as data need to be proportionately sampled from the different subdistributions of the data. As a result, we also need to add parameters indicating the number of classes in the dataset and their respective sizes. This is done with parameters *numClasses* and *classSize*. *numClass* indicates the number of classes in the dataset. *classSize* is a vector of size *numClass* that lists the size of each class. Listing 5.10 gives the code for stratified *k*-fold cross-validation.

Listing 5.10: Sample R code for executing stratified *k*-fold cross-validation.

```
#Stratified k-fold Cross-Validation
stratcv = function(k, dataSet, setSize, dimension, numClasses,
                   classSize, classifier1, classifier2) {
# Intialize
numFolds <- k
BaseSamp <- 1:setSize

# We assume that the instances are sorted by classes and we
# create subsets of the entire dataset containing homogeneous
# classes
DatasetList <- list()
currentPosition <- 1
for(i in 1:numClasses){
 SubSamp <- currentPosition:(currentPosition+classSize[i]-1)
 oneDataset <- dataSet[SubSamp, 1:dimension]
  DatasetList <- c(DatasetList, list(oneDataset))
  currentPosition <- currentPosition+classSize[i]
}
# We create a different shuffling and BaseSamps of the
# instances for each class
shuffledInstanceList <- list()
baseSampList <-list()
for(c in 1:numClasses){
  testFoldSize[c] <- classSize[c]/numFolds
  shuffledInstance <- sample(classSize[c], classSize[c],
                          replace=FALSE)
  shuffledInstanceList <- c(shuffledInstanceList,
                          list(shuffledInstance))
  baseSampList <- c(baseSampList, list(1:classSize[c]))
 }
# This function builds the training and testing pairs for a
# given fold and a given class. The sets built for different
# classes within each fold will then be bound together to form
# single training and testing sets for this fold.
getTestTrainSubset = function(i, c) {
```

```
    SubSamp <- shuffledInstanceList[[c]][((i-1)*testFoldSize
                                    [c]+1):(i*testFoldSize[c])]
    Test <- DatasetList[[c]][SubSamp, 1:dimension]
    Train <- DatasetList[[c]][setdiff(baseSampList[[c]],
                                    SubSamp), 1:dimension]
    list(Test, Train)
}
# This double loop creates the actual training and testing sets
# for each fold
TestList <- list()
TrainList <- list()
for (i in 1:numFolds) {
  testFold <- list()
  trainFold <- list()
  for (c in 1:numClasses) {
        testTrainPair <- getTestTrainSubset(i, c)
        testSubset <- testTrainPair[[1]]
        trainSubset <- testTrainPair[[2]]
          testFold <- c(testFold, list(testSubset))
          trainFold <- c(trainFold, list(trainSubset))
  }
TestList <- c(TestList, list(testFold))
TrainList <- c(TrainList, list(trainFold))
}

# Perform stratified k-Fold CrossValidation
classifier1ResultArray <- numeric(numFolds)
classifier2ResultArray <- numeric(numFolds)
for(i in 1:numFolds){
    oneTrain <- rbind(TrainList[[i]][[1]], TrainList[[i]][[2]],
                    TrainList[[i]][[3]])
    oneTest <- rbind(TestList[[i]][[1]], TestList[[i]][[2]],
                    TestList[[i]][[3]])
    classifier1Model <- classifier1(class~., data=oneTrain)
    classifier2Model <- classifier2(class~., data=oneTrain)
    classifier1Evaluation <- evaluate_Weka_classifier(
                                    classifier1Model,
                                    newdata=oneTest)
    classifier1Accuracy <- as.numeric( substr(
                    classifier1Evaluation$string, 70,80))
    classifier2Evaluation <- evaluate_Weka_classifier(
                                    classifier2Model,
                                    newdata=oneTest)
    classifier2Accuracy <- as.numeric(substr(
                    classifier2Evaluation$string, 70,80))
    classifier1ResultArray[i] <- classifier1Accuracy
    classifier2ResultArray[i] <- classifier2Accuracy
}
return(list(classifier1ResultArray, classifier2ResultArray))
}
```

Listing 5.11 next provides the function definition for the associated *t* test. Note that this is similar to the one provided earlier in Listing 5.8 except that the resampling method invoked is *stratcv()* instead of *nonstratcv()*.

Listing 5.11: Sample R code for executing stratified *k*-fold cross-validation followed by a paired *t* test.

```
stratcvTtest = function(k, dataSet, setSize, dimension,
                        numClasses, classSize, classifier1,
                        classifier2) {
  allResults <- stratcv (k, dataSet, setSize, dimension,
                        numClasses, classSize, classifier1,
                        classifier2)
    print("mean accuracy of classifier 1:")
    print(mean(allResults[[1]]))
    print("mean accuracy of classifier 2:")
    print(mean(allResults[[2]]))
  t.test(allResults[[1]], allResults[[2]], paired=TRUE)
}
```

Listing 5.12 invokes the two methods to output the results. Please note that stratified cross-validation is not necessary on the Iris dataset, given that the classes have the same size. The procedure, however, was also tested on classes of different sizes.

Listing 5.12: Invocation and results of the stratified cross-validation/*t* test.

```
> library (RWeka)
>
> NB <- make_Weka_classifier("weka/classifiers/bayes/
                        NaiveBayes")
> iris <- read.arff(system.file("arff", "iris.arff",
                        package = "RWeka"))
> stratcvTtest(10, iris, 150, 5, 3, c(20,50,80), NB, J48)
[1] "mean accuracy of classifier 1:"
[1] 95.998
[1] "mean accuracy of classifier 2:"
[1] 93.997

        Paired t-test

data:   allResults[[1]] and allResults[[2]]
t = 1.1523, df = 9, p-value = 0.2789
alternative hypothesis: true difference in means is not equal
    to 0
95 percent confidence interval:
 -1.927188   5.929188
sample estimates:
mean of the differences
                2.001

>
```

The mean accuracy of NB is 95.998% whereas that of C45 is 93.997%. Just as was the case earlier, however, the difference in the performance of the two classifiers is not found to be statistically significant in this case.

5.8.2 Leave-One-Out Cross-Validation

The code for leave-one-out cross-validation is basically similar to that of non-stratified k-fold cross-validation presented in Listing 5.7, except that the k parameter is now set to $k = setSize$, (i.e., 150 in the case of the Iris dataset). Listing 5.13 shows the function call and the results obtained.

Listing 5.13: Invocation and results of the leave-one-out/t-test code.

```
> library(RWeka)
Loading required package: grid
> NB <- make_Weka_classifier("weka/classifiers/bayes/
                             NaiveBayes")
> iris <- read.arff(system.file("arff", "iris.arff",
                    package = "RWeka"))
> nonstratcvTtest(150, iris, 150, 5, NB, J48)
[1] "mean accuracy of classifier 1:"
[1] 95.33333
[1] "mean accuracy of classifier 2:"
[1] 95.33333

        Paired t-test

data:   allResults[[1]] and allResults[[2]]
t = 0, df = 149, p-value = 1
alternative hypothesis: true difference in means is not equal
    to 0
95 percent confidence interval:
 -3.237626   3.237626
sample estimates:
mean of the differences
                0

>
```

Since the accuracies here are identical, the statistical significance of performance difference cannot be established.

5.8.3 Random Subsampling

The basic code for random subsampling, prior to the calculation of the simple or corrected t test, is given in Listing 5.14. The parameters of the *randomSubsamp()* method are the same as those used in cross-validation. The function outputs a vector containing the differences in the proportion of test examples misclassified by *classifier1* and *classifier2* at each iteration. This quantity is then used in the computation of the subsequent *t* test.

Listing 5.14: Sample R code for executing random subsampling.

```
randomSubsamp = function(iter, dataSet, setSize, dimension,
                         classifier1, classifier2){
proportions <- numeric(iter)

for(i in 1:iter) {
Subsamp <-  sample(setSize, (2*setSize)/3, replace=FALSE)
Basesamp <- 1:setSize
  oneTrain <- dataSet[Subsamp ,1:dimension ]
oneTest <- dataSet[setdiff(Basesamp,Subsamp), 1:dimension]
classifier1Model <- classifier1(class~., data=oneTrain)
classifier2Model <- classifier2(class~., data=oneTrain)
  classifier1Evaluation <- evaluate_Weka_classifier(
                                  classifier1Model,
                                  newdata=oneTest)
  classifier1Accuracy <- as.numeric( substr(
                  classifier1Evaluation$string, 70,80))
  classifier2Evaluation <- evaluate_Weka_classifier(
                                  classifier2Model,
                                  newdata=oneTest)
  classifier2Accuracy <- as.numeric(substr(
                  classifier2Evaluation$string, 70,80))
pclassifier1 <- (100-classifier1Accuracy)/(setSize/3)
pclassifier2 <- (100-classifier2Accuracy)/(setSize/3)
proportions[i]= pclassifier2 -pclassifier1
}
return(proportions)
}
```

Simple Random Subsampling

The following code shows how the basic code of Listing 5.14 can be used in the computation of the simple resampled *t* test. The function takes the same parameters as the previous one and outputs the *t* value obtained.

Listing 5.15: Sample R code for executing the simple random subsampling *t* test.

```
simpleResampttest = function(iter, dataSet, setSize, dimension,
                         classifier1, classifier2){

proportions <- randomSubsamp(iter, dataSet, setSize, dimension,
                         classifier1, classifier2)
averageProportion <- mean(proportions)

sum=0
for (i in 1:iter) {
    sum = sum + (proportions[i]-averageProportion)^2
}
```

```
# Simple resampled t-test
t= (averageProportion * sqrt(iter))/ sqrt(sum/(iter -1))

print('The t-value for the simple resampled t-test is')
print(t)
}
```

This code can be invoked as follows (with 30 iterations).

Listing 5.16: Invocation and results of the simple resampling *t*-test code.

```
> library(RWeka)
Loading required package: grid
>
> NB <- make_Weka_classifier("weka/classifiers/bayes/
                              NaiveBayes")
> iris <- read.arff(system.file("arff", "iris.arff",
                                 package = "RWeka"))
> simpleResampttest(30, iris, 150, 5, NB, J48)
[1] "The t-value for the simple resampled t-test is"
[1] 1.409362
```

The preceding yields a value of $t = 1.4$, which is lower than $t_{29,0.975} = 2.04523$, which signifies that the null hypothesis suggesting that C45 and NB perform similarly on the Iris dataset cannot be rejected at 95% significance level. In the next chapter, we consider an improved version of this test known as corrected random subsampling.

5.8.4 Bootstrapping

The $\epsilon 0$ Bootstrap

We demonstrate the $\epsilon 0$ bootstrap by using C45 and NB on the Iris data, with respect to accuracy. RWeka can be tuned in many different ways, but this was not the purpose of this illustration, which is why we chose a very simple example. (For instance, we did not use the labor data because missing values in the dataset caused problems for the R interface with RWeka; similarly, we used accuracy rather than AUC, because the Iris domain is a three-class problem. Although these various issues could have been dealt with, we feel that they fall beyond the purpose of this subsection.) Listings 5.17 and 5.18 present, respectively, the method and the code it invokes for the $\epsilon 0$ bootstrap.

Listing 5.17: Sample R code for executing the $\epsilon 0$ bootstrap on two different classifiers.

```
e0Boot = function(iter, dataSet, setSize, dimension,
                   classifier1, classifier2){

classifier1e0Boot <- numeric(iter)
```

```
classifier2e0Boot <- numeric(iter)
  for(i in 1:iter) {
  Subsamp <- sample(setSize, setSize, replace=TRUE)
  Basesamp <- 1:setSize
    oneTrain <- dataSet[Subsamp ,1:dimension ]
  oneTest <- dataSet[setdiff(Basesamp,Subsamp), 1:dimension]
  classifier1model <- classifier1(class~., data=oneTrain)
  classifier2model <- classifier2(class~., data=oneTrain)
      classifier1eval <- evaluate_Weka_classifier(
                              classifier1model ,newdata=oneTest)
    classifier1acc <- as.numeric(
                        substr(classifier1eval$string , 70,80))
      classifier2eval <- evaluate_Weka_classifier(
                            classifier2model , newdata=oneTest)
        classifier2acc <- as.numeric(
                          substr(classifier2eval$string , 70,80))
  classifier1e0Boot[i]= classifier1acc
  classifier2e0Boot[i]= classifier2acc
  }
return(rbind(classifier1e0Boot, classifier2e0Boot))
}
```

The code just listed is invoked as follows, with 200 iterations. The result shown is then analyzed.

Listing 5.18: Invocation and results of the $\epsilon 0$ bootstrap followed by a t test.

```
> library(RWeka)
> NB <- make_Weka_classifier("weka/classifiers/bayes/
                              NaiveBayes")
> iris <- read.arff(system.file("arff", "iris.arff",
                              package = "RWeka"))
> setSize <- 150
> dimension <- 5
> iterations <- 200
>
>
> e0Bootstraps <- e0Boot(iterations , iris , setSize ,
                         dimension , NB, J48)
>
> e0NB <- mean(e0Bootstraps[1,])
> e0J48 <- mean(e0Bootstraps[2,])
>
> e0NB
[1] 95.0564
> e0J48
[1] 93.8675
>
> t.test(e0Bootstraps[1,], e0Bootstraps[2,], paired=TRUE)

        Paired t-test
```

```
data:   e0Bootstraps[1, ] and e0Bootstraps[2, ]
t = 5.3329, df = 199, p-value = 2.613e-07
alternative hypothesis: true difference in means is not equal
      to 0
95 percent confidence interval:
 0.7492774 1.6285226
sample estimates:
mean of the differences
                 1.1889
```

>

Unlike previous resampling methods, the *t* test applied to the results of the $\epsilon 0$ bootstrap rejects the hypothesis stipulating that NB and C45 perform equivalently. NB is thus the preferred classifier on this dataset.

The .632 Bootstrap

Listings 5.19 and 5.20 present the code of the .632 bootstrap method and its invocation (with 200 iterations), respectively.

Listing 5.19: Sample R code for executing the .632 bootstrap on two different classifiers.

```
e632Boot = function(iter, dataSet, setSize, dimension,
                    classifier1, classifier2){

classifier1appModel <- classifier1(class~., data=dataSet)
classifier1appEvaluation <- evaluate_Weka_classifier(
                                 classifier1appModel)
classifier1appAccuracy <- as.numeric(
        substr(classifier1appEvaluation$string, 70,80))
classifier1FirstTerm = .368 * classifier1appAccuracy

classifier2appModel <- classifier2(class~., data=dataSet)
classifier2appEvaluation <- evaluate_Weka_classifier(
                                 classifier2appModel)
classifier2appAccuracy <- as.numeric(
        substr(classifier2appEvaluation$string, 70,80))
classifier2FirstTerm = .368 * classifier2appAccuracy

e0Terms = e0Boot(iter, dataSet, setSize, dimension,
                    classifier1, classifier2)

classifier1e632Boot <- classifier1FirstTerm + .632 * e0Terms
      [1,]
classifier2e632Boot <- classifier2FirstTerm + .632 * e0Terms
      [2,]

return(rbind(classifier1e632Boot, classifier2e632Boot))
}
```

Listing 5.20: Invocation and results of the .632 bootstrap followed by a *t* test.

```
> library (RWeka)
> NB <- make_Weka_classifier ("weka/ classifiers / bayes /
                                NaiveBayes")
> iris <- read. arff (system . file ("arff", "iris . arff",
                        package = "RWeka"))
>
> setSize <- 150
> dimension <- 5
> iterations <- 200
>
> e632Bootstraps <- e632Boot(iterations , iris , setSize ,
                                dimension , NB, J48)
>
> e632NB <- mean( e632Bootstraps [1 ,])
> e632J48 <- mean( e632Bootstraps [2 ,])
>
>   e632NB
[1] 95.5517
> e632J48
[1] 95.39294
>
>   t. test(e632Bootstraps [1 ,], e632Bootstraps [2 ,], paired=TRUE)

        Paired t-test

data:  e632Bootstraps[1, ] and e632Bootstraps[2, ]
t = 1.1533, df = 199, p-value = 0.2502
alternative hypothesis: true difference in means is not equal
    to 0
95 percent confidence interval:
 -0.1126972   0.4302052
sample estimates:
mean of the differences
            0.158754

>
```

The *t*-test outcome does not reject the null hypothesis stipulating that the two classifiers obtain equivalent results.

5.8.5 *The Permutation Test*

In this subsection, we consider the example of Chapter 2 in which three classifiers, c45, NB, and RIP were compared on the labor dataset. Ten runs of 10-fold cross-validation were performed, and the results were recorded for each run and each fold. i.e., three tables of 100 values each were built (Tables 2.2, 2.3, and

2.4). Using the *t* test, we found that NB was significantly more accurate than
c4.5. We now repeat this experiment using the permutation test.

We run the permutation tests over accuracy of two classifiers. In particular,
we show the code (Listing 5.21) for a comparison between c4.5 (classifier1) and
NB (classifier2) on the results of 10 runs of 10-fold cross-validation. The null
hypothesis is that the mean accuracies of the observations of the two classifiers
are equal.

Listing 5.21: R code for executing the permutation test.

```
permtest = function(iter, classifier1Results,
                            classifier2Results) {

classifier1_mean = mean(classifier1Results)
classifier2_mean = mean(classifier2Results)

mobt = abs(classifier1_mean - classifier2_mean)
alldata = c( classifier1Results, classifier2Results)
count=0

for (i in 1:iter) {
    # Shuffle the results from the two classifiers
    oneperm= sample(alldata)
    # Assign the first half of this data to the first 'bogus'
    # classifier and the second half, to the second.
    pretend_classifier1 = oneperm[1:(length(alldata)/2)]
    pretend_classifier2 = oneperm[(((length(alldata)/2)+1):
                                    (length(alldata))]
    # Compute the absolute value of the difference between the
    # mean accuracy of the two 'bogus' classifiers
    mstar = abs(mean(pretend_classifier1) -
                mean(pretend_classifier2))
    # Increase the counter if that difference is greater than
    # the real observed difference.
    if (mstar > mobt)
        {count= count+1}
}

probability_of_mobt = count/iterations

return(rbind(mobt, probability_of_mobt))
}
```

The code just listed is invoked as follows, with 5000 iterations. The result shown
is then analyzed.

Listing 5.22: Invocation and results of the permutation test.

```
>
> classifier1= c(.2456, .1754, .1754, .2632, .1579, .2456,
                  .2105, .1404, .2632, .2982)
```

```
> classifier2= c(.0702, .0702, .0175, .0702, .0702, .0526,
                                .1579, .0351, .0351, .0702)
> iterations = 5000;
>
> permtestresults <- permtest(iterations, classifier1,
                                        classifier2);
>
> print('The difference in means obtained is')
[1] "The difference in means obtained is"
> print(permtestresults[1])
[1] 0.15262
> print('The probability of obtaining that mean is')
[1] "The probability of obtaining that mean is"
> print(permtestresults[2])
[1] 0
>
>
```

The observed difference between the two means was found to be 0.15262. Given that the permutation test tells us that the probability of obtaining a mean of 0.15262 under the null hypothesis (i.e., if the two means are indeed equal) is 0; this allows us to strongly reject the hypothesis that the two classifiers perform similarly on the labor data.

We repeated the same experiment in a different context: that of comparing NB and SVM on several datasets (see Subsection 6.8.2 in the next chapter). The data for this comparison are the following with NB standing for classifier1 and SVM standing for classifier2. The running and results of this test are shown in Listing 5.23.

Listing 5.23: Data preparation for the permutation test.

```
>
> classifier1= c(96.43, 73.42, 72.3, 71.7, 71.67, 74.36,
                                70.63, 83.21, 98.22, 69.62)
> classifier2= c(99.44, 81.34, 91.51, 66.16, 71.67, 77.08,
                                62.21, 80.63, 93.58, 99.9)
> iterations = 5000;
>
> permtestresults <- permtest(iterations, classifier1,
                                        classifier2);
>
> print('The difference in means obtained is')
[1] "The difference in means obtained is"
> print(permtestresults[1])
[1] 4.196
> print('The probability of obtaining that mean is')
[1] "The probability of obtaining that mean is"
> print(permtestresults[2])
[1] 0.4552
>
```

In this case, the obtained observed difference in means is 4.196, but this time the probability of obtaining such a mean under the null hypothesis that stipulates that the two means are equal is found to be 0.4552; i.e., 45.52%. This suggests that we cannot reject the null hypothesis because there is almost a one in two chance to obtain the observed difference under it (note that calculations here are done over percentages).

5.9 Summary

In this chapter, we focused on the issue of error-estimation and studied various error-estimation techniques along with the relationship of their bias–variance behavior to factors such as dataset size and classifier complexity. One of the main limitations of robust holdout-based estimation has long been the unavailability of a large enough amount of data, leading to inaccurate estimates. Resampling methods alleviate this problem by giving alternatives to utilize the limited available data to obtain relatively robust estimates when the holdout approach cannot be employed. We discussed both simple and multiple resampling schemes. Although the former, including techniques such as k-fold cross-validation and leave-one-out among others, tend to avoid reusing the examples for testing (i.e., tests each examples only once), the latter, including methods such as bootstrap and randomization, do not limit themselves in this manner. Of course, there are both advantages and limitations to these two strategies. They were discussed both directly and in a relative sense in various places. Our discussion highlighted a common line of understanding with regard to these techniques in that they are dependent on not only the classifier under consideration, but also on the domain of application, of course, in addition to the basic empirical data charateristics such as dimensionality and size. Once a robust estimate of error (or of any other performance measure) is obtained, statistical significance tests enable us to verify if the observed difference is indeed statistically significant (e.g., as in the t-test examples previously shown). This battery of tests is our focus in the next chapter.

5.10 Bibliographic Remarks

A discussion on resampling methods can be found in (Yu, 2003). Traditionally, error estimation was performed by using the resubstitution error or, more reliably, the holdout method. Rigorous guarantees on the expected risk of the classifier can be established in the case of the holdout estimate such as the one shown in Subsection 5.2.1. The bound and the corresponding proof have been known for a while and are standard in the statistical learning theory literature. The version shown here is along the lines of those of Shah (2006).

Resampling techniques make statistical inferences about quantities to be estimated based on repeated sampling within the same sample. These methods stem from Monte Carlo simulations, but differ from them in that they are based on some real data. Monte Carlo simulations, on the other hand, could be based on completely hypothetical data. Although the use of resampling methods in the machine learning context is relatively recent (owing especially to increased computational capability), some of them have been known for a while. For example, permutation tests were developed by Fisher and described in his book published and republished between 1935 and 1960 (Fisher, 1960). Cross-validation was first proposed by Kurtz (1948) and the jackknife (or leave-one-out) was first invented by Quenouille (1949).

The discussion of the goals of error estimation with regard to taking into account different variations discussed in Section 5.1 is based on (Dietterich, 1998). With regard to multiple resampling, the study of Dietterich (1998) also maps the problem of accounting for the preceding variations to statistical significance testing, especially the type I error and the power of the tests employed. We focus on these in the next chapter.

Weiss and Kulikowski (1991) and Witten and Frank (2005b) discuss the computational complexity of the k-fold CV and other resampling methods and also suggest stratification in the event of class imbalance. As discussed by Weiss and Kulikowski (1991), the leave-one-out estimate is not recommended for very small samples (fewer than 50 cases). On the other hand, it is recommended for sample sizes between 50 and 100 cases, as it may yield more reliable estimates than 10-fold cross-validation in such cases. Above that, the leave-one-out estimate may be computationally too expensive to be worth applying as it does not provide particular advantages over cross-validation. Irrespective of the sample size, there are a couple of special cases, however, for which the leave-one-out estimate is particularly useful, and that is when there is wide dispersion of the data distribution or when the dataset contains extreme scores (Yu, 2003). In such cases, the estimate produced by leave-one-out is expected to be better than the one produced by k-fold cross-validation. However, the k-fold cross-validation estimate, which uses the same principle as leave-one-out cross-validation, is easier to apply and has a lesser computational cost.

The discussion on the relationship between bootstraping and cross-validation is largely based on the empirical studies of Weiss and Kulikowski (1991), Efron (1983), Bailey and Elkan (1993), Kohavi (1995), Reich and Barai (1999), and Jain et al. (1987). Margineantu and Dietterich (2000) also discuss bootstrapping in cost-sensitive settings. These studies were all done in the context of the accuracy measure. Currently an *open question*, it would be interesting to see the results in the context of, and their dependence on, other performance measures. There are many variants of resampling methods. See (Weiss and Kapouleas, 1989, Mitchell, 1997), and (Kibler and Langley, 1988) for resampling and other evaluation methods.

Replicability of the results was emphasized as a necessary characteristic for an error estimator by Bouckaert (2003, 2004), who noticed that random subsampling and k-fold cross-validation both suffer from low replicability. This was also noticed earlier by Dietterich (1998), who suggested replacing 10-fold cross-validation with 5×2-fold cross-validation to improve the stability of the test. Bouckaert (2003) suggested that k-fold cross-validation repeated multiple times could be even more effective than 5×2-fold cross-validation. In particular, he investigated the use of 10×10-fold cross-validation. An *open question* would be to investigate if this approach can be generalized to a $k \times p$-fold cross-validation approach. With regard to statistical testing too, it would be interesting to see if the problems posed by a single k-fold cross-validation-based testing can be alleviated by averaging over numerous trials.

The randomized method is seldom used in the machine learning community (see, e.g., Jensen and Cohen, 2000). The description that was made in the text was based on that of Yu (2003) and Howell (2007).

Finally, the RWeka package used to illustrate the implementation of resampling techniques is available at http://cran.r-project.org/web/packages/RWeka/index.html.

Appendix: Proof of Equation (5.5)

Consider an algorithm A that, given some training set S, outputs a classifier $f = A(S)$. We wish to estimate the true risk $R(f)$ in terms of the risk on a distinct test sample T (disjoint from training set S). We can define the empirical risk of f on test set T as

$$R_T(f) \stackrel{\text{def}}{=} \frac{1}{m'} \sum_{i=1}^{m'} L(y_i, f(\mathbf{x}_i)),$$

where $m' = |T|$ is the number of examples in the testing set. Note that the test set $T = \mathbf{z}_1, ..., \mathbf{z}_{m'}$ of m' samples is formed from the instantiation of the variables $\mathbf{Z}^{m'} \stackrel{\text{def}}{=} \mathbf{Z}_1, \ldots, \mathbf{Z}_{m'}$. Every $\mathbf{Z}_i$ is distributed according to some distribution D that generates the sample S. Each $\mathbf{z}_i$ consists of an example $\mathbf{x}_i$ and its label y_i. Each example $\mathbf{x}_i$ can hence be considered an instantiation of a variable $\mathbf{X}_i$ and its label y_i as an instantiation of variable Y_i.

Hence, over all the test sets generated from the instantiations of variables $\mathbf{Z}^{m'}$, the risk of some classifier f can be represented as

$$R(\mathbf{Z}^{m'}, f) \stackrel{\text{def}}{=} \frac{1}{m'} \sum_{i=1}^{m'} L(Y_i, f(\mathbf{X}_i)),$$

where $L()$ is again the loss function over the misclassification. Now consider the loss function $L = L_z$ such that L_z is a Bernoulli variable; then the true risk can be expressed as

$$R(f) = \{\Pr(L_z(Y_i, f(\mathbf{X}_i)) = 1\} \stackrel{\text{def}}{=} p.$$

To bound the true risk $R(f)$, we make use of the Hoeffding's inequality, stated in the following theorem.

Theorem 5.1. *(Hoeffding: Bernoulli case). For any sequence $Y_1, Y_2, \ldots, Y_{m'}$ of variables obeying a Bernoulli distribution with $\Pr(Y_i = 1) = p$ $\forall i$, we have*

$$\Pr\left[\left|\frac{1}{m'}\sum_{i=1}^{m'} Y_i - p\right| > \epsilon\right] \le 2\exp(-2m'\epsilon^2).$$

This implies that

$$\Pr\left[\left|\frac{1}{m'}\sum_{i=1}^{m'} Y_i - p\right| \le \epsilon\right] \ge 1 - 2\exp(-2m'\epsilon^2).$$

Now, because $L_z(f(\mathbf{X}), Y)$ is a Bernoulli variable, we have

$$\Pr\left[\left|R(\mathbf{Z}^{m'}, f) - R(f)\right| \le \epsilon\right] \ge 1 - 2\exp(-2m'\epsilon^2).$$

Equating the right-hand side of the preceding equation to $1 - \delta$, we get

$$t_{1-\delta} = \epsilon = \sqrt{\frac{1}{2m'}\ln\left(\frac{2}{\delta}\right)}.$$

Hence, for any classifier f, the true risk $R(f)$, with probability $1 - \delta$ and test error $R_T(f)$ on some test set T, satisfies

$$\left|R_T(f) - R(f)\right| \le t_{1-\delta} = \sqrt{\frac{1}{2m'}\ln\left(\frac{2}{\delta}\right)}.$$

Therefore, with probability $1 - \delta$,

$$R(f) \approx R_T(f) \pm t_{1-\delta}.$$

Hence it can be seen that the convergence of the empirical risk to the true risk depends on the sample size m' and the true risk $R(f)$.

6

Statistical Significance Testing

The advances in performance measure characterization discussed in Chapters 3 and 4 have armed researchers with more precise estimates of classifier performance. However, these are not by themselves sufficient to fully evaluate the difference in performances between classifiers on one or more test domains. More precisely, even though the performance of different classifiers may be shown to be different on specified sets of data, it needs to be confirmed whether the observed differences are statistically significant and not merely coincidental. Chapter 5 started to look at this issue, but focused primarily on the objectivity and stability of the results. This can be construed as the first step to assessing the significance of a difference. Only in the case of the comparison of two classifiers on a single domain did the discussion actually move on to significance issues. Statistical significance testing, which is the subject of this chapter, enables researchers to move on to more precise assessments of significance of the results obtained (within certain constraints). The importance of statistical significance testing hence cannot be overstated. Nonetheless, the use of available statistical tools for such testing in the fields of machine learning and data mining has been limited at best. Researchers have concentrated on using the paired t test, many times inappropriately, to confirm the difference in classifiers' performance. Moreover, this has sometimes been done at the cost of excluding other, more appropriate, tests. Thus, although we have at our disposal a vast choice of tools to perform such testing, it is unarguably important for researchers in the field to be aware of these tests and, even more so, to understand the framework within which they operate. In particular, for each statistical strategy aimed toward performing significance testing, it is important for the user to have a thorough understanding of the assumptions that underlie each test and the issues that need to be addressed so as to be able to apply these strategies in practice. Furthermore, we need to develop an understanding of what each statistical strategy has to offer so that no unreasonable expectations from these tests are raised. This is precisely the purpose of this chapter:

to develop an understanding of various statistical significance testing strategies most relevant to assessing the performance of learning algorithms, their underlying assumptions, and the appropriateness of their application in any given scenario. These are not necessarily the only nor the ultimate tools available. Indeed, this approach to significance testing has many caveats that need to be understood. However, it is important to know that some of these caveats are not attributable to the inherent nature of the tests but rather to their inappropriate application. Applying a test outside the constraints in which it works is indeed a negligence on the part of the researcher rather than an inherent limitation of the test itself. This observation further emphasizes the need to develop a better understanding of these tests.

In this chapter, we focus on the concept of null-hypothesis statistical testing, popularly abbreviated as NHST, and on the related statistical tests that are relevant to classifier evaluation in machine learning settings. In addition to describing the conditions under which they apply and their mechanics, we also provide code and illustrations in R to demonstrate their application. But, before immersing ourselves in the discussion of various statistical tests, let us discuss the aspects of NHST that have made such testing prone to criticism. As we will see, part of such objections appears as a result of the lack of understanding of the tests, leading to unreasonable expectations and inappropriate interpretation of the test results. However, this discussion is aimed at both raising an awareness about the statistical tests and their limitations and, perhaps more important, increasing our understanding so as to avoid misrepresentations and misinterpretations of the subsequent results.

6.1 The Purpose of Statistical Significance Testing

Typically, researchers are interested in the following three, related tasks:

1. Assessing the performance of a learning algorithm of interest against that of existing algorithms on a specific problem. This is typically the case in which the aim is to demonstrate the utility of a particular (or novel) algorithm on a given learning problem of interest.
2. Assessing the performance of a learning algorithm of interest against that of existing algorithms on benchmark datasets. This is often useful in cases in which the aim is to demonstrate the effectiveness of a generic learning algorithm against existing approaches.
3. Assessing the performance of multiple classifiers on benchmark datasets or a given problem of interest. This is useful in case a broad analysis of learning strategies is required on either benchmark datasets (w.r.t. their general learning characteristics) or a specific domain of interest (w.r.t. finding the approach that is best suitable, given a learning domain).

Performing these tasks necessitates considering other issues such as deciding which evaluation metrics to use or whether graphical visualization and analysis methods should be employed. We have already discussed the most prominent of these approaches in earlier chapters. In addition, and as important, certain other questions need to be answered:

- Can the observed results be attributed to real characteristics of the classifiers under scrutiny or are they obtained by chance?
- Are the datasets representative of the problems to which the classifier will be applied in the future?

Unfortunately, because of the inductive nature of the problem, such questions cannot be fully answered. The user should instead accept that no matter what evaluation procedures are followed, they only allow us to gather some evidence into the classifiers' behavior. They are almost never conclusive.

Let us now look in more detail at the specific questions that the statistical tests are able to answer. Consider the following examples:

Example 6.1. Consider the results of running C4.5 (C45) and naive Bayes (NB) algorithms on the breast cancer dataset and using the root-mean-square error (RMSE) as our performance evaluation metric. Table 3.4 of Chapter 3 presented these results. We saw that C45 obtained a RMSE of 0.4324 and NB obtained a RMSE of 0.4534. Without statistical analysis, we would simply conclude that C45 performs better than NB on the breast cancer domain. This, however, is not necessarily the case because this result could have been obtained by chance.

What do we mean, though, when we say that the results may have been obtained by chance? Well, what we are really interested in is whether C45 is *consistently* better than NB on this domain. If it is not and if this lack of difference between the two algorithms can be detected by a null-hypothesis statistical test that makes small enough type I errors in this kind of situation, then we will know about the failure of C45 to surpass NB because the statistical test will inform us that we cannot reject the null hypothesis.

Informally stated, statistical tests work by observing the consistency of the difference in classifier performance, implicitly or explicitly. Such consistency estimates can either be obtained over multiple test cases (generally, test sets) or by performing multiple trials over a given test set. Such consistency would then indicate that the performance difference between two or more classifiers was not merely a chance result. Consider the following hypothetical example.

Example 6.2. Assume that classifiers f_A and f_B were tested on a test set of size 5, using RMSE, and that classifiers f_A and f_B obtained the following squared error results, on each testing instance, respectively. Classifier f_A: 0.012, 0.015, 0.02, 0.26, 0.009, and classifier f_B: 0.061, 0.054, 0.055, 0.062, 0.050. The RMSE for classifier f_A is thus 0.0632, and the RMSE for classifier f_B is thus 0.0564. A simple look at the RMSEs of the two classifiers would thus suggest that classifier f_B, the one with the lowest RMSE, exhibits better performance than classifier f_A. Would you agree with this conclusion? Probably not. Classifier f_A usually performs significantly better than classifier f_B, because it typically obtains squared errors in the [0.009, 0.02] interval whereas classifier f_B obtains squared errors in the [0.050, 0.062] interval. There was only one instance for which classifier f_A performed miserably and obtained a squared error of 0.26.

Given that the classifiers of the preceding example were tested on so few points, can we really conclude what the RMSE results suggest? That is, are the preceding test points enough to make any conjectures about the consistency of the classifier performances? It would perhaps be warranted if classifier f_A were shown on a large testing set to obtain such bad results relatively often while classifier f_B were shown to remain more stable. However, it is also possible that on a large sample, classifier f_B would also have obtained bad results once in a while. Perhaps it is only by chance that our size 5 sample did not contain a point on which classifier f_B did not fail miserably. Perhaps the point on which classifier f_A failed is the only point where classifier f_A would ever fail, and it happened, quite by chance, to show up in our sample. Either way, we can see the problems caused by the sole display of the average RMSE results. Whatever they show is not the whole story.

The purpose of statistical significance testing is thus to help us gather evidence of the extent to which the results returned by an evaluation metric are representative of the general behavior of our classifiers. The best way would be to look at the isolated results themselves, as we just did. But this is not realistic, given the size of the testing sets that need to be used to obtain sufficient information about the classifiers.[1] Statistical significance tests thus summarize this information. In doing so, however, they often make a number of assumptions that need to be considered before the test is applied to make sure that the results represent the situation accurately.

The remainder of this chapter discusses a number of statistical tests used in the case of learning problems and states their assumptions clearly. The reason for choosing to describe this particular subset of tests is that their assumptions are most in tune with the situations typically encountered in the field. It should be noted that we could not consider all possible situations a researcher is likely to encounter. The reader should thus take into consideration the fact that, in some cases, he or she may have to look beyond this book and into the statistics literature to find a more appropriate test. What we hope this book does in this vein, however, is to attempt to provide the reader with an appropriate launchpad by providing the necessary tools and understanding to make informed choices.

Note as well that, although statistical tests play an important part in assessing the validity of the results obtained, it is a mistake to believe that favorable

---

[1] Please note that looking at individual scores is not always useful either. In our example 6.2, for instance, we just do not have a sufficient number of observations to draw any conclusions. This, in fact, corresponds to cases in which statistical tests could be neither conclusive nor applied. (See the following section on the limitations of statistical significance testing.)

statistical results are all that is needed to answer the questions asked earlier. This is not the case. The choice and availability of the datasets, the way in which these datasets are resampled, and the testing regimen, as well as the number of experiments run, are all considerations that should also be kept in mind.

Prior to embarking onto the main matter of this chapter, though, we discuss yet another, more fundamental, limitation of statistical testing.

6.2   The Limitations of Statistical Significance Testing

The usefulness and validity of statistical testing and, in particular, of NHST (recall our discussion on the topic from Subsection 2.2.4 of Chapter 2), have been put into question in various studies (see, for instance, Meehl, 1967; Cohen, 1994; Schmidt, 1996; and Harlow and Mulaik, 1997). We highlight, in this section, some of the main objections to NHST.

As discussed by Drummond (2006) and Demšar (2008), and, before them, by Gigerenzer (2004) (see Chow, 1998, p. 199, and Gill and Meir, 1999, in the field of psychology), NHST can be construed as an inconsistent hybrid of Fisher's and Neyman–Pearson's ideas. As a result, the process is often misinterpreted, usually giving more credence to the hypothesis under test than it should (Gill and Meir, 1999). Let us discuss some common misinterpretations of NHST and their results.

Common Misinterpretations of NHST Previously Reported in the Literature
As noted by Demšar (2008), NHST does not tell us all that we need to know and what many researchers believe it conveys. Ideally, when comparing some new classifier f_A with some other existing classifier f_B, and being successful in rejecting the hypothesis that the difference between the two classifiers is nonexistent at significance level $p = 0.01$, we are often hoping that the result of NHST means that new classifier f_A is better than classifier f_B with probability 99%.[2,3]

Unfortunately, this is not the case. Our wish, assuming the hypothesis H that "classifier f_A is better than classifier f_B" with S being "the evidence from our experiments," is that $(1 - p)$ represents $P(H|D)$, the probability that f_A is better than f_B given our experimental observations, with p being the p value of the statistical test. In fact, this is not what $(1 - p)$ represents; $(1 - p)$ represents $P(S|H)$, i.e., the probability that the evidence from our experiments is correct if it is true that classifier f_A is better than classifier f_B. This syllogism is nicely exemplified by Cohen (1994, 2007), as further reported by Demšar (2008), who

---

[2] Of course, not everyone makes this error, as many researchers are aware of the true meaning of the test.

[3] While we use α for significance level elsewhere in the book, we retain p for this discussion in accordance with its common usage in such references. This should not be confused with other use(s) of p in the book.

noted that this error is similar to the absurd mistake of assuming that, because only a small proportion of U.S. citizens are members of Congress, then if some man is a congressman, one could conclude that he is probably not a U.S. citizen.

This is, hence, confusing the likelihood over H with posterior on H in the Bayesian sense. Now, of course, Bayes rule can enable us to derive $P(S|H)$ from $P(H|S)$, but one of the main obstacles in doing so is the lack of any knowledge of the priors over H and S (Demšar, 2008). In fact, as noted by Drummond (2006), both Fisher and Neyman–Pearson categorically rejected the use of Bayesian reasoning in NHST.

Another related misinterpretation of NHST is the assumption that $(1 - p)$ is the probability of successful replication of our experimental results. Yet the p value is not related to the issue of replication (Goodman, 2007).

Uncertainty in a clear interpretation over the NHST outcome has been cited as a reason for a discontinuation of its use (Hubbard and Lindsay, 2008). Confidence intervals have been suggested as alternatives to using NHST, along with effect sizes (Gardner and Altman, 1986). We introduced the concepts of confidence intervals and effect size in Chapter 2, along with some examples. However, there are counterarguments that could (and should) be made to these suggestions, as we will see a bit later.

Unfortunate Possibility of Manipulating the Results of the NHST Approach
Another issue that limits the value of NHST is the fact that any difference between two alternatives, no matter how small, can always be shown to be significant, provided that enough data are used (see Cohen, 2007, for example). The amount of data necessary can be determined by power analysis, as discussed in Chapter 2. This means that researchers can very often find a significant positive difference in favor of their respective algorithms, even if this difference is very small. Hence, in this view, the question should not be one of statistically significant difference, but rather, one of practical difference. This argument once again suggests that we abandon NHST in favor of other more commonsense means of evaluation.

Is Statistical Testing Necessary?
As a result of the two limitations of NHST just discussed, it has sometimes been suggested that statistical testing is not necessary and is even ill-advised in scientific research. This is because NHST is not a sound process, and it leads to overvalued results. The consequence of this is too much confidence in the results, further limiting the necessary experiments from being carried out.

An argument has been made in favor of exploratory experiments rather than confirmatory ones (Drummond, 2006) (recall our discussion on conformatory versus exploratory data analysis from Subsection 2.2.4). This would enable exploring novel ideas, discovering relationships, and comparing alternatives, in addition to hypothesis testing. In echoing similar views, suggestions have also been made for an Internet-based solution in which a sort of democratic process would distinguish the truly useful algorithms from the incremental ones (Demšar, 2008). This would be done by a direct publishing of results on the Web and their subsequent evaluation and citations, thus leading to a democratic approval of novel approaches.

Of course, arguments can easily be made against these specific suggestions. For instance, the exploratory approach still does not enable us to quantify our confidence in the suitability of a particular learning strategy in a given scenario. Such a quantification, or at least confirmation, is indeed required in some way when these strategies are put in practice. This can be considered a purely pragmatic take on the issue but is nevertheless important because this is where the utlimate utility of the approaches lies. Similarly, the Internet-based approach would enable broader evaluations of the algorithms simply owing to the fact that they would be available for a wider community for study and assessment. However, the question of quantifying the *goodness* of an approach over others, given some domain(s) of interest, is inevitable and still open, in addition to the issue of a possible preferential bias. This is of course in addition to the possibility of an overflow of sub-marginal improvements or even incorrect approaches that, even if discarded, would nonetheless result in significant waste of time and resources employed in evaluating them.

As we mentioned earlier, other suggestions to discontinue the use of NHST appear as a result of the uncertainty in the interpretation of its outcome. However, this uncertainty can, at least in big part, be attributed to a lack of proper understanding of these tests and their underlying assumptions. A better understanding would certainly help ameliorate this situation. Moreover, the alternative suggestion, the confidence interval approach, comes with its own set of issues, as we showed in Chapter 2 while introducing it. We will discuss these issues at some length later, in a comparative context with the novel approaches of using risk bounds on the true risk of the classifier, for classifier evaluation in Chapter 8. Briefly, these issues stem from the modeling assumptions over the distribution of the performance measures, generally the empirical risk of the classifier, and they also suffer from unrealistic outputs. For instance, the classical confidence interval approach, which reports the interval around the empirical error based on a measure of observed standard deviation of these errors, makes an asymptotic *normality* assumption over their distribution and, further, is not, in itself, designed to restrict the output to the desired $[0, 1]$ interval. As a result, we can easily obtain unrealistic confidence intervals. For instance, a confidence interval on a performance measure, such as 0.7 ± 0.5, can be an overly optimistic (or pessimistic, depending on how it is perceived) estimate.

Statistical testing can be useful if applied properly and understood correctly. Both researchers and practitioners should be aware of how to properly verify that all the underlying assumptions are met, and they should be aware of what their results truly mean. They should thus refrain from overvaluing such results and, further, make sure to apply and interpret them (only) in apt contexts. Indeed, however small a contribution, the role of NHST cannot be dismissed. At the very least, the impossibility of rejecting a null hypothesis *while using a reasonable effect size* is telling: It helps us guard against the claim that our algorithm is better than others when the evidence to support this claim is too weak. This is important, and the fact that nothing very specific can be concluded in the case in which the null hypothesis gets rejected does not take away the value of knowing that it was not accepted.

In addition, pragmatically speaking, the use of NHST is quite unlikely to disappear in the foreseeable future, despite the criticisms. This is not to say, however, that such tests are inevitable and that better alternatives do not exist or will never appear. Indeed, scientific progress is pinned on such discoveries (if some such alternatives already exist out there) and inventions (if we can come up with better, more-disciplined alternatives). But until this is done, we are indeed better off with at least utilizing the benefits that the current practices have to offer while trying to minimize the related costs. And this can be done only by a thorough understanding of these practices and the contexts in which they operate.

Keeping all the preceding critical observations and associated suggestions in mind, we thus choose to present the various approaches to NHST so as to at least help users apply them properly when deemed necessary. Finally, there is also a social aspect to our motivation in assuming this position. Science practice, although idealized as a search for the truth, is not independent of social implications. As such, advising new students or practitioners to go against the norm in their field might result in their ideas not getting considered. Such changes progress gradually. In the meantime, we are better off training the new cohorts as carefully as possible within the confines of the society they work in, while warning them of the limitations of its customs and hence encouraging a positive change.

6.3 An Overview of Relevant Statistical Tests

In this book, we restrict our focus to the evaluation of classifiers and, more generally, to the evaluation of inductive learning algorithms, i.e., algorithms that induce specific classifiers from a labeled dataset. We consider, in particular, the following most relevant cases:[4]

- the comparison of two algorithms on a single domain,
- the comparison of multiple algorithms on a single domain,
- the comparison of multiple algorithms on multiple domains.

---

[4] Note that Kononenko and Kukar (2007) used a similar breakdown of classifier evaluation approaches, although in a more limited context than the elaborate one that we present here.

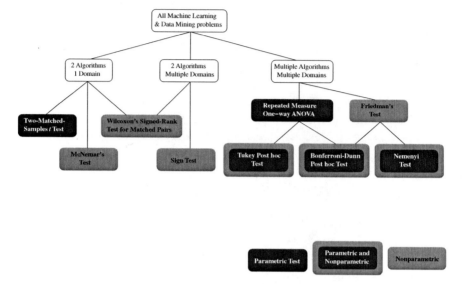

Figure 6.1. Overview of the statistical tests considered in this chapter.

In every case, we consider two categories of approaches: *parametric approaches* that make strong assumptions about the distribution of the population and *nonparametric approaches* whose assumptions are not as strong. As well, we assume that, in all cases, the algorithms are tested on the same domains (matched samples). Statistical tests are also available for the case in which they are not (unmatched samples), but given that it is most common for machine learning researchers to use the same domains in their comparisons, we decided to omit them here.

The field of statistics is very wide. Many tests have a great number of variations, depending on the details of the circumstances. Consider, for example, the very well-known procedure "analysis of variance" (ANOVA). ANOVA is not a single method, but rather a family of methods. Some of the variations of interest include one-way ANOVA, which tests the difference observed in more than two independent groups; one-way repeated measures ANOVA, which is the same as one-way ANOVA except for the fact that several measurements were made on each subject in the group; and n-way ANOVA, in which the analysis is done with respect to n independent variables. In this book, rather than describing the entire families of processes, we pick the specific ones that are relevant to the kind of situations that arise in inductive learning problems and focus on them specifically. This is true for ANOVA as well as for all the other families of processes we consider.

Figure 6.1 overviews all the statistical tests discussed in this chapter. This is by no means an exhaustive list of all the statistical tests that could be used for our situation, but it represents the tests more appropriate for use in classification problems.

Several points are worth noting:

- In the case of two algorithms compared on multiple domains, we do not consider any parametric solution. Actually, this is not quite the case because the paired t test was considered but immediately dismissed for the reasons discussed in Section 6.5.
- The same test, Wilcoxon's Signed-Rank test for matched pairs, can be used in the two distinct situations of two algorithms compared on a single domain and two algorithms compared on multiple domains.
- Both ANOVA and Friedman's test, in the case of multiple algorithms compared on multiple domains, should be followed (when the null hypothesis is rejected) by a post hoc test, in order to establish where the difference was located.

Note that all the tables associated with the tests discussed in this chapter are included in Appendix A. In most cases, these tables are reproductions from (Lindley and Scott, 1984), though in a few cases, we had to go to a different source, which is indicated on the page containing the table. We note that all the tables taken from (Lindley and Scott, 1984) list values corresponding to the one-sided test (meaning that, for a two-sided test, the p values corresponding to these values need to be multiplied by two). Also, it is important to note that the p values shown are the actual p values multiplied by 100 (this was done to make the connection to the confidence level in percentages clear). So, when looking in the column corresponding to $p = 5$, for example, we are actually looking at the case of a p value of 0.05. Last, the list that we present along with the tests we discuss in this chapter are not exhaustive but representative of what can be employed in a given scenario. Moreover, with regard to comparing two classifiers on a single domain, a dependency on the error-estimation technique used was discovered by Dietterich (1998), among others, who proposed modified versions of some tests that can be applied over multiple runs of simple resampling schemes for error estimation. We have not included these methods explicitly in Figure 6.1, but they are discussed in Section 6.8. These methods differ from the parametric tests used for comparing two classifiers on a single domain, although their basic principle is similar. The main difference between these two families of methods lies in the manner in which the estimates of classifier performance are obtained.

6.4 A Note on Terminology

Throughout the rest of this chapter, the tests and their null hypotheses are presented with respect to the *means* of the *samples*. These means represent the (average) performance measures (i.e., samples) of the classifiers that are output by the respective learning algorithms on the concerned datasets. Because the datasets are generally assumed to come from some arbitrary distribution, the samples or the performance measures can also be considered as coming from some *population*. The performance measure of a classifier f is denoted by $pm(f)$ and can mean any monotonic measure of classifier performance on a given dataset. As discussed in Chapter 2, by monotonic performance measure, we mean a measure of classifier performance that, when ordered, also orders the classifiers in the order of respective performances. For instance, classification accuracy $Acc(f)$ of a classifier f is a monotonic performance measure. When the accuracies of k classifiers $f_1, f_2, \ldots, f_k$ are ordered such that, $Acc(f_1) > Acc(f_2) > \cdots > Acc(f_k)$ then this implies that we can order the classifiers in that order with the meaning that classifier f_1 performs better than classifier f_2 which in turn performs better than classifier f_3, and so on. Similarly, misclassification error orders the classifiers in reverse order of their performances.

When considered as means, these measures represent an empirical estimation of the true mean over these performance measures. Consequently the tests that make assumptions on the distribution of the population in fact make assumptions over the distribution of these performance measures. This was explained in Chapter 2, for the general case, in the section on sampling distributions. We illustrate this idea now in the context in which the error rate (risk) of the classifier is used as a performance measure. The mean of this risk, which we also refer to as the error rate or the empirical risk of the classifier, is the average misclassification error over all examples in the dataset (generally the test set). Hence an assumption made over the distribution of the underlying population that generated this mean would basically refer to the distribution of the error rate made on individual examples (or a subset of examples, as the case may be) in the test set.

In the case of multiple hypothesis testing such as ANOVA, a common approach is to make use of blocking statistics. A block refers to an arrangement of the samples in groups according to some criterion of interest. This is generally done with regard to controlling the variability of the resulting subgroups. However, in classifier evaluation, we are interested in classifiers tested on the same datasets. That is, performance assessments of more than one classifier on a given test set corresponds to the same measure. This particular case is referred to as *repeated-measures design*. We use this design with regard to the multiple hypothesis testing for machine learning purposes. The analogous design in the case of single hypothesis testing (i.e., testing two classifiers) is referred to as the *"matched-samples"* or *"matched-pairs" design*. Hence, in the case of the comparison of two classifiers, we present the matched-pairs versions of the respective tests.

Other than that, the naming conventions are straightforward, with "domain" basically referring to a dataset and the "null hypothesis" generally referring to the hypothesis that the two (or more) means (and hence the performance measures) resulting from the application of two or more classifiers come from the same distribution. The premises necessary to understand the philosophy of hypothesis testing, along with one- and two-sided tests, were discussed in Chapter 2.

6.5   Comparing *Two Classifiers* on a *Single Domain*

This section presents statistical hypothesis tests that are useful for the case in which two classifiers are tested on a single domain. The first one of these tests is the well-known two-matched-samples t test. It is a parametric test. We then discuss a nonparametric test called McNemar's test. In the next subsection, we discuss more nonparametric tests applied to testing two classifiers on multiple domains and show how these can be adapted to the present case of a single domain. Similarly, at the end of this section, we discuss how the tests presented in this section can be extended to multiple-domain scenarios. The nonparametric tests, including McNemar's, are seldom used in the field, despite the fact that they are appropriate in the cases in which the parametric assumptions of tests, such as the t test, are not met. Let us start with the t test. We present the version that applies to two matched samples, as discussed in Section 6.4.

6.5.1 *Two-matched-samples* t *Test*

Because of its prominence in the machine learning community, we decided to take the space to carefully review the t test and specifically focus on its shortcomings, while emphasizing the situations in which it is appropriate to use. The t test comes in various flavors. However, the one most relevant in our context is the two-matched-samples version with unknown variances, which is the one discussed here. For a more complete description of the t test, please refer to statistical textbooks such as (Howell, 2002) and (Hill and Lewicki, 2007).

The two-matched-samples t test can be useful to find out whether the difference between two means is meaningful. As previously mentioned, we consider only the case of two matched samples. This test can be considered to be a specific case of the more general t test known as Welch's t test, which is applicable in the case of two independent samples.

Given two matched samples, we want to test whether the difference in means between these two samples is significant, i.e., whether the two samples come from the same population. We do so by looking at the difference in observed means and standard deviations (i.e., the first and the second moments of the samples) between these two samples. As discussed in Chapter 2, hypothesis testing consists of assuming a null hypothesis, H_0, the opposite of what we are interested in showing by confirming whether the null hypothesis can be rejected based on our evidence.

In this case, we hope to find a significant difference between the sample distributions from which the means were calculated. We are thus going to assume that, on the contrary, the two samples come from the same distribution. Therefore we will assume that the difference between these means is zero and see whether this null hypothesis H_0 can be rejected. To see whether the hypothesis can be rejected, we need to find out what kind of differences between two samples can be expected because of chance alone. We can do this by considering the mean of every possible sample of the same size as our sample coming from the first population and comparing it with the mean of every other possible sample of the same size coming from the second population, i.e., we are looking at the distribution of differences between sample means. Such a distribution is a sampling distribution (see Chapter 2) and will tend to *normality* (a normal distribution) as the sample size increases.

Given this normality assumption, we would expect the mean difference to deviate from zero according to the normal distribution centered at zero. We now check if the obtained difference (along with its variance) indeed displays this behavior. This is done with the following t statistic:[5]

$$t = \frac{\bar{d} - 0}{\frac{\bar{\sigma}_d}{\sqrt{n}}},$$ (6.1)

or, equivalently,

$$t = \frac{\overline{pm}(f_1) - \overline{pm}(f_2)}{\frac{\bar{\sigma}_d}{\sqrt{n}}},$$ (6.2)

where $\bar{d} = \overline{pm}(f_1) - \overline{pm}(f_2)$ represents the difference of our means of performance measures obtained by applying classifiers f_1 and f_2, and $\bar{\sigma}_d$ denotes the sample standard deviation of this mean difference, which can be defined by the following formula:

$$\bar{\sigma}_d = \sqrt{\frac{\sum_{i=1}^{n} (d_i - \bar{d})^2}{n - 1}},$$ (6.3)

where d_i is the difference between the performance measures of classifiers f_1 and f_2 at trial i, i.e., $d_i = pm_i(f_1) - pm_i(f_2)$.

Note that $\overline{pm}(f)$ is the average performance measure of the classifier f:

$$\overline{pm}(f) = \frac{1}{n} \sum_{i=1}^{n} pm_i(f),$$

where n is the number of trials.

We then find the probability that the t we just calculated is as large as the value obtained from the table listing the probability with which different

[5] We know that the distribution of differences between sample means is zero, but we do not know what its standard deviation σ is. Therefore we need to estimate it. We do so by using our sample variance. This leads to an overestimate of the value that would have been obtained if σ had been known. This is why the distribution of z, perhaps familiar to some of the readers, cannot be used to accept or reject the null hypothesis. Instead, we use the Student's t distribution, which corrects for this problem, and we compare t with the t table with degree of freedom $n - 1$.

mean differences are observable in the situation in which the two means come from samples emanating from the same distribution. The t table is found in Appendix A.2.

We output this probability if we are solely interested in a one-tailed test, and we multiply it by two before outputting it if we are interested in a two-tailed test (see Chapter 2). If this output probability, the p value, is small (by convention, we use the threshold of 0.05 or 0.01), we would reject H_0 at the 0.05 or 0.01 level of significance. Otherwise, we would state that we have no evidence to conclude that H_0 does not hold.

The following example illustrates the use of the t test as is done in many cases currently. However, along with demonstrating the practical calculations, the following examples also demonstrate the caveats that one should keep in mind before such an application.

Example 6.3. In this example, we compare the performance of the decision tree classifier c45 (the WEKA implementation of the c4.5 algorithm) and the NB classifier on the labor dataset. The results were presented in Table 2.3 of Chapter 2 and represent the average number of errors made by the classifier on the testing fold. The results were obtained by performing multiple trials by random resampling of data and performing a 10-fold cross-validation on each set (trial). Because each cell in Table 2.3 represents the error rate obtained by a given classifier in one fold within one run of the evaluation procedure, to compute the average error rate of this classifier for that run, we simply average the results obtained by a classifier at each fold of one run. For example, consider the first row of Table 2.3, which corresponds to the first cross-validation run of c4.5 on the labor dataset. The values in this row are 0.5, 0, 0.3333, 0, 0.3333, 0.3333, 0.3333, 0.2, 0.2, and 0.2. We take the average of these values, yielding 0.24332, which represents the value of $pm_1(c45)$ in our t test setting. The same calculation is repeated for all the runs of c45 and NB to yield the other pm_i (c45) and pm_i (NB) values.

Our overall average performance measures are the average of the cross-validated error rates of the respective classifiers in each trial and were computed in Chapter 2 as the mean of the continuous random variables representing the performance of each classifier. We recall that the values obtained for c4.5 and NB were

$$\overline{pm}(c45) = 0.2175,$$

$$\overline{pm}(NB) = 0.0649.$$

For $n = 10$, we thus get

$$\bar{d} = 0.2175 - 0.0649 = 0.1526,$$

and, from Table 2.3, we can compute the various d_i values as

$$d_1 = pm_1(\text{C45}) - pm_1(\text{NB}) = 0.2433 - 0.0733 = 0.17$$
$$\vdots \qquad\qquad \vdots \qquad\qquad\qquad \vdots \qquad\qquad\qquad \vdots$$
$$d_{10} = pm_{10}(\text{C45}) - pm_{10}(\text{NB}) = 0.2967 - 0.0733 = 0.2234.$$

and thus

$$\bar{\sigma}_d = \sqrt{\frac{\sum_{i=1}^n (d_i - \bar{d})^2}{n-1}} = \sqrt{\frac{0.0321}{10-1}} = 0.05969,$$

so that

$$t = \frac{\bar{d} - 0}{\frac{\bar{\sigma}_d}{\sqrt{n}}} = \frac{0.1526 - 0}{\frac{0.05969}{\sqrt{10}}} = 8.0845.$$

The degree of freedom is $n - 1 = 9$. A look at the t table in Appendix A.2 reveals that 8.0845 is much larger that the value shown for a degree of freedom of 9 and $p = 0.005$ (a value of 3.25), $p = 0.001$ (a value of 4.297), or $p = 0.0005$ (a value of 4.781). Because the one-sided test should be sufficient here, given that NB performs consistently better than C4.5, we could safely reject the null hypothesis, which states that the two algorithms do not behave differently from one another with that test. If, however, the user would prefer using a two-tailed test for more safety, the null hypothesis would be rejected with $p = 0.01$, $p = 0.002$, or $p = 0.001$ (the preceding p values multiplied by 2). If all the assumptions of the t test are met, one way or another, we could then conclude that the evidence from our experiments strongly suggest that, given the number of empirical risk of the two classifiers, NB performs better than C4.5 on the labor dataset (one-tailed test), or more generally NB and C4.5 show a statistically significant performance difference on the labor dataset (two-tailed test).

   The preceding example is repeated using R code in Subsection 6.9.1. The actual result obtained for t is slightly different because of precision differences in manual and R calculations.

   Finally, as mentioned earlier, a more general version of the t test is Welch's t test, which also applies in case of two unmatched samples of size n_1 and n_2. In this case, the t statistic is calculated as

$$t = \frac{\overline{pm}(f_1) - \overline{pm}(f_2)}{\sqrt{\frac{\sigma_1^2}{n_1} + \frac{\sigma_2^2}{n_2}}},$$

where σ_1^2 and σ_2^2 are the sample variances of the performance measures of the two classifiers and n_1 and n_2 are their respective number of trials.

Effect Size

The t test determines whether the observed difference in the performance measures of the classifiers is statistically significant. However, it cannot confirm whether this difference, although statistically significantly different, is also of any practical importance. That is, it does measure the *effect* but not the *size* of this effect. This can be done using one of the available *effect-size* measuring statistics. Many methods of assessing effect sizes can be found in the statistics literature such as Pearson's correlation coefficient, Hedges' G, and coefficient of determination. The effect size in the case of the t test is generally determined with Cohen's d statistic. Please refer back to Chapter 2 for more details on effect size and associated statistics. The Cohen's d statistic in the case of two matched samples was briefly mentioned in Chapter 2. Here we describe it in greater detail. More specifically, given classifiers f_1 and f_2, Cohen's d statistic can be calculated as follows (we denote the Cohen's d statistic with the notation d_{cohen} to avoid ambiguity):

$$d_{\text{cohen}} = \frac{\overline{\text{pm}}(f_1) - \overline{\text{pm}}(f_2)}{\sigma_p},$$

where σ_p, the pooled standard deviation estimate, is defined as

$$\sigma_p = \sqrt{\frac{\sigma_1^2 + \sigma_2^2}{2}},$$

and σ_1^2 and σ_2^2 represent the variances of distributions of the respective measures $\text{pm}(f_1)$ and $\text{pm}(f_2)$. A typical interpretation proposed by Cohen for this effect-size statistic was the following discretized scale:

- A d_{cohen} value of around 0.2 or 0.3 denotes a small effect, but is probably meaningful.
- A d_{cohen} value of about 0.5 signifies a medium effect that is noticeable.
- A d_{cohen} value of 0.8 signifies a large effect size.

Note, however, that d_{cohen} need not lie in the $[0, 1]$ interval and can indeed be even greater than 1, as we subsequently see.

We apply the formula for d_{cohen} with the values obtained in the previous example. In particular, we compute $\sigma_1^2 = \sigma_{\text{C4.5}}^2$ and $\sigma_2^2 = \sigma_{\text{NB}}^2$, using R as follows.[6]

---

[6] Note that we cannot use the variances obtained in Chapter 2 because these were based on a sample size of 100; here we made the problem more manageable by averaging the results obtained on the 10 folds of each run and reducing the problem to a sample size of 10. Please note that, even when using the 100 values instead of the 10 values when calculating d_{cohen}, we obtain a value greater than 0.8 (1.1221).

Listing 6.1: Variance calculation for C4.5 and NB.

```
> c45 = c(0.2433, 0.1733, 0.1733, 0.2633, 0.1633, 0.2400,
    0.2067, 0.1500, 0.2667, 0.2967)
> nb = c(0.0733, 0.0667, 0.0167, 0.0700, 0.0733, 0.0500,
    0.1533, 0.0400, 0.0367, 0.0733)
> var(c45)
[1] 0.002608929
> var(nb)
[1] 0.001334905
>
```

We thus have

$$d_{\text{cohen}} = \frac{0.2175 - 0.0649}{\sqrt{\frac{0.00261+0.00133}{2}}} = 3.4381.$$

From Cohen's guidelines, we conclude that, because $d_{\text{cohen}} > 0.8$, the effect size is large. That is, the difference in the means of the two populations and hence the performances of the two classifiers do differ (as confirmed by the t test), and the difference is practically important as further confirmed by an estimate of the size of this difference using the Cohen's d statistic (d_{cohen}).

When Is It and Is It Not Appropriate to Use the t Test?

As illustrated in the previous example, the t test is quite easy to use. An important issue, however, is that the t test relies on three basic assumptions that must all be verified for the test's results to be valid. Unfortunately, these do not always hold. These assumptions are as follows.

Normality or Pseudo-Normality. The t test requires that the samples come from normally distributed populations. The t test is, fortunately enough, quite robust to this assumption, and the simple requirement that the sample size of the testing set be greater than 30 is usually sufficient to ensure that the t test can be applied.[7] Alternatively, the normality of the samples can be confirmed with goodness-of-fit tests for normal distributions, more generally known as the normality tests, such as the Kolmogorov–Smirnov test (KS test), the Shapiro–Wilk test, or the Anderson–Darling test.[8] We do not discuss these tests here, but their description can be found in any standard statistics text.

Randomness of the Samples. The t test assumes that the samples from which the means are estimated are representative of the underlying population. That

---

[7] The sample size requirement of 30 is widely found in the literature as a minimum required sample size so as to approximate the sample by use of normal distribution. This number comes from a wide number of simulation studies that show how various distributions can converge to a normal distribution with increasing samples and is used as an empirical guide.

[8] As discussed later, however, one caveat of these tests is that they require a large sample size, which, if available, would make these tests unnecessary.

is, it assumes the performance measures to be representative of the underlying distributions. Because these are obtained from the application of a classifier on data instances, this assumption implicitly makes it imperative that the instances in the testing set be randomly chosen from their underlying, even though arbitrary, distribution. This is necessary because the t test relies on sample statistics such as the mean and the standard deviation with the assumption that these are unbiased estimates of the population parameters.

Equal Variances of the Populations. The paired t test assumes that the two samples come from populations with equal variance. This is necessary because we use the sample information to estimate the entire population's standard deviation.

The first assumption is easy to verify because it requires us to verify only that our algorithms are applied to testing sets that consists of enough samples for the assumption to hold. We discussed the sample size requirement in Chapter 2. Recall that, as a rule of thumb, each set should contain at least 30 samples. Further implication of this requirement is felt in our resampling strategy. Because we usually run 10-fold cross-validation experiments, this sample size requirement of 30 or more suggests that the datasets should be at least of size $10 \times 30 = 300$ for individual trials.

The second assumption is usually difficult for machine learning researchers to verify for the simple reason that they are typically not the people who gathered the data used for learning and testing. They must thus trust that the people responsible for this task built truly random samples and try to gather enough information about the dataset construction process to pass a judgment. There are cases, however, when true randomness is difficult to achieve, and this trust can be problematic. Note that, by randomness, we mean choosing the samples in an i.i.d. manner. This does not mean making an assumption about the data distribution. The data can come from any arbitrary distribution. However, the assumption is based on the notion of i.i.d. sampling from this distribution, which is indeed hard to verify.

We could verify the third assumption either by observing the calculated variances or by plotting the two populations (the measures on which the t test is to be applied) and visually deciding whether they indeed have (almost) equal variance. Alternatively, the similarity of variances can be tested with the F test, Bartlett's test, Levene's test, or the Brown–Forsythe test. Again, these can be found in many statistics texts.

The procedure that can be used in R is illustrated in the following example, where we question whether our use of the t test on the labor dataset was warranted or not.

Example 6.4. Given the assumptions just discussed, were we warranted in applying the t test to the labor data, as we did in the previous subsection?

- The first assumption requires an original dataset containing a minimum of 300 examples. However, labor contains only 57 instances altogether. The first assumption is thus violated because it is not known whether the distribution of the results obtained by applying c4.5 or NB on the labor data obeys a normal distribution. An alternative argument generally made in such a scenario is that, because we perform cross-validated trials for each trial, the classifier is ultimately tested on all of the test examples. Further, because we can consider each performance measure on a single example as a sample, the normality violation is indeed not violated because in this case the sample size exceeds the magic number of 30. However, it should be kept in mind that, while doing this, we also dramatically increase the degree of freedom for our calculations, and hence the t-test results should be evaluated in this light. Again, an application of the normality tests such as the KS test could be used to verify the normality of the samples (i.e., performance measures).
- As discussed previously, the second assumption can never be verified fully. The description of the labor dataset on the UCI website says, "The data includes all collective agreements reached in the business and personal services sector for locals with at least 500 members (teachers, nurses, university staff, police, etc) in Canada in 87 and first quarter of 88." Because all the collective agreements were reached for a given period, and because there is no reason to believe that 1987–1988 was a particularly favorable or unfavorable period for these kinds of transactions, we would be tempted to say that, in this case, we can consider the sample to be a random one.
- With regard to the last assumption, we can verify the similarity of the variance of each population, as previously mentioned, by using tests such as the F test or Bartlett's test. Alternatively, we can use R to visualize the sample variances, as subsequently done. To do so, we use the command of Listing 6.2 to obtain the two side-by-side box plots shown in Figure 6.2. Note that the scale of variances is shown with respect to the number of samples in each fold of each trial (with corresponding calculations). Figure 6.2 suggests that the variance of the two populations cannot be considered (almost) equal.

Listing 6.2: Generating box plot between c4.5 and NB performance in R.

```
> boxplot(c45, nb)
```

Hence, in the case of this experiment, we conclude that the requirements needed to use the t-test are not met.

Variations of t-*Test Design*

Further, there are other subtle design issues involved that affect the distributional assumptions.

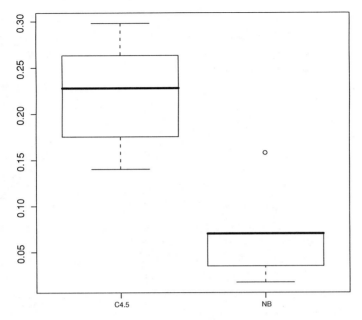

Figure 6.2. c4.5 and NB size-by-side box plots.

What we have illustrated in the preceding example is a form of the use of the *t* test known as the *resampled matched-pair t test* on cross-validated runs in each resampling. However, each cross-validated run involves using overlapping training sets. Hence, even though cross-validation has an advantage in the sense that in each fold, a high number of examples relative to the dataset size are available for training, the overlapping training sets bias the resulting classifiers. This effect, popularly known as correlated measurements (because each classifier is obtained on correlated sets instead of on independent ones), is further aggravated when multiple trials are performed over these cross-validated runs. As a result, the preceding version of the *t* test shows a very high type I error probability. Another version of this test is the *twofold resampled matched-pair t test*, in which, in each trial, the dataset is divided into a training set and a test set. In each trial, the algorithms to be compared are trained on the training set and tested on the test set. As a result of single training and testing (and hence no overlaps) in *individual trials*, this method results in relatively less bias and type I error probabilities. However, the issues of overlapping datasets for both training and testing across trials combined with difficulties in estimating the variances across overlapping sets still figure in this design because, to be effective, the twofold test is typically repeated multiple times.

The main issue in various cross-validated versions is the problem of estimating the variance of the performance across folds. The overlapping training sets in such cases generally result in an underestimation of this variance. This consequently results in a high type I error probability. This problem becomes more serious when multiple trials are involved, for instance, in the case of the preceding example. On the other hand, cross-validation results in larger training sets, rendering the tests more powerful. This is quite beneficial in the case of limited training data availability. In the limit, a t-test design over a single trial, known as the *cross-validated t test* (the version used in the preceding labor data example), is considered the most powerful as a result of high training-set sizes. Here, a trial is replaced with a performance measure calculation over each individual fold in the cross-validation. The rest of the calculations follows accordingly. However, this also suffers from a high type I error probability.

A trade-off between the number of trials and the number of folds in each trial was proposed empirically by Dietterich (1998), who limits the number of trials to five and uses a twofold cross-validation in each trial, resulting in the well-known 5×2-CV t test. We present these versions of t-test applications in Section 6.8. The 5×2-CV t test was then further improved by Alpaydn (1999), who proposed a 5×2-CV F test that has still higher power and a lower type I error probability. To deal with the underestimation of variance in the cross-validation versions, Nadeau and Bengio (2003) proposed a corrected resampled t test, a version of the twofold resampled matched-pair t test that incorporates the overlap into the variance estimation. These and further considerations are discussed in more detail in Section 6.8.

Getting back to the example, from the preceding observations, we cannot yet form any formal judgment as to whether or not the difference we observed in the two means (that obtained from C4.5 and that obtained from NB) is meaningful, based on the t test. An alternative method to confirm this would be to use tests that do not make assumptions on the sample distributions, the so-called nonparametric tests. One of the well-known nonparametric tests that fits the bill in our present scenario is McNemar's test.

6.5.2 McNemar's Test

The t test described in the previous subsection is a *parametric* test because it makes assumptions on the distribution over the performance measures. In particular, it assumes that the distribution of the performance measures is normal or pseudo-normal. Let us discuss a *nonparametric* alternative, McNemar's test, that does not make such assumptions. This test is generally applied to compare the classification errors of two classifiers. However, it can be customized to any monotonic measure of performance of classifiers.

We first divide the sample into a training set S_{train} and a test set S_{test} (just as in the case of the holdout method). Consider two learning algorithms A_1 and A_2 that yield the classifiers f_1 and f_2, respectively, on a training set S_{train}. We then test these classifiers on S_{test} and compute the following McNemar's contingency

Table 6.1. *McNemar's contingency matrix*
of classifiers f_1 and f_2

		Classifier f_2	
		0	1
Classifier f_1	0	c_{00}^{Mc}	c_{01}^{Mc}
	1	c_{10}^{Mc}	c_{11}^{Mc}

matrix $C_{Mc}(f_1, f_2)$ as shown in Table 6.1, where

$$c_{00}^{Mc} = \sum_{i=1}^{|S_{test}|} [I(f_1(\mathbf{x}_i) \neq y_i) \wedge I(f_2(\mathbf{x}_i) \neq y_i)],$$

$$c_{01}^{Mc} = \sum_{i=1}^{|S_{test}|} [I(f_1(\mathbf{x}_i) \neq y_i) \wedge I(f_2(\mathbf{x}_i) = y_i)],$$

$$c_{10}^{Mc} = \sum_{i=1}^{|S_{test}|} [I(f_1(\mathbf{x}_i) = y_i) \wedge I(f_2(\mathbf{x}_i) \neq y_i)],$$

$$c_{11}^{Mc} = \sum_{i=1}^{|S_{test}|} [I(f_1(\mathbf{x}_i) = y_i) \wedge I(f_2(\mathbf{x}_i) = y_i)],$$

with the rest of the notations as before. That is, c_{00}^{Mc} denotes the number of examples in S_{test} misclassified by both f_1 and f_2; c_{01}^{Mc} denotes the number of examples in S_{test} that are misclassified by f_1 but correctly classified by f_2; c_{10}^{Mc} denotes the number of examples in S_{test} that are misclassified by f_2 but correctly classified by f_1; and c_{11}^{Mc} denotes the number of examples in S_{test} that are classified correctly by both f_1 and f_2.

The null hypothesis assumes that both f_1 and f_2 have the same performance and hence the same error rates. That is, $c_{01}^{Mc} = c_{10}^{Mc} = c_{null}^{Mc}$. The next step is to compute the following statistic that is approximately distributed as χ^2:

$$\chi_{Mc}^2 = \frac{(|c_{01}^{Mc} - c_{10}^{Mc}| - 1)^2}{c_{01}^{Mc} + c_{10}^{Mc}}.$$

The χ_{Mc}^2 is then looked up against the table of χ^2 distribution values (See Appendices A.3.1 and A.3.2) and the null hypothesis is rejected if the obtained value exceeds that used in the table for the desired level of significance.

The χ_{Mc}^2 basically tests the goodness of fit that compares the observed counts with the expected distribution of counts if the null hypothesis holds. If this statistic is larger than $\chi_{1,1-\alpha}^2$, (the first subscript denotes the degrees of freedom), then we reject the null hypothesis with an α significance level or $1 - \alpha$ confidence.

For example, if the observed χ^2_{Mc} is larger than $\chi^2_{1,0.05} = 3.841$ (See the table in Appendix A.3.2), then we can reject the null hypothesis with 95% confidence, or 0.05 significance level, and thus conclude that the classifiers f_1 and f_2 have error rates that are statistically significantly different.

Note that if c^{Mc}_{01}, c^{Mc}_{10}, or both, are small ($c^{\text{Mc}}_{01} + c^{\text{Mc}}_{10} < 20$), then McNemar's statistic is not approximated by the χ^2 distribution but should rather be approximated by use of a binomial distribution. Specialized χ^2 tables are available for McNemar's test that use this approximation when the size of the $c^{\text{Mc}}_{01} + c^{\text{Mc}}_{10}$ diagonal in the contingency matrix is small. Alternatively, a sign test, which is a form of binomial test, can be used (see Subsection 6.6.1). We describe the sign test in the context of comparing two classifiers on multiple domains because this is the scenario in which the sign test is generally applied. However, later in that subsection, we also illustrate the use of sign test in a single-domain scenario.

Let us now illustrate McNemar's test on the labor dataset.

Example 6.5. In this example, we apply the C4.5 (C45) and NB classifiers on the labor data. Our default resampling method is 10-fold cross-validation, and we thus look at the results obtained on 10 different folds. (This means that we end up testing the algorithms on the entire dataset, because we add up the errors made by each classifier on all the folds.[9]) The specifics of the data, i.e., the actual classification of each example by both classifiers, are given in Appendix B.

From the listing in Appendix B, we can see that C4.5 (classifier f_1) makes errors on the instances numbered $1, 4, 5, 8, 11, 22, 23, 24, 31, 34, 38, 49, 53, 55, 57$; NB (classifier f_2) makes errors on instances numbered $1, 7, 11, 22, 24, 40$. Therefore the populated McNemar's contingency matrix is (see Table 6.2) such that for $|S_{\text{test}}| = 57$, we have

$$c^{\text{Mc}}_{00} = 4, \quad c^{\text{Mc}}_{01} = 11, \quad c^{\text{Mc}}_{10} = 2, \quad c^{\text{Mc}}_{11} = 40$$

and hence, $\chi^2_{\text{Mc}} = \dfrac{(|11 - 2| - 1)^2}{11 + 2} = 64/13 = 4.92.$

Because $4.92 > 3.841$ (where $\chi^2_{1,0.05} = 3.841$ per the table in Appendix A.3.2), we reject the null hypothesis and claim that C4.5 and NB classify the dataset differently. However, as mentioned previously, it turns out that McNemar's test should not be used in this case because $c^{\text{Mc}}_{01} + c^{\text{Mc}}_{10} = 11 + 2 < 20$, and the sign test that is discussed in Subsection 6.6.1 should be used instead.

An example using R is given in Section 6.9.1.

[9] Note that Dieterich (1998) did not mention this use of the McNemar test. In his paper, he considered McNemar's test applied to a testing set proper (not cross-validated) and compared this technique with the 10-fold cross-validated approach, among others. We, on the other hand, decided to separate the issues of statistical testing and resampling in this book. We use stratified cross-validation as a default, unless otherwise stated, in all our experiments. The issue of resampling was discussed in Chapter 5.

Table 6.2. *McNemar's contingency matrix*
for NB *and* C4.5 *examples*

		NB	
		0	1
c4.5	0	4	11
	1	2	40

Issues with This Example

As we mentioned earlier, McNemar's test is ideally applied over an independent test set for performance assessment and the consequent contingency matrix generation. However, the availability of a very limited number of examples in the labor data prohibits using a separate subset of examples as a test set because then the classifiers would not have sufficient training examples, resulting in classifier bias (even potential underfitting or overfitting). However, the advantage of more training examples comes at the cost of potentially biased performance estimates as a result of data overlap in each training fold. Another factor to keep in mind here is that the test is aimed at a matched pair. That is, it should be made sure, while the classifier performances are averaged, that the two classifiers use the same training and test sets during each fold of the cross-validation run. Finally, the constraint over the minimum size of the $c_{01}^{Mc} + c_{10}^{Mc}$ diagonal should also be kept in mind during such an application. And naturally, this size requirement also has potential implications on the size of the test set. This is reflected in our preceding example too. In the case of smaller sizes of disagreements between the classifiers, a binomial distribution is a better approximation of their behavior. Hence a sign test, which is a form of binomial test, can be better suited in such cases.

6.5.3 Extending the Tests to Multiple Domains

The matched-pair t test can be, and has been, extended to the case of testing two classifiers on multiple domains. However, such an application raises some issues. The first issue is that of commensurability of performance measures. The t test assumes the commensurability of performance measures, meaning that any two pairs of performance measures across different domains can be meaningfully compared and are proportionate to their actual performance in the concerned domains. However, this might not necessarily be the case because the domains on which the classifiers are tested are generally never similar. This is precisely the weakness of the approach consisting of averaging the classifier performances that we mentioned in Chapter 1. Note that this assumption does not have such strong implications in the single-domain case in which the classifiers' performances are measured on different subsets of a given data or averaged on multiple trials.

With regard to the testing of normality using the KS test or the Shapiro–Wilk test, as mentioned earlier, these tests work well when the sample size is large. However, for smaller samples, as is generally the case when two classifiers are tested on multiple domains (generally fewer than 30), these tests are not so powerful. Hence, as Demšar (2006, p. 6) pointed out, the irony is that, "*for using the t-test we need Normal distributions because we have small samples, but the small samples also prohibit us from checking the distribution shape.*"

Finally, the t test in this setting is also susceptible to outliers. That is, rare classifier performances that deviate largely from the performance on other domains will tend to skew the distribution, thereby affecting the power of the t test because they increase the estimated standard deviation of the performance measures.

With regard to McNemar's test, which works on nominal variables[10] as can easily be seen in the use of the contingency matrix in this case, extending the test to the case of multiple domains is not straightforward. There are other tests available, for instance, Cochran's test, that aims at extending this approach to multiple-classifier testing on multiple domains. However, as we will see later, we have better alternatives to perform such testing. Finally, also note that McNemar's test works on binary classification data. The related extension to the multiclass case would be the marginal homogeneity test, which we do not describe here, but can be found in many standard statistical hypothesis testing texts.

6.5.4 The t Test versus McNemar's Test

The main differences between the t test and McNemar's test can be cast along the lines of the respective assumptions that these make and the type of performance measures that they apply to. As previously mentioned, the t test is a parametric test and hence makes certain assumptions on the distribution of the classifiers' performance measures obtained on the datasets. We previously discussed these assumptions and their consequent implications. Being a nonparametric test, McNemar's test makes no such assumptions. On the other hand, the difference between the two should also be considered with regard to the type of performance measures that these tests take into account. Unlike the t test that can work on interval variables, McNemar's test works on nominal performance measures, as already mentioned. That is, the performance measures dealt with by McNemar's test can take into account only whether the data (or instances) were classified correctly or not, much like an indicator function, and do not give any quantification of such measures. Nonparametric alternatives that take interval variables into account are discussed in the next section, where we also show how they can be modeled to the current settings.

---

[10] This corresponds to classifying data into two categories but not quantifying the extent of classification.

Qualitatively, these two tests have been compared on the grounds of their respective powers and type I error probabilities too. As mentioned previously, Dieterich (1998) compared McNemar's test applied to a testing set proper (with no cross-validation) to various cross-validated versions of the t test. In his experiments, McNemar's test was thus at a disadvantage with respect to the t test. Yet he concluded that McNemar's test has as low, if not a lower, probability of making a type I error than the other tests in the study, including the t test. McNemar's test was also shown to have slightly less power than the 5×2-CV t test and a lot less power than the cross-validated t test (but the cross-validated t test had a higher probability of making a type I Error).[11] Dietterich's conclusions thus suggest that McNemar's test may be a good alternative to the t test; however, it is important to recall that McNemar's test applies only under the condition in which the number of disagreements between the two classifiers is large (generally, $c_{01}^{Mc} + c_{10}^{Mc} \geq 20$), as previously discussed.

6.6 Comparing *Two Classifiers* on *Multiple Domains*

Let us now further our discussion to the more practical situation in which classifiers are compared according to their performance on multiple domains. Whereas this section considers the case in which *two* classifiers are compared on various domains, the next section considers the more general case in which *several classifiers* are compared on multiple domains. To compare two classifiers on multiple domains, a natural approach would be to extend the tests that compare them on individual domains. We considered this case in Subsection 6.5.3 and the issues therein. Another approach would be averaging over the performance of classifiers over various domains. However, such averaging of the performance of each classifier on all the domains is not very meaningful because the domains are, in almost any practical scenario, quite different from one another. In addition, averages are susceptible to outliers, which can understandably be present in such a situation.

Hence, in this section, we present two nonparametric tests, the sign test and Wilcoxon's Signed-Rank test, which do not make assumptions such as commensurability of performance measures and are relatively robust to outliers. We then compare these two approaches to discuss their respective pros and cons. Let us start with the simpler one, the sign test.

6.6.1 The Sign Test (Wins, Losses, and Ties)

The sign test is perhaps the simplest of all statistical tests with the added advantage of being nonparametric. The sign test is an estimate of the number of

[11] We recall that a type I error of a statistical test corresponds to the probability of incorrectly detecting a difference when no such difference exists and that the power of a test corresponds to the ability of the test to discover a difference when such a difference does exist. Please refer to Chapter 2 for further details about these concepts.

trials on which an algorithm outperforms the other based on some performance measure. Hence if we have n datasets (trials) and two classifiers f_1 and f_2, we calculate the number of datasets on which f_1 outperforms f_2 (call this n_{f_1}) and the number of datasets on which f_2 outperforms f_1 (call this n_{f_2}).[12] Hence we have $n_{f_1} + n_{f_2} \leq n$. The inequality holds in case we have an odd number of ties as we subsequently see.

The null hypothesis states that the classifiers being compared are equivalent and hence, on average, win $n/2$ number of times over all the trials. Note that the number of trials on which the classifiers perform equally well is split between the two counts evenly (except when this number is odd, in which case one count can be ignored). Hence, if the null hypothesis were to hold, then the number of wins should follow a binomial distribution. A lookup in the table of critical values (See the table in Appendix A.4) shows the critical number of datasets (trials) for which one algorithm should outperform another to be considered statistically significantly better at the α significance level. More specifically, a classifier should perform better on at least w_α datasets relative to the total number of datasets used in the experiment to be considered statistically better at the α significance level.

When scaled to a greater number of trials than the 100 shown in the table of Appendix A.4, the null hypothesis assumes them to be normally distributed with mean $n/2$ and variance $\sqrt{n}/2$. In this case, a z statistic[13] (for classifier f_1) can be computed whereby an algorithm is significantly better with $p < \alpha$ if the number of wins for this algorithm n_{f_1} is such that

$$n_{f_1} \geq \frac{n}{2} + z_\alpha \frac{\sqrt{n}}{2}.$$

The values of z_α are found in Appendix A.1.

Finally, for each dataset, we can summarize the classifier performance by using any linear performance measure, e.g., the average 10-fold cross-validation error or accuracy. Let us illustrate the sign test with an example.

Example 6.6. We use Table 6.3[14] for our example, which lists the performance of eight classifiers on 10 different domains. From the table, we see that NB wins 4 times over SVM, ties once, and loses 5 times. Conversely, SVM wins 5 times, ties once, and loses 4 times. Because the table of critical values in Appendix A.4 shows that, for 10 datasets, a classifier needs to win at least 8 times for the null hypothesis to be rejected with significance level $\alpha = 0.05$ (or $\alpha = 0.1$ in the two-tailed test), we cannot reject the null hypothesis with the sign test. It cannot

[12] This can also be scaled up for comparing multiple classifiers by constructing a matrix of pairwise comparisons.
[13] A z statistic corresponds to the standard (or unit) normal distribution assumption.
[14] Please note that the results in the table are listed in percentages that are easily readable. These numbers will be divided by 100 in the context of certain statistical tests, as will be further discussed.

Table 6.3. *Several classifiers applied to several datasets*

Dataset	NB	SVM	1NN	ADA(DT)	BAG(REP)	C4.5	RF	RIP
Anneal	96.43	99.44 v	99.11 v	83.63*	98.22	98.44 v	99.55 v	98.22 v
Audiology	73.42	81.34	75.22	46.46*	76.54	77.87	79.15	76.07
Balance scale	72.30	91.51 v	79.03	72.31	82.89 v	76.65	80.97 v	81.60 v
Breast cancer	71.70	66.16	65.74*	70.28	67.84	75.54	69.99	68.88
Contact lenses	71.67	71.67	63.33	71.67	68.33	81.67	71.67	75.00
Pima diabetes	74.36	77.08	70.17	74.35	74.61	73.83	74.88	75.00
Glass	70.63	62.21	70.50	44.91*	69.63	66.75	79.87	70.95
Hepatitis	83.21	80.63	80.63	82.54	84.50	83.79	84.58	78.00
Hypothyroid	98.22	93.58*	91.52*	93.21*	99.55 v	99.58 v	99.39 v	99.42
Tic-tac-toe	69.62	99.90 v	81.63 v	72.54 v	92.07 v	85.07 v	93.94 v	97.39 v
Average	78.15	82.35	77.69	71.19	81.42	81.92	83.40	82.05 v
t test		3/6/1	2/6/2	1/5/4	3/7/0	3/7/0	4/6/0	4/6/0

Notes: A "v" indicates the significance test's success in favor of the corresponding classifier against NB while a "*" indicates this success in favor of NB. No symbol indicates the result between the concerned classifier and NB were not found to be statistically significantly different.

be rejected with significance level $\alpha = 0.05$ with a one-tailed significance test, either.

From Table 6.3, we now compare RF with ADA and see that RF beats ADA on 8 domains, ties on 1, and loses on 1. The sign test score for RF is thus of 8.5, which indicates that, in this case, the null hypothesis can be rejected with significance level $\alpha = 0.1$, as well as with significance level $\alpha = 0.05$, for the two-sided test.

The sign test is not illustrated in R because its computation is very simple to perform manually.

6.6.2 Wilcoxon's Signed-Rank Test

The Wilcoxon's Signed-Rank test for matched pairs (for paired scores) abides by the following *logic*:

> Given the same population tested under different circumstances C1 and C2. If there is improvement in C2, then most of the results recorded in C2 will be greater (better) than those recorded in C1 and those that are not greater will be smaller by only a small amount.

Also known as Wilcoxon's T test, this test is useful when a comparison is to be made between two circumstances $C1$ and $C2$ under which a common population is tested.[15] Wilcoxon's Signed-Rank test can thus be used as a nonparametric alternative to the matched-pair t-test. We denote the T statistic for Wilcoxon's test as T_{wilcox} to avoid ambiguity with the usage of T for a test set.

---

[15] This corresponds to testing the performance of two classifiers on some given datasets.

To see this, we revert to the same convention we used in the t test. Let us consider two classifiers f_1 and f_2 and the two conditions corresponding to their performance measures $\text{pm}(f_1)$ and $\text{pm}(f_2)$. The procedure is as follows:

- For each trial $i, i \in \{1, 2, \ldots, n\}$, we calculate the difference in performance measures of the two classifiers $d_i = \text{pm}_i(f_2) - \text{pm}_i(f_1)$, where the subscript i denotes the corresponding quantity for the ith trial.
- We rank all the absolute values of d_i. That is, we rank $|d_i|$. In the case of ties, we assign average ranks to each tied d_i.
- Next, we calculate the following sum of ranks:

$$W_{s1} = \sum_{i=1}^{n} I(d_i > 0)\text{rank}(d_i),$$

$$W_{s2} = \sum_{i=1}^{n} I(d_i < 0)\text{rank}(d_i).$$

- Assuming that there are r differences whose values are zero, there are two approaches to dealing with this issue. The first is to ignore these differences, in which case n takes on the new value of $n - r$. And all the further calculations follow in the same manner, as previously stated. Another approach is to split the ranks of these r zero-valued differences between W_{s1} and W_{s2} equally. If r is odd, we just ignore one of the zero-valued differences. Hence, in this case, n retains its original value (except when r is odd, where $n = n - 1$). The W_{s1} and W_{s2} are defined as

$$W_{s1} = \sum_{i=1}^{n} I(d_i > 0)\text{rank}(d_i) + \frac{1}{2} \sum_{i=1}^{n} I(d_i = 0)\text{rank}(d_i),$$

$$W_{s2} = \sum_{i=1}^{n} I(d_i < 0)\text{rank}(d_i) + \frac{1}{2} \sum_{i=1}^{n} I(d_i = 0)\text{rank}(d_i).$$

- Next, a T_{wilcox} statistic is calculated as $T_{\text{wilcox}} = \min(W_{s1}, W_{s2})$.
- In the case of smaller n's ($n \leq 25$), exact critical values of T can be looked up from the tabulated critical values of T_{wilcox} to verify if the null hypothesis can be rejected.
- In the case of larger n's, the T_{wilcox} distribution can be approximated normally. We compute the following z statistic as

$$z_{\text{wilcox}} = \frac{T_{\text{wilcox}} - \mu_{T_{\text{wilcox}}}}{\sigma_{T_{\text{wilcox}}}}$$

where $\mu_{T_{\text{wilcox}}}$ is the mean of the normal approximation of the distribution of T_{wilcox} when the null hypothesis holds:

$$\mu_{T_{\text{wilcox}}} = \frac{n(n+1)}{4};$$

Table 6.4. *Classifiers* NB *and* SVM *data ran on 10 realistic domains and used in the Wilcoxon test example*

Domain no.	NB accuracy	SVM accuracy	NB–SVM	|NB–SVM|	Ranks (|NB–SVM|)	± Ranks (|NB–SVM|)
1	0.9643	0.9944	−0.0301	0.0301	3	−3
2	0.7342	0.8134	−0.0792	0.0792	6	−6
3	0.7230	0.9151	−0.1921	0.1921	8	−8
4	0.7170	0.6616	+0.0554	0.0554	5	+5
5	0.7167	0.7167	0	0	Remove	Remove
6	0.7436	0.7708	−0.0272	0.0272	2	−2
7	0.7063	0.6221	+0.0842	0.0842	7	+7
8	0.8321	0.8063	+0.0258	0.0258	1	+1
9	0.9822	0.9358	+0.0464	0.0464	4	+4
10	0.6962	0.9990	−0.3028	0.3028	9	−9

and $\sigma_{T_{\text{wilcox}}}$ is the standard deviation of normally approximated T_{wilcox} when the null hypothesis holds:

$$\sigma_{T_{\text{wilcox}}} = \sqrt{\frac{n(n+1)(2n+1)}{24}}.$$

- Next, we look up the table for normal distribution to assess if the null hypothesis can be rejected for the desired significance level.
- In both cases, i.e., for smaller n's as well as large n's, the null hypothesis is rejected if T_{wilcox} is smaller than the critical values listed for n and the appropriate significance test considered in the respective tables.

Let us now illustrate this test with the following example that compares the NB and the SVM classifiers on 10 domains, as per the first two columns of Table 6.3, but divided by 100 to obtain accuracy rates in the [0, 1] interval. The results of the analysis performed to apply the Wilcoxon test are shown in Table 6.4.

The sum of signed ranks is then computed, yielding the values of $W_{S1} = 17$ and $W_{S2} = 28$. According to the algorithm previously listed,

$$T_{\text{wilcox}} = \min(W_{S1}, W_{S2}) = 17.$$

We look through the Wilcoxon table in Appendix A.5 for $n = 10 - 1 = 9$ degrees of freedom and find that the critical value V, which must be larger than T_{wilcox} for the null hypothesis (which states that the two classifiers are not significantly different) to be rejected at the 0.05 level, is $V = 8$ for the one-sided test and $V = 5$ for the two-sided test. In both cases, we thus conclude that the hypothesis cannot be rejected at significance level $p = 0.05$.

This example is repeated in R in Subsection 6.9.2.

6.6.3 Sign Test versus Wilcoxon's Signed-Rank Test

As we saw previously, unlike Wilcoxon's test, the sign test generally takes only ordinal variables into account (that is, win/loss/ties) and not interval variables (which can quantify the performances). The sign test takes into account only how often the two performance measures differ with regard to the median difference, that is, whether these differences lie above or below the median. However, it does not take into account the extent or even the direction (sign) of this difference. In contrast, Wilcoxon's Signed-Rank test does factor in this information. Consequently, Wilcoxon's Signed-Rank test is more powerful than the sign test. For the sign test to reject the null hypothesis, a classifier needs to be better than the other on almost all the datasets. Moreover, Wilcoxon's Signed-Rank test assumes qualitative commensurability of performance measures in the sense that the larger differences are considered more important. However, the extent (magnitude) of these differences is not taken into account. On the other hand, the sign test does not make this commensurability assumption on the performance measures. Even though the sign test could be used with interval variables, Wilcoxon's test remains a preferred choice. In the case of ordinal variables, the sign test can be used to replace the McNemar's test for the case in which the classifier disagreements are relatively few and hence not approximated by a χ^2 distribution.

When applied to comparing two classifiers on multiple domains, the t test can be more powerful than the Wilcoxon's Signed-Rank test when the parametric assumptions made by the t test are met. However, Wilcoxon's test is the method of choice when this is not the case.

6.6.4 Adapting the Tests to a Single-Domain Environment

Just as we showed how we can extend the t test to multiple domains, we can also customize, at least in principle, the sign test and the Wilcoxon's Signed-Rank test to the case of comparing classifiers on a single domain. This can be done if multiple trials can basically be made on the concerned domain. Methods of interest would include either permuted repetition (i.e., multiple trials over a dataset with examples randomly permuted or reordered) or some sort of resampling method such as cross-validation. The resulting classifier performance measures over each trial can then be used for comparison in the two tests. The multiple trials, however, violate the independent domain assumption because practically all the datasets on which the measures are obtained would overlap. This results in a high bias in the performance estimates. Moreover, the tests compare the respective performances of the two classifiers on each trial. Hence there is a very high probability that one classifier consistently outperforms the other (especially if the learning algorithm is robust to permutations of the training data). This would result in unfairly skewing the test results in favor of this classifier. A relatively better method, hence, would be to use a single trial of cross-validation because in this case the performances of classifiers over each fold can be compared, resulting in (relatively) independent performance assessments, unlike the multiple-trial version. However, it should be noted that, even in this case, the training sets of various folds can have a significant overlap, especially in the case of small sample sizes and larger numbers of folds considered in the cross-validated resampling regimen. We subsequently illustrate an example of how the sign test and Wilcoxon's test can be used in the single-domain scenario.[16]

The Sign Test on a Single Domain

In the setting of two classifier comparisons over a single domain, the basic principle of the sign test remains the same, except that we now compare the classifier performances over individual folds of a cross-validated trial over a single dataset. This is in contrast to the comparison of performances on individual datasets in the mutiple-domain setting. Let us illustrate this with an example.

Example 6.7. In this example, we again compare the performance of c45 and NB classifiers on the labor data, but this time, we do so over a single 10-fold cross-validated run. Recall that the data were presented in a single 10-fold cross-validated run from Table 2.3 of Chapter 2 (the first trial). Let us consider the first and third lines of trial 1 in this table. From these results obtained on the 10 folds of the first run of the experiment for both c45 and NB, we can see that NB wins 7 times over c45, that the two classifiers tie 2 times, and that it loses 1 time. Splitting the 2 ties between the two classifiers gives NB $(7 + 1) = 8$ wins, over 10 folds.

To find out whether the hypothesis that the two algorithms perform equally well is rejected at the 0.05 level, we check the table in Appendix A.4 for the number of trials $n = 10$. The critical value obtained at that level for both a one-sided and a two-sided test at significance level 0.05 is 8. Because the number of wins should technically be strictly higher than the critical value, we cannot reject the null hypothesis at the 0.05 level. On the other hand, because the values are equal, it might be acceptable to issue a borderline rejection at that level. This goes on to show the relative weakness of the sign test as discussed in Subsection 6.6.3, because, as will be subsequently seen the Wilcoxon Signed-Rank test will have no difficulty rejecting the null hypothesis.

As previously mentioned, the sign test is easily computed manually and does not require the R statistical software's assistance.

---

[16] This, however does in no way condone the view that these tests should be used in a single-domain scenario.

Table 6.5. *Classifiers* c45 *and* nb *data used for the Wilcoxon test example on a single cross-validation run*

Domain no.	c45 scores	NB scores	c45–NB	|c45–NB|	Ranks (|c45–NB|)	± Ranks (|c45–NB|)
1	0.5	0.1667	+0.3333	0.3333	6.5	+6.5
2	0	0	0	0	Remove	Remove
3	0.3333	0	+0.3333	0.3333	6.5	+6.5
4	0	0	0	0	Remove	Remove
5	0.3333	0	+0.3333	0.3333	6.5	+6.5
6	0.3333	0.1667	+ 0.1666	0.1666	1	+1
7	0.3333	0	+0.3333	0.3333	6.5	+6.5
8	0.2	0.4	−0.2	0.2	3	−3
9	0.2	0	+0.2	0.2	3	+3
10	0.2	0	+0.2	0.2	3	+3

Wilcoxon's Signed-Rank Test for a Single Domain

We illustrate this process on the same example as the one used for the sign test, i.e., we consider the first and third lines in trial 1 of Table 2.3 in Chapter 2.

Example 6.8. In this example, we are comparing c4.5 and NB on the labor dataset on the first of the 10 runs presented in Table 2.3, trying to establish whether the two classifiers behave significantly differently from one another. In more detail, Table 6.5 lists the fold number in the first column; the error rate of c4.5 on this fold in the first run in the second column; the error rate of NB on this fold in the first run is in the third column; the difference between the two scores just listed, in the fourth; the absolute value of this difference in the fifth; the rank of this absolute value in the sixth (with the folds for which no difference is found, removed); and the signed rank of this absolute value (where the sign of column 4 is added to the rank of column 6), in column 7.

The sum of signed ranks is then computed, yielding the values of $W_{S1} = 33$ and $W_{S2} = 3$. According to the algorithm previously listed,

$$T_{\text{wilcox}} = \min(W_{S1}, W_{S2}) = 3.$$

We look through the Wilcoxon table in Appendix A.5 for $n = 10 - 2 = 8$, the number of trials in our example, and find the critical value V, which must be larger than T_{wilcox} for the null Hypothesis to be rejected. At the 0.05 level, $V = 5$ for the one-sided test and $V = 3$ for the two-sided test. We thus conclude that the hypothesis can be rejected with significance $p = 0.05$ whether we use a one-sided or a two-sided test (though we are right at the limit for the two-sided test).

The same example using R is presented in Subsection 6.9.2.

6.7   Comparing *Multiple Classifiers* on *Multiple Domains*

We now move to an even more common situation in classifier evaluation in which large studies pit multiple classifiers on multiple domains. As mentioned previously, the t test can be appropriate for the comparison of two classifiers on a single domain, but it should not be used in simultaneous comparisons of various classifiers on multiple domains. However, it is not uncommon for the t test to be repeated in machine learning studies. The problems arising as a result of this usage have also been pointed out (Salzberg, 1997; Demšar, 2006). These problems can be traced to two main reasons. The first reason is quite practical in the sense that performing such pairwise testing requires too many tests for two classifiers to be performed in order to conduct all the pairwise comparisons possible in these experiments. Furthermore, analyzing the results in a unified manner is also rendered impractical. However, of grave concern is the second reason, an implication of performing such pairwise comparisons. The more the pairwise tests are performed, the greater the chance of committing a type I error. For example, if one test gives us a 5% probability of making a type I error, then two tests will give us a 10% chance of doing so. Ten tests give us a 40% chance of doing so (see, for instance, Hinton, 1995, p. 105).

Statistics offers solutions so as to avoid performing such pairwise testing and subsequently dealing with the issues such testing causes. In particular, there is a family of statistical tests specifically designed for multiple hypothesis testing. Both parametric and nonparametric alternatives to perform multiple hypothesis testing are available with their respective strengths and limitations within this family. The general methodology for performing such tests is twofold.[17] The first step is to use multiple hypothesis tests, also known as omnibus tests. These are aimed at confirming whether the observed differences between various classifier performances are statistically significantly different. That is, omnibus tests, by rejecting the null hypothesis, convey whether there exists at least one pair of classifiers with significantly different performances. This confirmation, if obtained, is then followed by what are known as post hoc tests that enable identification of these significantly different pairs of classifiers.[18]

In this section, we look at two principal omnibus tests deemed most appropriate for the multiple-classifier evaluation. The first one is the very well-known parametric test for multiple hypothesis testing: the analysis of variance or ANOVA. The second is a less-utilized nonparametric alternative called the Friedman test. We also study the appropriate post hoc tests pertaining to both

---

[17] Sometimes threefold when some preanalysis is performed using the so-called pre-hoc tests.

[18] Salzberg (1997) suggests another approach to deal with the problem of multiple comparisons: the binomial test with the Bonferroni correction for multiple comparisons. However, he himself remarks that such a test does not have sufficient power and that the Bonferroni correction is too drastic. Demšar (2006) agrees that the field of statistics produced more powerful tests to deal with these conditions.

these cases. For the case of ANOVA, we detail two of the main versions as they both apply to the evaluation of learning approaches, the difference between which will be clear from the description.

6.7.1 One-Way Repeated-Measure ANOVA

The analysis of variance, or ANOVA, is similar to the t test in that it deals with differences between sample means. However, unlike the t test, which is restricted to the difference between two means, ANOVA allows assessing whether the differences observed between any number of means are statistically significant. If the performances of classifiers on various datasets are organized as groups (i.e., the performance of all classifiers on dataset 1, as one group; the performance of classifier f on all the domains, as another group, and so on) then ANOVA monitors three different kinds of variations in the data:

- within-group variation,
- between-group variation, and
- total variation = within-group variation + between-group variation.

Each of the preceding variations is represented by sums of squares (SS) of the variations, as we will see further. This is a generalization of the paired t test and can compare performance measures of various classifiers across various datasets to see if the difference observed is statistically significant. The null hypothesis, in this case, is that the difference in the performance measures of the classifiers across the datasets is statistically insignificant.

We can partition the basic deviation between the individual performance measures and the overall mean of the performance measures in the experiment. Let us consider n different datasets and k different classifiers whose performances are to be compared on these n datasets.

We adopt the following notations: $\overline{\overline{pm}}$ refers to the overall mean of the performance measures of all the classifiers across all the datasets; pm_{ij} refers to the performance measure of classifier f_j on dataset S_i; $\overline{pm}_{i.}$ refers to the mean performance measure across all classifiers for dataset S_i; $\overline{pm}_{.j}$ refers to the mean of performance measure for classifier f_j across all datasets.

ANOVA models the performance measure of a classifier f_j on the dataset S_i as

$$pm_{ij} = \overline{\overline{pm}} + \alpha_i + e_{ij},$$

where α_i represents the between-dataset performance measure variability assumed to be distributed normally with mean 0 and variance σ_A^2 and e_{ij} represents the within-dataset performance measure variability assumed to be normally distributed with mean 0 and variance σ^2. That is, this model studies whether there is an overall difference between the performance measures of various classifiers, and what percentage of the total variation is attributable to the variability of performance measures within datasets and performance measures between datasets.[19] Here each e_{ij} is assumed to be independent of α_i and any other e_{ij}'s.

It is assumed that the underlying mean of the performance measure for each dataset is given by $\overline{\overline{\text{pm}}} + \alpha_i$, where α_i is distributed normally with mean 0 and variance σ_A^2. Hence σ_A^2 basically represents the extent of the variance in the performance measures between datasets. Similarly, the variance in the performance measure within dataset (that is, on the same dataset) is given by σ^2. Hence, for classifiers, the performance measures on dataset S_i will be distributed normally with mean $\overline{\overline{\text{pm}}} + \alpha_i$ with variance σ^2.

Now, if the terms MS_{pm} and MS_{Error} represent the measures of variability between and within classifiers respectively, then it can be shown that

$$\sigma^2 = E(\text{MS}_{\text{Error}}),$$

where $E(\cdot)$ denotes the expected value. Further,

$$\sigma_A^2 = E\left(\frac{\text{MS}_{\text{pm}} - \text{MS}_{\text{Error}}}{n}\right).$$

Before we define MS_{pm} and MS_{Error}, we need to define some measures of variations.

The variation that is due to the classifiers is quantified by the SS of the classifiers' performance measures (with degrees of freedom $= k - 1$):

$$\text{SS}_{\text{pm}} = \sum_{j=1}^{k}\sum_{i=1}^{n}(\overline{\text{pm}}_{.j} - \overline{\overline{\text{pm}}})^2 = n\sum_{j=1}^{k}(\overline{\text{pm}}_{.j} - \overline{\overline{\text{pm}}})^2.$$

Similarly the variation within datasets over various classifiers' performances is quantified by the SS of this block of interest[20] (with degrees of freedom $= n - 1$):

$$\text{SS}_{\text{Block}} = \sum_{j=1}^{k}\sum_{i=1}^{n}(\overline{\text{pm}}_{i.} - \overline{\overline{\text{pm}}})^2 = k\sum_{i=1}^{n}(\overline{\text{pm}}_{i.} - \overline{\overline{\text{pm}}})^2.$$

The next term, denoted as the Sum of Squares Total, defines the total variation over the classifiers' performances on all datasets (with degrees of freedom $= kn - 1$):

$$\text{SS}_{\text{Total}} = \sum_{j=1}^{k}\sum_{i=1}^{n}(\text{pm}_{ij} - \overline{\overline{\text{pm}}})^2.$$

The variation in the error follows naturally as the difference between the total variation and the combined variation accounted for by SS_{Block} and SS_{pm} [with

---

[19] Note, however, that we are not interested in quantifying these variabilities.
[20] See Section 6.4 for an explanation on blocking experiment design.

degrees of freedom $= (n-1)(k-1)]$:

$$SS_{Error} = SS_{Total} - (SS_{Block} + SS_{pm}).$$

Let us now define the quantities that enable us to model the variations of classifiers' performance measures over datasets. The first quantity, the between mean squares (MS), is a measure of variability *between* classifiers:

$$MS_{pm} = \frac{SS_{pm}}{k-1},$$

where $k-1$ are the degrees of freedom for SS_{pm}.

The second quantity, the within mean squares or mean-squares error, measures the variability *within* classifiers:

$$MS_{Error} = \frac{SS_{Error}}{(n-1)(k-1)},$$

where $(n-1)(k-1)$ are the degrees of freedom of SS_{Error}.

Finally, the statistic of interest, the F ratio, can be obtained as

$$F = \frac{MS_{pm}}{MS_{Error}}.$$

This F ratio can then be looked up in the table of critical value for F ratios to assess whether the null hypothesis can be refuted for the desired significance level. The degrees of freedom used are $df_1 = df_{SS_{pm}} = k-1$ and $df_2 = df_{MS_{Error}} = (n-1)(k-1)$. Note that the null hypothesis is rejected if the F ratio previously obtained is greater than the critical value in the lookup table. That is, larger F's demonstrate greater statistical significance than smaller ones. As with the z and t statistics, there are tables of significance levels associated with the F ratio. (Please refer to Appendix A.6 for these tables.)

Briefly summarizing, the goal of ANOVA is to discover whether the differences in means (the classifiers' performances) between different groups (i.e., over different datasets) are statistically significant. To do so, ANOVA partitions the total variance into variance caused by random error (the within-group variation) and variance caused by actual differences between means (the between-group variation). If the null hypothesis holds, then the within-group SS should be about the same as the between-group SS. We can compare these two variations by using the F test, which checks whether the ratio of the two variations, measured as mean squares, is significantly greater than one.

An Illustration

We illustrate this process with the following hypothetical example:

Assume that classifiers f_A, f_B, and f_C obtain the percentage accuracy results shown in Table 6.6 on domains 1–10 (we assume that each entry in the table is the result of 10-fold cross-validation).

Table 6.6. *Sample accuracy results for classifiers f_A, f_B, and f_C on 10 domains*

Domain	Classifier f_A	Classifier f_B	Classifier f_C
1	85.83	75.86	84.19
2	85.91	73.18	85.90
3	86.12	69.08	83.83
4	85.82	74.05	85.11
5	86.28	74.71	86.38
6	86.42	65.90	81.20
7	85.91	76.25	86.38
8	86.10	75.10	86.75
9	85.95	70.50	88.03
10	86.12	73.95	87.18

Dividing all the results by 100 to obtain an accuracy rate estimate that can be modeled by the statistical tests for Table 6.6, we have $\overline{\overline{pm}} = \frac{81.47}{100} = 0.8147$ and the corresponding $pm_{i.}$ and $pm_{.j}$ values as shown in Tables 6.7 and 6.8 respectively. Let us calculate the relevant quantities:

$$SS_{pm} = n \sum_{j=1}^{k} (\overline{pm}_{.j} - \overline{\overline{pm}})^2$$

$$= 10 \sum_{j=1}^{3} (\overline{pm}_{.j} - 0.8147)^2$$

$$= 10 \left[(0.8605 - 0.8147)^2 + (0.7286 - 0.8147)^2 + (0.8550 - 0.8147)^2 \right]$$

$$= 0.11135,$$

$$SS_{Block} = k \sum_{i=1}^{n} (\overline{pm}_{i.} - \overline{\overline{pm}})^2$$

$$= 3 \sum_{i=1}^{10} (\overline{pm}_{i.} - 0.8147)^2$$

$$= 3 \left[(0.8196 - 0.8147)^2 + (0.8166 - 0.8147)^2 + (0.7968 - 0.8147)^2 \right.$$

$$+ (0.8166 - 0.8147)^2 + (0.8246 - 0.8147)^2 + (0.7784 - 0.8147)^2$$

$$+ (0.8285 - 0.8147)^2 + (0.8265 - 0.8147)^2 + (0.8149 - 0.8147)^2$$

$$\left. + (0.8242 - 0.8147)^2 \right]$$

$$= 0.006555.$$

Table 6.7. $\overline{\mathrm{pm}}_{i.}$ for the 10 domains on
results of Table 6.6

Domain	$\overline{\mathrm{pm}}_{i.}$
1	0.8196
2	0.8166
3	0.7968
4	0.8166
5	0.8246
6	0.7784
7	0.8285
8	0.8265
9	0.8149
10	0.8242

Similarly, we get

$$
\mathrm{SS}_{\mathrm{Total}} = \sum_{j=1}^{k} \sum_{i=1}^{n} (\mathrm{pm}_{ij} - \overline{\overline{\mathrm{pm}}})^2
$$

$$
= \sum_{j=1}^{3} \sum_{i=1}^{10} (\mathrm{pm}_{ij} - 0.8147)^2
$$

$$
= 0.1249,
$$

$$
\mathrm{SS}_{\mathrm{Error}} = \mathrm{SS}_{\mathrm{Total}} - (\mathrm{SS}_{\mathrm{Block}} + \mathrm{SS}_{\mathrm{pm}})
$$

$$
= 0.1249 - (0.006555 + 0.11135)
$$

$$
= 0.006995,
$$

$$
\mathrm{MS}_{\mathrm{pm}} = \frac{\mathrm{SS}_{\mathrm{pm}}}{k - 1}
$$

$$
= \frac{0.111350}{3 - 1}
$$

$$
= 0.055675,
$$

Table 6.8. $\overline{\mathrm{pm}}_{.j}$ for the 3 classifiers on
results of Table 6.6

Domain	$\overline{\mathrm{pm}}_{.j}$
f_A	0.8605
f_B	0.7286
f_C	0.8550

$$MS_{Error} = \frac{SS_{Error}}{(n-1)(k-1)}$$

$$= \frac{0.006995}{(10-1)(3-1)}$$

$$= 0.000389.$$

Finally,

$$F = \frac{0.055675}{0.000389}$$

$$= 143.12.$$

We compare $F = 143.12$ with the value we find in the F table of Appendix A.6.2 for a p value $= 0.05$ and $df_1 = 2$ and $df_2 = 18$: 3.555 for a one-sided test and 4.560 for a two-sided test. Because $143.12 > 4.560 > 3.5546$, we reject the null hypothesis at significance level 0.05, using both the one-tailed and the two-tailed test. We can thus conclude that at least one group is different from the others.

The procedure is also illustrated using R on this example and on a larger and more realistic one in Subsection 6.9.3.

6.7.2 One-Way ANOVA

The model in the case of one-way ANOVA is a linear model trying to assess if the difference in the performance measures of classifiers over different datasets is statistically significant, just as the preceding one-way repeated-measures ANOVA does, but does not distinguish between the performance measures variability within datasets and the performance measure variability between datasets. That is, both these variabilities are analyzed in a combined manner. This results in a simpler model:

$$pm_{ij} = \overline{\overline{pm}} + \alpha_i + e_{ij},$$

where $\alpha_i = \overline{pm}_{.j} - \overline{\overline{pm}}$ and e_{ij} refers to the random error in the performance measures and is distributed normally with mean 0 and variance σ^2. Hence it follows that the performance measures for the classifiers over each dataset S_i are distributed normally about the mean $\overline{\overline{pm}} + \alpha_i$ with variance σ^2.

In terms of the calculation, the only difference with regard to the one-way repeated-measures ANOVA previously described is that we do not subtract the block variability (that is, variability of performance measures over all classifiers within datasets) from SS_{Error}. And all calculations proceed accordingly.

Note that the degrees of freedom for SS_{Error} become $nk - k$ because

$$SS_{Error} = SS_{Total} - SS_{pm}.$$

As a result, the mean-squares error becomes

$$MS_{Error} = \frac{SS_{Error}}{(nk - k)}. \tag{6.4}$$

The F ratio is, as before,

$$F = \frac{MS_{pm}}{MS_{Error}},$$

but with the *new* MS_{Error} term of Equation (6.4).

Finally, as before, this F ratio can be looked up in the table of critical F-ratio values, and the null hypothesis can be refuted if it is found to be greater than the F value in the lookup table for the desired significance level.

As we will see in Subsection 6.7.4, one-way ANOVA is not as powerful as one-way repeated-measures ANOVA and also does not deal with correlated settings (i.e., when the correlation of the performance measure by virtue of being measured on matched datasets is taken into account). It will still be illustrated in R in Subsection 6.9.3.

6.7.3 A Case for N-Way ANOVA

Looking at the preceding application of one-way ANOVA procedures, a natural question that arises is whether it is possible to utilize more sophisticated methods such as N-way ANOVA (more specifically N-way repeated-measure ANOVA) to obtain statistical significance testing over more than one performance measure for the learning algorithms to be compared. This has, so far, not been done in the machine learning and data mining community and is currently an open research question.

6.7.4 A Brief Discussion on ANOVA

The Difference Between One-Way and Repeated-measures ANOVA

In the sense of dealing with the variations, the repeated-measures ANOVA functions in a manner similar to that of the matched-samples t test. Just as the t test weighs the t statistic by the variations in the means so as to take into account the variations not attributed to the actual classifier performance (variations intrinsic to the data), the repeated-measures ANOVA removes such variations by explicitly removing the within-dataset variation over classifiers' performance from the total variation. This is not the case for one-way ANOVA. Hence, in this sense, one-way repeated-measures ANOVA is more powerful in discerning performance differences compared with the one-way ANOVA. Also note the difference in the assumptions made by these two tests. One-way ANOVA assumes the samples to be independent, unlike the repeated-measures

ANOVA, in which the correlation of the samples, i.e., classifiers' performance measures obtained on the same datasets, is taken into account. Hence, in general, one-way repeated-measures ANOVA is the best-suited parametric test in most scenarios pertaining to classifier evaluation. However, before it is employed, the user should be well advised about the assumptions that ANOVA makes and that should be verified for violations (or conformity).

Finally, note that the degrees of freedom with regard to the lookup for sampling distribution of the F ratio differs in the two tests. Unlike earlier tests that use sampling distributions with a 1-degree-of-freedom value, the F distribution results in a sampling distribution dependent on the two values of degrees of freedom corresponding to the mean-square variability between and within the classifiers, i.e., MS_{pm} (the numerator in the F ratio) and MS_{Error} (the denominator in the F ratio), respectively. Further, the one-way ANOVA and the repeated-measures ANOVA treat the MS_{Error} term differently. Consequently the respective sampling distributions of the F statistic in the two cases also differ as a result of this difference in the treatment of the *within* variability term.

Assumptions Made by ANOVA

The repeated-measures ANOVA makes assumptions similar to those made by the matched-samples t test. The samples are assumed to be drawn i.i.d. from a normal (or pseudo-normal) distribution, and the variances between the classifier performances are assumed equal. Finally, on the correlated samples, ANOVA assumes an equal-interval scale on which the variable of interest, i.e., the performance measure, is measured. The datasets used to evaluate the classifiers are generally of the same size. Hence the latter assumptions are generally satisfied in the case of one-way repeated-measures ANOVA. Note that one-way ANOVA further assumes that the classifier performances are noncorrelated across the datasets.

Finally, ANOVA also has an analogue to the equal-variance assumption of the t test. This is generally referred to as the homogenous covariance assumption.[21] The homogenous covariance assumption, just as its equal-variance t-test counterpart, assumes that all types of correlations existing between the interrelated variable of interest (the performance measures) are similar and equal to a considerable degree. This is generally done by assuming that all possible correlation coefficients that quantify such correlations among performances of various classifiers are positive and (approximately) equal in magnitude. In the case of repeated-measures ANOVA, this assumption takes the form of sphericity, stating that the various performance measures have equal variances. This assumption of sphericity made by repeated-measures ANOVA is probably the most difficult to acertain and has potential implications for the post hoc tests too.

---

[21] Although other terms can also be found such as *circularity* and *compound symmetry*.

The Need for a Nonparametric Alternative

Generally, given enough samples, repeated-measures ANOVA is robust to the violations of its normality assumptions to a significant extent. However, as previously mentioned, the difficulty in ascertaining the sphericity assumption has prompted some researchers to discourage the use of ANOVA to perform classifier evaluation (see, for instance, Demšar, 2006). There can be other scenarios in which the underlying assumptions made by ANOVA can be violated. One of the most obvious scenarios would be the case of ranking classifiers. Another can be the case in which the performance measure is only categorical (and not continuous). Further, the assumption also does not hold in cases in which the performance measures, unlike conventional measures such as accuracy, are not monotonic (hence potentially violating the equal-interval assumption and quite possibly also the normality assumption). In such cases, an alternative worth considering would be a nonparametric method of comparing classifier performances. One of the better nonparametric tests available is the Friedman test, which we describe next.

6.7.5 Friedman Test

The Friedman test is the nonparametric counterpart of the repeated-measures one-way ANOVA test. As in the case of Wilcoxon's test, the nonparametric counterpart of the t test, the analysis is based on the ranks of each classifier on each dataset and not on the explicit performance measures. Again, consider n datasets and k classifiers to evaluate. The evaluation proceeds as follows:

- Each algorithm is ranked for each dataset separately, according to the performance measure pm, in ascending order, from the best-performing classifier to the worst-performing classifier. Hence, for dataset S_i, the classifier f_j such that $\text{pm}_{ij} > \text{pm}_{ij'} \forall j', j, j' \in \{1, 2, \ldots, k\}, j \neq j'$, is ranked 1.[22] In the case of a d-way tie just after the rank r, assign a rank of $[(r + 1) + (r + 2) + \cdots + (r + d)]/d$ to each of the tied classifiers.
- Let R_{ij} be the rank of classifier f_j on dataset S_i.
- We compute the following quantities:
  - The mean rank of classifier f_j on all datasets:

$$\overline{R}_{.j} = \frac{1}{n} \sum_{i=1}^{n} R_{ij}.$$

---

[22] Note that here we make an implicit assumption that a higher value of the performance measure (e.g., accuracy) is always preferred. However, there are other performance measures, such as classification error $R_s(f)$ of classifier f, for which a lower value is an indicator of better performance. In this respect, the statement $\text{pm}_{ij} > \text{pm}_{ij'}$ should be interpreted as a representation of this criterion. That is, the classifier f_j will be considered to outperform $f_{j'}$ when f_j *performs better*. In the case of a measure such as accuracy, this would hold when $\text{Acc}(f_j) > \text{Acc}(f_{j'})$, whereas in the case of a measure such as classification error, this would hold when $R_s(f_j) < R_s(f_{j'})$. In this sense, a better representation would be $\text{pm}_{ij} \succ \text{pm}_{ij'}$.

– The overall mean rank:

$$\overline{R} = \frac{1}{nk} \sum_{i=1}^{n} \sum_{j=1}^{k} R_{ij}.$$

– The "sum of squares total" denoting the variation in the ranks:

$$SS_{\text{Total}} = n \sum_{j=1}^{k} (\overline{R}_{.j} - \overline{R})^2.$$

– The "sum of squares error" denoting the error variation:

$$SS_{\text{Error}} = \frac{1}{n(k-1)} \sum_{i=1}^{n} \sum_{j=1}^{k} (R_{ij} - \overline{R})^2.$$

• The test statistic, also called the Friedman statistic, is calculated as

$$\chi_F^2 = \frac{SS_{\text{Total}}}{SS_{\text{Error}}}.$$

• According to the null hypothesis, which states that all the classifiers are equivalent in their performance and hence their average ranks $R_{.j}$ should be equal, the χ_F^2 follows a χ^2 distribution with $k-1$ degrees of freedom for large n (usually > 15) and k (usually > 5).
• Hence, in the case of large n and k, χ_F^2 can be looked up in the table for χ^2 distribution (Appendix A.3). A p value, signifying $P(\chi_{k-1}^2 \geq \chi_F^2)$, is obtained and, if found to be less than the critical value for the desired significance level, the null hypothesis can be rejected.
• In the case of smaller n and k, the χ^2 approximation is imprecise and a table lookup is advised from tables of χ_F^2 values approximated specifically for the Friedman test (Appendix A.7).

Note that the preceding χ_F^2 statistic can be simplified to

$$\chi_F^2 = \left[\frac{12}{n \times k \times (k+1)} \times \sum_{j=1}^{k} (R_{.j})^2 \right] - 3 \times n \times (k+1).$$

An Illustration

To better explain the test, we illustrate our discussion with the example used previously in Table 6.6 in Subsection 6.7.1. We rewrite Table 6.6 in terms of the rank obtained by each classifier on each domain to produce Table 6.9, i.e., we look across each row and assign attribute values 1, 2, or 3 to the largest, the second-largest, and the third-largest accuracies, respectively, that we find. We use average ranks for ties. If there were no differences between the algorithms, we would expect the ranks to be evenly spread among the datasets, i.e., on some datasets, algorithm A would win, on others, algorithm B or C would win, i.e.,

Table 6.9. *Rewriting Table 6.6 as ranks*

Domain	Classifier f_A	Classifier f_B	Classifier f_C
1	1	3	2
2	1.5	3	1.5
3	1	3	2
4	1	3	2
5	2	3	1
6	1	3	2
7	2	3	1
8	2	3	1
9	2	3	1
10	2	3	1
Rank Sums ($R_{.j}$)	15.5	30	14.5

we could not notice any patterns. (f_A, f_B and f_C denote the classifiers output by the algorithms A, B and C respectively).

Consider the example previously used in the case of ANOVA. In our example, we see a pattern: Classifier f_B is always ranked third, whereas Classifiers f_A and f_C share the first and second places more or less equally. (There may not be any difference between f_A and f_C, but this is not what is getting tested here. This question is considered in the next subsection, which discusses post hoc tests.)

We then compute the following statistics for the Friedman test:

$$\chi_F^2 = \left[\frac{12}{n \times k \times (k+1)} \sum_{j=1}^{k} (R_{.j})^2 \right] - 3 \times n \times (k+1),$$

with $k - 1$ degrees of freedom and where k is the number of algorithms and n is the number of domains. In our example, this gives

$$\chi_F^2 = \left[\frac{12}{10 \times 3 \times (3+1)} \sum_{j=1}^{3} (R_{.j})^2 \right] - 3 \times 10 \times (3+1)$$

$$= \left\{ \frac{1}{10} \times [(15.5)^2 + (30)^2 + (14.5)^2] \right\} - 120$$

$$= 15.05,$$

with 2 degrees of freedom.

The critical values for the χ_F^2 distribution for $k = 3$ and $n = 10$ are 6.2 for a 0.05 level of significance and 9.6 at the 0.01 level of significance for a single-tailed test; and 7.8 for a 0.05 level of significance and 12.60 for a 0.002 level of significance for a two-tailed test. Because 15.05 is larger than all these values, we can confidently conclude that there is a significant difference among the three algorithms on these datasets.

An example of the application of Friedman's test using R can be found in Subsection 6.9.3.

6.7.6 Post Hoc Tests

We just described some "omnibus" statistical tests to compare multiple classifiers. These tests give an assessment if the differences in the classifiers' performances on the datasets are statistically significant. However, to have a zoomed-in view of what these differences correspond to precisely, we need to perform a deeper analysis to pinpoint the specific differences.

Post hoc tests are performed when a statistical test comparing multiple classifiers rejects the null hypothesis that the classifiers being compared are alike. These tests help in finding which classifiers actually differ. We describe here some of the prominent post hoc tests that can be used to identify these classifiers. Just as is the case with the omnibus tests, the post-hoc tests can also be categorized as parametric and nonparametric based on their respective assumptions (or lack thereof) on the distribution of classifiers' performance measures. Naturally, the tests designed for one-way repeated-measures ANOVA tend to be parametric whereas those designed for the Friedman test tend to be nonparametric. We start with the post hoc tests that can be utilized in the case of the ANOVA procedure previously described. Note that a repeated-measures setting is recommended for classifier evaluation. Hence the post hoc tests should be used in this setting too.[23]

6.7.7 Post Hoc Tests for ANOVA

Tukey Test

The Tukey test makes pairwise comparisons of algorithms' performance measures to find out whether their difference is significant. Like the t test, the Tukey test attempts to detect the random variation that can be found between *any* pair of means. By comparing a specific difference between two means with this random variation, we get a new statistic that tells us how big the difference between these two means is compared with the general random variation between means (Hinton, 1995).

The critical difference is that, unlike the t test, in which a standard error for each pair of means is used, the Tukey test uses a "general-purpose" standard error for any pair of means. As a result, the Tukey test does not suffer from

---

[23] This generally corresponds to utilizing the measures and respective degrees of freedom based on repeated-measures ANOVA when the respective post hoc test is applied.

the higher risk of type I error encountered by use of multiple t tests. The null hypothesis, as before, states that the performance of two classifiers being compared is equivalent (i.e., not statistically significantly different). The test is performed in the following manner:

- Compute the means of the performance measures of various classifiers for each dataset. That is, compute (in fact reuse) $\overline{pm}_{.j}$, $j \in \{1, 2, \ldots, k\}$.
- Calculate the standard error as

$$SE = \sqrt{\frac{MS_{Error}}{n}},$$

where MS_{Error} is as defined in one-way ANOVA (or one-way repeated-measures ANOVA, as the case may be).
- Calculate the q statistic for any two classifiers, say, f_{j1} and f_{j2}:

$$q = \frac{\overline{pm}_{.j_1} - \overline{pm}_{.j_2}}{SE}. \tag{6.5}$$

- Compare the $|q|$ just calculated with the critical value q_α in the table of critical q values for the desired significance level α and $(n-1)(k-1)$ degrees of freedom and number of groups $= k$ for repeated-measures one-way ANOVA (degree of freedom $nk - k$ for one-way ANOVA). This table is available in Appendix A.8.
- Reject the null hypothesis if $|q| > q_\alpha$.

The mean difference in the numerator of Equation (6.5) can also be characterized in terms of a statistic commonly known as the HSD (honestly significant difference) between means. That is, when expressed by Equation (6.5) as

$$HSD = q_\alpha SE,$$

the HSD denotes the minimum required mean difference between the two means of interest so as to be statistically significantly different at the significance level α. Hence any pair of classifiers with a mean difference greater than the HSD would imply a statistically significant difference.

Note that, in the case of unequal sample sizes, which is generally not the case in classifier evaluation, the Scheffe test can be used as an alternative equivalent of the Tukey test.

Example of the Tukey Test. To illustrate the process involved in the Tukey test, we go back to the comparison of the three classifiers, f_A, f_B, and f_C, over 10 domains listed in Table 6.6 used in Subsection 6.7.1 (recall that the accuracies are divided by 100). In that example, we recall the means for classifiers $f_A(j = 1)$, $f_B(j = 2)$, and $f_C(j = 3)$, over every domain:

$$\overline{pm}_{.1} = 0.8605, \overline{pm}_{.2} = 0.7286, \text{ and } \overline{pm}_{.3} = 0.8550.$$

We also have

$$SE = \sqrt{\frac{MS_{Error}}{n}} = \sqrt{\frac{0.000389}{10}} = 0.006237.$$

We compute the q statistics for the three pairs of classifiers and obtain

$$q_{12} = \frac{\overline{pm}_{.1} - \overline{pm}_{.2}}{SE} = \frac{0.8605 - 0.7286}{0.006237} = 21.15,$$

$$q_{13} = \frac{\overline{pm}_{.1} - \overline{pm}_{.3}}{SE} = \frac{0.8605 - 0.8550}{0.006237} = 0.882,$$

$$q_{23} = \frac{\overline{pm}_{.2} - \overline{pm}_{.3}}{SE} = \frac{0.7286 - 0.8550}{0.006237} = -20.27,$$

where $q_\alpha = 3.61$ for $\alpha = 0.05$, $df = (n-1)(k-1) = 9 \times 2 = 18$, and the number of groups $k = 3$, so we conclude that the null hypothesis can be rejected in both the cases of q_{12}, the comparison of classifiers f_A and f_B, and q_{23}, the comparison of classifiers f_B and f_C, but not in the case of q_{13}, the comparison of classifiers f_A and f_C. This is also true for $\alpha = 0.05$, because the critical value in this case is 4.70.

The calculation could also have been done using the HSD statistics. We demonstrate it here for the case in which $\alpha = 0.05$:

$$HSD = q_\alpha \times SE = 3.61 \times 0.006237 = 0.0225,$$

which is exceeded by both

$$|\overline{pm}_{.1} - \overline{pm}_{.2}| = |0.8605 - 0.7286| = 0.1319$$

and

$$|\overline{pm}_{.2} - \overline{pm}_{.3}| = |0.7286 - 0.8550| = 0.1264,$$

but not by

$$|\overline{pm}_{.1} - \overline{pm}_{.3}| = |0.8505 - 0.8550| = 0.0055.$$

The Tukey test is also illustrated in R later on in the chapter, in Subsection 6.9.3, but only in the case of the simple one-way ANOVA procedure, as the Tukey Test implemented in R does not apply to the repeated-measures one-way ANOVA case.

Dunnett Test

In the case in which the comparisons of various means of interest are to be made against a control classifier, the Dunnett test can be applied. Hence this test is performed when the difference in the performance of each classifier f_j, $j \in \{1, 2, \ldots, k\} \setminus \{c\}$ is measured with respect to the control classifier f_c.

For instance, the control classifier f_C can be the baseline classifier against which the comparisons might be needed. We calculate the following t statistic:

$$t_d = \frac{\overline{pm}_{.j} - \overline{pm}_{.c}}{\sqrt{\frac{2MS_{Error}}{n}}},$$

with the usual meanings for the notations. The null hypothesis that classifier f_j performs equivalently to the control is refuted by a table lookup for comparing the obtained t statistic for a degree of freedom $nk - k$ (the degree of freedom for MS_{Error} for one-way ANOVA), $(n - 1)(k - 1)$ (for one-way repeated-measures ANOVA), and for number of groups $= k$. The table is given in Appendix A.9.

Example of the Dunnett Test.   Assume that classifier f_B in Table 6.6 used in Subsection 6.7.1 is our control classifier. Then, we compare classifier f_A with classifier f_B by computing

$$t_{AB} = \frac{\overline{pm}_{.j} - \overline{pm}_{.c}}{\sqrt{\frac{2MS_{Error}}{n}}} = \frac{0.8605 - 0.7286}{\sqrt{\frac{2 \times 0.000389}{10}}} = 14.96$$

and classifier f_C with f_B by computing

$$t_{CB} = \frac{\overline{pm}_{.j} - \overline{pm}_{.c}}{\sqrt{\frac{2MS_{Error}}{n}}} = \frac{0.8550 - 0.7286}{\sqrt{\frac{2 \times 0.000389}{10}}} = 14.33.$$

For $df = (10 - 1)(3 - 1) = 18$ and $\alpha = 0.05$, we get the value 2.40 from the table in Appendix A.9. Because our obtained values for both comparisons of f_A and f_C with control algorithm f_B are greater than 2.40, we can reject the hypothesis that f_A and f_B are equivalent and f_B and f_C are equivalent at the $\alpha = 0.05$ significance level. In fact, it can also be rejected at the $\alpha = 0.01$ level because the critical value in the table is 3.17, which is still lower than our obtained values.

Bonferroni Test
Another alternative to discover the pairs with significant mean differences is to use the Bonferroni correction for multiple comparisons. This involves calculating a t statistic as

$$t_b = \frac{\overline{pm}_{.j_1} - \overline{pm}_{.j_2}}{\sqrt{\frac{2MS_{Error}}{n}}}.$$

That is, the Bonferroni correction is similar to the Dunnett test except that, in this case, the pairwise comparisons are made.

Example of the Bonferroni Test.   This test is the same as the Dunnett test, and its results were already calculated for classifiers f_A and f_B and f_B and f_C. We need to compute only the results for comparing algorithms f_A and f_C:

$$t_{AC} = \frac{\overline{pm}_{\cdot 1} - \overline{pm}_{\cdot 2}}{\sqrt{\frac{2MS_{Error}}{n}}} = \frac{0.8605 - 0.8550}{\sqrt{\frac{2 \times 0.000389}{10}}} = 0.624.$$

Because $0.624 < 2.40$ (2.40 was the critical value for $\alpha = 0.05$ that we obtained in the previous section when discussing the Dunnett test), we cannot reject the null hypothesis that states that f_A and f_C perform equivalently.

Performing all pairwise comparisons, however, has a drawback. As the number of comparisons increases, so does the probability of making a type I error. Bonferroni's correction for multiple comparisons (Salzberg, 1997) attempts to address the issue by using a tighter scaling of the t_b statistic (compare this with the t test, for instance). But, although this method may work fine for a small number of comparisons, it becomes more and more conservative as the number of comparisons increases. A refinement to the Bonferroni approach to deal with this issue has been proposed and is known as the Bonferroni–Dunn test or simply the Dunn test.

Bonferroni–Dunn Test

The Bonferroni–Dunn test is basically the same as the Bonferroni test except that the significance level α is divided by the number of comparisons made. That is, the lookup for the q statistic is performed not in comparison with q_α but rather with $q_{\frac{\alpha}{nc}}$, where nc is the number of comparisons made. This is especially beneficial when the comparisons are made against a control classifier because, in that case, the number of comparison nc is $k - 1$ unlike $\binom{k}{2} = \frac{k(k-1)}{2}$ when all pairwise comparisons are made.

Example of the Bonferroni–Dunn Test. In this example, the only thing that will change is the value with which the calculated t statistics will be compared. Because we made three comparisons in the Bonferroni test, we divide $\alpha = 0.05$ by 3 and obtain 0.017. A look at the t table shows that the value for $df = (10 - 1)(3 - 1) = 18$ and $\alpha = 0.01$ (which is close to 0.017) is 3.17.

Even with this correction, we can reject the hypotheses that suggests that f_A and f_B and f_C and f_B behave equivalently (because their values computed in the example associated with the Dunnett test are both greater than 3.17), but we cannot reject the hypothesis suggesting that f_A and f_C perform equivalently. We cannot run the test for $\alpha < 0.05$ because the table does not show the critical values for the significance level we would need in that case.

6.7.8 Post Hoc Tests for Friedman's Test

As in the case of parametric ANOVA, the Bonferroni–Dunn test can be used after the Friedman test on the absolute mean differences. An alternative, however, is to discover if the rank differences obtained as a result of the Friedman test are, indeed, significant. This can be done using the Nemenyi test.

The Nemenyi Test

The Nemenyi test computes a q statistic over the difference in average mean ranks of the classifier.

- Recall the ranking done in the Friedman test: Each algorithm is ranked for each dataset separately, according to the performance measure pm, in ascending order from the best-performing classifier to the worst-performing classifier. Hence, for dataset S_i, classifier f_j such that $pm_{ij} > pm_{ij'} \forall j', j, j' \in \{1, 2, \ldots, k\}, j \neq j'$, is ranked 1.[24] In the case of a d-way tie just after rank r, assign a rank of $[(r + 1) + (r + 2) + \cdots + (r + d)]/d$ to each of the tied classifiers.
- Let R_{ij} be the rank of classifier f_j on dataset S_i.
- We compute the mean rank of classifier f_j on all datasets:

$$\overline{R}_{.j} = \frac{1}{n} \sum_{i=1}^{n} R_{ij}.$$

- For any two classifiers f_{j1} and f_{j2}, we compute the q statistic as

$$q = \frac{\overline{R}_{.j_1} - \overline{R}_{.j_2}}{\sqrt{\frac{k(k+1)}{6n}}}.$$

- The null hypothesis is rejected after a comparison of the obtained q value with the q value for the desired significance table for critical q_α values, where α refers to the significance level.[25] Reject the null hypothesis if the obtained q value exceeds q_α.

Note the similarity in the statistic with the Tukey test. However, if expressed as a critical difference (CD) over ranks analogous to the HSD statistic, this CD would represent a different quantity (not the absolute mean difference but the rank difference). Also, q_α would correspond to the q values from the Tukey test but scaled by dividing it by $\sqrt{2}$. In this respect, the Nemenyi test works by computing the average rank of each classifiers and taking their difference. In the cases in which these average rank differences are larger than or equal to the CD just computed, we can say, with the appropriate amount of certainty, that the performances of the two classifiers corresponding to these differences are significantly different from one another.

Example of the Nemenyi Test. To illustrate the process of the Nemenyi test, as for the other post hoc tests, we go back to the comparison of the three classifiers,

---

[24] See footnote 22 in the Friedman Test.
[25] The critical values of q basically are a studentized range statistic scaled by a division factor of $\sqrt{2}$.

f_A, f_B, and f_C, over 10 domains. This time, however, rather than computing the average performance of each classifier on the 10 domains, we compute their average ranks. We thus have $R_{.A} = 15.5$, $R_{.B} = 30$, and $R_{.C} = 14.5$, as per Table 6.9. The difference in average rank between f_A and f_B is thus 14.5, that between f_B and f_C is 15.5, and that between f_A and f_C is 1. To answer the question of which of these differences are significant in the context of the Friedman and Nemenyi tests, we compute the critical difference by using the preceding formula. We get the following three q statistics:

$$q_{12} = \frac{\overline{R}_{.1} - \overline{R}_{.2}}{\sqrt{\frac{3(3+1)}{6 \times 10}}} = \frac{15.5 - 30}{\sqrt{\frac{3(3+1)}{6 \times 10}}} = \frac{-14.5}{0.45} = -32.22,$$

$$q_{13} = \frac{\overline{R}_{.1} - \overline{R}_{.3}}{\sqrt{\frac{3(3+1)}{6 \times 10}}} = \frac{15.5 - 14.5}{\sqrt{\frac{3(3+1)}{6 \times 10}}} = \frac{1}{0.45} = 2.22,$$

$$q_{23} = \frac{\overline{R}_{.2} - \overline{R}_{.3}}{\sqrt{\frac{3(3+1)}{6 \times 10}}} = \frac{30 - 14.5}{\sqrt{\frac{3(3+1)}{6 \times 10}}} = \frac{15.5}{0.45} = 34.44.$$

We recall from Appendix A.8 that $q_\alpha = 3.61$ for $\alpha = 0.05$ and $df = (n - 1)(k - 1) = 9 \times 2 = 18$ for the Tukey test. For the Nemenyi test, we divide this value by $\sqrt{2}$. This yields $q_\alpha = 2.55$. So we conclude that the null hypothesis can be rejected in both the cases of q_{12}, the comparison of classifiers f_A and f_B, and q_{23}, the comparison of classifiers f_B and f_C, because the absolute values of these q statistics are greater than 2.55, but not in the case of q_{13}, the comparison of classifiers f_A and f_C, because $2.22 < 2.55$. Please note that 2.22, however, is not that far from 2.55, which suggests that the Nemenyi test may consider the difference between f_A and f_C to be more significant than the Tukey test did, and thus be more sensitive.

Other Methods

Other methods exist that basically compute a statistic similar to those previously discussed but scale the significance level values so as to account for the family-wise error rate over multiple-classifier comparisons. Some examples include Hommel's test, Holm's test, and Hochberg's test. Hommel's test (Hommel, 1988) is a slightly more powerful nonparametric post hoc test. However, its practical use is difficult as a result of the added complexity in implementing it. Hence we have not discussed it here. Interested readers are encouraged to look these up in statistics texts.

6.7.9 Discussion on ANOVA and Friedman Tests

We have already outlined the critical assumptions that ANOVA makes. To reiterate, although ANOVA can be relatively robust to the normality assumption, it is practically impossible to ascertain the sphericity assumption in the case of repeated-measures ANOVA applicable to the machine learning experiment settings. Further, ANOVA can be shown to be theoretically more powerful when the assumptions are satisfied, but Friedman's test takes over when this is not the case. Further, even when the assumptions are met, the two tests do not show much practical difference as shown by Friedman (1940) and almost always agree. In addition to the advantages that the Friedman test has to being a non-parametric test, it is also easier to implement and yields a better presentation and interpretability of the results across a common range.

Finally, there can be cases in which, even though omnibus tests indicate a difference in performance, post hoc tests might not detect these. These results are mostly attributable to the lack of power of the respective post hoc tests. In such cases, the only conclusion that can be arrived at is that some algorithms among the ones tested do differ in performances, but it is not possible to identify which ones as a result of the limited power of available post hoc tests. Another issue that has been pointed out is with the use of overall measures (e.g., MS_{Error} in the case of post hoc ANOVA tests). It has been suggested that, instead of using overall measures that can be too sensitive to the violations of assumptions (e.g., homogeneity of covariance or sphericity), the measures used should take into account variability only because of the conditions of interest (i.e., with respect to the two classifiers and not others included in the omnibus test). See (Howell, 2007) for a discussion. With regard to a measure for quantifying the effect size in the case of ANOVA, the Cohen's f^2 measure was suggested.

Let us now discuss some variations of the tests to compare two classifiers on a single domain when resampling methods are used for error estimation.

6.8   Statistical Tests for Two Classifiers on a Single Domain Based on Resampling Techniques

This section discusses a few statistical tests that use resampling techniques to improve on the simple version of the paired t test presented in Subsection 6.5.1 of this chapter. We first discuss tests based on repetitions of random subsampling. We then move on to tests based on repeated k-fold cross-validation schemes. All the tests are illustrated in R in Subsections 6.9.5 and 6.9.6.

6.8.1 Multiple Trials of Simple Resampling and Associated Significance Tests

Random Subsampling
Dietterich (1998) describes the resampled paired t test as a test in which several trials n (usually $n = 30$) are conducted that each randomly divide the dataset into a training set, usually containing 2/3 of the data and a testing set containing

the remaining cases. He devised a hypothesis test following this resampling technique, as follows.[26]

This test consists of performing n trials by splitting the dataset S into a training set S_{train} and a test set S_{test}. Each time, a classifier is obtained on S_{train} and tested on S_{test}. Let the performance of the two learning algorithms A_1 and A_2 be compared on S_{test}^i, the test set on ith trial be $\text{pm}_{f_{1i}}^i$ and $\text{pm}_{f_{2i}}^i$ where f_{1i} and f_{2i} are the classifiers obtained from algorithms A_1 and A_2, respectively, by learning on S_{train}^i during trial i. Hence the difference in the average performance of the learning algorithms is

$$d_i = \text{pm}_{f_{1i}}^i - \text{pm}_{f_{2i}}^i.$$

The average difference is

$$\bar{d} = \frac{1}{n} \sum_{i=1}^{n} d_i.$$

The t statistic to be computed is the same as before:

$$t = \frac{\bar{d}\sqrt{n}}{s},$$

with

$$s = \sqrt{\frac{\sum_{i=1}^{n} (d_i - \bar{d})^2}{n - 1}}.$$

The degree of freedom is $n - 1$, so for a significance level $\alpha = 0.025$, the null hypothesis can be rejected if $|t| > t_{n-1,0.975}$. For a typical $n = 30$, the threshold is $t_{29,0.975} = 2.04523$.

Dietterich (1998) notes that there are two issues with this approach: First, the d_i's do not have a normal distribution, and second, they are not independent. The first issue relates to the fact that the training sets overlap, thus leading to $\text{pm}_{f_{1i}}^i$'s and $\text{pm}_{f_{2i}}^i$'s that are not independent; and the second issue relates to the fact that the testing sets overlap. As a result, this test shows a high probability of type I error, which actually increases as the number of trials increases.

Corrected Random Subsampling

To address the preceding shortcomings, Nadeau and Bengio (2003) proposed the corrected version of this test, reasoning that the high type I error observed in the original version is caused as a consequence of an underestimation of the variance that is due to overlapping samples. This was also noted by Bouckaert (2003). They correct the variance estimate by multiplying it by $\frac{1}{n} + \frac{|S_{\text{train}}|}{|S_{\text{test}}|}$ instead of $\frac{1}{n-1}$ (the quantity used to get an unbiased estimate of variance), with n being the number of trials and $|S_{\text{train}}| = |S_{\text{train}}^i|$ and $|S_{\text{test}}| = |S_{\text{test}}^i|$ for all $i \in \{1, \ldots, n\}$.

---

[26] Chapter 5 already described the random subsampling scheme. Here we focus on the ensuing t test.

Hence the corrected version of the preceding t statistic becomes

$$t = \frac{\bar{d}\sqrt{n}}{\sqrt{(\frac{1}{n} + \frac{|S_{train}|}{|S_{test}|}) \sum_{i=1}^{n} (d_i - \bar{d})^2}}.$$

In their experiments, Nadeau and Bengio (2003) show that the corrected resampled t test has an acceptable probability of type I error and has much better power than the cross-validated t test, simple resampled t test, and Dietterich's 5×2 CV, subsequently described.

6.8.2 Multiple Trials of k-Fold Cross-Validation and Associated Significance Tests

These tests are similar to the resampled paired t test except that, in this case, instead of dividing S randomly into training and test sets in each of the n trials, a k-fold cross-validation is performed. The training set S is randomly divided into k disjoint subsets $S_1, S_2, \ldots, S_k$. k runs of algorithms A_1 and A_2 are performed with the subset S_i acting as the test set and $S \setminus S_i$ acting as the training set.[27] The performances of the classifiers obtained from the two algorithms in each run is recorded and the difference d_i, between the two algorithms, at trial i, computed. The rest of the procedure is the same as previously described.

5 × 2-CV Test for Comparing Two Classifiers

It has been observed that the k-fold cross-validated resampling scheme does not always estimate the mean of the difference between two learning algorithms properly. Dietterich's (1998) investigations led him to conclude that the difference between the two algorithms at a single fold of the process behaves better than the mean of these differences at each fold. He thus proposed a new estimate that makes use of this observation: the 5×2-CV estimate. The test consists of five repetitions of twofold cross-validation. In twofold cross-validation, the data are split at random into two sets of approximately the same size. A learning algorithm is trained on one set and tested on the other and the process is repeated after exchanging the roles of each subset. The two estimates obtained from this procedure are averaged together.

In this method, five runs are conducted, dividing the dataset S randomly into S_{train} and S_{test} each time. Let the sets obtained in trial i be denoted by S_{train}^i and S_{test}^i. Moreover, two sets of estimates are obtained for each learning algorithm's performance. A classifier, say, $f_{1_{i_1}}$, is obtained by training the algorithm A_1 on the set S_{train}^i of trial i. This yields a performance measure $pm(f_{1_{i_1}})$ when tested on S_{test}^i. Similarly, the performance estimate $pm(f_{1_{i_2}})$ is obtained when the algorithm A_1 is trained on S_{test}^i to yield the classifier $f_{1_{i_2}}$, which is then tested on the set S_{train}^i. Similarly, for algorithm A_2, the performance measures $pm(f_{2_{i_1}})$ and $pm(f_{2_{i_2}})$ are obtained. Thus, in each of the five trials, a twofold cross-validation is performed.

---

[27] $S \setminus S_i$ means the complement of S_i on S.

Next, for each trial, the two differences are calculated as

$$d_i^{(1)} = \text{pm}(f_{1_{i1}}) - \text{pm}(f_{2_{i1}}),$$

$$d_i^{(2)} = \text{pm}(f_{1_{i2}}) - \text{pm}(f_{2_{i2}}).$$

Next, an estimate of the variance is obtained as

$$s_i^2 = (d_i^{(1)} - \bar{d}_i)^2 + (d_i^{(2)} - \bar{d}_i)^2,$$

where

$$\bar{d}_i = \frac{d_i^{(1)} + d_i^{(2)}}{2}.$$

Finally, the following statistic is estimated:

$$\tilde{t} = \frac{d_1^{(1)}}{\sqrt{\frac{1}{5}\sum_{i=1}^{5} s_i^2}}.$$

Dietterich (1998) shows that, under the null hypothesis, $\tilde{t}$ follows a t distribution with 5 degrees of freedom. The null hypothesis is hence rejected by a t-table lookup (Appendix A.2) when $\tilde{t} > t$ for the desired level of significance.

Dietterich's (1998) experiments with this new test showed that its probability of issuing a type I error is lower than that of the k-fold CV paired t tests, but the 5×2-CV t test has less power than the k-fold CV paired t test.

The 5×2-CV F Test

Alpaydn (1999) noticed that the 5×2-CV test proposed by Dietterich (1998) has one deficiency: It is dependent on the $d_1^{(1)}$ chosen for the test. In fact, he ran experiments using other differences and showed that the test did not behave uniformly in such cases. In other words, the hypothesis was sometimes accepted and sometimes rejected. He surmised that a test should not depend on a random choice and proposed a more robust version of Dietterich's (1998) test. His test is defined as follows:

$$f = \frac{\sum_{i=1}^{5}\sum_{j=1}^{2}(d_i^{(j)})^2}{2\sum_{i=1}^{5} s_i^2}.$$

This test is approximately F distributed with 10 and 5 degrees of freedom.

Experimental results suggest that the 5×2-CV F test has a lower chance of making a type I error than the 5×2-CV t test and is more powerful. The test, however, was not compared with the k-fold cross-validated paired t test.

$r \times k$ CV

The preceding method of the 5×2-CV t test is a special case of the general $r \times k$ cross-validation approach. In such an approach, r runs of a k-fold cross-validation are performed on a given dataset for the two algorithms, and the empirical differences of their performance, along with its statistical significance, are studied. Increasing the number of runs as well as folds, depending on the dataset size, can help in addressing issues such as replicability. Indeed, Bouckaert (2003, 2004) studied the 5×2-CV test with an emphasis on replicability and found the method wanting.[28] He proposed a version with $r = k = 10$. We first describe the method in its general form, and then we focus on the specific strengths and limitations of different versions of 10×10-CV tests.

Let d_{ij} represent the difference in performance of the classifiers obtained from algorithms A_1 and A_2 on the test set represented by the ith fold in the jth run.

For r runs of k-fold cross-validation, we can obtain the average difference of the empirical error estimates as

$$\bar{d} = \frac{1}{k} \sum_{i=1}^{k} \frac{1}{r} \sum_{j=1}^{r} d_{ij}.$$

Note that the average difference $\bar{d}$ is basically an extension of the 5×2-CV version. However, estimating the variance is not straightforward because its estimate can be affected by the different manners in which the averages over folds and over runs can be obtained. Four main ways, among others, have been suggested to be relevant in obtaining variance estimates in these settings:

1. **Use all the data:** This scheme obtains a variance estimate over all the folds and all the runs as

$$\hat{\sigma}^2 = \frac{\sum_{i=1}^{k} \sum_{j=1}^{r} (d_{ij} - \bar{d})^2}{kr - 1}.$$

2. **Average over folds:** In this scheme, the overall performance of the two algorithms averaged over the folds of a single k-fold CV run is taken into account:

$$\hat{\sigma}^2 = \frac{\sum_{j=1}^{r} (d_{.j} - \bar{d})^2}{r - 1},$$

where $d_{.j}$ is marginalized over the folds, i.e., $d_{.j} = \frac{1}{k} \sum_{i=1}^{k} d_{ij}$.

3. **Average over runs:** This scheme is analogous to the preceding one except that the estimates over the same folds across all the runs are obtained:

$$\hat{\sigma}^2 = \frac{\sum_{i=1}^{k} (d_{i.} - \bar{d})^2}{k - 1},$$

where $d_{i.}$ is defined as $\frac{1}{r} \sum_{j=1}^{r} d_{ij}$.

4. **Average over sorted runs:** This scheme is similar to *average over runs* except for the fact that, before averaging is performed on each fold over all the runs, the estimates of k folds in every single run are sorted in ascending order. Let $d_{o(i).}$ denote the averaged difference over all the runs for the ith

---

[28] A formal definition of replicability is given in the Bibliographic Remarks section at the end of this chapter.

fold after the ordering has been obtained by sorting the folds in each run. Hence this averages the fold with the ith lowest performance in each run. Then the variance is obtained as

$$\hat{\sigma}^2 = \frac{\sum_{i=1}^{k}(d_{o(i).} - \bar{d})^2}{k - 1}.$$

Based on the variance obtained from any of the preceding methods, a Z score can be computed as

$$Z = \frac{\bar{d}\sqrt{f_d + 1}}{\sigma},$$

where f_d denotes the degrees of freedom which is $k \times r - 1$ for the *use-all-data* scheme, $r - 1$ for the *average-over-folds* scheme, and $k - 1$ for both *average-over-runs* and *average-over-sorted-runs* schemes.

Let us now look at some specific findings for the special case in which $r = k = 10$.

10 × 10 CV

Bouckaert (2003) investigated the previously mentioned four variations in the context of variance estimation in the case in which $r = k = 10$ in an attempt to establish its reliability. Other variations were also considered but turned out to be either similar or less appropriate, in practice, than the four just considered.

In the use-all-data scheme, a degree of freedom $k \times r - 1$ would give $f_d = 99$. However, Bouckaert (2004) suggests the use of a calibrated paired t test with $f_d = 10$ instead of 99 because this choice shows excellent replicability. All the versions of the 10 × 10-CV tests typically do not yield a higher expected probability of type I errors than predicted for the experiments, although their type I error is higher than that of simple 10-fold cross-validation. However, the 10 × 10-CV scheme was shown to have as much, and often more, power. Based on the empirical observations, a 10 × 10-CV method with the use-all-data scheme for variance estimation with $f_d = 10$ seems more appropriate when the aim is to have a test with high power rather than a low type I error. When replicability is important though, a 10 × 10 CV with the average-over-sorted-runs scheme for variance estimation seems more suitable. Finally, just as a parametric test is used for significance testings, a nonparametric alternative can also be used.

6.9 Illustration of the Statistical Tests Application Using R

This section illustrates the application of all the tests considered in this chapter using the R software package. The subsections differ slightly from the subdivisions made in the earlier part of the chapter, but we hope that the parallels will be easy to make. More specifically, the examples of this section are organized with respect to the tests for two classifiers on a single domain, those for two classifiers on multiple domains, those for multiple classifiers on multiple domains, post hoc tests, and tests based on resampling. Please note that the R default for all the tests for which it is relevant is to run a two-tailed test. We used this default in all these cases. It is possible to change this default by specifying "one-sided" as per the R manual for statistical test commands. For rejecting the null hypothesis, we choose α with the highest confidence level based on the associated p-value.

6.9.1 Two Classifiers *on a* Single Domain

In this section, we consider three of the four tests described for the case of the comparison of two classifiers on a single domain:

- the two-matched-samples *t* test, along with the calculation of the effect size,
- McNemar's test, and
- Wilcoxon's Signed-Rank test for matched pairs.

The fourth test, the sign test, is easy to compute manually.

The two-matched-samples t Test

We recall the example from Chapter 2 that compared the results obtained by c4.5 (c45) and NB on the labor data. Different versions of the *t* test are implemented in R. In our specific case of two matched samples, all we need to do is call the "t.test" function, with the flag "paired=TRUE" raised. In Listing 6.3, "c45" and "nb" were the vectors defined in R in Chapter 2. This example was also presented in Subsection 6.5.1.

Listing 6.3: Sample R code for executing the matched *t* test.

```
> c45 = c(0.2433, 0.1733, 0.1733, 0.2633, 0.1633,
          0.2400, 0.2067, 0.1500, 0.2667, 0.2967)
> nb = c(0.0733, 0.0667, 0.0167, 0.0700, 0.0733,
         0.0500, 0.1533, 0.0400, 0.0367, 0.0733)
> t.test(c45, nb, paired=TRUE)


        Paired t-test

data:  c45 and nb
t = 8.0701, df = 9, p-value = 2.064e-05
alternative hypothesis: true difference in means is not equal
    to 0
95 percent confidence interval:
 0.1096298 0.1950302
sample estimates:
mean of the differences
            0.15233
```

From the p value we thus reject the null hypothesis, at the 0.01 level of significance, that C4.5 and NB perform similarly to one another. If all the assumptions of the t test were met (which they were not, as discussed in Subsection 6.5.1), we would conclude that if NB indeed classifies the domain better than C4.5, then the results we observed most probably did not occur by chance. In addition, please notice that this procedure also returns the 95% confidence interval of this difference in means. This result corroborates the one obtained manually in Subsection 6.5.1.

Let us now obtain the value of effect size (Listing 6.4).

Listing 6.4: Sample R code for computing the effect size using Cohen's d statistic.

```
> c45 = c(0.2433, 0.1733, 0.1733, 0.2633, 0.1633,
          0.2400, 0.2067, 0.1500, 0.2667, 0.2967)
>  nb = c(0.0733, 0.0667, 0.0167, 0.0700, 0.0733,
          0.0500, 0.1533, 0.0400, 0.0367, 0.0733)
> d= abs(mean(c45)-mean(nb))/sqrt((var(c45)+var(nb))/2)
> d
[1] 3.430371
```

The R calculation returns the same result as the manual calculation, and we thus conclude, as before, that the effect size is large because it is greater than 0.8.

McNemar's Test

R implements the McNemar test and can be used as shown in Listing 6.5, where x is the contingency matrix. We use the same example as the one calculated by hand in Subsection 6.5.2 and obtain the same result, which tells us that the null hypothesis can be rejected with a p value of 0.0265.

Listing 6.5: Sample R code for executing McNemar's test.

```
> x <- matrix(c(4, 11, 2, 40), nrow=2, ncol=2, byrow=TRUE)
> x
      [,1] [,2]
[1,]    4   11
[2,]    2   40
> mcnemar.test(x, correct=TRUE)

        McNemar's Chi-squared test with continuity correction

data:   x
McNemar's chi-squared = 4.9231, df = 1, p-value = 0.0265
```

Wilcoxon's Signed-Rank Test for Matched Pairs

We now show how R can be used to run Wilcoxon's test on the data resulting from the application of c45 and NB to the labor data. We recall that, in Subsection 6.6.4, we considered the 10-fold cross-validation results obtained on the first run of this experiment and summarized in Table 2.3 of Chapter 2. Once again, various versions of Wilcoxon's test are available in R. We use the one that implements the signed-rank test discussed in Subsection 6.6.4. The R code and results are presented in Listing 6.6. The results are the same as in the manual treatment of the example: We are able to reject the null hypothesis that states that c45 and NB perform similarly on the labor dataset at the 0.05 significance level.

Listing 6.6: Sample R code for Wilcoxon's test on the comparison of c4.5 and NB on the labor data, using the first run of 10-fold cross-validation results of Table 2.3.

```
> c4510folds= c(0.5, 0, 0.3333, 0, 0.3333, 0.3333, 0.3333, 0.2,
    0.2, 0.2)
> nb10folds= c(0.1667, 0, 0, 0, 0, 0.1667, 0, 0.4, 0, 0)
> wilcox.test(nb10folds, c4510folds, paired= TRUE)

        Wilcoxon signed rank test with continuity correction

data:  nb10folds and c4510folds
V = 3, p-value = 0.04030
alternative hypothesis: true location shift is not equal to 0
```

We point out, however, that there are two causes for concern with regard to the R statistical software's implementation of Wilcoxon's test. The first one is the fact that the order in which the data are presented to the test seems to matter. For example, in Listing 6.6, it should be noted that we listed the results of NB (the better-performing classifier) before those of c4.5. This yielded $V = 3$. Had we listed c4.5 before NB, we would have obtained $V = 33$, which represents the maximum, rather than the minimum, of the two sums of signed ranks. This is erroneous, although the p value indicated by the system is the same in both cases, meaning that the conclusion drawn by R is the same whatever order is used.

The second cause for concern has to do with the set of warnings R issues along with their meaning. In our preceding example, two such warning were issued as in Listing 6.7:

Listing 6.7: R warning messages.

```
Warning messages:
1: In wilcox.test.default(nb10folds, c4510folds, paired = TRUE):
    cannot compute exact p-value with ties
2: In wilcox.test.default(nb10folds, c4510folds, paired = TRUE):
    cannot compute exact p-value with zeroes
```

Table 6.10. *Results of (NB) and SVM on several datasets*

Dataset	NB	SVM
Anneal	96.43	99.44 v
Audiology	73.42	81.34
Balance scale	72.30	91.51 v
Breast cancer	71.70	66.16
Contact lenses	71.67	71.67
Pima diabetes	74.36	77.08
Glass	70.63	62.21
Hepatitis	83.21	80.63
Hypothyroid	98.22	93.58*
Tic-tac-toe	69.62	99.90 v
Average	78.15	82.35

This suggests that the p value issued is not fully reliable. It might thus be best for the user to run "wilcox.test" twice, using a different order in the presentation of the algorithms' results each time, to select the smallest V value issued by these two runs and to use the Wilcoxon table in Appendix A.5 to compute the p value manually.

6.9.2 Two Classifiers *on* Multiple Domains

In this Subsection, which illustrates the comparison of two classifiers on multiple domains by use of R, we illustrate the use of the Wilcoxon's Signed-Rank test on this problem. As mentioned before, the sign test is easy to compute manually and does not require the use of a statistical package.

Wilcoxon's Signed-Rank Test for Matched Pairs
Table 6.10 considers 10 datasets and two classifiers, NB and SVM (partial results from Table 6.3). Once again, we use R to apply Wilcoxon's test on the results listed in Table 6.10, as illustrated in Listing 6.8. Prior to applying the test, please note the division of the classifiers' results by 100 in order for them to be in the [0, 1] range.

Listing 6.8: Sample R code for Wilcoxon's test comparing NB and SVM on 10 datasets.

```
> nbDatasets= c(.9643, .7342, .723, .717, .7167, .7436, .7063,
    .8321, .9822, .6962)
> SVMdatasets=c(.9944, .8134, .9151, .6616, .7167, .7708,
    .6221, .8063, .9358, .999)
> wilcox.test(nbDatasets, SVMdatasets, paired=TRUE)

    Wilcoxon signed rank test with continuity correction
```

```
data:    nbDatasets and SVMdatasets
V = 17, p-value = 0.5536
alternative hypothesis: true location shift is not equal to 0

Warning message:
In wilcox.test.default(nbDatasets, SVMdatasets, paired = TRUE):
  cannot compute exact p-value with zeroes
>
```

The p value returned by R is very high; thus we do not reject the null hypothesis. Indeed, for $N = 10$, the number of datasets included in our study, the critical values from the Wilcoxon table are 8 and 10 for the two-sided and one-sided 95% confidence tests, respectively. These two values are smaller than the value of 17 returned by the R procedure, and so the hypothesis cannot be rejected. This is the same conclusion as the one that was obtained in Subsection 6.6.2.

6.9.3 Multiple Classifiers *on* Multiple Domains

This subsection illustrates the tests described in the context of multiple classifiers on multiple domains, using R. In particular, we illustrate the two omnibus tests: one-way repeated-measures ANOVA and its nonparametric alternative, the Friedman test. This is followed by a short illustration of R's very restricted procedures for the post hoc tests.

One-Way Repeated-Measures ANOVA

We show two examples of the use of R for the one-way repeated-measures ANOVA. Although the first was computed manually in Subsection 6.7.1, the second is too large to compute manually with ease. It is based on the results obtained by eight classifiers on 10 domains recorded in Table 6.3.[29] In both cases, note that we divide the results by 100.

The R code and output for the first example are presented in Listing 6.9, and the R code and output for the second are presented in Listings 6.10 and 6.11. In both cases, we import the data from a .csv file (summarized in the first figure of both cases). The second listing shows how to run repeated-measures ANOVA in R, in the second example. Note that the data format shown in these listings is the same as the one used in the .csv files. The function *read.table*() simply copies the table from the .csv file to the R interpreter.

There are two aspects of the R code we would like to point out and explain here. First, function *aov*() is the function that calls ANOVA in R. It can be used for *(simple) one-way ANOVA* or *repeated-Measures one-way ANOVA*. What

---

[29] Note that we chose one approach to executing repeated-measures one-way ANOVA in R. That is the approach we considered to be the simplest. Other means of doing so are also possible in R.

makes the difference between the two is the inclusion of the term + Error(X), where X takes the values "datasets" or "factor(datasets)." With this term, R performs repeated-measures one-way ANOVA. Without it, it performs one-way ANOVA.

In our second example, the formula inside $aov()$ is

$$\text{value } classifier + \text{Error(dataset)}.$$

In effect, this formula can be translated as meaning that we are trying to establish whether the various classifiers differ in accuracy and explicitly removing the within-dataset variation that may affect accuracy. If the term "+ Error(dataset)" were not included, we would simply be trying to establish whether the various classifiers differ in accuracy (with no worries about the correlations of the samples, i.e., the fact that classifiers' accuracies obtained on the same datasets have a measure of correlation). That is, we would be performing (simple) one-way ANOVA.

In our first example, the formula inside $aov()$ is slightly more complicated as it is:

$$\text{value } classifier + \text{Error(factor(dataset))}.$$

The difference between the two formulas lies in the use of the function "factor()." The reason why this function did not need to be used in the second example and needed to be used in the first is simple: In the second example, our database used the dataset names, anneal, audio, etc. In the first database, we specified the datasets numerically, using values 1, 2, 3, and so on. To signify to R that we wanted these numerical values treated as categories, we had to specify "factor(dataset)" every time "dataset" occurred in the formula of the first example. This was not necessary in the second example. With respect to the classifiers, because both examples referred to them as categorical values: classA, classB, or classC in the first example or the actual name of the classifiers in the second; there was no need to use the function *factor()*. However, had we referred to classifiers numerically (1, 2, 3, etc.) we would have needed to use factor(classifier) in the formulas.

Listing 6.9: Sample R code for executing repeated-measures ANOVA on the hypothetical dataset evaluating the three classifiers classA, classB, and classC on 10 domains.

```
> tt <- read.table ("rmanova-example.csv", header=T, sep=",")
> attach(tt)
> tt
   dataset  accuracy  classifier
1        1    0.8583      classA
2        2    0.8591      classA
3        3    0.8612      classA
4        4    0.8582      classA
```

```
5          5      0.8628      classA
6          6      0.8642      classA
7          7      0.8591      classA
8          8      0.8610      classA
9          9      0.8595      classA
10        10      0.8612      classA
11         1      0.7586      classB
12         2      0.7318      classB
13         3      0.6908      classB
14         4      0.7405      classB
15         5      0.7471      classB
16         6      0.6590      classB
17         7      0.7625      classB
18         8      0.7510      classB
19         9      0.7050      classB
20        10      0.7395      classB
21         1      0.8419      classC
22         2      0.8590      classC
23         3      0.8383      classC
24         4      0.8511      classC
25         5      0.8638      classC
26         6      0.8120      classC
27         7      0.8638      classC
28         8      0.8675      classC
29         9      0.8803      classC
30        10      0.8718      classC
>
> summary(aov(accuracy ~ classifier + Error(factor(dataset))))

Error: factor(dataset)
            Df       Sum Sq      Mean Sq  F value  Pr(>F)
Residuals    9    0.0065593   0.0007288

Error: Within
            Df       Sum Sq    Mean Sq  F value     Pr(>F)
classifier   2     0.111307   0.055653   142.42   9.26e-12  ***
Residuals   18     0.007034   0.000391
___
Signif. codes:    0  ***  0.001  **  0.01  *  0.05  .  0.1      1
>
```

Listing 6.10: Sample R code showing the data used for repeated-measures ANOVA on the realistic experiments of Table 6.3.

```
> tt <- read.table("rmanova-complex-example.csv", header=T,
    sep=",")
> attach(tt)
> tt
        dataset  accuracy  classifier
1       Anneal    0.9643        NB
```

2	Audio	0.7342	NB
3	Balance	0.7230	NB
4	Breast—C	0.7170	NB
5	Contact—L	0.7167	NB
6	Pima	0.7436	NB
7	Glass	0.7063	NB
8	Hepa	0.8321	NB
9	Hypothyr	0.9822	NB
10	Tic—tac—toe	0.6962	NB
11	Anneal	0.9944	SVM
12	Audio	0.8134	SVM
13	Balance	0.9151	SVM
14	Breast—C	0.6616	SVM
15	Contact—L	0.7167	SVM
16	Pima	0.7708	SVM
17	Glass	0.6221	SVM
18	Hepa	0.8063	SVM
19	Hypothyr	0.9358	SVM
20	Tic—tac—toe	0.9990	SVM
21	Anneal	0.9911	IB1
22	Audio	0.7522	IB1
23	Balance	0.7903	IB1
24	Breast—C	0.6574	IB1
25	Contact—L	0.6333	IB1
26	Pima	0.7017	IB1
27	Glass	0.7050	IB1
28	Hepa	0.8063	IB1
29	Hypothyr	0.9152	IB1
30	Tic—tac—toe	0.8163	IB1
31	Anneal	0.8363	ADA–DT
32	Audio	0.4646	ADA–DT
33	Balance	0.7231	ADA–DT
34	Breast—C	0.7028	ADA–DT
35	Contact—L	0.7167	ADA–DT
36	Pima	0.7435	ADA–DT
37	Glass	0.4491	ADA–DT
38	Hepa	0.8254	ADA–DT
39	Hypothyr	0.9321	ADA–DT
40	Tic—tac—toe	0.7254	ADA–DT
41	Anneal	0.9822	BAG–REP
42	Audio	0.7654	BAG–REP
43	Balance	0.8289	BAG–REP
44	Breast—C	0.6784	BAG–REP
45	Contact—L	0.6833	BAG–REP
46	Pima	0.7461	BAG–REP
47	Glass	0.6963	BAG–REP
48	Hepa	0.8450	BAG–REP
49	Hypothyr	0.9955	BAG–REP
50	Tic—tac—toe	0.9207	BAG–REP
51	Anneal	0.9844	C45

52	Audio	0.7787	C46
53	Balance	0.7665	C47
54	Breast—C	0.7554	C48
55	Contact—L	0.8167	C49
56	Pima	0.7383	C50
57	Glass	0.6675	C51
58	Hepa	0.8379	C52
59	Hypothyr	0.9958	C53
60	Tic—tac—toe	0.8507	C54
61	Anneal	0.9955	RF
62	Audio	0.7915	RF
63	Balance	0.8097	RF
64	Breast—C	0.6999	RF
65	Contact—L	0.7167	RF
66	Pima	0.7488	RF
67	Glass	0.7987	RF
68	Hepa	0.8458	RF
69	Hypothyr	0.9939	RF
70	Tic—tac—toe	0.9394	RF
71	Anneal	0.9822	Jrip
72	Audio	0.7607	Jrip
73	Balance	0.8160	Jrip
74	Breast—C	0.6888	Jrip
75	Contact—L	0.7500	Jrip
76	Pima	0.7500	Jrip
77	Glass	0.7095	Jrip
78	Hepa	0.7800	Jrip
79	Hypothyr	0.9942	Jrip
80	Tic—tac—toe	0.9739	Jrip

```
>
```

Listing 6.11: Sample R code (using data in Listing 6.10) for executing repeated-measure ANOVA.

```
> summary(aov(accuracy ~ classifier + Error(dataset)))

Error: dataset
           Df  Sum Sq  Mean Sq
classifier  9  0.82480  0.09164

Error: Within
           Df   Sum Sq   Mean Sq F value  Pr(>F)
classifier 16  0.128039  0.008002  2.0802  0.02344 *
Residuals  54  0.207734  0.003847
___
Signif. codes:  0 *** 0.001 ** 0.01 * 0.05 . 0.1   1
>
```

The results obtained on the first example corroborate those obtained manually in Subsection 6.7.1, save for the rounding error. We thus strongly reject the hypothesis that classifiers f_A, f_B and f_C all perform similarly on domains 1–10.

We did not treat the second example manually because of its size. However, the R treatment of this example concludes that we can reject the hypothesis that the eight classifiers perform similarly on the 10 domains considered at the 95% significance level (but not at a higher level of significance, as in the first example.)

The Friedman Test

We illustrate the Friedman test by using the same two examples as those used to illustrate the one-way repeated-measures ANOVA in the previous section. We thus recall that the first example is the one that we treated manually in Subsection 6.7.5. The R code and its output for this example are shown in Listing 6.12 (the WEKA classifiers' outputs are divided by 100, as we did previously).

Listing 6.12: Sample R code for executing Friedman's test on a hypothetical dataset containing three classifiers and 10 domains.

```
>   classA= c(85.83, 85.91, 86.12, 85.82, 86.28, 86.42, 85.91,
       86.10, 85.95, 86.12)/100
>   classB= c(75.86, 73.18, 69.08, 74.05, 74.71, 65.90, 76.25,
       75.10, 70.50, 73.95)/100
>   classC= c(84.19, 85.90, 83.83, 85.11, 86.38, 81.20, 86.38,
       86.75, 88.03, 87.18)/100
>   t=matrix(c(classA, classB, classC), nrow=10, byrow=FALSE)
>   t
            [,1]    [,2]    [,3]
  [1,]  0.8583  0.7586  0.8419
  [2,]  0.8591  0.7318  0.8590
  [3,]  0.8612  0.6908  0.8383
  [4,]  0.8582  0.7405  0.8511
  [5,]  0.8628  0.7471  0.8638
  [6,]  0.8642  0.6590  0.8120
  [7,]  0.8591  0.7625  0.8638
  [8,]  0.8610  0.7510  0.8675
  [9,]  0.8595  0.7050  0.8803
 [10,]  0.8612  0.7395  0.8718
>   friedman.test(t)

        Friedman rank sum test

data:   t
Friedman chi-squared = 15, df = 2, p-value = 0.0005531


>
```

We can see in the first example that the R results corroborate those we obtained manually. The Friedman test thus also concludes that there is a difference in performance of the three classifiers, f_A, f_B, and f_C, on the 10 hypothetical datasets.

For the second example, we recall that we did not treat it manually as it is too large because it is based on the results obtained by eight classifiers on 10 domains, as recorded in Table 6.3. We obtain the results shown in Listing 6.13 for this example.

Listing 6.13: Sample R code for executing Friedman's test on a real dataset containing eight classifiers and 10 domains.

```
> nbDatasets <- c(96.43, 73.42, 72.30, 71.70, 71.67, 74.36,
      70.63, 83.21, 98.22, 69.62)/100
> SVMDatasets <- c(99.44, 81.34, 91.51, 66.16, 71.67, 77.08,
      62.21, 80.63, 93.58, 99.90)/100
> IB1Datasets <- c(99.11, 75.22, 79.03, 65.74, 63.33, 70.17,
      70.50, 80.63, 91.52, 81.63)/100
> AdaboostDatasets <- c(83.63, 46.46, 72.31, 70.28, 71.67,
      74.35, 44.91, 82.54, 93.21, 72.54)/100
> BaggingDatasets <- c(98.22, 76.54, 82.89, 67.84, 68.33,
      74.61, 69.63, 84.50, 99.55, 92.07)/100
> C45Datasets <- c(98.44, 77.87, 76.65, 75.54, 81.67, 73.83,
      66.75, 83.79, 99.58, 85.07)/100
> RFDatasets <- c(99.55, 79.15, 80.97, 69.99, 71.67, 74.88,
      79.87, 84.58, 99.39, 93.94)/100
> JRipDatasets <- c(98.22, 76.07, 81.60, 68.88, 75.00, 75.00,
      70.95, 78.00, 99.42, 97.39)/100
> table=matrix(c( nbDatasets, SVMDatasets, IB1Datasets,
      AdaboostDatasets,
BaggingDatasets, C45Datasets, RFDatasets, JRipDatasets),nrow
      =10, byrow=FALSE)
> table
           [,1]    [,2]    [,3]    [,4]    [,5]    [,6]    [,7]    [,8]
 [1,]  0.9643  0.9944  0.9911  0.8363  0.9822  0.9844  0.9955  0.9822
 [2,]  0.7342  0.8134  0.7522  0.4646  0.7654  0.7787  0.7915  0.7607
 [3,]  0.7230  0.9151  0.7903  0.7231  0.8289  0.7665  0.8097  0.8160
 [4,]  0.7170  0.6616  0.6574  0.7028  0.6784  0.7554  0.6999  0.6888
 [5,]  0.7167  0.7167  0.6333  0.7167  0.6833  0.8167  0.7167  0.7500
 [6,]  0.7436  0.7708  0.7017  0.7435  0.7461  0.7383  0.7488  0.7500
 [7,]  0.7063  0.6221  0.7050  0.4491  0.6963  0.6675  0.7987  0.7095
 [8,]  0.8321  0.8063  0.8063  0.8254  0.8450  0.8379  0.8458  0.7800
 [9,]  0.9822  0.9358  0.9152  0.9321  0.9955  0.9958  0.9939  0.9942
[10,]  0.6962  0.9990  0.8163  0.7254  0.9207  0.8507  0.9394  0.9739
> friedman.test(table)

        Friedman rank sum test

data:  table
Friedman chi-squared = 20.6872, df = 7, p-value = 0.004262

>
```

The results show that we can reject the hypothesis that all the algorithms are the same at the 0.005 level, which is a higher significance level than the one obtained with the repeated-measures one-way ANOVA, suggesting a greater sensitivity for the Friedman test in this particular case.

6.9.4 Post Hoc Tests

The only post hoc test clearly implemented in R is Tukey's test. However, it is not implemented on repeated-measures one-way ANOVA. For the sake of completeness, we thus demonstrate how this test is used for (simple) one-way ANOVA. However, the reader is reminded that (simple) one-way ANOVA is usually not the most powerful test to use in this context (see Subsection 6.7.4) and the procedure shown here is not recommended. Instead, we suggest that the user apply the post hoc tests following repeated-measures one-way ANOVA and the Friedman test manually, as shown in Subsections 6.7.7 and 6.7.8.[30]

Listing 6.14 illustrates the application of (simple) one-way ANOVA to the three-classifier 10-domain hypothetical example that was first treated manually in Subsection 6.7.1. In this case the results of simple ANOVA corroborates with those of repeated-measures ANOVA as the null hypothesis gets rejected with a very high significance level. Listing 6.15 illustrates the application of the Tukey test on this result. The results of the Tukey test show that although we can reject the hypothesis that classifier f_B performs similarly to f_A and f_C, we cannot reject the hypothesis that f_A and f_C perform similarly on these three domains.

Listing 6.16 illustrates the application of (simple) one-way ANOVA to the eight-classifiers and 10-domain realistic problem described in Table 6.3. In this example, the low power of simple one-way ANOVA relative to repeated-measures ANOVA is clearly apparent because (simple) one-way ANOVA cannot reject the null hypothesis (which was rejected by both repeated-measures one-way ANOVA and the Friedman test). There was *no* need to apply the Tukey test in this case, but we did it anyway to illustrate what the procedure returns. This is shown in Listing 6.17, where it is clear that no hypothesis in the overall comparison can be rejected.

We did not find a simple implementation of the Nemenyi test in R. The restrictions on the post hoc tests for ANOVA in the case of repeated measures should not apply to the case of the Nemenyi test. So altogether, the Friedman test followed by the Nemenyi test is an appealing nonparametric alternative in the

---

[30] That being said, David Howell (2007) suggests that the major reason why statistical software does not implement simple off-the-shelf post hoc tests for repeated-measures tests is that "unrestrained use of such procedures is generally unwise" (sic). His reason is basically that, although the omnibus tests are often robust enough to violation of certain constraints, the ensuing post hoc tests are not. It is thus suggested that the manual computations for post hoc tests for repeated-measures one-way ANOVA presented in Subsection 6.7.7 be used only with extreme caution.

case of comparisons of multiple classifiers on multiple domains, as was already
suggested by Demšar (2006).

Listing 6.14: Sample R code for executing (simple) one-way ANOVA on the
hypothetical example.

```
> classA= c(85.83,  85.91,  86.12,  85.82,  86.28,  86.42,  85.91,
     86.10,  85.95,  86.12)/100
> classB= c(75.86,  73.18,  69.08,  74.05,  74.71,  65.90,  76.25,
     75.10,  70.50,  73.95)/100
> classC= c(84.19,  85.90,  83.83,  85.11,  86.38,  81.20,  86.38,
     86.75,  88.03,  87.18)/100
> df = stack(data.frame(classA ,classB ,classC ))
> summary(x <- aov(values ~ ind , data=df ))
            Df   Sum Sq   Mean Sq  F value      Pr(>F)
ind          2  0.111307  0.055653   110.54   9.914e-14 ***
Residuals   27  0.013593  0.000503

Signif. codes:  0 *** 0.001 ** 0.01 * 0.05 . 0.1   1
>
```

Listing 6.15: Sample R code for executing Tukey's test on the results of
Listing 6.14.

```
> TukeyHSD(x)
   Tukey multiple comparisons of means
     95% family-wise confidence level

Fit: aov(formula = values ~ ind , data = df)

ind
                   diff           lwr           upr       p adj
classB-classA   -0.13188   -0.15675964   -0.10700036   0.0000000
classC-classA   -0.00551   -0.03038964    0.01936964   0.8478002
classC-classB    0.12637    0.10149036    0.15124964   0.0000000
```

Listing 6.16: Sample R code for excuting one-way ANOVA on the eight-
classifier and 10-domain realistic example of Table 6.3.

```
>
>   nbDatasets= c(96.43,  73.42,  72.3,  71.7,  71.67,  74.36,  70.63,
      83.21,  98.22,  69.62)/100
>   SVMDatasets=c(99.44,  81.34,  91.51,  66.16,  71.67,  77.08,
      62.21,  80.63,  93.58,  99.9)/100
>   IB1Datasets=c(99.11,  75.22,  79.03,  65.74,  63.33,  70.17,
      70.5,  80.63,  91.52,  81.63)/100
>   AdaboostDatasets=c(83.63,  46.46,  72.31,  70.28,  71.67,  74.35,
      44.91,  82.54,  93.21,  72.54)/100
>   BaggingDatasets=c( 98.22,  76.54,  82.89,  67.84,  68.33,
      74.61,  69.63,  84.50,  99.55,  92.07)/100
```

```
>   C45Datasets=c(98.44, 77.87, 76.65, 75.54, 81.67,
    73.83,66.75, 83.79, 99.58, 85.07)/100
>   RFDatasets= c(99.55,79.15, 80.97, 69.99, 71.67, 74.88,
    79.87, 84.58, 99.39, 93.94)/100
>   JRipDatasets=c(98.22, 76.07, 81.60, 68.88, 75.00, 75.00,
    70.95, 78.00, 99.42, 97.39)/100
> df = stack(data.frame(nbDatasets,SVMDatasets,IB1Datasets,
        AdaboostDatasets,BaggingDatasets,C45Datasets,RFDatasets,
        JRipDatasets))
>
> summary(x <- aov(values ~ ind, data=df))
            Df   Sum Sq  Mean Sq  F value  Pr(>F)
ind          7  0.11294  0.01613   1.1088  0.3671
Residuals   72  1.04763  0.01455
>
```

Listing 6.17: Sample R code for executing Tukey's test for Listing 6.16.

```
> TukeyHSD(x)
    Tukey multiple comparisons of means
      95% family-wise confidence level

Fit: aov(formula = values ~ ind, data = df)

ind
```

	diff	lwr	upr	p adj
BaggingDatasets−AdaboostDatasets	0.10228	−0.06612666	0.2706867	0.5581351
C45Datasets−AdaboostDatasets	0.10729	−0.06111666	0.2756967	0.4964397
IB1Datasets−AdaboostDatasets	0.06498	−0.10342666	0.2333867	0.9280210
JRipDatasets−AdaboostDatasets	0.10863	−0.05977666	0.2770367	0.4801609
nbDatasets−AdaboostDatasets	0.06966	−0.09874666	0.2380667	0.8991796
RFDatasets−AdaboostDatasets	0.12209	−0.04631666	0.2904967	0.3280533
SVMDatasets−AdaboostDatasets	0.11162	−0.05678666	0.2800267	0.4443862
C45Datasets−BaggingDatasets	0.00501	−0.16339666	0.1734167	1.0000000
IB1Datasets−BaggingDatasets	−0.03730	−0.20570666	0.1311067	0.9969888
JRipDatasets−BaggingDatasets	0.00635	−0.16205666	0.1747567	1.0000000
nbDatasets−BaggingDatasets	−0.03262	−0.20102666	0.1357867	0.9987155
RFDatasets−BaggingDatasets	0.01981	−0.14859666	0.1882167	0.9999531
SVMDatasets−BaggingDatasets	0.00934	−0.15906666	0.1777467	0.9999997
IB1Datasets−C45Datasets	−0.04231	−0.21071666	0.1260967	0.9934440
JRipDatasets−C45Datasets	0.00134	−0.16706666	0.1697467	1.0000000
nbDatasets−C45Datasets	−0.03763	−0.20603666	0.1307767	0.9968180
RFDatasets−C45Datasets	0.01480	−0.15360666	0.1832067	0.9999936
SVMDatasets−C45Datasets	0.00433	−0.16407666	0.1727367	1.0000000
JRipDatasets−IB1Datasets	0.04365	−0.12475666	0.2120567	0.9920847
nbDatasets−IB1Datasets	0.00468	−0.16372666	0.1730867	1.0000000
RFDatasets−IB1Datasets	0.05711	−0.11129666	0.2255167	0.9631438
SVMDatasets−IB1Datasets	0.04664	−0.12176666	0.2150467	0.9882591
nbDatasets−JRipDatasets	−0.03897	−0.20737666	0.1294367	0.9960429
RFDatasets−JRipDatasets	0.01346	−0.15494666	0.1818667	0.9999967

SVMDatasets−JRipDatasets	0.00299	−0.16541666 0.1713967	1.0000000
RFDatasets−nbDatasets	0.05243	−0.11597666 0.2208367	0.9769766
SVMDatasets−nbDatasets	0.04196	−0.12644666 0.2103667	0.9937668
SVMDatasets−RFDatasets	−0.01047	−0.17887666 0.1579367	0.9999994

>

6.9.5 Tests Based on Multiple Runs of Random Subsampling

In this Subsection, we use the Iris data from the UCI Repository for machine learning. We apply the WEKA classifiers to these data and retrieve accuracy results. As in some previous examples, these accuracies are expressed in percentages rather than in their equivalents in the [0, 1] range. However, simple and corrected random subsamplings both compute proportions that are in the [0,1] range. It is these proportions that are used in the statistical test that follows the resampling scheme, so there is no need in that case to convert the accuracies to their equivalent [0, 1] range equivalents.

Simple Random Subsampling
The R code for the *t* test applied to the result of simple random subsampling was already shown in Chapter 5. Therefore we do not repeat it here. Instead, we move on to the improved version of that test, called the corrected random subsampling.

Corrected Random Subsampling
The corrected random subsampling test uses exactly the same idea and thus the same code as the simple random subsampling test, except for the calculation of *t*, which is done according to a different formula. The code for the corrected random subsampling *t* test is given in Listing 6.18. Please note that this procedure differs from that for the simple random subsampling resampling *t* test at only two places.

Listing 6.18: Sample R code for executing the corrected random subsampling *t* test.

```
correctedResampttest = function(iter, dataSet, setSize, dimension,
                                classifier1, classifier2){

proportions <- randomSubsamp(iter, dataSet, setSize, dimension,
                             classifier1, classifier2)

averageProportion <- mean(proportions)

sum=0
for (i in 1:iter) {
```

```
    sum = sum + (proportions[i]−averageProportion)^2
}

# Corrected resampled t−test

t= (averageProportion * sqrt(iter))/sqrt(((1/iter)+
    ((2/3)/(1/3)))*sum)

print('The t−value for the corrected resampled t−test is')
print(t)
}
```

The code just listed is invoked as in Listing 6.19, with 30 iterations. The result shown is then analyzed.

Listing 6.19: Invocation and results of the corrected resampling t test code.

```
> library(RWeka)
Loading required package: grid
>
> NB <− make_Weka_classifier("weka/classifiers/bayes/NaiveBayes")
> iris <− read.arff(system.file("arff", "iris.arff",
                    package = "RWeka"))
> correctedResampttest(30, iris, 150, 5, NB, J48)
[1] "The t−value for the corrected resampled t−test is"
[1] 0.5005025
```

Using this correction on the previous example, we obtain a value of $t = 0.5005$, which is smaller than $t_{29,0.975} = 2.04523$, which signifies that the null hypothesis suggesting that c45 and NB perform similarly on the Iris dataset cannot be rejected at the $\alpha = 0.025$ level.

6.9.6 Tests Based on Multiple Runs of Cross-Validation

As in the previous case, this section uses the Iris data from the UCI Repository for Machine Learning with WEKA, yielding percentage accuracies. We used these accuracies after dividing them by 100 (see the code for Tikcv below).

5×2-CV t and F Tests

Dietterich (1998) came up with the 5×2 cross-validated resampling scheme followed by the t test. Alpaydn (1999) used the same resampling scheme, but refined the statistical test that follows it. In particular, he devised an F test for this resampling scheme. The code for the resampling scheme along with both statistical tests is given here. Because the F test reuses a lot of the same code, we present the two schemes together.

We first show the code common to both procedures. Specifically, we first show the code for the resampling scheme proper, which takes as input the same parameters as stratcv() as well as parameter *iter*, which indicates the number of desired iterations of k-fold cross-validation. This code is defined in the function titled Tikcv() (Listing 6.20), which outputs an *iter* $\times$ *k* table listing the differences in accuracy between the two classifiers compared (classifier1 and classifier2) at each fold of each iteration. This piece of code is also used in all the resampling tests that involve 10×10-CV resampling. The second piece of code common to both the 5×2-CV test procedures is defined in the function titled T52cvVariance(), which takes as input the output of the previously described function and outputs a vector of size 5 containing the estimated variances at each iteration, as defined by Dietterich and Alpaydn for their two tests. The code for these two functions is shown in Listing 6.20.

Listing 6.20: Sample R code for executing multiple runs of stratified k-fold cross-validation.

```
# TikCV performs ixk CV resampling and outputs the difference
# in accuracy between classifier1 and classifier2 at each of
# the k fold of each of the i iterations.
Tikcv = function(iter, k, dataSet, setSize, dimension,
               numClasses, classSize, classifier1, classifier2){
allResults = list()
for (r in 1:iter){
    allResults <- c(allResults, list(stratcv(k, dataSet, setSize,
        dimension, numClasses, classSize, classifier1, classifier2)))
}


# We transform the percentage accuracies returned by Weka into their
# equivalent in the [0,1] interval in order for these values to
# be proper continuous random variables. cl is the classifier number.
for (i in 1:iter)
    for (j in 1:k)
        for (cl in 1:2)
            allResults[[i]][[cl]][j] <- allResults[[i]][[cl]][j]/100


#p[i,j] represents the difference between NB's accuracy and J48's
# accuracy (NB-J48) on fold i for dataset j. There are 5 folds
# and 2 datasets
p <- matrix(1:(iter*k), nrow=iter)
for (i in 1:iter)
    for (j in 1:k)
        p[i, j] <- (allResults[[i]][[1]][j] - allResults[[i]][[2]][j] )

return(p)
}
```

```
# T52cvVariance takes as input the outut of T52cv and outputs a
# vector containing the estimated variance as calculated by the
# 5x2cv t-test and f-test for each of the 5 iterations
T52cvVariance = function(p) {
# pBar contains the average on replication i
pBar <- numeric(5)
for (i in 1:5)
pBar[i] <- (p[i,1] + p[i,2])/2

# Estimated Variance
sSquared <- numeric(5)
for (i in 1:5)
    sSquared[i] <- (p[i,1]-pBar[i])^2 + (p[i,2]-pBar[i])^2

return(sSquared)
}
```

We now show, in Listing 6.21, the code used to calculate the results of the 5×2-CV test introduced by Dietterich (1998).

Listing 6.21: Sample R code for executing the 5×2-CV t test.

```
# T52cvttest calls both T52cv and T52cvVariance and returns
# the t-value as per Dietterich's 5x2CV t-test.
T52cvttest = function(dataSet, setSize, dimension, numClasses,
                      classSize, classifier1, classifier2) {

p <- T1kcv(5 ,2 ,dataSet, setSize, dimension, numClasses,
           classSize, classifier1, classifier2)
sSquared <- T52cvVariance(p)

#calculating the value of t's denominator
denom <- 0
for (i in 1:5)
    denom <- denom + sSquared[i]
denom <- sqrt(denom/5)

#calculating t

 t <- p[1,1]/denom
 print('The t-value is equal to')
print(t)

}
```

This code is invoked as per the next description in Listing 6.22 and returns the output shown in the listing.

Listing 6.22: Invocation and results of the the 5 × 2-CV *t* test.

```
> library (RWeka)
> NB <- make_Weka_classifier("weka/ classifiers /bayes/ NaiveBayes")
> iris <- read.arff(system.file("arff", "iris.arff",
                    package = "RWeka"))
> T52cvttest(iris, 150, 5, 3, c(50,50,50), NB, J48)
[1] "The t-value is equal to"
[1] 1.518816
>
```

Because this *t* is approximately *t* distributed with 5 degrees of freedom, we could reject the hypothesis that the two classifiers have the same error rate with 95% confidence if *t* is greater than 2.571. Because *t* is smaller than 2.571, this hypothesis cannot be rejected.

The code for the 5 × 2-CV *F* test is identical to that of the Listing 6.22 *t* test, except for the computation of the *F* statistic itself. Both the denominator and the numerator are different. The code is given in Listing 6.23.

Listing 6.23: Sample R code for executing the 5 × 2-CV *F* test.

```
# F52cvftest calls both Tikcv and T52cvVariance and returns the
# f-value as per Alpaydin's 5x2CV f-test.
F52cvftest = function(dataSet, setSize, dimension, numClasses,
                      classSize, classifier1, classifier2) {

p <- Tikcv(5, 2, dataSet, setSize, dimension, numClasses,
           classSize, classifier1, classifier2)
sSquared <- T52cvVariance(p)

#calculating the value of f's denominator
denom <- 0
for (i in 1:5)
   denom <- denom + sSquared[i]
denom <- (2 * denom)

#calculating the value of f's numerator
numer <- 0
for (i in 1:5)
for (j in 1:2)
   numer <- numer + (p[i,j])^2

#calculating f

 f <- numer/denom
 print('The f-value is equal to')
 print(f)

}
```

When the 5×2-CV F test is applied to the Iris data as follows (Listing 6.24) we get the following results.

Listing 6.24: Invocation and results of the 5×2-CV F test.

```
> library(RWeka)
> NB <- make_Weka_classifier("weka/classifiers/bayes/NaiveBayes")
> iris <- read.arff(system.file("arff", "iris.arff",
                    package = "RWeka"))
> F52cvftest(iris, 150, 5, 3, c(50,50,50), NB, J48)
[1] "The f-value is equal to"
[1] 0.768631
>
```

Alpaydn (1999) showed that the preceding f is approximately F distributed with 10 and 5 degrees of freedom. This means, for example, that we can reject the null hypothesis with 0.95 confidence if the statistic f is greater than 4.74. It is not the case in our example, so the hypothesis cannot be rejected at that level of confidence.

10×10-CV Schemes

All the 10×10-CV schemes described by Bouckaert (2004) run the same 10×10-CV resampling scheme and compute the mean value of this resampling in the same manner. What changes from scheme to scheme is the computation of the variance and of the Z value of the hypothesis test that follows the resampling. The resampling, per se, is invoked using the function that was already defined in the context of the 5×2-CV tests, namely, Tikcv(), although this time the values of parameters *iter* and k are 10 and 10, respectively, rather than 5 and 2. The mean of this resampling is simply calculated by the code in Listing 6.25.

Listing 6.25: Mean of the 10×10-CV resampling strategy.

```
# Compute the mean
meanVal = function(x){
m <- 0
for (i in 1:10){
    mint <- 0
    for (j in 1:10)
        mint <- mint + x[i,j]
    mint <- mint/10
    m <- m + mint
}
m <- m/10
return(m)
}
```

We now show the specific code for each of the four 10×10-CV schemes discussed in this book (these vary in how the sample variance is calculated).

10 × 10-CV Use-All-Data

The code for the 10 × 10-CV use-all-data scheme is given in Listing 6.26.

Listing 6.26: Sample R Code for executing 10 × 10 CV use-all-data.

```
# 10 x 10 CV Use All data
T1010cvAlldata = function(dataSet, setSize, dimension, numClasses,
                    classSize, classifier1, classifier2){

x <- Tikcv(10, 10, dataSet, setSize, dimension, numClasses,
               classSize, classifier1, classifier2)
m <- meanVal(x)

# Compute the variance
v <- 0
for (i in 1:10)
   for (j in 1:10)
      v <- v + (x[i,j]-m)^2
v <- v/99

# Compute Z
z <- m/(sqrt(v)/sqrt(100))

print('The difference in means between classifier1 and
      classifier2 is')
print(m)
print('The variance of this difference in means is')
print(v)
print('The Z Value obtained in the 10x10CV Use All Data
      Scheme is')
print(z)
}
```

The code is invoked as follows in Listing 6.27 and yields the results shown.

Listing 6.27: Invocation and results of 10 × 10-CV use-all-data.

```
> library(RWeka)
> NB <- make_Weka_classifier("weka/classifiers/bayes/NaiveBayes")
> iris <- read.arff(system.file("arff", "iris.arff",
  + package = "RWeka"))
> T1010cvAlldata(iris, 150, 5, 3, c(50,50,50), NB, J48)
[1] "The difference in means between classifier1 and\n
                                           classifier2 is"
[1] 0.018004
[1] "The variance of this difference in means is"
[1] 0.002951864
[1] "The Z Value obtained in the 10x10CV Use All Data\n      Scheme is"
[1] 3.313758
>
```

The Z value is located between 3.2905 and 3.7190, which corresponds to levels of confidence between 99.9% and 99.98%. We thus conclude that the difference in means between the two classifiers is statistically significant at the 99.9% confidence level.

10 × 10 CV Average over Folds

The 10×10-CV average-over-fold test starts in the same manner as the 10×10-CV use-all-data scheme, but differs in the calculation of the variance. This is reflected in the code in Listing 6.28.

Listing 6.28: Sample R Code for executing 10×10-CV average-over-folds.

```
# 10 x 10 CV Average Over Folds
T1010cvFolds = function(dataSet, setSize, dimension, numClasses,
                        classSize, classifier1, classifier2){

x <- Tikcv(10, 10, dataSet, setSize, dimension, numClasses,
                        classSize, classifier1, classifier2)
m <- meanVal(x)

# Compute xDotj
xDotj <- numeric(10)
for (j in 1:10) {
    xDotj[j] <- 0
    for (i in 1:10)
        xDotj[j] <- xDotj[j] + x[i,j]
    xDotj[j] <- xDotj[j]/10
}

# Compute the variance
v <- 0
for (j in 1:10)
        v <- v + (xDotj[j]-m)^2
v <- v/9

# Compute Z
z <- m/(sqrt(v)/sqrt(10))

print('The difference in means between classifier1 and
        classifier2 is')
print(m)
print('The variance of this difference in means is')
print(v)
print('The Z Value obtained in the 10x10CV Average over
        Folds Scheme is')
print(z)
}
```

Listing 6.29 shows the results obtained when the code is invoked.

Listing 6.29: Invocation and results of 10×10-CV average-over-fold.

```
> library (RWeka)
> NB <- make_Weka_classifier("weka/classifiers/bayes/NaiveBayes")
> iris <- read.arff(system.file("arff", "iris.arff",
+                       package = "RWeka"))
> T1010cvFolds(iris, 150, 5, 3, c(50,50,50), NB, J48)
[1] "The difference in means between classifier1 and\n
                                        classifier2 is"
[1] 0.009333
[1] "The variance of this difference in means is"
[1] 0.0003971674
[1] "The Z Value obtained in the 10x10CV Average over\n
                                        Folds Scheme is"
[1] 1.480930
>
```

This time, the Z value is located between 1.28 and 1.64, which corresponds to levels of confidence between 80% and 90%. Because 1.64 is not reached, we cannot reject the hypothesis that the difference in means between the two classifiers is statistically significant at the 90% confidence level.

10×10-CV Average-Over-Runs

The 10×10-CV average-over-runs scheme is very similar to the 10×10-CV average-over-folds scheme. The code is given in Listing 6.30.

Listing 6.30: Sample R Code for executing 10×10-CV average-over-runs.

```
# 10 x 10 CV Average Over Runs
T1010cvRuns = function(dataSet, setSize, dimension, numClasses,
                    classSize, classifier1, classifier2){

x <- Tikcv(10, 10, dataSet, setSize, dimension, numClasses,
                classSize, classifier1, classifier2)
m <- meanVal(x)

# Compute xDoti
xDoti <- numeric(10)
for (i in 1:10) {
    xDoti[i] <- 0
    for (j in 1:10)
        xDoti[i] <- xDoti[i] + x[i,j]
    xDoti[i] <- xDoti[i]/10
}

# Compute the variance
v <- 0
for (j in 1:10)
    v <- v + (xDoti[i]-m)^2
v <- v/9
```

```
# Compute Z
z <- m/(sqrt(v)/sqrt(10))

print('The difference in means between classifier1 and
        classifier2 is ')
print(m)
print('The variance of this difference in means is ')
print(v)
print('The Z Value obtained in the 10x10CV Average over Runs
        Scheme is ')
print(z)
}
```

This code is invoked as in Listing 6.31.

Listing 6.31: Invocation and results of 10×10-CV average-over-runs.

```
> library(RWeka)
> NB <- make_Weka_classifier("weka/classifiers/bayes/NaiveBayes")
> iris <- read.arff(system.file("arff", "iris.arff",
+                     package = "RWeka"))

> T1010cvRuns(iris, 150, 5, 3, c(50,50,50), NB, J48)
[1] "The difference in means between classifier1 and\n
                                    classifier2 is"
[1] 0.006002
[1] "The variance of this difference in means is"
[1] 4.002667e-05
[1] "The Z Value obtained in the 10x10CV Average over Runs\n
                                    Scheme is"
[1] 3
>
```

In this test, the Z value is slightly below 3.09, which means that we can not reject the hypothesis that the two classifiers perform similarly at the 95% confidence level.

10×10-CV Average-Over-Sorted-Runs

The code for the 10×10-CV average-over-sorted-runs variation modifies the code for the 10×10-CV average-over-runs only very slightly. These modifications occur in only a few places. First, the return/last line of the stratcv() function is replaced with the following line that sorts the results obtained by each classifier at each iteration. The function is renamed stratsortedcv() and is identical to stratcv() in all other respects:

```
return(list(sort(classifier1ResultArray),
    sort(classifier2ResultArray)))
```

The only other difference occurs in function T1kcv(), which now calls stratsortedcv() rather than stratcv() on line 3. The rest of the code is identical in all respect to that used in the 10×10-CV average-over-runs except for the first print statement which now states

```
print('The Z Value obtained in the 10x10CV Average over
    Sorted Runs Scheme is')
```

We renamed the earlier T1010cvRuns() as T1010cvSortedRuns() to reflect the little changes just outlined in two of the functions it calls and its print statement. We now show how to invoke this new function and show the results it obtains on the Iris dataset, in Listing 6.32.

Listing 6.32: Invocation and results of 10×10-CV average-over-sorted-runs.

```
> #Stratified and Sorted
> library(RWeka)
Loading required package: grid
>
> NB <- make_Weka_classifier("weka/classifiers/bayes/NaiveBayes")
> iris <- read.arff(system.file("arff", "iris.arff",
                    package = "RWeka"))
> T1010cvSortedRuns(iris, 150, 5, 3, c(50,50,50), NB, J48)
[1] "The difference in means between classifier1 and\n
                                          classifier2 is"
[1] 0.005335
[1] "The variance of this difference in means is"
[1] 0.0002389580
[1] "The Z Value obtained in the 10x10CV Average over Runs\n
                                          Scheme is"
[1] 1.091374
> T1010cvSortedRuns(iris, 150, 5, 3, c(50,50,50), NB, J48)
[1] "The difference in means between classifier1 and\n
                                          classifier2 is"
[1] 0.00667
[1] "The variance of this difference in means is"
[1] 2.708339e-34
[1] "The Z Value obtained in the 10x10CV Average over Runs\n
                                          Scheme is"
[1] 1.281664e+15
> T1010cvSortedRuns(iris, 150, 5, 3, c(50,50,50), NB, J48)
[1] "The difference in means between classifier1 and\n
                                          classifier2 is"
[1] 0.005334
[1] "The variance of this difference in means is"
[1] 1.95364e-06
[1] "The Z Value obtained in the 10x10CV Average over Runs\n
                                          Scheme is"
[1] 12.06787
> T1010cvSortedRuns(iris, 150, 5, 3, c(50,50,50), NB, J48)
[1] "The difference in means between classifier1 and\n
                                          classifier2 is"
[1] 0.004
[1] "The variance of this difference in means is"
```

```
[1]  0.0001264988
[1]  "The Z Value obtained in the 10x10CV Average over Runs\n
                                                Scheme  is"
[1]  1.124649
>
```

We ran this code four times. In two out of four of the runs, the difference in the mean of the two classifiers appears highly significant (ridiculously highly significant in one case!). However, this is not the case in the other two runs which show less than 80% confidence.

Note that, in all the other 10×10-CV schemes, we also found the results to be somewhat unstable. It would thus be important to investigate these methods more thoroughly before using them systematically.*

6.10   Summary

This chapter discussed the philosophy of null-hypothesis statistical testing (NHST) along with its underlying caveats, objections, and advantages with the perspective of evaluation of machine learning approaches. We also looked at the common misinterpretations of the statistical tests and how such occurrences can be avoided by raising our understanding of the statistical tests and their frame of application. Building on the notions of machine learning and statistics reviewed in Chapter 2, we then looked at various statistical tests as applied in the classifier evaluation settings. The description of relevant statistical tests was studied in four parts. The first part covered the tests relevant to (and used in) assessing the performances of two classifiers on a single domain. In particular, we reviewed the most widely employed two-matched-samples t test. An important place was given to the description of the assumptions on which the t test is built and that need to be verified for it to be valid. More general shortcomings of the t test, as used by machine learning practitioners, were also discussed. A nonparametric alternative, called McNemar's test, was then also discussed. We also showed how these tests can be extended to the case in which two classifiers are evaluated on multiple domains, the evaluation setting, which was the subject of the second part. In the second part, we discussed two nonparametric tests, the sign test and Wilcoxon's Signed-Rank test, discussing their advantages and limitations, both overall and relative to each other. Also, we showed how these can be applied in a single-domain setting and the underlying caveats. The third part then focused on the more general setting of comparing multiple classifiers on multiple domains. In particular, we focused on the parametric test ANOVA and its nonparametric equivalent, Friedman's test. We also showed how these are omnibus tests that indicate whether at least one classifier performance difference among all the comparisons being made is statistically significant. The identification of the particular differences, however, cannot be achieved by the omnibus

---

* A possible cause for such behavior could also be the manner in which the R environment handles variables in consecutive runs. This should also be verified.

tests and is, rather, accomplished using the post hoc tests that we discussed next. We covered major post hoc tests for both ANOVA and the Friedman tests along with their assumptions, advantages, and limitations. The fourth and final part discussed how multiple runs of the simple resampling techniques from Chapter 5 can improve on conventional statistical tests for comparing two classifiers on a single domain, discussed in this chapter. In particular, it discussed tests based on multiple runs of random subsampling and tests based on multiple runs of k-fold cross-validation.

Finally, the chapter concluded with an illustration of all the tests using the R statistical package.

6.11   Bibliographic Remarks

The main objections toward NHST appear in (Meehl, 1967, Harlow and Mulaik, 1997), and (Ioannidis, 2005). Drummond (2006) and Demšar (2008) discuss these objections in the context of machine learning. In particular, they detail and explain the various misuses of NHST that derive from the inconsistency in its interpretation. The main criticism about the overvalued results from NHST and its questionable soundness has come from Drummond (2006) and Demšar (2008). Thus statistical testing tends to give researchers too much confidence in results that may not be correct. Because of this confidence, Drummond (2006) and Demšar (2008) argue that a lot of worthwhile experiments are not carried out. Drummond (2008) argues that, rather than being confirmatory, our experiments should remain exploratory. He believes that our current practice limits experimental testing to hypothesis testing or, even worse, that statistical hypothesis testing impoverishes our field. The Internet-based solution to the necessity of statistical testing has been put forth by Demšar (2008). This democratic publishing process would be Web-based and work as follows: Rather than being judged by conference committees and journal editors and reviewers, papers would be published by their authors on the Web and get evaluated in a collaborative Web-based way. Good papers would get informally referred to and cited on the Web and thus be democratically elected. This view can, however, be contested in view of the limited incentives that the participants will have to validate the contents on the Web and also in the view of preferential biases leading to ignoring certain contents in favor of unfair coverage of others.

The t test was proposed by William Sealy Gossett in 1908 under the pen name Student and hence became known as Student's t test. The ANOVA procedures were discussed in detail in (Fisher, 1959). Wilcoxon's Signed-Rank test was proposed by Wilcoxon (1945). Finally, the nonparametric Friedman test was proposed by Friedman (1937, 1940). The Kruskal–Wallis test (Kruskal and Wallis, 1952) is the nonparametric equivalent of the one-way ANOVA. Holm's test was proposed by Holm (1979), and Hommel's test was proposed by Hommel (1988). A nice empirical comparison of ANOVA and the Friedman test as well as a power analysis of various post hoc tests with regard to classifier evaluation can be found in (Demšar, 2006).

The random subsampling t test and 5×2-CV t test are discussed and compared in terms of their type I error and power in (Dietterich, 1998). The corrected resampled t test comes from Nadeau and Bengio (2003), and the 5×2-CV F test was described in (Alpaydyn, 1999). The various repetitions of 10-fold cross-validated tests are compared in (Bouckaert, 2004).

Along the lines of Bouckaert (2003), replicability is formally defined as follows.

Definition 6.1. *The* replicability *of an experiment is the probability that two runs of the experiment on the same dataset, with the same pair of algorithms and the same method of sampling the data, produce the same outcome.*

Although the type I error states the probability that a difference in outcome is found over all datasets, replicability states this probability over a single dataset. It can be quantified as

$$\hat{R}_2(e) = \sum_{1 \leq i < j \leq n} \frac{I(e_i = e_j)}{n.(n-1)/2},$$

where $e = e_1, \ldots, e_n$ are the outcomes of n experiments with different randomizations on the dataset; I is the indicator function. $\hat{R}_2(e)$ has been shown to be unbiased and argued to be the best estimator of replicability possible because it exhibits minimal variance. Naturally the repeated trials of simple resamplings will yield better replicability because of the averaging effect over the variances. This was also confirmed by Bouckaert (2003), who shows that calibrated repeated tests are actually preferable to the corrected resampled t test as they show much better replicability.

7

Datasets and Experimental Framework

We have discussed different aspects and components pertaining to the evaluation of learning algorithms. Given one or more fixed domains, we have discussed various performance measures, a number of sampling and resampling methods designed to estimate the outcome of these performance measures in a reliable manner and tests allowing us to estimate the statistical significance of the observed results. Many other aspects linked to each of these steps were also surveyed along the line, such as the notion of bias and variance and the debate on the need to practice statistical significance testing. The only aspect of evaluation that was not questioned, so far, is the issue of determining an appropriate testbed for our experiments. All the components that we discussed so far in this book made the implicit assumption expressed in the second sentence of this chapter: *"Given one or more fixed domains."* It is now time to expand on this issue because the application, results, and subsequent interpretation of the different components of the evaluation process depend critically on the domains on which these are assessed and quantified. Furthermore, selecting datasets for evaluating the algorithms is certainly a nontrivial issue.

One important result connected to the choice of datasets on which to evaluate learning algorithms is summarized in Wolpert's "No Free Lunch" theorems. These theorems show the importance of evaluating algorithms on a large number of problems, because, if only a small sample of problems is considered, the results could be biased. Indeed, these theorems show that if one learning algorithm tends to perform better than another on a given class of problems, then the reverse will be true on a different class of problems. In other words, no algorithm is better than any other on *all* possible problems. Interestingly, the fact that even mediocre learning approaches can be shown to be competitive by selecting the test domains carefully has been quite elegantly demonstrated by LaLoudouana and Tarare (2003).

The purpose of dataset selection in an evaluation framework thus should not be to demonstrate an algorithm's superiority to another in all cases, but rather to identify the areas of strengths of different algorithms with respect to domain characteristics or on specific domains of interest.

Keeping this important observation in mind, we first categorize the learning algorithms into two groups: generic algorithms and task-specific algorithms. As the name suggests, generic algorithms are realizations of some general learning principles. These algorithms are either intended as proof of concepts or as all-purpose learning algorithms, requiring very minor tuning in terms of parameters or algorithmic design. In either case, it is desirable that such generic algorithms demonstrate their utility across a range of varied domains so as to prove their robustness and applicability to any general classification task (i.e., domain).

On the other hand, task-specific learning algorithms are either customized realizations of the generic algorithms or algorithms whose learning premises are based on some domain-specific knowledge, or a combination of the two. These algorithms are typically customized to address a specific class of learning problem(s). They can be either fine-tuned versions of general learning principles (say, a generic algorithm) to a certain problem, or are designed, specifically keeping in view the problem of interest. Note that this fine-tuning does not refer to incorporating a bias in the learning process. Rather, it refers to making the algorithm sensitive to the specific aspects of the domain of application. Such knowledge typically comes from detailed know-how and expertise in the field. Various examples can be found for both generic as well as task-specific algorithms. Typically, any new learning theoretic principle results in a generic algorithm such as an SVM. On the other hand, task-specific algorithms or customized versions of generic algorithms appear frequently in various applied fields. Consider, for instance, the algorithms aimed at performing image segmentation for human brain magnetic resonance imaging (MRI), machine translation for specific language pairs, or learning from time-series microarray data, among others.

Validating any algorithm would require a large number of datasets whether from similar domains (in the case of task-specific algorithms) or a variety of domains (for generic algorithms). The domains needed to validate task-specific algorithms are very specific and so are the requirements over algorithms' desired performance on them. Generally, considerable expert knowledge and interpretation capability is needed in such cases. More relevant to our discussion, here, however is the evaluation of generic algorithms which involves comparing the novel algorithm to other computing approaches on a number of benchmark datasets.

Experience, for instance insights from the no-free-lunch theorems, suggests that many datasets are necessary to properly evaluate classifiers, unless the user is ultimately interested in classification on one particular domain of interest (e.g., a particular medical or industrial application). Further, if one is interested in testing some specific characteristics of the learning algorithms, then these requirements translate into some desired data characteristics. For instance, if an algorithm assumes a Gaussian prior distribution over the data, then one might seek a dataset specifically fulfilling this requirement to validate the algorithm.

On the other hand, one might specifically be interested in failure analysis and hence might put a strict requirement on the dataset, that the distribution of the instances be non-Gaussian. Even for generic algorithms, it is sometimes desirable to assess their performance on particular data characteristics such as robustness to particular noise models.

Such requirements on the data have resulted in at least two different approaches to addressing the problem. The first is what we call the data repository approach and the second is the synthetic or artificial data approach. Both approaches have been followed widely, either by themselves or in conjunction with each other. However, just as with any other component that we have discussed in the book, it should not come as a surprise that both these approaches have their respective advantages and shortcomings. Let us discuss these two approaches along with their benefits and limitations in a balanced manner, and then move on to some recent proposals for both dataset collection and dissemination and overall evaluation benchmark design.

7.1   Repository-Based Approach

The need for many domains to be used as testbeds for evaluation was understood long before it was formalized by Wolpert's theorems. Having their origin in the early 1990s, many data repositories have appeared, aimed at gathering datasets for the purpose of replication, access and subsequent comparison of results. One of the early initiatives in this direction with regard to machine learning was the data repository project at the University of California, Irvine. This repository is commonly referred to as the UCI Repository or the UCI Repository for Machine Learning. Other attempts at creating data repositories have also been made and resulted in projects such as DELVE in the context of large evaluation projects, Statlog, meta learning evaluation environment METAL, and so on. With regard to task-specific algorithms too, repositories of data on particular domain of interests have appeared. Examples include the GEO repository for microarray data, the Internet brain segmentation repository (IBSR), the Stanford microarray database, and so on. Table 7.1 shows a list of major machine learning and data mining repositories or organizations that store these repositories and their current hyperlink.

7.1.1   The UCI Repository

Among the machine learning repositories, UCI tends to subsume them all and remains the most complete and authoritative repository of domains for machine learning. It is still maintained and often expanded to include new contributed datasets. The UCI Repository is widely used. As must be obvious by now, all the examples presented in the book, so far, were based on datasets extracted from it. Such use of UCI data is quite widespread for performance assessment and evaluation of learning algorithms in the field. The commonplace use of

Table 7.1. *Some of the general machine learning and data mining repositories*

Name of the Repository	Hyperlink
UCI Repository	http://archive.ics.uci.edu/ml/
StatLib	http://lib.stat.cmu.edu/
StatLog	http://www.the-data-mine.com/bin/view/Misc/StatlogDatasets
METAL	http://www.metal-kdd.org/
DELVE	http://www.cs.toronto.edu/ delve/
NASA's datasets	http://nssdc.gsfc.nasa.gov/
CMU Data Repository	http://www.cs.cmu.edu/afs/cs/project/ai-repository/ai/areas/learning/0.html

the UCI Repository can be understood by looking at its impact in the field
in terms of the number of citations that the paper introducing the repository
has received. With over 1000 citations and growing, it is one of the top "100"
most cited papers in all of computer science. New domains are constantly
added to the repository, which receives active maintenance. Along with the UCI
Repository comes the UCI Knowledge Discovery in Databases (KDD) Archive,
which complements the UCI Repository by specializing in large datasets and
is not restricted to classification tasks. The archive includes very large datasets
including high-dimensional data, time series data, spatial data, and transaction
data. The creators of this database recognize the positive impact that the UCI
Repository has had on the field, but they lament that the datasets it contains
are not realistic for data mining because of limited size both in terms of the
number of samples and in terms of dimensionality, as well as narrow scope.
The UCI KDD Archive addresses these two issues and others, also expanding the type of datasets to problems other than classification (e.g., regression,
time series analysis) and different objects (e.g., images, relational data, spatial
data).

Although a few criticisms and some defense of these datasets have been
voiced, the question of what datasets we should use has not received significant
attention in the community. In addition, although the advantages brought on by
such repositories have been noted, the disadvantages in terms of both the explicit
issues as well as unintended consequences have not received the attention they
deserve. In this section, we aim to bring the trade-off between the advantages
and limitations of the repository-based approach into perspective. Let us start
with the positives.

7.1.2 Advantages of Repository-Based Approach

The main and most obvious advantages of the repositories are twofold. First,
they act as a source of databases that researchers can use immediately with
neither an in-depth knowledge of the data domain nor any worry concerning

data standardization or preprocessing. Second, they allow researchers to apply their algorithms to the same domains, thus simplifying comparative studies. This expands the reach of benchmark domains not only to machine learning and data mining researchers – who may not otherwise have access to such data – but it also makes evaluating these approaches easier for external researchers.

Another advantage concerns the data-acquisition process. Because the main thrust of repositories such as UCI is on obtaining real-world data, less reliance is placed on synthetic data generation. In this sense – which is sometimes limited, as we subsequently discuss – evaluations are performed in real-world settings with the assumptions that the characteristics of the data, including both their distribution and the inevitable noise model associated with it, tend to mimic the types of behavior found in real-world applications.

Moving further, the repositories are also a valuable source when it comes to replication of results. Having access to the same datasets makes replicating the published or previously known results easier as well as verifiable with regard to the available learning methods. Not only this, but the repositories also act as uniform testbeds. That is, access to the same datasets both over time and across researchers makes comparative evaluations more reliable. Such comparative evaluations can be made between different approaches as well as novel approaches assessed against the state of the art. This not only allows for performance comparisons on a common benchmark, but also helps identify strengths, limitations, and issues that arise with respect to the application of various learning approaches to a real-world setting. In this respect, Bay et al. (2000, p. 85) rightly state that

> The UCI ML repository revolutionized the way research is conducted in machine learning by improving the quality and thoroughness of experimental evaluation.

The UCI KDD Archive creators gathered more complex datasets as a means to achieve the same quality of research in data mining. Their efforts were supported by the NSF Information and Data Management program, which indicates that practically motivated institutions concur in recognizing the usefulness of such repositories.

There are other advantages, as well, that were actually mentioned by some of the UCI Repository's most ardent critiques. For example, Saitta and Neri (1998) concede that evaluating algorithms on these datasets can provide important insights. Holte (1993) found the repository useful in showing that, although some real-world datasets are hard, many others are not, including a large number in the UCI Repository, which were shown to be representative of practical domains.

Finally, another feature of the UCI Repository, which can also be construed as an advantage is that the repository keeps on evolving with new datasets contributed to it on a regular basis. As well, its scope has widened through the addition of the UCI KDD Archive to incorporate datasets reflecting new concerns such as massive databases.

Given all these advantages that make researchers' life easier, why should we then be cautious when using such wonderful resources? Let us look at some counterarguments now.

7.1.3 Disadvantages of Repository-Based Approach

Despite the obvious (and less-obvious) advantages provided by data repositories, a number of disadvantages have also been pointed out. Let us study some of the main lines of arguments against an all-out use of such repositories.

The Problem of Generalizing Results

One of the main arguments against the use of data repositories stipulates that their use does not guarantee generalization to other datasets. Consider the experiment conducted by Holte (1993). On noting that his very simple 1R algorithm performed almost as well as c45 on 16 domains, including 14 from UCI, a concern can be raised about the fact that a simple classifier does so well on such a "wide" range of datasets. Holte (1993, p. 73) states that

> One does not intuitively expect 'real' classification problems to be solved by very simple rules. Consequently, one may doubt if the datasets used in this study are 'representative' of the datasets that actually arise in practice.

On further analysis, Holte notes that the domains that were used did not represent the whole range of problems expected to appear in real-world scenarios (noting that there are some real problems that are particularly "hard" for machine learning classifiers). However, he concedes that "the number and diversity of the datasets indicates that they represent a class of problems that often arises."

Another criticism of repository-based research has come in terms of their representativeness of the data mining process. For instance, Saitta and Neri (1998) contend that the UCI Repository contains only "ready-to-use" datasets that present only a small step in the overall data mining process. Although researchers agree that evaluating learning algorithms on these datasets can be useful, as it can provide interesting insights, the main objections are made along the following lines:

- Because the evaluations are typically done, even though on a common platform, by different researchers (and possibly over different implementations of the same learning approaches), unintentional or even unconcious tuning of some of the learning parameters can give unfair advantages to the algorithms most familiar to the researchers (e.g., the researchers who originally designed the approaches being tested).

- Because the goal of the comparison is not to use the learned knowledge (which would be what is useful in real-world settings), it is not clear that the results reported on these domains are of any use.
- In an effort to make repository datasets usable off the shelf, they are usually vastly oversimplified, resulting in datasets of limited size and complexity, with the difficult cases often set aside.

The first point is not easy to dismiss. In fact, it has profound implications. As a very trivial example, many studies report results concerning novel algorithms or algorithms of interest pitted against other competitive approaches. These other approaches are typically run using their "default" parameters (generally from a machine learning toolbox implementation such as WEKA), whereas the algorithm of interest to the study is carefully tuned. This can be in part due to the limited familiarity of the researchers with the other approaches, even if we discount intentional attempts (which is not entirely impossible). As a result, such assessments may not reflect a true comparison.

The second point stresses the need for domain knowledge that, indeed, must be involved or accounted for in any real-world application in order to obtain meaningful results. Although the point is certainly valid in terms of real-world applicability, it is relatively less troubling when generic approaches are compared because, in these cases, the main objective is to demonstrate a wide-ranging utility of the proposed approaches on a common testbed. However, when it comes to task-specific algorithms, this concern is indeed more serious. Nevertheless, using general repositories, such as the UCI, for evaluating task-specific approaches may not be a good idea altogether. Keeping such points in perspectives, various task- or domain-specific repositories are now appearing that provide a more meaningful set of data to evaluate approaches designed for these specific classes of problems.

The final point on the list is indeed true in many cases. However, with novel datasets being added regularly, especially as a result of data acquisitions from new and more mature technology, we hope that such reservations will be addressed in the near future. Furthermore, a full disclosure on the part of researchers as well as data submission groups would make it easier to interpret the subsequent results of learning approaches accordingly and be aware of the caveats implicit in such validation. We must keep in mind, however, that this issue gains more relevance when the scalability of the algorithms to the real world is concerned. In this respect, views such as those of Saitta and Neri (1998) suggest that a good performance on general repository data should be seen as a means to obtaining good results, but not as the goal of the research. Hence it is not sufficient to demonstrate better performance of some algorithms against others on these datasets, but rather it is both important and more relevant to analyze the reasons behind the different behaviors.

The Community Experiment Effect

Another major criticism of the repository-based approach appears in the form of the "community experiment effect." Simply stated, it is claimed that the very familiarity with these datasets has led to evaluation overfitting. The term overfitting has a broad connotation in this context. It is generally argued that, if very many experiments were run on the same datasets, some of these, by chance, would yield statistically significant outcomes. This can be true notwithstanding the correctness of the experiments or the careful handling of statistical tests. Consider the following illustration: Suppose that 100 different experiments are run aimed at comparing the accuracy of two learning algorithms A and B. Let us assume that A and B have the same mean accuracy over a very large population of datasets. Then, when studying the results of these algorithms statistically with a significance level of 0.05, we can expect, by chance alone, to observe five experiments that might show a statistically significant difference between the performances of A and B. Such statistically significant results then would have a higher chance of appearing in the literature, even though these may not be representative of A's and B's actual performance difference.

To account for this shortcoming, we need to go back to the previous limitation of the repository-based approach, i.e., the problem of generalizing results. Verifying any statistically significant result requires replication of experiments to assess if indeed the observed difference did not occur by chance. However, reasonable replication of experiments is easier said than done. In addition to some aspects of difficulties in replication that we discussed earlier, we also note that proper duplication requires drawing a new random sample from the population and repeating the study. Both at the instance level as well as the dataset level, this is very difficult owing to the static nature and relatively small size of the benchmark database.

Some counterclaims have also appeared in the form of empirical attempts to verify the said overfitting (see pointers in Section 7.6), although the results of such attempts remain inconclusive.

The Multiplicity Effect

The final criticism that we discuss with regard to repository-based evaluation is an extension of the previous argument. It focuses on two main community resources: The first are, of course, the data repositories and second are the general libraries (such as WEKA), implementing various learning approaches that can then be used off the shelf for comparative purposes. Referred to as the "multiplicity effect," the main argument made by this criticism is that, owing to the simplicity afforded by the two previous resources, running a large number of experiments and subsequently interpreting the results requires the establishment of more stringent statistical significance requirements than doing so over a few number of experiments. However, unlike the case of the previous two criticisms, the current issue can be to a great extent addressed by making the underlying statistical framework more robust (for instance, by using higher significance levels).

7.2   Making Sense of Our Repositories: Metalearning

Efforts aimed at understanding the dependencies and correlation between the data characteristics and the learning algorithms have resulted in a new branch of study commonly referred to as metalearning. Let us very briefly look at some such attempts in the context of classification.

The purpose of metalearning in this context is to map dataset characteristics to the algorithms that show strengths on these characteristics. The first attempts at metalearning came in the early 1990s with the works of researchers like Aha (1992), Rendell and Cho (1990), and Brodley (1993). These earlier works focused on studying dataset characteristics such as the number of instances, the number of classes, the number of instances per classes, the number of relevant and irrelevant attributes, and so on. Both static as well as run-time approaches were used to select the learning algorithms. Whereas the static approaches (such as those used by Rendell and Cho, and Aha) chose an algorithm a priori, the run-time approach (such as that of Brodley) typically performed a dynamic search for the best algorithm, recognizing, at run time, if an algorithm did not perform well and choosing a different one.

Large-scale attempts at metalearning, in order to understand the relationship between the data characteristics and learning algorithms, appeared later in the context of projects such as Statlog and METAL. More sophisticated features were utilized in these cases, which included statistical and information-theoretic features, in addition to the simpler features used in earlier attempts. The Statlog project covered a total of 22 datasets (all from UCI Repository) and 23 machine learning algorithms (belonging to the broad categories of machine learning, neural networks, and statistical classification algorithms). A decision tree was used to learn the mapping of domains to algorithms and resulted in a binary outcome for each classifier. The METAL project extended this study even further, using 53 datasets from the UCI Repository and other sources and 10 learning algorithms (the number of learning algorithms was reduced as it turned out that many algorithms could be treated together in the context of learning a mapping between domains and algorithms). Whereas the Statlog project used accuracy to measure performance, METAL used both accuracy and time performance in a multicriteria type measure. The results in the case of METAL were based on 10-fold cross-validation (which was not the case in the Statlog project). The features used to describe the domains were the same for both these projects. One difference between the two projects, however, was that the binary outcome of Statlog was replaced with an algorithm ranking approach in METAL.

Some recent attempts at metalearning have also been made, such as the work of Ali and Smith (2006), that increased the number of characteristic features and classification domains and used more sensitive performance measures than those of the earlier studies. However, the research in this direction has been limited and has not gained community-wide attention. One of the reasons for such limited focus on these studies is probably the limited applied use of machine learning methods up until very recently. Consequently such studies were either deemed not very practical to perform on a large scale or not very relevant because of perceived lack of novelty. However, as the applications of learning approaches increase in various fields and on a variety of problems, such empirical studies, although limited in their novelty value, not only offer some interesting insights into both the learning process and the data characteristics, but also expand our understanding of the nature of the domains and algorithms, as well as their impact on evaluation. This issue is increasingly important with the rise in both the number and size of data repositories and libraries of learning algorithms aimed as standardizing the evaluation process to a significant extent.

The typical approach to selecting datasets to evaluate the algorithms have focused on either choosing these datasets from a repository (typically UCI), at random (of course with minor considerations on size and dimensionality), or using the ones that have appeared in earlier studies in similar contexts. The verdict on the best approach to choosing the most suited datasets for evaluation is not yet out. An argument can be made for choosing the sets that demonstrate the strength of (or are most difficult for) a learning approach. Another argument can also be made for the choice of random but wide-ranging domains for evaluating generic algorithms, because eventually the purpose of testing such algorithms is precisely to demonstrate their applicability across the board. The insights obtained from metalearning approaches as well as other empirical studies, however, can have some more profound implications in the direction of our increased understanding.

As the applied thrust for learning approaches gains momentum, more such studies are needed. Until that is done, though, let us shift our attention toward another approach to dataset selection, the artificial data approach.

7.3 Artificial Data Approach

One of the common threads that runs through the criticism of the repository-based approach goes along the following line: The datasets from the repository are not representative enough so as to reliably mimic the real world. Extending this argument further suggests that, because the precise distribution over the data and possible associated noise are unknown, the conclusions drawn from repository experiments, both in absolute and comparative terms, are questionable at best. This has, in fact, been the main line of argument against the repository-based approach. As repositories evolve with time in terms of the number, variety, and size of datasets, the classical criticism over the unrepresentativeness of the real world has lost some ground. However, in some cases, it indeed might be necessary to evaluate algorithms on domains whose behavior is known and hence for which, the resulting predictions can be reliably verified.

One scenario for which such a requirement is in fact necessary is for the proof of concept implementations of algorithms. Consider, for instance, a Bayesian classifier that assumes the underlying data-generating distribution to be Gaussian (a probably more-than-common scenario), maybe with some known model of noise. Such a priori assumptions on data and noise can come from various sources, including expert knowledge of the domain, empirical model fitting over validation data, and noise modeling outcomes. However, once a classifier is built, it is indeed logical, as a first step, to evaluate its behavior on the a priori basis used to obtain the learning approach.

A common approach in such cases then is to validate the algorithm on artificial datasets that demonstrate the desired traits. In cases in which the real-world observations are known, or alternatively their main behavior traits are known, then the artificial datasets built accordingly would ensure relevance to the actual conditions of the application. Moreover, they also provide customized test benchmarks, giving the user control over the test conditions. Another advantage of such an approach is to guard against evaluation overfitting, as discussed in the previous section, as new datasets can always be generated, owing to the fact that both the data- and (possibly) noise-generating distributions are known. Using metalearning techniques affords an added advantage because the sampling can be done in conjunction with the metalearning process. This is especially beneficial when either the available real data are extremely limited and hence not fully representative of the domain or it is prohibitively expensive to obtain additional samples. In such cases, known models can be used to generate additional samples, and when such models are not known, empirical models can be built over the data in order to expand them.[1]

The limitations of this approach are quite obvious from the preceding discussion too. Indeed, a natural argument is that, because we often contend that the real-world domains are not very predictable (in the sense that they do not necessarily obey some fixed distributional models) and are prone to external exacting circumstances, isn't it too optimistic to expect data generated according to some fixed model, even when considering some (well-behaved) noise, to mimic the real-world domain of application? The answer is affirmative. Moreover, such a process can certainly be biased in favor of approaches that can model data more closely than others. Even when it suggests the strength of the winning algorithms in modeling such data, it does not necessarily depict their absolute or even comparative superiority in real applied settings for obvious reasons.

---

[1] However, this argument should be taken with a grain of salt because the underlying assumption is that the limited data is not representative of the actual domain. Hence empirical models obtained from such data would inevitably face similar issues and the resulting samples would indeed, at best, be grossly approximate, if at all.

In the wake of such serious objections, why then bother about artificial data at all? Well, as a rule of thumb, while looking at any approach, it is necessary to check if we are asking the right questions. This should, in fact, be viewed as a general rule, at least in evaluation. Throughout the book, when discussing various concepts, we have explicitly or implicitly highlighted this concern. Indeed, knowing the basic assumptions of any process, the constraints under which it is applied and the proper interpretation of the results has been a common theme in all our discussions. The same principle applies in this case too. Is the aim of the artificial-data-based approach to give a verdict on superiority of some particular algorithm? Is such an approach capable of discerning statistically significant differences over the generalization performance of the classifiers compared? We would, at least in a broader sense, answer both these questions in the negative. What is important is the ability to control various aspects of the evaluation process in an artifical data approach.

This trait gives us the ability to perform specific experiments aimed at assessing algorithms' behavior on certain parameters of interest while controlling for others in a relatively precise manner. Such flexibility is typically impossible in any real-world setting. Consider the problem of assessing the impact of changing environments on classifier performance. The topic of changing environments has led to a new line of research in statistical machine learning. In the relatively limited sense that it is pursued currently, the problem of changing environments refers to the scenario in which the distributions on which the algorithm is eventually tested (deployed) differs from the domain distribution on which it has been trained. Theoretical advancements have been made in this direction. However, such efforts have currently focused on limited scenarios (which are controlled to track for changing distributions). Although the problem is ubiquitous in the practical world, very few datasets are publicly available that address this issue. Given both the dearth of appropriate real-world data and the extremely limited tuning flexibility over them, a controlled study is almost impossible. Accordingly, the artificial data approach has been immensely helpful in obtaining such preliminary but encouraging and verifiable results. The work of Alaiz-Rodriguez and Japkowicz (2008) has relied on generating artificial datasets to study *empirically* the behavior of various algorithms' performance. Such observations can potentially complement the theoretical insights obtained by learning theoretic approaches, as well as understanding the premise of the problem itself. In particular, their empirical study relied on the artificial data approach to validate a version of the Occam's razor hypothesis, which states that, all other things being equal, simple classifiers are preferable over complex ones. More specifically, the study was aimed to test the hypothesis emphasized by Hand (2006) that simple classifiers are more robust to changing environments than complex ones. They in fact found that, in many cases, Hand (2006)'s hypothesis was not verified. Artificial datasets have been significantly relied on in this case because the major repositories do not contain datasets that are reasonably representative of such scenarios, even though it is frequently encountered in practice (can this be considered to be evidence in favor of the limited real-world representativeness of repository data?).

A suggestion to make the artificial data approach more acceptable has come in the form of proposing frameworks that can verify the realistic nature of artificially generated data and the effect of the data-generation method on this behavior. Efforts such as the framework proposed by Ganti et al. (2002) have recently appeared in this direction. These efforts have, in their preliminary form, concentrated on comparing the obtained artificial data with the real-world data and hence still require the real-world data at hand. However, if such methods do succeed, this requirement can be, to some extent, relaxed.

Another approach to complement this is a bottom-up approach. That is, it states that one can start with whatever limited real-world data are available and then extend it by using reliable artificial data-generation methods so as to have the datasets represent realistic conditions not represented in the actual domain. This is then viewed as a potential solution to limited availability and hence representativeness of real-world data. For instance, one can create an artificial dataset generator that takes as input a real domain, analyzes it automatically, and generates deformations of this dataset that follow certain high-level characteristics. Such high-level characteristics can represent, for instance, a particular noise injection, creating or reducing imbalances and so on. One such approach was proposed in the work of Narasimhamurthy and Kuncheva (2007). Although it may seem that obtaining the high-level characteristics can be troublesome, the upside is that, once reasonably verified, such characteristics in conjunction with this bottom-up bootstrap-type approach can provide practically unlimited data points.

7.4 Community Participation: Web-Based Solutions

Even though the generic as well as task-specific data repositories remain the main sources of datasets for evaluation purposes, there is a growing realization of the need to push forward in the direction of more meaningful, verifiable, and robust evaluation of learning approaches. Even though it can in some cases complement the evaluation efforts, the artificial data approach poses significant concerns, limiting its use to full proof evaluation. Some novel ideas such as metalearning and extending real datasets by artificial methods have appeared that aim to amalgamate the strengths of the two approaches while ameliorating their limitations to a significant extent. However, these approaches still face hurdles. For instance, as previously mentioned, extending the real-world datasets using artificial data generators is easier said than done because there is limited real-world data available to begin with, not to mention the extremely limited knowledge about the application domain. Even when this limitation does not exist (that is, reasonably sufficient data are available to obtain empirical models), this does not necessarily mean that efficient data generators can be obtained to expand on these empirical observations.

There have also been proposals, based on community participation, so as to develop access to data, learning algorithms, and their implementation, as well as methodologies to perform coherent algorithm evaluation that not only can scale up to real-world situations, but are also robust and statistically verifiable. Among the proposals recently put forward to address the issue, an interesting argument is that of community participation in the process. Taking inspiration from the success of collaborative projects such as Wikipedia, in which the collaboration comes from the effort of the community, this line of argument proposes partic- ipation of relevant researchers as well as groups in the evaluative process. An example of such a proposal is that by Japkowicz (2008). In this, she contends that the World Wide Web can be a powerful tool in facilitating such an effort. The basic idea underlying the argument is that the resources for the evaluative pro- cess can be made available in collaboration with various groups with a stake in the process. For instance, data mining and other groups (e.g., hospitals, clinical research centers, news groups) could contribute real-world data for evaluation and outline their goals clearly. Meanwhile, the machine learning community could offer public releases of algorithmic implementations, with comprehen- sive documentation. Participants from the statistical analysis community could provide guidelines for robust statistical evaluation and assessment techniques in concordance with the data provider's stated purpose. Performing subsequent evaluation of approaches as well as other studies and analysis, for instance in data characterization or the effects of statistical analysis techniques, could not only benefit respective communities, but could also provide important insights to other participating parties with regard to real-world implications of their work. For instance, data-gathering groups could analyze their data in order to make their respective data-acquisiton process more robust (e.g., when the concerns regarding missing values or noisy data are realized), whereas the statistically ori- ented groups would gain insight into the empirical applications of their analysis techniques. The learning community could also obtain a deeper understanding of the real-world application settings and the ways to make their approaches amenable to these applications in a robust and reliable manner. Of course, for such projects to succeed, it would be imperative for each party to provide as much precision and detail about their contributed components as possible.

With a growth in participating groups and proper organization, such efforts could have profound implications, not only on specific elements of the overall evaluation process, but also on the interrelationships among various disciplines. This could also bolster an appreciation of their strengths and the limitations under which they operate. This would hence not only facilitate the evaluation, but also strengthen the foundation of interdisciplinary research, the future of science. Such arguments have been voiced earlier too, as evidenced by the very existence of the UCI Repository itself.

7.5   Summary

This short chapter was aimed at discussing both the practical as well as a (partially) philosophical argument both in favor and against different approaches to selecting and using domains of application for the purpose of evaluating learning algorithms. The main approaches currently employed for generic evaluation in different studies include choosing the datasets from general repositories such as the UCI Repository for Machine Learning or using synthetic datasets. Both these methods have their respective advantages and limitations. In the case of the former, real-world datasets can better characterize the settings and the challenges that the learning algorithm can face when applied in such a setting, but also suffer from limitations such as the community experiment effects and limited control over the test criteria with regard to the algorithm of interest. The latter approach, on the other hand, enables evaluating specific aspects of the learning algorithms because the data behavior can be precisely controlled, but is limited in its ability to replicate real-world settings. Repositories have also appeared for approaches designed to address a specific task of interest (e.g., image segmentation). Analogous arguments can be made with regard to their utility and alternatives of simulated data as well. Relatively novel arguments for coming up with better approaches for domain selection and usage have appeared in the form of community participation over Web-based solutions. The jury is still out on such new proposals.

   This chapter completes the discussion of the various components of the evaluation framework for learning algorithms that we started in Chapter 3 with performance measures. With regard to different components, such as performance measures, error estimation, statistical significance testing and dataset selection, we mainly focused on the approaches that have become mainstream (although in a very limited use) in the sense that their behavior, advantages, and limitations against competing approaches are relatively well understood. In the next chapter, we present a brief discussion on the attempts either to offer alternative approaches to address different components or extensions of the current approaches that have appeared relatively recently. These attempts can be important steps forward in developing our understanding of a coherent evaluation framework.

7.6   Bibliographic Remarks

The most recent description of the UCI Repository for Machine Learning can be found in (Asuncion and Newman, 2007). The UCI KDD Archive is discussed in (Bay et al., 2000). Although there may have been a few attempts at creating other repositories in the context of large evaluation projects [e.g., DELVE (http://www.cs.toronto.edu/~delve/), StatLog (http://www.the-data-mine.com/bin/view/Misc/StatlogDatasets) and METAL (http://www.ofai.at/~johann.petrak/MLEE/mlee/doc/metal-mlee/)], UCI tends to subsume them all and remains the most complete and authoritative repository of domains for machine learning. It is still maintained and often expanded to include new contributed datasets. Other application-specific repositories have also appreared such as the IBSR (http://www.cma.mgh.harvard.edu/ibsr/), the GEO database (http://www.ncbi.nlm.nih.gov/geo/), and the Stanford microarray database (http://smd-www.stanford.edu/).

The no-free-lunch theorems were formulated in (Wolpert, 1996) and then with regard to optimization in (Wolpert and Macready, 1997).

The question of how relevant the UCI Repository domains are to data mining research was scientifically investigated by Soares (2003). To do so, he compared the distribution of the relative performance of various algorithms on a set of data known to be relevant to data mining research with that on a large subset of datasets contained in the UCI Repository. His statistical analysis revealed that there is no evidence that the UCI domains (at least, those containing over 500 samples) are less relevant than the domains known to be relevant. Soares (2003) also investigated the claim that machine learning researchers overfit the UCI Repository. In particular, Soares (2003) tested whether an algorithm overfits the Repository by testing whether its rank is higher in the repository than it is in the domains that are not included in the repository. Once again, his study revealed that there is no statistical evidence that suggests that algorithms rank higher in the repository than in the other datasets, and thus there is no evidence that supports the claim of overfitting. However, more research needs to be done to guarantee reliability of the employed statistical framework.

The community experiment effect has been discussed by, among others, Salzberg (1997) and Bay et al. (2000).

Smith-Miles (2008) gives a comprehensive survey of metalearning research for algorithm selection. Although she looks at various kinds of algorithms, we focused on only classification algorithms here as we followed her discussion. Other references to metalearning approaches can be found in the works of Rendell and Cho (1990), Aha (1992), Brodley (1993), and, more recently, Ali and Smith (2006).

The study by Ganti and colleagues referred to in the text can be found in (Ganti et al., 2002). Deformations of real data and their extension by use of artificial methods discussed in the text refers to (Narasimhamurthy and Kuncheva, 2007).

8

Recent Developments

We reviewed the major components of the evaluation framework in the last chapters and described in detail the various techniques pertaining to each, together with their applications. The focus of this chapter is to complement this review by outlining various advancements that have been made relatively recently, but that have not yet become mainstream. We also look into some approaches aimed at addressing problems arising from the developments on the machine learning front in various application settings, such as ensemble classifiers.

Just as with the traditional developments in performance evaluation, recent attempts at improving as well as designing new performance metrics have led the way. These have resulted in both improvements to existing performance metrics, thereby claiming to ameliorate the issues with the current versions, and proposals for novel metrics aimed at addressing the areas of algorithm evaluation not satisfactorily addressed by current metrics. We discuss in brief some of these advancements in Section 8.1. In Section 8.2, we focus on the attempts at unifying these performance metrics as well as studying their interrelation in the form of both theoretical and experimental frameworks. A natural extension to such studies is the design of more general or broader measures of performance, either as a result of insights obtained from the theoretical framework or by combining existing metrics based on observations from the experimental frameworks. Such metric combinations for obtaining general measures are the focus of Section 8.3. Then, in Section 8.4, we outline some advancements in statistical learning theory, the branch of machine learning aimed at characterizing the theoretical aspects of learning algorithms, that can potentially lead to more informed algorithm evaluation approaches that can take into account not just the empirical performance, but also the specific properties of the learning algorithms. Finally, in Section 8.5, we discuss recent findings and developments with regards to other aspects of algorithmic evaluation.

8.1   Performance Metrics

This section surveys two different types of advances in the study and design of performance metrics. The first ones continue to address the traditional performance criteria already discussed in Chapters 3 and 4, whereas the second moves beyond these criteria to include qualitative considerations. Let us now discuss these in turn.

8.1.1   Quantitative Metrics

Various attempts have been made to study the characteristics of individual performance metrics and to identify their limitations. In addition, attempts have also been made to study the interrelation between pairs of performance metrics in the hope of studying their suitability in various scenarios and applications. The measure that received the most attention naturally has been accuracy (and hence, indirectly, the misclassification error) because it has long been the metric of choice for reporting the empirical performance of classifiers. This then is followed by studies on the area under the ROC curve (AUC), which subsequently replaced accuracy as the metric of choice for reporting results on scoring classifiers because of its ability to summarize the performance of algorithms over different cost ratios. Inevitably, this led to studies that focused on investigating the comparative behavior of the two metrics, yielding some interesting insights. Among the representative attempts at studying this pair of metrics have been those of Provost and Domingos (2003), Ferri et al. (2003), and Cortes and Mohri (2004). An interesting insight was also obtained by Rosset (2004), who experimentally showed how optimizing AUC on a validation set yields better accuracy on the test set. This was an interesting finding in terms of the interrelation between the performance metrics and their potential agreement. Other studies have focused on alternative metric pairs for comparison (e.g., Davis and Goadrich, 2006, compares ROC and PR curves). Efforts at studying the statistical characteristics of some extensions to AUC in specific settings have also been made (see, for instance, He and Frey, 2008, and references therein for medical imaging applications). Performance guarantees over the AUC and ROC curves in general have also been studied in terms of confidence bounds (see, for instance, Cortes and Mohri, 2005, for confidence bounds on AUC, Macskassy et al., 2005, for pointwise confidence bounds on ROC, and references therein for more general confidence bands around ROCs, and Yousef et al., 2005, on another approach to studying the uncertainty of the mean AUC). Yousef et al. (2006) also use AUC and its statistical properties to assess classifiers.

These and other efforts have also enabled a better understanding of measures such as the AUC and identifying their limitations. The limitations of AUC in particular have been studied in (Vanderlooy and Hüllermeier, 2008) and Hand

(2006, 2009), among others. These are indeed clearly articulated by Hand (2009), who also proposes an alternative summary statistic called the H measure to alleviate these limitations.[1] This measure depends on the class priors, unlike the AUC, and addresses one of the main concerns of the AUC, that of treating the cost considerations as a classifier-specific problem. This indeed should not be the case because relative costs should be the property of the problem domain, independently of the learning algorithm applied.

Other novel metrics have also been proposed such as the scored AUC (abbreviated SAUC) (Wu et al., 2007) aimed at addressing the dependency of AUC on score imbalances (fewer positive scores than negative, for instance), implicitly mitigating the effects of class imbalance. In a similar vein, Klement (2010) shows how to build a more precise scored ROC curve and calculate a SAUC from it. Santos-Rodríguez et al. (2009) investigates the utility of the adjusted RAND index (ARI), a commonly used measure in unsupervised learning, for performance assessment as well as model selection in classification. These and other novel metrics have yet to be rigorously studied and validated against current measures and so are not yet mainstream.

The issue of asymmetric cost, in which the cost of misclassifying an instance of one class differs from that of other class(es), has also received considerable attention, albeit in the context of specific metrics. The inherent difficulty in obtaining specific cost has long been appreciated by the machine learning community leading, in part to cost- or skew-ratio approaches such as ROC analysis, based on the premise that even though quantifying specific misclassification costs might be difficult, it might be possible to provide relative costs. Other efforts have also been made with regard to cost-sensitive learning, as it is quite often referred to. See, for instance (Santos-Rodríguez et al., 2009) with regard to using Bregman divergences for this purpose (Zadrozny and Elkan, 2002, Lachiche and Flach, 2003), and (O'Brien et al., 2008) for cost-sensitive learning using Bayesian theory (Zadrozny et al., 2003), and (Liu and Zhou, 2006) for approaches based on training instance weighting, and (Landgrebe et al., 2004) for examples of such attempts in experimental settings. Previous attempts to perform cost-sensitive learning with regard to individual classifiers include ones such as (Bradford et al., 1998, Kukar and Kononenko, 1998), and (Fan et al., 1999).

Other proposed metrics include extensions to existing metrics and new measures for ensemble classifiers. Various approaches with regard to combination of classifiers and their subsequent evaluation have been proposed. Some specific works include those of Kuncheva et al. (2003) and Melnik et al. (2004) for analyzing accuracy-based measures, and Lebanon and Lafferty (2002), Freund et al. (2003), and Cortes and Mohri (2004) for alternative measures in such scenarios. Theoretical guarantees and analysis have also been proposed with

---

[1] The R code for estimating the H measure is also available.

regard to these measures. See, for instance (Narasimhamurthy, 2005) for theoretical bounds over the performance of ensemble classifiers and (Murua, 2002) for bounds on error rates for linear combinations of classifiers.

The relationship between performance metrics and their use for model selection have also been investigated. In addition to the work done on ROC curves for this purpose (see Bibliographic Remarks of Chapter 4), probabilistic measures have been investigated by Zadrozny and Elkan (2002). Also see (Yan et al., 2003) for the use of the Wilcoxon–Mann–Whitney statistic for model selection. Learning-theoretic attempts have also been made to assess classifier performance by use of risk bounds and then using these to subsequently guide the learning process (see, for instance, Shah, 2006, and Laviolette et al., 2010). We discuss some insights from such approaches with regard to algorithmic evaluation in Section 8.4.

Our overview of approaches for designing, analyzing, comparing, and characterizing performance metrics in various settings is not meant to be comprehensive, but to be representative of the work currently pursued in this area. Constant advances are being made, and we have inevitably missed some complementary approaches, not to mention approaches related to reinforcement learning, active learning, online learning, and so on, for which performance assessments take on different meanings with regard to the assessment criteria of interest. In such scenarios, various performance metrics have either been adapted from the existing ones or novel measures have been proposed to address the specific concerns of evaluation. However, these methods are beyond the scope of this book.

8.1.2 Qualitative Metrics

The performance criteria studied so far aim at evaluating the algorithms empirically on various kinds of data. These, however, do not provide the means for performing any kind of qualitative evaluation. Drummond (2006) recently emphasized the need to look at criteria of importance that cannot be easily assessed because of their qualitative nature in conjunction with the traditional empirical performance criteria in order to assess and compare learning algorithms properly. These criteria include, e.g., understandability, usability, novelty, and interestingness of the discovered rules. Such concerns with regard to qualitative evaluation have in fact been raised before. Nakhaeizadeh and Schnabl (1998), for instance, looked at the issue of qualitative criteria earlier and broadly categorized these as nominal or ordinal. Whereas the nominal criteria, those that assign a category to the performance, are not directly comparable, the ordinal criteria, those that can be ordered (and hence, ranked), can be used to quantify the differences. Criteria such as understandability or usability can belong to the latter category even if the scale used in judging the quality is human based and subjective as opposed to the objective nature of quantitative criteria. For instance, the user can rate the understandability of a classifier on a scale from

1 to 5, 1 being the worst and 5 the best. More sophisticated classifiers, such as neural networks, can be rated as 1 on the scale whereas simple decision rules can be rated as 5. However, the relationships between different scale values may not be easy to interpret. For example, what about a rule-learning system, which is often more understandable than a neural network? Should it be given a 5? Should both the decision tree and the rule learner be given 5 or should the decision tree be demoted to 4? How about naive Bayes? Does it belong at 3, perhaps? If so, is the difference between 4 (the decision tree) and 5 (the rule-based learner) the same as the difference between 3 (naive Bayes) and 4 (the decision tree)? Probably not. Decision trees and rule-based learners may seem closer in understandability than naive Bayes and decision trees; again, this is a subjective opinion. Consequently the representation of the scale itself for such criteria is important. For instance, Nakhaeizadeh and Schnabl (1998) suggest the following raw scale for understandability:

```
0   0   1   ==>  Low  understandability
0   1   1   ==>  medium  understandability
1   1   1   ==>  high  understandability
```

Although the scale can be simplified to the first two bits, the third bit can be used to denote finer scale values. Increasing the number of bits can result in a finer resolution, but the approach can become impractical with too many ordinal values. Alternatively, a single output taking natural number values can be used, but again this representation remains arbitrary (because the differences between 1 and 2, and 3 and 4 are not necessarily equal, even though they are in this representation) and is not robust (if someone arranged the scale from 0 to 4 rather than 1 to 5, the values would not be correct anymore).

Taking into account qualitative criteria along with the empirical-performance-based assessment of classifier performance can indeed be more insightful. However, striking a proper balance between their trade-offs, which is inevitable, has not been properly formalized yet. Some attempts have been made at combining such criteria, as we will briefly see a little later. For now, however, we shift our focus toward some attempts at studying the performance measures in a unified manner and studying their interrelationship both theoretically and experimentally.

8.2   Frameworks for Performance Metrics

Various frameworks, both theoretical and empirical, have been explored to analyze the behavior of the different metrics in assessing the classifier performance as well as to study their interrelationships. Some frameworks have also aimed at unifying the metrics under a common paradigm and use the insights from this exercise to come up with more-informed or finer measures.

8.2.1 Theoretical Frameworks

On the theoretical front, the studies of Huang and Ling, Flach, and Buja (see subsequent discussion) are three examples that have aimed at performing such an analysis, each within a different framework. Whereas the first tries to develop a general framework that can encompass not just the quantification of the evaluation measures, but also some qualitative aspects, the second and third ones are purely quantitative.

The approach of Ling et al. (2003) and Huang and Ling (2007) of coming up with a framework for comparing different metrics is aimed at characterizing the metrics while taking into account their qualitative "goodness." To quantify this, two criteria called the *consistency* and the *discriminancy* of the measures are defined as follows:

Definition 8.1. Consistency: *For two measures* pm_1 *and* pm_2 *on domain S,* pm_1 *and* pm_2 *are strictly consistent if there exist no two points* $x_1, x_2 \in S$ *such that* $pm_1(x_1) > pm_1(x_2)$ *and* $pm_2(x_1) < pm_2(x_2)$.

Definition 8.2. Discriminancy: *For two measures* pm_1 *and* pm_2, pm_1 *is strictly more discriminating than* pm_2 *if there exists two points on domain S,* $x_1, x_2 \in S$ *such that* $pm_1(x_1) > pm_1(x_2)$ *and* $pm_2(x_1) = pm_2(x_2)$, *and there exist no two points* $x_1, x_2 \in S$ *such that* $pm_2(x_1) > pm_2(x_2)$ *and* $pm_1(x_1) = pm_1(x_2)$.

Given these, they provide the following definitions:

Definition 8.3. Degree of consistency: *For two measures* pm_1 *and* pm_2 *on domain S, let*

$$C_R = \{(x_1, x_2)|x_1, x_2 \in S, pm_1(x_1) > pm_1(x_2); pm_2(x_1) > pm_2(x_2)\}$$

and let

$$C_S = \{(x_1, x_2)|x_1, x_2 \in S, pm_1(x_1) > pm_1(x_2); pm_2(x_1) < pm_2(x_2)\}.$$

Then the degree of consistency of pm_1 *and* pm_2 *is Con, where*

$$Con = \frac{|C_R|}{|C_R| + |C_S|}.$$

Definition 8.4. Degree of disciminancy: *For two measures* pm_1 *and* pm_2 *on domain S, let*

$$D_P = \{(x_1, x_2)|x_1, x_2 \in S, pm_1(x_1) > pm_1(x_2); pm_2(x_1) = pm_2(x_2)\}$$

and let

$$D_Q = \{(x_1, x_2)|x_1, x_2 \in S, pm_2(x_1) > pm_2(x_2); pm_1(x_1) = pm_1(x_2)\}.$$

The degree of disciminancy for pm_1 *over* pm_2 *is Dis, where*

$$Dis = \frac{|D_P|}{|D_Q|}.$$

Based on these quantities, the goodness of a measure can then be characterized as follows:

Definition 8.5. Goodness of a measure: *A measure* pm_1 *is statistically consistent and more discriminating than* pm_2 *iff* Con > 0.5 *and* Dis > 1. *In such cases, we say that* pm_1 *is a better measure than* pm_2.

They define two versions of their concepts of consistency and discriminancy. The first one is a strict Boolean definition, which looks for perfect instances of these concepts, whereas the second version relaxes the strict definition by adding a probabilistic component to it. Informally, two measures, pm_1 and pm_2, are *consistent* with each other if whenever pm_1 decides that A is a strictly better algorithm than B, then pm_2 does not stipulate that B is better than A. pm_1 is also thought of as more discriminating than pm_2 if pm_1 can sometimes tell that there is a difference between algorithms A and B, whereas pm_2 cannot. The study then, in keeping with the more general tradition of comparing AUC with accuracy, does just that, and shows that AUC is statistically consistent and more discriminating than accuracy. From a practical point of view, they use the finer metric AUC to optimize a model and show that the resulting model performs better on accuracy than the model optimized using accuracy. Notice that this is in line with the finding of Rosset (2004). However, in a followup, Huang et al. (2008) suggest that this result is not statistically significant and that in fact one is better off optimizing a model by using the metric that is to be used in the deployed system.

Another interesting analysis for studying the interrelationship between performance measures was done by Flach (2003), who focuses on the ROC space and its role in characterizing various performance metrics. We discussed the main components of this framework, including the isometrics, in Chapter 4. By considering the generalized 3D ROC space, Flach (2003) and then Fuernkranz and Flach (2005) study various metrics such as AUC, accuracy, F measure, and so on, in this space.

Finally, Buja et al. (2005) consider a Fisher consistency of the performance metrics and verify whether they can be characterized as proper scoring rules. The focus of the study is on scoring rules that can yield probability estimates on the data in a Fisher-consistent manner. The analysis is beyond the scope of this book, and we refer the interested readers to the original study.

8.2.2 Experimental Frameworks

On the experimental front, various attempts have been made at analyzing the relationship between two or more performance metrics. Two independent large-scale experimental evaluation studies are especially worth noting.

Caruana and Niculescu-Mizil (2004) studied nine different performance metrics for binary classification, using two different tools: a visual tool (or projection approach), *multidimensional scaling (MDS)*, and a statistical tool, *correlation analysis*. The metrics were compared according to the results they obtained on seven learning models and seven different domains from the UCI Repository and other sources. The study was thus quite extensive. The metrics were organized into three families (which correspond, roughly, to the categories we formed in Chapters 3 and 4 but in terms of the information utilized):

1. **Threshold Metrics:** These are metrics, such as accuracy, for which a threshold is set ahead of time within the classifier and for which the distance from the threshold does not matter. All that matters is whether the classifier issues a value above or below the threshold.
2. **Ordering or Rank Metrics:** These are metrics, such as AUC, for which the test examples are assumed to be ordered according to the predicted values output by the classifier. These metrics measure to what extent the classifiers ranked positive instances above the negative ones. Another way to interpret such measures is to think of them as summaries of the classifiers' performances over all possible thresholds.
3. **Probability Metrics:** These are metrics, such as RMSE, that compute how far the truth lies from the predicted values output by the classifiers. They do not directly compare results with a threshold, like the threshold metrics, nor do they directly compare the instances' ranks from one another, the way ordering metrics do it. However, they could be thought of as performing these two tasks indirectly.

The MDS and correlation analysis showed that all the ordering metrics cluster close to one another in metric space and are highly correlated. Accuracy, on the other hand, did not seem to correlate with the other threshold metrics. Instead, it was often closely related to RMSE, a probability metric. An important observation was made in noting that RMSE is a very robust metric, well correlated to all the others. Caruana and Niculescu-Mizil (2004) recommended it for general-purpose experiments in which no specific practical outcome is sought. In fact, a new combination metric, discussed in the next section, was also proposed but was found to be highly correlated with RMSE.

Another large-scale experimental framework was developed in (Ferri et al., 2009), which is similar to that of Caruana and Niculescu-Mizil (2004) in some respects but expanded the latter to the multiclass case and studied the sensitivity of metrics to different domain characteristics, in particular, misclassification noise (changes in class threshold), probability noise (change in calibration with no effect on the ranking), ranking noise (changes in ranks that do not affect the classification), and changes in class frequency. While retaining the categorization of metrics in the three categories as done by Caruana and Niculescu-Mizil (2004), the framework considered a total of 18 metrics, doubling the number from the previous study, including the variations of common metrics especially in multiclass settings. The 30 small- and medium-sized test domains from the

UCI Repository consisted of a balanced set of binary and multiclass as well as balanced and imbalanced domains. Groupwise correlation analysis was subsequently performed.

The findings show the various ranking measures to be similar, whereas the classification and reliability measures were found to be more correlated. The two sets, ranking measures on the one hand and the classification and reliability measures on the other, were found to be farther apart in their groupwise behavior. This then justified the use of AUC as a different view on the problem. One difference of note with the study of Caruana and Niculescu-Mizil (2004) was the relatively lower correlation of RMSE in the multiclass setting (as opposed to the binary setting considered earlier). While in binary domains, RMSE is more closely correlated to the ranking metrics than it is to the classification metrics; this relationship is reversed in the multiclass setting.

The results obtained on balanced versus imbalanced domains supported very well the intuitive notion that the choice of metrics is important in imbalanced datasets. Indeed, we see that the classification metrics behave fairly similarly in the balanced case, whereas they behave quite differently in the imbalanced case. This is true for all the other categories and across categories as well. With respect to small versus large domains, the correlation results show that classification and ranking metrics are closer to each other than to the reliability metrics in the small-domain case, but that, in the case of large domains, ranking metrics are quite separated from classification and reliability metrics, which are more closely related.

The classification measures are found to be relatively better behaved than the ranking and reliability measures in the presence of class noise. If probability noise is present, then classification metrics are not reliable. On the other hand, ranking metrics seem quite robust to this kind of distortion. The reliability measures' performance in this scenario falls midway between those of the classification and the ranking metrics. When ranking noise is present, once again, the classification metrics are the ones that are most affected, whereas ranking and reliability metrics are more robust. Finally, ranking metrics are found to be more sensitive to variations in class frequency and seem to be unreliable when a particular class is represented by only very rare cases. On the other hand, as long as these measures take into consideration the proportion of examples in each class, the classification and reliability metrics seem well behaved. Some of these results could have been expected from the characterization of the performance metrics that we outlined in earlier chapters and in fact place these insights into a practical perspective.

8.2.3 Do More-Informed Metrics Give Us Better Information Regarding Classification?

The question that may be asked after considering the wealth of evaluation metrics available is how useful the more-sophisticated metrics are in algorithmic evaluation. A simple strategy for selecting measures could be to use classification measures when the goal of the exercise is pure classification, a ranking measure when ranking is necessary, and possibly a probabilistic measure when building classifier ensemble methods. Nonetheless, metrics have been assessed across domains. In particular, based on the observation that ROC-based methods are not sensitive to prior class distributions the way accuracy is, AUC, a measure that summarizes the results of ROC analysis, is often used in place of accuracy, especially in class imbalance problems, but, most lately, even as a general measure. As a matter of fact, there is merit in crossing such boundaries: The more information we can gather about the classifiers, the better off we are. The only problem, however, is that it is not entirely clear how to interpret this information. Intuitively, it would seem that the more-informed metrics should give us better insights about the behavior of the classifiers on future data, but very few studies to date have asked this question (see Bellinger et al., 2009, for instance). As we discussed earlier, Rosset (2004) and Huang and Ling (2007) looked at the relation of using one measure (AUC) to train the algorithm and its effect on measuring the effectiveness of the algorithm in test domains using another measure (accuracy). Reliability metrics such as RMSE and Kononenko and Bratko information score, while generally slightly less appropriate than accuracy on binary classification tasks, sometimes fare slightly better than it in multiclass or imbalanced domains.

The attempts at analyzing the performance metrics in a unified manner under the constraints of a framework have not only resulted in the characterization of their behavior, but have also provided some understanding as to how these can either be improved or combined to obtain finer measures of performance. We now move on to the attempts that have been made to obtain metrics by combining the existing ones.

8.3 Combining Metrics

The attempts at combining metrics can be categorized into mainly three groups. The first stems from the evaluation frameworks discussed in Section 8.2. The second group consists of measures that aim to combine the qualitative considerations with the quantitative measures of performance. These approaches are commonly known as multicriteria metrics. The final group consists of approaches inspired from visualization by the way of projection of metrics on a common space.

8.3.1 Framework-Based Combination Metrics

Evaluation frameworks such as those of Ling et al. (2003) or Flach (2003) can give important insights into the conceptually different but complementary nature of the performance measures in their respective settings. A natural extension to such an analysis would then be to investigate whether combining measures or coming up with more sophisticated measures can result in better assessments of classifier performance. Not surprisingly then, attempts have been made to this effect. Consider for instance the SAR metric derived from the experimental framework of Caruana and Niculescu-Mizil (2004), which linearly combines the most prominent member of each of the categories they devised, namely, squared error(S), accuracy (A), AUC, and ROC Area (R), in an attempt to obtain a more informative measure (and hence the name SAR). Their measure takes the following form:

$$\text{SAR} = \frac{[\text{Accuracy} + \text{AUC} + (1 - \text{RMSE})]}{3}.$$

Similarly, a combined metric was also proposed as a consequence of derivation from the framework of Ling et al. (2003) in the form of AUC:acc, which is an instance of the general two-level framework discussed in Huang and Ling (2007). The basic idea is that, when two algorithms are compared, AUC is the first measure used. If a tie is observed when AUC is used, then the comparison is done using accuracy instead. This is different from the linear combination proposed by Caruana and Niculescu-Mizil (2004). It also applies more generally with AUC and acc being replaced with any other two performance metrics. In general, Huang and Ling (2007) show that the two-level measure is consistent with, and finer than, the two measures it is based on. When used with AUC and acc, it is also shown to correlate with RMSE better than either AUC or accuracy. These combined metrics, however, have yet to be extensively evaluated and studied for their adherence to their expected behavior. For instance, SAR, although apparently more powerful than individual metrics, was found not to present much advantage over the simple RMSE that correlates very well with it.

8.3.2 Multicriteria Metrics

Considerable effort has been devoted to investigating metrics that can, in addition to measuring the performance of classifiers under the criterion of interest, weigh it against the gains in other complementary, even qualitative criteria. The best algorithm under this setting would then be the one that achieves an optimal trade-off of the assessment criteria of interest. We explain, in some detail, the main measures proposed along these lines. Three main approaches of multicriteria evaluation were proposed: The efficiency method, the simple and intuitive measure, and the measure-based method. Lavesson and Davidsson (2008b) further attempt to synthesize the three to propose the candidate evaluation function. We briefly discuss each of these in turn. These approaches should not be confused with the combination metrics such as SAR and AUC:acc, discussed in the previous section, which do not generalize to take qualitative criteria into account. In the current settings, we consider all performance metrics to be normalized in a specific interval, typically [0, 1], with necessary sign adjustments so that higher values are better.

The Efficiency Method

Motivated from the operations research concept of data envelopment analysis (DEA), the efficiency method introduced by Nakhaeizadeh and Schnabl (1997) aims to weight the positive metrics (whose higher values are desirable) against the negative metrics (whose lower values are desirable). The positive metrics can be the ones such as accuracy, whereas the negative ones can be characteristics such as computational complexity or execution time. Even qualitative metrics such as *interestingness* of an algorithm can be included. On a given dataset S, the efficiency of a classifier f, denoted as $\mathcal{E}_S(f)$, is given by

$$\mathcal{E}_S(f) = \frac{\sum_i w_i \mathrm{pm}_i^+(f)}{\sum_j w_j \mathrm{pm}_j^-(f)},$$

where the index i runs through positive metrics and j runs through negative metrics.

As can be easily seen here, assigning w_i's is, unfortunately, nontrivial. Nakhaeizadeh and Schnabl (1997) propose to set them by optimizing the efficiency of all the algorithms simultaneously. These efficiencies should be as close to 100% as possible and none should exceed 100%. This optimization problem can then be solved with linear programming techniques. In addition to this general idea, Nakhaeizadeh and Schnabl (1998) go on to discuss how the approach deals with subjective judgments of how the different criteria are assessed. This is implemented by applying restrictions on the automatic weight computations previously discussed that correspond to the user's preferences.

The Simple and Intuitive Measure (SIM)

The simple and intuitive measure (SIM) proposed by Soares et al. (2000) considers the combined effect of the distance between an evaluated algorithm's performance measure and the optimally obtainable result on that measure. The combination, in the form of a product, is typically unweighted. Let $\mathcal{I}$ denote the set of different performance metrics. Then SIM is defined as

$$\mathcal{S}_S(f) = \prod_{i \in \mathcal{I}} \left| \mathrm{pm}_i(f) - \mathrm{pm}_i^o \right|,$$

where pm_i^o denotes the optimal value of performance measure pm_i.

Obviously it is desirable that the distance measures reflect the possiblity of discrepancy in case the results on one or more measures are unacceptable. The distance for those measures should then go out of bounds, and so does the result of the combination, thus signaling a bad algorithm. The following bounded version of the measure aims to achieve this, in which each performance measure $\mathrm{pm}_i(f)$ is expected to lie in a respective interval:

$$\mathcal{S}_S^B(f) = \begin{cases} \mathcal{S}_S(f) & \text{if } \forall i \left(\mathrm{pm}_i(f) \in \left[\mathrm{pm}_i^l, \mathrm{pm}_i^u\right]\right) \\ \infty & \text{otherwise} \end{cases}.$$

Finally, in a comparative setting, the result can be normalized to generate a score for the algorithm as

$$\mathcal{S}_S^{\mathcal{N}}(f) = \frac{\mathcal{S}_S^B(f)}{\prod_i |\mathrm{pm}_i^u - \mathrm{pm}_i^l|}.$$

SIM can also be used in an exploratory way as it can be represented graphically so that the user may interact with it on the fly, trying different settings. The advantage of this approach over the efficiency method of Nakhaeizadeh and Schnabl (1997) is that it uses no weights, which are typically difficult to set. Instead, it combines quantities that the user knows should not exceed certain bounds. The different criteria on which the evaluation is based are assumed to have the same weight, that is, they are considered to be equally important. As a result, SIM is able to handle uncertainty in the estimates of the criteria, which the efficiency approach could not account for. Nonetheless, by the same argument, the efficiency approach has the advantage of being more precise as it allows certain criteria to be considered more important than others.

The Measure-Based Method

The measure-based method proposed by Andersson et al. (1999) attempts to define measure functions denoting the algorithm-neutral aspects of the problem that we want to optimize. These measure functions get evaluated on algorithm-application pairs, and their results are combined in a weighted linear fashion. Again, let $\mathcal{I}$ denote the set of different performance metrics. The measure function, denoted as $\mathcal{M}_S(f)$ of a classifier f over dataset S, is defined as

$$\mathcal{M}_S(f) = \sum_{i \in \mathcal{I}} w_i \times \mathrm{pm}_i(f).$$

The measure-based method decomposes the evaluation problem into simpler components of the evaluation, such as whether the training instances are classified correctly, whether similar examples are classified similarly and how simple the partition learned by the algorithm is. Each component is evaluated separately, and these components are then combined linearly, by the user who can choose to weigh some components more than others, at will. Accordingly, the pm_i's in this measure need not concern themselves only with standard performance measures as before, but rather refer to the components under consideration. This method presents some similarity with the efficiency method of Nakhaeizadeh and Schnabl (1997), but it focuses on the learned model rather than the learning algorithm and is more concerned with generalizing issues than with qualitative ones.

The Candidate-Evaluation Function

The candidate-evaluation function proposed by Lavesson and Davidsson (2008b) (also see Lavesson and Davidsson, 2008a) extends the measure-based method by incorporating elements of the simple and intuitive measure, namely, its bounds to yield the following measure:

$$C_S(f) = \begin{cases} \sum_i w_i \mathrm{pm}_i(f) & \text{if } \forall i \left(\mathrm{pm}_i(f) \in \left[\mathrm{pm}_i^l, 1\right]\right) \\ 0 & \text{otherwise} \end{cases},$$

such that $\sum_{i \in I} w_i = 1$, ensuring boundedness of $C_S(f)$, that is, $C_S(f) \in [0, 1]$. The aim of the approach is to verify that the application domain constraints are not violated (as ascertained by SIM) while at the same time being able to perform the component-wise evaluation as the measure-based method. SIM's normalization is also adopted to ensure that all the combined measures are in the same range, as this is a necessary prerequisite to meaningful weighting. Lavesson and Davidsson (2008a) suggest the use of a taxonomy of performance quality attributes that could be subdivided into time, space, and accuracy components. Further quality attributes such as comprehensibility, complexity, and interestingness can also be included. However, operationalizing these ideas is difficult for the same reason that quantifying a qualitative measure of interest is nontrivial.

8.3.3 Visualization-Based Combination Metrics

The argument behind the visualization approach proposed by Alaiz-Rodríguez et al. (2008) is that, in conventional methods of combining metrics, the information is lost at two stages, first when scaling the individual metrics and then when these scaled metrics are combined. The metrics combination issue in this approach is addressed by means of a graphical projection and has the advantage over other combination methods to provide a component-wise comparison of different classifiers applied to different domains and evaluated by different metrics.[2]

The approach works by recording all the results associated with a single classifier on the various domains considered and with all the performance metrics selected by the user into a single vector. Every classifier compared in the study is thus represented by a vector whose entries comprise the values of the performance measures used. This organization in vector form guarantees that there is a pairwise correspondence of each vector component from one classifier to the next. By use of a distance measure (the Euclidean distance) and a projection method (multidimensional scaling), the vectors are then projected onto a 2D space. Figure 8.1 illustrates the approach and compares it with the traditional

---

[2] A recent implementation of this approach, by Alexandre Kouznetsov, is available for downloading from *http://www.site.uottawa.ca/~nat/Visualization_Software/visualization.html*.

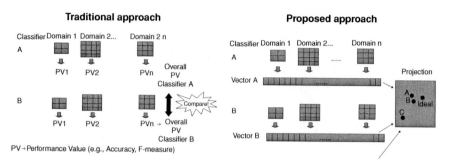

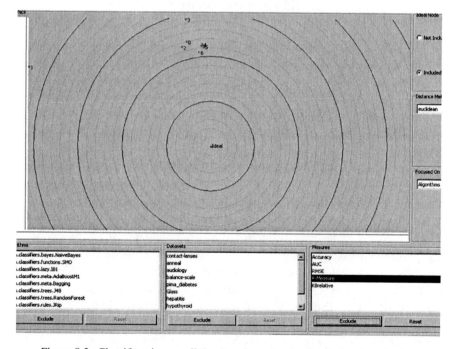

Figure 8.1. The traditional and proposed approaches to classifier performance evaluation. *Source*: (Japkowicz et al., 2008).

metric combination. As opposed to aggregating the performance measures and then comparing these across classifiers, the visualization approach preserves these in original form, simply concatenated into a vector. The transformation is delayed until the projection is applied. This means that, in the visualization approach, information is lost only once, in the projection phase. In the traditional approach, information is lost with each such aggregation. The resulting projections can then be visualized and their relationship over classifiers studied in this projected space. Figure 8.2 illustrates a typical result from a study illustrated in Chapter 9. The graph displays the results obtained by eight

Figure 8.2. Classifier view on all the domains using the five evaluation metrics.

classifiers on 10 domains and using five performance measures. In other words, the results are based on five 8×10 tables that list in each cell the result obtained by a single classifier on a single domain by a single evaluation metric. Instead of showing these tables, the visualization approach combines the results into a single compact graph. The plot also shows how far from the ideal classifier and from one another each of the eight classifiers used in the study is with respect to the domains they were tested on and the performance measures that were used. In particular, it shows what classifiers are clustered together and how far these clusters are from the ideal classifier. For example, the graph shows that the four tree- or rule-based classifiers – bagging trees (4), C4.5 (5), random forests (6), and Ripper (7) – are clustered together and are closest to the ideal classifier. Then the NB and 1NN are not far behind, with RF being closest to ideal.

Note, however, the dependency of the approach on the distance measure (Euclidean distance) as well as on the projection method. Wildly varying measures can adversely affect the distances in such cases because the resulting distances can be skewed. Similarly, the relationship would also depend on how well behaved the projections are in preserving the relationship of different classifier performances. These points were considered by Japkowicz et al. (2008), who compared the results of two projection methods, including a distance-preserving projection and two distance measures. However, more research is needed to accumulate a better understanding of this approach.

8.4 Insights from Statistical Learning Theory

One of the main directions that the field of statistical learning theory has contributed to, in relation to classifier evaluation, is the study of the behavior of learning algorithms in terms not only of their empirical performance, but also of other information available from the data and the learning algorithms' predisposition to select one classifier over another, i.e., the classical problems of model selection and learning bias. Some of the main quantities of interest in the learning theory context include the algorithms' future performance guarantees, the nature of the classifier space explored, and the complexity of the final classifier output by the learning algorithm on a given dataset, along with the corresponding trade-offs involved. In particular, attempts have been made at characterizing the performance of the classifier as well as the guarantees over its future performance. Such results have generally appeared in the form of generalization error bounds. These guarantees basically provide upper (and sometimes lower) bounds on the deviation of the true error of the classifier from its empirical error and take into account the precise quantities that a classifier learns from the data. Being able to characterize the algorithms in a common framework can have distinct advantages. If we know that the algorithms share comparable learning biases or work under similar constraints, then we can go beyond merely measuring their performance on the test data. We can in fact also make inferences, based on the nature of the classifiers that these algorithms output. That is, we can quantify some of the qualitative criteria, describing the performance of the learning algorithms on the domains of interest. Indeed, different learning algorithms can have different learning biases owing to the different classifier spaces that they explore. However, the fact that they operate under similar optimization constraints can be telling in terms of their respective abilities to yield general results. Consider, for instance, a framework within which the quality of an algorithm (in terms of how well the resulting classifier will generalize to future data) is judged, by combining the performance it obtains on some training data with a measure that quantifies the complexity of the resulting classifier. Among the many ways in which such complexity can be characterized, one is the extent to which the algorithm can compress the training data (i.e., identify the most important examples enough to represent the classifier). This is the classical sample compression framework of learning. Characterizing two learning algorithms, such as decision trees and decision lists, within this framework would then enable measuring their relative performances with regard to *both* the empirical risk *and* compression constraints. That is, this will essentially enable a user to characterize which algorithm manages to obtain the most meaningful trade-off between these quantities under its respective learning bias. Training-set bounds that characterize the generalization error of learning algorithms in terms of their empirical risk, compression, and possibly other criteria of interest (priors on data, for instance) can be used to compare the performances of learning algorithms. These give rise to the so-called, *algorithm-dependent* approach to evaluation. Even though various training-set bounds have appeared for learning algorithms under various learning frameworks, these, with very few exceptions, generally work in asypmtotic limits. We subsequently discuss a practical bound.

Providing generalization error bounds on a classifier also involves characterizing an algorithm within a probabilistic framework (akin to demonstrating the confidence in the presented results). In the context of the approaches presented in this book with regard to both reliability as well as hypothesis testing, the probably approximately correct (PAC) framework draws a close parallel. It provides approximate guarantees on the true error of a classifier with a given confidence parameter δ (similar to the α confidence parameter but not necessarily with the same intepretation), as can be seen in the sample bounds subsequently presented. With regard to the dependence that these guarantees have on the algorithm and the framework that characterizes it, the generalization error bounds or risk bounds can be categorized as *the training-set bounds* and *the test-set (holdout) bounds*. The training-set bounds typically rely on two aspects: the error of the algorithm on the training set and the properties of the algorithm itself. The first aspect obviously results from the limited data availability, requiring the empirical risk on the training set to approximate the true risk. However, an insight into the algorithm's behavior can prove to be a significant help in reducing our reliance solely on the training error and hence helps avoid overfitting so as to yield better estimates on the true risk.

The holdout bounds, on the other hand, are the guarantees on the true error of the classifier obtained on a given test set and can be obtained without reference to the learning algorithm in question. With regard to this algorithm-independent way of doing evaluation (as we have done so far) too, learning theory gives more meaningful results in the form of alternative confidence bounds on the test-set performance of the classifier. We briefly presented one such bound in Chapter 2, which was based on Hoeffding's inequality. Let us take a look at a tighter version of this bound, based on the binomial tail inversion, and see how these can better model the hold out error of the classifier.

As it must be obvious by now, although the test-set bounds can readily be utilized for performance assessments, there are many challenges with regard to training-set bounds owing to the difficulties in efficiently characterizing different algorithms in the theoretical frameworks of interest.

8.4.1 Holdout Risk Bounds as an Alternative to Confidence Intervals

As we discussed earlier, one of the most common techniques for measuring the performance of a machine learning algorithm is to do so on a separate set of test examples (not used for training the algorithm). This is generally referred to as holdout testing. A learning algorithm is trained on the training set, using an apt model selection strategy, to output a classifier. This classifier is then tested on the heldout dataset. Providing a confidence interval (or alternatively an upper and a lower bound) around the empirical risk of the classifier can be done as discussed in Chapter 2. That approach relies on the assumption that the empirical risk of the classifier on the test data can be modeled in the limit as a Gaussian. Based on this assumption, the necessary statistics are obtained from testing the classifier on the test data. That is, the mean classification error and its corresponding variance on the test examples are obtained. A confidence interval is then provided, in terms of a Gaussian, around the mean empirical risk with its tails removed at the limits of the critical region. This is typically twice the standard deviation estimate on either sides (effectively a two-sided 95% confidence interval).

This approach relies strongly on the Gaussian assumption motivated by the central limit theorem (see Chapter 2 for detailed discussion). Under this setting, however, the Gaussian assumption holds on a *fixed underlying statistic and that too asymptotically*. However, this does not typically hold for the empirical risk of the classification it aims to model. The risk, in the case of classification, is modeled as a zero–one loss. This is equivalent then to having an indicator function that is true when the classifier errs on an example. This would lead to a binomial distribution over a number of trials (i.e., it would test the classifier on a number of samples). Further, the aim of learning is to obtain as low an empirical risk as possible. That is, we are not interested in modeling random variables merely in the [0, 1] interval, but rather in modeling the empirical risk of the classifier for lower values (values closer to zero). However, for smaller values of empirical risk, a binomial distribution cannot be approximated by a Gaussian. This observation was also made by Langford (2005). Consequently, applying a Gaussian assumption results in estimates that are overly pessimistic when obtaining an upper bound and overly optimistic when obtaining a lower bound around the empirical risk. Langford (2005) also showed a comparison between the behavior of the two distributions with an empirical example of upper bounds on the risk of a decision tree classifier on test datasets. Let us derive a holdout risk bound and illustrate this effect empirically. To do so, we use the holdout bound derived by Shah (2008) and Shah and Shanian (2009) by using a binomial tail inversion argument (the derivation of these bounds is provided at the end of this chapter).

We define the binomial tail inversion to be the largest true error such that the probability of observing λ or fewer errors is at least δ as

$$\overline{\text{Bin}}(m, \lambda, \delta) = \max\{p : \text{Bin}(m, \lambda, p) \geq \delta)\}.$$

Now, if each of the examples of a test set is obtained i.i.d from some arbitrary underlying distribution D, then an upper bound on the true risk of the classifier $R(f)$, output by the algorithm, can be defined as follows:

Theorem 8.1. *For all classifiers f, for all $\mathcal{D}$, for all $\delta \in (0, 1]$:*

$$\Pr_{T \sim D^m}(R(f) \leq \overline{\text{Bin}}(m, \lambda, \delta)) \geq 1 - \delta.$$

From this result, it follows that $\overline{\text{Bin}}(m, \lambda, \delta)$ is the smallest upper bound that holds with probability at least $1 - \delta$ on the true risk $R(f)$ of any classifier f with an observed empirical risk $R_T(f)$ on a set of m examples.[3]

In an analogous manner, a lower bound on $R(f)$ can be derived:

Theorem 8.2. *For all classifiers f, for all $\mathcal{D}$, for all $\delta \in (0, 1]$:*

$$\Pr_{T \sim D^m}(R(f) \geq \min_{p}\{p : 1 - \text{Bin}(m, \lambda, p) \geq \delta\}) \geq 1 - \delta$$

We present an illustration of the advantage of this approach in the Appendix to this chapter.

8.4.2 Training-Set Bounds

The idea of training-set bounds is more involved. Various theoretical frameworks can be utilized to characterize the behavior of a learning algorithm and bound the true risk of the classifier. Most of these are built on the PAC framework previously mentioned with a confidence measure δ. The lower the δ, the higher

---

[3] $R_T(f)$ is represented by λ errors over m examples.

the confidence in the estimate of the true risk (and by consequence, the looser the bound) and vice versa. Such models generally provide these guarantees over the future classifier performance in terms of its empirical performance and possibly some other quantities obtained from training data and some measure of the complexity of the classifier space that the learning algorithm explores. Such measures have appeared in the form of Vapnik–Chervonenkis dimension (VC dimension), Rademacher complexities, and so on (see, for instance, Herbrich, 2002, for discussion). Bounds on specific resampling techniques have also appeared with the prominent of these being the leave-one-out error bounds (see, e.g., Vapnik and Chapelle, 2000). There are other learning frameworks that do not explicitly include the algorithm's dependence on the classifier space complexity in the risk bound and hence have an advantage over conventional bounds that do. This is because the complexity measure grows with the size (and complexity) of the classifier space and many times results in unrealistic bounds. A brief introduction to statistical learning theory can be found in Bousquet et al. (2004).

Successful attempts in the direction of attaining practical, realizable bounds have appeared, although few of them are specifically designed within the sample compression framework (see, for instance, Shah, 2006). Briefly, this framework relies on characterizing a classifier in terms of two complementary sources of information, viz., a compression set S_i, and a message string σ. The compression set is a (preferably) small subset of the training set S, and the message string is the additional information that can be used to reconstruct the classifier from the compression set. Consequently this requires the existence of such a reconstruction function that can reconstruct the classifier solely from this information. The risk bound that we subsequently present as an example bounds the risk of the classifier represented by $f = (\sigma, S_i)$ over all such reconstruction functions. The bound presented is due to Laviolette et al. (2005), who also utilized this bound to perform successful model selection in the case of the SCM algorithm.

Theorem 8.3. *For any reconstruction function $\mathcal{R}$ that maps arbitrary subsets of a training set and message strings to classifiers, for any prior distribution $P_\mathcal{I}$ on the compression sets and for any compression-set-dependent distribution of messages $P_{\mathcal{M}(S_i)}$ (where $\mathcal{M}$ denotes the set of messages that can be supplied with compression set S_i), and for any $\delta \in (0, 1]$, the following relation holds with probability $1 - \delta$ over random draws of $S \sim D^m$:*

$$\forall f: R(f)$$
$$\leq 1 - \exp\left\{\frac{-1}{m - |S_i| - mR_S(f)}\left[\ln\binom{m - |S_i|}{mR_S(f)} + \ln\left(\frac{1}{P_\mathcal{I}(\mathbf{i})P_{\mathcal{M}(S_i)}(\sigma)\delta}\right)\right]\right\},$$
$$(8.1)$$

where $R_S(f)$ is the mean empirical risk of f on $S\backslash S_i$ (i.e., on the examples that are not in the compression set).

As can be seen, the preceding bound will be tight when the algorithm can find a classifier with a small compression set (a property known as sparsity) along with a low empirical risk. The preceding bounds apply to all the classifiers in a given classifier space uniformly, unlike the test-set bound. Hence the training-set bound focuses precisely on what the learning algorithm can learn (in terms of its reconstruction) and its empirical performance on the training data. As also discussed before, training-set bounds such as the one shown above, also provide an optimization problem for learning, and, theoretically, a classifier that minimizes the risk bound should be selected. However, this statement should be considered more carefully. As also discussed by Langford (2005), choosing a classifier based on the risk bound necesarily means that this gives a better worst-case bound on the true risk of the classifier. This is different from obtaining an improved estimate of true risk. Generally measures such as the empirical risk that guide the model selection have a better behavior. Some successful examples of learning from bound minimization do exist, however. See for instance, Laviolette et al. (2005) and Shah (2006).

8.4.3 Bounds for Classifier Evaluation?

With the progress on the learning theory front in providing tighter risk bounds for classifiers, there lies a potential in utilizing these bounds for classifier evaluation too. Performing successful model selection with bounds appears to be an encouraging advancement. The test-set bounds appear to be a more direct method for such classifier comparisons and can result in more meaningful confidence estimates around the observed empirical behavior of the classifier. The training-set bounds' utilization for this purpose, however, warrants a deeper understanding as well as addressing various issues before successful application. A standardized optimal framework can result in the specification of learning algorithms and may enable inter-algorithm comparisons on a common platform, although it remains to be seen how this can be done meaningfully. Many issues remain to be addressed. For instance, if algorithm A (e.g., SCM) is characterized within a certain framework, then is this framework optimal too for characterizing algorithm B (e.g., SVM) with which we wish A to be compared? That is, when such a characterization is possible at all.

A concrete example can be seen in the case of the sample compression framework previously described above. A necessity is to have a reconstruction function that can reconstruct the classifier from compression sets and message strings. Many algorithms confirm to the existence of such reconstruction functions, whereas there are algorithms for which such a direct reconstruction scheme does not exist. For instance, algorithms such as the set covering machine (SCM) (Marchand and Shawe-Taylor, 2002) have been designed with sparsity considerations in mind and can be successfully characterized in this framework. Similarly, algorithms such as the SVMs can also be represented within this framework. So can algorithms such as decision trees (see, e.g., Shah, 2007). However, algorithms such as SVM, although characterizable within the sample compression framework, are not originally designed with sparsity as the learning bias. Hence such a comparison will always yield biased estimates. On the other hand, sample compression algorithms, such as the SCM, consider the classifier space that is defined *after* having the training set at hand (because each classifier is defined in terms of a subset of the training set), a notion widely known as data-dependent settings. Therefore a complexity measure such as the VC dimension, defined without reference to the data and applicable in the case of SVMs, cannot characterize the complexity of the classifier space that sample compression algorithms explore.

Other considerations also come into play here, such as the resulting nature of the optimization problem when such frameworks are used. Also, how to obtain tight-enough training-set bounds currently remains an active research question. Examples such as those previously shown are few. It would be interesting to see advances on this front in the near future and their impact on the field of classifier evaluation. The test-set bounds, on the other hand, provide a readily favorable alternative to the confidence-interval-based approaches in terms of more meaningful characterization of a classifier's empirical performance.

8.5 Other Developments

In addition to the wide efforts undertaken with regard to a performance-measure-based analysis and research, and some novel insights from fields such as statistical learning theory discussed so far, there have also been efforts, although not as numerous, in studying some other components of the evaluation framework. For instance, Neville and Jensen (2008) extend the bias–variance analysis to the relational domain to study the behavior of performance metrics. Webb (2007) looks at statistical approaches to reduce type I error in pattern discovery approaches. Analyses on the ROCs have also been extended in other ways. For instance, Jin and Lu (2009) have recently looked into using the Mann–Whitney statistic on the ROC to demonstrate the competitiveness of discriminant functions in a permutation test setting. The Wilcoxon–Mann–Whitney statistic has also been used to optimize classifier performance by Yan et al. (2003). Under similar settings, Marrocco et al. (2008) also use AUC for model selection in the context of nonparametric linear classifiers.

On the error-estimation front, an interesting resampling approach has appeared in the form of progressive validation (Blum et al., 1999) that allows for a large part of the holdout set for training (important, naturally, in the limited dataset size scenario) while maintaining the guarantees of the holdout bound. The aim was hence to mitigate the adverse effects of resampling approaches in limiting the size of holdout sets and hence affect the respective theoretical guarantees. The approach of Dietterich (1998) has also been another attempt at addressing some of the shortcomings of the classical resampling methods and also correcting accordingly for statistical significance testing. Other works such as that of Micheals and Boult (2001) have also looked at alternative sampling strategies such as stratified resampling for evaluation. Sahiner et al. (2008) study the resampling schemes in the context of neural networks.

Other avenues with regard to various aspects of evaluation continue to be explored, not only in the context of classification but also in other learning approaches. Our aim here was just to give a snapshot of some of the main directions that the recent efforts have taken. Again, it must be reiterated that this list of works is not at all meant to be comprehensive but merely representative. The main aspect that we should emphasize here is how the approaches can exploit varied insights and how, while doing this, there may be other caveats (even implicit assumptions) that may seep in, which should be taken into account while both using these approaches as a part of the evaluation framework and interpreting the subsequent outcomes.

8.6   Summary

This chapter provided a glimpse into the different developments taking place in various directions of machine learning research that can have a direct or indirect impact on the issue of evaluation of learning algorithms. We have tried, instead of being exhaustive, to discuss some of the main threads in this direction, and have provided details for which we felt that the issues discussed are important and can have a long-term impact in the evaluation context. Among the advancements we discussed are, in addition to some important isolated advancements and analysis efforts, the approaches in the broad direction of general frameworks characterizing performance measure, metrics combination approaches, and insights from the statistical learning theory. However, a definitive word on the status of various approaches is still awaited and so is their import in the mainstream evaluation framework. The reader is encouraged to follow the references provided in the text and the ever-growing literature in the field to obtain details regarding these and other developments.

In the next chapter, we wrap up our discussion from the chapters so far by putting into perspective how these different components and areas of evaluation constitute different components of a complete evaluation framework. We will also emphasize how the interdependencies of these components need to be taken into account when choices are made at different stages of evaluation.

Appendix: Proof of Theorems 8.1 and 8.2

We consider binary classification problems in which the input space $\mathcal{X}$ consists of an arbitrary subset of $\mathbb{R}^n$ and the output space $\mathcal{Y} = \{-1, +1\}$. An example $\mathbf{z} \overset{\text{def}}{=} (\mathbf{x}, y)$ is an input–output pair, where $\mathbf{x} \in \mathcal{X}$ and $y \in \mathcal{Y}$. We adopt the PAC setting, in which each example $\mathbf{z}$ is drawn according to a fixed, but unknown, probability distribution D on $\mathcal{X} \times \mathcal{Y}$. Recall from Chapter 2 that the true risk $R(f)$ of any classifier f is defined as the probability that it misclassifies an example drawn according to D:

$$R(f) = \Pr_{(\mathbf{x},y) \sim D}(f(\mathbf{x}) \neq y) = \mathbf{E}_{(\mathbf{x},y) \sim D} I(f(\mathbf{x}) \neq y),$$

where $I(a) = 1$ if predicate a is true and 0 otherwise. The *empirical risk* $R_T(f)$ of classifier f on a test set $T = \{\mathbf{z}_1, \ldots, \mathbf{z}_m\}$ of m examples is defined as

$$R_T(f) = \frac{1}{m} \sum_{i=1}^{m} I(f(\mathbf{x}_i) \neq y_i) \stackrel{\text{def}}{=} \mathbf{E}_{(\mathbf{x},y) \sim T} I(f(\mathbf{x}) \neq y).$$

Now we model $R_T(f)$ as binomial. The distribution is defined as the probability of λ errors on a set of m examples with the true risk of the classifier f being $R(f)$:

$$\Pr_{T \sim D^m}(m R_T(f) = \lambda | R(f)) = \binom{m}{\lambda} (R(f))^{\lambda} (1 - R(f))^{m-\lambda}.$$

We use the cumulative probability, which is the probability of λ or fewer errors on m examples:

$$\text{Bin}(m, \lambda, R(f)) = \Pr_{T \sim D^m}(m R_T(f) \leq \lambda | R(f))$$

$$= \sum_{i=0}^{m} \binom{m}{\lambda} (R(f))^{i} (1 - R(f))^{m-i}.$$

We define the binomial tail inversion (Langford, 2005) as

$$\overline{\text{Bin}}(m, \lambda, \delta) = \max\{p : \text{Bin}(m, \lambda, p) \geq \delta)\}$$

which is the largest true error such that the probability of observing λ or fewer errors is at least δ.

Then, the risk bound on the true risk of the classifier is defined as (Langford, 2005) follows.

For all classifiers f, for all D, for all $\delta \in (0, 1]$,

$$\Pr_{T \sim D^m}(R(f) \leq \overline{\text{Bin}}(m, \lambda, \delta)) \geq 1 - \delta.$$

From this result, it follows that $\overline{\text{Bin}}(m, \lambda, \delta)$ is the smallest upper bound that holds with probability at least $1 - \delta$, on the true risk $R(f)$ of any classifier f with an observed empirical risk $R_T(f)$ on a set of m examples.

In an analogous manner, a lower bound on $R(f)$ can be found as follows:

$$\Pr_{T \sim D^m}(R(f) \geq \min_{p}\{p : 1 - \text{Bin}(m, \lambda, p) \geq \delta\}) \geq 1 - \delta.$$

Table 8.1. *Dataset description for the illustration of holdout bound of Subsection 8.4.1.*

Dataset	$|T|$	$|S|$	Dim
Bupa	175	170	6
Credit	300	353	15
HeartS	147	150	13
Sonar	103	105	60
Breast cancer	343	340	9
Wdbc	284	285	30
Tic-tac-toe	479	479	9
Ionosphere	175	176	34
Letter_OQ	1036	500	16
Letter_DO	1055	500	16
Mushroom	4062	4062	22

Illustration of Holdout Bound of Subsection 8.4.1

To illustrate the difference in the confidence interval and the bound of Theorems 8.1 and 8.2, we compared six learning algorithms on 11 different datasets. The learning algorithms compared are the SVM equipped with a radial basis function kernel, the SCM for learning conjunctions of data-dependent balls (Marchand and Shawe-Taylor, 2002), Adaboost with decision stumps, decision trees, decision lists and the NB algorithms. Each dataset was divided into two parts, a training set S and a test set T. The training set was used to train the learning algorithm and perform model selection to obtain the best parameters from a predefined set of parameter values. The algorithms were then trained with the chosen parameter values on the training set. The final classifier output by each algorithm was then tested on the test set. The details of the datasets are provided in Table 8.1. Columns $|S|$ and $|T|$ refer to the number of examples in the training and the test sets, respectively. Column Dim refers to the number of attributes (dimensionality) in each dataset. The results of testing each of the classifiers on these datasets are presented in Table 8.2. The column labeled R_T denotes the empirical risk of the classifier on the test set, and columns CI_l and CI_u denote the lower and upper limits of the confidence interval obtained by use of the asymptotic Gaussian assumption on the sampling distribution of the empirical risk. These limits are the two standard deviation limits around the empirical risk. The variance of the risk is obtained on the test-set data samples, with the empirical risk assumed as the mean of the distribution. Finally, the B_u and B_l columns denote, respectively, the upper and lower intervals generated from computing the upper and lower risk bounds of Theorems 8.1 and 8.2 with $\delta = 0.025$. This value of δ is chosen to obtain intervals comparable to the two standard deviation intervals obtained with the Gaussian assumption approach (two-sided 95% confidence interval).

Table 8.2. *Results of various classifiers on UCI Datasets illustrating the difference between the traditional confidence interval approach and the hold out bound based on characterization of empirical error using a binomial distribution.*

Dataset	A	R_T	B_l	B_u	CI_l	CI_u
Bupa	SVM	0.352	0.235	0.376	−0.574	1.278
	ADA	0.291	0.225	0.364	−0.620	1.202
	DT	0.325	0.256	0.400	−0.614	1.264
	DL	0.325	0.256	0.400	−0.614	1.264
	NB	0.4	0.326	0.476	−0.582	1.382
	SCM	0.377	0.305	0.453	−0.595	1.349
Credit	SVM	0.183	0.141	0.231	−0.592	0.958
	ADA	0.17	0.129	0.217	−0.582	0.922
	DT	0.13	0.094	0.173	−0.543	0.803
	DL	0.193	0.150	0.242	−0.598	0.984
	NB	0.2	0.156	0.249	−0.603	1.003
	SCM	0.19	0.147	0.239	−0.596	0.976
HeartS	SVM	0.204	0.142	0.278	−0.604	1.012
	ADA	0.272	0.202	0.351	−0.621	1.165
	DT	0.197	0.136	0.270	−0.601	0.995
	DL	0.156	0.101	0.225	−0.574	0.886
	NB	0.136	0.085	0.202	−0.552	0.824
	SCM	0.190	0.130	0.263	−0.598	0.978
Sonar	SVM	0.116	0.061	0.194	−0.528	0.760
	ADA	0.135	0.076	0.217	−0.553	0.823
	DT	0.365	0.099	0.251	−0.581	0.911
	DL	0.281	0.197	0.378	−0.622	1.184
	NB	0.262	0.180	0.358	−0.621	1.145
	SCM	0.310	0.223	0.409	−0.620	1.240
Breast cancer	SVM	0.038	0.020	0.063	−0.344	0.420
	ADA	0.049	0.029	0.078	−0.385	0.483
	DT	0.061	0.038	0.092	−0.419	0.541
	DL	0.046	0.026	0.074	−0.376	0.468
	NB	0.046	0.026	0.074	−0.376	0.468
	SCM	0.037	0.020	0.063	−0.345	0.419
Wdbc	SVM	0.070	0.043	0.106	−0.442	0.582
	ADA	0.042	0.022	0.072	−0.361	0.445
	DT	0.052	0.029	0.085	−0.396	0.500
	DL	0.059	0.035	0.094	−0.416	0.534
	NB	0.049	0.027	0.081	−0.384	0.482
	SCM	0.056	0.032	0.089	−0.406	0.518
Tic-tac-toe	SVM	0.062	0.042	0.088	−0.423	0.547
	ADA	0.016	0.007	0.326	−0.240	0.272
	DT	0.135	0.106	0.169	−0.550	0.820
	DL	0.048	0.030	0.071	−0.372	0.468
	NB	0.340	0.297	0.384	−0.608	1.288
	SCM	0.106	0.080	0.137	−0.511	0.723

(continued)

Table 8.2. *(continued)*

Dataset	A	R_T	B_l	B_u	CI_l	CI_u
Ionosphere	SVM	0.045	0.019	0.088	−0.373	0.463
	ADA	0.091	0.053	0.144	−0.487	0.669
	DT	0.091	0.053	0.144	−0.487	0.669
	DL	0.142	0.094	0.203	−0.559	0.843
	NB	0.16	0.109	0.222	−0.574	0.894
	SCM	0.24	0.178	0.310	−0.617	1.097
Letter-OQ	SVM	0.010	0.005	0.018	−0.195	0.215
	ADA	0.043	0.031	0.057	−0.364	0.450
	DT	0.077	0.061	0.095	−0.457	0.611
	DL	0.055	0.041	0.070	−0.401	0.511
	NB	0.157	0.135	0.180	−0.571	0.885
	SCM	0.109	0.090	0.129	−0.514	0.732
Letter-DO	SVM	0.013	0.007	0.022	−0.215	0.241
	ADA	0.024	0.016	0.035	−0.286	0.334
	DT	0.061	0.047	0.077	−0.420	0.542
	DL	0.054	0.042	0.070	−0.402	0.510
	NB	0.080	0.064	0.098	−0.464	0.624
	SCM	0.061	0.047	0.077	−0.420	0.542
Mushroom	SVM	0	0	0.0009	0.0	0.0
	ADA	0	0	0.0009	0.0	0.0
	DT	0	0	0.0009	0.0	0.0
	DL	0	0	0.0009	0.0	0.0
	NB	0.091	0.083	0.101	−0.486	0.668
	SCM	0.025	0.020	0.304	−0.287	0.337

As can be seen in Table 8.2, the limits of intervals in the classical Gaussian confidence interval approach are not restricted to the [0, 1] intervals, rendering them meaningless in most scenarios. Indeed, the empirical risk of the classifier, by definition, should always be constrained in the [0, 1] range, and so should its true risk. Hence obtaining confidence intervals that spill over this known interval does not make much sense. On the other hand, the risk bound approach is guaranteed to lie in the [0, 1] interval. The confidence interval technique is also limited in a zero-empirical-risk scenario and cannot yield a confidence interval in this case. This can be seen directly because the resulting Gaussian in this case has both a zero mean and a zero variance. Hence, in the case of zero empirical risk, the confidence interval technique becomes overly optimistic. The risk bound, on the other hand, still yields a finite upper bound [of course very small because $R_T(f) = 0$].

9

Conclusion

We conclude the discussion on various aspects of performance evaluation of learning algorithms by unifying these seemingly disparate parts and putting them in perspective. The *raison d'être* of the following discussion is to appreciate the breadth and depth of the overall evaluation process, emphasizing the fact that such evaluation experiments should not be put together in an ad hoc manner, as they are currently done in many cases, by merely selecting a random subset of some or all of the components discussed in various chapters so far. Indeed, a careful consideration is required of both the underlying evaluation requirements and, in this context, of the correlation between the different choices for each component of the evaluation framework.

This chapter attempts to give a brief snapshot of the various components of the evaluation framework and highlights some of their major dependencies. Moreover, for each component we also give a template of the various steps necessary to make appropriate choices along with some of the main concerns and interrelations to take into account with respect to both, other steps in a given component and other evaluation components themselves. Unfortunately, because of the intricate dependencies between various steps as well as components, it might seem necessary to make simultaneous choices and check their compatibility.

The general model evaluation framework should serve as a representative template and not as a definitive guide. Relationships and dependencies between different components may exist, or be discovered, that do not seem obvious and may even appear as a result of advances in evaluation research. However, the framework should serve as an important basic building block in this direction. Along the way, we consider the advantages and limitations of some practical choices that can be made at each step, as illustrations. However, making concrete recommendations at each step is not necessarily possible without knowledge of the problem at hand and the choices made at other steps of the evaluation. Following the description of the framework, we consider two sample

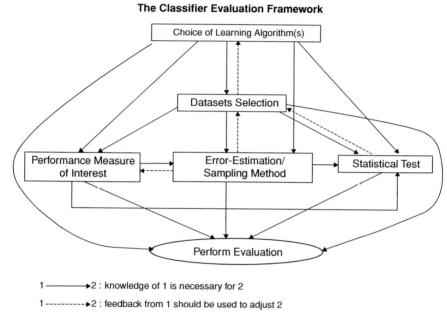

Figure 9.1. Overview of the classifier evaluation procedure.

case studies to highlight some of the practical implications of this framework in Appendix C.

9.1 An Evaluation Framework Template

The overall evaluation exercise can essentially be broken down into broad components along the lines of the framework of Figure 9.1.

As can be seen, each step in the framework of Figure 9.1 corresponds to one of the evaluation components discussed in this book. An implicit assumption made in this framework is that the final aim (though not necessarily the outcome) of the evaluation exercise is known. Given this knowledge, the first step naturally is to decide which algorithms to include in the evaluation exercise. Different considerations need to be addressed while making this choice, for instance, whether a novel algorithm is to be evaluated or whether a testbed of interest exists on which a best algorithm needs to be identified, and so on. One main component-level dependency for algorithm selection exists with the dataset selection implicitly highlighting issues such as whether a generic algorithm is evaluated or an application-specific evaluation is to be performed. The next step is to identify the domains on which the evaluation is to be performed if they did not already guide the algorithm selection step (e.g., in the applications case). For the generic algorithm case or the testing of a novel approach, considerations are made accordingly. The important issues to be addressed at this step may include whether a general characterization of the algorithm is required or some specific criteria of interest need to be tested, whether some specific domain characteristics are desired, and so on. Consequently the dataset selection is not independent of other components because it would affect the error estimation (e.g., because of its size) as well as performance measure selection (e.g., because of issues such as class imbalance). In the same manner, the dataset selection also exerts dependence relationships in other components of the framework. Selecting a performance measure to assess the classifiers will have a high degree of dependence on choices made on the datasets, not to mention the algorithm selection. The choices thus made on the performance measures will also affect the choices made in the subsequent statistical significance testing components and vice versa. The error-estimation step involves making choices that would ensure that the criteria of interest characterizing a classifier's performance are assessed effectively and in as unbiased a manner as possible. A natural dependence of this component would fall on the choices made on the datasets because the characteristics (one of the main ones being the size) of the chosen datasets would decide which error-estimation methods are applicable.

Furthermore, each component of the evaluation framework itself requires careful considerations of the available options and their respective assumptions, constraints of application, advantages, and limitations. Let us now consider each of these components in turn. But before we jump into these, recall that we made the assumption that the aim of evaluation in this whole exercise are well understood. The need for evaluation of learning algorithms can arise broadly from one of the following objectives:

1. Comparison of a *new algorithm* with other (may be generic or application specific) algorithms on a *specific domain* (e.g., when proposing a novel learning algorithm).
2. Comparison of a *new generic algorithm* with other generic ones on a set of *benchmark domains* (e.g., to demonstrate general effectiveness of the new approach against other approaches).
3. Characterization of *generic algorithms* on *benchmarks domains* (e.g., to study the algorithms' behavior on general domains for subsequent use).
4. Comparison of *multiple algorithms* on a *specific domain* (e.g., to find the best algorithm for a given application task).

Of course, in some contexts objectives 1 and 2 can be mapped to objectives 4 and 3, respectively. However, there will be situations in which these cases need to be differentiated.

Notation

Within this context, we consider the different components of the evaluation framework of Figure 9.1. Note that we show dependencies in graphical form for various components of the evaluation with the exception of the learning algorithms selection, in which case the considerations are largely qualitative and not only depend on the evaluation requirements but also characterize the evaluation process itself.

With regard to the representation of the process and dependencies in other components (Figures 9.2 to 9.5), we use the following conventions: The components are represented by dash-dotted boxes, and the arrows denote the dependencies on the processes of the component with the originating arrow. Solid black boxes represent the information from the corresponding process or step, and the diamond boxes represent a test or verification step. The solid black arrows represent dependencies on the information, (output of) process, or the verification step. Hence, arrows are of two types: solid and dashed. The solid arrows indicate the *requirement* of the information of the process or components *from which they originate*, to enable the action, process or component *to which they point*. Dashed arrows, on the other hand, refer to the feedback *from the components or process* of their origination. For instance, a dashed arrow from a diamond box to an oval box may signify the feedback of the decision or verification action that the diamond box represents on the possible actions represented by the oval box. In this sense, we should use a bidirectional relationship notation for such feedback, but we use single dashed arrows instead to keep the figures simple. Note that a black box inside a dash-dotted box denotes the information or process that exerts dependencies on the current component, but are themselves part of the component denoted by the dash-dotted box that encloses them.

Let us start discussing each component, starting with algorithm selection.

9.1.1 Selecting Learning Algorithms

Choosing the candidate learning algorithms for the evaluation experiment depends largely on, among other factors, the overall goal of the evaluation. Broadly, this boils down to whether one wishes to perform a general evaluation or test a specific algorithm. The objectives of a general evaluation and accordingly the subsequent algorithms utilized can be many. For instance, one might be interested in determining a general-purpose classifier effective across a variety of tasks. Even for a given specific problem(s) of interest, one might wish to find the most efficient algorithm. Testing a specific algorithm, on the other hand, tends to narrow down the criteria of selecting other learning algorithms against which the effectiveness of the algorithm of interest is to be evaluated. An example can be to evaluate a novel approach in relation to the existing or state-of-the-art approaches. In case the algorithm of interest (possibly a novel approach) is a generic one, the evaluation would include the most effective generic learning algorithm(s). On the other hand, if the algorithm of interest is application specific, the evaluation should include the most efficient state-of-the-art approaches for the given application.

The preceding description makes the algorithm selection process look pretty straightforward. However, this is certainly not the case because of various practical hassles. Not all approaches claimed to be effective and projected as serious candidates for various domains have their implementations available. This shifts the onus of developing an implementation from the original inventor of the approach onto the researcher carrying out the evaluation. However, even when making the effort of implementing the claimed approach(es) seems worthwhile, the issue of the limited familiarity of the researcher carrying out the evaluation to the nitty-gritties of the algorithm or its implementation makes it extremely difficult. In many cases, such details may not be available at all in the public domain. Hence it turns out that including all possible candidate algorithms in the evaluation may not be feasible, even not possible, after all. This optimal alternative then needs to be traded off in favor of approaches deemed close in performance to the claimed state of the art, even though they are not quite as strong. Such problems are very common in the case of applied research, in which the proposed approaches are composed of independent or interdependent components put together in a processing pipeline. Implementing these then involves difficulties not only in terms of the availability of the various components, but also in figuring out the exact nature of their relationship to other components of the processing pipeline. If the learning algorithm happens to be only one of the components of such a pipeline, then even more care needs to be taken to make sure that the other components are controlled before making any inference on the performance behavior of the algorithm.

The next natural question in selecting the candidate algorithms is that of how many algorithms need to be included in the evaluation. Of course, it would be easy to answer this question if there were a universal winner, i.e., an algorithm that proved to be better (on the criteria of interest, of course) than all other candidates. Evaluating the algorithm of interest against this universal winner would possibly be sufficient, at least as a first step in the evaluation. However, this evidently is almost never the case. As a result, the answer to this question becomes highly subjective. For instance, when a specific application domain is involved, one might want to include the state-of-the-art approaches to evaluate the algorithm of interest against. Of course, there can be cases in which no (or very few) approaches have been proposed with the chosen application in mind. As a result, even though there may be multiple algorithms that can be applied to the domain, they may not be optimal, at least in their classical form. This may give an unfair advantage to the application-specific approach (optimized with the application of interest in mind). Both the evaluation and interpretation of the subsequent results, at the very least (if optimizing the candidate algorithms is not possible), should bear this caveat in mind. Similarly, if the overall goal of evaluation is to determine the best algorithm for a given domain or a set of domains, then a reasonable first step is to include algorithms with a wide range of learning biases (e.g., linear classifiers, decision-based classifiers). Accordingly,

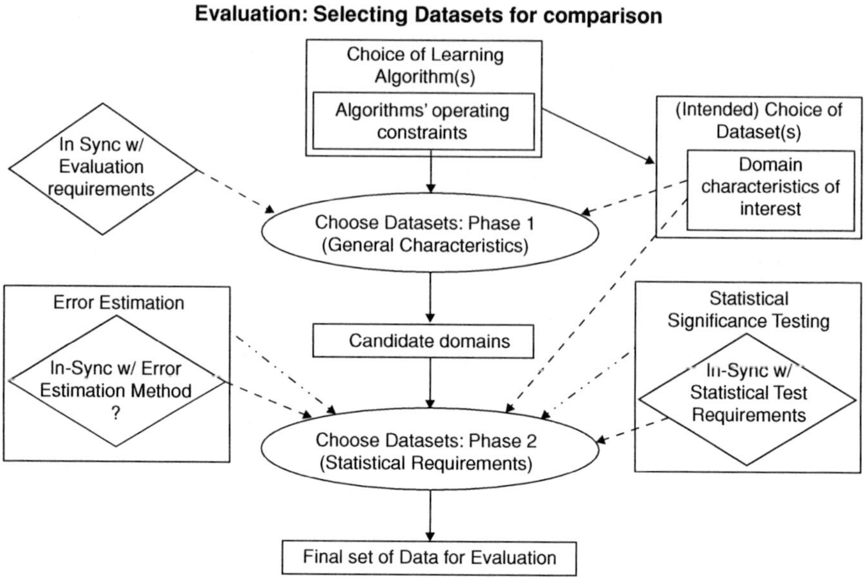

Evaluation: Selecting Datasets for comparison

Figure 9.2. Overview of the dataset selection process.

evaluating a novel generic algorithm would necessitate testing it against a range
of other generic algorithms on a variety of domains. Other relevant issues concern
the characteristics of the domain(s) utilized as well. For instance, an optimal
binary classifier may not be the best choice if the goal is multiclass classification,
or an algorithm known to be most effective in balanced class scenarios may not
be the best choice for domains with highly skewed class distributions. As can be
noted, all these considerations also highlight the dependence of the algorithm
selection component with other components of the evaluation framework, most
notably the dataset selection, which we discuss next.

9.1.2 Selecting Datasets

Figure 9.2 provides an overview of the decision process involved in the dataset
selection component of the evaluation framework.

As discussed a few times now, the choice of the datasets for evaluation
depends, in great part, on the purpose of the evaluation. Naturally, evaluating
generic learning algorithms would necessitate including a variety of datasets
with various characteristics of interest, keeping in mind the purpose and limits of
evaluation. On the other hand, an application-specific evaluation would require
realistic datasets from the domains of interest.

In the application-specific context, great care should be taken while selecting the datasets as well as other components of the evaluation. Effects such as
those of external validity should be kept in mind because the learning system

selected will probably not be deployed on the exact same domain. The desired application area can even be broad such as text classification. Consequently the domains considered would need to cover a broad spectrum of the variabilities in data characteristics such as dimensionality, class distributions, noise levels, class overlaps, and so on. In the context of generic learning algorithms, these variabilities need to be considered in the more general context of various domains too.

In both cases, the dependence on the other evaluation framework components, such as the intended performance measures and error estimation, should also be kept in mind. For instance, measuring accuracy may not bode well with a domain with skewed class distributions. Similarly, the size of the dataset would also affect the error-estimation process. Reverse dependencies exist as well with regard to related concerns. In the case in which a leave-one-out error estimation is of interest (say, because of concerns over theoretical guarantees) for instance, a very large dataset may not only prove to be computationally prohibitive, but also may result in highly biased estimates. A 10-fold cross-validation method, on the other hand, would require at least a reasonably sized dataset to enable reliable estimates. The choice of the number of datasets would also in turn affect the resulting statistical testing. Although the large number of domains would help in making more concrete inferences on the broad effectiveness of the approaches, the size and other characteristics of these domains affect the confidence in their performances' statistical differences.

A simple two-stage approach, as shown in Figure 9.2, can be effective. Whereas the first stage enables filtering out the domains not relevant to the goals of the evaluation and other compatibility issues based on algorithm selections, the second stage allows for further refinement, based on finer considerations on domain characteristics and their dependence on other components such as error estimation and statistical testing. Other issues can appear when multiple approaches and widely varying domains are evaluated. For instance, in a generic evaluation, if the chosen domains are too different from one another, the results can reflect this variability in the performances of the algorithms, rendering them less meaningful. Averaging these performances does not help in such cases, because such estimates highlight marginal (if any) differences. Approaches such as clustering algorithms based on their performance along domain characteristics of interest can be useful in such scenarios. Even visualization methods (e.g., Japkowicz et al., 2008) can be useful because such methods allow the decoupling of classifier performance from the dependence on the domains. However, such issues are naturally quite subjective and will need to be addressed in their respective contexts.

Questions also arise in addition to the ones discussed in detail in Chapter 7. First comes the obvious question of how many datasets are sufficient for evaluation so that clear inferences can be made about the algorithms' performances. Second, one can ask where the datasets can be obtained from? In other words, what is the availability of the required datasets? And finally, one can wonder how the relevance of some domains over all the other available ones can be determined.

The answer to the first question is, in some sense, both related to and affects the third concern. In a generic approach it is felt that, the more varied the datasets, the better the performance analysis. However, it should be noted that the more varied the datasets are, the greater are the chances of obtaining high performance variance in the algorithms, thus jeopardizing sensible interpretation of their comparison. On the other hand, conclusions based on too few datasets may be prone to coincidental trends and may not reflect the true difference in the performance of the algorithms. Interestingly, with a large number of domains too, the issue of the multipicity effect becomes significant, as discussed in Chapter 7. In cases in which a wide variety of datasets is considered, a cluster analysis can prove to be better. The datasets are grouped in clusters (say of 3–5 as a rule of thumb) representing their important common characteristics so as to yield fewer variant performance estimates across them. Algorithms' behavior can then be studied over these individual groupings.

The second question of how to obtain datasets was discussed at length in Chapter 7, where we analyzed the effects of using application-specific datasets, repository-based data, and synthetic data with characteristics of interest in the wake of either the unavailability of real-world data (say because of copyright or privacy issues) or to evaluate the algorithms' performance over specific criteria of interest.

Finally, the answer to the last question, that of selecting a subset of datasets from all those that fulfill the previously mentioned initial requirements, would depend on both the nature of the algorithms and the evaluation requirements and goals [e.g., discarding ones with high missing attribute values in case these result in asymmetric performance (dis)advantages for algorithms].

The next issue, once the algorithms and the dataset(s) are decided on, is that of deciding on the yardstick(s) on which the performances of the algorithms are to be measured and subsequently analyzed. Let us then take a peek at the issues involved in choosing the performance measure(s) of interest.

9.1.3 Selecting Performance Measure(s)

The selection of a performance measure is illustrated in Figure 9.3.

Once again, we suggest dividing the selection process into two stages: first, a broad filter based on dependencies on other components in the evaluation framework, followed by a second stage of finer filtering based on the synchronization requirements with the error estimation as well as other specific requirements on the chosen measures.

The first stage of filtering of the candidate performance measures is basically guided by the previous choices in algorithm selection and dataset selection

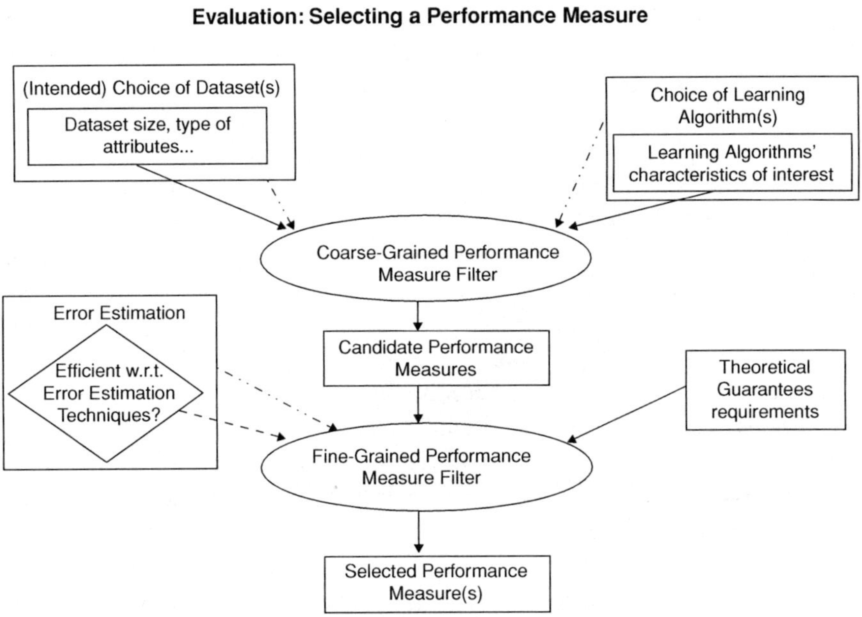

Evaluation: Selecting a Performance Measure

Figure 9.3. Overview of the performance measure selection process.

components, as well as the characteristics of interest in the evaluation, either because of the algorithms' properties or the requirements imposed by the application domain. The choice of learning algorithms can have a crucial effect on the choices that can be made over the performance measures. For instance, this problem occurs when two algorithms with different degrees of reliance on the respective thresholds are compared. Hence, in the event of limited data, an effective threshold setting procedure would be extremely difficult to optimize.[1] A threshold-sensitive point measure such as accuracy would be less recommended in such cases against measures such as ROC that can characterize the behavior over the full operating range (of course within the constraint of limited dataset size). The selection of datasets also imposes certain constraints on the possible performance measure choices. We saw the relationship between these two components above too. However, the constraints on the choices of performance measures are also imposed in other ways. If, for example, some of the selected datasets are multiclass domains, it will be impossible to use a one-class focused measure such as precision or recall without collapsing some of the classes together. Such a collapsing action is, of course, not always desirable, and, as a result, a measure that applies to multiclass domains, such as accuracy, would have to be employed. Similar is the case of hierarchical classification where specialized hierarchical measures must be employed. The characteristic(s) of interest in the evaluation are very important too, for obvious reasons. In

---

[1] Similar problems will of course be faced in model selection over algorithms.

medical applications, for example, the sensitivity and specificity of a test matter much more than its overall accuracy. The performance measure will, thus, have to be chosen appropriately.

Once several candidate performance measures have been chosen, a finer-grained filter needs be applied to ensure that they are in synchronization with our choice of an error estimation technique and that it is associated with appropriate confidence measures or guarantees. The ease as well as computational complexity of calculating a performance measure would play a crucial role when assessing its dependence on the error-estimation technique. Other guarantees on the performance measures might be desirable too, in certain scenarios. Consider, for instance, performance guarantees in the form of either confidence intervals or upper bounds on the generalization performances. Not all performance measures have means of computing the tight confidence intervals associated with them. For example, although point-wise bounds over ROC curves as well confidence bands around the ROCs have been suggested as measures of confidence for ROC analysis, in many cases such bands are not very tight (Elazmeh et al., 2006). Similarly, the learning-theoretic analysis that we discussed briefly in Chapter 8 is relevant over only few measures, most specifically the empirical risk. Further, subsequent validation (or significance testing) over such measures can affect their choice.

We discussed different viewpoints as well as specific performance measures in Chapters 3 and 4. These two chapters discussed the various strengths, limitation, and the context of application of these measures that would be helpful in making the required choices. Given the performance measures of interest, the next issue will be selecting techniques best suited to obtain their estimate(s) objectively. Hence we turn our focus on the issue of selecting the error-estimation method.

9.1.4 Selecting an Error-Estimation and Resampling Method

Chapter 5 discussed the importance as well as implications of choosing a proper error-estimation method in any given problem context. However, in addition to the general reliance on these methods to strike a suitable trade-off between the bias–variance behavior of the performance measure, there are other dependencies that need to be taken into account. Figure 9.4 illustrates a template of the decision process involved in choosing an apt error-estimation method.

The two-stage method of error-estimation method selection is a bit different from the two-stage filtering performed in other components of the evaluation framework. The first stage decides which of the basic error-estimation methods is needed for reliable estimation of the performance measures. The second stage then fine-tunes this method (e.g., decides on the parameters) based on the requirements of the evaluation process. For instance, the first stage can decide that resampling is necessary and that a k-fold cross-validation is the method of choice. The second stage can then decide over the value of k and determine

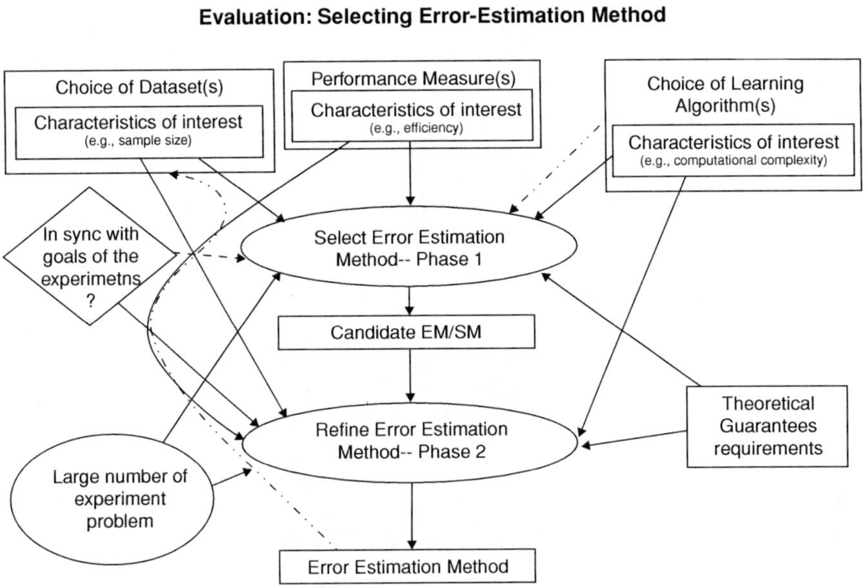

Evaluation: Selecting Error-Estimation Method

Figure 9.4. Overview of the error-estimation selection process.

whether stratified cross-validation is needed. However, note that the factors affecting the choice of the error-estimation method in the first stage also affect the fine-tuning choices made in the second stage. The main dependence on the error-estimation components is exerted from the algorithm selection, dataset selection, as well as the performance measure selection components of the evaluation framework. The choice of the algorithm can affect the error estimation in terms of algorithmic behavior, computational complexity, and so on, in tandem with similar considerations over the error-estimation methods themselves. Further, the reliance of the error-estimation method on the chosen dataset is easy to note, with the most obvious dependency exerted by the size of the dataset. Other properties of the datasets can further affect the fine-tuning stage. For instance, stratified resampling may be deemed important in cases in which the dataset is imbalanced. The problem of large numbers of experiments, also known as the multiplicity effect, refers to the fact that, if too many experiments are run, there is a greater chance that the observed results occur by chance. Some of the ways to deal with this problem involve the choice of an error-estimation technique. For example, randomization testing may prove to be effective in this case. With regard to performance measure too, similar considerations need to be made. Consider, for instance, the need to compute guarantees on the performance measures. The holdout risk bound discussed earlier necessitates a separate testing set, which might not be possible if the dataset is already too small, making it impossible for the algorithm to learn reliably. Other performance measure guarantees may be considered in such cases, for instance, training-set

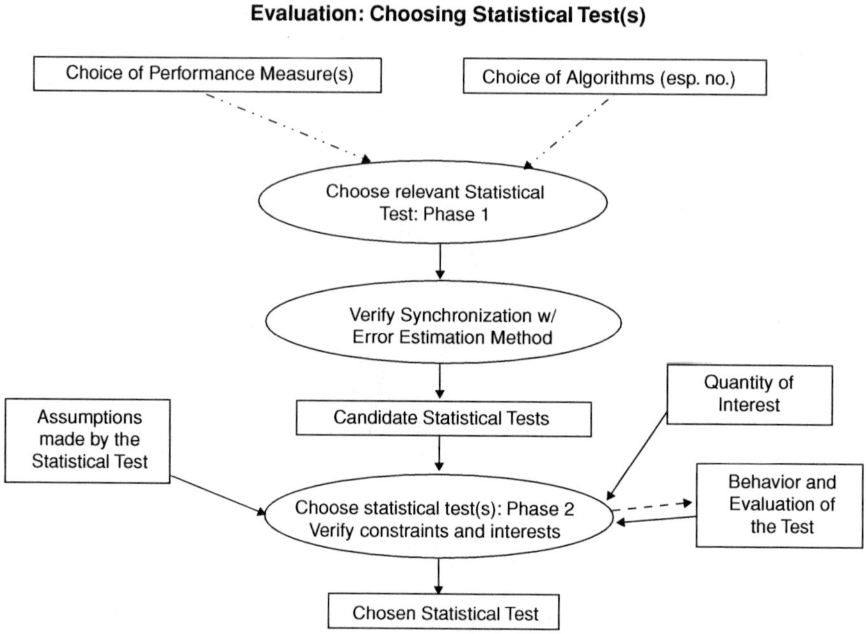

Evaluation: Choosing Statistical Test(s)

Figure 9.5. Overview of the statistical test selection process.

bounds in the case in which a proper learning-theoretic characterization of the algorithm can be obtained or is already available. Considerations also need to be made with respect to statistical significance testing. For example, as we saw earlier, the statistical guarantees that are derived from bootstrapping have much lower power than those derived from t tests applied after resampling methods were run. If power is of importance for the particular application, then a resampling error-estimation regimen is preferred to a bootstrapping one. In fact, the issues of selecting an error-estimation method and associated statistical significance testing are very closely related. We explore this relationship briefly in the discussion of the next component: selecting statistical test(s).

9.1.5 Selecting Statistical Test(s)

The final component that completes the evaluation framework makes the call on choosing the method best suited to determine the statistical significance of the difference in performance of the learning algorithms in the evaluation study. The process is depicted in Figure 9.5.

Analogous to the previous steps, the process of selecting the best-suited tests for assessing the statistical significance of the performance differences consists of two stages. The first stage chooses a subset of candidate statistical tests, based on the dependencies of other components, and the second stage filters out the tests from this subset that do not meet the more specific criteria of interest or other requirements or constraints of evaluation. The first and foremost dependence on the choice of the statistical test comes from the algorithm selection component. For instance, when multiple algorithms are chosen that need to be compared as a group, pairwise tests such as the t test may not be suitable. Similar dependencies exist with other components, such as those of error estimation (and, by implication, the dataset selection) as well as performance measure selection. Consider the case of error estimation that yields multiple, relatively independent, estimates of performance measurements, in which case a parametric statistical test might be considered. On the other hand, if correlated estimates are obtained or the evaluation requires a ranking estimation, nonparametric statistical tests may seem more suitable. The first stage of the component takes into consideration such coarse-grained dependencies. Once a number of candidate tests have been selected by the first stage, a second-stage filter is applied to restrict the choice to a single (or a few) tests, taking into account the user's constraints and preferences, as well as procedural constraints. The criteria thus considered might include the evaluation requirement on the quantity (performance measure) of interest with respect to the statistical justification sought. For instance, one might be interested only in determining whether the difference in the performances are statistically significant, or one might require a quantification of the degree of such a statistically significant difference. Other considerations, such as focus on type I or type II error of the test, may also need to be taken into account. And last but not least, the chosen test will need to be verified with regard to the assumptions, constraints, and their context of application. For instance, if the results over the classifiers' performance cannot be approximated relatively well with a normal distribution, the t test may be rendered meaningless.

Error Estimation and Statistical Test Selections

As mentioned previously, the issues of selecting an error-estimation method and a statistical test are intimately related. For example, if the size of the dataset is large enough, and if the statistics of interest to the user is parameterizable, one should consider using a standard cross-validation with a parametric test for obtaining statistical significance. The latter can be a t test, for instance, in the case of comparing two classifiers on a single domain, and ANOVA, as discussed in Chapter 6, in the case of multiple classifiers over multiple domains. On the other hand, if the dataset is prohibitively small, one might consider resampling methods such as bootstrapping or randomization. The same goes if the statistics of interest does not have statistical tests associated with it. If such techniques are too computationally expensive, then nonparametric tests based on ranking could be used.[2]

---

[2] Note that the rank test and the randomization test are indeed related in that randomization tests can be interpreted as a brute-force version of rank tests. Hence randomization tests should not be used when an exact solution exists in the form of a rank test (Cohen, 1995).

Another important aspect to consider is that of the robustness of the error-estimation procedure, which affects the confidence in the reported significance levels. But robustness does not answer the question of whether efficient use is made of the data so that a false null hypothesis can be rejected. Such a question is answered by considering the notion of whether a statistical procedure is powerful. The power of a test depends on some intrinsic nature of that test, but also on the properties of the population to which it is applied (that is, the sampling distribution of the performance measures). For example, parametric tests based on the normal distribution assumption are generally as or more powerful than nonparametric tests based on ranks in the case of distribution functions with lighter tails than the normal distribution. Such parametric tests, however, are less powerful than nonparametric ones in the case in which the tails of the distribution are heavier than those of the normal distribution (an important kind of data that present such distributions are data containing outliers). Note that the relative power of parametric and nonparametric tests does not change as a function of sample size, even if a test is asymptotically distribution free (i.e., if it becomes more and more robust as the sample size increases). Computer-intensive nonparametric tests are more powerful than their non-computer-intensive counterparts.

One general rule of thumb in making this choice is that a simpler and computationally inexpensive test is preferable among the ones with comparable power. With that in mind, if the assumptions underlying a parametric test are verified, then this parametric test is probably more powerful than its nonparametric counterparts.

A nonparametric combination of error estimation and statistical test should be considered once it has been established that the parametric route could not be followed (e.g., based on exploratory analysis of the sampling distribution in case previous steps do not resolve the ambiguities). There are two scenarios in which a nonparametric test should be preferred: Either there is no parametric sampling distribution for the statistics of interest (e.g., the statistic of interest is the median, rather than, say, the mean) or the assumptions underlying the parametric statistical tests of interest are violated. In either case, one can use a non-computer-intensive nonparametric test applied to the population generated by simple resampling methods or a computer-intensive nonparametric test over bootstrapping or randomization. The sign test described in Chapter 6 is an example of such a nonintensive nonparametric test that could be applied on the population generated by a cross-validation experiment. In general, it might be a good idea to use several statistical tests to confirm the results obtained by a single one in case there are multiple tests satisfying the required criteria. We follow this route (especially because this will allow us to highlight the differences between these tests on a concrete example) in the case studies that are presented in Appendix C. In particular, these case studies illustrate the reasoning we discussed with regard to the various components of the evaluation framework.

In the meantime, we conclude this discussion, and, indeed, the entire book with the following remarks.

9.2 Concluding Remarks

The aim of this book was not only to educate researchers and practitioners who are not familiar with the evaluation process, its underlying assumptions, and its context of application, but also, more broadly, to help the community realize the importance of the evaluation process itself. We tried to emphasize, by dividing the complete process of evaluation into its basic components, the issues that need to be addressed while choices are made at different stages of the evaluation exercise, and the fact that these seemingly disparate components are indeed highly correlated. We illustrate this decision process in the two case studies presented in Appendix C. The choices made in any given component hence need to respect the context of application of other components. Ignoring such intercomponent dependencies can result in misleading outcomes of evaluation with grave consequences. Of course, these dependencies have to be considered together with more fundamental concerns within each component, which are not often acknowledged. The lack of concern for these dependencies, discussed in detail in this chapter, can eventually result in their inappropriate application to the evaluation of learning algorithms. Moreover, a lack of proper understanding and appreciation of the context in which the different components of the evaluation framework operate, discussed in Chapters 3–7, may also lead to a misinterpretation of the evaluation outcomes.

We hope that the discussions in this book leave the reader with an increased understanding and appreciation of the evaluation process as well as improved insights that will prove helpful in making informed choices in practical settings. Even though we limited our discussion to binary classification algorithms in most cases, we hope that we gave a necessary understanding in terms of the underlying evaluation principles that will be useful in expanding one's understanding of and application on the cases not specifically covered in this book.

Indeed, we hope that the elaborate discussions in the various chapters have successfully emphasized the fact that the evaluation process is not simply a matter of making ad hoc choices or adhering to a panacea approach. The various choices at different stages and aspects of evaluation need to be made with care, and their effects and implications, not just on the other components, but on the entire evaluation process, be kept in perspective. This is not to say that such an evaluation will change the fundamental results we have come to accept over time, partly because this understanding is obtained as a consequence of wide empirical verification and validation in a community-wide effort. However, better evaluation can indeed suggest modest changes or highlight initial discrepancies that may have gone unnoticed until practical problems arise in the future. More important perhaps, following the principle that a scientist should fully understand his or her practices, we hope that this book sheds light into the underlying reasons for these practices. With a greater integration of learning-based approaches in various applications, this will, incidentally, facilitate an interdisciplinary dialogue. We thus hope that this book fills the existing void in this area in the machine learning and data mining literature and proves to be a productive first step toward meaningful evaluation.

9.3   Bibliographic Remarks

Our discussion on the relationship between error estimation and statistical test selections in Section 9.1.5 is based, in great part, on Conover (1999, pp. 114–119) and Cohen (1995, pp. 175–183).

The dataset used in the first case study that is reported in Appendix C was designed for the 2008 ICDM Data Contest and is available at http://www.cs.uu.nl/groups/ADA/icdm08cup/data.html.

The visualization algorithm used in the second case study that is also reported in Appendix C was proposed by Alaiz-Rodríguez et al. (2008), as discussed in Chapter 8. A software implementation is available online at http://www.site.uottawa.ca/\~nat/Visualization_Software/visualization.html.

Appendix A

Statistical Tables

This appendix presents all the statistical tables necessary for constructing the confidence intervals or for running a hypothesis test of the kind discussed in this book. In particular, we present seven kinds of tables, although, in some cases, the table is broken up into several ones. More specifically, the following nine tables are presented:

1. the Z table
2. the t table
3. the χ^2 table (two subtables)
4. the table of critical values for the signed test
5. the Wilcoxon table for signed-rank test
6. the F-ratio table (4 subtables)
7. the Friedman table
8. critical values for the Tukey test
9. critical values for the Dunnett test

A.1   The Z Table

Table A.1. *Percentage points of the normal distribution*

P	x(P)	P	x(p)	P	x(P)	P	x(P)	P	x(P)	P	x(P)
50	0.0000	5.0	1.6449	3.0	1.8808	2.0	2.0537	1.0	2.3263	0.10	3.0902
45	0.1257	4.8	1.6646	2.9	1.8957	1.9	2.0749	0.9	2.3656	0.09	3.1214
40	0.2533	4.6	1.6849	2.8	1.9110	1.8	2.0969	0.8	2.4089	0.08	3.1559
35	0.3853	4.4	1.7060	2.7	1.9268	1.7	2.1201	0.7	2.4573	0.07	3.1947
30	0.5244	4.2	1.7279	2.6	1.9431	1.6	2.1444	0.6	2.5121	0.06	3.2389
25	0.6745	4.0	1.7507	2.5	1.9600	1.5	2.1701	0.5	2.5758	0.05	3.2905
20	0.8416	3.8	1.7744	2.4	1.9774	1.4	2.1973	0.4	2.6521	0.01	3.7190
15	1.0364	3.6	1.7991	2.3	1.9954	1.3	2.2262	0.3	2.7478	0.005	3.8906
10	1.2816	3.4	1.8250	2.2	2.0141	1.2	2.2571	0.2	2.8782	0.001	4.2649
5	1.6449	3.2	1.8522	2.1	2.0335	1.1	2.2904	0.1	3.0902	0.0005	4.4172

A.2   The t Table

Table A.2. *Percentage points of the t distribution*

P	40	30	25	20	15	10	5	2.5	1	0.5	0.1	0.05
$v=1$	0.3249	0.7265	1.0000	1.3764	1.963	3.078	6.314	12.71	31.82	63.66	318.3	636.6
2	0.2887	0.6172	0.8165	1.0607	1.386	1.886	2.920	4.303	6.965	9.925	22.33	31.60
3	0.2767	0.5844	0.7649	0.9785	1.250	1.638	2.353	3.182	4.541	5.841	10.21	12.92
4	0.2707	0.5686	0.7407	0.9410	1.190	1.533	2.132	2.776	3.747	4.604	7.173	8.610
5	0.2672	0.5594	0.7267	0.9195	1.156	1.476	2.015	2.571	3.365	4.032	5.893	6.869
6	0.2648	0.5534	0.7176	0.9057	1.134	1.440	1.943	2.447	3.143	3.707	5.208	5.959
7	0.2632	0.5491	0.7111	0.8960	1.119	1.415	1.895	2.365	2.998	3.499	4.785	5.408
8	0.2619	0.5459	0.7064	0.8889	1.108	1.397	1.860	2.306	2.896	3.355	4.501	5.041
9	0.2610	0.5435	0.7027	0.8834	1.100	1.383	1.833	2.262	2.821	3.250	4.297	4.781
10	0.2602	0.5415	0.6998	0.8791	1.093	1.372	1.812	2.228	2.764	3.169	4.144	4.587
11	0.2596	0.5399	0.6974	0.8755	1.088	1.363	1.796	2.201	2.718	3.106	4.025	4.437
12	0.2590	0.5386	0.6955	0.8726	1.083	1.356	1.782	2.179	2.681	3.055	3.930	4.318
13	0.2586	0.5375	0.6938	0.8702	1.079	1.350	1.771	2.160	2.650	2.012	3.852	4.221
14	0.2582	0.5366	0.6924	0.8681	1.076	1.345	1.761	2.145	2.624	2.977	3.787	4.140
15	0.2579	0.5357	0.6912	0.8662	1.074	1.341	1.753	2.131	2.602	2.947	3.733	4.073
16	0.2576	0.5350	0.6901	0.8647	1.071	1.337	1.746	2.120	2.583	2.921	3.686	4.015
17	0.2573	0.5344	0.6892	0.8633	1.069	1.333	1.740	2.110	2.567	2.898	3.646	3.965
18	0.2571	0.5338	0.6884	0.8620	1.067	1.330	1.734	2.101	2.552	2.878	3.610	3.922
19	0.2569	0.5333	0.6876	0.8610	1.066	1.328	1.729	2.093	2.539	2.861	3.579	3.883
20	0.2567	0.5329	0.6870	0.8600	1.064	1.325	1.725	2.086	2.528	2.845	3.552	3.850
21	0.2566	0.5325	0.6864	0.8591	1.063	1.323	1.721	2.080	2.518	2.831	3.527	3.819
22	0.2564	0.5321	0.6858	0.8583	1.061	1.321	1.717	2.074	2.508	2.819	3.505	3.792
23	0.2563	0.5317	0.6853	0.8575	1.060	1.319	1.714	2.069	2.500	2.807	3.485	3.768
24	0.2562	0.5314	0.6848	0.8569	1.059	1.318	1.711	2.064	2.492	2.797	3.467	3.745
25	0.2561	0.5312	0.6844	0.8562	1.058	1.316	1.708	2.060	2.485	2.787	3.450	3.725
26	0.2560	0.5309	0.6840	0.8557	1.058	1.315	1.706	2.056	2.479	2.779	3.435	3.707
27	0.2559	0.5306	0.6837	0.8551	1.057	1.314	1 703	2.052	2.473	2.771	3.421	3.690
28	0.2558	0.5304	0.6834	0.8546	1.056	1.313	1.701	2.048	2.467	2.763	3.408	3.674
29	0.2557	0.5302	0.6830	0.8542	1.055	1.311	1.699	2.045	2.462	2.756	3.396	3.659
30	0.2556	0.5300	0.6828	0.8538	1.055	1.310	1.697	2.042	2.457	2.750	3.385	3.646
32	0.2555	0.5297	0.6822	0.8530	1.054	1.309	1.694	2.037	2.449	2.738	3.365	3.622
34	0.2553	0.5294	0.6818	0.8523	1.052	1.307	1.691	2.032	2.441	2.728	3.348	3.601
36	0.2552	0.5291	0.6814	0.8517	1.052	1.306	1.688	2.028	2.434	2.719	3.333	3.582
38	0.2551	0.5288	0.6810	0.8512	1.051	1.304	1.686	2.024	2.429	2.712	3.319	3.566
40	0.2550	0.5286	0.6807	0.8507	1.050	1.303	1.684	2.021	2.423	2.704	3.307	3.551
50	0.2547	0.5278	0.6794	0.8489	1.047	1.299	1.676	2.009	2.403	2.678	3.261	3.496
60	0.2545	0.5272	0.6786	0.8477	1.045	1 296	1.671	2.000	2.390	2.660	3.232	3.460
120	0.2539	0.5258	0.6765	0.8446	1.041	1.289	1.658	1.980	2.358	2.617	3.160	3.373
∞	0.2533	0.5244	0.6745	0.8416	1.036	1.282	1.645	1.960	2.326	2.576	3.090	3.291

A.3   The χ^2 Table

Table A.3. *Percentage points of the χ^2 distribution*

P	99.95	99.9	99.5	99	97.5	95	90	80	70	60
$v = 1$	0.0^63927	0.0^51571	0.0^43927	0.0^31571	0.0^39821	0.003932	0.01579	0.06418	0.1485	0.2750
2	0.001000	0.002001	0.01003	0.02010	0.05064	0.1026	0.2107	0.4463	0.7133	1.022
3	0.01528	0.02430	0.07172	0.1148	0.2158	0.3518	0.5844	1.005	1.424	1.869
4	0.06392	0.09080	0.2070	0.2971	0.4844	0.7107	1.064	1.649	2.195	2.753
5	0.1581	0.2102	0.4117	0.5543	0.8312	1.145	1.610	2.343	3.000	3.655
6	0.2994	0.3811	0.6757	0.8721	1.237	1.635	2.204	3.070	3.828	4.570
7	0.4849	0.5985	0.9893	1.239	1.690	2.167	2.833	3.822	4.671	5.493
8	0.7104	0.8571	1.344	1.646	2.180	2.733	3.490	4.594	5.527	6.423
9	0.9717	1.152	1.735	2.088	2.700	3.325	4.168	5.380	6.393	7.357
10	1.265	1.479	2.156	2.558	3.247	3.940	4.865	6.179	7.267	8.295
11	1.587	1.834	2.603	3.053	3.816	4.575	5.578	6.989	8.148	9.237
12	1.934	2.214	3.074	3.571	4.404	5.226	6.304	7.807	9.034	10.18
13	2.305	2.617	3.565	4.107	5.009	5.892	7.042	8.634	9.926	11.13
14	2.697	3.041	4.075	4.660	5.629	6.571	7.790	9.467	10.82	12.08
15	3.108	3.483	4.601	5.229	6.262	7.261	8.547	10.31	11.72	13.03
16	3.536	3.942	5.142	5.812	6.908	7.962	9.312	11.15	12.62	13.98
17	3.980	4.416	5.697	6.408	7.564	8.672	10.09	12.00	13.53	14.94
18	4.439	4.905	6.265	7.015	8.231	9.390	10.86	12.86	14.44	15.89
19	4.912	5.407	6.844	7.633	8.907	10.12	11.65	13.72	15.35	16.85
20	5.398	5.921	7.434	8.260	9.591	10.85	12.44	14.58	16.27	17.81
21	5.896	6.447	8.034	8.897	10.28	11.59	13.24	15.44	17.18	18.77
22	6.404	6.983	8.643	9.542	10.98	12.34	14.04	16.31	18.10	19.73
23	6.924	7.529	9.260	10.20	11.69	13.09	14.85	17.19	19.02	20.69
24	7.453	8.085	9.886	10.86	12.40	13.85	15.66	18.06	19.94	21.65
25	7.991	8.649	10.52	11.52	13.12	14.61	16.47	18.94	20.87	22.62
26	8.538	9.222	11.16	12.20	13.84	15.38	17.29	19.82	21.79	23.58
27	9.093	9.803	11.81	12.88	14.57	16.15	18.11	20.70	22.72	24.54
28	9.656	10.39	12.46	13.56	15.31	16.93	18.94	21.59	23.65	25.51
29	10.23	10.99	13.12	14.26	16.05	17.71	19.77	22.48	24.58	26.48
30	10.80	11.59	13.79	14.95	16.79	18.49	20.60	23.36	25.51	27.44
32	11.98	12.81	15.13	16.36	18.29	20.07	22.27	25.15	27.37	29.38
34	13.18	14.06	16.50	17.79	19.81	21.66	23.95	26.94	29.24	31.31
36	14.40	15.32	17.89	19.23	21.34	23.27	25.64	28.73	31.12	33.25
38	15.64	16.61	19.29	20.69	22.88	24.88	27.34	30.54	32.99	35.19
40	16.91	17.92	20.71	22.16	24.43	26.51	29.05	32.34	34.87	37.13
50	23.46	24.67	27.99	29.71	32.36	34.76	37.69	41.45	44.31	46.86
60	30.34	31.74	35.53	37.48	40.48	43.19	46.46	50.64	53.81	56.62
70	37.47	39.04	43.28	45.44	48.76	51.74	55.33	59.90	63.35	66.40
80	44.79	46.52	51.17	53.54	57.15	60.39	64.28	69.21	72.92	76.19
90	52.28	54.16	59.20	61.75	65.65	69.13	73.29	78.56	82.51	85.99
100	59.90	61.92	67.33	70.06	74.22	77.93	82.36	87.95	92.13	95.81

Table A.3 *(cont.)*

P	50	40	30	20	10	5	2.5	1	0.5	0.1	
$v = 1$	0.4549	0.7083	1.074	1.642	2.706	3.841	5.024	6.635	7.879	10.83	12.12
2	1.386	1.833	2.408	3.219	4.605	5.991	7.378	9.210	10.60	13.82	15.20
3	2.366	2.946	3.665	4.642	6.251	7.815	9.348	11.34	12.84	16.27	17.73
4	3.357	4.045	4.878	5.989	7.779	9.488	11.14	13.28	14.86	18.47	20.00
5	4.351	5.132	6.064	7.289	9.236	11.07	12.83	15.09	16.75	20.52	22.11
6	5.348	6.211	7.231	8.558	10.64	12.59	14.45	16.81	18.55	22.46	24.10
7	6.346	7.283	8.383	9.803	12.02	14.07	16.01	18.48	20.28	24.32	26.02
8	7.344	8.351	9.524	11.03	13.36	15.51	17.53	20.09	21.95	26.12	27.87
9	8.343	9.414	10.66	12.24	14.68	16.92	19.02	21.67	23.59	27.88	29.67
10	9.342	10.47	11.78	13.44	15.99	18.31	20.48	23.21	25.19	29.59	31.42
11	10.34	11.53	12.90	14.63	17.28	19.68	21.92	24.72	26.76	31.26	33.14
12	11.34	12.58	14.01	15.81	18.55	21.03	23.34	26.22	28.30	32.91	34.82
13	12.34	13.64	15.12	16.98	19.81	22.36	24.74	27.69	29.82	34.53	36.48
14	13.34	14.69	16.22	18.15	21.06	23.68	26.12	29.14	31.32	36.12	38.11
15	14.34	15.73	17.32	19.31	22.31	25.00	27.49	30.58	32.80	37.70	39.72
16	15.34	16.78	18.42	20.47	23.54	26.30	28.85	32.00	34.27	39.25	41.31
17	16.34	17.82	19.51	21.61	24.77	27.59	30.19	33.41	35.72	40.79	42.88
18	17.34	18.87	20.60	22.76	25.99	28.87	31.53	34.81	37.16	42.31	44.43
19	18.34	19.91	21.69	23.90	27.20	30.14	32.85	36.19	38.58	43.82	45.97
20	19.34	20.95	22.77	25.04	28.41	31.41	34.17	37.57	40.00	45.31	47.50
21	20.34	21.99	23.86	26.17	29.62	32.67	35.48	38.93	41.40	46.80	49.01
22	21.34	23.03	24.94	27.30	30.81	33.92	36.78	40.29	42.80	48.27	50.51
23	22.34	24.07	26.02	28.43	32.01	35.17	38.08	41.64	44.18	49.73	52.00
24	23.34	25.11	27.10	29.55	33.20	36.42	39.36	42.98	45.56	51.18	53.48
25	24.34	26.14	28.17	30.68	34.38	37.65	40.65	44.31	46.93	52.62	54.95
26	25.34	27.18	29.25	31.79	35.56	38.89	41.92	45.64	48.29	54.05	56.41
27	26.34	28.21	30.32	32.91	36.74	40.11	43.19	46.96	49.64	55.48	57.86
28	27.34	29.25	31.39	34.03	37.92	41.34	44.46	48.28	50.99	56.89	59.30
29	28.34	30.28	32.46	35.14	39.09	42.56	45.72	49.59	52.34	58.30	60.73
30	29.34	31.32	33.53	36.25	40.26	43.77	46.98	50.89	53.67	59.70	62.16
32	31.34	33.38	35.66	38.47	42.58	46.19	49.48	53.49	56.33	62.49	65.00
34	33.34	35.44	37.80	40.68	44.90	48.60	51.97	56.06	58.96	65.25	67.80
36	35.34	37.50	39.92	42.88	47.21	51.00	54.44	58.62	61.58	67.99	70.59
38	37.34	39.56	42.05	45.08	49.51	53.38	56.90	61.16	64.18	70.70	73.35
40	39.34	41.62	44.16	47.27	51.81	55.76	59.34	63.69	66.77	73.40	76.09
50	49.33	51.89	54.72	58.16	63.17	67.50	71.42	76.15	79.49	86.66	89.56
60	59.33	62.13	65.23	68.97	74.40	79.08	83.30	88.38	91.95	99.61	102.7
70	69.33	72.36	75.69	79.71	85.53	90.33	95.02	100.4	104.2	112.3	115.6
80	79.33	82.57	86.12	90.41	96.58	101.9	106.6	112.3	116.3	124.8	128.3
90	89.33	92.76	96.52	101.1	107.6	113.1	118.1	124.1	128.3	137.2	140.8
100	99.33	102.9	106.9	111.7	118.5	124.3	129.6	135.8	140.2	149.4	153.2

A.4   The Table of Critical Values for the Signed Test

Table A.4. *Critical values of T for the sign test*

Two-sided	0.10	0.05	0.02	0.01	Two-sided	0.10	0.05	0.02	0.01
One-sided	0.05	0.025	0.01	0.005	One-sided	0.05	0.025	0.01	0.005
n					n				
1	–	–	–	–	31	11	13	15	17
2	–	–	–	–	32	12	14	16	16
3	–	–	–	–	33	11	13	15	17
4	–	–	–	–	34	12	14	16	16
5	5	–	–	–	35	11	13	15	17
6	6	6	–	–	36	12	14	16	18
7	7	7	7	–	37	11	13	17	17
8	6	8	8	8	38	12	14	16	18
9	7	7	9	9	39	13	15	17	17
10	8	8	10	10	40	12	14	16	18
11	7	9	9	11	45	13	15	17	19
12	8	8	10	10	46	14	16	18	20
13	7	9	11	11	49	13	15	19	19
14	8	10	10	12	50	14	16	18	20
15	9	9	11	11	55	15	17	19	21
16	8	10	12	12	56	14	16	18	20
17	9	9	11	13	59	15	17	19	21
18	8	10	12	12	60	14	18	20	22
19	9	11	11	13	65	15	17	21	23
20	10	10	12	14	66	16	18	20	22
21	9	11	13	13	69	15	19	23	25
22	0	12	12	14	70	16	18	22	24
23	9	11	13	15	75	17	19	23	25
24	10	12	14	14	76	16	20	22	24
25	11	11	13	15	79	17	19	23	25
26	10	12	14	14	80	16	20	22	24
27	11	13	13	15	89	17	21	23	27
28	10	12	14	16	90	18	20	24	26
29	11	13	15	15	99	19	21	25	27
30	10	12	14	16	100	18	22	26	28

Level of significance α (both halves)

356 Appendix A

A.5 The Wilcoxon Table

Table A.5. *Percentage points of Wilcoxon's Signed-Rank distribution*

P	5	2.5	1	0.5	0.1	P	5	2.5	1	0.5	0.1
n = 5	0	–	–	–	–	n = 45	371	343	312	291	249
6	2	0	–	–	–	46	389	361	328	307	263
7	3	2	0	–	–	47	407	378	345	322	277
8	5	3	1	0	–	48	426	396	362	339	292
9	8	5	3	1	–	49	446	415	379	355	307
10	10	8	5	3	0	50	466	434	397	373	323
11	13	10	7	5	1	51	486	453	416	390	339
12	17	13	9	7	2	52	507	473	434	408	355
13	21	17	12	9	4	53	529	494	454	427	372
14	25	21	15	12	6	54	550	514	473	445	389
15	30	25	19	15	8	55	573	536	493	465	407
16	35	29	23	19	11	56	595	557	514	484	425
17	41	34	27	23	14	57	618	579	535	504	443
18	47	40	32	27	18	58	642	602	556	525	462
19	53	46	37	32	21	59	666	625	578	546	482
20	60	52	43	37	26	60	690	648	600	567	501
21	67	58	49	42	30	61	715	672	623	589	521
22	75	65	55	48	35	62	741	697	646	611	542
23	83	73	62	54	40	63	767	721	669	634	563
24	91	81	69	61	45	64	793	747	693	657	584
25	100	89	76	68	51	65	820	772	718	681	606
26	110	98	84	75	58	66	847	798	742	705	628
27	119	107	92	83	64	67	875	825	768	729	651
28	130	116	101	91	71	68	903	852	793	754	674
29	140	126	110	100	79	69	931	879	819	779	697
30	151	137	120	109	86	70	960	907	846	805	721
31	163	147	130	118	94	71	990	936	573	831	745
32	175	159	140	128	103	72	1020	964	901	858	770
33	187	170	151	138	112	73	1050	994	928	884	795
34	200	182	162	148	121	74	1081	1023	957	912	821
35	213	195	173	159	131	75	1112	1053	986	940	847
36	227	208	185	171	141	76	1144	1084	1015	968	873
37	241	221	198	182	151	77	1176	1115	1044	997	900
38	256	235	211	194	162	78	1209	1147	1075	1026	927
39	271	249	224	207	173	79	1242	1179	1105	1056	955
40	286	264	238	220	185	80	1276	1211	1136	1086	983
41	302	279	252	233	197	81	1310	1244	1168	1116	1011
42	319	294	266	247	209	82	1345	1277	1200	1147	1040
43	336	310	281	261	222	83	1380	1311	1232	1178	1070
44	353	327	296	276	235	84	1415	1345	1265	1210	1099
45	371	343	312	291	249	85	1451	1380	1298	1242	1130

A.6   The *F*-ratio Table

Table A.6(a). *10% points of the F distribution*

$v_1 =$	1	2	3	4	5	6	7	8	10	12	24	∞
$v_2 = 1$	39.86	49.50	53.59	55.83	57.24	58.20	58.91	59.44	60.19	60.71	62.00	63.33
2	8.526	9.000	9.162	9.243	9.293	9.326	9.349	9.367	9.392	9.408	9.450	9.491
3	5.538	5.462	5.391	5.343	5.309	5.285	5.266	5.252	5.230	5.216	5.176	5.134
4	4.545	4.325	4.191	4.107	4.051	4.010	3.979	3.955	3.920	3.896	3.831	3.761
5	4.060	3.780	3.619	3.520	3.453	3.405	3.368	3.339	3.297	3.268	3.191	3.105
6	3.776	3.463	3.289	3.181	3.108	3.055	3.014	2.983	2.937	2.905	2.818	2.722
7	3.589	3.257	3.074	2.961	2.883	2.827	2.785	2.752	2.703	2.668	2.575	2.471
8	3.458	3.113	2.924	2.806	2.726	2.668	2.624	2.589	2.538	2.502	2.404	2.293
9	3.360	3.006	2.813	2.693	2.611	2.551	2.505	2.469	2.416	2.379	2.277	2.159
10	3.285	2.924	2.728	2.605	2.522	2.461	2.414	2.377	2.323	2.284	2.178	2.055
11	3.225	2.860	2.660	2.536	2.451	2.389	2.342	2.304	2.248	2.209	2.100	1.972
12	3.177	2.807	2.606	2.480	2.394	2.331	2.283	2.245	2.188	2.147	2.036	1.904
13	3.136	2.763	2.560	2.434	2.347	2.283	2.234	2.195	2.138	2.097	1.983	1.846
14	3.102	2.726	2.522	2.395	2.307	2.243	2.193	2.154	2.095	2.054	1.938	1.797
15	3.073	2.695	2.490	2.361	2.273	2.208	2.158	2.119	2.059	2.017	1.899	1.755
16	3.048	2.668	2.462	2.333	2.244	2.178	2.128	2.088	2.028	1.985	1.866	1.718
17	3.026	2.645	2.437	2.308	2.218	2.152	2.102	2.061	2.001	1.958	1.836	1.686
18	3.007	2.624	2.416	2.286	2.196	2.130	2.079	2.038	1.977	1.933	1.810	1.657
19	2.990	2.606	2.397	2.266	2.176	2.109	2.058	2.017	1.956	1.912	1.787	1.631
20	2.975	2.589	2.380	2.249	2.158	2.091	2.040	1.999	1.937	1.892	1.767	1.607
21	2.961	2.575	2.365	2.233	2.142	2.075	2.023	1.982	1.920	1.875	1.748	1.586
22	2.949	2.561	2.351	2.219	2.128	2.060	2.008	1.967	1.904	1.859	1.731	1.567
23	2.937	2.549	2.339	2.207	2.115	2.047	1.995	1.953	1.890	1.845	1.716	1.549
24	2.927	2.538	2.327	2.195	2.103	2.035	1.983	1.941	1.877	1.832	1.702	1.533
25	2.918	2.528	2.317	2.184	2.092	2.024	1.971	1.929	1.866	1.820	1.689	1.518
26	2.909	2.519	2.307	2.174	2.082	2.014	1.961	1.919	1.855	1.809	1.677	1.504
27	2.901	2.511	2.299	2.165	2.073	2.005	1.952	1.909	1.845	1.799	1.666	1.491
28	2.894	2.503	2.291	2.157	2.064	1.996	1.943	1.900	1.836	1.790	1.656	1.478
29	2.887	2.495	2.283	2.149	2.057	1.988	1.935	1.892	1.827	1.781	1.647	1.467
30	2.881	2.489	2.276	2.142	2.049	1.980	1.927	1.884	1.819	1.773	1.638	1.456
32	2.869	2.477	2.263	2.129	2.036	1.967	1.913	1.870	1.805	1.758	1.622	1.437
34	2.859	2.466	2.252	2.118	2.024	1.955	1.901	1.858	1.793	1.745	1.608	1.419
36	2.850	2.456	2.243	2.108	2.014	1.945	1.891	1.847	1.781	1.734	1.595	1.404
38	2.842	2.448	2.234	2.099	2.005	1.935	1.881	1.838	1.772	1.724	1.584	1.390
40	2.835	2.440	2.226	2.091	1.997	1.927	1.873	1.829	1.763	1.715	1.574	1.377
60	2.791	2.393	2.177	2.041	1.946	1.875	1.819	1.775	1.707	1.657	1.511	1.291
120	2.748	2.347	2.130	1.992	1.896	1.824	1.767	1.722	1.652	1.601	1.447	1.193
∞	2.706	2.303	2.084	1.945	1.847	1.774	1.717	1.670	1.599	1.546	1.383	1.000

Appendix A

Table A.6(b). *5% points of the F distribution*

$v_1 =$	1	2	3	4	5	6	7	8	10	12	24	∞
$v_2 = 1$	161.4	199.5	215.7	224.6	230.2	234.0	236.8	238.9	241.9	243.9	249.1	254.3
2	18.51	19.00	19.16	19.25	19.30	19.33	19.35	19.37	19.40	19.41	19.45	19.50
3	10.13	9.552	9.277	9.117	9.013	8.941	8.887	8.845	8.786	8.745	8.639	8.526
4	7.709	6.944	6.591	6.388	6.256	6.163	6.094	6.041	5.964	5.912	5.774	5.628
5	6.608	5.786	5.409	5.192	5.050	4.950	4.876	4.818	4.735	4.678	4.527	4.365
6	5.987	5.143	4.757	4.534	4.387	4.284	4.207	4.147	4.060	4.000	3.841	3.669
7	5.591	4.737	4.347	4.120	3.972	3.866	3.787	3.726	3.637	3.575	3.410	3.230
8	5.318	4.459	4.066	3.838	3.687	3.581	3.500	3.438	3.347	3.284	3.115	2.928
9	5.117	4.256	3.863	3.633	3.482	3.374	3.293	3.230	3.137	3.073	2.900	2.707
10	4.965	4.103	3.708	3.478	3.326	3.217	3.135	3.072	2.978	2.913	2.737	2.538
11	4.844	3.982	3.587	3.357	3.204	3.095	3.012	2.948	2.854	2.788	2.609	2.404
12	4.747	3.885	3.490	3.259	3.106	2.996	2.913	2.849	2.753	2.687	2.505	2.296
13	4.667	3.806	3.411	3.179	3.025	2.915	2.832	2.767	2.671	2.604	2.420	2.206
14	4.600	3.739	3.344	3.112	2.958	2.848	2.764	2.699	2.602	2.534	2.349	2.131
15	4.543	3.682	3.287	3.056	2.901	2.790	2.707	2.641	2.544	2.475	2.288	2.066
16	4.494	3.634	3.239	3.007	2.852	2.741	2.657	2.591	2.494	2.425	2.235	2.010
17	4.451	3.592	3.197	2.965	2.810	2.699	2.614	2.548	2.450	2.381	2.190	1.960
18	4.414	3.555	3.160	2.928	2.773	2.661	2.577	2.510	2.412	2.342	2.150	1.917
19	4.381	3.522	3.127	2.895	2.740	2.628	2.544	2.477	2.378	2.308	2.114	1.878
20	4.351	3.493	3.098	2.866	2.711	2.599	2.514	2.447	2.348	2.278	2.082	1.843
21	4.325	3.467	3.072	2.840	2.685	2.573	2.488	2.420	2.321	2.250	2.054	1.812
22	4.301	3.443	3.049	2.817	2.661	2.549	2.464	2.397	2.297	2.226	2.028	1.783
23	4.279	3.422	3.028	2.796	2.640	2.528	2.442	4.375	2.275	2.204	2.005	1.757
24	4.260	3.403	3.009	2.776	2.621	2.508	2.423	2.355	2.255	2.183	1.984	1.733
25	4.242	3.385	2.991	2.759	2.603	2.490	2.405	2.337	2.236	2.165	1.964	1.711
26	4.225	3.369	2.975	2.743	2.587	2.474	2.388	2.321	2.220	2.148	1.946	1.691
27	4.210	3.354	2.960	2.728	2.572	2.459	2.373	2.305	2.204	2.132	1.930	1.672
28	4.196	3.340	2.947	2.714	2.558	2.445	2.359	2.291	2.190	2.118	1.915	1.654
29	4.183	3.328	2.934	2.701	2.545	2.432	2.346	2.278	2.177	2.104	1.901	1.638
30	4.171	3.316	2.922	2.690	2.534	2.421	2.334	2.266	2.165	2.092	1.887	1.622
32	4.149	3.295	2.901	2.668	2.512	2.399	2.313	2.244	2.142	2.070	1.864	1.594
34	4.130	3.276	2.883	2.650	2.494	2.380	2.294	2.225	2.123	2.050	1.843	1.569
36	4.113	3.259	2.866	2.634	2.477	2.364	2.277	2.209	2.106	2.033	1.824	1.547
38	4.098	3.245	2.852	2.619	2.463	2.349	2.262	2.194	2.091	2.017	1.808	1.527
40	4.085	3.232	2.839	2.606	2.449	2.336	2.249	2.180	2.077	2.003	1.793	1.509
60	4.001	3.150	2.758	2.525	2.368	2.254	2.167	2.097	1.993	1.917	1.700	1.389
120	3.920	3.072	2.680	2.447	2.290	2.175	2.087	2.016	1.910	1.834	1.608	1.254
∞	3.841	2.996	2.605	2.372	2.214	2.099	2.010	1.938	1.831	1.752	1.517	1.000

Table A.6(c). *2.5% points of the F distribution*

$v_1 =$	1	2	3	4	5	6	7	8	10	12	24	∞
$v_2 = 1$	647.8	799.5	864.2	899.6	921.8	937.1	948.2	956.7	968.6	976.7	997.2	1018
2	38.51	39.00	39.17	39.25	39.30	39.33	39.36	39.37	39.40	39.41	39.46	39.50
3	17.44	16.04	15.44	15.10	14.88	14.73	14.62	14.54	14.42	14.34	14.12	13.90
4	12.22	10.65	9.979	9.605	9.364	9.197	9.074	8.980	8.844	8.751	8.511	8.257
5	10.01	8.434	7.764	7.388	7.146	6.978	6.853	6.757	6.619	6.525	6.278	6.015
6	8.813	7.260	6.599	6.227	5.988	5.820	5.695	5.600	5.461	5.366	5.117	4.849
7	8.073	6.542	5.890	5.523	5.285	5.119	4.995	4.899	4.761	4.666	4.415	4.142
8	7.571	6.059	5.416	5.053	4.817	4.652	4.529	4.433	4.295	4.200	3.947	3.670
9	7.209	5.715	5.078	4.718	4.484	4.320	4.197	4.102	3.964	3.868	3.614	3.333
10	6.937	5.456	4.826	4.468	4.236	4.072	3.950	3.855	3.717	3.621	3.365	3.080
11	6.724	5.256	4.630	4.275	4.044	3.881	3.759	3.664	3.526	3.430	3.173	2.883
12	6.554	5.096	4.474	4.121	3.891	3.728	3.607	3.512	3.374	3.277	3.019	2.725
13	6.414	4.965	4.347	3.996	3.767	3.604	3.483	3.388	3.250	3.153	2.893	2.595
14	6.298	4.857	4.242	3.892	3.663	3.501	3.380	3.285	3.147	3.050	2.789	2.487
15	6.200	4.765	4.153	3.804	3.576	3.415	3.293	3.199	3.060	2.963	2.701	2.395
16	6.115	4.687	4.077	3.729	3.502	3.341	3.219	3.125	2.986	2.889	2.625	2.316
17	6.042	4.619	4.011	3.665	3.438	3.277	3.156	3.061	2.922	2.825	2.560	2.247
18	5.978	4.560	3.954	3.608	3.382	3.221	3.100	3.005	2.866	2.769	2.503	2.187
19	5.922	4.508	3.903	3.559	3.333	3.172	3.051	2.956	2.817	2.720	2.452	2.133
20	5.871	4.461	3.859	3.515	3.289	3.128	3.007	2.913	2.774	2.676	2.408	2.085
21	5.827	4.420	3.819	3.475	3.250	3.090	2.969	2.874	2.735	2.637	2.368	2.042
22	5.786	4.383	3.783	3.440	3.215	3.055	2.934	2.839	2.700	2.602	2.331	2.003
23	5.750	4.349	3.750	3.408	3.183	3.023	2.902	2.808	2.668	2.570	2.299	1.968
24	5.717	4.319	3.721	3.379	3.155	2.995	2.874	2.779	2.640	2.541	2.269	1.935
25	5.686	4.291	3.694	3.353	3.129	2.969	2.848	2.753	2.613	2.515	2.242	1.906
26	5.659	4.265	3.670	3.329	3.105	2.945	2.824	2.729	2.590	2.491	2.217	1.878
27	5.633	4.242	3.647	3.307	3.083	2.923	2.802	2.707	2.568	2.469	2.195	1.853
28	5.610	4.221	3.626	3.286	3.063	2.903	2.782	2.687	2.547	2.448	2.174	1.829
29	5.588	4.201	3.607	3.267	3.044	2.884	2.763	2.669	2.529	2.430	2.154	1.807
30	5.568	4.182	3.589	3.250	3.026	2.867	2.746	2.651	2.511	2.412	2.136	1.787
32	5.531	4.149	3.557	3.218	2.995	2.836	2.715	2.620	2.480	2.381	2.103	1.750
34	5.499	4.120	3.529	3.191	2.968	2.808	2.688	2.593	2.453	2.353	2.075	1.717
36	5.471	4.094	3.505	3.167	2.944	2.785	2.664	2.569	2.429	2.329	2.049	1.687
38	5.446	4.071	3.483	3.145	2.923	2.763	2.643	2.548	2.407	2.307	2.027	1.661
40	5.424	4.051	3.463	3.126	2.904	2.744	2.624	2.529	2.388	2.288	2.007	1.637
60	5.286	3.925	3.343	3.008	2.786	2.627	2.507	2.412	2.270	2.169	1.882	1.482
120	5.152	3.805	3.227	2.894	2.674	2.515	2.395	2.299	2.157	2.055	1.760	1.310
∞	5.024	3.689	3.116	2.786	2.567	2.408	2.288	2.192	2.048	1.945	1.640	1.000

Table A.6(d). *1% points of the F distribution*

$v_1 =$	1	2	3	4	5	6	7	8	10	12	24	∞
$v_2 = 1$	4052	4999	5403	5625	5764	5859	5928	5981	6056	6106	6235	6366
2	98.50	99.00	99.17	99.25	99.30	99.33	99.36	99.37	99.40	99.42	99.46	99.50
3	34.12	30.82	29.46	28.71	28.24	27.91	27.67	27.49	27.23	27.05	26.60	26.13
4	21.20	18.00	16.69	15.98	15.52	15.21	14.98	14.80	14.55	14.37	13.93	13.46
5	16.26	13.27	12.06	11.39	10.97	10.67	10.46	10.29	10.05	9.888	9.466	9.020
6	13.75	10.92	9.780	9.148	8.746	8.466	8.260	8.102	7.874	7.718	7.313	6.880
7	12.25	9.547	8.451	7.847	7.460	7.191	6.993	6.840	6.620	6.469	6.074	5.650
8	11.26	8.649	7.591	7.006	6.632	6.371	6.178	6.029	5.814	5.667	5.279	4.859
9	10.56	8.022	6.992	6.422	6.057	5.802	5.613	5.467	5.257	5.111	4.729	4.311
10	10.04	7.559	6.552	5.994	5.636	5.386	5.200	5.057	4.849	4.706	4.327	3.909
11	9.646	7.206	6.217	5.668	5.316	5.069	4.886	4.744	4.539	4.397	4.021	3.602
12	9.330	6.927	5.953	5.412	5.064	4.821	4.640	4.499	4.296	4.155	3.780	3.361
13	9.074	6.701	5.739	5.205	4.862	4.620	4.441	4.302	4.100	3.960	3.587	3.165
14	8.862	6.515	5.564	5.035	4.695	4.456	4.278	4.140	3.939	3.800	3.427	3.004
15	8.683	6.359	5.417	4.893	4.556	4.318	4.142	4.004	3.805	3.666	3.294	2.868
16	8.531	6.226	5.292	4.773	4.437	4.202	4.026	3.890	3.691	3.553	3.181	2.753
17	8.400	6.112	5.185	4.669	4.336	4.102	3.927	3.791	3.593	3.455	3.084	2.653
18	8.285	6.013	5.092	4.579	4.248	4.015	3.841	3.705	3.508	3.371	2.999	2.566
19	8.185	5.926	5.010	4.500	4.171	3.939	3.765	3.631	3.434	3.297	2.925	2.489
20	8.096	5.849	4.938	4.431	4.103	3.871	3.699	3.564	3.368	3.231	2.859	2.421
21	8.017	5.780	4.874	4.369	4.042	3.812	3.640	3.506	3.310	3.173	2.801	2.360
22	7.945	5.719	4.817	4.313	3.988	3.758	3.587	3.453	3.258	3.121	2.749	2.305
23	7.881	5.664	4.765	4.264	3.939	3.710	3.539	3.406	3.211	3.074	2.702	2.256
24	7.823	5.614	4.718	4.218	3.895	3.667	3.496	3.363	3.168	3.032	2.659	2.211
25	7.770	5.568	4.675	4.177	3.855	3.627	3.457	3.324	3.129	2.993	2.620	2.169
26	7.721	5.526	4.637	4.140	3.818	3.591	3.421	3.288	3.094	2.958	2.585	2.131
27	7.677	5.488	4.601	4.106	3.785	3.558	3.388	3.256	3.062	2.926	2.552	2.097
28	7.636	5.453	4.568	4.074	3.754	3.528	3.358	3.226	3.032	2.896	2.522	2.064
29	7.598	5.420	4.538	4.045	3.725	3.499	3.330	3.198	3.005	2.868	2.495	2.034
30	7.562	5.390	4.510	4.018	3.699	3.473	3.304	3.173	2.979	2.843	2.469	2.006
32	7.499	5.336	4.459	3.969	3.652	3.427	3.258	3.127	2.934	2.798	2.423	1.956
34	7.444	5.289	4.416	3.927	3.611	3.386	3.218	3.087	2.894	2.758	2.383	1.911
36	7.396	5.248	4.377	3.890	3.574	3.351	3.183	3.052	2.859	2.723	2.347	1.872
38	7.353	5.211	4.343	3.858	3.542	3.319	3.152	3.021	2.828	2.692	2.316	1.837
40	7.314	5.179	4.313	3.828	3.514	3.291	3.124	2.993	2.801	2.665	2.288	1.805
60	7.077	4.977	4.126	3.649	3.339	3.119	3.953	2.823	2.632	2.496	2.115	1.601
120	6.851	4.787	3.949	3.480	3.174	2.956	2.792	2.663	2.472	2.336	1.950	1.381
∞	6.635	4.605	3.782	3.319	3.017	2.802	2.639	2.511	2.321	2.185	1.791	1.000

A.7   The Friedman Table

Table A.7. *Upper percentage points of Friedman's distribution*

k = 3

P	10	5	2.5	1	0.1
n = 3	6.000	6.000	–	–	–
4	6.000	6.500	8.000	8.000	–
5	5.200	6.400	7.600	8.400	10.00
6	5.333	7.000	8.333	9.000	12.00
7	5.429	7.143	7.714	8.857	12.29
8	5.250	6.250	7.750	9.000	12.25
9	5.556	6.222	8.000	9.556	12.67
10	5.000	6.200	7.800	9.600	12.60
11	5.091	6.545	7.818	9.455	13.27
12	5.167	6.500	8.000	9.500	12.67
13	4.769	6.615	7.538	9.385	12.46
14	5.143	6.143	7.429	9.143	13.29
15	4.933	6.400	7.600	8.933	12.93
16	4.875	6.500	7.625	9.375	13.50
17	5.059	6.118	7.412	9.294	13.06
18	4.778	6.333	7.444	9.000	13.00
19	5.053	6.421	7.684	9.579	13.37
20	4.900	6.300	7.500	9.300	13.30
21	4.952	6.095	7.524	9.238	13.24
22	4.727	6.091	7.364	9.091	13.45
23	4.957	6.348	7.913	9.39I	13.13
24	5.083	6.250	7.750	9.250	13.08
25	4.880	6.080	7.440	8.960	13.52
26	4.846	6.077	7.462	9.308	13.23
27	4.741	6.000	7.407	9.407	13.41
28	4.571	6.500	7.714	9.214	13.50
29	5.034	6.276	7.517	9.172	13.52
30	4.867	6.200	7.400	9.267	13.40
31	4'839	6.000	7.548	9.290	13.42
32	4.750	6.063	7.563	9.250	13.69
33	4.788	6.061	7.515	9.152	13.52
34	4.765	6.059	7.471	9.176	13.41
∞	4.605	5.99I	7.378	9.210	13.82

k = 4

P	10	5	2.5	1	0.1
n = 3	6.600	7.400	8.200	9.000	–
4	6.300	7.800	8.400	9.600	11.10
5	6.360	7.800	8.760	9.960	12.60
6	6.400	7.600	8.800	10.20	12.80
7	6.429	7.800	9.000	10.54	13.46
8	6.300	7.650	9.000	10.50	13.80
9	6.200	7.667	8.867	10.73	14.07
10	6.360	7.680	9.000	10.68	14.52
11	6.273	7.691	9.000	10.75	14.56
12	6.300	7.700	9.100	10.80	14.80
13	6.138	7.800	9.092	10.85	14.91
14	6.343	7.714	9.086	10.89	15.09
15	6.280	7.720	9.160	10.92	15.08
16	6.300	7.800	9.150	10.95	15.15
17	6.318	7.800	9.212	11.05	15.28
18	6.333	7.733	9.200	10.93	15.27
19	6.347	7.863	9.253	11.02	15.44
20	6.240	7.800	9.240	11.10	15.36
∞	6.251	7.815	9.348	11.34	16.27

k = 5

P	10	5	2.5	1	0.1
n = 3	7.467	8.533	9.600	10.13	11.47
4	7.600	8.800	9.800	11.20	13.20
5	7.680	8.960	10.24	11.68	14.40
6	7.733	9.067	10.40	11.87	15.20
7	7.771	9.143	10.51	12.11	15.66
8	7.700	9.200	10.60	12.30	16.00
9	7.733	9.244	10.67	12.44	16.36
∞	7.779	9.488	11.14	13.28	18.47

k = 6

P	10	5	2.5	1	0.1
n = 3	8.714	9.857	10.81	11.76	13.29
4	9.000	10.29	11.43	12.71	15.29
5	9.000	10.49	11.74	13.23	16.43
6	9.048	10.57	12.00	13.62	17.05
∞	9.236	11.07	12.83	15.09	20.52

A.8 The Table of Critical Values for the Tukey Test

Table A.8. *Critical values of the Studentized Range Statistic[1] for use with Tukey test*

df$_{WG}$	α	Number of Groups								
		2	3	4	5	6	7	8	9	10
5	.05	3.64	4.60	5.22	5.67	6.03	6.33	6.58	6.80	6.99
	.01	5.70	6.98	7.80	8.42	8.91	9.32	9.67	9.97	10.24
6	.05	3.46	4.34	4.90	5.30	5.63	5.90	6.12	6.32	6.49
	.01	5.24	6.33	7.03	7.56	7.97	8.32	8.61	8.87	9.10
7	.05	3.34	4.16	4.68	5.06	5.36	5.61	5.82	6.00	6.16
	.01	4.95	5.92	6.54	7.01	7.37	7.68	7.94	8.17	8.37
8	.05	3.26	4.04	4.53	4.89	5.17	5.40	5.60	5.77	5.92
	.01	4.75	5.64	6.20	6.62	6.96	7.24	7.47	7.68	7.86
9	.05	3.20	3.95	4.41	4.76	5.02	5.24	5.43	5.59	5.74
	.01	4.60	5.43	5.96	6.35	6.66	6.91	7.13	7.33	7.49
10	.05	3.15	3.88	4.33	4.65	4.91	5.12	5.30	5.46	5.60
	.01	4.48	5.27	5.77	6.14	6.43	6.67	6.87	7.05	7.21
11	.05	3.11	3.82	4.26	4.57	4.82	5.03	5.20	5.35	5.49
	.01	4.39	5.15	5.62	5.97	6.25	6.48	6.67	6.84	6.99
12	.05	3.08	3.77	4.20	4.51	4.75	4.95	5.12	5.27	5.39
	.01	4.32	5.05	5.50	5.84	6.10	6.32	6.51	6.67	6.81
13	.05	3.06	3.73	4.15	4.45	4.69	4.88	5.05	5.19	5.32
	.01	4.26	4.96	5.40	5.73	5.98	6.19	6.37	6.53	6.67
14	.05	3.03	3.70	4.11	4.41	4.64	4.83	4.99	5.13	5.25
	.01	4.21	4.89	5.32	5.63	5.88	6.08	6.26	6.41	6.54
15	.05	3.01	3.67	4.08	4.37	4.59	4.78	4.94	5.08	5.20
	.01	4.17	4.84	5.25	5.56	5.80	5.99	6.16	6.31	6.44
16	.05	3.00	3.65	4.05	4.33	4.56	4.74	4.90	5.03	5.15
	.01	4.13	4.79	5.19	5.49	5.72	5.92	6.08	6.22	6.35
17	.05	2.98	3.63	4.02	4.30	4.52	4.70	4.86	4.99	5.11
	.01	4.10	4.74	5.14	5.43	5.66	5.85	6.01	6.15	6.27
18	.05	2.97	3.61	4.00	4.28	4.49	4.67	4.82	4.96	5.07
	.01	4.07	4.70	5.09	5.38	5.60	5.79	5.94	6.08	6.20
19	.05	2.96	3.59	3.98	4.25	4.47	4.65	4.79	4.92	5.04
	.01	4.05	4.67	5.05	5.33	5.55	5.73	5.89	6.02	6.14
20	.05	2.95	3.58	3.96	4.23	4.45	4.62	4.77	4.90	5.01
	.01	4.02	4.64	5.02	5.29	5.51	5.69	5.84	5.97	6.09
24	.05	2.92	3.53	3.90	4.17	4.37	4.54	4.68	4.81	4.92
	.01	3.96	4.55	4.91	5.17	5.37	5.54	5.69	5.81	5.92
30	.05	2.89	3.49	3.85	4.10	4.30	4.46	4.60	4.72	4.82
	.01	3.89	4.45	4.80	5.05	5.24	5.40	5.54	5.65	5.76
40	.05	2.86	3.44	3.79	4.04	4.23	4.39	4.52	4.63	4.73
	.01	3.82	4.37	4.70	4.93	5.11	5.26	5.39	5.50	5.60
60	.05	2.83	3.40	3.74	3.98	4.16	4.31	4.44	4.55	4.65
	.01	3.76	4.28	4.59	4.82	4.99	5.13	5.25	5.36	5.45
120	.05	2.80	3.36	3.68	3.92	4.10	4.24	4.36	4.47	4.56
	.01	3.70	4.20	4.50	4.71	4.87	5.01	5.12	5.21	5.30
∞	.05	2.77	3.31	3.63	3.86	4.03	4.17	4.29	4.39	4.47
	.01	3.64	4.12	4.40	4.60	4.76	4.88	4.99	5.08	5.16

[1]This table is abridged from Table 29 in E.S. Pearson and H.O. Hartley (Eds.), *Biometrika tables for statisticians* (3rd ed., Vol 1), Cambridge University Press, 1970.

A.9 The Table of Critical Values for the Dunnett Test

Table A.9. *Critical values of the Dunnett test*[2]

		Number of Groups, Including Control Group								
n	α	2	3	4	5	6	7	8	9	10
5	.05	2.57	3.03	3.29	3.48	3.62	3.73	3.82	3.90	3.97
	.01	4.03	4.63	4.98	5.22	5.41	5.56	5.69	5.80	5.89
6	.05	2.45	2.86	3.10	3.26	3.39	3.49	3.57	3.64	3.71
	.01	3.71	4.21	4.51	4.71	4.87	5.00	5.10	5.20	5.28
7	.05	2.36	2.75	2.97	3.12	3.24	3.33	3.41	3.47	3.53
	.01	3.50	3.95	4.21	4.39	4.53	4.64	4.74	4.82	4.89
8	.05	2.31	2.67	2.88	3.02	3.13	3.22	3.29	3.35	3.41
	.01	3.36	3.77	4.00	4.17	4.29	4.40	4.48	4.56	4.62
9	.05	2.26	2.61	2.81	2.95	3.05	3.14	3.20	3.26	3.32
	.01	3.25	3.63	3.85	4.01	4.12	4.22	4.30	4.37	4.43
10	.05	2.23	2.57	2.76	2.89	2.99	3.07	3.14	3.19	3.24
	.01	3.17	3.53	3.74	3.88	3.99	4.08	4.16	4.22	4.28
11	.05	2.20	2.53	2.72	2.84	2.94	3.02	3.08	3.14	3.19
	.01	3.11	3.45	3.65	3.79	3.89	3.98	4.05	4.11	4.16
12	.05	2.18	2.50	2.68	2.81	2.90	2.98	3.04	3.09	3.14
	.01	3.05	3.39	3.58	3.71	3.81	3.89	3.96	4.02	4.07
13	.05	2.16	2.48	2.65	2.78	2.87	2.94	3.00	3.06	3.10
	.01	3.01	3.33	3.52	3.65	3.74	3.82	3.89	3.94	3.99
14	.05	2.14	2.46	2.63	2.75	2.84	2.91	2.97	3.02	3.07
	.01	2.98	3.29	3.47	3.59	3.69	3.76	3.83	3.88	3.93
15	.05	2.13	2.44	2.61	2.73	2.82	2.89	2.95	3.00	3.04
	.01	2.95	3.25	3.43	3.55	3.64	3.71	3.78	3.83	3.88
16	.05	2.12	2.42	2.59	2.71	2.80	2.87	2.92	2.97	3.02
	.01	2.92	3.22	3.39	3.51	3.60	3.67	3.73	3.78	3.83
17	.05	2.11	2.41	2.58	2.69	2.78	2.85	2.90	2.95	3.00
	.01	2.90	3.19	3.36	3.47	3.56	3.63	3.69	3.74	3.79
18	.05	2.10	2.40	2.56	2.68	2.76	2.83	2.89	2.94	2.98
	.01	2.88	3.17	3.33	3.44	3.53	3.60	3.66	3.71	3.75
19	.05	2.09	2.39	2.55	2.66	2.75	2.81	2.87	2.92	2.96
	.01	2.86	3.15	3.31	3.42	3.50	3.57	3.63	3.68	3.72
20	.05	2.09	2.38	2.54	2.65	2.73	2.80	2.86	2.90	2.95
	.01	2.85	3.13	3.29	3.40	3.48	3.55	3.60	3.65	3.69
24	.05	2.06	2.35	2.51	2.61	2.70	2.76	2.81	2.86	2.90
	.01	2.80	3.07	3.22	3.32	3.40	3.47	3.52	3.57	3.61
30	.05	2.04	2.32	2.47	2.58	2.66	2.72	2.77	2.82	2.86
	.01	2.75	3.01	3.15	3.25	3.33	3.39	3.44	3.49	3.52
40	.05	2.02	2.29	2.44	2.54	2.62	2.68	2.73	2.77	2.81
	.01	2.70	2.95	3.09	3.19	3.26	3.32	3.37	3.41	3.44
60	.05	2.00	2.27	2.41	2.51	2.58	2.64	2.69	2.73	2.77
	.01	2.66	2.90	3.03	3.12	3.19	3.25	3.29	3.33	3.37

[2]This table is abridged from C.W. Dunnett, New tables for multiple comparisons with a control, *Biometrics*, 1964, 482–491.

Appendix B

Additional Information on the Data

Tables B.1 and B.2 show the results obtained using 10-fold cross validation by c45 and NB on each instance of the labor data respectively as output by WEKA. The first column lists the instance number; the second column lists the instance label, where class 1 corresponds to class "bad" and class 2 corresponds to class "good"; the third column lists the predicted class, using the same naming convention; column 4 uses the "+" symbol to indicate whether the predicted label differs from the actual one and a blank if they are in agreement; finally, the last two values, which are complementary and add up to 1, indicate the confidence of their prediction. The first value indicates how much the classifier believes the instance to be of class 1 (bad), and the second indicates how much the classifier believes the instance to be of classs 2 (good). The dominant value is preceded by a "*" symbol and corresponds to the value of the predicted label.

Please note that the numbers denoting the instances in the first column are not sequential. After number 6 or 7 is reached, a 1–6 or 1–7 sequence is repeated. This is because every 1–6 or 1–7 sequence represents a different fold. Indeed, it can be seen that 10 different sequences are present in each classifier run, corresponding to the 10 folds of 10-fold cross-validation. Note, however, that despite the repetition, the instances are different. For example, instance 2 of fold 1 is different from instance 2 of fold 2. In fact, it can be seen that the number of instances present in each classifier run corresponds to the number of examples in the dataset. That is because cross-validation tests each instance exactly once, as discussed in Chapter 5.

Table B.1.   *c45 applied to the labour data: Predictions on test data*

Inst	Actual	Predicted	Error	Probability distribution	
1	1:bad	2:good	+	0	*1
2	1:bad	1:bad		*0.762	0.238
3	2:good	2:good		0.082	*0.918
4	2:good	1:bad	+	*0.762	0.238
5	2:good	1:bad	+	*0.762	0.238
6	2:good	2:good		0	*1
1	1:bad	1:bad		*0.85	0.15
2	1:bad	2:good	+	0	*1
3	2:good	2:good		0	*1
4	2:good	2:good		0.14	*0.86
5	2:good	1:bad	+	*0.85	0.15
6	2:good	2:good		0.14	*0.86
1	1:bad	1:bad		*0.83	0.17
2	1:bad	1:bad		*0.83	0.17
3	2:good	2:good		0.185	*0.815
4	2:good	2:good		0.185	*0.815
5	2:good	2:good		0.185	*0.815
6	2:good	2:good		0.185	*0.815
1	1:bad	1:bad		*0.98	0.02
2	1:bad	1:bad		*0.98	0.02
3	2:good	2:good		0.033	*0.967
4	2:good	1:bad	+	*0.98	0.02
5	2:good	1:bad	+	*0.925	0.075
6	2:good	1:bad	+	*0.98	0.02
1	1:bad	1:bad		*0.83	0.17
2	1:bad	1:bad		*0.83	0.17
3	2:good	2:good		0.037	*0.963
4	2:good	2:good		0.037	*0.963
5	2:good	2:good		0.037	*0.963
6	2:good	2:good		0.037	*0.963
1	1:bad	2:good	+	0.123	*0.877
2	1:bad	1:bad		*0.92	0.08
3	2:good	2:good		0.123	*0.877
4	2:good	1:bad	+	*0.92	0.08
5	2:good	2:good		0.236	*0.764
6	2:good	2:good		0.123	*0.877
1	1:bad	1:bad		*0.84	0.16
2	1:bad	2:good	+	0.163	*0.837
3	2:good	2:good		0.163	*0.837
4	2:good	2:good		0.163	*0.837
5	2:good	2:good		0.163	*0.837
6	2:good	2:good		0.163	*0.837

(continued)

Table B.1   *(continued)*

Inst	Actual	Predicted	Error	Probability distribution	
1	1:bad	1:bad		*0.933	0.067
2	1:bad	1:bad		*0.933	0.067
3	2:good	2:good		0.295	*0.705
4	2:good	2:good		0.027	*0.973
5	2:good	2:good		0.197	*0.803
1	1:bad	1:bad		*0.797	0.203
2	1:bad	2:good	+	0.14	*0.86
3	2:good	2:good		0.14	*0.86
4	2:good	2:good		0.14	*0.86
5	2:good	2:good		0.14	*0.86
1	1:bad	2:good	+	0	*1
2	1:bad	1:bad		*0.915	0.085
3	2:good	1:bad	+	*0.654	0.346
4	2:good	2:good		0	*1
5	2:good	1:bad	+	*0.654	0.346

Table B.2.   *Naive Bayes applied to the labor data: Predictions on test data*

Inst	Actual	Predicted	Error	Probability distribution	
1	1:bad	2:good	+	0.351	*0.649
2	1:bad	1:bad		*0.963	0.037
3	2:good	2:good		0	*1
4	2:good	2:good		0	*1
5	2:good	2:good		0.015	*0.985
6	2:good	2:good		0	*1
1	1:bad	2:good	+	0.016	*0.984
2	1:bad	1:bad		*0.969	0.031
3	2:good	2:good		0.001	*0.999
4	2:good	2:good		0	*1
5	2:good	1:bad	+	*0.511	0.489
6	2:good	2:good		0	*1
1	1:bad	1:bad		*0.928	0.072
2	1:bad	1:bad		*1	0
3	2:good	2:good		0.003	*0.997
4	2:good	2:good		0.001	*0.999
5	2:good	2:good		0	*1
6	2:good	2:good		0.004	*0.996
1	1:bad	1:bad		*1	0
2	1:bad	1:bad		*0.999	0.001
3	2:good	2:good		0.004	*0.996
4	2:good	1:bad	+	*0.749	0.251
5	2:good	2:good		0.056	*0.944
6	2:good	1:bad	+	*0.647	0.353

Inst	Actual	Predicted	Error	Probability distribution	
1	1:bad	1:bad		*1	0
2	1:bad	1:bad		*0.926	0.074
3	2:good	2:good		0.35	*0.65
4	2:good	2:good		0.001	*0.999
5	2:good	2:good		0	*1
6	2:good	2:good		0	*1
1	1:bad	1:bad		*0.996	0.004
2	1:bad	1:bad		*1	0
3	2:good	2:good		0	*1
4	2:good	2:good		0	*1
5	2:good	2:good		0	*1
6	2:good	2:good		0	*1
1	1:bad	1:bad		*1	0
2	1:bad	1:bad		*1	0
3	2:good	2:good		0	*1
4	2:good	1:bad	+	*1	0
5	2:good	2:good		0	*1
6	2:good	2:good		0	*1
1	1:bad	1:bad		*0.718	0.282
2	1:bad	1:bad		*1	0
3	2:good	2:good		0.04	*0.96
4	2:good	2:good		0	*1
5	2:good	2:good		0	*1
1	1:bad	1:bad		*0.98	0.02
2	1:bad	1:bad		*1	0
3	2:good	2:good		0.013	*0.987
4	2:good	2:good		0	*1
5	2:good	2:good		0	*1
1	1:bad	1:bad		*0.998	0.002
2	1:bad	1:bad		*0.997	0.003
3	2:good	2:good		0.333	*0.667
4	2:good	2:good		0.051	*0.949
5	2:good	2:good		0	*1

Appendix C

Two Case Studies

This appendix is a companion to Chapter 9. In particular, it discusses two case studies that illustrate the evaluation framework laid out in that chapter and whose details were discussed all throughout the book. The first case study focuses on a practical (albeit semiartificial) domain; the second uses datasets from the UCI Repository for Machine Learning. The two studies are now discussed in turn.

C.1 Illustrative Case Study 1

In this case study, we used the dataset generated by Health Canada for the 2008 ICDM Data Contest. The purpose of the data is to serve as a basis for construction of automated learning systems able to monitor the amount of a few particular xenon isotopes (radioxenon) released in the atmosphere in an effort to verify compliance of the global ban on nuclear tests (the Comprehensive Nuclear Test Ban Treaty or CTBT). These isotopes, when released in some given pattern, are characteristic of nuclear explosions. What makes the problem difficult, however, is that the monitoring stations are typically not located at the site of the explosion. Instead, the isotopes are transported, over days or weeks, through various weather systems, toward these stations and, in the process, lose their characteristic pattern. This is further complicated by the fact that xenon isotopes in various quantities are present in the atmosphere at the sites of the monitoring stations. This is due to the release of such gases by perfectly legal civil nuclear plants such as medical isotope production facilities and nuclear power plants. In the case of illegal nuclear-weapon-testing activities somewhere in the world, once the radioxenon reaches the monitoring stations, the releases caused by this activity are mixed with the regular background releases. One interesting aspect of this dataset is that it is seminatural and semiartificial. Because most countries have abided by the CTBT, current releases of radioxenon that are due to weapon-testing activities are extremely rare. Therefore, to construct their datasets, Health Canada has to rely on the data available from nuclear tests that took place prior to the political push to eradicate nuclear proliferation. As well, they have to construct weather model systems to simulate the transport of radioxenon to the monitoring stations. On the other hand, all the background data are readily available in large quantity at each monitoring station. The explosion part of the dataset is thus constructed from both sources, whereas the background data correspond to the actual readings done at the monitoring stations. In more detail, the data are composed of radioxenon measurements from four or five CTBTO monitoring sites. Each data point is represented by a quadruplet representing the four activity concentrations of Xe-131m, Xe-133m, Xe-133, and Xe-135 for a given air sample. An additional feature represents the class of the point and corresponds to either the class "Background" or the class "Background plus Explosion."

One difficulty in this dataset is its small dimensionality, showing that the data are quite convoluted. Adding to this difficulty is the fact that the dataset is highly imbalanced with 8072 explosions (positive) versus 623 normal background (negative) samples. Learning from such imbalanced domains is, in itself, a problem of interest in machine learning and has led to several interesting findings. However, a detailed discussion on these is beyond the current scope of the book. We, for the purpose of this case study based on a preliminary exploratory analysis, downsampled the positive class samples so as to obtain balanced classes with 623 examples each. Readers interested in more details on data processing and algorithmic techniques for dealing with class imbalances on this problem is referred to (Stocki et al., 2008). Another reason for balancing the dataset is that, although we discussed the performance measures that are recommended in the case of class imbalances, we did not want to shift the focus of the study to dealing with class imbalances only. Therefore, although we demonstrate the use of the performance measures most appropriate for class imbalances, we do not have to restrict our attention solely to them.

The purpose of the study was to compare the performance of the decision tree classifier (c45) with that of AdaBoost (ADA) on this domain. However, to illustrate the difficulty of the learning domain, we subsequently give the results of typically strong classifiers with nevertheless simpler biases than c45. Applying Naive Bayes (NB) and k-Nearest Neighbors (IBK) along with c45 and ADA for a preliminary analysis gives the results for various performance metrics of interest as shown in Table C.1. These results were obtained from WEKA that, by default, uses 10×10-fold stratified cross-validation as its error-estimation method. We used this default procedure as well as all of WEKA's default classifier's parameter values in this study.

Table C.1 shows that, even when the results of NB and IBK can seem reasonable on some isolated metrics (e.g., TPR, recall, and F measure for IBK and FPR for NB), their results show an exceptionally high degree of variation between metrics, even over a balanced domain. Indeed, characterizing their behavior over their full operating ranges against that of c45 using the ROC analysis further

Table C.1. *Initial results of c45, NB, and IBK on the 2008 ICDM
Data Mining Contest Health Canada dataset*

Measure	NB	c45	IBK	AdaBoost
Accuracy	0.503	0.62	0.523	0.611
InfoScore	8.50	146.1	43.59	100.7
RMSE	0.519	0.478	0.658	0.482
TPR	0.059	0.408	0.523	0.581
FPR	0.053	0.167	0.477	0.36
Precision	0.529	0.709	0.523	0.618
Recall	0.059	0.408	0.523	0.581
F measure	0.107	0.518	0.523	0.599
AUC	0.503	0.649	0.515	0.641

confirmed this fact. Drawing the ROC curves for these classifiers (using the
RWeka and ROCR packages in R), as shown in Figure C.1, further confirms that
the performances of NB and IBK are indeed not too far from that of a random
classifier (which is expected to appear along the diagonal). In fact, the relatively marginally better performances of c45 and ADA themselves demonstrate
the difficulty of learning the domain. We hence exclude NB and IBK from further consideration in this study and focus on a comparative evaluation of c45
against ADA. On the other hand, drawing ROC performances of c45 and ADA

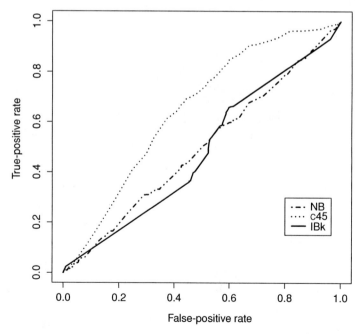

Figure C.1. ROC Curves for NB, c45 and IBk. Only the curve for c45 lifts above the random
line.

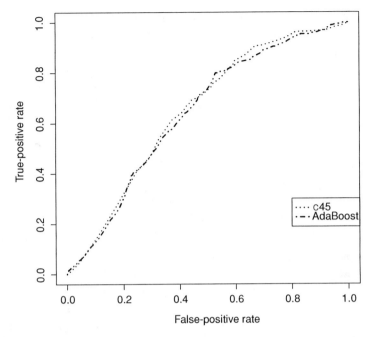

Figure C.2. ROC Curves for c45 and ADA. The two curves are very similar, although c45 seems to dominates more often than ADA. However, it is not clear whether this dominance is statistically significant.

(see Figure C.2) shows that these two classifiers trade off performances across different portions of the operating range. However, the information yielded by the ROC curve is not very useful because of the highly overlapping nature of the classifiers.

Hence, let us focus on metrics that can highlight their performances on individual classes, in particular, sensitivity, specificity, positive predictive value (PPV) and negative predictive value (NPV). The results are listed in Table C.2.

Note that, as mentioned in Chapter 3, although WEKA may not seem to output these values, it actually does so in some hidden ways. In particular, in the part titled "Detailed Accuracy By Class," the "yes" TPR corresponds to sensitivity; the "no" recall corresponds to specificity; the "yes" precision corresponds to

Table C.2. *Results obtained with additional measures*

Measure	c45	ADA
Sensitivity	0.408	0.581
Specificity	0.833	0.64
PPV	0.709	0.618
NPV	0.502	0.605

the PPV; and the "no" precision corresponds to the NPV. We can verify this by comparing the ADA entries in Table C.2 and the partial WEKA output for ADA, shown in Listing C.1.

Listing C.1: WEKA output on AdaBoost.

```
=== Detailed Accuracy By Class ===

TP Rate   FP Rate   Precision   Recall   F—Measure   ROC Area   Class
   0.581     0.36        0.618    0.581       0.599      0.641    yes
   0.64     0.419        0.605    0.64        0.622      0.641    no
```

For the problem of detecting nuclear explosions, it is important to detect as many true explosions as possible while at the same time controlling the number of false alarms. Sensitivity and specificity seem then to be the pair of interest with regard to measuring the performance of the classifiers over these criteria. Recall from Chapter 3 that sensitivity tells us what percentage of actual explosions are rightly predicted by the classifier and that specificity tells us what percentage of the time the classifier rightly tells us that no explosions occurred. Table C.2 seems to suggest that ADA does a better job than c45 on sensitivity and thus detects more actual explosions than c45. However, c45 seems to be stronger on specificity, and thus more often correct when suggesting that no explosion took place. Just as we discussed analyses involving alternative curves of interest in Chapter 4 (e.g., PR curves), we can also draw the sensitivity–specificity curve over the operating ranges of these classifiers, as shown in Figure C.3 (the ROCR

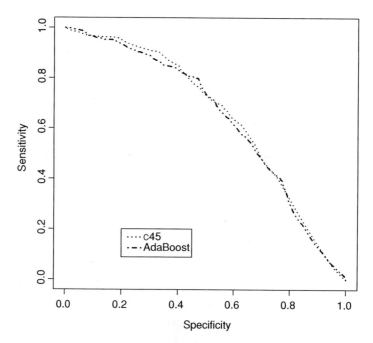

Figure C.3. Sensitivity and specificity Curves for c45 and Adaboost.

package in R can be used for this purpose). It can be noted in Figure C.3 that, even if overall c45 seems to dominate ADA on this graph, around a specificity of 0.5, ADA is more sensitive than c45.

Let us then verify if the performances of the two classifiers in terms of the sensitivity and specificity pair are indeed statistically significant (over the default threshold used by WEKA and that we also relied on). However, note that a model selection could have been further performed in order to choose the optimal threshold.

This then brings in the question of which is the most suitable statistical test for this purpose. Note that, for this part of the study, we still did not vary the error-estimation method and remained with WEKA's default 10 × 10-fold stratified cross-validation. Two additional error-estimation methods were also experimented on, as will be subsequently seen. Clearly, because we are interested in comparing two classifiers on a single domain (over individual metrics of sensitivity and specificity), the three candidate statistical tests are the paired t test and its nonparametric alternatives, McNemar's test and Wilcoxon's Signed-Ranks test. Because McNemar's test does not have straightforward ways to integrate the measures of interest here (sensitivity and specificity) in its computations, we focus on the other two tests.

As just mentioned, we also decided to use two additional error-estimation strategies that yield additional measures of statistical significance from Chapter 5: bootstrapping and the permutation test.

Listings C.2 and C.3 show, for sensitivity and specificity respectively, the results of the paired t test and its corresponding effect size using Cohen's d statistic, Wilcoxon's Signed-Ranks test, and .632 bootstrap and permutation (randomization) test estimates.

Listing C.2: Statistical significance testing results in R between AdaBoost and c45 over sensitivity (AdaBoost is the leading classifier).

```
#     For Sensitivity
#     ─────────────────

#1)            Paired t-test

data:  j48 and AdaBoost
t = -4.1275, df = 9, p-value = 0.002569
alternative hypothesis: true difference in means is not equal to 0
95 percent confidence interval:
 -0.27462727 -0.08017273
sample estimates:
mean of the differences
            -0.1774

#2) Cohen's d Statistic

> d
```

[1] 1.896586   (>.8, thus of practical significance)

#3)   Wilcoxon signed rank test with continuity correction

data: j48 and AdaBoost
V = 0, p−value = 0.02225
alternative hypothesis: true location shift is not equal to 0

#4) .632 Bootstrapping

> b632J48
[1] 0.4157718
> b632Adaboost
[1] 0.5523992
>

#5) Permutation Test
> mobt
[1] 0.1065
> probability_of_mobt
[1] 0.019   (We reject with probability .019 the
                             hypothesis that J48 and Adaboost
                             display the same sensitivity)

Listing C.3: Statistical significance testing results in R between Adaboost and
c45 over specificity (c45 is the leading classifier).

For Specificity
─────────────────
#1)   Paired t−test
data: j48 and AdaBoost
t = 6.9867, df = 9, p−value = 6.418e−05
alternative hypothesis: true difference in means is not equal to 0
95 percent confidence interval:
 0.1090069 0.2133931
sample estimates:
mean of the differences
                0.1612
#2) Cohen's d Statistic

> d
[1] 2.388927   (>.8, thus of practical significance)

#3)   Wilcoxon signed rank test with continuity correction

data: j48 and AdaBoost
V = 55, p−value = 0.005793
alternative hypothesis: true location shift is not equal to 0

#4)   .632 Bootstrapping

```
> b632J48
[1]  0.8228896
> b632Adaboost
[1]  0.7028262

#5)
> mobt
[1]  0.1695
> probability_of_mobt
[1]  0.0026        (We reject with probability .0026 the hypothesis that
                   J48 and Adaboost display the same specificity)
```

As can be seen from the results, all tests concur over the finding that c45's performance is indeed statistically significantly different (better) than that of AdaBoost with high certainty with regard to specificity whereas the reverse is true with regard to sensitivity. Hence the analysis suggests that AdaBoost would be the classifier of choice (among the ones evaluated) when the goal is high sensitivity (at the expense of some false alarms) whereas c45 would be more apt (again among the ones evaluated) when the issue of false alarm (possibly leading to unjustified implications of forbidden testing of nuclear weapons) is more important. Note that this remains an illustrative exercise and is in no way representative of the actual approaches utilized for the purpose, which are significantly more sophisticated and rigorously validated before being deployed. The interesting aspect of this study, however, is the demonstration of the flexibility that the tools discussed in this book provide us. We now turn to our second case study in which several generic domains are involved.

C.2   Illustrative Case Study 2

To highlight some other aspects of evaluation studies and the interrelationship between the various components, we go back to the illustration of Chapter 1 that focused on comparing eight classifiers on 10 application domains chosen from the UCI Repository for Machine Learning. The eight classifiers considered were the WEKA implementations of naive Bayes (NB), support vector machines with polynomial kernel (SVMs), 1-Nearest Neighbors (1NN), AdaBoost (ADA), bagging (BAG), c4.5 (c45), random forests (RF), and Ripper (RIP). The UCI domains that were selected were anneal, audiology, balance scale, breast cancer, contact-lenses, Pima diabetes, glass, hepatitis, hypothyroid, and tic-tac-toe.

Recall that the average accuracy estimates of each classifier were obtained over all domains. Results over the generalized t test used in a pairwise fashion were then used to infer that RF and SVM are the two leading classifiers, closely followed by RIP, c4.5, and BAG. NB and 1NN are a little bit behind, with ADA appearing to be the weakest classifier of the lot. However, the results varied quite a bit from domain to domain. In general, it was found that anneal, hypothyroid,

Table C.3. *Results obtained on eight classifiers and 10 domains, using accuracy*

Domains	NB	1NN	SVM	ADA	BAG	C45	RF	RIP	AVG
Contact lenses	76.17	72.17	72.5	72.17	75.67	83.5	75.67	80.67	76.065
Anneal	85.59	99.13	97.46	83.63	98.76	98.58	99.41	98.26	95.1025
Audiology	72.64	75.29	80.77	46.46	76	77.27	77.09	73.11	72.32875
Balanced scale	90.53	78.16	87.57	71.77	83.37	77.82	80.11	80.3	81.20375
Pima diabetes	75.76	70.62	76.8	74.92	75.66	74.49	74.44	75.18	74.73375
Glass	49.45	69.95	57.36	44.89	72.48	67.63	76.16	66.78	63.0875
Hepatitis	83.81	81.4	85.77	81.37	82	79.22	82.47	78.13	81.77125
Hypothyroid	95.31	91.52	93.58	92.97	99.56	99.54	99.19	99.42	96.38625
Breast cancer	72.7	68.59	65.52	71.62	69.1	74.28	69.7	71.45	70.37
Tic-tac-toe	69.64	80.85	98.33	72.72	90.98	85.28	93	97.55	86.04375
AVG	77.16	78.77	81.57	71.252	82.358	82.724	82.085		

and tic-tac-toe were the domains that were generally easy to classify. SVM, RF, C45, RIP, and BAG were the systems shown to win and tie most often in the aggregated t tests against each of the other classifiers.

Let us now redo the evaluation analysis with the perspectives obtained from this book. The results used in Chapter 1 were all based on the accuracy measure alone. The results on the accuracy estimates are shown here in Table C.3.[1] However, in the absence of knowledge of the best performance measure to use or a concrete measure of interest, one would be inclined to take into account more generic measures that can characterize the performances of the classifiers. In particular, in addition to accuracy, we use the RMSE, the AUC, the F measure, and the Kononenko and Bratko (KB) relative information score. The results of applying these measures are shown in Tables C.4 (RMSE), C.5 (AUC), C.6 (F), and C.7 and C.8 (KB). Before we go further, let us see what a visual exploratory analysis can show us over the performance of these classifiers.

C.2.1 Visualization Analysis

We make use of the visualization system discussed in Chapter 8 for a preliminary qualitative analysis of different aspects of the classifier performance and their dependence of the application domains as well as performance measures. This allows us to put the performances in an easy-to-interpret form as well as perform a preliminary aggregation of the results in a relatively reliable manner. Note that we use these results here as an exploratory analysis, and hence the results should be viewed with all the qualifications of the system as discussed in Chapter 8 (reliance on the Euclidean distance metric and the associated aggregation methodology). Once some insight is obtained into the important factors, we can possibly utilize this in our subsequent fine-grained evaluation.

---

[1] Note, however, that the numbers in Table C.3 do not match exactly with those in Chapter 1 because all the experiments were rerun from scratch for this analysis.

Table C.4. *Results obtained on eight classifiers and 10 domains, using RMSE*

Domains	NB	1NN	SVM	ADA	BAG	C45	RF	RIP	AVG
Contact lenses	0.2965	0.3052	0.3741	0.2904	0.3028	0.2333	0.2587	0.267	0.291
Anneal	0.2028	0.0384	0.3111	0.269	0.0573	0.0571	0.0474	0.0664	0.1312
Audiology	0.1355	0.1417	0.1934	0.1724	0.123	0.1208	0.1216	0.1343	0.1428
Balanced scale	0.2785	0.3791	0.345	0.3602	0.2857	0.3574	0.3102	0.3333	0.3312
Pima diabetes	0.4194	0.5402	0.4793	0.4157	0.403	0.4388	0.4199	0.4274	0.4430
Glass	0.337	0.29	0.3162	0.3026	0.2366	0.2832	0.2175	0.2759	0.2824
Hepatitis	0.3459	0.2902	0.3435	0.3601	0.3522	0.404	0.3419	0.4077	0.3557
Hypothyroid	0.1379	0.2904	0.3214	0.1216	0.0422	0.0385	0.0651	0.0488	0.1332
Breast cancer	0.4512	0.2904	0.5477	0.4355	0.4505	0.444	0.4663	0.4494	0.4419
Tic-tac-toe	0.4308	0.2904	0.1103	0.3011	0.2843	0.3344	0.275	0.1376	0.2705
AVG	0.3036	0.2856	0.3342	0.3029	0.2538	0.2712	0.2524	0.2548	

Table C.5. *Results obtained on eight classifiers and 10 domains, using AUC*

Domains	NB	1NN	SVM	ADA	BAG	C45	RF	RIP	AVG
Contact lenses	0.95	0.765	0.915	0.835	0.935	0.945	0.975	0.94	0.9075
Anneal	0.9954	0.9375	0.9826	0.831	0.9655	0.931	0.9676	0.755	0.9207
Audiology	0.7033	0.5	0.5	0.5	0.5	0.5	0.5	0.5	0.5254
Balanced scale	0.9934	0.8598	0.9261	0.889	0.9596	0.8448	0.9577	0.8619	0.9115
Pima diabetes	0.815	0.6677	0.7131	0.8049	0.8218	0.7514	0.7945	0.7195	0.7610
Glass	0.729	0.7984	0.7783	0.7083	0.9063	0.7938	0.9209	0.8019	0.8046
Hepatitis	0.8567	0.6785	0.7685	0.8326	0.8257	0.6678	0.8378	0.6224	0.7613
Hypothyroid	0.9317	0.6709	0.5918	0.9914	0.9965	0.9962	0.9986	0.988	0.8956
Breast cancer	0.7025	0.6043	0.5836	0.6991	0.6416	0.6063	0.6471	0.5975	0.6353
Tic-tac-toe	0.7443	0.7851	0.9759	0.8021	0.9726	0.9013	0.9792	0.9738	0.8918
AVG	0.8421	0.7267	0.7735	0.7893	0.8525	0.7938	0.8578	0.776	

Table C.6. *Results obtained on eight classifiers and 10 domains, using the F measure*

Domains	NB	1NN	SVM	ADA	BAG	C45	RF	RIP	AVG
Contact lenses	0.3767	0.31	0.3867	0.4017	0.3667	0.4767	0.3867	0.4733	0.3973
Anneal	0.6317	0.7	0.6833	0	0.495	0.5067	0.7	0.3767	0.5117
Audiology	0	0	0	0	0	0	0	0	0
Balanced scale	0.9421	0.8475	0.9115	0.746	0.8727	0.8267	0.8773	0.8356	0.8574
Pima diabetes	0.8183	0.7785	0.8339	0.8145	0.8177	0.8063	0.8119	0.8159	0.8121
Glass	0.5762	0.7248	0.5276	0.6269	0.7519	0.6957	0.7852	0.6834	0.6715
Hepatitis	0.6405	0.4691	0.6297	0.4846	0.3678	0.4085	0.4578	0.3646	0.4778
Hypothyroid	0.9767	0.9563	0.9665	0.9737	0.9986	0.9983	0.9961	0.9977	0.9830
Breast cancer	0.8131	0.7811	0.7974	0.8066	0.8017	0.8378	0.7953	0.8126	0.8057
Tic-tac-toe	0.4868	0.718	0.9749	0.5976	0.857	0.779	0.8959	0.9642	0.7842
AVG	0.6262	0.6285	0.6712	0.5452	0.6329	0.6336	0.6706	0.6324	

Table C.7. *Results obtained on eight classifiers and 10 domains, using KB relative information score*

Domains	NB	1NN	SVM	ADA	BAG	C45	RF	RIP	AVG
Contact lenses	112.48	128.15	87.72	43.45	113.88	166.62	140.28	148.32	117.6125
Anneal	6079.01	8533.8	−4486.12	2187.18	8275.9	8383.68	8400.66	8199.38	5696.68625
Audiology	1299.53	1465.61	204.69	569.62	1483.31	1589.65	1398.76	1386.1	1174.65875
Balanced scale	2941.12	3506.62	2104.95	1534.14	3187.15	3216.25	3568.65	3195.98	2906.8575
Pima diabetes	2793.16	2512.03	3597.15	2368.57	2472.69	2489.41	2435.09	2039.3	2588.425
Glass	862.8	1308.59	276.1	596.08	1200.5	1250.15	1385.06	1072.85	994.01625
Hepatitis	619.19	526.32	764.25	450.32	257.37	298.73	383.58	204.84	438.075
Hypothyroid	16533.44	8311.91	−179227	22044.55	34802.82	35498.28	30242.13	34768.23	371.795
Breast cancer	555.38	549.69	619.1	367.74	136.22	320.52	275.03	268.84	386.565
Tic-tac-toe	1770.41	5356.4	9208.81	3280.18	5336.09	6044.11	5555.74	8881.55	5679.16125
AVG	3356.65	3219.91	−16685.04	3344.18	5726.59	5925.74	5378.50	6016.54	

Table C.8. *Results obtained on eight classifiers and 10 domains, using KB relative information scores that were mapped to the [0,1] range using the procedure described in Footnote 2*

Domains	NB	1NN	SVM	ADA	BAG	c45	RF	RIP	AVG
Contact lenses	0.4782	0.5448	0.3729	0.1847	0.4841	0.7083	0.5964	0.6305	0.5
Anneal	0.5188	0.6393	0	0.3277	0.6266	0.6319	0.6328	0.6229	0.5
Audiology	0.5532	0.6238	0.0871	0.2425	0.6314	0.6766	0.5954	0.59	0.5
Balanced scale	0.5059	0.6032	0.3621	0.2639	0.5482	0.5532	0.6138	0.5497	0.5
Pima diabetes	0.5395	0.4852	0.6949	0.4575	0.4776	0.4809	0.4704	0.3939	0.5
Glass	0.434	0.6582	0.1389	0.2998	0.6039	0.6288	0.6967	0.5397	0.5
Hepatitis	0.7067	0.6007	0.8723	0.514	0.2938	0.341	0.4378	0.2338	0.5
Hypothyroid	0.545	0.5221	0	0.5603	0.5959	0.5978	0.5832	0.5958	0.5
Breast cancer	0.7184	0.711	0.8008	0.4757	0.1762	0.4146	0.3557	0.3477	0.5
Tic-tac-toe	0.1558	0.4716	0.8108	0.2888	0.4698	0.5321	0.4891	0.7819	0.5
AVG	0.5155	0.586	0.414	0.361	0.4907	0.5565	0.5471	0.5286	

The plot of Figure C.4 shows an aggregate view of the classifier performance on all five evaluation measures over all the domains.

Let us explain how the plot should be read. The classifiers are listed in the window at the bottom left, the domains used are listed in the bottom middle. The performance measures used are listed in the bottom right window. The algorithms, domains, and measures are numerically labeled starting at 0 in the

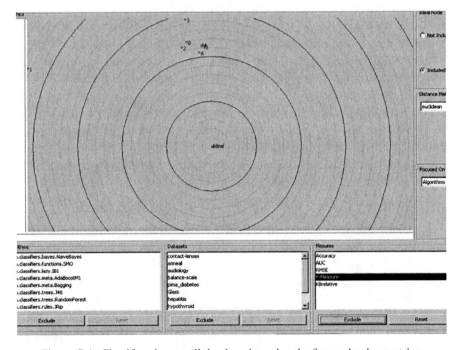

Figure C.4. Classifier view on all the domains using the five evaluation metrics.

order in which they appear in the respective windows. That is, NB is classifier 0, SVM (SVM) is classifier 1, and so on for the classifiers. Similarly, over the domains, contact lenses is domain 0, anneal is domain 1, and so on. Note, however, that the domain labeling is not relevant in this plot because we are focusing on the classifier view, as indicated by the tab titled "Focused on" on the right. The plot depicts the relative distances (under the Euclidean metric) of the classifiers in terms of their aggregate performance as well as their distance to the ideal classifier (in terms of the best performance over the aggregate measures).

Some simple observations can be made. RF (classifier 6) and SVM (classifier 1) represent the two extremes of performances in this framework, with the former being the closest to the ideal classifier. The other classifiers tend to cluster in between these two, with the exception of ADA (classifier 3), which trails behind the cluster. Although these results show some similarities to the earlier findings, there are some interesting differences. For instance, as in Chapter 1, we see that NB (classifier 0) and 1NN (classifier 2) are slightly behind the tree or rule-based classifiers (C4.5, RF, RIP, and BAG) and that ADA (classifier 3) is even further back; the SVM, unlike in Chapter 1, where it was considered the second best, is shown to be inferior in terms of the aggregate performance over all the domains. This demonstrates the dependence of these results on the evaluation measures, the manner in which these are aggregated, or both.

Let us then see if the domains can be clustered (in fact, ranked) in this framework in terms of the ease or difficulty of learning from them as measured by the aggregate measures. Figure C.5 plots this analysis.

The domain view of the analysis, as indicated by the "Focused on" tab on the right, shows that the easiest domains to classify are domains 3, 4, 8, and 9, corresponding to balance scale, pima diabetes, breast cancer, and tic-tac-toe. The domains with an intermediate level of difficulty are domains 0, 1, 5, and 6, corresponding to contact lenses, anneal, glass, and hepatitis. And the two most difficult domains to classify are domains 2 and 7, corresponding to audiology and hypothyroid. Keep in mind, however, that these results depend on the classifiers and the metrics involved in the study. Were these to change, so would the ranking. Again, note the difference with interpretations drawn solely on accuracy in Chapter 1, indicating anneal, hypothyroid, and tic-tac-toe as the easiest to classify, further emphasizing the reliance of the findings on the performance measures and the aggregation process.

From this, we can then break down the plot of Figure C.4 to study classifier performances in terms of domain difficulty. Considering the three broad groups of domains with easy, intermediate, and high levels of difficulty in learning them, as previously identified, we did a similar analysis (figures not shown) to discover some interesting characteristics of classifier performances. In terms of the aggregate performances and within the framework of analysis, we can note that all classifiers seem to be almost equally effective (with the exception of perhaps NB and ADA) on easy domains whereas SVM and ADA show a marked deterioration in performances with increasing difficulty of domains. Overall, RF

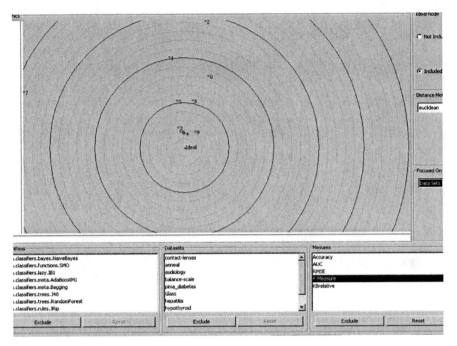

Figure C.5. Domain view using all the classifiers and the five evaluation metrics.

seems to be the better-performing classifier throughout the spectrum of domain difficulty.

In view of these findings, we focus on RF in our subsequent finer analysis. However, before that, let us perform a concrete quantitative analysis to see if indeed the performances of the classifiers on different domains are statistically significant. As is easy to note, we are interested in determining whether the performances of *multiple classifiers on multiple domains* differ in a statistically significant manner. Referring back to the candidate methods suggested to do so, we see that the one-way repeated-measures ANOVA and Friedman's test fit the bill. In the absence of a concrete knowledge on the effectiveness of the parametric ANOVA test as well as to illustrate the use of the nonparametric tests, we choose to use both these omnibus tests for our purpose. We run these tests over each performance measure of Tables C.3–C.7.[2] In case the tests return affirmative results in terms of statistical significance (rejecting the null hypothesis), we

---

[2] Please note that the data used in ANOVA were different from those in these tables for the accuracy and the information scores. In particular, in both these cases, the data were mapped into the [0,1] range. This was easy in the case of accuracy as all the values could simply be divided by 100. In the case of the information score, the mapping was trickier. In particular, for each dataset, the average value reported in the last column (AVG) of Table C.7 was considered to have a mapped value of 0.5. All the other values for this dataset were then multiplied by $\frac{0.5}{\text{AVG}}$. However, if any of the values in Table C.7 was negative, then, prior to applying the preceding step, we began by shifting the scores by the negative amount (so that that negative value became 0 and all the others were shifted by that amount), and then proceeded as in the other cases. The transformed data from Table C.7 is shown in Table C.8.

follow these with the respective post hoc tests (the Dunnett test for ANOVA and the Nemenyi test for Friedman's test in our case).

Let us start with the one-way repeated-measures ANOVA, whose results are listed in Listing C.4.

Listing C.4: The results of the omnibus ANOVA test on the eight classifiers, 10 domains, and five evaluation measures. (Values are imported from respective csv files for each measure)

```
> tt <- read.table("rmanova-chapter9-accuracy.csv",
                   header=T, sep=",")
> attach(tt)
> summary(aov(Accuracy ~ classifier + Error(dataset)))

Error: dataset
            Df  Sum Sq Mean Sq F value Pr(>F)
Residuals    9 0.81416 0.09046

Error: Within
            Df   Sum Sq  Mean Sq F value    Pr(>F)
classifier   7 0.108316 0.015474  4.2245 0.0007091 ***
Residuals   63 0.230757 0.003663

Signif. codes:  0 *** 0.001 ** 0.01 * 0.05 . 0.1   1

~~~~~~~~~~~~~~~~~~~~~~~~~~~~~~~~~~~~~~~~~~~~~~~~~~~~~~~~~~~~~~~~~

> tt <- read.table("rmanova-chapter9-RMSE.csv",
                   header=T, sep=",")
> attach(tt)
> summary(aov(RMSE ~ classifier + Error(dataset)))

Error: dataset
            Df  Sum Sq Mean Sq F value Pr(>F)
Residuals    9 0.99017 0.11002

Error: Within
            Df   Sum Sq  Mean Sq F value  Pr(>F)
classifier   7 0.061714 0.008816  1.9412 0.07767 .
Residuals   63 0.286119 0.004542

Signif. codes:  0 *** 0.001 ** 0.01 * 0.05 . 0.1   1
>

~~~~~~~~~~~~~~~~~~~~~~~~~~~~~~~~~~~~~~~~~~~~~~~~~~~~~~~~~~~~~~~~~

> tt <- read.table("rmanova-chapter9-AUC.csv",
                   header=T, sep=",")
> attach(tt)
```

```
> summary(aov(AUC ~ classifier + Error(dataset)))

Error: dataset
          Df  Sum Sq Mean Sq F value  Pr(>F)
Residuals  9 1.29361 0.14373

Error: Within
          Df  Sum Sq Mean Sq F value   Pr(>F)
classifier 7 0.14657 0.02094  3.3505 0.004243 **
Residuals 63 0.39370 0.00625
___
Signif. codes:  0 *** 0.001 ** 0.01 * 0.05 . 0.1   1
>
```

~ ~

```
> tt <- read.table("rmanova-chapter9-FMeasure.csv",
                    header=T, sep=",")
> attach(tt)
> summary(aov(Fmeasure ~ classifier + Error(dataset)))

Error: dataset
          Df Sum Sq Mean Sq F value Pr(>F)
Residuals  9 6.0324  0.6703

Error: Within
          Df  Sum Sq Mean Sq F value Pr(>F)
classifier 7 0.10585 0.01512  1.3814 0.2289
Residuals 63 0.68962 0.01095
>
```

~ ~

```
> tt <- read.table("rmanova-chapter9-KBRelative.csv",
                    header=T, sep=",")
> attach(tt)
> summary(aov(KBRel ~ classifier + Error(dataset)))

Error: dataset
          Df    Sum Sq    Mean Sq F value Pr(>F)
Residuals  9 2.5602e-13 2.8447e-14

Error: Within
          Df  Sum Sq Mean Sq F value Pr(>F)
classifier 7 0.40546 0.05792   1.656 0.1364
Residuals 63 2.20353 0.03498
>
```

From the results, we can reject the hypothesis that the results are all similar for the eight classifiers at the 99% significance level for accuracy and AUC.

For RMSE, this hypothesis can be rejected only at the 90% significance level, and it cannot be rejected for the F measure and KB's information score. Let us then follow up this with Dunnett's post hoc test on the results of accuracy, AUC, and RMSE. Note that the degree of freedom for these experiments is $(10 - 1)(8 - 1) = 63$ (10 domains and eight classifiers) and the significance level $\alpha = 0.05$. Accordingly, we get the value of approximately 1.671 for the one-tailed test or of approximately 2.0 for the two-tailed test (i.e., looking at $\alpha = 0.025$) from the t table of Appendix A[3] for the resulting Dunnett test statistic. Under the assumption that RF is superior to the other algorithms, we can use the one-tailed test, and thus the value of 1.671. Consequently, if the absolute value of Dunnett's t statistic (denoted t_{f_1, f_2} for classifiers f_1 and f_2) is smaller than 1.671, then we cannot reject the hypothesis that both classifiers perform equivalently.

For the accuracy measure, we then get the following results:

- $t_{NB,RF} = \frac{0.7716 - 0.8272}{\sqrt{\frac{2 \times 0.003663}{10}}} = -2.05$
- $t_{1NN,RF} = -1.46$
- $t_{SVM,RF} = -0.43$
- $t_{ADA,RF} = -4.24$
- $t_{BAG,RF} = -0.14$
- $t_{C45,RF} = -0.35$
- $t_{RIP,RF} = -0.23$

These results thus suggest (we take their absolute value) that, as far as accuracy is concerned, RF performs significantly better (at significance level 0.05) than two classifiers: NB and ADA.

Similarly, for AUC, we get the following results, suggesting that RF performs significantly better, at a significance level of 0.05, than 1NN, SVM, ADA, C45, and RIP.

- $t_{NB,RF} = \frac{0.8421 - 0.8578}{\sqrt{\frac{2 \times 0.00625}{10}}} = -0.45$
- $t_{1NN,RF} = -3.75$
- $t_{SVM,RF} = -2.41$
- $t_{ADA,RF} = -1.96$
- $t_{BAG,RF} = -0.15$
- $t_{C45,RF} = -1.83$
- $t_{RIP,RF} = -2.34$

Finally, the following post hoc test results for RMSE shows RF to be significantly better than NB, SVM, and ADA at a significance level 0.05.

- $t_{NB,RF} = \frac{0.3036 - 0.2524}{\sqrt{\frac{2 \times 0.004542}{10}}} = 1.71$

---

[3] The table does not list a value for degree of freedom 63, so we chose the closest: degree of freedom 60.

- $t_{\text{INN,RF}} = 1.11$
- $t_{\text{SVM,RF}} = 2.73$
- $t_{\text{ADA,RF}} = 1.68$
- $t_{\text{BAG,RF}} = 0.05$
- $t_{\text{C45,RF}} = 0.63$
- $t_{\text{RIP,RF}} = 0.08$

Overall, based on ANOVA–Dunnett, it then seems that RFS are slightly more effective than a number of other classifiers, at least with respect to AUC and, to some extent with respect to RMSE for the chosen domains.

Let us now investigate the effect of paramteric assumptions in the preceding findings by using a potentially more sensitive nonparamteric test, Friedman's, and follow it with Nemenyi's post hoc test in the event of null-hypothesis rejections. Listings C.5, C.6, C.7, C.8 and C.9 give the results of running Friedman's test in R for the results on accuracy, AUC, RMSE, F measure, and KB information score, respectively.

Listing C.5: The results of the omnibus Friedman test on the eight classifiers and 10 domains, using accuracy.

```
>
> NBaccuracy  = c(.7617, .8559, .7264, .9053, .7576, .4945,
                  .8381, .9531, .727, .6964)
> IB1accuracy= c(.7217, .9913, .7529, .7816, .7062, .6995,
                  .814, .9152, .6859, .8085)
> SVMaccuracy= c(.725, .9746, .8077, .8757, .768, .5736,
                  .8577, .9358, .6552, .9833)
> Adaaccuracy= c(.7217, .8363, .4646, .7177, .7492, .4489,
                  .8137, .9297, .7162, .7272)
> Bagacuracy=  c(.7567, .9876, .76, .8337, .7566, .7248, .82,
                  .9956, .691, .9098)
> J48accuracy= c(.835, .9858, .7727, .7782, .7449, .6763,
                  .7922, .9954, .7428, .8528)
> RFaccuracy=  c(.7567, .9941, .7709, .8011, .7444, .7616,
                  .8247, .9919, .697, .93)
> JRIPaccuracy= c(.8067, .9826, .7311, .803, .7518, .6678,
                  .7813, .9942, .7145, .9755)

> t=matrix(c(NBaccuracy, IB1accuracy, SVMaccuracy, Adaaccuracy,
            Bagacuracy, J48accuracy, RFaccuracy, JRIPaccuracy),
            nrow=10, byrow=FALSE)
>
> friedman.test(t)

        Friedman rank sum test

data:  t
Friedman chi-squared = 15.6205, df = 7, p-value = 0.02882
```

Listing C.6: The results of the omnibus Friedman test on the eight classifiers and 10 domains, using AUC.

```
>
> NBAUC = c(0.95,  0.9954,0.7033,0.9934,0.815,0.729,0.8567,
            0.9317,0.7025,0.7443)
> IB1AUC= c(0.765,0.9375,0.5,0.8598,0.6677,0.7984,0.6785,
            0.6709,0.6043,0.7851)
> SVMAUC= c(0.915,0.9826,0.5,0.9261,0.7131,0.7783,0.7685,
            0.5918,0.5836,0.9759)
> AdaAUC= c(0.835,0.831,0.5,0.889,0.8049,0.7083,0.8326,
            0.9914,0.6991,0.8021)
> BagAUC= c(0.935,0.9655,0.5,0.9596,0.8218,0.9063,0.8257,
            0.9965,0.6416,0.9726)
> J48AUC= c(0.945,0.931,0.5,0.8448,0.7514,0.7938,0.6678,
            0.9962,0.6063,0.9013)
> RFAUC=  c(0.975,0.9676,0.5,0.9577,0.7945,0.9209,0.8378,
            0.9986,0.6471,0.9792)
> JRIPAUC=c(0.94,0.755,0.5,0.8619,0.7195,0.8019,0.6224,0.988,
            0.5975,  0.9738)
> t=matrix(c(NBAUC, IB1AUC, SVMAUC, AdaAUC,  BagAUC, J48AUC,
             RFAUC, JRIPAUC), nrow=10, byrow=FALSE)
>
> friedman.test(t)

        Friedman rank sum test

data:  t
Friedman chi-squared = 24.5, df = 7, p-value = 0.0009302
```

Listing C.7: The results of the omnibus Friedman test on the eight classifiers and 10 domains, using RMSE.

```
>
> NBRMSE=  c(0.2965,0.2028,0.1355,0.2785,0.4194,0.337,0.3459,
             0.1379,0.4512,0.4308)
> IB1RMSE= c(0.3052,0.0384,0.1417,0.3791,0.5402,0.29,0.2902,
             0.2904,0.2904,0.2904)
> SVMRMSE= c(0.3741,0.3111,0.1934,0.345,0.4793,0.3162,0.3435,
             0.3214,0.5477,0.1103)
> AdaRMSE= c(0.2904,0.269,0.1724,0.3602,0.4157,0.3026,0.3601,
             0.1216,0.4355,0.3011)
> BagRMSE= c(0.3028,0.0573,0.123,0.2857,0.403,0.2366,0.3522,
             0.0422,0.4505,0.2843)
> J48RMSE= c(0.2333,0.0571,0.1208,0.3574,0.4388,0.2832,0.404,
             0.0385,0.444,0.3344)
```

```
> RFRMSE=   c(0.2587,0.0474,0.1216,0.3102,0.4199,0.2175,0.3419,
             0.0651,0.4663,0.275)
> JRIPRMSE=c(0.267,0.0664,0.1343,0.3333,0.4274,0.2759,0.4077,
             0.0488,0.4494,0.1376)
> t=matrix(c(NBRMSE, IB1RMSE, SVMRMSE, AdaRMSE,  BagRMSE,
             J48RMSE, RFRMSE, JRIPRMSE), nrow=10, byrow=FALSE)
>
> friedman.test(t)

        Friedman rank sum test

data:  t
Friedman chi-squared = 13.9333, df = 7, p-value = 0.05238

>
```

Listing C.8: The results of the omnibus Friedman test on the eight classifiers and 10 domains, using the F measure.

```
>
>
> NBFMEAS=   c(0.3767,0.6317,0,0.9421,0.8183,0.5762,0.6405,0.9767,
              0.8131,0.4868)
> IB1FMEAS=  c(0.31,0.7,0,0.8475,0.7785,0.7248,0.4691,0.9563,
              0.7811,0.718)
> SVMFMEAS=  c(0.3867,0.6833,0,0.9115,0.8339,0.5276,0.6297,0.9665,
              0.7974,0.9749)
> AdaFMEAS=  c(0.4017,0,0,0.746,0.8145,0.6269,0.4846,0.9737,
              0.8066,0.5976)
> BagFMEAS=  c(0.3667,0.495,0,0.8727,0.8177,0.7519,0.3678,0.9986,
              0.8017,0.857)
> J48FMEAS=  c(0.4767,0.5067,0,0.8267,0.8063,0.6957,0.4085,0.9983,
              0.8378,0.779)
> RFFMEAS=   c(0.3867,0.7,0,0.8773,0.8119,0.7852,0.4578,0.9961,
              0.7953,0.8959)
> JRIPFMEAS=c(0.4733,0.3767,0,0.8356,0.8159,0.6834,0.3646,0.9977,
              0.8126,0.9642)
> t=matrix(c(NBFMEAS, IB1FMEAS, SVMFMEAS, AdaFMEAS, BagFMEAS,
             J48FMEAS, RFFMEAS, JRIPFMEAS), nrow=10, byrow=FALSE)
>
> friedman.test(t)

        Friedman rank sum test

data:  t
Friedman chi-squared = 5.691, df = 7, p-value = 0.5763
```

Listing C.9: The results of the omnibus Friedman test on the eight classifiers
and 10 domains, using the KB relative information score.

```
>
> NBKB=   c(0.4781805,  0.5187728,  0.5531521,  0.5058934,
            0.5395482,  0.4339969,  0.7067169,  0.5449937,
            0.7183527,  0.1558427)
> IB1KB=  c(0.5447975,  0.6393088,  0.6238450,  0.6031634,
            0.4852430,  0.6582337,  0.6007191,  0.5221051,
            0.7109930,  0.4715869)
> SVMKB=  c(0.3729195,  0.0000000,  0.0871274,  0.3620662,
            0.6948530,  0.1388810,  0.8722821,  0.0000000,
            0.8007708,  0.8107599)
> AdaKB=  c(0.1847168,  0.3276748,  0.2424619,  0.2638829,
            0.4575311,  0.2998341,  0.5139759,  0.5603366,
            0.4756509,  0.2887929)
> BagKB=  c(0.4841322,  0.6266453,  0.6313791,  0.5482123,
            0.4776437,  0.6038634,  0.2937511,  0.5958554,
            0.1761929,  0.4697988)
> J48KB=  c(0.7083431,  0.6319375,  0.6766433,  0.5532177,
            0.4808735,  0.6288378,  0.3409576,  0.5977915,
            0.4145745,  0.5321341)
> RFKB=   c(0.5963652,  0.6327713,  0.5953899,  0.6138330,
            0.4703806,  0.6966989,  0.4378017,  0.5831585,
            0.3557358,  0.4891372)
> JRIPKB=c(0.6305452,  0.6228880,  0.5900011,  0.5497311,
            0.3939268,  0.5396542,  0.2337956,  0.5957591,
            0.3477294,  0.7819474)
> t=matrix(c(NBKB, IB1KB, SVMKB, AdaKB, BagKB, J48KB, RFKB,
            JRIPKB), nrow=10, byrow=FALSE)
>
> friedman.test(t)

        Friedman rank sum test

data:   t
Friedman chi-squared = 14.7667, df = 7, p-value = 0.03911

>
```

The p values obtained for all these tests tell us that, although for the F measure, the hypothesis that all classifiers perform similarly cannot be rejected, it
can be rejected at the 95% confidence level for accuracy, AUC, and KB information score, and at the 90% confidence level for the RMSE. To discover these
differences we apply Nemenyi's post hoc test. We start by calculating each of the
algorithms' rank sums over each evaluation measure. The resulting rank sums
for the classifiers on all domains are tabulated for each performance measure
in Tables C.9 (accuracy), C.10 (RMSE), C.11 (AUC), and C.12 (KB score).
Following each of these tables is the corresponding Nemenyi test calculations

Table C.9. *Rank-sum results obtained on eight classifiers and 10 domains,*
using accuracy

Domains	NB	1NN	SVM	ADA	BAG	C45	RF	RIP
Contact lenses	3	7.5	6	7.5	4.5	1	4.5	2
Anneal	7	2	6	8	3	4	1	5
Audiology	7	5	1	8	4	2	3	6
Balanced scale	1	6	2	8	3	7	5	4
Pima diabetes	2	8	1	5	3	6	7	4
Glass	7	3	6	8	2	4	1	5
Hepatitis	2	5	1	6	4	7	3	8
Hypothyroid	5	8	6	7	1	2	4	3
Breast cancer	2	7	8	3	6	1	5	4
Tic-tac-toe	8	6	1	7	4	5	3	2
Rank sums	44	57.5	38	67.5	34.5	39	36.5	43

Table C.10. *Rank-sum results obtained on eight classifiers and 10 domains, using RMSE*

Domains	NB	1NN	SVM	ADA	BAG	C45	RF	RIP
Contact lenses	5	7	8	4	6	1	2	3
Anneal	6	1	8	7	4	3	2	5
Audiology	5	6	8	7	3	1	2	4
Balanced scale	1	8	5	7	2	6	3	4
Pima diabetes	3	8	7	2	1	6	4	5
Glass	8	5	7	6	2	4	1	3
Hepatitis	4	1	3	6	5	7	2	8
Hypothyroid	6	7	8	5	2	1	4	3
Breast cancer	6	1	8	2	5	3	7	4
Tic-tac-toe	8	5	1	6	4	7	3	2
Rank sums	52	49	63	52	34	39	30	41

Table C.11. *Rank-sum results obtained on eight classifiers and 10 domains, using AUC*

Domains	NB	1NN	SVM	ADA	BAG	C45	RF	RIP
Contact lenses	2	8	5	7	6	3	1	4
Anneal	1	5	2	7	4	6	3	8
Audiology	1	5	5	5	5	5	5	5
Balanced scale	1	7	4	5	2	8	3	6
Pima diabetes	2	8	7	3	1	5	4	6
Glass	7	4	6	8	2	5	1	3
Hepatitis	1	6	5	3	4	7	2	8
Hypothyroid	6	7	8	5	3	4	2	1
Breast cancer	1	6	8	2	4	5	3	7
Tic-tac-toe	8	7	2	6	4	5	1	3
Rank sums	30	63	52	51	35	53	25	51

Table C.12. *Rank-sum results obtained on eight classifiers and 10 domains, using KB relative information score*

Domains	NB	1NN	SVM	ADA	BAG	C45	RF	RIP
Contact lenses	6	4	7	8	5	1	3	2
Anneal	6	1	8	7	4	3	2	5
Audiology	6	3	8	7	2	1	4	5
Balanced scale	6	2	7	8	5	3	1	4
Pima diabetes	2	3	1	7	5	4	6	8
Glass	6	2	8	7	4	3	1	5
Hepatitis	2	3	1	4	7	6	5	8
Hypothyroid	6	7	8	5	2	1	4	3
Breast cancer	2	3	1	4	8	5	6	7
Tic-tac-toe	8	5	1	7	6	3	4	2
Rank sums	50	33	50	64	48	30	36	49

focusing on discovering the differences of RF's performance with that of other classifiers for the respective metrics.

Starting with the accuracy, we apply the Nemenyi test, using RF as the control to obtain the following results:

- $q_{NB,RF} = \dfrac{\bar{R}_{NB} - \bar{R}_{RF}}{\sqrt{\frac{k(k+1)}{6n}}} = \dfrac{44 - 36.5}{\sqrt{\frac{8 \times 9}{60}}} = 6.85$
- $q_{1NN,RF} = 19.18$
- $q_{SVM,RF} = 1.37$
- $q_{ADA,RF} = 28.31$
- $q_{BAG,RF} = -1.83$
- $q_{C45,RF} = 2.28$
- $q_{RIP,RF} = 5.94$

Tukey's critical value for degree of freedom $(n - 1)(k - 1) = 9 \times 7 = 63$ is $q_\alpha = 4.31$ for $\alpha = 0.05$ (from table A.8). Recall that, for Nemenyi's test, we must divide the q_α value by $\sqrt{2}$, yielding the value of 3.048. It can be seen that ADA, 1NN, and RIP, whose q value exceeds 3.048, are thus the three classifiers displaying statistically significant differences with RF.

Similarly, for RMSE, the Nemenyi test calculations using RF as control yield the following results:

- $q_{NB,RF} = \dfrac{\bar{R}_{NB} - \bar{R}_{RF}}{\sqrt{\frac{k(k+1)}{6n}}} = \dfrac{52 - 30}{\sqrt{\frac{8 \times 9}{60}}} = 20.08$
- $q_{1NN,RF} = 17.34$
- $q_{SVM,RF} = 30.12$
- $q_{ADA,RF} = 20.08$
- $q_{BAG,RF} = 3.65$
- $q_{C45,RF} = 8.22$
- $q_{RIP,RF} = 10.04$

All the results are significant in the case of RMSE because all of the q values exceed the value of 3.048. Note the contrast with the previous Dunnett's test, for which a significant difference is found in only some of the comparisons.

Moving on to the AUC, we obtain the following results for the Nemenyi test calculations for AUC, again using RF as control:

- $q_{\text{NB,RF}} = \dfrac{R^-_{\text{NB}} - R^-_{\text{RF}}}{\sqrt{\frac{k(k+1)}{6n}}} = \dfrac{30-25}{\sqrt{\frac{8\times9}{60}}} = 4.56$
- $q_{\text{1NN,RF}} = 34.69$
- $q_{\text{SVM,RF}} = 24.65$
- $q_{\text{ADA,RF}} = 23.73$
- $q_{\text{BAG,RF}} = 9.13$
- $q_{\text{C45,RF}} = 25.56$
- $q_{\text{RIP,RF}} = 23.73$

Once again, as with the RMSE, all the results are found to be statistically significant in the case of AUC because all of the q values exceed the value of 3.048.

Finally, on the KB scores, with RF as control, the Nemenyi test calculations give these results:

- $q_{\text{NB,RF}} = \dfrac{R^-_{\text{NB}} - R^-_{\text{RF}}}{\sqrt{\frac{k(k+1)}{6n}}} = \dfrac{50-36}{\sqrt{\frac{8\times9}{60}}} = 12.78$
- $q_{\text{1NN,RF}} = -2.73$
- $q_{\text{SVM,RF}} = 12.78$
- $q_{\text{ADA,RF}} = 25.56$
- $q_{\text{BAG,RF}} = 10.95$
- $q_{\text{C45,RF}} = -5.48$
- $q_{\text{RIP,RF}} = 11.87$

Because all the (absolute) values but one ($q_{\text{1NN,RF}}$) exceed 3.048, they are all deemed significant with respect to the KB relative information score, except for the comparison between 1NN and RF.

Several remarks can be made concerning this study as compared to that of Chapter 1. First and foremost, the use of several metrics, and not just accuracy alone, is an eye-opener with respect to the strengths and weaknesses of each method. That a classifier, such as SVM, can jump from the top position to the bottom is certainly indicative of the caveats in using a single metric such as accuracy. Second, the use of visualization methods presents a nice advantage by providing a quick summary of results thereby allowing us to focus immediately on the points of interest (and even identifying them). This obviates the need to track individual results over each classifier. Obtaining conclusions that are relevant is hence rendered easier once the criteria of interest are identified. In the current case, we focused on the strength of RF compared with other classifiers on various measures. Making use of omnibus tests for statistical significance followed by relevant post hoc tests was not only less cumbersome but also more sensible given the large number of pairwise comparisons required. Hence, we see how a broader understanding of various evaluation methods and the tools available at our disposal allow us to perform relatively more principled evaluation.

Bibliography

N. M. Adams and D. J. Hand. Comparing classifiers when the misallocation costs are uncertain. *Pattern Recognition*, 32:1139–1147, 1999.

D. Aha. Generalizing from case studies: A case study. In *Proceedings of the 9th International Workshop on Machine Learning (ICML '92)*, pp. 1–10. Morgan Kaufmann, San Mateo, CA, 1992.

R. Alaiz-Rodriguez and N. Japkowicz. Assessing the impact of changing environments on classifier performance. In *Proceedings of the 21st Canadian Conference in Artificial Intelligence (AI 2008)*, Springer, New York, 2008.

R. Alaiz-Rodríguez, N. Japkowicz, and P. Tischer. Visualizing classifier performance on different domains. In *Proceedings of the 2008 20th IEEE International Conference on Tools with Artificial Intelligence (ICTAI '08)*, pp. 3–10. IEEE Computer Society, Washington, D.C., 2008.

S. Ali and K. A. Smith. Kernel width selection for svm classification: A meta learning approach. *International Journal of Data Warehousing Mining*, 1:78–97, 2006.

E. Alpaydn. Combined 52 f test for comparing supervised classification learning algorithms. *Neural Computation*, 11:1885–1892, 1999.

A. Andersson, P. Davidsson, and J. Linden. Measure-based classifier performance evaluation. *Pattern Recognition Letters*, 20:1165–1173, 1999.

J. S. Armstrong. Significance tests harm progress in forecasting. *International Journal of Forecasting*, 23:321–327, 2007.

A. Asuncion and D. J. Newman. *UCI machine learning repository*. University of California, Irvine, School of Information and Computer Science, 2007. URL: http://www.ics.uci.edu/ mlearn/MLRepository.html.

T. L. Bailey and C. Elkan. Estimating the accuracy of learned concepts. In *Proceedings of the 1993 International Joint Conference on Artificial Intelligence*, pp. 895–900. Morgan Kaufmann, San Mateo, CA, 1993.

S. D. Bay, D. Kibler, M. J. Pazzani, and P. Smyth. The UCI KDD archive of large data sets for data mining researc and experimentation. *SIGKDD Explorations*, 2(2):81–85, December 2000.

C. Bellinger, J. Lalonde, M. W. Floyd, V. Mallur, E. Elkanzi, D. Ghazi, J. He, A. Mouttham, M. Scaiano, E. Wehbe, and N. Japkowicz. An evaluation of the value added by informative metrics. In *Proceedings of the Fourth Workshop on Evaluation Methods for Machine Learning*, 2009.

E. M. Bennett, R. Alpert, and A. C. Goldstein. Communications through limited response questioning. *Public Opinion Q*, 18:303–308, 1954.

K. J. Berry and P. W. Mielke, Jr. A generalization of Cohen's kappa agreement measure to interval measurement and multiple raters. *Educational and Psychological Measurements*, 48:921–933, 1988.

A. Blum, A. Kalai, and J. Langford. Beating the hold-out: Bounds for k-fold and progressive cross-validation. In *Proceedings of the 12th Annual Conference on Computational Learning Theory (COLT '99)*, pp. 203–208. Association for Computing Machinery, New York, 1999. doi: http://doi.acm.org/10.1145/307400.307439.

R. R. Bouckaert. Choosing between two learning algorithms based on calibrated tests. In T. Fawcett and N. Mishra, editors, *Proceedings of the 20th International Conference on Machine Learning*. American Association for Artificial Intelligence, Menlo Park, CA, 2003.

R. R. Bouckaert. Estimating replicability of classifier learning experiments. In C. Brodley, editor, *Proceedings of the 21st International Conference on Machine Learning*. American Association for Artificial Intelligence, Menlo Park, CA, 2004.

O. Bousquet, S. Boucheron, and G. Lugosi. Introduction to statistical learning theory. In *Advanced Lectures on Machine Learning*, pp. 169–207. Vol. 3176 of Springer Lecture Notes in Artificial Intelligence. Springer-Verlag, Berlin, 2004.

J. P. Bradford, C. Kunz, R. Kohavi, C. Brunk, and C. E. Brodley. Pruning decision trees with misclassification costs. In *Proceedings of the European Conference on Machine Learning*, pp. 131–136. Springer, Berlin, 1998.

P. Bradley. The use of the area under the ROC curve in the evaluation of machine learning algorithms. *Pattern Recognition*, 30:1145–1159, 1997.

L. Breiman, J. H. Friedman, R. A. Olshen, and C. J. Stone. *Classification and Regression Trees*. Chapman & Hall, CRC, 1984.

C. E. Brodley. Addressing the selective superiority problem: Automatic algorithm/model class selection. In *Proceedings of the 10th International Conference on Machine Learning*, pp. 17–24, Morgan Kaufmann, San Mateo, CA, 1993.

A. Buja, W. Stuetzle, and Y. Shen. Loss functions for binary class probability estimation: Structure and applications. 2005. http://www-stat.wharton.upenn.edu/ buja/PAPERS/paper-proper-scoring.pdf.

J. R. Busemeyer and Y. M. Wang. Model comparisons and model selections based on generalization test methodology. *Journal of Mathematical Psychology*, 44:171–189, 2000.

T. Byrt, J. Bishop, and J. B. Carlin. Bias, prevalence and kappa. *Journal of Clinical Epidemiology*, 46:423–429, 1993.

R. Caruana and A. Niculescu-Mizil. Data mining in metric space: An empirical analysis of supervised learning performance criteria. In *Proceedings of KDD*. Association for Computing Machinery, New York, 2004.

M. R. Chernik. *Bootstrap Methods: A Guide for Practitioners and Researchers*. 2nd ed. Wiley, New York, 2007.

S. L. Chow. Precis of statistical significance: Rationale, validity, and utility. *Behavioral And Brain Sciences*, 21:169–239, 1998.

M. Ciraco, M. Rogalewski, and G. Weiss. Improving classifier utility by altering the misclassification cost ratio. In *Proceedings of the 1st International Workshop on Utility-Based Data Mining (UBDM '05)*, pp. 46–52. Association for Computing Machinery, New York, 2005.

J. Cohen. A coefficient of agreement for nominal scales. *Educational and Psychological Measurements*, 20:37–46, 1960.

J. Cohen. The earth is round (p ¡ .05). *American Psychologist*, 49:997–1003, 1994.

J. Cohen. The earth is round (p ¡ .05). In L. L. Harlow and S. A. Mulaik, editors, *What If There Were No Significance Tests?* Lawrence Erlbaum, Mahwah, NJ, 1997.

P. R. Cohen. *Empirical Methods for Artificial Intelligence*. MIT Press, Cambridge, MA, 1995.

W. J. Conover. *Practical Nonparametric Statistics*. 3rd ed. Wiley, New York, 1999.

C. Cortes and M. Mohri. AUC optimization vs. error rate minimization. In *Advances in Neural Information Processing Systems*, Vol. 16. MIT Press, Cambridge, MA, 2004.

C. Cortes and M. Mohri. Confidence intervals for the area under the ROC curve. In *Advances in Neural Information Processing Systems,* Vol. 17. MIT Press, Cambridge, MA, 2005.

J. Davis and M. Goadrich. The relationship between precision-recall and ROC curves. In *Proceedings of the International Conference on Machine Learning*, pp. 233–240. Association for Computing Machinery, New York, 2006.

J. J. Deeks and D. G. Altman. Diagnostic tests 4: Likelihood ratios. *British Medical Journal*, 329:168–169, 2004.

G. Demartini and S. Mizzaro. A classification of IR effectiveness metrics. In *Proceedings of the European Conference on Information Retrieval*, pp. 488–491. Vol. 3936 of Springer Lecture Notes. Springer, Berlin, 2006.

J. Demšar. Statistical comparisons of classifiers over multiple data sets. *Journal of Machine Learning Research*, 7:1–30, 2006.

J. Demšar. On the appropriateness of statistical tests in machine learning. In *Proceedings of the ICML'08 Third Workshop on Evaluation Methods for Machine Learning*. Association for Computing Machinery, New York, 2008.

L. R. Dice. Measures of the amount of ecologic association between species. *Journal of Ecology*, 26:297–302, 1945.

T. G. Dietterich. Approximate statistical tests for comparing supervised classification learning algorithms. *Neural Computation*, 10:1895–1924, 1998.

P. Domingos. A unified bias-variance decomposition and its applications. In *Proceedings of the 17th International Conference on Machine Learning*, pp. 231–238. Morgan Kaufmann, San Mateo, CA, 2000.

C. Drummond. Machine learning as an experimental science (revised). In *Proceedings of the AAAI'06 Workshop on Evaluation Methods for Machine Learning I*. American Association for Artificial Intelligence, Menlo Park, CA, 2006.

C. Drummond. Finding a balance between anarchy and orthodoxy. In *Proceedings of the ICML'08 Third Workshop on Evaluation Methods for Machine Learning*. Association for Computing Machinery, New York, 2008.

C. Drummond and N. Japkowicz. Warning: Statistical benchmarking is addictive. Kicking the habit in machine learning. *Journal of Experimental and Theoretical Artificial Intelligence*, 22(1):67–80, 2010.

B. Efron. Estimating the error rate of a prediction rule: Improvement on cross-validation. *Journal of the American Statistical Association*, 78:316–331, 1983.

B. Efron and R. J. Tibshirani. An Introduction to the Bootstrap, Chapman and Hall, New York, 1993.

W. Elazmeh, N. Japkowicz, and S. Matwin. A framework for measuring classification difference with imbalance. In *Proceedings of the 2006 European Conference on Machine Learning (ECML/PKDD 2008)*. Springer, Berlin, 2006.

W. Fan, S. J. Stolfo, J. Zhang, and P. K. Chan. Adacost: Misclassification cost-sensitive boosting. In *Proceedings of the 16th International Conference on Machine Learning*, pp. 97–105. Morgan Kaufmann, San Mateo, CA, 1999.

T. Fawcett. ROC graphs: Notes and practical considerations for data mining researchers. Technical Note HPL 2003–4, Hewlett-Packard Laboratories, 2004.

T. Fawcett. An introduction to ROC analysis. *Pattern Recognition Letters*, 27:861–874, 2006.

T. Fawcett and A. Niculescu-Mizil. PAV and the ROC convex hull. *Machine Learning*, 68 (1):97–106, 2007. doi: http://dx.doi.org/10.1007/s10994-007-5011-0.

C. Ferri, P. A. Flach, and J. Hernandez-Orallo. Improving the AUC of probabilistic estimation trees. In *Proceedings of the 14th European Conference on Machine Learning*, pp. 121–132. Springer, Berlin, 2003.

C. Ferri, J. Haernandez-Orallo, and R. Modroiu. An experimental comparison of performance measures for classification. *Pattern Recognition Letters*, 30:27–38, 2009.

R. A. Fisher. *Statistical Methods and Scientific Inference*. 2nd ed. Hafner, New York, 1959.

R. A. Fisher. *The Design of Experiments.* 2nd ed. Hafner, New York, 1960.

P. A. Flach. The geometry of ROC space: Understanding machine learning metrics through ROC isometrics. In *Proceedings of the 20th International Conference on Machine Learning*, pp. 194–201. American Association for Artificial Intelligence, Menlo Park, CA, 2003.

P. A. Flach and S. Wu. Repairing concavities in ROC curves. In *Proceedings of the 19th International Joint Conference on Artificial Intelligence (IJCAI'05)*, pp. 702–707. Professional Book Center, 2005.

J. L. Fleiss. Measuring nominal scale agreement among many raters. *Psychological Bulletin*, 76:378–382, 1971.

G. Forman. A method for discovering the insignificance of one's best classifier and the unlearnability of a classification task. In *Proceedings of the First International Workshop on Data Mining Lessons Learned (DMLL-2002)*, 2002.

M. R. Forster. Key concepts in model selection: Performance and generalizabilty. *Journal of Mathematical Psychology*, 44:205–231, 2000.

Y. Freund, R. Iyer, R. E. Schapire, and Y. Singer. An efficient boosting algorithm for combining preferences. *Journal of Machine Learning Research*, 4:933–969, 2003.

M. Friedman. The use of ranks to avoid the assumption of normality implicit in the analysis of variance. *Journal of the American Statistical Association*, 32:675–701, 1937.

M. Friedman. A comparison of alternative tests of significance for the problem of *m* rankings. *Annals of Mathematical Statistics*, 11:86–92, 1940.

J. Fuernkranz and P. A. Flach. Roc 'n' rule learning – Towards a better understanding of covering algorithms. *Machine Learning*, 58:39–77, 2005.

V. Ganti, J. Gehrke, R. Ramakrishnan, and W. Y. Loh. A framework for measuring differences in data characteristics. *Journal of Computer and System Sciences*, 64:542–578, 2002.

M. Gardner and D. G. Altman. Confidence intervals rather than p values: Estimation rather than hypothesis testing. *British Medical Journal*, 292:746–750, 1986.

L. Gaudette and N. Japkowicz. Evaluation methods for ordinal classification. In *Proceedings of the 2009 Canadian Conference on Artificial Intelligence*. Springer, New York, 2009.

L. Geng and H. Hamilton. Choosing the right lens: Finding what is interesting in data mining. In F. Guillet and H. J. Hamilton, editors, *Quality Measures in Data Mining*, pp. 3–24. Vol. 43 of Springer Studies in Computational Intelligence Series, Springer, Berlin, 2007.

G. Gigerenzer. Mindless statistics. *Journal of Socio-Economics*, 33:587–606, 2004.

J. Gill and K. Meir. The insignificance of null hypothesis significance testing. *Political Research Quarterly*, pp. 647–674, 1999.

T. R. Golub, D. K. Slonim, P. Tamayo, C. Huard, M. Gaasenbeek, J. P. Mesirov, H. Coller, M. L. Loh, J. R. Downing, M. A. Caligiuri, C. D. Bloomfield, and E. S. Lander. Molecular classification of cancer: Class discovery and class prediction by gene expression monitoring. *Science*, 286:531–537, 1999.

S. N. Goodman. A comment on replication, p-values and evidence. *Statistics in Medicine*, 11:875–879, 2007.

W. S. Gosset (pen name: Student). The probable error of a mean. *Biometrika*, 6:1–25, 1908.

K. Gwet. Kappa statistic is not satisfactory for assessing the extent of agreement between raters. *Statistical Methods for Inter-Rater Reliability Assessment Series*, 1:1–6, 2002a.

K. Gwet. Inter-rater reliability: Dependency on trait prevalence and marginal homogeneity. *Statistical Methods for Inter-Rater Reliability Assessment Series*, 2:1–9, 2002b.

D. J. Hand. Classifier technology and the illusion of progress. *Statistical Science*, 21:1–15, 2006.

D. J. Hand. Measuring classifier performance: A coherent alternative to the area under the ROC curve. *Machine Learning*, 77:103–123, 2009.

D. J. Hand and R. J. Till. A simple generalisation of the area under the ROC curve for multiple class classification problems. *Machine Learning*, 45:171–186, 2001.

J. A. Hanley and B. J. McNeil. The meaning and use of the area under a receiver operating characteristic (ROC) curve. *Radiology*, 143:29–36, 1982.

L. L. Harlow and S. A. Mulaik, editors. *What If There Were No Significance Tests?* Lawrence Erlbaum, Mahwah, NJ, 1997.

T. Hastie, R. Tibshirani, and J. Friedman. *The Elements of Statistical Learning: Data Mining, Inference and Prediction.* Springer-Verlag, New York, 2001.

J. He, A. H. Tan, C. L. Tan, and S. Y. Sung. On quantitative evaluation of clustering systems. In W. Wu and H. Xiong, editors, *Information Retrieval and Clustering.* Kluwer Academic, Dordrecht, The Netherlands, 2002.

X. He and E. C. Frey. The meaning and use of the volume under a three-class ROC surface (vus). *IEEE Transactions Medical Imaging*, 27:577–588, 2008.

R. Herbrich. *Learning Kernel Classifiers.* MIT Press, Cambridge, MA, 2002.

T. Hill and P. Lewicki. STATISTICS Methods and Applications. StatSoft, Tulsa, OK, 2007.

P. Hinton. *Statistics Explained.* Routledge, London, 1995.

S. Holm. A simple sequentially rejective multiple test procedure. *Scandinavian Journal of Statistics*, 6(2):65–70, 1979.

R. C. Holte. Very simple classification rules perform well on most commonly used data sets. *Machine Learning*, 11:63–91, 1993.

G. Hommel. A stagewise rejective multiple test procedure based on a modified Bonferroni test. *Biometrika*, 75:383–386, 1988.

L. R. Hope and K. B. Korb. A Bayesian metric for evaluating machine learning algorithms. In *Australian Conference on Artificial Intelligence*, pp. 991–997. Vol. 3399 of Springer Lecture Notes in Computer Science. Springer, New York, 2004.

D. C. Howell. *Statistical Methods for Psychology.* 5th ed. Duxbury Press, Thomson Learning, 2002.

D. C. Howell. *Resampling Statistics: Randomization and the Bootstrap.* On-Line Notes, 2007. URL http://www.uvm.edu/ dhowell/StatPp./Resampling/Resampling.html.

J. Huang and C. X. Ling. Constructing new and better evaluation measures for machine learning. In *Proceedings of the 20th International Joint Conference on Artificial Intelligence (IJCAI '07)*, pp. 859–864, 2007.

J. Huang, C. X. Ling, H. Zhang, and S. Matwin. Proper model selection with significance test. In *Proceedings of the European Conference on Machine Learning (ECML-2008)*, pp. 536–547. Springer, Berlin, 2008.

R. Hubbard and R.. M. Lindsay. Why p values are not a useful measure of evidence in statistical significance testing. *Theory and Psychology*, 18:69–88, 2008.

J. P. A. Ioannidis. Why most published research findings are false. *Public Library of Science Medicine*, 2(8):e124, 2005.

P. Jaccard. The distribution of the flora in the alpine zone. *New Phytology*, 11(2):37–50, 1912.

A. K. Jain, R. C. Dubes, and C. Chen. Bootstrap techniques for error estimation. *IEEE Transactions on Pattern Analysis and Machine Intelligence*, 9:628–633, 1987.

N. Japkowicz. Classifier evaluation: A need for better education and restructuring. In *Proceedings of the ICML'08 Third Workshop on Evaluation Methods for Machine Learning*, July 2008.

N. Japkowicz, P. Sanghi, and P. Tischer. A projection-based framework for classifier performance evaluation. In *Proceedings of the 2008 European Conference on Machine Learning and Knowledge Discovery in Databases (ECML PKDD '08) – Part I*, pp. 548–563. Springer-Verlag, Berlin, 2008.

D. Jensen and P. Cohen. Multiple comparisons in induction algorithms. *Machine Learning*, 38:309–338, 2000.

H. Jin and Y. Lu. Permutation test for non-inferiority of the linear to the optimal combination of multiple tests. *Statistics and Probability Letters*: 79:664–669, 2009.

M. Kendall. A new measure of rank correlation. *Biometrika*, 30:81–89, 1938.

D. F. Kibler and P. Langley. Machine learning as an experimental science. In *Proceedings of the Third European Working Session on Learning (EWSL)*, pp. 81–92. Pitman, New York, 1988.

W. Klement. Evaluating machine learning methods: Scored receiver operating characteristics (sROC) curves. Ph.D. thesis, SITE, University of Ottawa, Canada, May 2010.

R. Kohavi. A study of cross-validation and bootstrap for accuracy estimation and model selection. In *Proceedings of the 14th International Joint Conference on Artificial Intelligence (IJCAI '95)*, pp. 1137–1143. Morgan Kaufmann, San Mateo, CA, 1995.

I. Kononenko and I. Bratko. Information-based evaluation criterion for classifier's performance. *Machine Learning*, 6:67–80, 1991.

I. Kononenko and M. Kukar. *Machine Learning and Data Mining: Introduction to Principles and Algorithms*. Horwood, Chichester, UK, 2007.

H. C. Kraemer. Ramifications of a population model for κ as a coefficient of reliability. *Psychometrika*, 44:461–472, 1979.

W. J. Kruskal and W. A. Wallis. Use of ranks in one-criterion variance analysis. *Journal of the American Statistical Association*, 47:583–621, 1952.

M. Kubat, R. C. Holte, and S. Matwin. Machine learning for the detection of oil spills in satellite radar images. *Machine Learning*, 30:195–215, 1998.

M. Kukar, I. Kononenko, and S. Ljubljana. Reliable classifications with machine learning. In *Proceedings of 13th European Conference on Machine Learning (ECML 2002)*, pp. 219–231. Springer, Berlin, 2002.

M. Z. Kukar and I. Kononenko. Cost-sensitive learning with neural networks. In *Proceedings of the 13th European Conference on Artificial Intelligence (ECAI-98)*, pp. 445–449. Wiley, New York, 1998.

L. I. Kuncheva, C. J. Whitaker, C. A. Shipp, and R. P. W. Duin. Limits on the majority vote accuracy in classifier fusion. *Pattern Analysis and Applications*, 6:22–31, 2003.

A. K. Kurtz. A research test of Rorschach test. *Personnel Psychology*, 1:41–53, 1948.

N. Lachiche and P. Flach. Improving accuracy and cost of two-class and multi-class probabilistic classifiers using ROC curves. In *Proceedings of the 20th International Conference on Machine Learning*, pp. 416–423. American Association for Artificial Intelligence, Menlo Park, CA, 2003.

D. LaLoudouana and M. B. Tarare. Data set selection. In *Proceedings of the Neural Information Processing System Workshop*. MIT Press, Cambridge, MA, 2003.

T. Landgrebe, P. Pacl'ik, D. J. M. Tax, S. Verzakov, and R. P. W. Duin. Cost-based classifier evaluation for imbalanced problems. In *Proceedings of the 10th International Workshop on Structural and Syntactic Pattern Recognition and 5th International Workshop on Statistical Techniques in Pattern Recognition*, pp. 762–770. Vol. 3138 of Springer *Lecture Notes in Computer Science*. Springer-Verlag, Berlin, 2004.

J. Langford. Tutorial on practical prediction theory for classification. *Journal of Machine Learning Research*, 3:273–306, 2005.

N. Lavesson and P. Davidsson. Towards application-specific evaluation metrics. In *Proceedings of the Third Workshop on Evaluation Methods for Machine Learning (ICML'2008)*. 2008a.

N. Lavesson and P. Davidsson. Generic methods for multi-criteria evaluation. In *Proceedings of the Eighth SIAM International Conference on Data Mining*. Society for Industrial and Applied Mathematics, Philadelphia, 2008b.

F. Laviolette, M. Marchand, and M. Shah. Margin-sparsity trade-off for the set covering machine. In *Proceedings of the 16th European Conference on Machine Learning (ECML 2005)*, pp. 206–217. Vol. 3720 of Springer *Lecture Notes in Artificial Intelligence*. Springer, Berlin, 2005.

F. Laviolette, M. Marchand, M. Shah, and S. Shanian. Learning the set covering machine by bound minimization and margin-sparsity trade-off. *Machine Learning*, 78(1-2):275–301, 2010.

N. Lavrač, P. Flach, and B. Zupan. Rule evaluation measures: A unifying view. In S. Dzeroski and P. Flach, editors, *Ninth International Workshop on Inductive Logic Programming (ILP '99)*, pp. 174–185. Vol. 1634 of Springer Lecture Notes in Computer Science. Springer-Verlag, Berlin, 1999.

G. Lebanon and J. D. Lafferty. Cranking: Combining rankings using conditional probability models on permutations. In *Proceedings of the Nineteenth International Conference on Machine Learning (ICML '02)*, pp. 363–370. Morgan Kaufmann, San Mateo, CA, 2002.

M. Li and P. Vitányi. *An Introduction to Kolmogorov Complexity and Its Applications*. 2nd ed. Springer-Verlag, New York, 1997.

D.V. Lindley and W.F. Scott. *New Cambridge Statistical Tables*. 2nd ed. Cambridge University Press, New York, 1984.

C. X. Ling, J. Huang, and H. Zhang. AUC: A statistically consistent and more discriminating measure than accuracy. In *Proceedings of the Eighteenth International Joint Conference on Artificial Intelligence (IJCAI '03)*, pp. 519–526. Morgan Kaufmann, San Mateo, CA, 2003.

X. Y. Liu and Z. H. Zhou. Training cost-sensitive neural networks with methods addressing the class imbalance problem. *IEEE Transactions on Knowledge and Data Engineering*, 18:63–77, 2006.

S. A. Macskassy, F. Provost, and S. Rosset. Pointwise ROC confidence bounds: An empirical evaluation. In *Proceedings of the Workshop on ROC Analysis in Machine Learning (ROCML-2005) at ICML '05*. 2005.

M. Marchand and M. Shah. PAC-Bayes learning of conjunctions and classification of gene-expression data. In L. K. Saul, Y. Weiss, and L. Bottou, editors, *Advances in Neural Information Processing Systems*, Vol. 17, pp. 881–888. MIT Press, Cambridge, MA, 2005.

M. Marchand and J. Shawe-Taylor. The set covering machine. *Journal of Machine Learning Reasearch*, 3:723–746, 2002.

D. D. Margineantu and T. G. Dietterich. Bootstrap methods for the cost-sensitive evaluation of classifiers. In *Proceedings of the Seventeenth International Conference on Machine Learning*, pp. 583–590. Morgan Kaufmann, San Mateo, CA, 2000.

C. Marrocco, R. P. W. Duin, and F. Tortorella. Maximizing the area under the ROC curve by pairwise feature combination. *Pattern Recognition*, 41:1961–1974, 2008.

A. Martin, G. Doddington, T. Kamm, M. Ordowski, and M. Przybocki. The DET curve in assessment of detection task performance. *Eurospeech*, 4:1895–1898, 1997.

P. E. Meehl. Theory testing in psychology and physics: A methodological paradox. *Philosophy of Science*, 34:103–115, 1967.

O. Melnik, Y. Vardi, and C. Zhang. Mixed group ranks: Preference and confidence in classifier combination. *IEEE Transactions on Pattern Analysis and Machine Intelligence*, 26:973–981, 2004.

R. J. Micheals and T. E. Boult. Efficient evaluation of classification and recognition systems. In *Proceedings of IEEE Conference on Computer Vision and Pattern Recognition: IEEE Computer Society*, pp. 50–57. Washington, DC, 2001.

T. Mitchell. *Machine Learning*. McGraw-Hill, New York, 1997.

A. Murua. Upper bounds for error rates of linear combinations of classifiers. *IEEE Transactions on Pattern Analysis and Machine Intelligence*, 24:591–602, 2002. doi: http://dx.doi.org/10.1109/34.1000235.

C. Nadeau and Y. Bengio. Inference for the generalization error. *Machine Learning*, 52: 239–281, 2003.

G. Nakhaeizadeh and A. Schnabl. Development of multi-criteria metrics for evaluation of data mining algorithms. In *Proceedings of KDD-97*, pp. 37–42. American Association for Artificial Intelligence, Menlo Park, CA, 1997.

G. Nakhaeizadeh and A. Schnabl. Towards the personalization of algorithms evaluation in data mining. In *Proceedings of KDD-98*, pp. 289–293. American Association for Artificial Intelligence, Menlo Park, CA, 1998.

A. M. Narasimhamurthy. Theoretical bounds of majority voting performance for a binary classification problem. *IEEE Transactions on Pattern Analysis and Machine Intelligence*, 27:1988–1995, 2005. doi: http://dx.doi.org/10.1109/TPAMI.2005.249.

A. M. Narasimhamurthy and L. I. Kuncheva. A framework for generating data to simulate changing environments. In *Proceedings of the 2007 Conference on Artificial Intelligence and Applications*, pp. 415–420. ACTA Press, 2007.

J. Neville and D. Jensen. A bias/variance decomposition for models using collective inference. *Machine Learning*, 73:87–106, 2008. doi: http://dx.doi.org/10.1007/s10994-008-5066-6.

D. B. O'Brien, M. R. Gupta, and R. M. Gray. Cost-sensitive multi-class classification from probability estimates. In *ICML 08: Proceedings of the 25th International Conference on Machine Learning (ICML '08)*, pp. 712–719. Association for Computing Machinery, New York, 2008.

F. Provost and P. Domingos. Tree induction for probability-based ranking. *Machine Learning*, 52:199–215, 2003. doi: http://dx.doi.org/10.1023/A:1024099825458.

F. Provost, T. Fawcett, and R. Kohavi. The case against accuracy estimation for comparing induction algorithms. In *Proceedings of the 15th International Conference on Machine Learning*. Morgan Kaufmann, San Mateo, CA, 1998.

M. Quenouille. Approximate tests of correlation in time series. *Journal of the Royal Statistical Society Series B*, 11:18–84, 1949.

R Development Core Team. *R: A Language and Environment for Statistical Computing*. R Foundation for Statistical Computing, Vienna, Austria, 2010. URL http://www.R-project.org.

Y. Reich and S. V. Barai. Evaluating machine learning models for engineering problems. *Artificial Intelligence in Engineering*, 13:257–272, 1999.

L. Rendell and H. Cho. Empirical learning as a function of concept character. *Machine Learning*, 5:267–298, 1990.

ROCR. Germany, 2007. Web: http://rocr.bioinf.mpi sb.mpg.de/.

S. Rosset. Model selection via the auc. In *Proceedings of the 21st International Conference on Machine Learning*. Association for Computing Machinery, New York, 2004.

S. Rosset, C. Perlich, and B. Zadrozny. Ranking-based evaluation of regression models. *Knowledge and Information Systems*, 12(3):331–353, 2007.

B. Sahiner, H. Chan, and L. Hadjiiski. Classifier performance estimation under the constraint of a finite sample size: Resampling schemes applied to neural network classifiers. *Neural Networks*, 21:476–483, 2008.

L. Saitta and F. Neri. Learning in the "real world." 1998 special issue: applications of machine learning and the knowledge discovery process. *Machine Learning*, 30:133–163, 1998.

S. L. Salzberg. On comparing classifiers: Pitfalls to avoid and a recommended approach. *Data Mining and Knowledge Discovery*, 1:317–327, 1997.

R. Santos-Rodríguez, A. Guerrero-Curieses, R. Alaiz-Rodríguez, and J. Cid-Sueiro. Cost-sensitive learning based on Bregman divergences. *Machine Learning*, 76:271–285, 2009. doi: http://dx.doi.org/10.1007/s10994-009-5132-8.

F. L. Schmidt. Statistical significance testing and cumulative knowledge in psychology. *Psychological Methods*, 1:115–129, 1996.

H. J. A. Schouten. Measuring pairwise interobserver agreement when all subjects are judged by the same observers. *Statistica Neerlandica*, 36:45–61, 1982.

W. A. Scott. Reliability of content analysis: The case of nominal scale coding. *Public Opinion Q*, 19:321–325, 1955.

M. Shah. *Sample Compression, Margins and Generalization: Extensions to the Set Covering Machine*. Ph.D. thesis, SITE, University of Ottawa, Canada, May 2006.

M. Shah. Sample compression bounds for decision trees. In *Proceedings of the 24th International Conference on Machine Learning (ICML '07)*, pp. 799–806. Association for Computing Machinery, New York, 2007. doi: http://doi.acm.org/10.1145/1273496.1273597.

M. Shah. Risk bounds for classifier evaluation: Possibilities and challenges. In *Proceedings of the 3rd Workshop on Evaluation Methods for Machine Learning at ICML-2008*. 2008.

M. Shah and S. Shanian. Hold-out risk bounds for classifier performance evaluation. In *Proceedings of the 4th Workshop on Evaluation Methods for Machine Learning at ICML '09*. 2009.

T. Sing, O. Sander, N. Beerenwinkel, and T. Lengauer. ROCR: Visualizing classifier performance in R. *Bioinformatics*, 21:3940–3941, 2005.

K. A. Smith-Miles. Cross-disciplinary perspectives on meta-learning for algorithm selection. *ACM Computing Surveys*, 41(1):article 6, 2008.

C. Soares. Is the UCI repository useful for data mining? In F. M. Pires and S. Abreu, editors, *Proceedings of the 11th Portuguese Conference on Artificial Intelligence (EPIA '03)*, pp. 209–223. Vol. 2902 of Springer *Lecture Notes in Artificial Intelligence*. Springer, Berlin, 2003.

C. Soares, J. Costa, and P. Bradzil. A simple and intuitive mesure for multicriteria evaluation of classification algorithms. In *Proceedings of the ECML 2000 Workshop on Meta-Learning: Building Automatic Advice Strategies for Model Selection and Method Combination*, pp. 87–96. Springer, Berlin, 2000.

S. Sonnenburg, M. L. Braun, C. S Ong, S. Bengio, L. Bottou, G. Holmes, Y. LeCun, K. Mller, F. Pereira, C. E. Rasmussen, G. Ratsch, B. Scholkopf, A. Smola, P. Vincent, J. Weston, and R. Williamson. The need for open source software in machine learning. *Journal of Machine Learning Research*, 8:2443–2466, 2007.

C. Spearman. The proof and measurement of association between two things. *American Journal of Psychology*, 15:72–101, 1904.

StatSoft Inc. *Electronic Statistics Textbook*. URL: http://www.statsoft.com/textbook/stathome.html.

T. Stocki, N. Japkowicz, K. Ungar, I. Hoffman, J. Yi, G. Li, and A. Siebes, editors. *Proceedings of the Data Mining Contest, Eighth International Conference on Data Mining*. IEEE Computer Society, Washington, D.C., 2008.

S. Vanderlooy and E. Hüllermeier. A critical analysis of variants of the AUC. *Machine Learning*, 72(3):247–262, 2008. doi: http://dx.doi.org/10.1007/s10994-008-5070-x.

V. Vapnik and O. Chapelle. Bounds on Error Expectation for Support Vector Machines. Neural Computation, 12:2013–2036, 2000.

G. I. Webb. Discovering significant patterns. *Machine Learning*, 68:1–33, 2007. doi: http://dx.doi.org/10.1007/s10994-007-5006-x.

S. M. Weiss and I. Kapouleas. An empirical comparison of pattern recognition, neural nets, and machine learning classification methods. In *Proceedings of the 11th International Joint Conference on Artificial Intelligence (IJCAI '89)*, pp. 781–787, Morgan Kaufmann, San Mateo, CA, 1989.

S. M. Weiss and C. A. Kulikowski. *Computer Systems That Learn*. Morgan Kaufmann, San Mateo, CA, 1991.

F. Wilcoxon. Individual comparisons by ranking methods. *Biometrics*, 1:80–83, 1945.

I. H. Witten and E. Frank. *Weka 3: Data Mining Software in Java*. 2005a. http://www.cs.waikato.ac.nz/ml/weka/.

I. H. Witten and E. Frank. *Data Mining: Practical Machine Learning Tools and Techniques*. Morgan Kaufmann, San Mateo, CA, 2005b.

D. H. Wolpert. The lack of a priori distinctions between learning algorithms. *Neural Computing*, 8:1341–1390, 1996.

D. H. Wolpert and W. G. Macready. No free lunch theorems for optimization. *IEEE Transactions on Evolutionary Computation*, 1:67–82, 1997.

S. Wu, P. A. Flach, and C. Ferri. An improved model selection heuristic for AUC. In *Proceedings of the 18th European Conference on Machine Learning*, Vol. 4701, pp. 478–487. Springer, Berlin, 2007.

L. Yan, R. Dodier, M. C. Mozer, and R. Wolniewicz. Optimizing classifier performance via the Wilcoxon–Mann–Whitney statistic. In *The Proceedings of the International Conference on Machine Learning (ICML)*, pp. 848–855. American Association for Artificial Intelligence, Menlo Park, CA, 2003.

W. A. Yousef, R. F. Wagner, and M. H. Loew. Estimating the uncertainty in the estimated mean area under the ROC curve of a classifier. *Pattern Recognition Letters*, 26:2600–2610, 2005.

W. A. Yousef, R. F. Wagner, and M. H. Loew. Assessing classifiers from two independent data sets using ROC analysis: A nonparametric approach. *IEEE Transactions on Pattern Analysis and Machine Intelligence*, 28:1809–1817, 2006.

C. H. Yu. Resampling methods: Concepts, applications, and justification. *Practical Assessment, Research and Evaluation*, 8(19), 2003.

B. Zadrozny and C. Elkan. Transforming classifier scores into accurate multiclass probability estimates. In *Proceedings of the 8th ACM SIGKDD International Conference on Knowledge Discovery and Data Mining (KDD '02)*, pp. 694–699. Association for Computing Machinery, New York, 2002. doi: http://doi.acm.org/10.1145/775047.775151.

B. Zadrozny, J. Langford, and N. Abe. Cost-sensitive learning by cost-proportionate example weighting. In *Proceedings of the 3rd IEEE International Conference on Data Mining*, p. 435. IEEE Computer Society, Washington, D.C., 2003.

Index